Our Long Island Ancestors
The first six generations of Daytons in America
1639-1807

A compilation of records by
Stephen Dayton & James P Dayton

IngramSpark
2016

FIRST EDITION

Researchers are also encouraged to provide feedback to the compilers, including questions about content. Send correspondence to: Stephen Dayton at bonacker1650@gmail.com or Jim Dayton at James.Paul.Dayton@gmail.com

Pages 390 and 391 in the paperback edition have been modified to reflect new information

"Not-for-Profit Commitment"

The compilers have no intention to collect monetary profit from the sale of this book. The advertised price was calculated to recover costs of publication and distribution. In order to uphold our commitment to those who assisted us, any revenue realized beyond our expense will be donated to historical societies and similar history-preserving organizations.

ACKNOWLEDGEMENTS

Over the last many years, my brother and I have developed a special attachment to Long Island and the many fine residents of the Townships of Brookhaven and Riverhead, and the Bellport area, as well as the south fork on the East End. We cherish many friendships made there. Our friends have been so gracious and helpful, welcoming us and making us feel at home. We wish to thank the Fire Place History Club and especially the following professionals for their hospitality, for sharing knowledge and expertise, and for giving of their time in granting interviews, for "showing us around," providing access to artifacts, and for answering our many questions.

Richard Barons
Steve Boerner
John Deitz
Beth Gates
Hugh King
Karen Martin

Fred Overton
Gina Piastuck
Barbara Russell
Ned Smith
Beverly Tyler
Martin Van Lith

We give our love and thanks to Joanne Klinger for the cover artwork.

We are especially grateful to our wives, Nancy (Steve) and Judy (Jim) for their patience, counsel and accommodation. Without their support and love, this compilation could never have come about.

TABLE OF CONTENTS

TABLE OF FIGURES

x

ABBREVIATIONS

Because of the heavy reliance upon town records, Barstow books and professional publications, the following are listed with the abbreviations used for each in our compilation.

Brookhaven Town Records	BTR
East Hampton Town Records	ETR
Southampton Town Records	STR
New Haven Town Records	NHTR
Setauket, Alias Brookhaven	SAB
New York Genealogical and Biographical Record	NYGBR
New England Historical and Genealogical Register	NEHGR

DEDICATION

This book is dedicated to our dad, Paul Dayton, who instilled in us a pride of family and heritage.

PREFACE

Our Long Island Ancestors

This work, like most genealogical or family-centered collections, is composed of material gathered over many years, from a host of sources. Those who love history are fortunate to have such detailed town records as are found on Long Island, and skillful historians to interpret them. The lengthy records for early New Haven, East Hampton, Southampton and Brookhaven, as well as the abundant references to Daytons in the work of author Belle Barstow must be recognized. Information has been gleaned from official documents—federal, state and county censuses, town meeting minutes, civil proceedings, deeds, ear mark and marriage registries, as well as from administration of wills, from estate inventories and loyalty oaths and military records. Other biographical data and information come from parish and church records—baptism, marriage, membership, death and burial records and still other sources include commercial ledger entries, diaries, cemetery memorial stone inscriptions, maps and artifacts including entries from a family Bible.

It has been observed that a great deal of information about our early families exists in somewhat diverse forms and many fragments remain scattered about, much in need of being gathered together into a convenient resource to aid those who would begin Dayton research. This was our purpose—to create a collection in order that it might encourage and help launch others with their investigations because, as one well respected historian told us, "a Dayton history is long overdue." Although this project is neither comprehensive nor exhaustive, it references most known primary or secondary sources for this topic and period. In our attempt to go beyond the genealogical lists and annotated genealogy, the first few chapters in particular include some historical, contextual information for those whom it may benefit.

Our family history begins with Ralph Deighton, who emigrated about 1639/40 from England, near Ashford, Kent. Five more generations in direct line follow until Ralph's great-great-great grandson David left Long Island, during or immediately after its occupation by British forces and settled in Hadley, NY.

A narrow and direct path was pursued, proceeding from father to son; from Ralph to Samuel, then to Abraham, to Henry, to David and finally to his son David who had been on Long Island before the rebellion, yet appeared in the first U.S. Census at Cambridge, NY in 1790.

Subsequent to the period covered by this book, three more generations would remain at the Dayton farm on Hadley Hill, at which time our grandfather Wilbur sold the homestead and moved downriver a few miles to the village of Corinth.

Chapter 1

More Interesting than Legend

Impressive, animated and self-affirming analyses are plentiful throughout the field of genealogy, and some histories of early Daytons are no exception. But our purpose was not to "join the crowd" and glorify our pedigree, but rather to honor and understand real people. In the process, it is our hope that we have not dishonored our forebearers. This is where studies in genealogy can be humbling, not always because one finds he or she doesn't measure up to the accomplishments of his or her ancestors, but because one confirms and accepts that at least a few of those ancestors were "ordinary" people.

Our study begins with a review of some sixteenth and seventeenth century background and contextual information before presenting a few possible origins of the Dayton name and examination of records focusing on our Dayton ancestry.

Our American Progenitor

Ralph Dayton is the uncontested immigrant progenitor for Daytons in North America. *Merriam-Webster* defines progenitor as, "someone who first thinks of or does something; an ancestor of an individual in a direct line of descent along which some or all of the ancestral genes could theoretically have passed." It is said that most everyone with "Dayton blood," on this side of the ocean, can trace his or her lineage back to Ralph. Of this descent across America, to the year 1807 (or the first six generations), 3,245 descendants born with the last name "Dayton" have been identified.[1] Projecting the rate of growth to the nineteenth century, conservative

---

[1] (J. Dayton 2012)

mathematical calculations of Dayton blood descendants show the figure could have been close to 216,000 by 1900.[2]

Ralph lived in America about 18 years, just under half of that time on Long Island, until his death in 1658. It was not in Ralph's nature to draw attention to himself, but he apparently earned a respectable reputation so that his opinion mattered. During his years at Easthampton,[3] Ralph held positions of civic service where his good discretion and common sense were both fitting and applied. Even as the town's first constable seemed out of character for unpretentious Ralph, performance of some public duties, to the point of serving official capacities, was a precondition of community in the new settlements.

In contrast, we have become accustomed to reading sentimental, sanitized depictions of the Puritan, "Goodman" Dayton that, in amalgamated form, go something like this:

Ralph Deighton, son of William, though descended from English royalty, was an orphaned boy who found his way to Ashford from the plague-ridden streets of London. Ralph was apprenticed and later flourished at Ashford, Kent as a craftsman shoemaker. Pursuing religious freedom for his family, he left England with his sons in order to establish a home in the New World. In a few renditions, Ralph followed his step-daughter Bennett Tritton Stanley to Massachusetts Bay, where he then sent for his wife and daughters who arrived with other women from their congregation. After a few years at the Massachusetts Bay town of Lynn, the family headed out for the wilds of the Quinnipiac territory where Ralph helped organize New Haven Colony on Long Island Sound. Thriving at Connecticut, Ralph became a respected member of the community and his expertise as craftsman was again greatly in demand. From there, the family became pioneers to Long Island where Ralph and his son-in-law were founders of East Hampton. Thus Ralph established an inspiring legacy for his descendants.

At least, so the legend goes.

As with many family legends, threads of truth are found interwoven with wishful extrapolation based on generous interpretation of the record. Other elements are interesting supposition because they are not disproven. While the plot is satisfying and romantic elements are intriguing, other particulars in the story cannot be supported by irrefutable evidence or even by probability.

With this book, we purposed to gather what information could be found about our British ancestors and, with respectful but sober expectations, relay provenance

---

[2] Note: 3 male children are assumed, with 2.5 reaching childbearing age and 3 female children bearing the surname Dayton per generation. These accumulative counts include blood daughters but exclude mothers, and assume that child bearing age was 20 to 43.

[3] Note: East Hampton was spelled as one word "Easthampton" until shortly after *The East Hampton Star* spelled it as two words in its first publication in 1885. The modern spelling has been chosen for use in most of this book, except when a quotation uses the previous spelling.

that may also suggest other possibilities for the next researcher to explore. It was our purpose to compile a host of "official" records pertaining to our pedigree, including even some of the neglected and mundane entries, and to introduce some of the more difficult or perplexing passages in order to suggest explanations for those that are usually ignored. It is our hope that the inclusion of some banal (by themselves) passages will add value to the effort.

Admittedly, it could have been enjoyable and comforting to boast more about our ancestry, but our true goal was to contribute to the understanding of our legacy, while minimizing bravado. This is the dynamic process of genealogy; even when new information is recognized and accepted as knowledge, the serious genealogist learns and exercises restraint, acknowledging the possibility that a previous idea has to be later altered or even abandoned, when new knowledge modifies or replaces it. It can be a frustrating process, but a rewarding experience.

In our study, an attempt has been made to discover a genuine sense of character and identity, but for Ralph availability of records is largely limited to the last eighteen years of his life, beginning after he was about fifty years of age. In the last two decades of his life, it can be argued that Ralph was an ordinary man of his time; generally disciplined, practical, sober, but particularly cautious and calculated. Even so, out of his devotion to his family, he did take risk to purposely place himself and his family where they would benefit most, when opportunities presented themselves.

When compared among the core of men who established communities throughout New England and on Long Island, Ralph does not appear to have been particularly inclined toward risk without first hesitation, as he calculated the probable outcome. One author described Ralph as "discreet"[4] while at East Hampton, a reputation probably earned in the New Haven Colony, he being older than many in his company. Evidence is found to suggest that sometimes when Ralph became frustrated or faced significant resistance, he was not afraid to express his opinion or displeasure. But unlike his son Samuel, he might passively take another route, preferring not to prolong controversy. Illustrations include the circumstances of his departure from New Haven and his relinquishment of wife Mary's bequeathed property to her children. More will be said about those later.

Despite these characterizations, as one reads history of seventeenth century mankind and tries to imagine the hardships of everyday life and the constant perils threatening one's very existence, Ralph cannot be denied his achievement and those benefits transferred to posterity. It seems that even among some more reserved of his generation, much of modern man might struggle to compare in energy, fortitude or bravery.

Ralph appears to have been a man of superior character and it is our belief that the record relates Ralph's dedication to his family as his decisions empowered his

---

[4] (B. F. Thompson, History of Long Island Containing an Account of the Discovery and Settlement to the Present Time 1839)

children with opportunities heretofore inaccessible. Ralph remained of relatively simple position and we cherish this humble legacy.

On Creating History

In 2010, the compiler was privileged to interview Richard Barons, Executive Director of the East Hampton Historical Society, discussing difficulties, among other things, in interpreting history generally and genealogies specifically. Mr. Barons stated the challenge very well when he said, "The problem with the genealogies, so much of it is suspect, written at a time when people are remembering. Then of course, when you get to family stories…so much of it is folklore extraordinaire."[5]

It has since occurred to me that the interview location had actually been quite appropriate for this part of our discussion. The setting for the interview was inside *Home Sweet Home* where Hugh King, museum curator and East Hampton Town Crier hosted us. The house is situated on James Lane, on the east side of the beautiful Town Green, once believed by some to be the childhood home of John Howard Payne, located on the very lot where Ralph Dayton and his son Robert lived over 350 years ago. It is now believed that young Payne did not actually live there, but visited the house while his father taught at Clinton Academy. Early into our research, perhaps twenty-five years ago, we were excited and proud to learn that Robert Dayton had built that landmark house, a story that had been passed down and, at some point, became history. However, to their credit, and by means of diligent research and scientific analysis, the historical society determined that the house was probably built in the 1720's, about a decade after Robert Dayton's death and then retracted previous claims by others that the house existed in Robert's lifetime. One can imagine our disappointment when it was discovered that the Dayton name and claim had been removed from the museum's description. But the folks at East Hampton have modeled what is proper interaction with the process of studying and writing history.

In December of 2012, *Newsday* published a short piece that featured the contribution Hugh King has made to the community, especially as East Hampton's Town Crier.[6] In the abbreviated version, King was quoted as he warned,

> …there are dangers in going through old documents, and seeing the reality of East Hampton's history as more than just attractive windmills and wooden houses. Even the Colonial town government, thought by many as religious and proper, wasn't above doing business on Christmas Day in 1664. They met…to approve Samuel Dayton's pledge to give his son, Jacob, to his brother Thomas Backer and his wife for 14 years of servitude, in exchange for a promise the boy would get 'sufficient meate Drink and apparell & to Doe for him as his owne'…it illustrates why

---

[5] (Barons 2010)
[6] (Freedman 2012)

4

people should not boast about how long their family has lived in East Hampton until they check to see what their ancestors actually did when alive.

Mr. King's point was not to belittle Sam or his descendants, but to point out that Sam was not wealthy. Considering the harsh realities of the day, it is our opinion that Sam did what he felt he had to do, in the best interests of his sons.

My brother and I submit the Long Island history of our Dayton lineage with humility, and invite inquisitive readers to examine the information, ideas and source material. When our research is judged dubious or faulty, the reader is asked to advance the narrative by presenting his or her own research to refute or expand that which is questionable or deficient. While the purpose of our writing was not to disparage anyone, it is our obligation to call attention to the problem of erroneous or sloppy reporting, or agenda-laden histories that have only proliferated with use of the internet. At the same time, our own fallibility is recognized as is the extraordinary advantage of enormous amounts of information that are easily accessible and electronic resources that were unimagined just one generation ago. It is our desire to add to the body of knowledge.

Our hope is that this work will be helpful as a guide, a place to begin, for those interested family historians who follow us.

Stephen Dayton, 2015

Figure 1. Ralph Dayton's narrow lot at East Hampton (2012)

The compiler stands near Ralph Dayton's narrow lot at East Hampton, facing the green. Ralph occupied it beginning in 1650. Ralph probably lived close to where the St. Luke Episcopal Church is currently located, and his son Robert lived in close proximity to where the Home Sweet Home museum is seen, at the left, possibly in the same footprint. Thomas Baker's house was directly across the green.

Chapter 2

Reading Ancient Deighton Histories
Introductory Context

Phonetics

Reading early handwritten British American documents can be challenging. Recognizing letters and words requires a little practice, but even as the reader becomes conscious of syntax, diction and archaic spelling, the use of strange or different spellings of an ancestor's name can be particularly troubling at first.

During the period under consideration, spelling was not standardized so words were spelled phonetically.[7] For example, upon his arrival at New Haven, Ralph (or Ralfe) signed his own name "Dayghton," but it had been common to see the British spelling Dyghton possibly because the pronunciation of the "a" might sound more like an "i." Consequently, there is no reason for the reader to be concerned when a name is found with multiple spellings, even in the same document. This was almost the norm. In one version of Henry Dayton's will alone, his last name has five spellings. Therefore, the reader should be aware that "Dayton" can be encountered in many forms, such as Dyghttone, Ditton, Deighton, Digton, Dayghto' and, yes, occasionally "Dayton" in England as early as the 1620's. Ralph's last name was written as Drayton in his marriage record. A few examples from New Haven Colony include Dayghton, Datton, Daighton, Dyghton, Dighton and even Dightō. On Long Island, additional examples found at East Hampton were Daiton, Daytan, and Daitone and at Brookhaven, Dayten, Detten, Dateton, and Daitun, with the addition of Doyton in western Long Island. Records in New Jersey include Daten, Daton and Datten, which is misspelled as Patton[8] in the archives of New Jersey marriage records.

For simplification, the "Deighton" spelling is used in England unless in a quotation or in reference to a specific resource utilizing another spelling. Likewise,

---

[7] (G. Mason 2000)
[8] (Nelson, First Series, Documents Relating to the Colonial History of the State of New Jersey, Marriage Records, 1665-1800 1900)

in America, the "Dayton" spelling was favored unless inside a quotation or in reference to a specific resource.

What's In a Name?

Even though "Dayton" could be of Scandinavian origin,[9] the surname Deighton supposedly derived from the pre-10th century Anglo-Saxon word "dic" and later "deek," meaning a protective ditch or dyke, plus the suffix "tun" or the Anglo-Saxon "ton" meaning an enclosure, homestead or town; together, the parts might become something like "enclosure surrounded by a ditch" or perhaps a "manor with a dyke."[10] The postulation that the Deighton name originates from "de Deighton" (meaning something like "removed from Deighton") is likely because many surnames identified strangers with their birth place. So, it is likely that the first Dayton came from a place referred to as "Deighton," a settlement, perhaps a manor, identified with its moat.

Many Possible Origins

The picturesque county of Yorkshire, in the north of England, seems to be the most popularly identified geographic origin for our surname. The earliest accounts of place names for Deighton in Yorkshire are from the *Domesday Book*, compiled in 1086.

The *Domesday Book* is England's first public record,[11] created under William the Conqueror's command. His civil servants surveyed the entirety of England, including, "classifying and valuing mills, plough lands, ox teams, saltpans, fish ponds, vineyards, castles, agriculture and trade. Of the 13,418 places named, almost all are still occupied in some manner, but not as they were. Birmingham, for example, was merely a village, and Hampstead was valued at 5 shillings. We can still relate to, and trace, not only the place names but also those of people."[12] But in York, the identification of that distinct individual or family, the link that holds promise for our search, eludes us. In *Domesday*, place name Dictune was listed for Deighton (Northallerton), Diston and Distone for Deighton (Escrick, East Riding) and Distone for Kirk Deighton and North Deighton, both of North Yorkshire. Each possessed a moat.

By 1284-85, the survey of the county of York taken by John de Kirby lists Dighton and Dycton for Deighton (Northallerton), Dighton and Dyghton for

---

[9] (Pollick n.d.)
[10] (Parish 1888). 42.
[11] (Hallam n.d.)
[12] Ibid.

Deighton (Escrick), Magna Dighton and Suth Dithon for Kirk Deighton and Parva Dighton and North Dithon for North Deighton.[13]

One of the earliest recorded spellings of what could possibly be the family name has to be that of Thomas de Dicton in 1204, in the *Assize Court rolls of Yorkshire*, during the reign of King John, 1199-1216.[14] Other early records include Robert de Dighton, who appeared in the *Register of the Freeman of the City of York*, dated 1330, and a few de Dyghtons recorded in the *Poll Tax records of Yorkshire* in 1379 and William Dyghton in 1379-81.[15]

There has been speculation that Dayton is a variation of Drayton [Draiton, Drayson, Dreyton] or Dutton [Duttun], names found in the Court of Canterbury,[16] and plentiful in areas of London for many centuries. The surname could even be a variation from Deaton[17] or Ditton[18] and the name Ralph de Dittone can be found in *The Kent Lay Subsidy Roll of 1334/5*.[19] Despite these possibilities and others, none can yet be positively tied to our ancestry, but they are mentioned because the search piques our interest.

Initial Records near York

It is not unreasonable to believe that the Dayton line of ancestry might have an early association with any or all of the three Yorkshire villages called Deighton, found near the towns of York, Northallerton and Wetherby. One contender for the origin of the Deighton (pronounced Dee-ton) surname was near Huddersfield in West Yorkshire. Efforts to find the Huddersfield Deighton in *Domesday* were unsuccessful, but it is, "a settlement of considerable antiquity"[20] and has been espoused by researchers such as H. Deighton in 1938.[21] Searches in the records of *British History Online* frequently reveal the Deighton name in its many forms, as well as other similarly named places, scattered around England since the twelfth century. In all of these settlements, there is yet to be found any conclusive evidence suggesting nomenclature and connection to our ancestors.

---

[13] (De Kirby 1867)
[14] (Clay 1911)
[15] (McHardy 1977) 20-25.
[16] (Cowper 1894)
[17] (Deaton 2000)
[18] (Phillimore 1910)
[19] (Hanley 1961, rev. 2008) 115
[20] (Pollick n.d.)
[21] (Deighton 1938)

York

Of all the hamlets called Deighton, the one situated south of the city of York and just north of Escrick appeared to be an early favorite cited as the origin of our surname. In her 1902 book, Laura Dayton Fessenden proclaimed:

> The family…took its name from the hamlet or village of Deighton in the parish of Deighton, in the east riding of Yorkshire, England, and is about four and a half miles south, south east from the city of York. The Deightons appear to have been for generations tenants of a farm, on the Manor of Deighton, which was held by the Abbott of St. Mary's York, he being Lord of the Manor.[22]

This would be a significant discovery if it were proven. Unfortunately, the author cited no references to support her belief that this hamlet was the origin of our surname.

Deighton Hall and moat are still visible on this published 1855 Ordnance map, hand-drawn by the cartographers of the Ordnance Survey. Both are also present in the 1890-91 Ordnance map, available on UK government-sponsored websites.

Figure 2. Deighton Hall, 1855 Ordnance map

(Note: The *Swan Inn*, visible in the upper right of this map, is reportedly still in business today, and is known as the *White Swan*)

A record of this Deighton can readily be found back to the twelfth century, when the settlement became Anglican.

> [In 1086, Deighton] consisted of a single 4-carucate estate held by Count Alan. Between 1158 and 1184 Eudes the marshal, son of the Breton, gave the lordship of Deighton to St. Mary's abbey, a gift confirmed by Alan

---

[22] (Fessenden 1902)

10

son of Roald, constable of Richmond, who also gave whatever he himself had there. Thus Deighton, like Escrick, was in the honor of Richmond and the liberty of St. Mary's. The estate was granted by the abbey between 1161 and 1184 to Duncan Darel, who also received Geoffrey de Brettanby's land at Deighton and 2 bovates which Peter of Wheldrake had held of Thomas son of Erneis.[23]

There are records of a chapel at this Deighton in the thirteenth or early fourteenth century and a windmill at Deighton in 1447. In 1619, the manor house was described as 'fair and new built and moated round about' and in 1976, at the time Volume 3 of *'Escrick', A History of the County of York East Riding* was written, "the site is still moated."[24] Because the moat has apparently been filled-in and other buildings were constructed there subsequent to that writing, a map[25] illustrating the position of the moat in 1855 was located, and still, there is no indication as to the age of the original manor house nor is it known if an earlier manor existed close by.

Northallerton (Hambleton)

The settlement of Dedon is found in Northallerton parish in the *Calendar of Close Rolls* compiled under Henry VI in the mid fifteenth century.[26] The township of Deighton, about 40 miles directly north of Kirk Deighton and seven miles north of Northallerton in North Yorkshire, is situated on a road leading from Northallerton to Appleton Wiske. Today, the site boasts the remains of an ancient moat enclosing about four acres of land and is protected as a scheduled ancient monument. The site of the old manor-house[27] is shown in an Ordnance Survey and Google© satellite photo.

Figure 3. Deighton, Northallerton maps in the mid 1800s and today

[23] (Baggs 1976). 17-28
[24] Ibid.
[25] (Ordinance Map-Deighton Hall 1855)
[26] (Flower 1947)
[27] (Page 1914)

Kirk Deighton/North Deighton

At North Deighton, located about 20 miles south and east of Nidderdale and about one mile north of Kirk Deighton, Borough of Harrogate, there is a prehistoric earthwork probably of late Neolithic or early Bronze Age called Howe Hill Motte that may have eventually become the site of the original manor. By the mid-eleventh century, that place called 'Distone' in the Borgescire' region of 'Eurvicscire' (Yorkshire) was listed in the *Domesday* Survey under 'Land of Emeis de Bruen.'[28]

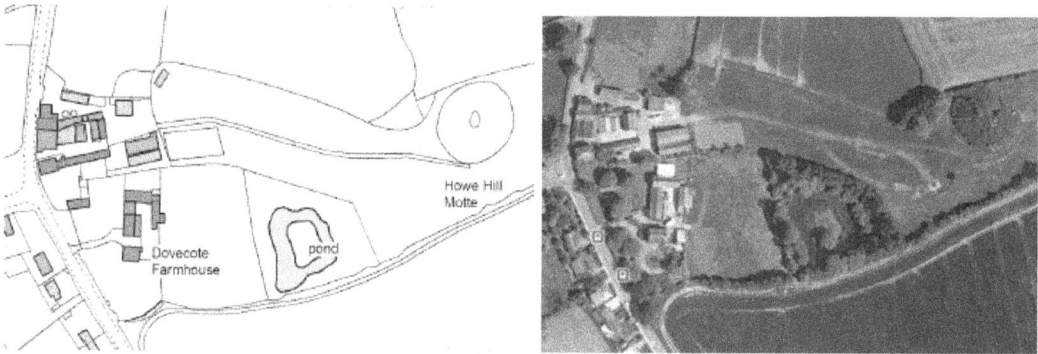

Figure 4. North Deighton, Harrogate Map.

The 2011 map on the left (figure 4) from the North Deighton Conservation Area Character Appraisal, Harrogate Borough Council, illustrates Howe Hill Motte while the Google© satellite photo on the right shows the earthwork in about the same year.

By the twelfth, thirteenth and fourteenth centuries, where inhabitant lists are found, there are examples of people possessing early versions of the surname Deighton. Of course, this is no indication how long these people had existed with an early form of the Deighton name, and no significant authority or land ownership was indicated. For example, in Kyrkdyghton (Kirk Deighton), the poll tax returns of King Richard Second 1378-79 include Petrus de Dighton, *Faber* (a smith) and Margareta de Dighton, *vidua* (could be widow or unmarried woman) and someone named Johannes *seruiens* (in servitude) to a Petri de Dighton. "The parish of Kirk Deighton…was very profitably cultivated in Saxon times, and its church, then existing, was well endowed on the Norman settlement."[29] "Up to the Norman invasion it was reckoned the most valuable of the King's manors in these parts."[30] *Domesday* records the immensity of the destruction occurring in the Norman invasion.

---

[28] (Harrogate Borough Council 2011)
[29] (Speight, Nidderdale, from Nun Monkton to Whernside: being a record of the history, antiquities, scenery, old homes, families, & c., of the beautiful valley of the Nidd 1906)
[30] (Speight, Nidderdale and the Garden of the Nidd: A Yorkshire Rhineland 1894)

Like the Deighton site south of York, just north of Escrick, the plot of land where a manor house once stood has not been identified. If there had once been a protective ditch at this site, it has been covered, probably after destruction of the manor. Had most of those inhabitants called "Distone" already been dispossessed by 1086? Nonetheless, it is intriguing to contemplate that, at some point, probably between the fifth century Saxon occupation and the eleventh century Norman invasion, someone here may have already had some early iteration of our surname.

Tradition of Sir Walter de Dyghton, Knights Templar

"There is a tradition that the pre-Conquest owner, Merlesuan, died at York and was buried in his church at Kirk Deighton. An incised coffin-slab, found there in 1872, and bearing a cross and sword of an early type, is believed to have covered his remains."[31] Another tradition, perhaps related, whose origin is also undocumented, identifies a Knights Templar, Sir Walter de Dyghton, the 1181 Knight Protector of Temple Newsham-York,[32] buried in the parish church of his native village.[33] Part of the story can be found in *Old Yorkshire*, where it is said that during a restoration of the church at Kirk Deighton, two ancient stones were recovered. It appeared that they had probably been covering two very early graves of Knights Templars because, "each slab has engraved upon it in a rather crude fashion the Templars' wheel cross and staff and sword." The stones were then placed into a wall at the church. The story continues that, "...Walter de Diton (clearly Deighton) was Preceptor of Xewsara as appears by a charter given before dates were inserted." This church today is probably the Church of All Saints, which dates from 1160-1170, located in Kirk Deighton, Harrogate, North Yorkshire, less than 40 miles south of the Deighton, Northallerton site. The Church of All Saints is situated less than 14 miles northwest of Wetherby, 19 miles west northwest of York and 200 miles north of London. The particulars of the ancient story are murky and may be a melding of legends.

Bedfordshire

Howell's 1887 *Genealogies*[34] implied that our immigrant ancestor Ralph might have been connected to Bedfordshire and the statement was repeated in Burke as well as in a publication of the National Society of the Daughters of the American Revolution where they proclaimed, "The Dayton family are English and the name a

---

[31] (Speight, Nidderdale, from Nun Monkton to Whernside: being a record of the history, antiquities, scenery, old homes, families, & c., of the beautiful valley of the Nidd 1906), 168

[32] (Deighton 1938), 1

[33] (W. E. Smith 1882)

[34] (Howell 1887)

Bedfordshire name."[35] The same is stated in Henry Whittemore's *Heroes* book.[36] Howell was again cited in Mather's *The Refugees of 1776 from Long Island to Connecticut* in 1913.[37] Of course, in 1897 and in 1913, there were Deightons living in Bedfordshire, just as there are Deightons living there today, but four hundred years ago there were countless Deightons living in many other communities throughout England, like Peter Daton, and his wife, who are listed with Dutch refugees in Maidstone, "[a] stranger dwelling in Maidstone 1585."[38]

By the sixteenth century, Bedfordshire records contained many Deightons. Burials between 1591 and 1601 include Rob Ditton and Alice Dytton in Cardington and Eliz Dyton, Alice Dyton and Jn Diton in Dunstable. Baptisms between 1580 and 1596 include a Marian Dyton, Ag Dyton, Helen Dytonne and even a Ralph Dytonne, all at Dunstable. In fact, variations of "Deighton" like these are plentiful in parish records throughout England so it is not known why Howell and others give preference to Bedfordshire unless they were somehow able to link this Ralph Dytonne. If no more information was uncovered, perhaps Bedfordsire was chosen because the name was still so abundant there in the nineteenth century.

London

Deighton records and potential Dayton-variant records also exist in and around the city of London. West Drayton, in the London Borough of Hillingdon, less than three miles north of present-day Heathrow Airport, was recorded as, "Drayton water-mill, belonging to the manor…in surveys of 1086 and 1222. It is known to have been in continuous existence from 1467 at the latest, and appears always to have occupied approximately the same site, a short distance upstream from Drayton Point, at the confluence of Drayton Stream and the Cowley Stream or Frays River. This location is confirmed by maps drawn in 1645 and 1694."[39] (Note: there is also a Drayton in Nottingham, about 15 miles west of Lincoln, variously known as Estdrayton, Draitune, Great Drayton, Drayton Magna, Draytone and Drayton cum Membry.[40] The oldest part of the St. Peter Church dates from the late 12th century).

About five miles northwest of Heathrow Airport, sits Ditton Manor, "on a 14-acre moated island."[41] No relationship to our family has been established, yet Ditton Park is worth mentioning because it, "is known to have been occupied for at least

---

[35] (The Dayton Family 1900)
[36] (Whittemore 1897). 35
[37] (F. G. Mather 1913)
[38] (Kent Online Parish Clerks; Dutch Refugees in Maidstone, 1585 2013)
[39] (S. E. Reynolds 1962)
[40] Ibid.
[41] (The National Gardens Scheme n.d.)

14

nine hundred years. Ditton Manor was first mentioned in the *Domesday Book* (1066) when it was owned by William, Son of Ansculf. By 1331 Sir John de Molyns was granted a license by Edward III to fortify his mansion and to build a park of 38 acres. In 1472 the property reverted to the crown and was at the time the residence of Cardinal Wolsey. Later in 1532, Anne Boleyn was Keeper of Ditton Park as part of her endowment from Henry VIII. His first daughter, the future Queen Mary I, spent some of her young childhood here.[42]

In London, 1587/88 William Dutton married Margerye Dunnedge at the bride's parish, St Mary Woolnoth at Lombard and King William Streets. The church is still there in 2013. Another London record has an Alice Dayton [Dalton] burial at Westminster, Middlesex, at St Margaret's, in June of 1587.

In another region, this time on England's east coast at Coltishall, Norfolk, Gulielmus Daden married Alicia Kempe in 1570 at St. John the Baptist Church. In the west, near the border with Wales, at Gloucestershire, Thornbury, William Dutton married Margaret Greene in 1584 at St Mary Church.[43] Although a great distance from both London and Ashford, perhaps this record has some connection with the William Deighton and Agnes Green marriage in London?

Summation

Our decision to identify and introduce a few locations called Deighton was to make a point. There were many Deightons scattered throughout England centuries before Ralph's parents were born, making the search for the origin of our surname seem all but impossible. When searching for the origin of our surname, the researcher can easily locate a handful of possible locations in Yorkshire alone, many with ancient moated sites. As a result, until more convincing evidence is uncovered, we are not prepared to present arguments that trace our ascendancy from 1617, through the evolution of our surname, to the English origin of our ancestors. What is probable—the original family that was identified by name, linking with a location called "Deighton," will never be known.

Calendar Styles

It is critical to familiarize one's self with calendar styles when trying to order historical events sequentially. In Chapter 9, the reader will find an example of two East Hampton town records that appear to be incorrectly sequenced, but with the calendar correction applied, it will be found that they are in fact ordered correctly. Today's calendar, the Gregorian calendar, observes January 1 as the first day of the New Year and is referred to as the "New Style" (N.S.). The Gregorian calendar was

---

[42] (NGS Gardens Open For Charity n.d.)
[43] W.P.W. Phillimore. Gloucestershire Parish Registers, Marriages XV, Phillimore's Parish Register Series. Vol XV. (London, 1908)

adopted by Roman Catholic countries in 1582 but was not officially adopted in England and the colonies until 1752. The previous calendar, the Julian calendar, observed March 25 as the first day of the New Year and is called the "Old Style" (O.S.). For a period of time between 1582 and 1752, Europe was using both calendars, generally depending upon whether the country was Roman Catholic or Protestant. England used two "first" days, March 25 and January 1 because the government still observed March 25th while most of the population observed January 1st. To remedy this obvious source of confusion, many people wrote dates using a system of "double dating" for dates between January 1 and March 25. So a date expressed in the old style calendar might include two years and look like January 10, $16\frac{39}{40}$ or January 10, 1639/40 or something similar.[44]

Various conversion equations are readily available on the internet, for example, at a Connecticut State Library website,[45] or with easy converting tools such as the one at the website "Converting between Julian and Gregorian Calendar in One Step," by Stephen P. Morse.[46]

The following examples are provided by The USGenWeb Project:

Julian or Old Style	Gregorian or New Style	Double Date
December 25, 1718	December 25, 1718	December 25, 1718
January 1, 1718	January 1, 1719	January 1, 1718/19
February 2, 1718	February 2, 1719	February 2, 1718/19
March 20, 1718	March 20, 1719	March 20, 1718/19
March 25, 1718	March 25, 1719	March 25, 1719

"By the time England and the colonies adopted the new calendar, the discrepancy between the calendars was eleven days. To resolve the discrepancy, the government ordered that September 2, 1752 be followed by September 14, 1752. Some people also added 11 days to their birth dates (a fact which is not noted on their birth certificates)."[47]

---

[44] (Old Calendar and Dating Information n.d.)
[45] (The 1752 Calendar Change n.d.)
[46] (Morse 2011)
[47] (Old Calendar and Dating Information n.d.)

Chapter 3

Seventeenth Century Kent
Additional Background Information

Our progenitor, Ralph Deighton can be traced to the parish at Ashford, Kent, in the Southeast of England. Kent contains the closest point across the English Channel from the continent, so it has been the favored place of traveler's arrival and departure for thousands of years. Consequently, Kent has enjoyed the benefits of trade and communication at its sea ports and in its towns and villages along the routes to London. The South East has also been subject to invasion and occupations since the Neolithic era. In modern days, Kent's Folkestone has become a terminus for the channel tunnel, the "chunnel" that runs to Calais, France.

The borough of Ashford is about fifteen miles inland from the English Channel, situated on the travel route to London. Ashford probably originated from a ninth century settlement on the Roman[48] road that passed through from the iron-making areas [i.e. "The Weald"] to Canterbury, placing Ashford at a crossroads. Ashford is identified on a variety of old maps that contain legends of churches and windmills. By the latter part of the eleventh century, the *Domesday Book* had listed the settlement having a church, two mills and a value of 150 shillings, under its original Saxon name of "Essetesford."[49] The small towns of Ashford and Maidstone flourished and Ashford's householders, innkeepers and merchants profited from the significant number of travelers passing through, steadily improving the status of the merchants in these towns.[50]

"Unlike many parts of England, the county of Kent had no single, powerful landowning family. Before the reformation much of the land was owned by the two cathedrals and nearly 80 other monasteries and religious houses established in Kent. Cities and towns also held land, yet some prominent family manors such as Esture, Licktop, Repton, and Wall did persist for centuries and their estates surrounded the town of Ashford."[51]

---

[48] For related reading: See (Hussey 1858)
[49] (Ashford Kent 2015)
[50] (Maidstone Kent 2015)
[51] (Education IT Services 2015)

"Gavelkind," the custom of dividing inheritance equally between sons, had been practiced in Kent since before 1293, when it was accepted as having the force of statute law. So, while many areas of England continued the system of primogeniture that required the eldest son to inherit the estate and preserve large land holdings, inheritances in Kent became smaller, as estates were divided. Over time, generation after generation, the custom enabled the emergence of the yeoman class in Kent.[52] This tradition might prove to be an important consideration when studying Dayton wills and other Puritan families from Kent. Yeomen were land-owning farmers, and in English society, they were below nobility and the gentry (gentlemen), but above most of the population who were either tenant farmers, craftsmen or laborers.

In Kent, each parish appointed an overseer of the poor, to assure provision was made for those who could not work. As shall be seen, the tradition of caring for those who could not care for themselves was carried to New England and Long Island towns settled by Kentish immigrants. Also, in Kent, the overseer had power to force administration of a special tax to help the poor and to set up apprenticeships for the children of the poor.[53] On Long Island, caregivers were sometimes acknowledged and compensated with town funds and apprenticeships were approved by the local courts.

By the early 1600's, Kent was one of the most wealthy counties in England and was becoming one of the more populous. "Its prosperity was largely based upon diversified agriculture." Grazing in the highlands around Maidstone and Ashford, varieties of cattle and sheep thrived and contributed to Ashford's reputation as a market town.[54]

The sandstone ridge between the towns of Maidstone and Ashford was known for its many hop gardens and the fertile hinterland was beneficial for cereals and grain. In England, hops were first grown in Kent, when they were introduced as a crop by Dutch farmers in the early sixteenth century. Until that time, the preferred drink in the British Isles had been Ale, brewed without hops, but the preserving qualities of hops were discovered and its use in brewing proliferated. As a result, the area around Ashford and Maidstone drew seasonal employment for hop pickers.

Kent also became the premier fruit growing area in England at a time when cider, another immensely popular drink, reached a peak during the seventeenth century. In fact, it is said that Appledore, an ancient village and administrative parish

---

[52] For Further information: Kent Archaeological Society, *Project Custumal of Kent Paper No. 2*, transcription from the Norman French text reproduced in William Lambarde, A Perambulation of Kent, London 1576. Translation by Karl Wittmer M.A. 2009.

[53] (T. Lambert, Society in 17th Century England 2013)

[54] (Leggitt n.d.)

in the district of Ashford, about 12 miles southwest of Ashford town, gets its name from a Saxon Apuldre, meaning an apple tree.

Kent also benefitted from its local supply of ragstone, in very short supply elsewhere in the southeast of England. The stone quarry near Maidstone had been used since Roman times and its stone can be found in many of England's most important buildings including the Tower of London, Hampton Court and the Rochester cathedral and castle.[55]

But, with all the economic advantage that came with its proximity to London, Ashford not only received trade, but was also the recipient of plague, probably from traffic to and from London.

> The plague, once thought to be transmitted by fleas that lived on rats, devastated London in 1603 and 1636. Emerging theories, made possible by DNA testing of unearthed skeletons in the Clerkenwell area of London in 2013, suggest that the plague spread so quickly because it was airborne.[56]

> [In the] summer of 1625, the plague raged dreadfully in this town [Ashford] and neighbourhood, insomuch, that the justices of the peace, finding the inhabitants unable to support and relieve the sick who were poor and in necessity, taxed this and the neighbouring hundreds for that purpose, according to the directions of the privy council; left, as was said, the sick should be forced, for the succour of their lives, to break forth of the towne, to the great danger of the country.[57]

While the direct impact of the plague on our family is uncertain, they must have had great fear, as friends and neighbors succumbed. At that time Ralph and Alice Deighton had three young children at home (Ralph Junior, daughter Alice and Samuel), all under 10 years of age, and mother Alice might have been pregnant with Ellen. The Black Death had beset England for centuries and first struck the poor of London, then spread to the point where even Royalty fled London to Oxford and Windsor Castle.

The Godly

At the beginning of the seventeenth century, James I ascended to the throne of England after unmarried Elizabeth I died. James, son of Queen Mary of Scots moved

---

[55] (History and Heritge n.d.)
[56] (Osborn 2014)
[57] (Pearman 1868)

from Scotland and became the first of the Stuart Kings of the combined kingdoms. He reigned until his death in 1625.

By law, everybody was supposed to belong to the Church of England. The king, who believing God had chosen him to rule, even commissioned the production of a new, pro-government Bible, the King James Version. The publication was meant to replace the Geneva Bible, used by the nonconformist group known today as the Puritans, with the king's authorized version in order to "correct" the commentaries of the Geneva Bible that were so disliked by the ruling Anglicans.[58] A majority of Puritans valued education and the ability to read and interpret the Bible without official sanction, believing the individual was directly responsible to God and that scripture is the only true law. Nearly two thirds of adult males could sign their own names.[59] This seems to be the case for most of the Ralph Deighton family also, as it appears that nearly all the men and probably most of the women were at least partially literate.

As many members of Parliament were Puritan, their beliefs were in opposition to James. Of course, many conflicts developed between Parliament and the King, but even when he was willing to work with the Puritan-controlled parliament, James still believed he possessed ultimate authority.

When James I died in 1625, his son Charles followed him to the throne. Like his father, Charles believed in the divine right of kings and deeply favored the Anglican form of worship. His leading advisor was William Laud, Archbishop of Canterbury who was strongly opposed to the Puritans and Charles supported him wholeheartedly.

Puritanism was a very large and significant part of the nonconformist movement, composed of a collection of distinctive subgroups who believed too much of the Catholic Church had been retained after the Reformation and who were united by their overriding belief in purity. These groups, though not all interchangeable in their beliefs, preferred to call themselves "the godly," as they believed that God applied to all of life,[60] not separating human existence into compartments of the sacred (church) and secular (government). In keeping with their belief, the Puritans felt called to ensure purity among earthly authorities. Among other groups was the Separatist, a more radical sect. Separatists wanted to separate themselves from the Church of England and their extremism necessitated exile in Holland before settling in the Americas. Two hundred years later, these separatists were given the name "Pilgrim" and are remembered most notably at Plymouth Plantation in 1620. Unlike the Separatist subgroup, a majority of Puritans sought to remain loyal to the Church of England, purifying the church from within, so some tolerance was afforded them.

---

[58] (Bible Translation Magazine 2014)
[59] (Fischer 1989)
[60] (Geree 1646)

At first, the Puritans had been an agitation to the king so he encouraged their emigration to New England, to rid himself of them. But as those outspoken Puritan leaders continued to disagree with the traditions and rituals of the Church of England, and the Puritan movement steadily grew, King Charles felt greatly threatened because he regarded them as rebellious to his personal authority. Some Puritan activists were not opposed to an open hostility to Anglican control, but history does not reveal if Ralph had contributed to the animosity. The king's tolerance of Puritan clergy deteriorated and he exerted pressure on outspoken leaders and placed limitations on emigration. When the Puritans finally gained control in Parliament, he dissolved it temporarily in 1626 and again in 1629, for the remainder of his rule.

Whether Ralph connected with the more entrenched dissenters or not, he apparently did support their views to the degree that he would eventually accompany them in their quest for religious independence. Records from the Ashford parish indicate Ralph remained in the parish at least 20 years, as he and Alice were married there and all five of their children were baptized there. When their parish was identified by Archbishop Laud as a hotbed for dissension, its stability for the family must have been compromised, as friends and associates in the parish continued to leave for New England.

Puritans then became a persecuted minority, and few ministers espoused Puritan beliefs and practices, their churches being indirectly under the control of the King. Charles sought to dampen the religious revolt by banning secret religious meetings and worship, and mandated church attendance on Sunday. This meant that everyone was required to attend their local Anglican parish church, and also had to accept whoever was preaching in the parish, however inadequate he may be. After the dissolution of the monasteries, the average English clergyman was not up to task, as described by Lori Stokes:

> …some having been shoemakers, barbers, tailors, even water-bearers, shepherds, and horse keepers. Even worse, to the Puritans, everyone who attended church was required to take communion. This anguished Puritans, who reported people stumbling drunk to the rail to receive the body of Christ. Known sinners—self-acknowledged liars, cheaters, and blasphemers—sat side-by-side with the faithful and made a mockery of the service and especially the sacrament of communion. Feeling they had no other choice, Puritans broke the law by removing themselves from their assigned parishes to hear sermons from Puritan ministers in other towns.[61]

The same author wrote:

> These Puritans believed that England's refusal to reform its church and its society was bringing God's wrath down on the kingdom…There was

---

[61] (Stokes 2013)

a real sense of urgency amongst Puritans in the early seventeenth century. Apocalypse seemed immediate. Two paths lay open to the Puritans: work even harder to reform the church and save the kingdom, or remove from England entirely and thus avoid God's wrath.[62]

So, with about 300 Puritans onboard, five ships departed in 1629 for the colony at Massachusetts Bay and religious independence. Later that year, the growing group of Puritans families in England elected Rev. John Winthrop as Governor of the Fleet and the Colony. They were joined by many other recruits through the winter as the London-based organizers sought respectable men with necessary trades in the counties surrounding London to sustain the colony, once established. The variety of men needed also included rural farmers. As more Puritans who had witnessed the mutilation and imprisonment of clergy[63] were themselves feeling threatened, the great migration intensified. By 1630 about 700 colonists began the voyage to New England, including the Rev. Winthrop in the flagship *Arabella*. "The seventeen vessels that sailed to Massachusetts in 1630 were the vanguard for nearly 200 ships altogether, each carrying about a hundred English souls."[64] Before 1631, there were already 2,000 resolute Puritans settled around the bay of Boston. The colonists came from a wide class of English society, i.e. tradesman, craftsman, wealthy country gentlemen, prominent men involved in commerce and industry, and active in civic affairs in England and some who had even served in Parliament.[65] "More than 40 percent were adult men and women over the age of 25 and about half of them were children under the age of 16. The gender ratio was about 150 men to 100 women. Very few were elderly and very few were servants."[66]

Author David Hackett Fischer claims, "The leaders of the great migration actively discouraged servants and emigrants of humble means." Some were urged to recruit 'honest men' and 'godly men' who were, "endowed with grace and furnished with means," insisting that, "they must not be of the poorer sort." When John Winthrop's son asked permission to send a servant named Pease, the governor replied:

'…people must come well provided, and not too many at once. Pease may come if he will, and such others as you shall think fit, but not many and let those be good, and but few servants and those useful ones…' As a

---

[62] Ibid.
[63] (Coffey 2006)
[64] (Fischer 1989)
[65] (Heinsohn 1998)
[66] (Fischer 1989)

result of this policy, nearly three-quarters of adult Massachusetts immigrants paid their own passage-no small sum in 1630.[67]

Most Puritans, even those on the trailing edge of the Great Migration, belonged to a classification spread across England's economic and social middle (falling short of using the term "middle class"), from yeomen to artisans, with many of the ministers who led them, "alumni of Emmanuel College, Cambridge. Few of the nobility and few of the desperately poor in the jails and slums, poorhouses and asylums, migrated to New England..."[68] Even though the colony benefitted from the Puritan work ethic (they viewed daily labor as worship unto God), this idealist standard and vision of community was not sustainable, and fairly quickly eroded to the realization that there was more than enough back-breaking and necessary menial work than could be performed without a supply of less expensive laborers.

Archbishop Laud was determined to contain and smother Puritan opposition so he sent commissioners into almost every parish to make sure the local churches came into line. "...In 1636 the bishops began visitations in their dioceses, silencing or suspending non-conformists. In the spiritual courts the non-conformists risked fines and imprisonments, ear-croppings and nose-slittings without the right to a trial by jury, to a writ of habeas corpus, or to being informed of their alleged offense."[69]

As the Puritans perceived that their attempts to reform the Anglican Church were not going to be successful, and also realizing the relative success of the Pilgrims in the Americas, many decided to join the company of wealthier and more educated Puritans seeking religious independence in New England under the guidance of their newly-created Massachusetts Bay Company. For the time being, the beliefs of the Massachusetts Puritans still appeared to be somewhat tolerated as long as they were practiced in the New World, and as long as they continued to profess allegiance to the Church of England and to the King. As will be discussed later, a large group from Kent and Herefordshire joined the Davenport Company just before the *Hector* set sail in 1637.[70] A second vessel was hastily arranged to join the *Hector* but, as many were becoming convinced that the situation in England was hopeless, the second vessel could not hold them all and the remainder were not able to leave for two more years.

Were Ralph and family among either of these groups? They have not officially been counted among those first immigrants, part of the Great Migration. These earlier movements were well documented and yet Ralph's record remains silent for nearly ten years after its beginning, until 1639. To the date of this writing (August 2015), the exhaustive *Great Migration Study Project*, under the leadership of Robert Charles Anderson, has not yet mentioned Daytons. We are eager to discover if Anderson will

---

[67] Ibid.
[68] (Jones 1968)
[69] (Jones 1968)
[70] (Atwater 1902)

include Puritans arriving at other New England ports along Long Island Sound and whether Daytons will be included with the next volume.

Between 1629 and 1640 the Massachusetts Colony grew to 4,000, encompassing a wide range of occupations. The leaders were men of good practical understanding, and had probably provided for their anticipated wants of an infant colony by bringing with them men of skill in such arts as were likely to be most needed.[71] In his *Genealogy Notes on the Founding of New England*, Ernest Flagg says that "of the 5,000 original, male progenitors, heads of family who came to New England between 1620 and 1640, less than 50, or not 1%, are known to have belonged to the upper gentry of England, and less than 250 more, or not quite 5% can be considered as from the minor mercantile or landed gentry." New England also became a reasonably safe haven for those Puritans who had been in exile in the Netherlands.

> This exodus was not a movement of attraction. The great migration was a great flight from conditions which had grown intolerable at home. It continued from 1629 to 1640, precisely the period that Whig historians called the 'eleven years tyranny' when Charles I tried to rule England without a parliament, and Archbishop William Laud purged the Anglican Church of its Puritan members. These eleven years were also an era of economic depression, epidemic disease, and so many sufferings that to John Winthrop it seemed as if the land itself had grown weary of her Inhabitants, so as man which is most precious of all the Creatures, is here more vile and base than the earth they tread upon.[72]

Back in England, the emergence of the First Civil War gave dissenters hope for more religious independence and greatly diminished the urgency to abandon their homeland and so the great migration of Puritans largely subsided. Oliver Cromwell, friend to the Puritan movement, had become commander of the English military and later assumed control of the Republic. By the time the revolution was over, nearly 21,000 of the Puritan philosophy had already immigrated to Massachusetts and David Hackett Fischer says that from that point on, growth occurred naturally from within the group. This is why it is said that once a person discovers an ancestor of seventeenth century New England, he or she is likely to find many other ancestors of like circumstance.

Once again, Fischer's book *Albion's Seed: Four British Folkways in America* is quoted:

> The emigrants who came to Massachusetts in the great migration became the breeding stock for America's Yankee population...[to] more than

---

[71] (Heinsohn 1998)
[72] (Fischer 1989). (Ackley 1997)

sixteen million by 1988—all descended from 21,000 English emigrants who came to Massachusetts in the period from 1629 to 1640.[73]

Charles I had lost the Second Civil War with the parliaments and was captured and then executed in 1649.

It is important to our story that the conditions not be misrepresented among the diversity of groups in the Puritan Movement as harmonious or achieving religious freedom within Puritan communities. "The Separatists saw the non-separating Puritans as compromisers who practiced their faith halfway, which was as bad as not practicing it at all."[74] The Puritans had sought religious independence and so now sought theocratic governance, therefore freedom of religion within their communities was not tolerated.

But while Puritan thought is routinely disparaged in our modern world, we are proud of and grateful for our heritage, flawed as it was, recognizing that post-Christian thought possesses its own conceit. In his escape from the "iron hand of Puritanism," as it is often described, modern man is simply trading masters, his supposed liberation leading him to places no less tyrannical.

---

[73] (Fischer 1989).
[74] (Stokes 2013)

Chapter 4

Ashford Connection

In the last quarter of the nineteenth century, extending into the twentieth century, studies and publications of genealogies were in vogue. For some society-minded people, it was important to reinforce one's social standing by establishing a dignified pedigree. For others, the craze sparked scholarly interest and a genuine desire to uncover and understand family heritage.

Constructing a genealogy required a great deal of perseverance. The search was tedious, access to resources was usually very difficult and sometimes expensive, and communication was slow. It appears that the immense challenge facing the authors of those popular Dayton histories written before the early twentieth century was the lack of Dayton records preceding the New Haven Colony, beginning in 1639. Despite their efforts, it appears that, until the early twentieth century, researchers failed to return lineage back to Great Britain, and beyond that, they leave very little evidence of European linkage. Histories of our Dayton line in England would be transformed with the discovery of Ralph and family in the records of the St. Mary's parish registry at Ashford in Kent.

Before The Discovery

Before connections were discovered in England, author Allen Rosenkrans published his book entitled *The Rosenkrans Family in Europe and America*.[75] In his 1900 work, he discussed an Elijah Rosencrantz,[76] born 1814, married to Caroline Livingston Dayton who was, "…connected with the Livingstons, who like the Daytons, were distinguished in our early history and of English descent, connected with the Royal family of England, through James 1st." The book included an, "authentic list of the Livingston-Dayton family descended from Robert de Deighton, born at Deighton, England, 1305 AD, furnished by William Dayton Rosencrantz,"

---

[75] (Rosenkrans 1900)
[76] Note: The various spellings of the last name are used as they are given

purported to be copied from the *Surtees Publication*.[77] This Robert appeared as Robertus de Digton in *Admissions to the Freedom of York-Temp*.[78]

As impressive as the Dayton pedigree was, Allen Rosenkrans claimed that W.D. Rosencrantz also possessed an astonishing list with the lineage of his mother that began with "Adam the son of God" and proceeded 153 generations.

Of particular interest to us, the William Dayton Rosencrantz list also contained claims, though yet unfounded, that pertained to our known ancestors in America.

> …Samuel Dayton, born 1630; son of Ralph Deighton, the emigrant, born at Deighton, 1589, who m[arried] Agnes Pool, and came to Boston. Ralph was the son of William; son of Robert; son of Henry; grandson of William born 1419; son of John; son of Robert; son of John; son of Robert; son of Robert de Deighton born 1305.[79]

Unfortunately, Rosencrantz did not provide documentation for any of these claims essentially presented as fact, so evaluating the authenticity of the pre-Ralph theory is impossible. As indicated by his pronouncements concerning Ralph and Samuel, W. D. Rosencrantz had not yet learned in 1900 of Samuel's baptism record in Ashford, so presumably someone calculated Samuel's birth backward from the first mention of Samuel's wife in 1653.[80] After considerable pursuit by the compilers, an explanation of where or why the theory of a wife named Agnes Pool originated remains unknown to us. The only Dayton/Poole connection discovered, although very weak, was in the will of Henry Poole[81] and the story of his death in 1643. Thomas Dighton was a fellow passenger aboard a ship, with Nehemiah Bourne, Wm. Davis and Robert Cooke when another passenger Henry Poole became very ill and died shortly after reaching Boston. In his will, Henry named Thomas Dayton one of his overseers for, "managing and composing of my affairs in New England."[82] William Dayton Rosencrantz probably had knowledge of the will by 1900, as its contents were disclosed in an 1892 publication of The New England Historic Genealogical Society.[83] A few years later, Margaret Ellen Poole's *The Poole Family of Poole Hall in Wirral* also included the 1643 letter sent back to England from Neh. Bourne, Wm. Davis, Robt. Cooke and Thomas Dighton informing Henry's wife:

> During the time of our viadge for y[e] greatest p[t] thereof God shined upon your husband with health when most of us all were under his hand of sickness and about 14 days before he landed God strooke him…

---

[77] (Collins, Register of the Freemen of the City of York: Vol 96 1897)
[78] (Collins, Admissions to the Freemen of York-Temp. Edward I (1272-1307): Register of the Freemen of the City of York: Vol. 1, 1272-1558 2002)
[79] (Rosenkrans 1900)
[80] In 1653, Samuel's wife was mentioned in the Southampton NY Town Records
[81] (Fogg 1892)
[82] (Poole 1902) 204
[83] (Fogg 1892)

For lack of a better theory, it is supposed that the idea of Agnes Pool's connection to Ralph Dayton may have been formed through Henry Poole's association with Thomas Dighton at Boston, the assumption being that Thomas was a relative of Ralph, and Henry was somehow related to Agnes. Without references or explanation, and this being written in 1900, it is only assumed by the compilers this was the case. As for Ralph's birth at a place called Deighton, the author provided no rationale to support the statement. In fact, it is presumed that several generations had been living south toward London and were scattered to the corners of England by 1589, Rosenkrans's (another spelling of the name) theoretical year for Ralph's birth.

Likewise, the 1902 book by Laura Dayton Fessenden entitled *Chronicle of a Branch of the Dayton Family*, still a popular source cited today, contains the lineage from Rosenkrans's work, but Fessenden inserted at least four more generations between Robert (b. 1305) and Ralph without documentation. The Fessenden book traced Ralph Dayton back to London and his baptism at St. Martin's in 1598, as well as his marriage to Agnes Pool in 1629 (the same year the Ashford Registry says that Ralph's youngest son Robert was baptized). Fessenden chose the settlement of Deighton, just south of York, as the origin of the surname.[84]

As the research process of genealogists and written histories go, the discovery and publication of the parish records at Ashford have exposed errors in the early works of Rosenkrans and Fessenden, as they pertain to Ralph Dayton. Fessenden might have claimed London for Ralph because Henry Poole was from London[85] and especially because *The Registers of the Parish of St. Martin in the Fields* contain an August 9, 1584 record of marriage for Guilielm' Dayghto' & Agnete Greene,[86] Fessenden's presumed parents of Ralph. It is not known to us why "William" has so often been the chosen name for Ralph's father, but this possible connection to Ralph is worthy of further research. The name "Guilielm" is Latin for William and "Agnete" comes from German or Swedish for Agnes—thus, William Dayton and Agnes Greene. It must be acknowledged that the marriage year for William and Agnes fits very nicely with the presumed year of Ralph's birth and it is our hope that future researchers can uncover evidence, beyond circumstantial, that will help to tell the story of Ralph's parents and how Ralph found his way to Ashford.

While searching *The Registers of the Parish of St. Martin in the Fields* for William and Agnes and/or a record of Ralph's baptism, the following notation was found for the year 1588, our presumed year of birth for Ralph:

In the old Register are wanting all the Baptismes from th'end of Jan: until the begin'inge of Julye.

---

[84] (Fessenden 1902)
[85] Ibid.
[86] (T. Mason 1898)

Since the idea of William as Ralph's father seems to be a preferred theory, another marriage record for a William Dayghton in London should be mentioned, occurring eighteen years after the St. Martin in-the-Fields entry, just two miles from St. Martin. In 1602, "William Dayghton of St. Bartholomew the Less, London, cordwainer & Jane Phillipps, of same, widow of Thomas Phillipps, late of same, cordwainer"[87] married. "The Less" in the name of the small 15th century parish of St. Bartholomew the Less distinguishes it from its senior neighbor, St. Bartholomew the Great. The date would work for a second marriage, but could be another red herring because the London year of marriage comes after the first mention of "Deighton" in the Ashford registry. While Fessenden failed to present evidence to connect Ralph to William Deighton or Agnes Pool, she also did not establish Ralph as a widower, or link Thomas and Nicholas, as brothers, to Ralph.

Fessenden claimed that Ralph immigrated to Boston with his brothers, Thomas and Nicholas. If Henry Poole's Thomas and Fessenden's Thomas were the same person, and Ralph was already in New England in early 1640, the 1643 voyage wasn't Thomas's first time crossing the ocean which may be supported by implication from an entry in Charles Henry Pope's *Pioneers of Massachusetts.* Interestingly, his lists include a record of [Deighton] "Thomas, merchant, Boston, witness to a document 1645" and includes the statement, "had acct. with Airs. Elizabeth Poole of Westminster, Eng 1640."[88] Perhaps Thomas worked for Nehemiah Bourne who, as a shipwright, shipped ships masts from New England to England. It should be noted here that parish registers at St. Nicholas Gloucester were searched back to 1640 by the Vicar and it was noted (not certified) that both a Thomas Deighton and Nicholas Deighton were found.[89] The register had Thomas baptized Aug 19, 1621 and Nicholas married to Alice Walker June 29, 1641 so it is concluded that Thomas was probably born too late to be Ralph's brother. No other evidence was found that Ralph was part of this family. In this regard, it is more than noteworthy to consider that some of the most revered researchers/compilers [Torrey, Savage, Bailey, and Farmer] don't even mention a Thomas, Nicholas or John when listing pre-1700 settlers in America.

Before leaving our discussion of Fessenden, two curious claims are mentioned—the first is hopefully unrelated to our work, but it may be of interest to some readers. Fessenden's claimed lineage includes a Jon de Deighton/John Dighton who was admitted as freeman in 1481, contemporary with the published account of a John Deighton who was named by Sir Thomas More to be an agent of Richard III, and murderer of Edward V.[90] The second claim has to do with yet another wife for

---

[87] (J. Foster 1887)
[88] (Pope 1900)
[89] (Holman 1932)
[90] (Markham 2011)

Ralph, in addition to Agnes Pool. Fessenden speculated that a subsequent wife named Dorothy Brewster died in childbirth in 1649, leaving an infant son, Brewster.[91] The observation is made by the compilers that the proud father would have been more than 60 years old by 1649. Minimal investigation to trace the origin for these claims has revealed possible confusion with a Dorothy Brewster who gave birth to Brewster Dayton in the middle of the eighteenth century in East Hampton. Our efforts have not gone far beyond this level of speculation.

Unfortunately in 1907, just five years after Fessenden, another publication, this time by distinguished historian and prolific author William Smith Pelletreau (1840-1918), repeated Fessenden's ancient lineage and included wives Agnes Pool and Dorothy Brewster.[92]

In fairness, it has been proposed by others that there might have been another Ralph Dayton at the same time, perhaps living in London and married to an Agnes Pool, but no basis is found to support the idea. Perhaps this and a few other modern propositions are the result of attempts to corroborate the pre-Edson Dayton theories and coordinate them with the discoveries at Ashford.

It is with mixed feelings that criticism is directed toward these works by Rosenkrans and Fessenden, and with humility that Pelletreau is questioned, he being a scholar to whom many recognize their indebtedness. Perhaps the authors' claims had what appeared to be strong foundations, but their lack of citation does not help to validate it. The works of these authors are rich in other areas, but for Dayton family information in England, they fall short. Again, an obligation to prospective researchers and other interested readers is acknowledged because Rosenkrans and Fessenden are cited in numerous Dayton research projects but we remind ourselves that many authorities consider uncited material no different than fiction.

The Ashford Connection Achieved

It is not clear who should rightfully receive credit for the discovery of the European origin of Ralph and when the connection was made.

Although Edson Dayton appears to have been in possession of the record in 1921, it seems that Ernest Flagg was the first to publish a European connection in 1926, when he presented the record of Ralfe and family preserved in the St. Mary's parish registry at Ashford. Taken together, the parish entries for the immigrant family span a period of at least twelve years, counting the last item as the 1629/30 record of Robert's (Robard) baptism. Of course, the Deighton record continues well beyond

---

[91] (Fessenden 1902)
[92] (W. S. Pelletreau, Historic Homes and Institutions and Genealogical and Family History of New York 1907)

1630 for oldest son Ralph Junior who remained at Ashford, and for the Tritton and Goldhatch families who were at the parish for generations.

While visiting the Long Island Collection at the East Hampton Public Library, the compilers were fortunate to view handwritten correspondence from September 9, 1944 between Osborne Shaw of Bellport, NY and an undisclosed recipient in a file entitled, "eight pages of Dayton material."[93] The letter includes discussion of the carefully documented 1931 work of Edson C. Dayton. In the same folder was found a typewritten paper with the heading: "From records by Edson C. Dayton of Clifton Springs, N.Y. privately printed in 1931, with additional data supplied by Osborn Shaw, the Historian of Brookhaven and Long Island records."[94] Immediately below the heading, Edson Dayton noted:

> *The following is from the Register of the Parish Church of St. Mary, the Virgin, Ashford, England. Ralph Dayton, q.v. born 1588/9* Great Bentley, Essex, England. *He married Alice (Goldhatch) Tritton widow both of the Parish, June 16, 1617. He died c. 1658. She died 1655. In 1656 he married Mary Haines, widow. Buried in an unmarked grave in Southampton.*
>
> > *Issue: June 28, 1618, Ralfe Dayton was baptized.*
> > *May 21, 1620, Alice was baptized.*
> > *Feb. 7, 1624, Samuel was baptized.*
> > *Dec. 3, 1626, Ellen was baptized.*
> > *Jan. 3, 1629, Robard was baptized.*
>
> *All of these entries certified correct from Parish Register of Ashford Church, Dec 21, 1921...by Harry W. Blackburne, Vicar.*

Clearly, the first paragraph above includes some of Edson Dayton's early private notes that remained unpublished and were not actually part of the Ashford record. This fact is also reinforced by his use of abbreviation 'qv' in the notes, indicating that Edson was referring to other notes he made regarding Ralph. These notes will be discussed in more detail later in this chapter.

It is assumed, from these notes, that either Edson Dayton had been in correspondence with the vicar at Ashford Parish in 1921 or he recorded the work of another researcher. Either way, Edson Dayton apparently knew of such research because he referenced and published his 1929 correspondence with Vicar Harry W Blackburne in his 1931 book.[95] In his chapter on Ashford, Dayton wrote:

---

[93] Note: Osborne Shaw was Brookhaven Town Historian at the time.

[94] Note: Unknown author, typewritten paper with the heading: "From records by Edson C. Dayton of Clifton Springs, N.Y. privately printed in 1931, with additional data supplied by Osborn Shaw, the Historian of Brookhaven and Long Island records."

[95] (E. C. Dayton, Genealogical and Biographical Account of One Branch of the Dayton Family in America 1931)

I AM glad to be able at the beginning of this narrative to give a reliable statement of the contents of the old parish registers in Ashford, County Kent, England, in so far as they relate to the Daytons who constitute the theme of this family monograph. It will serve to correct mistakes in names and dates which writers on the subject have unintentionally made, mistakes from which, so far as I know, no one of the many American publications concerning themselves with the Ashford sources, is entirely free.

Perhaps Edson Dayton was referring to Flagg who had identified Ralph "Drayton" in the marriage record[96] at St. Mary's just a few years earlier, but Dayton's statement relates to us that "many" American publications already knew of the Ashford references by 1931. Flagg published the record as part of his research in Stanley family records, including Bennet Tritton who married Thomas Stanley.

The Parish Registry at St. Mary's, Ashford

For centuries, the town of Ashford had been a local communications hub for its surrounding villages and the parish church, St. Mary the Virgin, sat prominently placed in the town. Two centuries after the first record of settlement, the Normans mentioned the Church of St. Mary the Virgin in their 1086 *Domesday Book*. In the *Domesday Book*, Ashford is called both Estefort and Essetesford, and in other ancient records, Eshetisford, taking its name from the river Esshe (or Esshet), which runs close to it.[97] The Ashford church building contains many family tombs including those of Fogge, Smyth and Whitfield. Parts of the current parish church date from the 13th century but the building was substantially restored in the 15th century with many alterations since.[98]

The first time we saw what was actually in the registry was in November of 2013, when photographs and a transcription was received from genealogist Celia Heritage, Heritage Family History, Tonbridge UK. The marriage record of Ralph and Alice, dated June 16, 1617 looks like this:

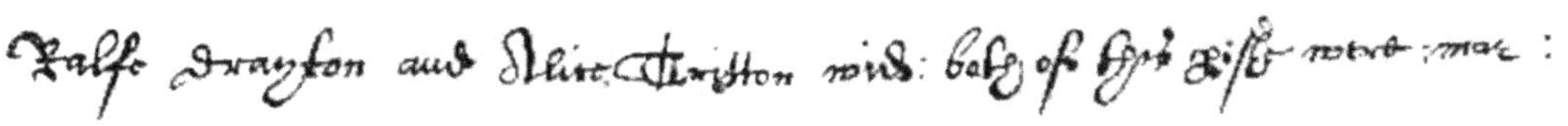

"Ralfe Drayton and Alice Tritton wid: both of this parish were mar:"

Figure 5. Marriage record of Ralph and Alice

---

[96] (Flagg, Parish Register Ashford, Kent 1926) 343
[97] (Hasted 1798)
[98] (Ashford Kent 2015)

The sum of all this seems to suggest that either the work of Earnest Flagg or the work of Edson Dayton was a first generation discovery of Ashford and that Shaw was drawing upon their work as the original authority. Edson Dayton's scholarship became a landmark publication for early Dayton research, although Flagg may have had a part if indeed it was Flagg who Edson Dayton referenced when he said, "American publications concerning themselves with the Ashford sources." Perhaps the Flagg research at Ashford followed Dayton's 1921 correspondence with the vicar?

It is interesting that after Edson Dayton's book in 1931, Donald Lines Jacobus, arguably America's best known genealogist,[99] still used Flagg's correct spelling (as found) when he commented, "The name was spelled 'Drayton' in the marriage entry at Ashford, perhaps because he was a newcomer in the parish and his name not well known there, but thereafter it was spelled Dayton." As was mentioned in chapter 2 of this book, the name 'Drayton' had been established for centuries near London's present-day Heathrow Airport.

Dr. Seversmith, in his account of the family,[100] suggests that Drayton may have been the original form of the name, but Jacobus says the signature (reference to Ralph's New Haven autograph, spelled Dayghton in figure 7) indicates rather that it was a variant of Deighton, a very ancient name with some prominent branches in England.[101] Indeed, just one year after the 1617 "Drayton" spelling in the marriage record, the spelling "Dayton" was used for Ralph Junior's baptism and two years after this, "Daighton" was used for daughter Alice's baptism. As anyone would expect, the Jacobus assessment is very good but it would have been beneficial if Jacobus had also discussed the important phrase, "both of the parish" which could conceivably contradict the theory that Ralph was new to the parish. Perhaps Ralph had recently arrived, but he had made it known that he intended to remain there.

Also stated in Jacobus is the fact that most subsequent spellings are *Dayton*, as is found in the entry of Sam's baptism written under the heading, "Parish of Ashford from the 29th of September 1623 to the 29th of September 1624 as follows:" Next to the word *February* appearing to the left, the entry reads, "Samuel the son of Ralph Dayton bapt." Just seven years after their marriage entry, the old spelling of Ralfe with an "f" was also changing, becoming "ph" through the influence of Anglo-French embellishment which began in the Renaissance. The same spelling continues in the

---

[99] Note: Jacobus was publisher of New Haven Genealogical magazine, compiler of Families of Old Fairfield, and renowned founder, publisher and contributing editor of The American Genealogist [TAG].

[100] (Seversmith, Colonial Families of Long Island, New York and Connecticut, Being the Ancestry & Kindred of Herbert Furman Seversmith 1939-1958)

[101] (D. Jacobus 1959)

burial record for Ralph Junior's wife Alice, October 13, 1681 and in the burial record of Ralph Junior himself, February 10, 1705.

In Britain, the word "parish" not only refers to an ecclesiastical parish, a unit of area committed to one pastor,[102] but can also refer to a civil division called an administrative parish, a territorial designation of local government inside a county. These parishes often coincide with an original ecclesiastical parish. In fact, many ancient boundaries that define current parishes came from the previous system of local administration in rural areas which was the system of manors. Alternatively, by resolution of its parish council, a civil parish can be known as a town, village, neighborhood or community. The meaning of the word "parish" becomes important for the next discovery.

While researching Ralph and Alice's possible connections before marriage, we happened upon an unusual claim regarding the location of Ralph and Alice's marriage. The fact had long been obvious to us that Ralph and Alice had been married at the parish in Ashford, dedicated to St. Mary the Virgin. After all, there are considerable records of Alice's family there (before her marriage to Ralph); the couple's marriage record and baptisms of all of their children, so there was no need to entertain any claim that would seem contrary to that fact. The curious claim, reportedly taken from an actual image of parish records at Ashford (recently indexed LDS microfilm #1736522), had "Ralfe Deayton" and widow Alice Tritton wed June 16, 1617 at Appledore Parish, Canterbury Diocese, Kent.[103] No other information was given. The settlement of Appledore is 12 miles south and west of Ashford.

Although the compilers acquired and viewed the film, the record was not found. Still, others should not be discouraged from searching the microfilm because it might be there.

To better understand how parish records work, the Kent Archaeological Society was consulted. Their website research launch page for Ashford, Kent states "this index includes the details of all known births, marriages (including those by license) and burials in Ashford of known persons, and also of those recorded in other parishes, but described as of Ashford."[104] Contacting the Kent Archaeological Society for clarification, it was learned that the records of the Ashford congregation may also contain entries of parishioners from nearby villages who sometimes used the church, even though every village around Ashford had its own church with its own records.[105] This is true for Kent registries from the late sixteenth century until the late nineteenth century and currently the records for the Church of St. Mary's date back to 1570.[106] Attempts to confirm that Appledore records were actually located at St. Mary's Church were unsuccessful.

---

[102] Merriam-Webster
[103] "Index-English Marriages, 1538-1973." FamilySearch.org. (https://familysearch.org/pal:/MM9.1.1/NNWX-4YX). FHL microfilm 1736522
[104] (Kent Archaelogical Society 2012)
[105] (Unknown, Helen 2013)
[106] (E. Dayton 1978) 4

As amicable as neighboring parishes might have been, after the Black Death had devastated London, they had to guard themselves against the inflow of vagabonds and beggars which would drive up their poor rates. These 'poor rates' were a form of tax, a mandatory collection for maintenance of the poor. In an email, the obliging people at the Kent Archaeological Society told us,

> A village could only afford to care for its parishioners, not those of strangers...poor rates of the time, paid by the community, kept parishioners within their parishes for births, marriages and burials. There were instances where poor travelling women in labour were carried over the boundary line into the next village due to the costs of the poor rates.[107]

Fortunately, there are organizations such as the Kent Archaeological Society, investing much effort in transcribing parish registers. Their website states their purpose, "to discover more about the history of the town...the parish registers were used to gather the basic information about many of the people who had contributed to the life and development of the town over the centuries."

In our minds, the extensive records over many years, including the Goldhatch and Tritton families' marriage and baptism records, indicate that the burden of proof falls on the side that tries to prove that Daytons did not belong to the congregation at St. Mary's. Nothing else has been found to suggest that Ralph Dayton's records belonged anywhere but with the St. Mary's congregation, at least after 1617. Our correspondence with the Kent Archaeological Society reinforced our belief when a representative stated, "the children to which you refer were baptised in Ashford and were more than likely to have been born there."[108]

The Earliest Reliable Connection

Taking into account all the information that has been gathered, benefitting from many years of research from highly qualified scholars, we are convinced that the earliest reliable and explicit Dayton record in our line of ancestry is the 1617 marriage of Ralfe Dayton and Widow Alice Goldhatch Tritton, found in St. Mary's Parish Records at Ashford.[109] Nearly ninety years have passed since the marriage record was discovered and was then published in Earnest Flagg's text and refined by Edson Dayton, Shaw and Jacobus, but there appears to be no link or association preceding 1617. Our conclusion has to be that, as of the time of this writing in 2015, it is not proper to represent any part of our Dayton story prior to 1617 as historical fact, until reasonable linkage can be established.

---

[107] (Unknown, Helen 2013)
[108] Ibid.
[109] (Vicar n.d.)

Next Steps

Many big questions remain. Among them are: Where was Ralph born? Who were his parents? How did he come to arrive at Ashford?

It seems logical to us that 1588, suggested by Donald Lines Jacobus and others, is probably very close to the correct birth year for Ralph (for context in history, this was also the celebrated year of the defeat of the Spanish Armada). Since it was customary for baptism to follow birth within six or eight weeks and since her baptism occurred September 24, 1587, Alice was about thirty at the time of marriage to Ralph. Ralph's birth has been frequently judged to be between 1585 to 1590, making him near to his wife's age, as seems to be the norm for subsequent generations. It is also reasonable that the places of his birth most often considered by earlier researchers are areas in or near London, particularly Maidstone in Kent or other parishes neighboring Ashford, and to a lesser extent, any one of the towns of Deighton. Still, compelling evidence to verify any one of these is lacking.

As mentioned earlier in the chapter, the 1584 marriage record for Guilielm' Dayghto' & Agnete Greene[110] was located but our search to find Ralph in the same registry was not successful. We excitedly turned to 1588 entries in the same book but found the note on page twenty that the old registry was missing baptisms between January and July of that year.

Edson Dayton's private notes, held at East Hampton Library, also contain the lines, "Ralph Dayton...born 1588/9 Great Bentley, Essex, England...both of the Parish." He isolated this notation by making use of the Latin abbreviation "q.v," (quod videre) to separate personal notes requiring investigation from actual record, coming before and after the phrase in question. Since Shaw said in his letter that Edson Dayton, "wanted proof of every statement he makes in his book," the fact that Edson didn't use this birthplace (Great Bentley, Essex) for Ralph in his book says to us that he did not believe it to be reliable. In this regard, microfilmed photography of the Great Bentley registry for that time period was secured and examined [courtesy LDS Family/History Library, Salt Lake City], but the pages were too tattered and faded to be legible. Perhaps the application of forensic science would yield a readable document. If the Great Bentley record were to ever be found in the church record, as unlikely as that is, we imagine it was as if Ralph told the vicar on the occasion of his marriage to Alice that he was born there. Great Bentley, Essex is located about halfway between Colchester and Clacton-On-Sea, about ten miles from each, and is about 100 miles north of Ashford, Kent.

One seemingly remote possibility is that Ralph had been apprenticed, in his youth, possibly to a shoemaker near Ashford. Perhaps he was even orphaned as a child, as some have suggested, as the plague was rampant around London. The theory that Ralph could have been indentured or apprenticed by his parents is not an unlikely

---

[110] (T. Mason 1898). 72

scenario since a pattern of this practice emerged for the next two generations of our Dayton line of ancestry, as will be developed later. A romantic's imagination could even place young Ralph in his future father-in-law's shoemaking shop near Ashford.

Using the presumed 1588 birth year, Ralph would have been about 29 when he married Alice, making the possibility of a previous marriage more likely than if he had been 21. If Ralph had been married previous to 1617, the couple probably lived at another location since there is no record of Ralph in the Ashford parish registries prior to his marriage to Alice at St. Mary's. To date, no workable theories have been explored to explain Ralph's age at marriage or his occasion to seek out a wife at Ashford (if he was not already living there). But the town was easily accessible and received many travelers because of its strategic location and offered opportunities in many fields of employment as discussed in chapter 3.

More likely, if Ralph was not living in Kent, he had been in a nearby town before marrying Alice and settling at Ashford. If a previous marriage is discovered, researchers will also be compelled to entertain the idea that Ralph might have had other children before 1617, although it is not our inclination to believe that Ralph had a surviving son before the birth of Ralph Junior.

But a peculiar Canterbury marriage entry for Ralph Junior was recorded that won't let our assumptions rest. The record says,

> Dayton, Ralph of Ashford, cordwainer…about 22 or 23 at his own govt., and Susan Burr of Walmer, v, 21 and upwards, whose parents are dead. At S. Margaret's, Cant. Robert Goldhatch of Ashford, husb., bonds Nov 27,1639.[111]

This marriage license record, of course, presents a problem because, using this information, Ralph's birth year is calculated to about 1616/1617, too early for his father's June 1617 marriage date. Even considering the possibility that Ralph Junior was the product of a previous marriage, the easier explanation for the discrepancy is that either Ralph represented himself as older than he was, or his estimated age was mistaken because he just looked older than his actual age.

The observation has been made that a few articles and perhaps a half dozen websites use June 16, 1616 as the marriage date for Alice Tritton and Ralph Dayton, and the source for the replicated error has not been determined. We surmise that it is an accommodation for the Canterbury record. For example, Ernest Flagg[112] claims the 1616 date but Edson C. Dayton[113] gives the marriage exactly one year later, June 16, 1617. The Edson Dayton book includes an entire chapter on the Ashford Records and the author communicated directly with the vicar of the Ashford Parish to

---

[111] (Cowper 1894). 277

[112] (Flagg, Genealogical Notes on the Founding of New England : My Ancestors Part in That Undertaking 1990). 343

[113] (E. C. Dayton, The Record of a Family Descent from Ralph Dayton and Alice (Goldhatch) Tritton, Married June 1617, Ashford, County Kent, England 1931)

document this information, including a letter from the vicar as validation, and, of course, our photo of the original record leaves no question that 1617 was recorded.

According to parish records, the family of Ralph Senior's bride had been of the congregation for quite some time. Alice was the daughter of Robert Goldhatch and Bennett Meade of the vicinity of Ashford, married about April 16, 1585. The record shows that Alice was baptized September 24, 1587 so she was probably born less than a month before that date, making her slightly older than Ralph, using 1588 as his birth year.

In his will, dated Jan 10, 1599, Alice's father Robert Goldhatche of Ashford, husbandman, left to his youngest son Robert Goldhatche, his house and

> …land there now in my occupation, containing 5 acres, after the death of Bennett my wife, he to pay to my daughter Alice, £10 in three years after the death of my said wife. If my said son Robert die before his mother, remainder to my eldest son Richard Goldhatch, he to pay, after the death of my wife, £10 to my daughter Alice Goldhatche. To my sons, Richard and William Goldhatche, 6s, 8d each, to be paid one month after my decease. All residue to my wife Bennett to bring up my two youngest children, she to be sole executrix.[114]

It is likely that Alice's father Robert died shortly after his will was recorded. Parish records show that widow Goldhatch then married widower Hugh Tryton May 11, 1601.[115]

The registries at Ashford that list the baptism of Alice's daughter Alice also tell us that daughter married Hugh's son, Daniel Tryttone (Tritton) April 14, 1607, making Daniel both her husband and step-brother. Burial records February 2, 1614 show that Daniel and Alice were married less than eight years when Alice became Daniel's widow at about age 27, she being left with two young daughters.

In this burial record, Daniel is listed as a "householder," as was his father, Hugh Tritton.

Figure 6. St.Mary's Church registry, Daniel Tritton householder buried

---

[114] (Flagg, Genealogical Notes on the Founding of New England : My Ancestors Part in That Undertaking 1990). (See also Arch. Of Canterbury, vol. 51, fol. 426) Proved July 19, 1600 by executrix.
[115] Note: Ashford Parish Records

Householders were similar to innkeepers except that their livelihoods were not derived primarily from their hospitality, but instead they had another means of income or occupation.[116] In this regard, it is noteworthy that the Parish Burial Record of November 26, 1619 lists Hugh as a householder, but he had been called a shoemaker just three weeks before, in his November 3, 1619 will.[117] Probably, like his father, Daniel did have another occupation, perhaps also as a shoemaker.

As stated, Daniel Tritton died before his father, perhaps unexpectedly, because no will has been found and the court made an account and ordered division of Daniel's estate March 1, 1614.[118] As a result, after debts, fees and court charges, the remainder of Daniel's estate went to Alice and her two daughters, £2 each to the girls and more than £13 to Alice.

As difficult as it is for us to conceive in our day, it was a common custom for a widow's young children of a previous marriage to be removed from the dwelling at the time of their mother's next marriage, as can be illustrated or implied in many documents of the day. Therefore, it is possible that Grandfather Hugh provided care for the girls upon Widow Alice's marriage to Ralph Drayton (Dayton). Daniel's father's will dated November 3, 1619 provided, "To Bennet and Rose Tritton, daughters of my son Daniel Tritton, deceased, £10 each at their ages of 17 years." By the time their mother married Ralph on June 16, 1617, daughter Bennett was about ten and Rose was about six years of age.

From Hugh's will, it is learned that Hugh called himself a shoemaker, he named his wife Bennett the executrix (she was also executrix when her first husband died) and he does not mention a house or dwelling. An extraordinary feature of the will was Hugh's attention to his wife's needs extended for her lifetime as well as his leaving her half of his household goods, despite the existence of male children. Possibly this had something to do with the fact that mother and daughter (Bennett and Alice) married father and son (Hugh and Daniel) bolstering bonds between Hugh, his wife Bennett, and Alice who was both his daughter-in-law and his step-daughter. Since common practice at the time was for a husband to provide for his widow only until her next marriage, the generosity to wife and step-daughter could be the same reason the will was objected to by most of the heirs before it was allowed December 15, 1620,[119] more than three years after Alice's marriage to Ralph, and after the birth of their first two children, Ralfe and Alice.

Along with Widow Bennett, is it possible daughter Alice, and new husband Ralph, were already de facto owners of the large house and shoemaking shop? If true, Ralph probably inherited the shoemaker's shop and tools. Is this where he or someone else apprenticed his son Ralph to become a shoemaker? If Ralph Senior hadn't been

---

[116] (Beale Jr., The Law of Innkeepers and Hotels 1906)
[117] (Flagg, Genealogical Notes on the Founding of New England : My Ancestors Part in That Undertaking 1990). 343
[118] Ibid. (See also Arch. Of Canterbury, Computi, vol. 24) 108.
[119] (Flagg, Genealogical Notes on the Founding of New England : My Ancestors Part in That Undertaking 1990). also see Arch of Canterbury, vol 66, p330

a shoemaker before the marriage, could his mere possession of the shop explain why Ralph was eventually referred to as a shoemaker when in America? Or, perhaps shoemaking had been his craft before his marriage to Alice and that is somehow the reason he knew the Trittons. Further research should be pursued to determine if this dwelling that had belonged to the Tritton family was the same seven hearth building Ralph Junior possessed at the 1664 Lady Day tax assessment. If Ralph Senior obtained the large dwelling from his marriage to Alice or if the two obtained it from her mother, perhaps it elevated newcomer Ralph's position in the community, initiating a pattern of financial betterment followed by Dayton widowers for a few more generations.

In addition to marriage records, the registry at Ashford also includes baptismal entries for all five of Ralph's known children in the parish; Ralfe June 28, 1618, Alice May 21, 1620, Samuel February 1, 1623 (could actually be 1623/24), Ellen December 3, 1626 and Robard [Robert] January 3, 1629, ending about ten years before Ralph is found in America. Even though no evidence has been found that the family remained in the Ashford parish in the decade before departure for New England, there is no reason to believe that Ashford or another nearby parish wasn't home until they gathered for departure. Also, no record of fellow parishioners fleeing to Leiden during this time can be found, other than those who were possibly clergy.

Below is a list of Dayton entries from the parish registry at St. Mary's, Ashford, Kent, as transcribed by volunteers for the Kent Archaeological Society, Maidstone.[120] Included are entries up to the death of Ralph Junior retrieved 11/26/13 from the Kent Archaeological Society website, in the section entitled *Research*.

DAYTON

1617 Jun 16 m	Ralfe & Alice Tritton, wid.
1618 Jun 28 c	Ralfe, son of -do-.
1620 May 21 c	Alice, dau. of -do-.
1623 Feb 1 c	Samuel, son of -do-.
1626 Dec 3 c	Ellen, dau. of -do-.
1629 Jan 3 c	Robard, son of -do-.
1639 Nov 27 l	Ralph, cordwainer 22 yrs., & Susan Burr, 21 yrs. of Walmer
1641 Jan 30 c	Robert, son of -do-. [date uncertain]
1651 Mar 26 c	Ralph, son of -do-.
1654 Jun 15 c	Thomas, son of -do-.
1656 Oct 22 c	Alice, dau. of -do-.
1658 Mar 23 c	James, son of -do-.
1662 Feb 19 m	Ralph & Alice Walter
1662 Mar 13 b	[Susan] wife of Ralph
1669 Jan 30 m	Robert & Hannah Philpott
1670 Nov 18 c	Susannah, dau. of -do-.
1672 Sep 8 c	Ralph, son of -do-.

---

[120] (Redboat Design 2012)

1674 Feb 11 c	Alice, dau. of -do-.
1677 May 20 c	Hannah, dau. of -do-.
1678 May 21 b	Alice, dau. of -do-.
1681 Jun 2 b	Thomas, a poor man.
1681 Oct 13 b	Alice, wife of Ralph.
1703 Sep 30 m	Ralph & Mary Goodale
1703 Mar 17 c	Elizabeth, dau. of -do-.
1705 Oct 8 c	George, about 7 yrs old.
1705 Feb 10 b	Ralph, aged 88 yrs.

bap/b- baptism, mar/m - marriage, dea/d - death from St Mary's Church Registers, lic/l - License

There is still much to be done with pre-1617 registry entries as additional information may be present, possibly informing the search for Ralph's past.

Dissent in the Parish

There can be no question that St. Mary's at Ashford and neighboring parishes contained significantly dissident congregations at the time Ralph was in attendance.

In his book *From Hothfield and Ashford to New England*,[121] R. W. Rivers wrote:

> It is known that the desire for religious change was particularly strong in Ashford. In 17th century Ashford it is stated that Dr. Comfort Starr, an Ashford resident with fanatical Puritan convictions, sailed for New England aboard the *Hercules* in 1635, leaving behind his brother Joyful Starr, no less extreme in his Puritanism, to be churchwarden at Ashford parish during the late 1630's. Ralph Dayton probably worshiped at this church and he may therefore have been influenced by the Puritan teachings of the minister.

As mentioned, the Dayton, Goldhatch and Tritton families were all part of the congregation of St. Mary the Virgin Parish at Ashford, or in congregations close to Ashford. There are no known records of the political or religious leanings of the Goldhatch family or the Tritton family, but it would be interesting to research these topics. It is assumed that the Trittons were Puritans because Jacobus tells us that Ralph's step-daughter, Bennett (Tritton) Stanley's husband and his two brothers sailed for New England[122] aboard the *Planter* in 1634/35 and made their home in Hartford. Bennett's sister, Rose Tritton, also came in 1634/35, on the *Hercules*.[123]

---

[121] (Rivers n.d.)

[122] (D. Jacobus 1959)

[123] Note: According to *Great Migration: Immigrants to New England, 1634-1635*, Volume VII, T-Y page 98. Peter Wilson Coldham, in *The Complete Book of Emigrants: 1607-1660*, 1987 lists "Rose Tritton of Ashford, servant" immediately following Isaac Cole of Sandwich, carpenter, but we do not know if any connection was implied (page 132 of our 1987 edition).

There is ample evidence that Ralph Dayton shared convictions as a non-conformist, today referred to as a dissident. In fact, this characteristic of independent thinking, along with a share of stubbornness, seems to run through the generations, as will be developed.

The situation in Kent was probably little better for Puritans than for dissidents in general. In fact, at one point, conditions in Kent may very well have been worse as attention from the crown was focused on the area. After the death of the Church of England's archbishop Abbot, the situation intensified significantly with Charles' appointment of Laud as the new Archbishop of Canterbury in 1633. "Abbot had shielded them [Puritans] in his own diocese, and had encouraged, at least indirectly, other bishops to do likewise… [But with Laud,] Puritan clergymen in larger numbers than ever were imprisoned."[124] Unlike Abbot's relative tolerance of Puritan views, Laud demanded conformity to high church policies and practices and this greatly alarmed the Puritans, escalating the departure of both separatists and Puritans evading certain persecution. "Though the clergy were more exposed than the laity to the storm of persecution, the latter were not exempt." For example, if a congregation was found by the spies of the High Commission to be nonconforming in their ceremony, the minister and all those in attendance were imprisoned until swearing off non-conformity.[125]

As Atwater tells it, dissenters in the parishes of Ashford and Egerton had reason to fear Charles I and flee Laud's administration as it is apparent Laud was concentrating efforts against dissenters and separatists around Ashford and Egerton, Kent. "[With] Laud, there was an immediate and radical change in the administration of the diocese. In the reports which he rendered annually to the king, the primate complains, both in 1634 and 1635, of a part of Kent around Ashford, as specifically infected with distemper against the church."[126] In Laud's 1636 account to the King, Laud expressed his contempt for the people of the parishes around Ashford:

> I have every year acquainted your majesty, and so must do now, that there are still about Ashford and Egerton divers Brownists and other Separatists. But they are so very mean and poor people that we know not what to do with them. They are said to be the disciples of one Turner and Fenner, who were long since apprehended by order of your Majesty's High Commission Court. But how this part came to be so infected with such a humour of Separation, I know not, unless it were by too much connivance at their first beginning. Neither do I see any remedy like to be, unless some of their chief seducers be driven to abjure the kingdom

---

[124] (Atwater 1902)
[125] Ibid.
[126] Ibid.

which must be done by the Judges at the Common Law, but is not in our power.

The king took note of Laud's report and, in the margin of the paper containing this account the King wrote, "Inform me of the particulars, and I shall command the Judges to make them abjure."[127]

In Her Majesty's Public Record Office is found a calendar of State Papers of the Reign of Charles I, including a *Book of Rough Notes* by Nicholas January 6, 1636 containing memoranda that show Laud's attempt to build a case against them, "That the statute of abjuration may be put in execution against some principal men. That the judges be spoken with against Fenner and Turner."[128]

It is interesting to note in the same *Book of Rough Notes*, the heading *A catalogue of books written by Anabaptists* that also appears in January, somewhere above the abjuration.[129] It is our opinion that the anxiety and resolve in Ashford that had been building was by 1636 approaching a level where a result or response would be imminent. So the exodus continued. Atwater says:

> If they had known that several wealthy merchants of London, inclined to non-conformity, had embarked their whole estates in the *Hector*, and were intending to go to New England with their families to find there a permanent residence, they would have found means to frustrate the undertaking. The number of nonconformists fleeing the king's rule grew so large by spring 1637, the king commanded that no one should leave without first taking oaths of supremacy and allegiance and conform to the discipline of the established church. By now, a feeling of desperation was overtaking the Puritans around Kent and even the royal proclamation from the king couldn't keep them from leaving.

Hurry Up and Wait

Dayton researchers should take particular note of the significant events over the next two years, as they begin to present possible scenarios for the Dayton crossing.

On July 26, 1637 the ship *Hector* again made landfall at Boston Harbor with Rev. Davenport aboard and, it is believed, members of his London congregation and wealthy merchants. Shortly before the *Hector* had set sail, a large group from Kent and Herefordshire joined the company which forced them to arrange for a second vessel to accompany the *Hector* on her voyage. Unfortunately, even the accompanying vessel was not adequate to accommodate the large numbers wishing

---

[127] Ibid.
[128] (Nicholas 1636/37)
[129] Ibid.

to leave. Atwater says, "Their departure was so hasty that many who wished to go were forced to wait for another opportunity, and came out two years afterward in the first ship which sailed from England direct to the harbor of New Haven."[130]

Meanwhile, other groups in the Thames River area continued to leave. But in March of 1638, the Privy Council ordered that eight ships on the Thames, full of passengers and bound to New England, be detained.[131] All objections against them were then answered by Mr. Godfrey, who lived remote from them, where all had taken the Oath of Allegiance and Supremacy; so that upon his plea, the order was rescinded and all the ships were cleared.[132]

On the 6th of April, in the same year, an order in council was passed that no person should be allowed to go to New England without a license. In consequence of this order, "many persons embarked ostensibly for Virginia, but really for Massachusetts." Again, the sense of urgency was validated as, "the strictest watch was placed upon all emigrants..."[133] Atwater speaks of the situation:

> Many found no difficulty in obtaining a bona-fide certificate of conformity, and it does not appear that any objected to the oaths of allegiance and supremacy. If unable to obtain a certificate from the minister of the parish where they had lived, they came, some clandestinely, and some under borrowed names and corresponding passports... If ever lists of the passengers in the *Hector* and her consort should be discovered, they will probably not contain the name of John Davenport or of Samuel Eaton.[134]

Is it possible then, even if passenger lists are found for the vessel that carried the Daytons, the family might not be identified because many escaped after April of 1638, concealed under borrowed names and authorization? Later a theory will be developed that the Dayton family crossed in 1639 but, considering these circumstances, the particulars of what really happened might never be known.

Whenever the Daytons were finally able to make their escape, especially if they departed in 1638 or 1639, the monetary expense must have been quite high, with estimates for a party of 10 traveling aboard the Ship *Jonathan* in 1639 from England at £76.8.0,[135] roughly the equivalent of at least three years' salary for a craftsman, working 6 days per week.[136] For a tenant farmer, the cost was much more burdensome

---

[130] (Atwater 1902)
[131] (Felt 1855)
[132] (Gardener 1660)
[133] Ibid.
[134] (Atwater 1902)
[135] (Powell 1963). 215
[136] Note: Calculated estimate taken from the website (The National Archives)
http://www.nationalarchives.gov.uk/currency

and often required payback by indenture upon arrival. Of course, this bill probably does not include any costs obtained acquiring covert documents. David Hackett Fischer, in *Albion's Seed*, said,

> The cost of outfitting and moving a family of six across the ocean was reckoned at £50 for the poorest accommodation, or £60 to £80 for those who wished a few minimal comforts. A typical English yeoman had an annual income of perhaps £40 to £60. A husbandman counted himself lucky to earn a gross income of £20 a year, of which only about £3 or £4 cleared his expenses. Most ordinary families in England could not afford to come to Massachusetts.[137]

Despite the hardship and sacrifice, the Dayton family made the voyage, probably all traveling together since there is no evidence to the contrary. Ralph's family would require passage for at least six including himself, wife Alice and children Alice, Samuel, Ellen and Robert. The Dayton family might have departed from the Thames in London where they, along with their group, would have had to find accommodations for themselves and any belongings until departure, making the financial burden sizable. Just as likely, the family could have left England from any one of the southeast ports such as Sandwich, where Dr. Comfort Starr and family and perhaps Thomas Osbourne of the same St. Mary's parish at Ashford had departed aboard the *Hercules* in 1634/35.[138]

Ralph probably carried little more than the supplies required to immediately sustain the family. But anything not carried with them from England would have to be purchased at extremely high cost upon arrival. Considering the challenges and uncertainties of the ordeal, it is understandable why parish families determined to travel together, relying on and supporting one another and perhaps sharing supplies to supplement their needs.

Records prove that at least five members of the family made it to New England. Eldest son Ralph Junior did not accompany his parents and, even though no records were found for Ralph Senior's wife Alice, the absence of record does not dictate her death. Instead, it is logical to assume that Alice was with the family since no record of another wife seems to exist for almost 15 years after the family's arrival. Ralph's wife [no name provided] was finally mentioned in 1653/54 when Robert received land in East Hampton. As for the children, since all who crossed were minors at the time, it is easy to accept their omission from the earliest New Haven record, since omitting minors (and women in general) from official records was still largely the practice of the day. Admittedly, most troubling is the complete omission of the name of Ralph's wife Alice in the records, from the crossing even to her death. This explains why some theorize that Ralph and sons journeyed without Alice and the girls.

---

[137] (Fischer 1989)
[138] (Starr 1879)

In New England, the first record of progenitor Ralph is found in 1639 or 1640 (debated), when husband and wife were more than 50 years old, Alice probably being slighter older than Ralph. Their eldest child Ralph Junior, their only adult child in 1639, decided to remain at Ashford for his lifetime. The second oldest was daughter Alice who was about 19, son Samuel was about 15 or 16 at the time of crossing, daughter Ellen, about 13 (not mentioned until her father's death), and youngest child Robard [Robert], was roughly 10 years of age.

Considering his responsibilities of family and unconventional age for relocation, we believe it is difficult to conceive or defend any other reason why Ralph would undertake the perilous journey, to a foreign land and uncertain future, if not for conscience and duty to God. While there is no way to know Ralph's heart, considering the risk and sacrifice, it is not likely that he would have exiled himself and family from their native land, and undertaken the pursuit for anything less.

Chapter 5

Some Parts Beyond the Seas

Massachusetts Bay or New Haven Colony?

That Ralph Dayton immigrated through Boston has been a fairly consistent ingredient of his story, at least since 1849 when the esteemed Henry P. Hedges declared it in his address, delivered at the bi-centennial anniversary celebration of the settlement of East Hampton. Quite early in his speech, Hedges proclaimed, "Ralph Dayton came from England to Boston and thence here."[139] At the end of the nineteenth century, author George Howell acknowledged Ralph's time at New Haven but clung to the claim that Ralph was at Boston, "Ralph Dayton was for a short time a resident of Boston, from whence he removed to New Haven in 1639."[140]

In the twentieth century, Laura Fessenden not only asserted the view that Ralph arrived at Boston in 1636, but she also advanced the idea that Ralph traveled with his brothers, perhaps settling at Lynn.[141] The Daughters of the American Revolution improved on Howell, saying that Ralph, "removed from Boston to New Haven in 1639, thence to South Hampton, Long Island."[142] Twomey ignored New Haven but said, "…Dayton had but a short time arrived from England, and learning on his landing in Boston that a settlement by his friends was undertaken on the east end of Long Island, he immediately proceeded there."[143] Among other assorted tales, Ralph's adventures in Boston advance in repetition with immunity, made possible by means of the internet. A more outrageous example of unfounded claims, pulled from the multi-volume work by Lewis Publishing *Hudson-Mohawk Genealogical and Family Memoirs*, states without reserve,

---

[139] (H. Hedges 1897)
[140] (Howell 1887). 229
[141] (Fessenden 1902). 136
[142] (Bouron 1900). 140
[143] (Twomey 2001). 128

In America the family begins with Ralph Dayton and the year 1636. He was born in St. Martin-in-the-Fields, London, England 1598; married there Agnes, daughter of Henry Pool, and by her two sons, Robert and Samuel. After the death of his wife he immigrated to New England (Boston).[144]

Since all these historians seem to know that Ralph landed in the vicinity of Boston Harbor, we set out to locate their source, but none could be found. Could it be that all had just assumed that Ralph landed at Boston, without consideration of other possibilities? After all, Boston was still the primary port of entry for New England, especially for the English Puritans, and numerous Kentish dissenters are found in or near Lynn, Massachusetts. Consequently, it is not surprising that Lynn (known as Saugus until November of 1637), the logical choice, was declared with confidence and it may seem almost foolish at first to even question it.

Wherever the Daytons made landfall, there is good reason to believe Ralph was among members of his Ashford congregation or like-minded neighboring communities until he made his way to Quinnipiac. By itself, the strongest evidence that Ralph did land at Boston is the fact that some Ashford acquaintances were found there and they likely made the journey, "between 1635 and 1639."[145] Other connections between Ralph and communities in the Massachusetts Bay area must also be acknowledged. Kent records show that Ralph's stepdaughter Bennet married Thomas Standley Aug 3, 1630 and the Kent Archaeological Society tells us that Bennet Tritton Stanley immigrated to New England with Thomas Stanley in 1634. Since this could have been as long as six years before Ralph followed, there was plenty of time for Bennet's reports of life in New England to make their way back to her mother and stepfather. Even though settlement "beyond the seas" often meant that family members would forever be separated, perhaps these messages were an encouragement to Alice and Ralph to undertake the odyssey.

There were also perhaps distant relatives already in Massachusetts like Francis Dighton Williams, through her father John Deighton of Uley, Gloucester. Although this line, still with Deighton surname, was not preserved in America, a form of the name might remain because it is said that the city of Dighton,[146] near Taunton, was named in honor of Francis. Her father's will, proved May 21, 1640 in England, mentions eldest son John who remained in England[147] and the three daughters who

---

[144] (C. Reynolds 1911). 1751
[145] (Frost 1912)
[146] (Emery 1893). 82
[147] (Roberts 2004). 259-261

settled in the area of Boston:[148] Jane,[149] Frances,[150] and Katherine.[151] [152] This information indicates that other Deightons, outside Ralph's immediate family at Ashford, were also Puritans and married into Puritan families. But still, none of the relationships indicate that Ralph landed at Boston.

The strongest argument for Ralph at Boston then, it seems to us, is the fact that congregations often traveled together and Kentish men, some from the Ashford and Hothfield congregations, are discovered to have been at Boston and Lynn in the mid-1630's. Unhappily, it has been reported that sometime after 1715, nearly all the early official record at Lynn had been lost[153] so if Ralph had been there, it might be difficult to prove.

Some effort was exerted to trace and document movements of other Kentish immigrants, especially from Ashford and surrounding parishes, in the hope of finding circumstantial evidence pointing to Ralph's probable entry point. The project quickly extended to include Puritan families from the south and the east of Britain and included many of the families that eventually show up at Quinnipiac, Southold, Southampton, North Sea and East Hampton. It was then apparent that in order to perform an adequate analysis, worthy of serious consideration, a great deal of additional effort would be required to accomplish the task. As a result, the project was abandoned for lack of time even though it is worthy of someone more skilled than ourselves.

As just implied, our preliminary findings were deemed of little value because, of those claimed to have been at Lynn, later planters of Southampton, or the original nine at East Hampton, there seems to be little commonality of location in the Old World. To complicate matters further, the known Kentish immigrants to the New World are scattered amongst numerous New England communities. It appears that they "trickled" out of their Old World communities, perhaps beckoned by personal reasons rather than a communal exodus organized by a charismatic leader. These preliminary findings seem to be at odds with what seems to be popular belief but obviously the study has not been adequately developed to form a conclusive hypothesis. This type of study should be extended to include all Kentish emigrants to Quinnipiac, Southampton, and East Hampton. As at least one expert advocated, it

---

[148] (Weis 2004). 90, 139, 177.

[149] (Roberts 2004). Note: Jane Deighton also migrated to Boston 1637-1638, died Boston after 1671.

[150] (Weis 2004). Note: Frances Deighton/Dighton d. Taunton MA Feb 1705

[151] Note: Catherine Deighton April 14, 1644 Boston MA married Thomas Dudley, son of Captain Roger Dudley and Susanna Thorne.

[152] (Ancestors of Gregory Thomas Wirt 2013)

[153] Note: Although nearly all Lynn records were lost, the town grant of 1638 has been found. The 1661 Essex Court case of William Longley (or Richard Langley) v Town of Lynn for land he claimed was granted to him by the town. One of the documents in the case was the 1638 town records of the complete town grant of 1638.

would be of great value to Dayton history if gifted and determined researchers would meticulously trace and document movements of other Kentish immigrants such as Richard Brook, Thomas James, (James left the colony in 1645) Benjamin Price and John Osbourne, especially from Ashford and surrounding parishes.

To believe that Ralph landed at Boston around 1639 is at first both easy and logical, but using the argument as some do that the first six of the original nine settlers of East Hampton, NY came from Lynn, Massachusetts and some had been from the area of Ashford, Kent[154] does nothing to support the theory that Ralph was ever at Lynn. What can explain the fact that Ralph and Thomas Baker joined this group who were already at East Hampton after Ralph had been in New Haven for ten years? Despite the consensus of belief, the lack of original source documentation or any other evidence that Ralph was first in the Massachusetts Bay causes us to pursue other possibilities because it is quite possible that Boston was not his destination.

Quinnipiac

Beginning with what can be proven, that Ralph was at Quinnipiac (now New Haven, CT) possibly as early as 1639, we traced backward, to try to understand how he got there. Most interesting are the references to Kentish Puritans arriving at Quinnipiac directly from their homeland in 1639, bypassing Boston for the settlement in Connecticut. Perhaps Ralph came a little bit later than many of the Kentish immigrants to Boston, and sailed directly to Quinnipiac, where the voyagers knew many who had already migrated. This scenario, of course, creates another set of questions but, for now, circumstances around Kentish immigrants in 1639 and the very first year Puritans who sailed directly from England to Quinnipiac will be explored.

The English had become acquainted with the land beyond the Connecticut River during the Pequot war in 1637, when the Native Americans fled south and west, along the sound. The Europeans, in pursuit, found the land and harbor at the mouth of the Quellipioak River particularly desirable and in a letter to Gov. Winthrop, Captain Stoughton said, "The providence of God guided us to so excellent a country…"[155]

By 1637, Davenport, Eaton and the more recently-arrived company shepherded by Peter Prudden in Massachusetts saw opportunities to establish a new colony, being ready to leave crowded Boston whose religious climate, some perceived, had become polluted. Upon hearing about desirable lands along the Connecticut River, Davenport sent an advance company to explore and select a suitable location to establish their new colony. The explorers selected a place called Quinnipiac, about 30 miles beyond the mouth of the Connecticut River and left a small group to remain there through

---

[154] (H. Hedges 1897)

[155] (Hutchinson, A Letter from Captain Israel Stoughton to the Governor of Massachusetts 1865). 70

the winter, near the harbor, in effect staking their claim in preparation of the main company to arrive in the spring.

In March or April of 1638, Rev. Davenport, with about 500 Puritans, sailed from Boston into Long Island Sound and arrived at their new home, Quinnipiac. That summer and fall were spent building houses to establish a more permanent colony, in preparation for all those expected to join them. In November they entered into an agreement with the Quinnipiac people who welcomed them as allies and sold the land in exchange for protection against the Pequots who were attacking them.[156]

Meanwhile, the preaching of another of Davenport's friends in England, the Rev. Henry Whitfield, had aroused the indignation of the high churchmen. Rather than face another censure, in 1638 Whitfield resigned his position as Vicar of Ockley Church and became an itinerant preacher traveling to parts of southern England. Like many of the charismatic ministers of the time, he formed a "Clerical Company" and gathered around him 25 families of young people, largely farmers of Surrey or Kent, to make plans to immigrate to the New World as a congregation.[157] Writing in his *Ecclesiastical History of New England*, Cotton Mather said Whitfield, "came over to New England in the year 1639, with a multitude of poor people, out of Surrey, Kent, and Sussex, who could not live without his ministry."[158] One wonders what percentage of the Whitfield people were actually "poor," and what was Mather's motivation to deride Whitfield's work by belittling his followers?

In his book, John Brooks Threlfall states [Rev. Whitfield] sold his personal estate…probably went to London and made contact with the Coleman Street Puritans…and formulated a plan for another expedition to New England.[159] Whitfield, his wife, and [at least] fifty others, including parishioners from Ockley and Coleman Street, Surrey and Kent, together with John Davenport's young son, set off across the Atlantic, to Davenport's new colony.[160]

Before the first of the Whitfield fleet arrived at New Haven at the beginning of June, the men aboard pledged their lives and futures toward the good of the entire party by signing the Plantation Covenant, dated June 1, 1639.[161] They were welcomed, upon arrival by Davenport, himself at New Haven, who proclaimed their ship to have been, "guided by God's hand to our town."[162]

No record indicating the total number of ships in the Whitfield fleet has been found, but apparently there were a relatively large number of immigrants in their company, possibly including others whose departure had been delayed. Davenport

---

[156] (Nash 1853).
[157] (Doude 1885)
[158] (C. Mather 1820)
[159] (Threlfall 1970)
[160] (Carpenter 2005)
[161] (Atwater 1902)
[162] (C. Mather 1820)

indicates in his July 28, 1639 letter to friend Lady Mary Vere who was still in Britain, that there were at least three ships in the Whitfield group. In the letter Davenport says, "…the ship came in, guided by God's own hand to our town. The sight of the harbor did so please the captain of the ship and all the passengers, that they called it the Fair Haven. Since that, another ship hath brought sundry passengers, and a third is expected daily."[163] In this same letter, Davenport indicates that Whitfield's is the first vessel to sail directly from England to Quinnipiac.

Atwater provides a list of 24 men who are believed to have arrived on the second ship[164] but the ships of that period would have accommodated approximately 100-125. "Unfortunately, information on women, children, indentured servants and males who are disenfranchised is limited."[165] Atwater says: "As the first ship brought only twenty-three of the first planters of Guilford, we must conclude that the others arrived in the second or in the second and third ships mentioned in Rev. Davenport's letter. If the first ship arrived in June, the second early in July, and the third soon after the date of the letter, it can be concluded that only preliminary steps were taken for selecting a site previous to the arrival of the last division of their company." Soon after all had arrived, a meeting was held in Mr. Newman's barn to form a government for the colony.

What is found thought-provoking is the fact that, given all that has been recorded of Davenport and company in Quinnipiac, almost nothing is known about the ships that followed Whitfield's arrival, bypassing Boston. Much of what is known of their existence comes from a single personal letter, not a chronicle, and if not for the residual content in the letter, the fact of these ships might have been lost to history. Does this indicate that there were probably many ships arriving at this time, supplying the settlements, most of which are not recorded in history? It appears, from the 1639 letter, that in addition to ships arriving from Boston, vessels were also arriving directly from England, perhaps more than one per month.

Since Ralph probably sailed in 1639, while ships were arriving at Quinnipiac directly from England, we see no reason why landfall at Connecticut isn't as likely as Boston. Of course, we are aware that this thesis may not be supported by the majority, so it was encouraging to learn that Isabel Calder had (long ago) suggested the same hypothesis. Calder said,

> In the two vessels which followed came…possibly David and Joshua
> Atwater of Royton in the parish of Lenham and Ashford, and Ralph
> Dayton of Ashford, Kent…acquiring the Indian title to Menunkatuck,
> strikingly similar to the rolling hills of Surrey and Kent from which they

---

[163] Note: Davenport letter to Lady Vere, Quinnipiac, CT. July 28, 1639
[164] (Atwater 1902)
[165] (Carpenter 2005) Comments by Michael McBride, curator of the Rev. Whitfield House Museum appear on the website.

came, the Whitfield company founded the plantation of Menunkatuck or Guilford, in its symmetry resembling New Haven. The group soon lost Thomas Naish and his family, the Caffinches, the Atwater's, and Ralph Dayton to New Haven.[166]

Calder had not agreed with Edward Atwater who claimed that the Atwaters came over in 1637 with Davenport. Solid evidence to support Calder's statements about the Atwaters or about Ralph was not found so we wonder what made Calder specifically choose Ralph Dayton to include in her list of whom she believed might be aboard.

"We came out of England in the year 1639"

As is generally agreed, the initial landed record of Ralph is his signature "Ralfe Dayghton" appended to the June 4, 1639 *Fundamental Agreement of the New Haven Colony*. A rather poor image of the autograph can be seen in the 1896 Myron A. Munson book about Captain Thomas Munson[167] so a cleaner re-creation is provided:

Figure 7. Autograph of Ralfe Dayghton from Fundamental Agreement

Since Ralph was among a second group of men who added their names sometime after the original document was created, they probably departed England, on the two month journey, sometime after the beginning of April, but before October. This timeline assumes Quinnipiac, and not Boston, was their desired port of entry. Alternatively, because the year 1639 extended to the end of March (using the old style calendar), it is possible but not probable that the Daytons left as late as March of 1639/40 and arrived about May of 1640. Either way, our relative assurance of a 1639 departure is based on the following five pieces of reasoning:

The centerpiece of our argument for a 1639 crossing is a handwritten record found inside the Baker family bible, belonging to Ralph's son-in-law, Thomas Baker. This bible is currently preserved in the Long Island Collection, housed in the East Hampton Public Library (all bible photos are courtesy of EHPL).

---

[166] (Calder 1934). 73
[167] (Munson 1896)

Figure 8. Thomas Baker family bible

Thomas was born in Hothfield, Kent in the parish of Ashford, where his October 1618 baptismal record is found at St. Margaret's Church. Thomas was the husband of Alice Dayton, Ralph's oldest daughter. One of the proofs of Thomas's relationship to Ralph is his testimony in a deposition taken November 13, 1657, that his, "…father in law, Ralph Daiton, had a coulte come of his mare wch had white feete & white about the face & walle eyes…"[168]

In the bible is a handwritten record, presumably in Thomas Baker's hand, stating "*we came out of England in the year 1639*" (photos courtesy of EHPL). The sentence can be found in the top half of the page (see arrow drawn in figure 9). While there might be a question of who "we" was referring to, it is reasonable to assume that Thomas was speaking for both himself and his wife Alice many years after the fact. Alice was probably making the voyage with her own family in the same year, conceivably months after Thomas. The voyage was about four years before their marriage, as recorded just below the records of birth for Thomas and Alice and above the "*we came out of England*" statement, and says, "*Thomas Backer and Alys his wife was married the 20 of June 1643.*" These two statements are believed to be the first and original entries on the page. Both entries appear to have been written in frail hand, perhaps when Thomas was either aged or had declining eyesight.

---

[168] (H. Hedges 1887)

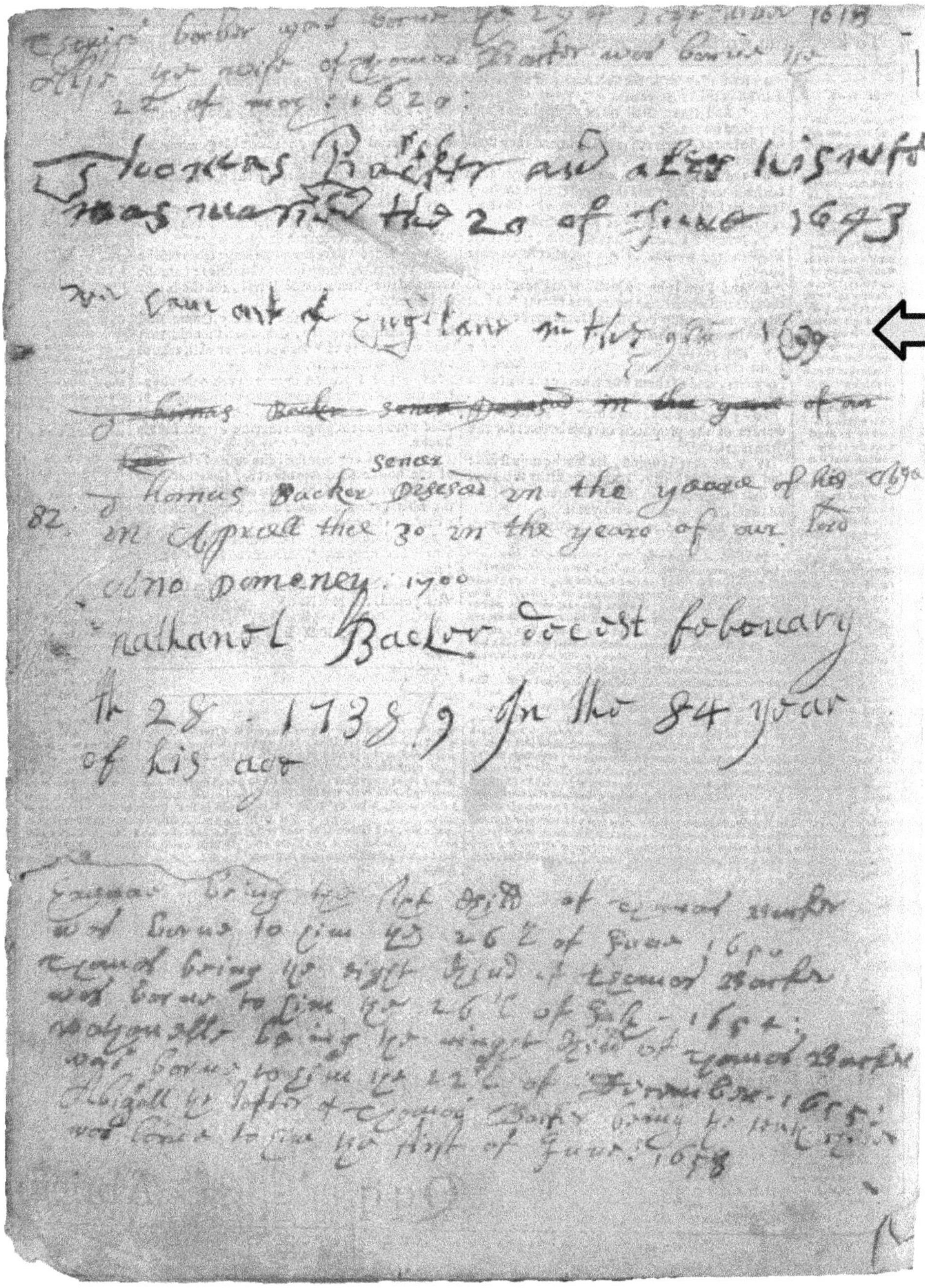

Figure 9. Family registry in Baker bible

It is interesting to note the writing of multiple generations on that single page, establishing an official record and a primary source, should the reader agree that the events were recorded close enough to the time of the event. In his chapter entitled *Entries in bibles—Inscriptions, etc*, Thomas Coventry says, "The circumstance of an

57

entry being in a family bible, to which all the family have access gives it a credibility."[169]

At the top of the page are the records of the birth of Thomas in 1618 and Alice in 1620. Obviously, these were recorded in the New World, and not by Thomas's father in England, who might have been the original owner of the bible. However, since it cannot be determined that any of the writing in the bible belongs to this Thomas Senior of England, it can be argued that Thomas may have purchased the costly bible sometime after his arrival in Connecticut or at East Hampton. At the bottom of the page is a listing of the children of Thomas and Alice that appears, to our amateur eyes, to be the same aged handwriting as that at the top.

It might be important to some that an irregularity is noted—the insertion of the identifier "senior" above the name of, "Thomas Backer deceased." The reader should be aware that Thomas Baker was actually a "junior," even though he was never referred to as such because his father remained in England. Therefore Thomas Baker III was referred to as "junior" and his father Thomas Baker, husband of Alice Dayton, was labeled "senior" in this bible. As the bible was handed down, either to Thomas or to Nathaniel, both sons of Thomas and Alice, one of them probably recorded their father's death, *Thomas Backer disesed in the year of his age 82 on April the 30 in the year of our Lord Ano Domeney: 1700,"* to which the word "senior" was added.

Below the notation of Thomas's death is the record, *"Nathaniel Baker decest [deceased] February the 28 1738/9 In the 84 year of his age,"* presumably written by the great-grandson of Thomas Senior. At the bottom of the page, there appears to be a record of children born to Thomas and Alice in 1650, 1654, 1655 and 1658, all in the hand of their father. This unmistakable handwriting matches the 1673 letter written by Thomas to Anthony Brockholles, the frontispiece of *Baker Ancestry*, compiled by Frank Baker.

The Baker family bible is a Geneva Bible, first printed in 1560 by English Protestants who had fled to Switzerland to escape Queen Mary's persecution. Baker's Geneva Bible was printed 1599, 19 years before the birth of Thomas, so it is possible that the bible could have been a parting gift from his family. The mere fact that this footnoted translation of the Geneva Bible belonged to the family is an indication of Bakers Calvinist or Puritan disposition. The translation was completed by Calvinist reformers, very much disliked by Anglicans and King James I whose response was to commission his own "authorized version."

The second piece of evidence affirms the first. It is Nathaniel Baker's attempt to clarify that 1639 is the correct year for both of his parents, Thomas and Alice, to have come from England. The account is passed to us in Frank Baker's book[170] where the author presents Nathaniel Baker's entries in an "account book" written before 1739, the year of Nathaniel's death. At the time of Frank Baker's writing in 1914, the

---

[169] (Coventry 1832). 143
[170] (F. Baker 1914)

account book was in the possession of John Baker Strong, a descendant of Nathaniel, and the owner by inheritance of his farm at Amagansett in the town of East Hampton. The book or manuscript were not found at the Long Island Collection at East Hampton in the fall of 2012. An image of the actual accounts appears near the front of Frank Baker's book and below are some of the more pertinent lines recorded by Nathaniel:

Nathaniel Backer was bornd the 22 day of December 1655.

Katherine Backer the wife of the said Nathaniel Backer was bornd the 9 day of Aprill 1656.

This is the account when my father and mother came out of Ingland before they were married. They came out of Ingland in the year 1639.

My father and mother was married the 20 day ac June. 1643.

Nathaniel's use of a two-part account specifically connecting the phrases, "my father and mother" and "they" convinces us that he was saying that both his mother and father, "came out of Ingland in the year 1639." It is also significant that Nathaniel chose to use the word "account," implying that this was a chronicle or testimony given for the benefit of future generations, shortly before he died.[171] The children may have listened to their father and mother's stories of the "old country" and the long journey crossing the ocean.

The third support for 1639 is one mentioned earlier, the Isabel Calder statement in her book *The New Haven Colony*. Undoubtedly this is the weakest of the five because it appears to be conjecture.

In the two vessels which followed [Whitfield] came Samuel Desborough of Eltisley in Cambridgeshire, related to Oliver Cromwell by the marriage of his brother to Jane Cromwell, and probably himself already married to Dorothy Whitfield; John Stevens perhaps from Ockley; Jasper Stillwell of Dorking nearby; John Scranton, William Boreman, Alexander Chalker, John Johnson, Thomas French, Thomas Betts, all with family names found at Cranbrook; Thomas Relf, and John, Samuel, and Thomas Caffinch from Tenterden, a short distance to the southeast of Cranbrook; and possibly David and Joshua Atwater of Royton in the parish of Lenham and Ashford, and Ralph Dayton of Ashford, Kent.

Though the reason why Calder specifically includes Ralph in one of the two vessels sailing with Reverend Whitfield directly to Quinnipiac is not given, it is interesting that she names only two or three passengers from the parish of Ashford,

---

[171] Note: The image of the transcript can be found in Baker Ancestry (F. Baker 1914)

conspicuously culling the Atwaters and Ralph Dayton. It is also very curious that Calder has arranged possible passengers by distance from Ashford: Cambridgeshire 113mi, Ockley 80-90mi, Dorking 66mi, Cranbrook 18mi, Tenterden 12mi, Royton 10mi and Ashford. We do not understand the significance of this arrangement[172] or if this was intentional. It is duly noted that Calder's notion is generally rejected by Atwater chroniclers who claim David and Joshua Atwater at Boston in 1637 with the Davenports even though, like Ralph, Joshua was an aftersigner.

The fourth basis for the 1639 theory is the fact that Ralph's eldest son Ralph, cordwainer, and Susan Burr of Walmer (30 miles from Ashford) obtained a marriage license November 27, 1639, as recorded in the Ashford parish records at St. Mary's. By late 1639, son Ralph would have been at least 21, even though one record implies 22. Certainly Ralph and family were not among the first of their congregation to leave. Instead, they may have delayed departure as long as they could, perhaps waiting for their first-born son to become of legal age to own property and to establish his own means of income. The marriage probably occurred very near the time his family left for the Americas, though it is difficult to ascertain timing of events based on the questionable christening date of Robert, their eldest son.

Ralph's oldest son Ralph Junior remained in or near Ashford all of his life because parish records tell us that Robert Goldhatch, living in Ashford, named Alice's eldest son Ralph Junior as his executor about 30 years later. In the will of Robert Goldhatch (son of Robert) of Ashford, yeoman February 1668/69, Robert made Ralph executor and left, "to cousin Ralph Dayton, mess[173] & land in Ashford & elsewhere…and residue."[174] It is also known that Ralph Junior's family remained in the parish as Lee C. Baker in *Chronicles of Family Baker* says, "He was twice married and died on February 10, 1705/06 at the age of eighty-eight. His two marriages, his death and his wives' two deaths are also in the Parish Records…"[175]

It seems appropriate that Ralph Junior would have waited until he acquired a home and means of income before marrying. He was already called a shoemaker at the time he and Susan obtained their marriage license, and being the eldest son, he had probably been preparing to receive his inheritance at the departure of his father. This being accepted, it can be deduced that the family departed for New England late 1639. Both of Susan's parents were deceased before her marriage and no record of assets she brought to the marriage is found but, judging from Ralph's tax assessment twenty five years later, it appears that the couple were successful in his trade. In the

---

[172] (Calder 1934)

[173] Note: One translation of the word "Mess" in this quote means buildings, gardens, orchards etc—basically everything on land except land itself

[174] (Ruderman 2011)

[175] (L. Baker n.d.)

Lady Day Hearth Tax Assessment for Kent in 1664, he is responsible for a very large building containing seven fireplaces in, "the towne of Ashford in the Lath of Scray."[176] The hearth tax was a tax on the number of fireplaces in a dwelling, the intent being that one fireplace would represent one family unit. It would be significant to determine if this house once belonged to his father.[177] A structure with seven hearths was larger than most houses in Ashford at the time, so son Ralph could have achieved elevated status by 1664, or perhaps he owned an inn or tavern, or was a householder. According to a parish map produced by the Centre for Hearth Tax Research, only 6-12% of households had between 5 and 9 hearths.[178] If Ralph Senior had been in possession of the large dwelling at the time his family left, it is reasonable to imagine that departure was delayed in order to maximize his son's opportunities through his inheritance. By 1639, the number of parishioners in the Dayton family's local congregation was shrinking and conditions were worsening to the point where Ralph determined he should leave.[179]

The fifth reason is the fact that Ralph's autograph "Ralph Dayghton," is the earliest record of a landed Dayton and appears to be appended to the June 4, 1639 Fundamental Agreement at Quinnipiac (later New Haven Colony).[180] It would be a mistake to emphatically attribute June of 1639 because Ralph was actually not a member of the original group of 63, however his signature does indicate he probably was in the New Haven territory by May 1640. Because his autograph is among the second group of 48 names, we assume he arrived about the same time as some members of that group. It is likely that the common mistake (we believe) of dating his signature to June 4th is born from the belief that Ralph relocated from Boston, where he had been for a year or two. What is not explained by those who espouse that theory is why, if he was in Boston, he would delay departure for Quinnipiac and sign with the second group?

Reverend Sylvester Nash, among others, claims that the original document was copied, names and all, into the Book of Records and afterwards was signed by 48 "after subscribers," probably added within the year, perhaps in a few weeks.[181] Ralph was one of the 48 "after subscribers." Chapter 7 of Atwater[182] says:

> It was with the arrival of the second group, after the first division was ordered, a second allotment was made, disposing by portions of common property laying outside the squares. When a general court was held in

---

[176] Laths were units containing Hundreds, used for judicial and taxation purposes until sometime in the 18th century and are no longer used. The Lath of Scray contained over 400 square miles. (see Hearth Tax Online www.hearthtax.org.uk)
[177] (Kent Hearth Tax Assessment Lady Day 1664 2000). 217
[178] (Center for Hearth Tax Research 2010)
[179] (Beale Jr., The Law of Innkeepers and Hotels 1906).
[180] (Thorpe 2008)
[181] (Nash 1853)
[182] (Atwater 1902)

October of 1640, it was 'ordered that in the second division every planter in the town shall have for every hundred pounds of estate given in, twenty acres of upland, and for every head, two acres and a half.' (Note: 'upland' is land at higher elevation)

If the second division of land, occurring in October 1640, was also meant to accommodate the arrival of some in the second group (those who did not receive "freely assigned" lots), it would indicate that the second group may have arrived as late as summer 1640. Since the year 1639 did not end until March, the timing of the division may not conflict with Nathaniel Baker's account that his parents left England in 1639. Still, we have some uneasiness about suggesting that they would have attempted a winter crossing.

Is it plausible to think that Ralph arrived almost a year after the original group of 63 signed the Fundamental Agreement (i.e. leaving March 1639/40 and arriving 2 months later, in May of 1640)? Nash believed the original document has probably been destroyed so visual analysis is impossible. If we understand Nash correctly, he believed the original document was copied before the second group added their actual signatures, so it seems more probable that some time had passed. As stated in Charless,[183] it appears that Ralph's autograph was appended to the original Compact, perhaps in 1640/41. This, we believe would bolster the theory of the direct New Haven landing and the possibility of Ralph being aboard a later vessel with Whitfield affiliation.

It was in November of 1639 that Thomas Baker was allowed free planter status at Milford and the same record establishes its first members.

Thomas should not be confused with at least two others with the same name, all living in New England at this time. Our Thomas, from Hothfield in Kent, and of Milford, Connecticut and East Hampton, Long Island, can actually be made distinct from the other two because he can be followed almost continuously and appears to relocate only twice after the initial records at New Haven in 1639. Thomas seems to be most often mistaken for a Thomas Baker of Roxbury, Massachusetts but is probably also confused with a third Thomas Baker, a child, who arrived in Boston with his father, aboard *The Rose of Yarmouth* on April 8, 1637.[184] Most famously, he is improperly attributed as early freeholder and inhabitant of Southold, at the very same time he is actually well documented at Milford.[185]

Five weeks after Davenport and Theophilus Eaton's company landed at Boston in 1637, another ship arrived with a group headed by Peter Prudden, a native of Hertfordshire. We'll visit Prudden again in the next chapter.

---

[183] (C. J. Hoadly, Records of the Colony and Plantation of New Haven From 1638 to 1649 1857). 18.
[184] (Lewis Publishing Staff 1896)
[185] (Whitaker 1881)

The new arrivals stayed in the Massachusetts Bay Colony for almost a year but Davenport and Prudden desired to establish their own colony, and when the possibilities at the mouth of the Quinnipiac River in Connecticut were verified, they decided that was the place to found their colony. In April, 1638, Peter Prudden and a number of his followers sailed with the Davenport group from Boston, bound for the Quinnipiac. A separate allotment, known as the Hertfordshire section, was granted to them. They cleared the land, built houses, and planted crops. From April, 1638, to the fall of 1639, the Prudden group was a part of the New Haven Colony. During the summer of 1638 Mr. Prudden preached at Wethersfield, and there attracted a devoted following, many of whom wished to found a new settlement where he would be their pastor. This crystallized the movement to found a separate colony among the Hertfordshire group in New Haven.[186]

At the arrival of Mr. Whitfield and company who eventually settled Guilford, they combined in the Fundamental Agreement. Both the churches of Guilford and Milford may have been organized on the same day, in August 1639 at New Haven.[187] Of the original settlers of Milford, Thomas Tapping, Robert Treat, John Sherman, Thomas Tibbals, John Fletcher, George Hubbard, Richard Miles and Andrew Benton were Wethersfield recruits. Zachariah Whitman, Benjamin Fenn, and Thomas Sandford, from Dorchester, Massachusetts, and Thomas Baker is listed with John Astwood, John Peacocke, Jasper Gunn, John Burwell, and Thomas Uffot from Roxbury. We believe Thomas Baker was at Milford and should not have been placed with the group from Roxbury because it appears he has been mistaken with that Thomas Baker living in Roxbury. These joined the Prudden group and in late 1639 went to the mouth of the Wepawaug, 10 miles west of New Haven. "The Milford Colony was thus a settlement of Mr. Prudden's followers, recruited from towns in England and New England where he had preached, and held together by personal devotion to their leader."[188] The position of Thomas Baker's lot is illustrated in George Hare Ford's *Historical Sketches of the Town of Milford.*[189]

It would be a romantic notion to imagine Alice Dayton becoming acquainted with Thomas Baker during their long ocean voyage or in August at the time the young congregations formed at Guilford or Milford, but neither was probably the case. Instead, the Daytons probably arrived on a later vessel, perhaps 4 to 8 months after Thomas.

---

[186] (F. Harrington 1939)
[187] Ibid.
[188] Ibid.
[189] (Ford 1914)

Chapter 6

Uncertain Beginnings at New Haven Colony

Among the sources utilized, three works of particular note in our study of the New Haven Colony belong to Hoadly, Atwater and Calder. These, more than any others, were repeatedly consulted to build an understanding of the years Ralph lived in Connecticut.

A few years before 1857, hundreds of pages of the original manuscript of New Haven Colony records was transcribed and reproduced under the direction of Charles J. Hoadly, State Librarian of Connecticut. *The Records of the Colony and Plantation of New Haven from 1638 to 1649* was published and includes the first settlements within the Connecticut Patent, the plantations of New Haven, Guilford and Milford as well as Stamford, Southold (Yennycock) and Branford (Totoket) up to the year 1650. Of all the works by Edward E. Atwater, his 1881 book *History of The Colony of New Haven to its Absorption into Connecticut* was consulted and referenced most often, and Isabel M. Calder's *The New Haven Colony*, published in 1934, was most helpful.

Absence 1639/40 to 1644

There is no doubt that Ralph Dayton was in New Haven Colony within a number of months after its founding, marked by the establishment of the Fundamental Agreement. However, curiously, no record of Ralph has been found between the 1641 drawing for "small" lots and his 1644 signing the Oath of Fidelity, a period of much activity in the colony.

The lack of account probably would be of little concern if not for the numerous theories of the whereabouts of Ralph's son Samuel, he not being recorded in New Haven until 1645. Reports of Samuel on eastern Long Island as early as 1641 have grabbed our attention, especially since Samuel was only about sixteen years of age when the family arrived in Connecticut.

If the Dayton family ventured away from New Haven and returned by 1644 they were most likely at one of the nearby plantations of Guilford or Milford, or less likely, at one of the early settlements on Long Island. The old jurisdiction of New Haven consisted of six plantations, some trying to establish their own distinct governments, but became united in order to better protect themselves against the

Native American threat. The six settlements of the colony of New Haven were New Haven, Milford, Guilford, Branford, Stamford and the Southold areas on Long Island.

There is little to indicate Ralph's financial status upon arrival, but that Ralph was not wealthy by 1641/42 seems apparent by examining the lot drawn for him at New Haven. As disagreeable as the prospect may be for some to consider, the possibility that members of Ralph's family were placed in short-term indentured servitude upon arrival cannot be eliminated. Most of the early Puritans who had made the voyage could afford to pay their own passage, but for those later arrivals who couldn't, like some with large families, this arrangement of work in return for passage to America concluded after four or five years at which time they became admitted freemen.[190] The possibility that Ralph put Samuel to indenture or apprenticeship in Connecticut or on Long Island cannot be dimissed simply because, as will be discussed, at least two of the first three generations in our direct line of ancestry "disposed" sons to other households. Lacking the ability to provide for them in December of 1664, Samuel himself would be forced to dispose his young sons Caleb and Jacob when his first wife died. Later, just as his father had done, Samuel's son Abraham disposed his young son Caleb in 1696 sometime after his wife Mary died. The interested reader should observe that there is no mention of Samuel in the New Haven records until just after he becomes 21 years of age, by custom, the age at which sons become active in town records, but it was also the common age to end some types of indenture.

Atwater comments that the social importance of each of the proprietors of the town, so far as the measure of his wealth determined it, could be studied in connection with the location of his house lot. In the first division, the proprietors of New Haven had laid out the town plot in a nine section grid, between the two creeks, with sections divided out by streets. This occurred within the first year. Eight sections of the grid were set aside for compatible family groups and were further divided into house lots, with the center section left as a common area. The pioneers who had arrived in April were probably already living on their house lots by the approach of winter, so some left their temporary shelters for new arrivals.

Between the time of the first and second divisions, the proprietors so desired to increase the population, they "freely assigned" small plots outside the town to every householder who wished to become a permanent resident. Atwater tells us that, "Besides the home-lots assigned to proprietors, thirty-two 'small lots' had been freely given to as many householders, before the second division of out lands was made." The name *Goodm Dighton* appears in this list for lots drawn outside this town plot, along the West Creek. His inclusion clearly indicates that he did not hold right of commonage, having invested little or nothing into the common stock, and further indicates his relative lack of wealth and social status in 1642. Since it was not uncommon for a surrogate drawing to take place in anticipation of the recipient's settlement, we cannot be assured Ralph was in attendance or if he chose to accept the

---

[190] (Brooke 2004)

lot drawn for him, located with twenty-four others between George Street and West Creek. The fact that no records of Ralph have been found between his arrival and the 1641/42 drawing and then, from the drawing to 1644 does not necessarily mean he wasn't living at New Haven during these periods, nor does it rule out the possibility that he may have been elsewhere, although Ralph's name does not appear on the lists for Milford, Guilford, Southold or Southampton.

It is interesting to note that Ralph was one of only a few men in the list referred to as *Goodm* or *Goodman*, a title of address from England. No useful meaning can be attributed to the title in this case because, in New England, the title took on different usages before it disappeared altogether. Could this indicate he was among the craftsman class? When he was visiting the Plymouth Colony in 1632, Governor John Winthrop had publically implied that *Goodman* meant, "worth as a citizen capable of serving his community in civic matters" while some clergy argued against its use for non-church members.[191] The wife of a Goodman was referred to as *Goodwife*, but very often the term was abbreviated to *Goody*. Today, it is common for writers to think of a Goodman in more broad terms, implying a respected member of the community, ranking socially somewhere between a freeman and a gentleman. To our knowledge, while he was at New Haven, Ralph never attained the formal title of Gentleman, a title often attributed to an owner and renter of land.

Throughout the study of the first few generations in New England and on Long Island, the reader will repeatedly encounter the practice of distributing land by "drawing." Although there are no records found to describe the actual method utilized by the Puritans of Connecticut and Long Island; assuredly, drawing provided an orderly process for decision-making. The actual physical procedure utilized by Puritans could have involved the throwing or drawing of pebbles or straw, or some other form of lottery popular at the time. The drawing or casting of lots as a way to make a decision was a tradition mentioned dozens of times in the bible's Old Testament alone. By casting lots, sailors determined that Jonah was the cause of their calamity on the seas. In addition, quoting from their 1599 Geneva Bible, Joshua 18:10 says, "Then Joshua cast lots for them in Shiloh before the Lord, and there Joshua divided the land unto the Children of Israel, according to their portions." The Geneva Bible also includes an insightful footnote for that verse, "That everyone should be content with God's appointment," implying that the results of the drawing come from the divine will of God, and for them, a predetermined course. In her book *Researching Your Colonial New England Ancestors,*[192] author Patricia Law Hatcher suggests that the practice also had the effect of creating random initial settlement patterns.

---

[191] (Dossena n.d.). 235
[192] (Hatcher 2006)

In New Haven, the town plan was for merchants, investors and other primary men to receive their lots within the nine square grid, and subsequent drawings for surrounding surveyed lots were performed according to the needs of the settlement.

When the English settled in New England, they arranged their communities similarly to their English towns with farms outside of the village. In his book, Atwater[193] refers to what he calls, "…a curious essay on the laying out of towns" by an unknown author that is without address or date. The essay to which Atwater refers seems to have been written before the settlement of New Haven, but lays down the same principles as ruled in the laying out of New Haven. "The meeting-house is to be, 'the centre of the circumference.' The houses are to be orderly placed about it. Then there is to be a first division of land extending from the centre one-half the distance to the outside boundary, to be improved in the earlier years of the settlement, before the second division comes into use."[194] This appears to be the model followed in New Haven. For more detail of the drawing and distribution of lands, see Isabel MacBeath Calder's *The New Haven Colony*.[195]

The assignment of lots at New Haven was chronicled as follows (the bold is ours):

> The land for the small lotts on ye banke side and by ye west creeke was appoynted to be layd out, as their lotts were drawne in order as followeth.

Steven Metcalfe	Another lott
2 Adam Nicolls	Goodm Hames
3 Nath: Merryman	**Goodm Dighton**
4 John Tompson	Good Pigge
5 Bro: Kimberleys bro:	17 Francis Browne
6 John Nash	George Larrymo
7 Mrs. Swinton	Tho: Beam
8 Goodman Davis	Tho: Leaver
9 Rich: Newm	John Vincent.
Tho: Mitchell	Joh: Hall
Tho: Morris	Will Russells
Goodm Peck	Christopher Tod
25 Thomas Mounson	A bricklayer
Ben: Willmott	Obadiah Barnes
Joh : Walker	Eliz : the washer
Ben: Pauling	Will Gibbons [196]

---

[193] (Atwater 1902). 247
[194] Note: Mass Hist Col XL p474 referred to in (Atwater 1902)
[195] (Calder 1934)
[196] (C. J. Hoadly, Records of the Colony and Plantation of New Haven From 1638 to 1649 1857)

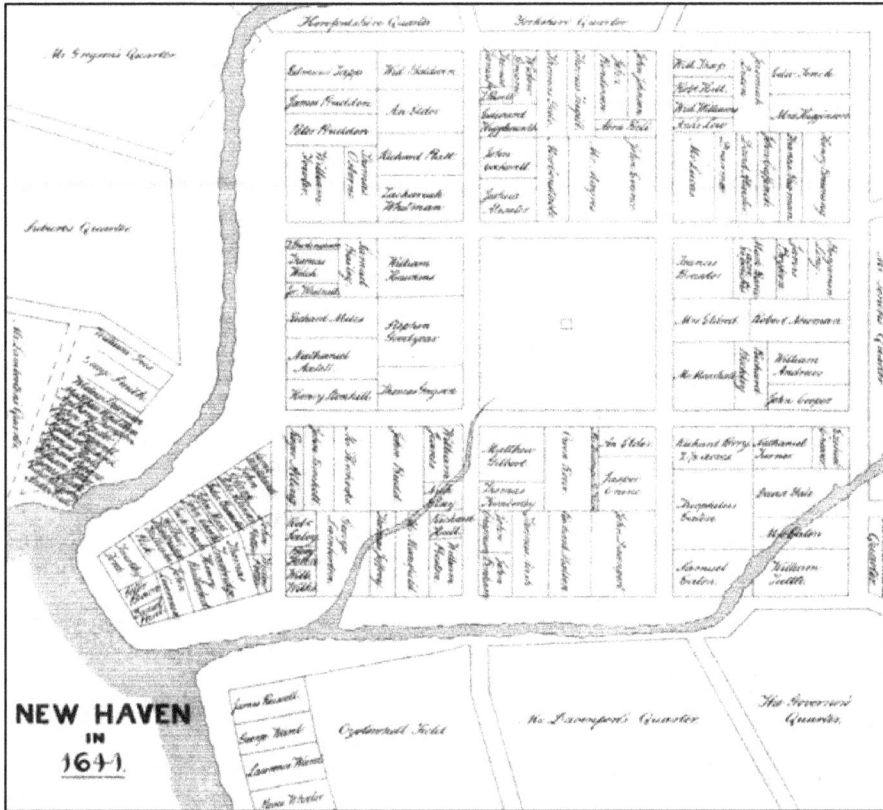

Figure 10. New Haven's Nine Squares and West Creek.

Brockett Map of 1641, New Haven Museum, New Haven Colony Historical Society

Only the general location of these lots can be identified today, but as Old West Creek no longer exists in New Haven, it is impossible to pinpoint the boundaries of the lots or to even imagine their appearance three hundred seventy five years ago. Today, a section of the creek bed is in the proximity of the 1.1 mile long Oak Street Connector, just as Frontage Street probably took its name from the old river bank. In the 1950's, the Connector project was partially conceived to replace old Oak Street (formerly Morocco Street) and rid the downtown of this very old and extremely poor area where leather workers had congregated along West Creek.[197]

A year after the first division among proprietors, unclaimed lots and other plots that had been drawn on behalf of those not yet arrived still remained empty and so it was proclaimed that these lots would remain reserved until the next ships arrived.[198]

---

[197] (New Haven Historic Resources Inventory Phase I: Central New Haven, City of New Haven Plan." n.d.)

[198] (C. J. Hoadly, Records of the Colony and Plantation of New Haven From 1638 to 1649 1857)

While this fact may not have any direct bearing on the distribution of "small lots" and Ralph, it does introduce the idea that Ralph may not have accepted his lot because, by some circumstance, he had gone elsewhere either before or after the drawing.

Calder seems to think that Ralph was in the Guilford group,[199] having come later and directly to Quinnipiac, but he was lost to New Haven shortly after the founding of Guilford. Guilford, just east of New Haven, was settled in 1639 by Surrey and Kent men, mostly farmers. Atwater has written, "As the first vessel is known to have brought about half of the Guilford families, the second would probably be sufficient for the transportation of the remainder. The third vessel sufficiently accounts for the presence at New Haven of the Southold Company…"[200] Atwater states that the accounting was unresolved, as the earliest Southold records are lost. If Ralph was at Guilford, he might have left before the official establishment of Guilford, because his name doesn't appear there. In fact, in 1639, forty planters are listed, but ten years later, there are still only forty-eight,[201] which leads us to believe that, despite the small increase, others left Guilford during this period.

On the other side of New Haven, to the west, was the settlement of Milford. Of the two, it is probably more likely that Ralph was at Guilford than at Milford since there are very few connections found except with Thomas Baker of Hothfield. Still, Thomas might be a significant consideration for determining where Ralph might have been in 1640 because he came from Hothfield, a community adjacent to Ashford, Kent. Milford men consisted largely of the Massachusetts group that followed Rev. Peter Prudden to New Haven, forming their church there, and another group from Wethersfield, Connecticut. Prudden had been preaching at Wethersfield, before the church there had filled their pulpit. As the Prudden group was looking to separate themselves and settle their own community, they were joined by others from Wethersfield who also wanted Prudden as their minister. Rev. Prudden's ordination as pastor of the Milford church came in April of 1640.[202] The core of original Milford settlers came from the area of Aylesbury in Buckinghamshire, Yorkshire and Herefordshire, where Prudden had preached. These are all some distance from Kent. Not being with either the Davenport group or the Wethersfield group, Thomas Baker seems to be an exception to those common origins. He was probably recruited in New Haven since he doesn't seem to belong to either group, being from Hothfield, near Ashford, Kent. Unlike the proprietors of the New Haven colony who were merchants

---

[199] (Calder 1934)
[200] (Atwater 1902)
[201] (H. Smith 1877). 89
[202] (Greene 1899)

from the area of London, the principle men of the Milford colony were workers of the land.[203]

The communities may have shared a meeting house in the beginning. The first meeting house in New Haven was built in 1640, Milford built theirs the following year and Guilford built theirs before 1646.[204] We wonder what role, if any, shared worship played in the eventual marriages of Alice to Thomas Baker of Milford in 1643 and of her sister Ellen to John Linley/Lindley of Guilford in 1645.[205]

On the other hand, in John W. Fowler's book, he tells us that the principle settlers of Milford were from Surrey, Sussex and Kent[206] when he proposed the idea that William Fowler's son may have left Guilford for Milford because of their previous connections with settlers there. Did Ralph attempt to do the same?

There has long been speculation that Ralph's son, Samuel had been on Long Island prior to 1645, actually before the first town record of him in New Haven can be found. This first town record was from June when, at about 21 years of age, he was called to a New Haven court, as were others, to answer an accusation of neglecting his responsibilities while on watch. This first account sets a period of about five years where the record of Sam is quiet, beginning at his theoretical arrival to New England, all the time still "not of legal age." The fact that the May 1648 Southampton record refers to Sam, "last lived at Flushing" has certainly helped to fuel speculation of an even earlier Long Island habitation.

There are actually many scenarios that could have directed Sam to Long Island, or even to the Cape May and Delaware Bay region of New Jersey when the Delaware Bay Company was founded in 1640. Merchants from the Colony of New Haven sought markets there to take up, "whatever opportunities the Delaware Bay had to offer."[207] Some of these theories have consumed much of our time and their studies are not fully included in this publication.

Most of those historians who placed Sam on Long Island very early have offered no evidence or source materials. In his book *The History of Long Island*, Benjamin Thompson provided a list of 47 people, including Samuel, who arrived within the first year [after 1639], but his claims have been refuted by Winans in his work *Early Southampton, Long Island, Inhabitants Lists*.[208] Winans was critical of

---

[203] Note: It is believed that traditional historians overestimate the percentage who practiced skilled crafts or were tradesmen, even upon arrival in the 1600's, but especially later when occupations are taken from lists such as the 1778 Oath of Allegiance where Long Islanders had incentive at time of war, to claim occupations the military needed at home.

[204] (Calder 1934). 90

[205] (Atwater 1902)

[206] (Fowler 1887)

[207] (History n.d.)

[208] (Winans 1911)

Thompson's list calling it, "artificial and based on inference." But even James Savage, former President of the Massachusetts Historical Society and Editor of *Winthrop's History of New England*, placed Samuel at Southampton in 1641,[209] supplying no sources. Our respect for these historians dictates our search for Sam and for clues and evidence that other pioneers not only came from Lynn to Southampton, but also from New Haven. John Rather in "Some Notable 'Firsts'; First Town Meeting," published Nov 15, 1998, *The New York Times* said of the early Southampton settlers, "[the] first South Fork settlers, [were] Puritans of rebellious Kentish stock..." Mr. Rather seems to be describing the likes of Sam, as some researchers have come to understand him.

There is an interesting account in the 1905 book, *The Post Family* where it is said that in June of 1644, "being of grete age," Arthur Post of Maidstone, Kent (near Ashford, Kent) disinherits his oldest son Richard, "being now of New England or some parts beyond the seas." The record of Richard in New England is first found with other settlers at Southampton in 1640 when Richard is about 23 years of age. The author of the Post book theorizes that when others from Lynn, Massachusetts migrated to Hartford, Connecticut with Rev. Thomas Hooker, "Richard Post evidently preferred to join the band going to Southampton." The author then provides the names of the settlers who arrived during the first twelve months and the list includes Samuel Dayton.[210]

To suggest that Ralph or Sam could have been at Southampton by 1640/41 may not be far-fetched when you consider one of the more popular and dramatic stories of English settlement on Long Island, the tale of the Lynn group who eventually settled Southampton. Governor Winthrop tells the story in his Journal and Governor Hutchinson, in his *History of Massachusetts*,[211] mention that in 1640, a number of families removed from Lynn Massachusetts to the West end of Long Island (probably Cow Bay in Manhasset) via Long Island Sound, having bought land there of James Farret, Agent to the Earl of Sterling. (The *Story of Bridgehampton* claims that the expedition occurred in 1639, not 1640, because the Dutch courts used their own calendar). The story continues that as they began to build their houses in territory that had been claimed by the Dutch, the "strollers and vagabonds" as the Dutch record called them, were detained and then forced to remove back to New Haven, to renegotiate with Farret for another location on Long Island. This time the group, who by now had grown in size, decided to move to the East end of Long Island, further distant from the Dutch.

In his book, Goddard[212] gives us a slightly different perspective and since we cannot improve on it, a lengthy quote from Goddard is provided:

---

[209] (Savage 1860)
[210] (M. Post 1905)
[211] (Hutchinson, History of Massachusetts 1795). 88
[212] (Goddard 2011)

The projected group of settlers met with James Farrett, probably at first in Boston and then later in New Haven, and agreed that they should plant themselves somewhere on Long Island. Between 1639 and 1640, Farrett gave them two and possibly three deeds, each of them slightly different, the last of which provided for an extremely generous sixty-four square miles of land ('eight miles square') between Canoe Place on the west and a line to the east extending south from 'Mr. ffarret's Island' (Shelter Island) to the ocean. (Farrett had mistakenly thought he had purchased the island for himself from its inhabitants, the Manhansett Indians. They later denied it claiming that they had merely let him live there.) This was a much larger tract than the Bay Colony was accustomed to granting, usually only six miles square or thirty-six square miles. The fortunate colonists then set sail from New Haven to North Sea Harbor in Peconic Bay with their families, belongings, probably a few servants, some essential livestock, building materials, and their copy of the Stirling patent. They arrived in June 1640. This story has been many times told and does not need repeating here but there is sufficient complexity in the events prior to the settlers' arrival in Southampton, as well as some problems with the dating of them, to suggest that there were at least two if not three failed attempts at Settlement in various Long Island locations before arriving at North Sea Harbor.

The Lynn group was much larger heading out for Long Island again, having gained recruits while at New Haven. The group drafted workers, servants and probably some adventurers. Sailing into Peconic Bay, they located an agreeable harbor at Conscience Point, North Sea (about 4 miles north of Southampton). Ogilby's *History of America*[213] says that the band of settlers were led by Native Americans from North Sea to a flat area near the ocean. "About the year 1640 a fresh supply of people…erected the town called Southampton, by the Indians, Agauam." Here they set up their first houses in an area later called Old Towne about ¾ of a mile east of present Main Street, near modern Southampton Hospital. The English were eager to explore Long Island and it was becoming an attractive option for settlement. Even before the original group from Lynn finished renegotiations with James Farret to settle Southampton, "a second group of settlers from Lynn came to settle at Oyster Bay. This second group was headed by Captain Edward Tomlins and his brother Timothy and was also quickly dispatched by the Dutch."[214] Perhaps Samuel took up with one of these groups or with a secondary group, delivering supplies to Southampton shortly after their 1640 landing.

---

[213] (Ogilby 1671)
[214] (Hammond 2003)

Many of these narratives tell us the Long Island-bound groups, headed for the north shore, spent some time at New Haven also. Was Sam recruited for the trip to Flushing or did Ralph join the group to Southampton in 1640? This idea is worthy of further research because this group from Lynn contained members later frequently interacting with Ralph Dayton.[215]

Attempts were also made to settle the south of New Jersey. *History of Cape May County* claims, "English colonists came from New Haven in 1638, to engage in whaling, and some of the descendants are among the present inhabitants of the country."[216] Was this the beginning of Sam's odyssey with the sea? Another publication suggests the first New Haven whalers even went to Cape May, New Jersey in 1640, and for a long time they sheltered their vessels there, not becoming permanent settlers until about 1685.[217]

> Besides the Quakers, Cape May included a number of New Haven people, the first of whom were there as early as 1640 under the leadership of George Lamberton and Captain Turner, seeking profit in whale fishing. They were not driven out by the Dutch or Swedes, as happened to their companions who attempted to settle higher up the river at Salem and the Schuylkill. About one-fifth of the old family names of Cape May and New Haven are similar, and there is supposed to be not a little New England blood not only in Cape May but in the neighboring counties of Cumberland and Salem.[218]

Paul Sturtevant Howe[219] says:

> Unlike the early history of the Pilgrim settlement at Massachusetts, the beginnings of history in Cape May County are involved in obscurity. No chronicler, like Governor Bradford, gives a complete history of the times, and the facts we are able to gather from diaries and records are fragmentary and disconnected. Until 1857 no attempt was made to write a history of the early days of the County, and to Dr. Maurice Beesley we owe the first outline—his careful work is still our authority for the period…The town of Southampton, Long Island, was settled in 1640, by colonists who came from Lynn, in Massachusetts Bay. Here the ancestors of many of the Cape May County families first came…the early history of Cape May is associated with the whaling occupation, and the first settlers came here in pursuit of that calling.[220]

---

[215] (H. Hedges 2001)
[216] (Heston 1924)
[217] (Planters and Traders of Southern Jersey 2006-2013)
[218] (Fisher 1920)
[219] (Howe 1921)
[220] Ibid.

Beginning with these and following with future generations, the Daytons would, in fact, become involved in whaling on Long Island and possibly at Great Egg Harbor, NJ.

Dayton Records in America

At this juncture, we pause to note how fortunate the descendants of Ralph Dayton are to have parish records in England and a number of town and court records in America, the bulk of which begin 1644 and proceed for generations on Long Island. The Puritans relied heavily upon public registers, town and court calendars to record abstracts, decrees, disagreements, transactions, taxation, regulations, maps and public registers containing earmarks. Analysis of these fragments enables us to peer into Puritan culture and the interaction of our ancestors with their communities. From this point, the remainder of the present compilation relies immensely on the records of the towns of New Haven, Southampton, East Hampton, and Brookhaven, and to a lesser extent, Oyster Bay, progressing chronologically through the records, as practicality allows.

Nearly every organized Puritan settlement kept careful public record. "The level of education and the quantity of writing the Puritans produced may have had a direct influence on the establishment of English as the primary language of North America." The *Norton Anthology of American Literature* continues,

> Since the English language arrived late to the New World, it was by no means inevitable that the English would dominate, even in their own colonies. But by 1700, the strength of the (mostly religious) literary output of New England had made English the preeminent language of early American literature. Boston's size, independent college and printing press at Harvard (founded in 1636), and non-nationalist, locally driven project of producing Puritan literature gave New England the publishing edge over the other colonies.[221]

Apparently, education was also important to the Dayton family. There is evidence to believe that every generation of our line on Long Island was literate, at least to the degree that they could read and write with some understanding, with the exception of Abraham whose abilities are questioned because he may have used a mark in place of his signature. For this, we reason that Abraham's schooling may have been interrupted by various family circumstances. To date, examples of original signatures for four of the first six generations have been identified. Almost nothing is known of formal schooling, but it is believed that each successive generation of men in our direct line of ancestry had some ability to read the Bible and it appears that at least Ralph, Sam, Henry and David Senior had enough ability to author documents, legal and otherwise. Although many records having to do with schooling

---

[221] (O'Connor n.d.)

and education on the East End were lost in the great fire at the New York State Library at Albany, we do know that the first school buildings were churches and many times the first teachers were ministers of the church. It also appears that many of the Dayton men paired themselves with strong, caring and dependable women. Not only do some of their wives appear to have been educated, but some also may have possessed strong moral character, equaling or exceeding that of their husbands' and many of the wives and mothers should be credited for the level of education the children received.

Ralph's deposition given February 8, 1654/55 is further evidence that he was literate. Ralph signed his autograph on at least two occasions, first to New Haven's Fundamental Agreement and he probably signed, though in feeble hand, his own will. In the February deposition Ralph states he was asked by John Cooper and Joshua Garlicke, "to make a letter of attornie." The ETR by Hedges says,

> The Deponant sayth that being at Josua Garlicks John Cooper. Coming in Desired A Lettr of attorney ffrom Josua Garlick about the payment of the boat which was to be payd part in Corne & otherwise According to their Discourse together whear vpon the aforesd John Cooper & Josua Garlick Desired the Deponant to make a Letter of attornie; but the Deponant Refusing of it the sd John Cooper; & Josua Garlick went to Giles Silvester for it to Lt Lion Gardeners & further the Deponant sayth not: this taken before Lion Gardener Robert Bond and Tho: Baker:

Sometimes the records can be bewildering, so we consulted Mr. Beverly Tyler, Three Village Historical Society Historian, writer and professional photographer. Mr. Tyler met us in the Emma S. Clark Memorial Library, across from historic Setauket Presbyterian Church, and he shared a bit of his knowledge and insight in response to our questions. We asked him about the significance of record and he gave us new perspective on seventeenth and early eighteenth century municipal documentation and testimony:

> …to have a record of whatever happened, I don't care what it was, it could be a horse dealing, it could be almost anything, you went to court and the court kept a record. The records of the town of Brookhaven and other towns are just loaded with this kind of thing because that is what you did, if you wanted it to be a record. If you had a property dispute, like even 6 inches or a foot or two feet, or a fence in the wrong place—you didn't go to court because you were nasty, you went to court because that was where things were written about and decided. So many people…couldn't write or read so they needed to go to court and have someone record the information for them and that became a permanent part of the town records.[222]

---

[222] (Tyler 2012)

Although the Puritans were an organized and prescribed society, it seems that records were not always arranged sequentially. They might have been reassembled at some point or transcribed to a different sequence. But this is understandable because the challenges of recording were often new to the recorder and methods and procedures were frequently experimental. In New England, the decisions of the Puritans were foundationally based on their interpretations of the Holy Scriptures, not on the ecclesiastical courts of the Church of England. Real property transactions, the transfer, setting and maintaining of boundaries represent a major portion of the official town records. Infringements and resulting land disputes presented new challenges for the early settlers of New England because back in Europe, ownership of land had been under the old feudal system.

One example of non-sequential records is the placement of a significant "schedule" of New Haven proprietors from its very first years. Atwater says this schedule was found among 1643 records but was probably prepared before the collection of the rate due in April 1641. In the schedule are found many names that have become familiar to us (Osborne, Goodyear, Miles, Tapp, Vale, Atwater), but Dayton is not there.

In our opinion, the first evidence that Ralph was living somewhere in Connecticut appeared on August 5, 1644, when New Haven Records indicate that Raiph Dightō was declared a free burgesse as the result of signing the Oath of Fidelity, a declaration administered by Governor Theophilus Eaton. But the fact that Ralph appears on the list does not confirm that he was a resident of the town at that time because Milford men are also found on the document. The account follows:

> The Governoʳ haveing allso received the oath of fidelity as followeth…promoting the publique good of the same whilest I shall continue an inhabitant there. And whensoever I shall be duely called as a free burgesse, according to the fundamentall order and agreemᵗ… to the best good of the same wᵗhout respect of persons, so help me God, &c. Then he gave itt to all those whose names are herevnder written…

Will White	James Bell	Joh: Benham
Raiph Lines	John Linley	Edw: Wiglsewor[th]
Robᵗ Bassett	Isaack Mould	Johnath: Marsh
Roger Knap	Joseph Alsop	**Raiph Dightō**
Robᵗ Mecar	Rich: Lambert	Mr. Bracie
Will Mecar	Edward Preston	Joh: Wakefi[eld]
John Beach	Edward Newtonl	Hen: Bish:p
John Hutchison	Will Bladen	Will Bradley
Joseph Peck	Rich: Webb	Abra: Stolyon
Tho: Robinson	John Mors	Geo: Warde
Will Fancie	John Kimber	Roger Betts.[223]

---

[223] (C. J. Hoadly, Records of the Colony and Plantation of New Haven From 1638 to 1649 1857)

As stated, Ralph's presence on the list, by itself, does not mandate his residency in any particular town. However, beginning soon after the oath, there is a procession of town records that involve Ralph which may indicate that the oath does, in fact, signal his arrival. If he had been absent before 1644, Ralph's return to New Haven probably occurred at least a few months before taking the oath. Ralph's daughter Alice had married Thomas in June of 1643 and the couple had, no doubt, returned to Milford where Thomas was well-established.

Thomas Baker would become an extraordinarily good friend and consistent ally to the Dayton family. We believe both parties were beneficiaries in this relationship, but clearly, Thomas demonstrated his loyalty and assistance time and time again, as examples inform us.

In March of 1644/45, about eight months after becoming a free burgesse of New Haven, Ralph went to the town officials and suggested a good place to graze the cattle, under or beyond the landmark known as West Rock, which was about 2.5 miles north and west of town. Today, the prominent feature is located within West Rock Ridge State Park.

Figure 11. West Rock

The painting of West Rock in figure 11 is by American painter Frederic Edwin Church, 1849 and is held in the New Britain Museum of American Art.

Just beyond the West Rock are a pond and lake, which certainly must have been a factor in Ralph's recommendation. Town officials then agreed that the area Goodman Dighton recommended should be viewed to determine if it was adequate for their needs. What incentive motivated Ralph to suggest this place? What were his intentions and under what circumstances did he become familiar with the area?

Less than two months later, May of 1645, Thomas Barnes went to court asking that Ralph compensate him for his cow that died while the herd was in the care of Ralph's son. This probably took place at the grazing ground recommended by Ralph. In a court held the 6th of May 1645,

> Thomas Barnes required satisfactiō of Raiph Dighton for a cow of his wᶜh perished as he conceives through his sons neglect who kept the heard thatt day, butt Ralph Dighton alleadged thatt a cow of thatt heard being swamped, his son came home to the towne to gett help, and left his partner wᵗh the cow in the interim, and before they had gott the cow out of the swamp itt was night and the heard was coming home, and they nott knowing of any dangerous place betwixt the bridge and the place where the cattell used to come over, did nott conceive itt necessary to follow the cattell, butt came over the bridge, and though they came on the other side of the river over against the place where his cow was afterwards found perished wᵗh her foote in a hole betwixt the banck and the roote of a tree, yett they did neither heare nor see her. Itt was testified by others that there was noe knowen place of danger in thatt place before menconed. The judgmᵗ of the Court was thatt itt was an afflicting providence of God wᶜh the said Barnes was to beare himselfe, and that the boy was innocent in the case.[224]

The "boy" was probably Robert, not Sam as some writers have proposed,[225] because Sam was probably twenty-one (baptized Feb 1623/24) while Robert was about fifteen (baptized Jan 1629/30). Since Ralph is the one compelled to court to answer for his son, it assures that his son was a minor at the time. The record provides no information about indenture, so we assume Robert and his "partner" were just fulfilling the family's responsibility, tending the herd, on the other side of the river, perhaps in that area near West Rock. Calder tells us that, "For about six months of the year the planters hired herdsmen to drive out and care for the milch cows, and either themselves took turns in driving the dry cattle to pasture or employed other herdsmen for that purpose."

June 1, 1645 is a significant date for it is the first time that Sam was mentioned in an "official" record in America, when he was 21. Just one month after Ralph's court appearance to respond to charges for Robert, the town record at New Haven says,

> Will Russells being mar of a watch, for suffering his watch to sleepe was fined 10s. The sentinell fined 5s and all the rest 1s a peece. John Hunter

---

[224] (C. J. Hoadly, Records of the Colony and Plantation of New Haven From 1638 to 1649 1857)
[225] Note: The common interpretation refers to Sam. Some renditions use the plural "his sons neglect" while others use the singular "his son's neglect."

fined 5s for neglecting his watch. Sam Dighton and Anthony Stevens respite.[226]

It was Anthony Stevens, the servant to Mr. Malbon, who was exhorted for his behavior by George Spencer, from the gallows, just before Spencer was executed.[227]

At this early time in the colony, it was required that many members of the community take their turns with the obligation of keeping watch. The admitted inhabitants ordered watches and wards to preserve the peace and provided armed guards during the church services. The watch often occurred inside a confined area like the town, after the animals were brought in for the night, for the purposes of safety.

Just how long Sam had been in town and what part, if any, he played in the offense for which they were charged are not known, but the charges against him and the charges against Stevens were suspended. The fact that Sam had just turned 21 years of age might bolster an argument that he may have just completed a period of indenture which many times was completed at age 21. He had probably only recently returned from somewhere outside this settlement, perhaps from Long Island, or he had been living with his sister in nearby Milford. His recent arrival might have temporarily afforded him a lesser amount of responsibility, especially since he probably hadn't yet been sufficiently armed, as we'll see, even by early 1646.

On October 22 of 1645, with the approach of winter, "Goodman Deighton [Ralph] was ordered to burne the playne with all convieneent speed." It is assumed that this was common pasture. It also is possible that he hadn't yet fulfilled his responsibility to take part in the burning of shared woodlands that neighbored his lands. To burn the undergrowth on the plain was the preferred maintenance method used by the Native Americans who had previously cleared the land. Typically, the reasons for clearing land in this manner would have been to improve the spring grasses, prepare it for cutting trees or planting in the spring, to fireproof the area or to control insects. It is interesting to note that there were fences close-by, suggesting that there were probably divisions of land in the plain or a highway passing through it.

If Sam had been residing in New Haven continuously since the June 1645 neglect charge, he was already there for about a year by early 1646 when the town record says, "Samuell Daighton wanting all amies [arms], but he being latly come to towne & at present provided, it was passed by." New Haven required all men to be furnished with adequate arms and ammunition, usually a gun and sword. When necessary, the particular weapon or items, like those desired by Sam, were provided by the town. In each area of the settlement, militia officers were ordered to inspect such arms at least quarterly, and to direct about six militia musters per year. If not

---

[226] (C. J. Hoadly, Records of the Colony and Plantation of New Haven From 1638 to 1649 1857)
[227] George Spencer, a servant, was described as a "habitual troublemaker" and is claimed to be the first non-native executed in Connecticut. More details of the charges against him are readily available.

80

exempted, any able-bodied man was fined if he failed to maintain his arms or to appear at musters. In fact, for many years, the Puritans were obliged to carry their arms to meeting but were not allowed to fire off charges on the Sabbath except for Indian or wolf.

Perhaps Sam received some relief of his charge because he had not yet declared his desire to become a resident, especially since there is no record of him owning land. Sam was yet to be established in the community and, whatever his real intentions were, Sam may have even been considered somewhat transient. The record implies that Sam probably did not reside there continuously after the initial court appearance in June of 1645 since he was still inadequately armed to comply with the order, without assistance. It is likely that court officials were of the opinion that Sam wasn't going to settle there so they weren't inclined to supply him. This uncertainty toward Sam might be explained if he had only been a frequent visitor, perhaps traveling between Connecticut jurisdictions, including settlements on Long Island. Perhaps this was a signal toward shunning if Sam hadn't followed protocol to procure permission to join the community. Less likely, Sam might have married by this time and brought his new bride back to New Haven, with the idea of settling there. If his wife was not of the Puritan group, the couple might have faced rejection. If she was not English, they could have faced hostility.

By October of the same year, less than one and a half years after Sam was first mentioned, the New Haven record tells us Sam, "was absent one squadron day and one Lord's day." He was to be fined 3 shillings 6 pence, "if he can not give satisfying answere." Apparently by October of 1646, Sam had accumulated enough time in New Haven to obligate him to civil responsibilities (usually about six months). We wonder if Sam had already tired of the community and perhaps he had already left New Haven because there is no recorded ending or conclusion to the action. At that time there was still fear of Native Americans and every able-bodied man from age 16 to 60 had to drill on squadron day. Perhaps Sam had not followed the existing procedure for leaving by not disclosing his departure to town officials.

By February of 1646/47 it was probably apparent to all that Sam was not returning, so William Meeker had an entry placed in the court record, that noted the loss of meal attributed to Sam. Meeker was probably either working at the mill where grains were ground or he was a transporter of grain because in October of 1646 he, "was propounded by the court to be loader to mill for a 12 month to goe in all seasons except vnreasonable weather."[228] The record says,

> Wm Meeker informed the court that 7 pecks of meale he hath received of Sam: Daighton, & that yet he doth want a sack & one peck, & he had order from the court to dispose of 6 pecks of meale, vntill the court se cause to order it to the partyes that did loose by Samuell Daighton.[229]

---

[228] (C. J. Hoadly, Records of the Colony and Plantation of New Haven From 1638 to 1649 1857)
[229] Ibid.

Lacking the ability to determine for certain what was explained in the court record, our thoughts and interpretations are offered. One possibility is that Sam had not paid for the grain Meaker had milled for him so Meaker was paid one peck as a down payment for his services and holding back 6 pecks in lieu of payment for processing them. Or, Sam might have been employed by the ferry man or as another transporter of grain across Long Island sound when some meal was lost or became contaminated. The British dry measure of a peck is 2 gallons so the small amount of meal lost could have been spillage.

To our knowledge, Samuel never returned to live at New Haven.

Order of Seating at the Meeting House

Atwater states that the first seating in the meeting house probably occurred in the first year or in 1640, when all the proprietors were placed. Alice Morse Earle tells us that it had become Puritan custom to sell "Spots for Pues." She says, "at first to some few rich or influential men who wished to sit in a group together, and each family of dignity or wealth sat in its own family pew.[230]

On March 10, 1646/47, a subsequent order of seating in the meeting house was read aloud in the General Court session, and on this occasion, included all heads of families.[231] The following is a lengthy summary of Earle's description of the Puritan process of selection, found in her amusing and informative book *The Sabbath in Puritan New England,*

> Perhaps no duty was more important and more difficult of satisfactory performance in the church work in early New England than 'seating the meeting-house.' Our Puritan forefathers, though bitterly denouncing all forms and ceremonies, were great respecters of persons; and in nothing was the regard for wealth and position more fully shown than in designating the seat in which each person should sit during public worship. A committee of dignified and influential men was appointed to assign irrevocably to each person his or her place, according to rank and importance. In many cases, the members of the committee were changed each year or at each fresh seating in order to obviate any of the effects of partiality through kinship, friendship, personal esteem or debt…A second committee was also appointed to seat the members of committee number one, in order that…there may be no grumbling at them for picking and placing themselves.

---

[230] (Earle 1891)
[231] (Atwater 1902)

The seating committee sent to the church the list of all the attendees and the seats assigned to them, and when the list had twice or thrice read to the congregation, and nailed on the meeting-house door, it became a law.[232]

Earle continues,

It is easy to comprehend what a source of disappointed anticipation, heart-burning jealousy, offended dignity, unseemly pride, and bitter quarrelling this method of assigning seats, and ranking thereby, must have been in those little communities. How the goodwives must have hated the seating committees! 'The inhabitants are to rest silent and sett down satysfyed.' Complaints and revolts were frequent...

It was found necessary, at a very early date to 'dignify the meeting,' which was to make certain seats, though in different localities, equal in dignity; thus could peace and contented pride be partially restored. For instance, the seating committee in the Sutton Church used their 'best discresing,' and voted that 'the third seat below be equal in dignity with the foreseat in the front gallery, and the fourth seat below be qual in dignity with the foreseat in the side gallery,' etc, thus making many seats of equal honor.

The public reading began with the Governor and then 99 men and 90 women listed in the congregation (not counting the clergy, trustees and a few other officials). Goodman Daighton's seating was given as the 5th row, "on the other side of the door," referring to the door on the side of the building. There were groups in front of the door, meaning to the front of the building, and there was a group of men situated beyond the door or, in the back. If the seating arrangements resembled Atwater's example chart of a typical meetinghouse[233] (see figure 12 for our rendering of Atwater's original), there were about six or seven rows, "on the other side of the door." Of course, the New Haven meetinghouse may have had a slightly different arrangement, but either way Ralph would have been seated a few rows from the back, which may have placed a pillar in his line of view to the front.

---

[232] (Earle 1891)
[233] (Atwater 1902).

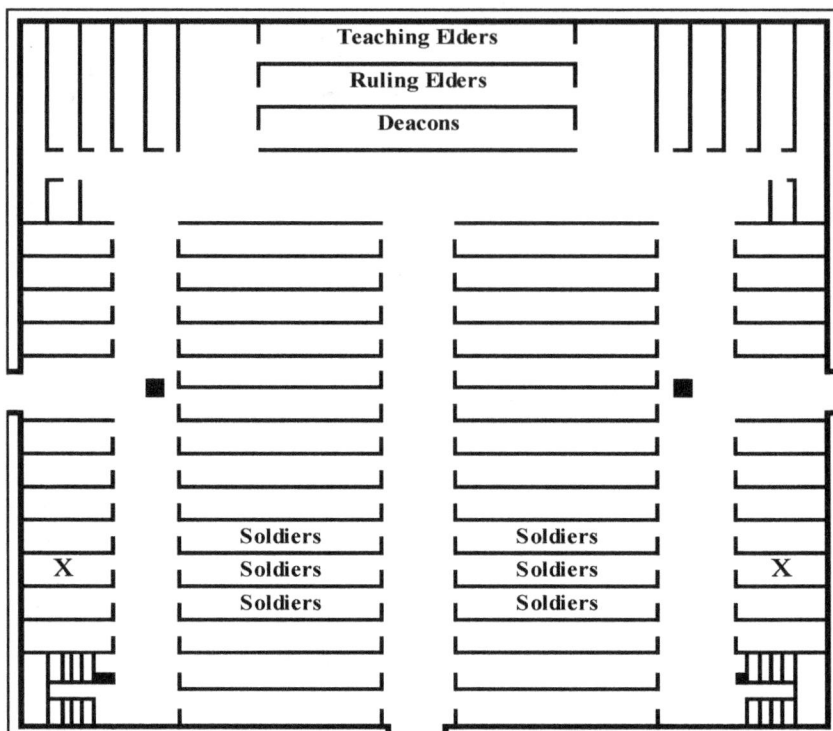

Figure 12. Ground plan of a meeting house

Atwater claims that no seats were assigned to persons inferior to a Goodman or Goodwife[234] and in reality, the seating of Ralph Dayton does not indicate the prominent social status that some authors have attributed to him. Instead, his approximate position indicated on the chart as "X" suggests that he was probably nearer the bottom half of the seated hierarchy, but still, "not inferior to goodman." From this, we submit that perhaps Ralph was not of the merchant class at this time and it may be reasonable to believe that he was no longer primarily of the trades at age fifty-seven or fifty-eight.

It is at this point that some researchers have theorized that because there was no mention of Ralph's wife in the seating, it is evidence Alice had died. We are not quick to agree. Ralph's wife Alice doesn't seem to have been a member of the church, just as her daughter Alice did not become a member of the Milford church, although her husband Thomas had been a member since 1639. So Alice could have been alive, but not a church member.

The perceived status of daughter Alice's membership at Milford is particularly awkward since her marriage to the respected Thomas Baker in June of 1643 provided

---

[234] Ibid.

84

stature in the community and made her actions ever more visible. Equally troubling is the unexplained excommunication of Ralph's son-in-law from the Milford church for two years, beginning January 1645/46. No reason was recorded for the censure in the Milford First Congregational Church Records,[235] but, "very often this discipline was leveraged against an unrepentant member to force him to succumb to a rule or tenant of the church in which he does not agree."[236] Cornelia Hughes Dayton wrote, "Each congregational church had the right to excommunicate a member for persistently defending religious ideas that departed from the fundamental tenets of *true religion* as expounded by the pastor and his cleric and magistrate colleagues."[237] This could have been the case with Thomas.

Since some parishioners didn't master reading or writing, they probably depended upon the pastor for reading and explaining scripture, giving him limited control of what the congregation believed. There is good reason to believe that Baker could read (as evidenced by his position and duties at East Hampton) and interpret the scriptures for himself. His well-worn bible attests to its use for generations. It is conceivable then that Baker had the opportunity to disagree with the Pastor's interpretations and conclusions more than some other persons in the congregation. Whatever the reason, to be excommunicated would have been a shameful thing to endure in the context of 1 Corinthians 5 that speaks of expelling the immoral brother and Matthew 18:15-19 that instructs the process of addressing sin in the church.

It is supposed that the remedies for offenses taken by Rev Peter Prudden or by any of the "Seven Pillars" of the Milford Church would be dealt with the support of civil authority since the leaders of the church were also the leaders in civil affairs. At least, that might have been the expectation. As was common among these Puritans, Thomas exhibited an independence and perhaps an outspokenness that may have offended the preacher and maybe even a few in the congregation.

Considering the stature Thomas would later possess, this event convinces us that Thomas was seen as a leader among men and as a man who may not have been afraid to challenge authorities on principle, although this event would come to haunt him thirty years later, in the form of a lingering grudge, as he ran for public office in East Hampton.[238] The grudge tends to support the idea that the censure was perhaps rooted in a personality conflict especially since no reason was given for the censure. It is fair to suggest that his offense was of minor nature and could have been the result of obstinance or disagreement with the Rev Prudden even though the stated

---

[235] (Theodore, Milford First Congregational Church Records-1639-1837 Jun 2009)
[236] (Brown 1994)
[237] (McLaren 1999)
[238] (F. Baker 1914)

justification might be "to strengthen and purify the church."[239] The fact of Thomas's continued stature in the community at East Hampton supports this.

The gripe in East Hampton[240] was expressed by the minister there, Reverend James, who was opposed to Thomas running for public office, saying he was unfit because he had been excommunicated so many years before. Other evidence suggests that the contention was more of a personal nature because in 1671 Thomas,

> in behalf of the people of Easthampton, protested to the Governor against the confirmation of a purchase of lands from the Montauk Indians by Mr. James and Mr. John Mulford, upon the ground that such purchase was against the order of Governor Nicoll and deprived the other people of the town of their right of commonage in the lands so purchased. (14 N. Y. Col. Rec. 650.) The town records show that there had been dealings in horses between Mr. James and Mr. Baker, and such dealings, or the above protest, rather than the ancient church trouble, may have been the real cause of Mr. James' opposition to Mr. Baker's appointment. The action of Governor Andros upon Mr. James' protest was well calculated to show what foundation, if any, there was for his charge against Mr. Baker.[241]

Thomas was appointed to the office and nothing further was heard from Mr. James on the subject.

On January 22 1647/48, Thomas Baker was officially received back into the Church of Milford. Because of the embarrassment, if indeed he was embarrassed, returning to the congregation who had found him guilty of a flagrant disregard for the tenants of the Christian faith had to have been difficult to endure. Even so, life at Milford was probably more difficult without membership, keeping in mind that Baker's house lot was #10, near West Main and River Street[242] on the plat of 1646, placing his house and family diagonally across the street from the First Congregational Church.[243] One can imagine that Thomas was forced to confess and requested absolution in anticipation of his future request for a letter of transfer. A letter of recommendation, as is typical in many denominations today, would have been used to transfer membership from one congregation to another, unavailable without reinstatement.

What is one to suppose? Since Baker's excommunication occurred about the same time that Lady Deborah Moody was passing through New Haven, is it possible that these difficulties were connected to the teachings of Anabaptists or the reception

---

[239] (Brown 1994)
[240] (Devlin 2012)
[241] (F. Baker 1914)
[242] (Abbot 1979)
[243] (E. R. Lambert 1838)

they received? Lady Moody was influential, especially with some women in the New Haven congregation, but was she equally as persuasive at nearby Milford? During her time visiting New Haven about 1645, on her way to establish Gravesend, Long Island, Moody managed to "infect" and convert Mrs. Eaton,[244] wife of the first governor of New Haven Colony, who conveyed her dissent to the congregation in "theatrical expressions." Did Lady Moody have any influence on Alice at New Haven or her daughter Alice Baker at Milford to dissent?

Anabaptism was a movement begun in 16th century Europe and is an ancestor of modern-day Amish, Hutterite and Mennonite movements. We spoke earlier of the situation when discussing Laude and the *Book of Rough Notes*.[245] Nothing has been found to suggest that anyone in Ralph's immediate family was an adherent to these sects but members may have been interacting with them socially or with followers in one of the other separatist sects to the degree that they were was in danger of being labeled. Mennonite archives have no reference to Anabaptists at Ashford before the mid 1620's, but Brownist and Barrowist separatists like Brewer, Fenner and Turner were at Ashford and Maidstone as late as 1638.[246]

Alice Morse Earle describes the impact of excommunication.[247] Earle says,

> In some communities, of which Lechford tells us New Haven was one, these unhouselled Puritans were allowed, if they so desired, to stand outside the meeting-house door at the time of public worship and catch what few words of the service they could. This humble waiting for crumbs of God's word was doubtless regarded as a sign of repentance for past deeds, for it was often followed by full forgiveness. As excommunicated persons were regarded with high disfavor and even abhorrence by the entire pious and godly walking community, this apparently spiritual punishment was more severe in its temporal effects than at first sight appears. From the Cambridge Platform, which was drawn up and adopted by the New England Synod in 1648, we learn that 'while the offender remains excommunicated the church is to refrain from all communion with him in civil things,' and the members were specially 'to forbear to eat and drink with him;' so his daily and even his family life was made wretched. And as it was not necessary to wait for the action of the church to pronounce excommunication, but the 'pastor of a church might by himself and authoritatively suspend from the Lord's table a brother suspected of scandal' until there was time for full examination, we can see what an absolute power the church and even the minister had over church-members in a New England community.

---

[244] (McLaren 1999)
[245] (Nicholas 1636/37)
[246] (Burrage 1912)
[247] (Earle 1891)

Between the Seating at the Meeting House in March of 1646/47 and the time Ralph finally left Connecticut in 1649 or 1650, there were six more records or references to Daytons in New Haven. Three had to do with land transactions, one was an unspecified dispute, one had to do with cattle and the last was a simple debt repayment in an estate settlement. The six entries are given as follows, beginning in 1647,

> Bro: Mitchell & Goodm[n] Daighton request the court to bestow a peice of spare grownd vpon them which lay betweene their howse lotts, with promise to mayntayne the highway before their dores or howselotts & stopp the currant that now spoyleth the way. And the grant of the land w'h a view of the conveyniency of it to the towne & them with the inconveyniences that may attend Goodman Buckingham was refferred vnto brother Ric[h] Myles & bro: W[m] Davis, & what they should doe therein the towne would allow of. The land to be devided in proportion to each as the committee see cause.[248]

One lot separated Mitchell and Dayton, and either the highway ran through the lot or the highway abutted all three lots. Since they may have lived on or near the river, perhaps storm runoff compromised the road or they maintained the crossing or bridge to town on this traveled road. The court said they would ask others how it might impact them—perhaps Buckingham, and even Myles and Davis were neighbors, and had businesses that would be impacted or were heavy users of the highway.

The next entry was vague and simply states: "A difference between Mr. Francis Newman, Tho. Mitchell and Goodman Dayton was presented to the court. Vpon the courts advize that 2 men might be chosen to end it, by consent Mr. Crayne & Goodman Myles wer chosen."[249] No other information was provided and so renders our speculation pointless.

Here again is another instance where Ralph was looking after cattle. In 1647, the record includes testimony from Ralph concerning a steer and it states:

> Henry Lions testimony vpon oath was read, wherin he testifieth that though they had indeauored to have driven back a beast of Mr. Ceffinches towards Newhaven, from Mr. Crayns penn onn the west side, they could not, but went with the cattle driven to Milford, & neere Mr. Tapps they parted Mr. Tapps cattle, & testifieth that Henry Whelply with the rest of his cattle drove away a stray beast of Mr. Ceffinches, &c.

> Goodm Daighton saith that hee looking with others for Mr. Bernards cattle, & finding them with strange cattle, mett Mr. Crayne who told them they had neede looke to it what they did to drive away Strañg cattle, for

---

[248] (C. J. Hoadly, Records of the Colony and Plantation of New Haven From 1638 to 1649 1857)
[249] Ibid.

he had smarted for it, but being at Mr. Crayns penn on the west side, some Milford cattle went away & Mr. Ceffinches bullocke w^{t}h them, then he told Henry Whelply, he would not have any hand in driveinge away Strang cattle & so came away. But he further affirmeth that about 3 weeks after he saw the same bullocke vnder the West Rocke.[250]

Mr. Knell informed the court that at the waterside at Poquanock ferry they did indeauour to have driven ouer their cattle, and then one ranne away but afterwards was fownd, and Mr. Cafiinch doubting it had bin his bullocke had the sight of it & liked it not, and indead all of them proved Mr. Bernards. Goodn Daighton testfied vpon oath what he had respectively testified."[251]

The finding of the court was that the damages must fall on, "the playntiffe, he being defective in proofe of his chardge, and ordred to allow 5s to Henry Whelply besids the charges of the court."

In 1648, "Francis Browne passeth ouer to Henry Glover 10 acre of land at the plaines, lying betwixt the land of Ralph Dayton & the common."[252] The common refers to the common pasture.

Nearing the end of the Dayton records at New Haven, on April 3, 1649, Richard Platt and Ralph were in a dispute over the terms of a sale of lands between them, disagreeing over how boundaries were represented or understood before the sale. This boundary dispute was serious enough that it may have accelerated Ralph's decision to remove to Long Island.

Richard Platt declareth that he sold a pcell of land to Ralph Dayton, pt of his first devission, & all his second, & 4 ac^{re} of meddow, & would haue passed it ouer to him in ye court, but he would not haue it passed ouer to him, because it would, (he said,) be some prejudice to him, but said he would take order with the treasurer to see ye rates should be paide. Ralph Dayton saith that he acknowledges he bought the land & they differ not aboute the paye, but he would haue ye land laid out & passed ouer to him, butted & bounded wher it lyes. The plant' said he told him it was not laid out, but he must take it wher it falles, but for the first devission, he ptly knew wher it was, on ye other side of ye West River. For ye meddow, it was pt in Mr. Malbons meddow and pt in Sollatarie Cove, and the second devident he thought might fall aboute ye sheppards penn, & produced Mr. Wakeman for a witnes, whoe saith that he cannot speakc to ye bargaine, but Goodman Dayton spake to him asking him wher it was, showing

---

250 Ibid.
251 Ibid.
252 Ibid.

thcrby that Goodman Platt did not determine the place, but mentioned the sheppards penn, as if Goodman Platt informed him that it might fall ther.[253]

The court told Goodman Dayton:

…it appeares by this testimoney that he bought Goodman Platts interest in this land, hopeing the 2[d] devident would fall aboute y[e] shepards penn, for if he bought land which he knew was not laid out, how could he looke to liaue it butted & bounded. He was asked if he had any witnes to cleare his case any more. Hee said no, whervpon the court ordered that Ralph Dayton take y[e] land sold him by Richard Piatt & haue it entred in the court & paye rates for it to the towne.[254]

Ralph lost the case and was forced to accept the land and to pay taxes on it. It appears that Ralph did take possession of the land because about ten years later, a few months after Ralph's death, Phillip Leeke referred to this same land he had bought from Ralph. Upon hearing of Ralph's death on Long Island, Leeke may have been concerned that the sale was not properly registered at the time of sale, so he wanted to assure that there was an adequate record, in order to protect it from Ralph's heirs. Could this indicate that Ralph had made a hasty sale and removal from New Haven?

February 1658/59: Phillip Leeke desired that an entry might be made of certaine parcells of land wh[ch] he bought of Ralph Deiton, * y[e] particulers whereof being exprest in a writeing subscribed by y[e] s[d] Deiton, witnessed by Gervase Boykin, wh[ch] begin read ye Court allowed of & ordered y[t] y[e] s[d] lands should be recorded as belonging to Phillipp Leeke, wh[ch] are as followeth: 8 akers of the first division within y[e] 2 mile; the whole 2[d] division, 48 akers; 3 akers meadow in M[r] Malbons meadow; & one aker in Solitary Cove, as he thinketh; wh[ch] lands sometimes appertained to Rich. Platt, as appears by a passage in Court, Aprill 3, 1649: also y[e] house & home lott belonging to y[e] s[d] Ralph Deiton at ye towne of Newhaven.[255]

We might assume that the Solitary Cove referred to in the New Haven record was the same Solitary Cove today known as Morris Cove, in East Haven. Perhaps this is the estate Ralph's heirs still felt was unsettled seventy-five years later, and they were entitled to part or all of it. In 1726, Ralph's grandson Abraham of Brookhaven returned to Connecticut to convey to his son-in-law Rogers,

---

[253] Ibid.
[254] Ibid.
[255] (Dexter 1917)

all such Right Estate Title Interest Claim and demand which I now have or ought to have of in and unto any Housing fences Lands Commons or common Rights or any other Estate by any ways or means what so ever belonging to me in the Township of New Haven[256]

Leeke's 1649 purchase of Ralph's assets in New Haven was apparently proved to the court and recorded almost 10 years after their sale, with Leeke's display of a legal document. The date of the purchase indicates that Ralph and family probably moved to Long Island in 1649.

One of the last records of Ralph in New Haven was in the estate of James Hayward, as debtor to over thirty others, on September 4, 1649. This occurred five months after losing the dispute with Richard Platt so it is probable that Ralph and the family had already made their way to Long Island, perhaps lodging near Sam while negotiating their move to East Hampton. The removal of the entire Dayton family to Long Island would be complete except that daughter Ellen remained in Connecticut with her husband.

An additional reference to Ralph in the NHTR in May of 1652 (after he had already removed to East Hampton) says, "Widdow Walker passeth over to Isacke Beecher 8 acre of land at the plaines, lying betwixt the land of Robert Pigg & Ralfe Dayton.[257] Is this evidence that Ralph's sale to Leeke was not adequately recorded with the town? This question will come back to us again later.

---

[256] Ibid.
[257] Ibid.

Chapter 7

Cordwainer or Cowboy?

If we had always been confident about one thing concerning Ralph, we knew he was a shoemaker. So, with determination to collect evidence, our job should have been an easy one, but instead we found nothing beyond one statement that referred to Ralph as shoemaker in America. Considering the volume of records for Ralph, shouldn't more be found to implicate him?

Was Ralph Dayton, our American progenitor, a shoemaker while in America? Yes, he was a shoemaker because the New Haven records once labeled him so.

> …some of the shooes thus made was brought from Mr. Evane, wh[ch] were some of the best of them, and the court called and dissiered Leivtenant Seely, Goodman Dayton, Goodman Groue of Millford, shoemakers, and Goodman Osborn and Seriant Jeffery, tanners, to take those shooes aside and veiwe them well…

But many men made shoes for their families. At the time, many of these same men were like Ralph, who was also a farmer, cow-keeper, shepherd, town constable and project supervisor, bee-keeper and probably even a logger, hunter, fisherman, weaver and carpenter. Nonetheless, the single account of Ralph as shoemaker in 1647 seems to have solidified the modern perception of Ralph's vocation.

Was Ralph's principle occupation that of a shoemaker? Circumstantial evidence suggests he most likely was a shoemaker in England and, as was customary tradition, his oldest son Ralph was also a shoemaker. His second son Sam even self-identified as a cordwainer when convenient, on occasions where it was beneficial to identify a trade which might have indicated a stable income. But to confirm that Ralph Senior or Sam were shoemakers, as their principle occupations in America, is not easy or convincing.

For perspective and context, Charles Andrews in *Puritans and Pilgrims* says of the early settlement:

> For the great majority there was little opportunity in these early years to practice a trade or a profession. …there was little else for any one to do than engage in farming, fishing, and trading with the Indians, or turn

carpenter and cobbler[258] according to demand. The artisan became a farmer, though still preserving his knack as a craftsman, and expended his skill and his muscle in subduing a tough and unbroken soil.[259]

A considerable search to locate supporting evidence or innuendo proved only marginally successful. No corroborating evidence such as mentioning customers, acquiring supplies for shoemaking, bartering with shoes or any other transaction having to do with Ralph's shoemaking in America could be detected. Settlers were always bartering what they had, yet Ralph and Sam are never found exchanging their skills or shoes for anything as was the case when Robert Smith and Samuel Ackerly dealt with John Roe, to plow four acres of land for compensation of eight shillings worth of shoes.[260] Still, Ralph's opinion was desired by the New Haven court because he was older than most of the men in the colony and his opinion in matters of his former trade was valued.

There might be little question that Ralph was not practicing the trade on this side of the ocean if not for the reference to "all my sowmaking tooles and cumeing tooles" [popularly interpreted as shoemaking and cutting tools] enumerated in his will to son Samuel. This piece of evidence is used frequently to connect both Ralph and Sam to shoemaking. How extensive a collection "all" refers to—a few household pieces or enough to fit a shop—is not indicated, but we contend that he may have been in possession of no more leather-working tools than the average man of his time. If Ralph had owned highly valued tools of the craft, they were no doubt left along with the shop and other necessary supplies to his son Ralph in Ashford or sold to collect funds for passage. Ralph's will states,

> Also my will is that my sonn Samuell shall have this house and land at Northampton [North Sea] and my cart and plow and two chanes and all my showmaking tooles and cumeing tooles and the sorill horse which I had of Jonas Wood.[261]

Thus, according to some, is given the first evidence of son Samuel becoming a shoemaker.

During the November 2010 discussion with Richard Barons in East Hampton, we posed the questions, "Should any conclusions about Ralph's occupation be drawn if he bequeathed to Samuel shoemaking and leather-cutting tools? Would this make Ralph a shoemaker?" (Mr. Barons spoke in a general sense because he did not have the benefit of being briefed on all the circumstances in this specific case)

He replied with this caution:

---

[258] Note: A cordwainer is a maker of shoes while a cobbler is a repairer of shoes
[259] (C. M. Andrews 1919)
[260] (Barstow, Setauket, Alias Brookhaven 2004)
[261] Note: Ralph's will, the original document, is held at the Long Island Collection, East Hampton Public Library, NY. An image is shown later in this compilation.

The problem with the shoemakers tools, remember, is that every male had shoemaking tools...they all worked with leather. You're eeking out anything you can possibly have. You are multitasking all the time.

In his book *Setauket 1655-1955 The First Three Hundred Years*, Adkins says of Setauket men,

> They were, of necessity, men of many occupations. Tailor, blacksmith, hunter, fisherman, farmer—all were necessary, and sometimes in the person of one individual most of these accomplishments were to be found. Illustrative of the many skills often displayed by one individual is the ledger of Thomas Hulse, who left an account of his transactions during the years 1739-40. Hulse did his own weaving of cotton and wool cloth, and fashioned this into suits of clothes. He worked in the fields for 6s a day, and wintered two cows for £1 6s. In addition, he engaged in trade with various kinds, including real estate.[262]

So, for whatever purpose the tools served, their existence in Ralph's will does not dictate the assignment of profession any more than does the existence of the cart, plow, chains and horse contribute evidence to suggest that Ralph's primary occupation was a grower of crops. Hedges remembers,

> The shoes, stockings, cap, straw hats, clothing, linen for the table and bedding, the harness, brushes and brooms were manufactured largely or wholly in the family. Within the memory of the writer there were residents in one-half the dwelling houses on East-Hampton Main Street a shoemaker member of the household who made the shoes for the family.[263]

Hedges goes on to provide us with additional context for the time:

> Nothing was bought that could be made at home. The spinning wheel was constantly running and carried in visits to neighbors. The farmer raised, and his wife and daughters spun the flax and wool that kept the family warm with clothing by day and covering by night. The family meal was eaten from wooden trenchers or pewter plates and platters, with the smallest possible allowance of tin and crockery ware. Corn and rye with very little wheat furnished flour for bread. Fish, beef and pork salted for the years supply were the chief items of animal food. Unceasing industry and toil occupied all the members of the family, young and old. Rigid economy ruled every expenditure. The simplest, cheapest diet satisfied

---

[262] (Adkins 1955)
[263] (H. Hedges 1897)

the appetite. The homespun apparel in summer and mostly in winter was then worn. For clothing the cost of buttons, for harness the price of buckles, bitts and trace irons were almost the only expenditure. Looking back three score years and ten it is simply astonishing how little money was sufficient to buy all that the then wants of a family required.[264]

With the passing of years, specialization and exchange grew as craftsmen were able to focus on the craft for which they were most gifted and exchange for supplies and necessities. This didn't seem to be the case for Ralph. We suppose this was because he was about fifty-two upon arrival and perhaps had failing vision, and he died before "the passing of years," being a member of the first generation in America.

Undeniable

Still, that undeniable evidence that links Ralph to a profession in leatherworking is the December 7, 1647 New Haven court account when Ralph was called to judge the quality of a sample pair of leather boots, in a manner of speaking "an expert witness," along with other workmen, both shoemakers and tanners. The plaintiff was suing over what he claimed were inferior quality boots and the record also involves a disagreement between the tanner providing the hides and Mr. Meges, the shoemaker, each blaming the other as the cause of the inferior shoes. Statements from other customers were read, testimony given, and after both plaintiff and defendant were finished speaking, the court debated and found both guilty of deception. The court ordered fines, satisfaction to all for damages, and required that none of the faulty shoes be carried into other jurisdictions, but rather should be burned. The account states:

> The court having heard those things on bothe sides did thinke there was a fault in bothe, and that the cuntery was much wronged in this wayc, therfore they were willing to call in some workmen, bothe shoemakers and tanners, that they might see it and judge whose the fault was, and so give into the courte what light they coulde. To this ppose, some of the shooes thus made was brought from Mr. Evanc, wh[ch] were some of the best of them, and the court called and dissiered Leivtenant Seely, Goodman Dayton, Goodman Groue of Millford, shoemakers, and Goodman Osborn and Seriant Jeffery, tanners, to take those shooes aside and veiwe them well, and if ther be cause, ripe some of them, that they maye give into the courte according to ther best light, the cause of this damadge. They did so, and returned this answer, Leivtenant speaking in the name of the rest. Wee aprehend this, that the leather is very bad, not tanned, nor fitt to be sold for servicable leather, but it wrongs the cuntry, nor can a man make good worke of a great deale of it. And wee find the

---

[264] Ibid.

workemanship bad allso, first ther is not sufficient stufe put in the thred, and instead of hemp it is flax, and the stiches are two longe, and the threds not drawne home, and ther wants wax on the thred, the aule is to bige for the thred. We ordinarily put in 7 threds, and hear is but 5; so that according to our best light wee laye the cause liothe vpon the workemanship and the badnesse of the leather. [265]

The entry is the sole reference found of Ralph as shoemaker. That is, to our knowledge, no others exist. From this record, it is observed that Ralph was grouped with shoemakers and not with the tanners. The term *cordwainer*, it seems, has consistently been interpreted as *shoemaker* for the Dayton men, despite the more general definition of cordwainer as *a worker of new leather*.[266] The men were not only judging the quality and construction of the boot by Goodman Meges, but also judging the quality of the leather by Goodman Gregory. Upon first review of the record, it seemed unclear if Ralph was from Milford but it was determined that he was probably from New Haven because Lieutenant Robert Seeley, in the same group, was clearly from New Haven[267] while Philip Groves was a shoemaker from Milford. As a result of the inferior boots and the deception perpetrated, the court introduced a rating system in order to declare the quality of hides for shoemaking purposes. This order was issued in January 1647/48. Mr. Groves later served as leather sealer for Stratford.[268]

Still, it is not only noteworthy but compelling to consider what seems like Ralph's continuous association with cattle and the work of tending livestock, as was mentioned or implied many times in town records from New Haven and East Hampton. It appears to us that Ralph spent considerable time farming and/or tending cattle. Perhaps Ralph occupied most of the year with farming and some of the winter months with leatherworking or shoemaking. It was very common for those who farmed to practice a trade as well, occupying their winters with trades such as weaving or even whaling.[269] This would seem true for the Daytons. One Long Island historian told us "...the majority of weaving would have been males during the wintertime because there wasn't quite as much farm work to do...The majority of textiles made wouldn't be for the household, but for barter. So they mostly made diaper cloth."

In mid-seventeenth century New England and Long Island, hard currency was in very short supply so nearly everything could be used to barter—whether produced,

[265] (C. J. Hoadly, Records of the Colony and Plantation of New Haven From 1638 to 1649 1857)
[266] (The Honourable Cordwainer's Company 1984)
[267] (Seeley Genealogical Society n.d.)
[268] (D. L. Jacobus, History and Genealogy of the Families of Old Fairfield 1991)
[269] Note: See accounts for Thomas Leaming. Historical Collections of the State of New Jersey; Containing a General Collection of the Most Interesting Facts, Traditions, Biographical Sketches, Anecdotes Etc Relating to History and Antiquities with the General Descriptions of Every Township in the State, John W. Barber and Henry Howe, 1844.

bred or harvested. Lumber, firewood, woven materials, boots, honey, cattle and whale oil many times replaced British currency or Native American currency (wampum). Perhaps Ralph worked with cattle belonging to others and bartered for hides to use for leatherworking or shoemaking as a winter occupation? Again, this is only conjecture and there is no attempt to defend the idea, but Ralph's ongoing associations with tanner Thomas Osborne deserve closer examination, perhaps aiding in the discovery of Ralph's work.

If Ralph did choose to identify himself as a shoemaker, why would he do so if he did not intend to continue this work in America? Our theory suggests that he probably perceived and calculated that his knowledge of leatherworking could work to his advantage at the plantations. In fact, he may very well have been skilled at shoemaking or shoe mending for his family and believed he could create a market for his wares. This theory contends that if he was identified on a ship's passenger list, he could have been listed as a shoemaker in reference to his acquisition of Tritton's shoemaking shop in Ashford, if that acquisition did in fact occur. Ralph's father-in-law Hugh Tritton had been a cordwainer and householder as was Hugh's son Daniel, Alice's first husband. Although a fanciful idea, is it possible that Ralph's association with Hugh began earlier as apprentice with the very tools his son Ralph Junior would inherit with his marriage to Susan Burr? The search to further develop this knowledge of family cordwainer connections in England would be a fascinating project for research and analysis.

Just like the abundance of "weavers" on Long Island at the time of the American Revolution, there are circumstances in history where prudence trumps modesty. When a Puritan community considered acceptance of a new member, it was pragmatic for the individual seeking inclusion to present his value and contribution in the best light, in order to satisfy a perceived need in the community. Naturally, if a prospective member wanted to join a community that already had a supply of poor farmers, if he could, he would claim another skill or occupation for which he might have enough knowledge or proficiency to prove himself during the test period. Is it possible that Ralph chose not to practice his supplemental craft once informed that shoemakers were already present at New Haven? Atwater says,

> The production of leather and the manufacture of shoes increased so rapidly, that, within nine years after the commencement of the plantation at New Haven, shoes were made for exportation. At first the tanners [Osborne is mentioned] spoiled many hides through ignorance, as they alleged, of the tan of the country.[270]

While sometimes merchants and select skilled craftsmen were given incentives to join a community, there was a fear of other craftsmen becoming itinerant, and so they received less favorable treatment and smaller pieces of land.[271] Perhaps this

---

[270] (Atwater 1902)
[271] (Calder 1934). 161

explains why Ralph is found in the suburbs, probably along the creek that later became an area populated by tanners.

No other craft has been attributed to Ralph Senior and Ralph Junior, although Junior may have been a householder. In England, Ralph Junior called himself a *cordwainer* when he obtained a marriage license in 1639. As stated earlier, Senior's second son Sam was self-reported as cordwainer three times in primary sources, even though no other allusion to shoemaking was ever advanced. The first record was in a 1655 court, when Sam was about 31 or 32, he being accused of theft aboard a Dutch vessel. Might he have made the claim as a type of "gainful employment" statement? The second was probably 1663, when he mortgaged his house and home lot in North Sea to Jonathan King of Boston. "If said Dayton shall pay to said King £17 2s 7d before the first of December next the above sale is void December 28, 1663." If our assumptions of this arrangement are correct, it was certainly in Sam's best interest to represent himself with another skill and means of livelihood. The third time was when Sam sold his house and accommodations at North Sea to John Cooper:

> Samuel Dayton of the North Sea belonging to Southampton cordwinder sells to John Cooper all that my house or tenement and accomodations at North Sea. Except two parcels of meadow which I sold to Henry Pierson being of the denomination of three quarters of a hundred pound allotment. The greater part of which accommodations lyeth in the Neck commonly called Cow Neck lying at the east end thereof with a pond and spring in it, and Mr. John Scotts land lying at the west end thereof and Mr. John Jennings land to the Southwest thereof. Dated March 27th 1666, witness Henry Pierson, Humphrey Hughes."[272]

By 1675, Samuel was called a husbandman[273] living in the town of Brookhaven or Setauket in the county of Yorkshire. A husbandman was usually an overseer of a farm. Samuel mortgaged his house to Benjamin Gibbs, merchant in Boston, but he continued to occupy the property until 1677.

In the end, we have no problem referring to Ralph as a shoemaker but, at the same time, we would have no problem referring to Ralph as herdsman or cow-keeper. It is very possible Ralph was once a gifted shoemaker, but any statement of the kind should be mitigated because it is likely that shoemaking was not his primary occupation, especially once having arrived in America.

---

[272] (W. W. Pelletreau 1910)
[273] (W. J. Weeks 1930)

Chapter 8

Island of Opportunity

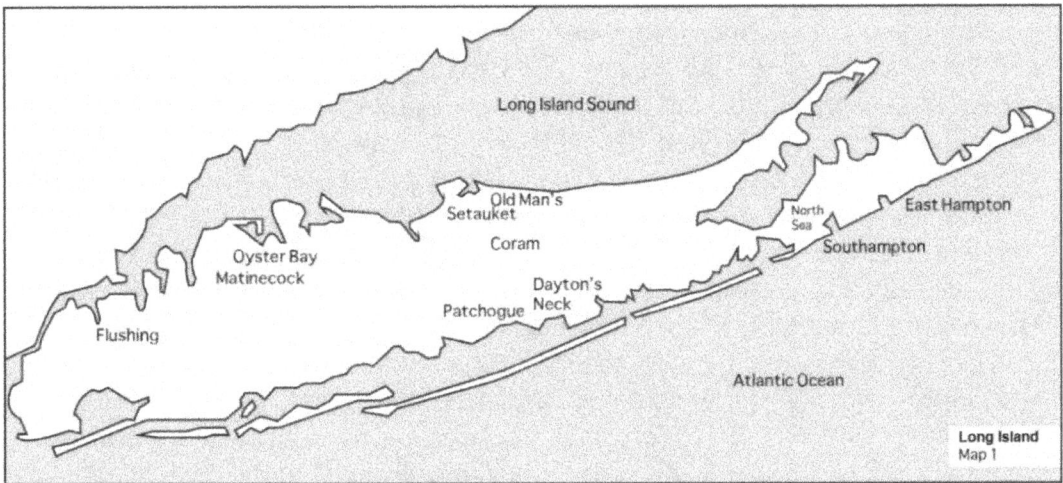

Figure 13. Long Island map

The first official record (primary source) of Sam in America was at New Haven, little more than five years after the family disembarked. Upon his reaching majority in 1645, the June record was the first of four New Haven records that emerged in a span of sixteen or seventeen months, presenting the possibility that Sam was present there for only that brief time. From what is later learned of Sam, he seemed to be possessed with a restlessness, as is his common characterization among writers, causing one to wonder where he was and what he had been doing during those five years before reaching legal adult status. Perhaps if Sam had been indentured, he had fulfilled the contractual agreement by June of 1645. After the last New Haven entry for Sam in 1646, there is again no word of him again until May of 1648 when he received a lot on the ocean shore of Long Island, at Southampton settlement. At the time of his acceptance there, it was disclosed that he had come from Flushing, on the west end and north shore of the Island. The reason for that diversion remains undiscovered.

As Sam appeared on Long Island and resided there, the focus of attention moves across the sound to Long Island records, beginning with Southampton Town Records (STR), leaning heavily on the editing and transcribing work of William Pelletreau.

Mr. Pelletreau, town clerk and distinguished historian, tirelessly interpreted original handwritten documents and published his first volume of Southampton Town Records in 1874.

Samuel Received at Southampton Plantation

Southampton and Southold were both settled in 1640, and each has claimed to be the oldest English town on Long Island. These settlements consisted of New Englanders who were not content to remain in the area of their initial dwellings and who sought greater independence (and distance) from their previous Massachusetts or Connecticut communities.

After being turned away from western Long Island, the small group of families from Lynn, Massachusetts (the same group discussed in chapter 6) returned to Long Island via the Great Peconic Bay and North Sea Harbor, and made their way down an old trail about six miles across the southern fork, from their landing at North Sea, to arrive at their chosen spot near the ocean. Perhaps the Native Americans led them to fertile ground, parts of which they had already cleared. There the families constructed temporary shelters that were probably nothing more than crude cellars dug into the ground, covered first with a few saplings to support branches, sod and salt hay woven together. For some families, this would be home until land divisions were established and more permanent structures could be built.

Probably within a year of settlement, the land was divided to its first inhabitants at Olde Town. Goddard, in *Colonizing Southampton* says "The settlers formed a church, built a small meetinghouse, hired a minister, and established minimal but effective civil government; but the main purpose of the enterprise was to allocate land to its subscribers for their productive use in an economically rational manner." Goddard continues,

> [Reverend Pierson] joined the settlers in December 1640, six months after their own arrival and after they had already constructed a small meetinghouse in readiness. Yet it must be stressed that, pious though they no doubt were, this small band did not leave Lynn or the Bay in general for religious reasons as perhaps they had left England. They left for land. Pierson lasted a few years only, a division within the church over the question of whether church membership was to be a prerequisite for the election of town officials having led to his departure. The town was firmly against it but a small number of his parishoners departed with him.

Howell says,

> Each man was entitled to a house lot of four acres (afterward changed to three acres), twelve acres for cultivation, and about thirty-four acres of meadow and upland, together with a certain number of shares or rights in the undivided common land, according to the amount of money he had disbursed toward the expenses of the settlement and the purchase of the

town. These were called Proprietor's Eights, and were handed down with inherited estate from father to son. There is no question but the land of the town was, from the first, and always down to the present time, owned in two distinct modes or tenures — first, as divided into certain lots, whether homesteads, meadows, uplands, arable lands or wood lands; and, secondly, the remainder of the undivided lands within the limits of the town was owned by the proprietors, their heirs, assigns or successors in joint tenantry.[274]

"The earliest complete list of male inhabitants at Southampton is the whale squads list of March 1644, forty–two names. It is especially to be noted that this list includes several landless servants, and also minors above 16 years. The list is not partial; it is for whale-oil dividends. It was some years before the full number of forty householders was reached."[275] No Daytons appear on the 1644 list.

By June 11, 1647, the seventh year of settlement, another land distribution was announced. The town had experienced significant growth and likewise, the harbor to the north, North Sea (then called New York: Feversham and Northampton), was increasingly busy with newcomers, supplies and trade. It was ordered by all the inhabitants that the town was to be divided, six thousand pounds into forty house lots, with the size of lots determined by the size of their contributed shares. This was the origin of the £150 lots.[276]

Within eight years of its founding, the small settlement was filled and a more suitable location was selected about a mile west, where Towne Street was laid out just east of Agawam Lake. Towne Street, later called Main Street, was connected to Old Towne by Toylsome Lane, the east-west road which is still known by the same name today. Beginning at North End Cemetery, Main Street connects with Southampton's oldest road, the old trail or North Sea Road, to extend south to the ocean. Just one month after the whole town was called together "to consider of a towne plot," Sam had arrived. The town,

> …ordered that Samuel Dayton shall be accepted as an inhabitant, & hath a fifty pound lot granted unto him provided the said Samuell (being a stranger to vs) weare of good aprobation in ye place where he last lived at flushing, & do demeane himself well heare for ye time of aprobation namely six months next to come.[277]

This May 6, 1648 record was the first of Sam at Southampton and the first record of Sam outside New Haven plantation. He was about 24 or 25 years old and

---

[274] (Howell 1887)
[275] (Winans 1911)
[276] (Adams 1918)

had probably left New Haven just over a year and a half earlier, but had come from Flushing because the Southampton record specifically states, "where he last lived." Whether Sam was referring to his place of residence before or after visiting his father at New Haven is not known. Nor is it discovered how Sam came to settle in Southampton, but since others were also accepted at that time, there might be clues found among the others. His decision to leave Flushing and settle at Southampton was probably not made without the influence of someone else. In that day, travel was most often by boat so the distance from Flushing to Southampton was at least doubled had they traveled over land, across 85 miles of "wilderness."

Newcomers to Southampton were cautiously vetted, but Sam seemed to receive a little extra attention in the official record by labeling him a stranger. Whether the language had special significance beyond the norm is not known, but he was accepted with the condition of a longer trial period, as was Thomas Robbinson on the same day.

Was there a stigma attached to Flushing that would make the settlers of Southampton hesitant to accept Sam, perhaps a repulsion to one of the new faiths practiced on the west end? Southampton was generally more tolerant of strangers than East Hampton later was, but

> One had to prove oneself respectable, God fearing and industrious. There was a vetting process. You needed credentials. If you had been a troublesome person in your previous community, you were not welcome. Did you have skills required by the town? Would you adhere to the faith and the rules of the community?[278]

Land available for habitation had already been distributed among the proprietors so in order to acquire it without an outright purchase, the outsider might exchange his services. If someone at the still young plantation had vouched for Sam's character, perhaps this person also arranged an exchange with Sam, should Sam's assets be inadequate. Anyway, with his acquisition of land, Samuel seems to be our Long Island Progenitor.

No marriage record can be found for Sam in Connecticut or Long Island, and there being no reference to Sam's wife until 1656, we cannot know if Sam brought his wife to Southampton or if he married her there. One can imagine Sam's impatience and his father urging him toward an acceptable wife at New Haven but, instead of settling there, Sam's adventurous and independent spirit would entice his retreat to Flushing, on the Dutch end of Long Island, where events would be less structured or managed, at least in the ways of Puritanism. Alice Morse Earle, the author of *The Sabbath in Puritan New England*, claimed,

---

[278] (P. Shillingburg n.d.)

Bachelors were so restricted and governed in the colonies...Single men could not live alone, but were forced to reside with some family to whom the court assigned them, and to do in all respects just what the court ordered. Thus, in olden times, a man had to marry to obtain his freedom.[279]

Assuming this dynamic can even be partially applied to Sam's case, it is possible that the town accepted Sam conditionally because he was unmarried (and did not hold sufficient currency). The environment of Southampton, though still Puritan, was a little more relaxed than strict New Haven and whatever had drawn him to New Haven didn't induce him to remain there.

Flushing

Is it possible that in 1646, when Sam left New Haven, he returned to a place and a people still omitted from our story of the Daytons in 1640 to 1643? Had he encountered something or someone that caused his heart and dreams to lay elsewhere? If true, it is possible that Sam left New Haven in pursuit of a less conventional union on western Long Island.

When considering why Sam had "last lived at Flushing," it is helpful to know what was happening at the west end of Long Island before 1648, to provide clues to some possibilities that might be considered.

European colonization of the part of Long Island now known as Queens began during the early seventeenth century when the Dutch government incorporated land purchased from Native American groups into New Netherlands. In 1639, officials of the Dutch West India Company acquired the area where Flushing and Jamaica are presently located, permitting the native inhabitants to remain on the land. Relations with the Native Americans, however, were not peaceful, and after several conflicts in the 1640s, the Dutch found themselves desperate for more settlers to help retain their holdings. English settlers who were not comfortable in New England fulfilled this need, and the Dutch administration granted charters for several English towns during this period. A patent was granted by Dutch governor William Kieft to the English colony of Mespat (Maspeth) in 1642, but this settlement was quickly dispersed by Native American raids. Three English towns were chartered by the Dutch before any Dutch towns were chartered: Hempstead in 1644, Vlissingen (Flushing) in 1645, and Gravesend in 1645[280] and later, New Englanders settled Oyster Bay in 1653. With Dutch farmers from Brooklyn settling among the English, "Queens" was a place of diverse cultural traditions from its beginnings.

---

[279] (Earle 1891)
[280] (Cohen 1992)

To illustrate possible scenarios for placing Sam on Long Island at this time, a few stories of Long Island settlement are offered in this chapter and additional scenarios will follow in subsequent chapters.

In 1642, brothers John and Richard Ogden, of Stamford, CT entered into a contract with the new director-general William Kieft and other church wardens of New Amsterdam to build a stone church in the fort, 72 by 50 ft., for the sum of 2500 guilders, to be paid in beaver, cash, or merchandise; 100 guilders to be added if the work proved satisfactory; and the use of the company's boat to be given the builders, for carrying stone, a month, six weeks if necessary.[281] The work was satisfactorily completed in 1645 and the church stood until it was destroyed in a slave insurrection in 1741. Today, the site of Fort Amsterdam is Battery Park located at the southern tip of Manhattan Island, 13 miles south and west of Flushing. No records of the Ogden brother's employees have come to light, to establish the identities of the "English carpenters," servants or apprentices, but it is evident that Sam was later associated with John Ogden in some of his ventures. This association with Ogden lasted a number of years, so the possibility of Sam's earlier indenture and employment by Ogden is not out of the question.

In 1643, the Ogden brothers joined with the Reverend Robert Fordham, the Reverend Richard Denton and others to buy land from the Native Americans on Long Island. The price was some large and small kettles, some wampum and cloth, a broadax, knives, gunpowder, lead, and a shirt for the chief. This they paid for all the land running from the North to the South Shore that now includes Hempstead and North Hempstead.[282] Flushing is situated less than 15 miles west of modern-day North Hempstead while Fort Amsterdam was about 25 miles west of both Hempstead and North Hempstead, with the perimeters of each territory much closer. Interestingly, *Ancestors of Chauncey Lemon Dayton*[283] has Sam at Flushing in 1643. The author, Lewis Scott Dayton, might have formed this idea from Edson C. Dayton who, according to Jacobus, made an error in the date.[284]

In 1644, Fordham and John Carmen confirmed their purchase with the Dutch governor William Kieft and with John Ogden as one of the Patentees. They removed early 1644 from Stamford and settled Hempstead, and brought about 30 families from Connecticut to settle. These settlers lived in Hempstead and used the Port Washington peninsula as a pasture for their cows, calling it "Hempstead: Cow Neck." The southern portion (now Manhasset) was later called "Hempstead: Little Cow Neck," and the bay "Hempstead: Cow Bay."[285]

After just three years at Hempstead, some in the group were beginning to reconsider their move, having grown tired of the tight control of the Dutch and, as

---

[281] (Hatfield 1868)

[282] (Hinkemeyer 2001)

[283] (L. S. Dayton 1949)

[284] (D. Jacobus 1959).

[285] (B. Thompson 1918)

some authors claim, disgusted with the callous treatment of Native Americans by the Dutch. After a few more years, many of Fordham's flock were ready to follow their pastor to Southampton, on Long Island's south fork. It appears that Ogden may have been negotiating a move as early as 1647, but it was not until 1649/50 that the town of Southampton voted to grant Ogden permission to plant a colony at North Sea (four miles north of Southampton town) with the provision that he plant at least six families. This is the same North Sea, bordering on the Great Peconic Bay, opposite Robbin Island where tradition says the Lynn company disembarked at "Conscience Point," on their way to Southampton in 1640.

It is intriguing to consider the fact that Sam appeared in the New Haven Colony records in 1645, the same year as the Ogdens finished construction of the church, and then he "disappeared" from the records in 1646, presumably for "Flushing" until 1648 (according to the STR), just a few months after Rev. Fordham determined to move to Southampton and Ogden was granted land at North Sea. At that point, Sam is accepted, with conditions, to inhabit the Town of Southampton. In fact, if this is a legitimate theory, Sam may have inhabited the lot that Pelletreau marked "John Ogden 1648" on his Southampton map of Main Street while developing his own land. However, this is only speculation.

Although Sam was not included on the March 8, 1649/50 "list of the perfect freemen," he apparently passed the probationary period because one year after his acceptance to the colony, he is among 26 others on the May 10, 1649 "list of all the tounsmen," found in Hedges and Pelletreau.[286]

Mr. Edward Howell	Mr. Gosmer	Mr. Raynor
Mr. Odell	Thomas Halsey	John Howell
John Cooper	Thomas Cooper	Thomas Sayre
Job Sayre	Edward Johnes	Josiah Stanborough
Thomas Talmage	**Samuel Dayton**	Thomas Vayle
Richard Post	Thomas Hildreth	Henry Pierson
JohnWhite	Ellis Cooke	Isaac Willman
Richard Barrett	Richard Smith	Thomas Burnet
George Wood	John Jessup	Wm Rogers

(Again, caution is advised against accepting Thompson's "names of the settlers who had arrived during the first twelve months" found in his *History of Long Island,* as S.R. Winans established in his 1911 critical analysis.[287])

A search for Sam's lot in Southampton did not result in its identification on Pelletreau's map of Main Street. The hope was that the search might help determine when Sam moved from there to North Sea. Winans provides the following guidance to locating the home lots of certain inhabitants of Southampton, taken directly from his work:

---

[286] (H. Hedges 1874). 56
[287] (Winans 1911)

Land division lists were naturally drawn by lot, and were usually recorded in that order. Certain of the lists—besides those noted by Howells—happily are in residence order, a fact not hitherto brought out. Such is the 'townmen' list of May 10, 1649, except that the gentry, the 'Mr.'s,' are named first; then read the names across (S.T.R., Vol 1, p 56). It goes from Thomas Halsey northward on the West side of the street, and from Samuel Dayton, South on the East side. Winans says,

> …the fencing list of 1651-2 (S.T.R., Vol 1, pp 143-4), is now found to be in house order. Set the columns of page 144 directly under those of page 143, and then read continuously. This list goes twice from North to South, first on West side, then South on East, with several appended names. These early lists, here cited, may now furnish supplementary material to the excellent street plan by Mr. W.S. Pelletreau, prefaced to S.T.R., Vol III.[288]

Since our copy of the STR, Vol III did not include the Pelletreau map (as some editions do), we communicated our need of the map to the Rogers Memorial Library in Southampton and were promptly accommodated by Beth Gates, Librarian, who sent us a copy of the map[289] from the Long Island Collection in East Hampton.

Pelletreau's long map arrived in four sections, and when assembled end-to-end, creates a picture of Main Street. Armed with the map and the list from Hedges and Pelletreau, Winans was consulted for instructions to identify Sam's home lot.

---

[288] Ibid.

[289] (W. S. Pelletreau, A Land Map of Main Street, Southampton, New York, from 1648-1878 Book of Records of the Town of Southampton 1878)

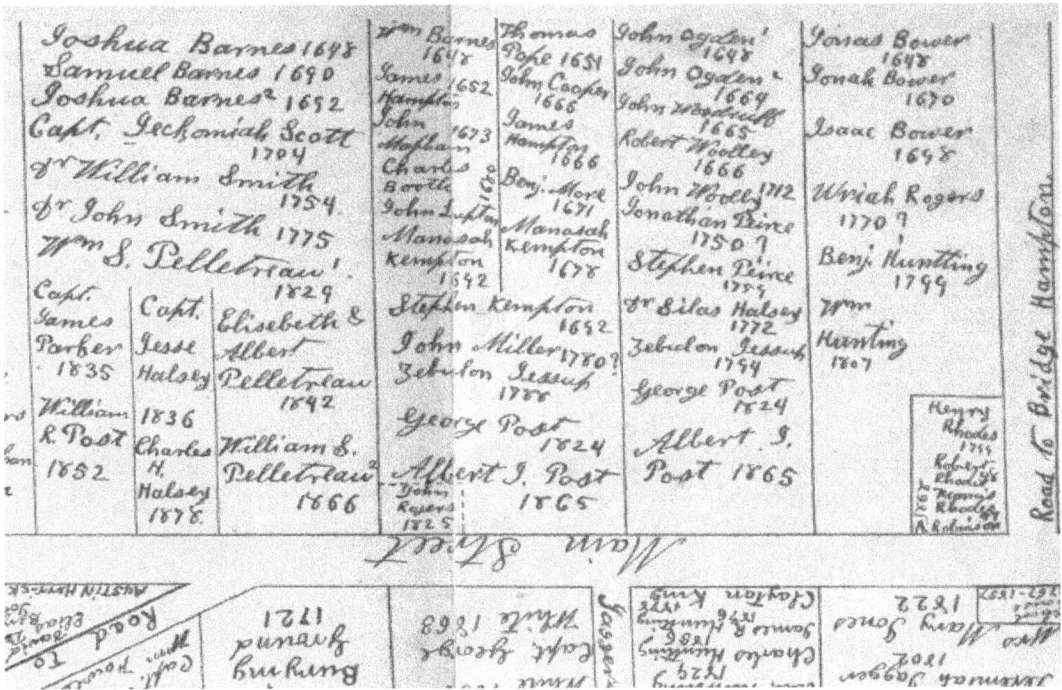

Figure 14. Land Map of Main Street, Southampton

Taken from multiple pages of *A Land Map of Main Street, Southampton* by William S. Pelletreau, 1878, this portion shows the east side of Main Street, with the road to Bridgehampton on the right (heading east) and the road to North Sea on the bottom left, heading north.

Since the settlement at Southampton began at the south end of Main Street and filled-in northward, one would expect Sam to be placed north when he was granted a home lot in 1648. STR says Sam was located on the northernmost lot, on the east side of street (as listed in the townsman list). "It goes from Thomas Halsey northward on the West side of the street, and from Samuel Dayton, South on the East side."

Using the list as a guide, Sam's plot falls just about where "John Ogden 1648" appears, which is very interesting because other sources had Ogden still in Hempstead until early in 1650. Is it possible that accommodations were granted for Ogden on Main Street in anticipation of the arrival of the group from Hempstead and Ogden's settlement at North Sea? Perhaps Pelletreau used the same information as stated in T.R. Vol 6, p.273 when he says "In 1647, the town granted to John Ogden and Company, Cow Neck and Jeffries Neck."[290] Referring to the group from

---

[290] (H. Hedges 1874) 48

Hempstead, James Thuslow Adams notes "...[Capt. Topping] probably came to Southampton with John Ogden, both of them being chosen freemen the same day, March 31, 1650."[291]

Among those who had followed Fordham from Hempstead was John Ogden, who, in 1649/50, was given permission by the town to found a 321-acre settlement at North Sea,[292] which included Cow Neck and Jefferies Neck granted to, "Mr. Ogden and his company" if, among other conditions, Ogden place six other families in the settlement.[293]

On the same day that Southampton accepted Sam, they also accepted Thomas Robbinson with 6 months' probation and six days later on May 12, 1648 they welcomed Robert Marden (Marvin) with 3 months' probation. As will be observed, these three men—Dayton, Robbinson and Marvin—seem to have some association in future events, so perhaps they traveled together.

By about 1649 or 1650, Sam's wife gave birth to their son Ralph, the first of six boys believed born to Medlin.[294] Based on the probable birth date of Ralph, we concur with Jacobus[295] that Samuel and Medlin likely married very close to the time of Sam's arrival at Southampton in 1648. But even so, it is still possible he could have married by 1645 when he was 21, before returning to New Haven, having found his wife on Long Island.

Following the ministry of Rev. Abraham Pierson at Southampton, Rev. Fordham's congregation was received from Hempstead and Fordham was installed as minister at Southampton in 1649. It is likely that Ogden had already been negotiating the move in 1648 and Pelletreau even attached that year on a Main Street lot for Ogden as part of his Southampton map. This was at the time when Ogden's company of "North Sea Proprietors" was establishing a community at North Sea. The North Sea settlement was to have all the meadow on Peconic Bay between Hog Neck Spring "and the brook by the Sachem's house." This brook is probably the one that empties into "Woolley's Pond," east of town. The complete list of land owners is lost to history but a few first settlers [of North Sea] are named: John Ogden, Samuel Dayton, Jonas Wood "of Oram," Vincent Meggs, Mark Meggs, (Calder says Meggs is a shoemaker) Samuel Clark, Fuller [Fulke] Davis, Edmond Shaw and Samuel Barker. "The North Sea line, which separates North Sea from Southampton, begins at a rock a few rods west of Mill Stone brook, at Seponack, and runs to a stone a few rods south of the head of Fish Cove. It crosses Great Fresh Pond."[296]

This list suggests that Samuel, as a "first settler" of North Sea, might have relocated there before 1650 from the ocean side settlement of Southampton. A letter from Josiah Stanborough of Southampton written to John Winthrop Junior on April

---

[291] (Adams 1918)
[292] (Howell 1887)
[293] (Adams 1918)
[294] (D. Jacobus 1959). 22
[295] Ibid.
[296] (Ross 1905)

4, 1650 suggested the need for another settlement, in support of Rev. Fordham's group at Southampton, to accommodate shipping, trading and his new whaling company. The letter reads,

> We have no newes heare being out of ye comon roade [or pticular is]; Southamp^t will be to strait [crowded] for Mr. Fordams friends. Easthampton is full, & Mr. Ogden begins a towne on or north side for tradein.[297]

Might this suggest that Sam had the opportunity to work for Mr. Ogden at the harbor, in shipping or some other field? This makes us wonder if perhaps Sam had gained shipping experience if he had worked for Ogden earlier, carrying materials, ferrying laborers, lumber or undressed quarry stone by company boat from the quarry to the building site at Fort Amsterdam.

> A number of enterprising men in Southampton and nearby East Hampton, like Ogden, were busily engaged in the sea trade. Their small shallops and pinnaces carried firewood, lumber, salt, hides, and farm produce throughout eastern and western Long Island. Using the small, shallow harbor at North Sea, Ogden also carried products from his whaling business to New Amsterdam, and probably to other ports in New England.[298]

Edwin Hatfield tells us that

> During his residence at Northampton, Ogden, by frequent visits as a trader to New Amsterdam, had kept up his acquaintance with his old friends and neighbors on the West End of the Island.[299] [300]

Another opportunity that may have occasioned Sam's removal to Long Island in the early 1640's was whaling. Southampton had an interest in whaling from its first years and was the first location where organized whaling by the English was recorded. In fact, whaling may have been the original attraction to that shore since it has been claimed that the Native American name for Southampton "Agauam" meant a *place abounding with fish.*

The harvest was so lucrative, the Bedford Whaling Museum website says "the first record of English colonists' attempts to organize community efforts to hunt drift whales was in Southampton, Long Island, in March of 1644/45." The website then claims "Over the next 30 years this organization developed into actual shore-whaling operations, where small boats were launched into the surf when whales were sighted

---

[297] (Adams 1918). 76
[298] (Harpster 2006)
[299] Note: Northampton is one of the early names for North Sea, still in use by Ralph Dayton in 1658
[300] (Hatfield 1868)

offshore."[301] Actually, we believe it would be more correct to say something like "before the end of the decade, this organization developed into actual shore-whaling operations..." but Bedford's self-interests are understood.

In *Colonizing Southampton*, Goddard wrote "...even here communal arrangements to establish whale watchers and a division of labor for processing whale carcasses quickly gave way to the development of small companies formed exclusively to hunt whales offshore for private profit."[302] What should be very interesting to Dayton researchers is, by 1650, one of the first whaling companies was formed: "the town voting that John Ogden, and his company, have the privilege of killing whales upon the south sea (the ocean) for a span of seven years."[303] The subject of Sam and the family interest in commercial whaling and future associations with Ogden will be continued later in the book.

Family Legend of the Indian Princess

There has long been a legend that Sam married a Native American princess, daughter of a minor sachem of the Montauks.

Recognizing that "the myth of the Cherokee Indian princess" is one of the most common of American family folklore, we resisted our early instincts to dismiss it as cliché and instead set out to search for the truth. It is apparently an old story and despite the absence of anything to substantiate the captivating tale, many variant accounts have been repeated in family genealogies, multiplying across the internet, especially popular with hobbyists. The stories seem to have grown out of attempts to solve the mystery of Medlin's identity.

The common core involves Samuel meeting his first wife Medlin, a Montauk, when he and his father Ralph treated with Native Americans and acted as interpreters. Quite often it has been stated that she was also known as Wilhelmina, a "Christian name bestowed on her by the Dutch." Other versions have Wilhelmina as a fourth wife. These stories are readily accessible on multiple family internet websites so none need be referenced here. The story of Sam's Native American princess bride has survived for at least a century, and conceivably longer. It appears that iterations of the tale have been embraced and sustained as contributors added interpretations of events based on what historical facts they knew, what they wanted to emphasize, and their desired image of the couple.

It is true that Sam lived close by Native Americans and had contact with them many times. In fact, there is good reason to believe he had built some kind of relationship with Native Americans both on the east end and middle of Long Island,

---

[301] (Chronology of American Whaling 2011)
[302] (Goddard 2011)
[303] (Ross 1905)

where more than once, they lived in very close proximity. It is also true that Sam was called upon to treat with the Native Americans, usually about land or whales. These occasions are recorded in town records and Pelletreau even called Sam "commissioner to the Indians."[304] However, a record of Sam treating with the Native Americans before the 1660's has not yet been found.

A century of investigation has already passed and still no evidence to substantiate a Native American wife has emerged. It is worthwhile to point out that no serious genealogist seems willing to defend the story in their writing. Accounts have been studied by Jacobus, among others, and nothing definitive has been found. After Edson C. Dayton followed another variation of the same story, he wrote his conclusion on page 22 of our copy of his 1931 publication "There is a tradition of a fourth wife, named Wilhelmina, and that she had Montauk blood. I have no authority...to substantiate this tradition."[305]

As some readers might also ponder the value of DNA testing to detect markers consistent for Native American blood, we learned that autosomal DNA testing could, in theory, detect relationships back to about the 6th or 7th generation (for us, that would be David Senior). In our case, Medlin is our 7th great-grandmother or 10 generations removed. At best, today's affordable technology severely limits what might be found once the percentage of DNA from the grandparent drops below the 1% threshold, or beyond 7 generations. The estimated percentage of DNA contribution from Medlin to my brother and I is minuscule, at only two-tenths of 1% and that is not even assured.

Theoretical Contributions

Generation	Relationship to the compiler	% DNA contribution and contributor	
2nd	Parent	50	
3	Grandparent	25	
4	Great GP	12.5	
5	GG-GP	6.25	Henry or Christie Anne
6	GGG-GP	3.13	David Junior or Chloe
7	GGGG-GP	1.56	David Senior or Anne
8	GGGGG-GP	.78	Henry or Abigail
9	GGGGGG-GP	.39	Abraham or Catherine
10th	GGGGGGG-GP	.2	Samuel or Medlin

We did not pursue the three types of genetic testing commonly used for genealogy, but opted for Single Nucleotide Polymorphism testing only.

According to Adam Rutherford, ancestry is messy.

Half of your genome comes from your mother and half from your father, a quarter from each of your grandparents. But because of the way the

---

[304] Ibid.
[305] (E. C. Dayton, The Record of a Family Descent from Ralph Dayton and Alice (Goldhatch) Tritton, Married June 1617, Ashford, County Kent, England 1931) 22

DNA deck is shuffled every time a sperm or egg is made, it doesn't keep halving perfectly as you meander up through your family tree. If you're fully outbred (which you aren't), you should have 256 great-great-great-great-great-great-grandparents. But their genetic contribution to you is not equal. Before long, you will find ancestors from whom you bear no DNA. They are your family, your blood, but their genes have been diluted out of your bloodline. Even though you are directly descended from Charlemagne, you may well carry none of his DNA.[306]

It is supposed that, at some point in the few hundred years after Medlin's death, an interested relative or inspired descendant/historian suggested that some of the circumstances or events in Samuel and Medlin's lives together could be explained if Medlin was Native American. Even the assumed time of her death (somewhere around 1664) has been cited in various works as evidence that she was Native American because Gardiner said the smallpox epidemic that swept across Long Island about the first half of the 1660's killed an estimated two-thirds of Native Americans there. "The East Hampton records indicate that the virulent disease was still raging among the Montauketts in 1664. The epidemic must have also taken the lives of many Unkechaugs, Sachem Warawakmy may also have been among the plague victims."[307] Admittedly, these circumstances do fit nicely into the puzzle but most of these "evidences" can be explained in equally legitimate ways, and most will be discussed in this book. It is supposed that, once recorded, the statements were repeated and eventually they evolved into a "memory" that had lost its origin. But where did the idea and selection of the name "Wilhelmina" come from?

In chapter 4, the point was made that some society-minded people in the last quarter of the nineteenth century sought to reinforce their social standing by establishing dignified pedigrees. This activity has always been popular in families, but it was especially fashionable and prominent near the turn of the twentieth century. Was the idea of creating "Wilhelmina" chosen in an attempt to dignify and romanticize Medlin by association with Princess Wilhelmina Helena Pauline Maria of the Netherlands, celebrated ruler of the time? Born in 1880, the only child of King Willem III, she became heiress presumptive when a child, and was crowned 1898, upon her coming of age.[308] Again, this is just an example of one possible explanation for selecting a name. No attempt is made to support this example.

In contemplation of how legends are born and nurtured, the book *Fellowship of the Ring*[309] comes to mind where J.R.R. Tolkien's ideas of history, legend, and oral tradition in Middle-Earth are eloquently expressed. Tolkien reminds us to take care with history, and to be attentive to the process of history and legend. Oral traditions have no doubt supplemented the written histories which allude to Sam's first wife.

---

[306] (Rutherford 2015)
[307] (J. A. Strong 2011)
[308] (The Statesman's Year-Book 1913)
[309] (Tolkien 1954)

Given Sam's independent thinking, as well as his reputation for adventures, there may still have been a mystique attributed to Sam by that time, handed down, but since lost. It is likely that, by 1931, when Edson C. Dayton was investigating the Native American story, the history had long ago become legend, and perhaps even the fashion and conceit of later years had been forgotten. In what appears to be a dispassionate attempt to determine the identity of the Native American wife, Edson C. Dayton begins to establish for us the probability that the Native American wife is not to be substantiated.[310]

When the compiler of this book had the privilege to interview Richard Barons at East Hampton in 2010, I gave a rendition of the family legend of Sam's Native American wife, and included what I thought were probably the justifications used to support it, particularly the idea that the couple did not receive warm receptions wherever they chose to live. Although we had earlier come to believe that it was more probable that Medlin was Dutch, Scottish or even English (but embracing one of the new religions), I asked Mr. Barons if it was possible or probable that Medlin was Native American. He was careful but self-assured in his response:

> It sounds so totally unlikely that she is Native American. If she was Dutch, she could be having a problem. Being Dutch, she would most certainly have been an outcast during that period. The only other Dutch wife was Lion Gardiner's...

Barons refers to the legendary Lion Gardiner about whom much is written. Gardiner wed his Dutch wife in Holland in 1625, while he was in the Dutch military. Gardiner, a military engineer and fortification expert, agreed to construct a fort for the English and design the layout of the town that would become Saybrook, Connecticut.[311]

Barons developed his response concerning marriage to a native person, and he also contemplated the charge of slander that was brought against Sam, upon the actions of his wife. Mr. Barons referenced East Hampton in his reply, but it is presumed Southampton would possess much of the same disposition toward Native Americans.

> I can't imagine anyone in East Hampton even thinking about suing a Native American, if it was a wife or anything. You wouldn't have to sue them...You could get an indemnity from them. You could get forty bushels of corn from them...There wasn't any equality. No, it doesn't make any sense. Why would you bother to marry her? It would tend to move you around though if you had this kind of relationship.

---

[310] (E. C. Dayton, The Record of a Family Descent from Ralph Dayton and Alice (Goldhatch) Tritton, Married June 1617, Ashford, County Kent, England 1931)
[311] (Culbertson 1987)

I don't know why, if you've come from England…it's not as if the kid has been born here. I mean, he's got all the traditions. It seems you'd really be a rebel marrying her, to spite society.

Mr. Barons offered a possible explanation for the imagined stories that created family legend, particularly at the time when publications of genealogies were very much in vogue. He explains:

> …and, of course, in the 1870's and 1880's, during the getting ready for and after the centennial, there was the romance about the Native Americans and most colonial families found it entertaining to decide that one of their relatives…that we have Native American blood. It was an entertaining thing. It was a conceit. Because it's at the same time, by 1900 or by the 1880's, is when we are coming up with this business about 'the last pure blood Indian died' and 'the last pure blood Montauketer died' and, of course, you know why they're doing that? To break treaties, if the last pure bred Native American is dead. They were waiting for the last one to die.[312]

In his writing, author John Strong told us that the "local newspapers always announced the death of an elderly Indian as the passing of the 'last pureblood.'" Strong continued, "When Mary Walkus died at the age of 100 in 1867, a town official solemnly noted that she was…*the last full-blooded squaw and oldest of the Shinnecocks.* When Wickham Cuffee died in 1915 he was anointed "last of the Shinnecocks" by historian John Morice." Strong also tells us that it happened again in 1936, when Mary Rebbeca Kellis died at the age of 102, she was heralded by the Long Island Press as "…the last full-blooded Indian living on Long Island."[313]

Our mitigated conclusion is that the tradition of Medlin as Native American, and particularly the legend of a princess bride are unfounded. They are both suspicious and problematic, a proliferation of romantic myth. We respectfully suggest that the legend of the Indian bride should no longer determine or even influence the direction of inquiry as Dayton researchers continue to search for the identity of Medlin. While the fantastic does stimulate conversations, the preoccupation of the romantic tale may impede or defeat interest in exploration of more realistic paths.

Medlin

As the much-loved Native American story has been disparaged, creating our own void, the search for a new story continues. If Sam's first wife was not the sachem's daughter, who was she?

---

[312] (Barons 2010)
[313] (J. Strong 1992) 39-73

116

Unfortunately, our knowledge of her continues to be almost exclusively limited to a few town records and it appears that most of the speculation around her, over the last century, has grown from attempts to make sense of these bits of information. First, Sam had a wife in 1653 because the STR from September 12 says Sam was sued on behalf of his [unnamed] wife. While it is not certain this wife was Sam's first and that she is indeed Medlin, it is supposed both are true. They would have been married about five years and already had their first three children —Ralph, Samuel and newborn Abraham.

Only one other record of this wife is found, STR dated December of 1656, where Medlin was mentioned by name. The record says, "John Howell bought of Medlin Dayton ye wife of Samuel Dayton with his consent 4 acres of ground in great plaines being next to the 4 acres of ground commonly called by the name of Harcres lot and the meadow belonging to it."

Working under the premise that the Native American story was discredited, our search for Medlin's identity began with examination of her name. Was "Medlin" her birth name, nickname, or perhaps a translation as suggested by those who prefer variations of Magdeline? Complicating the matter, one author claims that over forty spellings[314] of "Medlin" have been found. Was her name English, Scottish or departed Dutch, as one[315] who would suggest she could even be Magdalen, daughter of Cornelius Melyn, the Patroon of Staten Island in New Amsterdam? This theory is mentioned more for its interest than for its promise. The idea is that perhaps the name Medlin was assigned to her by the courts in order to associate her with her father or her husband's land, normally addressed as "widow Medlin." Some of the more interesting circumstances enhancing this unlikely theory include the names of Sam's sons—Abraham, Isaac and Jacob. Though these were common names, in a common sequence, children were often named after their relatives and Magdalen's siblings also happen to have been Abraham, Isaac and Jacob. Cornelius "escaped" from Dutch Long Island to New Haven and later died there. Also, it is claimed that Nathaniel Baker of East Hampton, nephew of Samuel, married Catherine Melyn, another daughter of Cornelius Melyn.[316]

Medlin is also a Scottish surname, and by tradition she could have received it, having been her mother's maiden name. Today, Medlins have a large family presence in America, particularly in the Carolinas, but thus far none have been identified in New England or on Long Island in the 1640's.

Next, family names of inhabitants in New Haven Flushing, Southampton and North Sea before 1650 were examined, in pursuit of anything that may point to her identity. Because the magnitude of this project makes it seem so daunting, focus was

---

[314] (O'Donnell 1976)

[315] Note: Extracted 2012 from comments on a genealogy discussion board, author and website unknown.

[316] (A. H. Davis 1888)

on daughters or widows and turned up some interesting finds but none offered resolution.

The founders of Southampton, settlers from Lynn, Massachusetts who had been driven out from Schout's Bay on western Long Island, established residence on lands obtained from the Shinnecock Indian Nation in 1640. The first settlers were landed near Conscience Point, at North Sea, by Captain Daniel Howe. The group was then led by Native Americans southward, less than four miles, to the spot by the ocean that the natives called Agauam. These men were Edmond Farrington, Edward Howell, Edmund Needham, Job Sayre, Thomas Sayre, Josiah Stanborough, Henry Walton and George Welbe but more families were added before they left Lynn: Allen Breed, John Cooper, Christian Connolly, John Farrington, Thomas Farrington, Thomas Halsey, William Harker, Daniel Howe, John Jessup, Nathaniel Kirtland, Philip Kyrtand, Thomas Newell, Richard Odell, Thomas Stephens and Thomas Terry. Still more were added from New Haven.

We often wonder if Samuel, as a young man of sixteen or seventeen, joined the group as indenture, when the company stopped enroute at New Haven in 1640. Was Medlin already in this group, as daughter of one of these inhabitants, or would she become a widow a few years later?

The name "Harcres," it seems, has become almost inseparable from conversations concerning the supposed identity of Medlin. The STR says that the Dayton land was "…in great plaines being next to the 4 acres of ground commonly called by the name of Harcres lot and the meadow belonging to it." Ever since the esteemed historian and genealogist Donald Lines Jacobus said, "Presumably this was land inherited by Samuel's wife, and it might be a clue to her identity" and he said, "'Harcres lot' evidently refers to William Harker, one of the original undertakers…,"[317] the association of Medlin with Harker has become fixed and perpetual. While it is understandable that so many would advocate the association only suggested by Jacobus, we don't believe it was his intention to limit the exploration to this possibility alone.

Like so many researchers before us, our investigation of William Harker did not yield any answers. In fact, it only created more questions. During the 1640 interrogation of Harker, he told the Dutch authorities he was 24,[318] meaning that Harker's children wouldn't be older than 19 by 1656 so William can likely be eliminated as Medlin's father or her husband since Harker was still living and she would be about eight years Sam's senior. How else might William Harker be some kind of benefactor for Medlin?

---

[317] (D. Jacobus 1959)
[318] (Howell 1887)

William Harck, Sheriff of Flushing, was also considered. He was banished to eastern Long Island[319] April 3, 1648. The investigation of Harck led us back to interesting stories of the Farringtons of Flushing and Southampton. Interested researchers might invest time attempting to connect or eliminate some of the conflicting stories of Thomas Farrington and the many husbands attributed to Helena Applegate. A few suggested sources to begin the undertaking are Cutter's *American Biography*,[320] Bolton's *A History of the County of Westchester*[321] and accounts by John E. Stillwell in 1914.

Medlin's presumed ownership of land has also been offered as evidence that Medlin was Native American. There is little doubt that, in the minds of those who support the idea of Medlin as Native American, Jacobus's suggestion that the land could have belonged to Medlin as an inheritance lent support to their argument. For those seeking evidence, their theory would be supported by the belief that it would be less likely for a Puritan woman to own land than for a Native American, especially a princess.[322]

Like other societies of their time, the Puritans placed restrictions on women, believing they should be culturally subservient to men. Women were to look to men for leadership, protection and direction (at least in public). Upon marriage, women almost always gave up property rights to their husbands so they were not allowed to buy or sell land, and many times were denied rights of inheritance. But these constraints did not always apply, especially to widows. Widows could own land, could sue and be sued, and were allowed to "discipline any children or servants in their households."[323]

There is also the counter-argument that Native Americans didn't own land, therefore she couldn't have been Native American. This idea comes from the common belief that individual land ownership did not exist among them. That is not exactly true. It was possible that a Native American woman could "own" land, but it would still be a very rare occurrence by 1656. Had Medlin been one of the few Native American women to own land, she most likely would have been of royalty, and if so, that information would probably have been gained from a Puritan record. Robert J. Miller of the Lewis & Clark Law School[324] said, "Most Indians did not consider that land could be privately owned but instead thought that tribal lands were communally owned." Miller argues,

> European and American colonists came to believe that Indians did not believe in or understand private property and capitalist principles... [but] American Indians were continuously involved in free market trade

---

[319] (Waller 1889) 56
[320] (Cutter 1922)
[321] (Bolton 1848)
[322] (J. A. Strong 2010)
[323] (Deering 2003)
[324] (Miller 2001)

situations before and after European contact and, while most of the land that Indians lived on was considered tribal land owned by the tribe or by all the tribe's members in common, almost all the tribes recognized various forms of permanent or semi-permanent private rights to land. Individual tribe members could, and did, acquire and exercise use rights over specific pieces of land (tribal and not), homes, and valuable plants like berry patches and fruit and nut trees, both through inheritable rights and by buying and selling.

There are a few instances where private "ownership" was recorded, as in the case of the female sachem or "sunksqua" named Catoneras, who passed a title to "land called Crab Meadow in the northeastern part of the Town of Huntington to her son, Jan." Roger Williams, in his 1643 guide *A Key to the Languages of America* described "sunksqua" as "queens" who had the same powers as the male sachems.[325]

With all these considerations in mind, it is our opinion that the town record should not contribute to the belief that Medlin was Native American. If one is to believe that Medlin actually did own the land, it is more likely she was a widow than Native American. Further, it is our belief that the record provides evidence that Medlin was not Native American because, you would expect the record to allude to those circumstances of ownership since it would not have been the norm. Ultimately, the interpretation of land ownership neither supports nor detracts from the argument of Medlin as Native American and actually, to us, the town record does not even allude to Medlin's ownership of the land. There is another logical, but simpler explanation.

Ned Smith[326] at the Suffolk County Historical Society was consulted, relating the account of Medlin selling land "with her husbands consent." Mr. Smith is the former Director of the Library and Research at the New York Genealogical and Biographical Society and as such, he possesses a wealth of knowledge and contextual insight. When Mr. Smith was asked if anything could be learned about Sam or Medlin from this unusual record his reply was almost immediate; he said, "Maybe he was out to sea." Smith's suggestion brought to our memories other instances where Sam was missing from significant events and these accumulative instances may give us a clue to his occupation that may have required some extended absence.

It is our conclusion that Medlin probably did not own the land. Instead, she acted on behalf of her husband, with his consent, probably because he did not have the ability to attend.

In some ways, 1650 was a transitional year for our ancestors. Sam and Medlin had their first child, a son whom they named after the boy's grandfather. That year, Sam probably found some kind of temporary accommodation for his parents, his

---

[325] (Williams 1973) 201
[326] (N. Smith 2012)

brother and his sister and her family in Southampton town, as the Daytons and Bakers, with their new baby, moved to Long Island. This was also the year that Sam's brother Robert would "come of age."

Just a few days after Josiah Stanborough wrote to John Winthrop Junior suggesting that Southampton was already crowded, Stanborough faced Sam in court. "An action of trespass entered upon the 11th day of Aprill 1650, by Josiah Stanborough plaintiff against Samuel Dayton defendant is to be tried by a particular court to be held upon the 14th day of Aprill next." Very often, these types of suits might involve a pig or some other domestic animal getting through a broken fence, to cause damage to a neighbor's property, especially a garden. Interestingly, the suit is then followed by a countersuit on the same day, with Sam as plaintiff. No completion of either case was found in the records so perhaps they settled their differences or further action was lost from the record.

Two years later, a most curious Southampton record says,

> Robert Mervin standeth bound vnto Thomas [word gone] and Capt Thomas Topping of Southampton, gentleman in the sum of ten pounds to prosecute a suite against Iohn Hubby in the next quarter court to be held in & vpon the first tuesday in december, for which the said Robert Mervin atacked a rapier in the hands of Samuel Dayton.[327]

A record that immediately followed was dated May 25, 1652. "An action of tresspass vpon the case entered by Robert Mervin plf against Iohn Hubby defendant, this action is not tryed but ye Cort forbear yet because of ye defendants absence."

Much time was invested mulling over the meaning of "atacked a rapier" until consulting Ned Smith of the Suffolk County Historical Society who suggested at least two possibilities,

> …the transcriber misread the original. Instead of *Mervin attacked a rapier in the hands of Samuel Dayton,* might it not really have been *Mervin attached a Papier [sic] in the hand of Samuel Dayton*? Perhaps Mervin was illiterate and needed someone else to write out his bond for him to submit to the court.

> The entry following the Mervin one was for another suit against John Hubby. This one was by John Cooper Junior and Thomas Vale against Hubby, and they were granted an attachment of Hubby's goods. [word gone] within the bounds of Southampton… that would be a lien against his property. Maybe the Mervin case involved just a lien against a sword owned by Hubby but in the temporary possession of Samuel Dayton. The difference in the value of the attachments might be because Cooper & Vale were seeking more in damages than Merwin was.[328]

---

[327] (H. Hedges 1874)
[328] (N. Smith 2012).

Once again, Mr. Smith made sense of a mysterious record, as supported by a similar East Hampton record dated September 15, 1653. This record, worded much the same as the Southampton record, shows us the common usage of the words, "attached…in the hands of." The example reads, "Vnto the Constabell of Easthampton you are by vertue here of to attach two Cowes and a Calfe of Captayne Daniel howes in the hands of Robert Bond…"

In the early days of Southampton, the Little Plains were fields located between Old Town Pond and Lake Agawam (known then as Town Pond), used as plough land. It is thought that perhaps these were fields whose fertility was previously nurtured by the Native Americans. Today, Little Plains Road bisects the once cultivated fields. The division of Little Plaine was determined by lottery drawn by the inhabitants in March of 1651/52. "Ellis Cook 100 drew No. 26. Samuel Dayton is to have a 50 share out of the same."[329] Then, the order of the fence for the little plaine lists each man's name and, as discussed earlier, this list was used with the Pelletreau map to locate Samuel's home lot, between Robert Mervin and George Wood.[330]

Further west, on the other side of Town Pond was farm land called general field or more commonly, the Great Plaines. This was probably the location of the "4 acres of ground in great plaines" that Medlin sold when Sam was absent. Today it is transversed east to west by Great Plains Road and Ox Pasture Road. The four necks of the Great Plains are referenced in the Southampton Town Records. Proceeding east to west, they are called First Neck, Cooper's Neck, Halsey's Neck, and Captain's Neck.

On September 12, 1653, Sam's unnamed wife was sued for slander by blacksmith Thomas Vail, who won the case and four days later a jury gave the plaintiff £3 damage with cost of Court. The record says, "An action of Slander entered by Tho. Vale against the wife of Samuel Dayton to £40 damage." The legal conclusion of the matter, on September 16, 1653 says,

> …at a purchased cort, the said action of Slander entered per Tho. Vale plf against Sam. Dayton defendant, tryed by 12 men namely Mr Richard Smith Mr Thurston Rayner Mr Richard Odell Thomas Halsey, Iohn Howell Richard Barret Christopher ffoster, Tho. Goldsmith Tho. Sayre Tho. Cooper Iohn Iessup Isack Willman. The said Jury finde for the plf. three pound damage, with increase of Cort charges.

Pelletreau notes,

> The term purchased court which is occasionally found in these records seems to be applied to courts held to try some particular case which for any reason could not be postponed until the setting of the regular quarter

---

[329] (H. Hedges 1874)
[330] Ibid.

court…for an instance in which Jonas Wood has a purchased court on account of his being about to remove from the town.

Sarah Vale, wife of Thomas, had a similar problem a few years earlier. Sarah Vale, on June 4, 1651, was, "sentenced to stand with her tongue in a cleft stick so long as the offense committed by her was read and declared."[331] George Wood, Sam's neighbor, was plaintiff. On October 23, 1650, a misdemeanor had been, "laid to their charge" and since Thomas and his wife Sarah were both ordered to appear, it is logical to assume the charge had something to do with Sarah.

William C. Armstrong, author of *Pioneer Families of Northwestern New Jersey*[332] writes of Sarah Vail, "The records of the Town of Southampton (p.80) reveal that this order was caused by a woman of strong mind, of precise speech and of positive character…It seems her offense was caused by just provocation and in this day she would not be blamed for defending and protecting herself with the only weapon a woman has." Armstrong continues to defend Sarah by saying, "However, the circumstances were as follows: George Wood, a neighbor, trespassed uninvited into the home of Thomas Veale, who complained to the Court. George Wood entered a cross action. The Court acquitted and dismissed both parties. After Court Mrs. Veale used the language for which she was punished." (Apparently the judge did not find "just provocation").

This is probably the same George Wood who had been, seven years earlier, the subject of an interesting court entry.

> March 4, 1644, Wheras George Wood and an Indian named by the name of Hope both of them being servants vnto Mr. Edward Howell of this towne of Southampton, haue consented to commit carnal filthiness together and the sayd Hope being begoten with child hath constantly affirmed the sayd George Wood to be the lawfull ffather of the sayd child. Both of them having receaued corporale punishment. The sayd George Wood and the sayd Indian named by the name of Hope, have both of them publickly in Court the daye and yeare aforesaid, Consented and agreede that the sayd child basely begoten being at this tyme a yeare old, shall continue to be the lawfull servant of the sayd Edward Houell, his heires or Assignes vntil the sayd child shall be of the age of thirty years before he shall be released of his aforesayd Apprenticeshippe, And the sayd Edward Houell doth promise for himself his heires and Assignes to prouide for the sayd child meat, drinke, and Apparel and necessaryes fit for such a servant dureing the sayd tyme. In witness whereof the parties aboue mentioned haue set to their hands this fourthe daye of March 1644.[333]

---

[331] Ibid. (Ancestors of Gregory Thomas Wirt 2013) 80
[332] (Armstrong 2009)
[333] (H. Hedges 1874) 80

In the case against Samuel and Medlin, one might wonder if the defense offered for Sarah by Armstrong could be utilized for Medlin's words against Sarah in 1653. Had Medlin been defending someone against Sarah? No mention of this case appears in Armstrong's book. The fact that the case against Sam (actually on account of Sarah and Medlin) took place in a purchased court, tried by 12 men, suggests that the accusation was judged especially serious or that the action was deemed necessary and couldn't wait until the time of scheduled court. There are a few ways to interpret what this meant...possibly town officers determined that what was described by Medlin was so troubling that, for the good of the town, the truth must be discovered. In modern politics and law, this argument is referred to as "the seriousness of the charge." Or, possibly the words were so shocking or deplorable that the very act of speaking them demanded punishment or what was described by Medlin so troubled town officers that they felt they must get at the truth. Another possibly is that the Vales were so offended that they sought relief as quickly as possible, seeking resolution because they expected that Sam may be out to sea for extended periods.

There is reason to believe that the Vails may have had ideas different than those of Puritans because one source claims Thomas's son Samuel was a Quaker minister while Armstrong says that Thomas's grandson, John was a Quaker preacher as well.[334] Subsequent generations were also Quaker. Some Vale researchers believe Thomas's move from Salem, Massachusetts to Long Island may have been due to the prosecution of those who possessed other religious convictions, including those forerunners of Quakerism in New England and this was the probable reason for the Vales going to Long Island. This theory could have also come from author William Armstrong who spoke about Quakers who had arrived on Long Island a decade after the Vales.

---

[334] (Armstrong 2009)

Chapter 9

The Settlement at Easthampton

Foundational source material for East Hampton is found in the two volumes entitled *Records of the Town of East Hampton, Long Island, Suffolk Co, N.Y.*, transcribed under the direction of the Town of East Hampton and published 1887. In the introduction, H.P.Hedges says, "The Records of the Town of East Hampton are more full, more clear, more continuous, more intelligent than are usually found in like early colonies...Every native of the old town, every careful student of our National History will rejoice that these records by publication have become an enduring memorial to the world, and thank the sons of her early settlers for this generous contribution to the history of our nation."

Proprietors

In 1902, author Peter Ross said that, "What time East Hampton was first settled is not certainly known. [It was] probably soon after Southampton."[335] Sherrill Foster says, "In 1648, John Mulford led 8 other entrepreneurs to the east of the South Fields, to be nearer to the livestock grazing lands of the Montauk peninsular, the area soon became known as East Hampe, or later East Hampton."[336] Mulford had been a resident of Southampton since 1643.[337] In the very first line of Hedges introduction to the 1887 publication of the town records, he states East Hampton was settled 1649.

Bob Hefner, historic preservation consultant for East Hampton, prefers 1648. Among other projects, Mr. Hefner planned and supervised preservative work on *Home Sweet Home* (that property so dear to Daytons), what he calls, "a seventeenth-century shingled cottage at 14 James Lane in East Hampton...perhaps the most shining example of early East Hampton architecture."[338] Hefner said,

---

[335] (Ross 1905)
[336] (S. Foster 2001)
[337] (H. Hedges 1874)
[338] (Hefner, Historic Preservation and Historic Districts 2002)

In 1648 the governors of the New Haven and Connecticut Colonies and their associates purchased from the Montauk Indians approximately 31,000 acres on Long Island's South Fork. The purchase extended from Southampton Town eastward to Nominicks, the first highlands of the Montauk peninsula. This group of investors in turn sold shares in their purchase to would-be settlers who originated from a number of different New England towns.[339]

The colonists wanted to establish their own settlement much like Southampton. While some of the group were already in Southampton in 1648, others arrived from New England, probably landing at North Sea because Northwest (which is much closer to East Hampton) may not have been developed. Northwest and Northwest Harbor were not mentioned in the records until four years later, in 1652. Of course, the landing at North Sea would have made Southampton a convenient terminal, as Hedges says, "It is not improbable that the preparing Pioneers stopped awhile at Southampton, proceeding from thence as a base to East Hampton."[340] So, by Southampton, Hedges may be referring to North Sea in addition to the settled town of Southampton.

Hedges said, "It has been said Tradition is the fragments which history loses on its way to eternity. The uniform tradition that East-Hampton was settled by a company from Lynn, until of late years, was unquestioned and is yet undisproved."[341] According to Gardiner, in his *Chronicles of Easthampton*,

> John Hand Senior, John Stretton Senior, Thomas Talmadge Junior, Robt. Bond, Daniel Howe, Robt. Rose, Thos. Tomson, Joshua Barnes, and John Mulford, commenced the first settlement, under the original contract, early in 1649. The first six of these came from Lynn, in Massachusetts, where they had remained for some time after their arrival from England...Howe was a sea captain, and held a military appointment under the magistracy of Salem. Hand was from the hamlet of Stanstede, in the county of Kent, England, where, for several years after his arrival here, he held an estate in lands. Barnes and Mulford had, but a short time previous to the purchase, arrived and settled at Southampton, from Salem. Most, if not all of them were from Maidstone, or the country in its vicinity, in the county of Kent, one of the richest agricultural districts in England. They first named the purchase Maidstone, after that town: a name which

---

[339] Ibid.
[340] (H. Hedges 1897)
[341] Ibid.

ought to have been retained, in preference to the one subsequently adopted and still used, as far more euphonious and exclusive...[342]

In regard to Gardiner's claims, Sherrill Foster contested,

> Now, we have to get over the notion that East Hampton was originally Maidstone. None of the original 9 settlers are from there or even from Kent. Those whose origins are known are from Devonshire, and Hampshire...That Maidstone legend can be traced to 1871 when David Johnson Gardiner published his essays about East Hampton. In the 19th century, the idea of Maidstone was eagerly taken up by the 'summer people' who named their club, their inns and other organizations with that name.[343]

Both views are given here for consideration, although Benjamin Thompson also mentioned "Maidstone" forty years before Gardiner.

Our research shows that, of the nine, only four have known origins and they are one each from Hampshire, Suffolk, Herfordshire and Kent. Those origins not confirmed may have been Devonshire (2), Suffolk (2) and Hampshire.

James Truslow Adams, in his *History of the Town of Southampton (East of Canoe Place)* gives the list of land allotments in Lynn, so far as it relates to the Southampton settlers was as follows—Edward Howell, Thomas Sayre, John Cooper, Christopher Foster, Allen Bread, Thomas Newhall, Edmund Farrington, [Wm] Harker, Josias Stanbury, Phillip Kirtland sen., Thomas Halsye, Phillip Kirtland jun., Job Sayre, George Wellbye, Daniel Howe. According to Ross, it was Pelletreau's opinion that East Hampton was really an overflow colony from Southampton. Of the men who purchased the territory, John Hand, Thomas Talmadge, Daniel Howe, Thomas Thompson, John Stratton, Robert Bond, Robert Rose, Joshua Barnes and John Mulford, all were originally settlers in Southampton, their names appearing in the early records of that township. "With the exception of Daniel How, not one had any previous residential connection with Lynn."[344] According to Hedges and others, Howe had resided in Southampton until 1643, at least part of this time ferrying people and supplies between Massachusetts and Southampton, a part of the agreement made in the Disposal of the Vessel.

---

[342] (D. Gardiner 1871)
[343] (S. Foster 2001)
[344] (Ross 1905)

Selecting the Spot

To the east of Southampton, about twelve miles distant from Towne Street, the proprietors selected the location for their settlement adjacent to the fertile coastal plain, just north of Hook Pond. East Hampton was the third English town established on eastern Long Island, after Southold and Southampton, eight years earlier. The town was laid out in New England Puritan fashion, composed of long, narrow house lots on both sides of a wide common, with houses placed at the front of each lot, leaving the remainder, behind the house, for cultivation and outbuildings. It is said that, at one time, the common was almost a mile long, extending all the way to Hook Mill Green, and contained a marshy area fed by a brook or spring. "This was probably on account of the convenience of getting water for themselves and cattle before they dug wells.[345]

Within the first year of settlement, the group had increased to thirty-four families, each distributed around the swampy area, probably in crude temporary dwellings at first. Each was on eight to twelve acres, but would be close enough to construct fences between buildings, forming a corral for their herds. "Of those who had joined the settlement during the first year several were from Gardiner's Island, where they had been farmers for Mr. Gardiner [Joshua Garlicke was one such farmer], and some from the settlement of Southampton, and others from several towns in New England, bordering on the sound."[346]

The expanse of lands outside the village of East Hampton provided a variety of important uses. Sources of fresh water, woodlands, meadow and fields for cultivation and pasturage, and ocean beaches for fishing and whale harvesting were in the south while harbors in the north provided access to fishing, travel and trade.

The Move to Long Island

When last discussed, our American progenitor was in New Haven, the date was April of 1649, and Ralph was in a court dispute where he had committed to buy land there, and buyer and seller had conflicting understandings of where the boundary should fall. Apparently Ralph purchased the land and discovered that the boundary was not where he had hoped. He was ordered by the court to take the land sold to him and pay taxes on it. As is normally the case, there was probably more to the story, and perhaps this decision and difficulty didn't set well with Ralph. If Ralph had tired

---

[345] Ibid.
[346] (D. Gardiner 1871) 19

of New Haven, he might have envisioned new opportunities on Long Island, for himself and for his youngest son Robert, who was about to become "of age."

By this time, Sam had already been in Southampton almost a year and sometime in the following year, Ralph's son-in-law Thomas Baker of Milford, CT would negotiate with Daniel Howe of East Hampton and Alexander Bryan of Milford to purchase Howe's very significant share in the East Hampton settlement.[347]

As one of the original six, Capt. Daniel Howe was also a proprietor, receiving his share of the division of 31,000 acres, according to his advance money. These investors sold shares to the settlers. If successful in the purchase, Baker could become one of the elite group in East Hampton, the men of substance who were set apart from the other inhabitants. By May 10, 1650, Baker began the purchase that was to be completed by September 29, 1650 when all of Howe's accommodations were to be turned over to him.

> Received this 10th day of May 1650 the sum of twentie pounds & is in full payment of the lot which was myne at Easthampton & now sould to Thomas Backer of Mylford I say recd by me Daniell How in full payment of my lott withall the accomodacons & convenyences belonging therevnto of my Cousin Alexander Bryan the sum of twentie pound & the lott & accomodacons to be delivered to and for the use of Thomas Backer the 29th of September next ensueing.[348]

Because Baker's purchase began so soon after the founding of East Hampton, there are random accounts that include him as an original founder in the patent of 1648. Sometimes, in these misconceptions, his name is even used in place of the original owner's name, Daniel Howe. For example, Ross tells us that in French's *Gazeteer*, "Settlement in the western part of the town was commenced in 1648 by a company of English families from Lynn, Mass. The trustees named in the patent were John Mulford, Thomas Baker, Thomas Chatfield, Jeremiah Concklyn, Stephen Hedges, Thomas Osborne sen., and John Osborne."[349]

The Bakers remained in Milford until the beginning of July 1650, for the baptism of newborn daughter Hannah. The record of Hannah's baptism[350] appears in the records of the Milford First Congregational Church, on a page that was charred and blackened in a 1922 fire, but can still be read, "June 30 Hannah: D of Thomas Baker."

---

[347] (L. Baker n.d.)
[348] (H. Hedges 1887)
[349] (Ross 1905)
[350] (Theodore, Milford First Congregational Church Records-1639-1837 Jun 2009)

Thomas satisfied payments to Howe by August of 1650, a few weeks before they were due. It appears that he did not travel to East Hampton to do this, but instead dealt with Howe's cousin in Milford, Alexander Bryan.

> Recd this 24th of August 1650 of Thomas Backer the sum of twentie pounds & is in full for the lott he bought of Capt. How at Easthampton. I say Recd in full for the lott £20 00s 00d. Pr me ALEXANDER BRYAN.[351]

Thomas was dismissed from the Milford Church in September and the Baker family left Connecticut for Long Island. Captain Howe eventually returned to England. It didn't take long for Thomas to become established in East Hampton because he was elected Townsman in October 1650.

The Problem of Southold

In *History of Southold, L.I. Its First Century*,[352] Rev. Epher Whitaker, pastor of the Southold Presbyterian Church, placed Thomas Baker prominently at the top of his list of inhabitants of Southold. Even though this claim seems to be his alone, out of respect for Whitaker's certainty, records were searched again for evidence that we may have overlooked. Despite the effort, nothing else was found that would support Whitaker's contention that Thomas was at Southold so, it has been concluded that Whitaker was mistaken. To complicate the matter, the earliest Southold records had, at some point, become lost and have never been found. In his book, Whitaker said,

> For nearly thirty years past I have been carefully making a list of the early settlers who left written evidence, (in the Town Records; in Deeds conveying lands, or other property; in Wills; on Tombstones, or other documents,) that they were full grown men here within the life-time of the first pastor. Nearly all named in the list which I have made were not only residents here, but also landowners. In the words of the Town Patent, they were 'Freeholders and Inhabitants.'[353]

Whitaker continued,

> Of the full-grown men—at least one hundred and thirty-eight—who lived here and left their record in the annals of this Town during the period of the ministry of the first pastor from 1640 to 1672, not a few removed to other places, and became important factors and elements in the settlement

---

[351] (H. Hedges 1887)
[352] (Whitaker 1881)
[353] Ibid.

and life of other Towns. Of these, Thomas Baker removed to Easthampton, Long Island. He was one of the settlers and representatives of that Town who obtained in 1649 the title from Gov. Eaton and Gov. Hopkins, these Governors having purchased it the previous year...

What was most unsettling for us was Whitaker's confidence to mention Thomas Baker first, almost set apart from the others on his list, but he provided no reference to validate the proclamation. In spite of our rather lengthy search, no other author has been found who spoke of Baker at Southold and no other reference or record to the same. Instead, the ETR, Vol I made it clear that Baker was of Milford, CT before he moved to East Hampton. There is equal confidence that Thomas, once settled and established at East Hampton, did not attempt a move elsewhere.

The ETR says, "Received this 10th day of May 1650 the sum of twentie pounds & is in full payment of the lot which was myne at Easthampton & now sould to Thomas Backer of Mylford..." Subsequent records in August and September concur that Baker was of Milford.

While it can't be proved that Thomas Baker never owned land at Southold, therefore saying that Whitaker was wrong on all accounts of Baker, we are inclined to believe that he did not.

Ralph at East Hampton

As for the Ralph Dayton family, when and how they made their way to East Hampton are not explicitly enumerated. The earliest record found with Ralph in East Hampton is on March 7, 1650, suggesting that he had already been there a while. Sam's sister, Ellen had married John Linley (Lindley/Linsley) in 1644 and remained in Guilford, CT[354] while her father, mother and her younger brother Robert made their way to Long Island, to settle on a lot that would later be directly across the green from Thomas and Alice. Ralph's home lot on the south or east side of the common, was later owned by his son Robert, and was then divided and now contains a bit of the Episcopal Church on one part[355] and *Home Sweet Home* museum on another. That house, made famous by John Howard Payne, was probably built shortly after Robert's death. If the Dayton lot hadn't been inhabited at some point before their arrival, the Dayton's temporary dwelling must have contrasted greatly with the Baker property on the north side of the street, where Howe may have already started construction of his dwelling. The Baker house was probably one of the larger buildings in early East Hampton because the house was used for church services before the meeting house was built.

---

[354] (Perry 1974)
[355] (F. Baker 1914)

Today, a remnant of what was probably Thomas Baker's second house (built about 1673) sits within a grand structure of 1911 English Arts and Crafts architecture called *The Baker House 1650*, a premier bed & breakfast.

What would influence Ralph's decision to move to East Hampton, and start over, when he was more than 60 years of age? Perhaps his 1649 purchase of additional land in the New Haven colony indicates that he was not planning to leave, but his subsequent sale to Leeke in that same year suggests a sudden change in plan. Robert was going to be 21 in 1650, so it is likely Ralph was purchasing land in New Haven with the interests of his son in mind, but the property dispute at New Haven might have been all the extra incentive Ralph needed to act.

This was a very common pattern of behavior in New England, among the Puritans, "if they had differences within the group, they would join with others and move on."[356] With such a grand opportunity at East Hampton for Ralph and then for Thomas, an opportunity that came about as a result of the original settlers of East Hampton beginning to leave, they both acted.

As is popularly suggested, Ralph's move to Long Island could have actually pre-dated his son-in-law's move, and he may have stayed with Sam in Southampton while negotiating and erecting his dwelling at East Hampton.

There is little doubt that East Hampton had a certain appeal for Ralph and family. "Raising Livestock, especially cattle, seems to have been the predominant aspect of East Hampton's agrarian economy."[357] Their daughter and son-in-law, with their new baby, were close by and there were many settlers moving to East Hampton who had come from Kent, even from their own Ashford parish. Richard Brook, Thomas James, Benjamin Price and John Osbourne appear in the Ashford parish registry, for example. In addition, John Hand of Maidstone, Kent could have been an acquaintance also because, "he had had property interests at Ashford, Kent."[358] The Bakers, Hedges and Strattons came from the Maidstone area. As well, "The Edwards family is said to have come originally from Wales, but left Maidstone for America. Mulford descendants are divided between claiming Devonshire or Maidstone as their place of origin. The Parsons family is said to have come from Devonshire too, but that family is represented in Maidstone today and very likely was in the 1600's. One settler named Miller certainly came from Maidstone."[359] Rattray points out there is some dispute within the Miller family concerning which Miller this was.

It has become tradition that Ralph stopped at Southampton, on his way to East Hampton. Certainly, it is likely he did stop there, especially because North Sea (part of Southampton) was the harbor commonly used for arrival, even to East Hampton.

---

[356] (Barons 2010)
[357] (Hefner, A Brief History of the Village of East Hampton, NY 2002)
[358] (Williston 2001)
[359] (Rattray 2001)

Besides, Sam could have afforded them accommodations on their way. Interestingly, Howell, in *History of Southampton*, placed Ralph at Southampton in 1649, but Howell does not provide his source. While Ralph could have been at Southampton as early as 1649, it is just as likely that he arrived there in 1650.

Occasionally, there are authors who claim Ralph Dayton was a founder or original settler of East Hampton. While he was most certainly a very early settler, he was probably not a founder. The idea that Ralph was a founder probably was derived in part from observations like Peter Ross's statement, "Excepting the Indian Deed for the Township, there is nothing of an earlier date on Record [than the Ralph Dayton record]."[360] Ross was referring to the first reference to Ralph after he left New Haven, found in East Hampton Town Records:

> It is ordered yt Ralph Daiton is to goe keneticot for to pcure evidence for our lands and for an Acquittance for the payment of money for tne purchase of our land and for a boddie of laws at a generall court houlden at Easthampton March 7, 1650…[361]

Ralph was apparently given the task of going to Connecticut to collect a receipt for "payment in full," perhaps even to acquire the deed for the East Hampton land the settlers had purchased. *Montauk Life*[362] said, "The settlers flourished, and by 1651 they finished paying their debt to the governors of Connecticut and New Haven, and received the final deed to their town." Hefner also says, "The thirty-four original settlers obtained full title to the land in 1651 from the Connecticut governors and their associates. By this time the new town was known as East Hampton."[363]

Ralph's mission was also to return with the set of laws which probably included rules of conduct and prescribed actions to enforce laws and redress wrongs. Thompson uses the same day but a much later year, "accordingly, on the 7th of March, 1658 ordered and determined by the general court, upon due consideration, that Ralph Dayton, one of their most discreet men, should go to Connecticut to procure the evidence for their lands, and a code of laws."[364] Obviously, the year 1658 was either a typographical or transcription error, but what intrigues us is Thompson's use of the word "discreet" to describe Ralph. This choice of words, it seems, belonged to Thompson, as the word, applied to Ralph, has not been located elsewhere. If "discreet" was to mean inconspicuous, it is very fitting, but other interpretations such as cautious, reserved and sensible are also qualities of demeanor we associate with Ralph.

---

[360] (Ross 1905)
[361] Ibid.
[362] (Montauk Indian Heritage 2004)
[363] (Hefner, A Brief History of the Village of East Hampton, NY 2002)
[364] (B. F. Thompson, History of Long Island 1839)

It appears that either Ralph was transported by Robert Bond or something may have prevented Ralph from going to Connecticut altogether because, just a few weeks later, Robert Bond was ordered to go for the same purpose. "…it is ordered by Joynt consent of the towne yt Roberd Bond shall goe the next opertunitie to the maine to Conecticot for to pcure the Evidence for our land & our combination & the bodie of laws and an Accquittance for our money." On April 1, 1651 (less than a month after March 7, 1650), Bond was reimbursed expenses for his service that had taken him fifteen days.

With guidance from these laws, East Hampton governed itself right from the beginning, until the Colony of New York took control in 1664. The existing East Hampton Town Records began in October of 1650 with a town meeting, then called "A Court of Election," where town officials were chosen. These earliest ETRs, at the time of self-governance, indicate that the only officials were the Townsmen, Constable and Recorder. Most of the earliest records were for the regulation of fencing and public lands, election of officers, and policing while a large part of court cases involved either defamation or small debts.

As alluded to, the East Hampton town and court records are rich with content because of the range and scope of life's activities included. For example, East Hampton used juries regularly, allowing many men in the community to participate in public life, even though New Haven and Southold had abolished trial by jury citing lack of Biblical precedent.[365] Author Peter Ross said,

> Their laws were enacted by all the citizens assembled in town meeting; this was styled 'the General Court' and a fine inflicted on such as did not attend [Besides three magistrates who were called Townsmen]. A Recorder and Constable were the only other public offices chosen…The Constable was always a reputable citizen and of great authority. He, by law, moderated the General Court. The Recorder, or Secretary, not only recorded all order of the General Court, but the decisions of the Magistrates…John Mulford, Robert Bone & Thos Baker [were] chosen by this Court for the execution of those Orders, complied with their trust for this year. Ralph Dayton, Constable and Benjn Price, Recorder.[366]

Perhaps, it was inevitable that Ralph, acting in official duty of Constable, be selected to go to Connecticut.

---

[365] (Murrin 1998)
[366] (Ross 1905)

134

The opportunity is taken now, as two sequential Town of East Hampton Records from Book 2, p 13 present themselves, to illustrate the importance of calendar conversion when studying pre-1752 American history.

The first of the two records appeared on the last day of the Julian year, March 24, 1650. Converted to new style, the Georgian calendar date was April 3, 1651.

—it is ordered yt the house lot lieinge on the north side of Goodman Daitons lot shall be Reserved for A man whom the Towne shall see mete to call to publike place.

The second record has the date April 1, 1651 or, when converted to new style, the Georgian calendar date was April 11, 1651.

—it is ordered by Joynt consent of the towne yt Roberd Bond shall goe the next opertunitie to the maine to Conecticot for to pcure the Evidence for our land & our combination & the bodie of lawes and an Accquittance for our money.

At a glance, it may appear that these two entries have been listed out of sequence, appearing that the first entry is more than a year older than the second entry, but in fact, these entries are actually sequenced correctly because the day after March 24, 1650 would begin 1651 on the Georgian calendar. So the April 1, 1651 entry occurs about one week after the previous March 24, 1650 entry, using the old style calendar.[367]

By 1651, elected officials were in place—John Mulford, Robert Bond & Thomas Baker were chosen as the three magistrates, also called Townsmen, and Ralph Dayton and Benjamin Price were chosen Constable and Recorder. Since Ralph was elected Constable in 1651, it is likely that he was also Constable when the court was created in 1650.[368]

It seems fitting to go back to the beginning of the records in East Hampton and begin our listing of the orders by the Court that specifically mention Ralph as well as some additional records that pertain to him.

The next record occurs at the November 17, 1651 meeting, the town prepared for the building of their meeting house.

It is ordered that the three men that are Chosen for towne affaires shal set out the place for the meetinge house and the five men that gett the thath shall fence the same nere that place...It is ordered and agreed vpon by vs

---

[367] Note: The Connecticut State Library provides a very good explanation of *The 1752 Calendar Change* on their website *http://www.cslib.org/CalendarChange.htm*
[368] (Hotchkiss 2001)

the Inhabitants that there shal be a meetinge house built 26 foote longe 20 foote broade and 8 foote stoode.

Apparently, before the meeting house was built (probably in 1652), religious services were held at the house belonging to Thomas Baker because his was probably the largest structure in East Hampton at the time and probably served as the village inn or public house in the beginning. For its use, the town felt obligated to compensate Baker as, "It is ordered that Thomas Baker shall have eighteene pence for evry Lords Day that the meetinge shalbe at his house." East Hampton already had their first pastor, Rev. Thomas James. The ETR shows that he had a town lot on April 22, 1651 but he may have arrived earlier.

The May 13, 1651 record tells us that fines collected from individuals not attending the town meeting were to be used to compensate the drummer for his responsibility to summon inhabitants to a public meeting. In those days, the drum would have been a more attractive alternative to the church bell, as a bell would come at a significant cost. The necessary ritual of "call to meeting" was popularly practiced throughout America until the twentieth century and still exists at some locations today.

It is at first surprising to find Ralph listed as a delinquent from the town meeting, he being a public official in General Court, but that fact may be the very reason he did not attend. But five months later, at an October 1652 town meeting it will be learned that the responsibilities of the constable consumed much of Ralph's time, and much of it without just compensation.

The Delinquents that did not appear at the Town metinge accordinge to warninge is Thomas Tallmage Senior his find paide 6d. Ralfe Daiton his find paide 6d John Mullford his fine 12d paid William Mullord his fine paid 1s both of them towards the Drum Richard Stratten paid 6d to the Drum, Luke Lillie 6d to the Drum Thomas Osborne paid 6d to the Drum Roberd Rose his fine 6d paid to the Drum.

The next day, the 14th of May, it was ordered that every house lot was to receive an addition to its rear, four acres for every £100 estate, according to their division in the plain. These additions were granted so that every addition could be accessed by its owner without trespassing on his neighbor's property.

For a very short time after the establishment of East Hampton, the grazing lands surrounding the village were shared among all, for common purpose, but as these systems usually go, the practice of the ideal apparently fell short of the goal and a series of land divisions commenced. Shillingburg says, "This experiment in communal ownership was not successful and was soon abandoned."[369] The order was given "…that John Hand Thomas Baker & Thomas Chatfield is to lay out the land vpon the great plaine that is not yet devided & that to be done between this & the last of may next Ensueing."[370]

Hefner provides descriptions of approximate boundaries for the divisions:

> The division of land was of the greatest importance to the proprietors. Each of the thirty-four proprietors owned a share in the 31,000 acres of land, harbors and ponds of the town, and the amount of that share would be the basis for all future allotments of valuable land. Until that time, much of the land was held in common. Divided at an early date was the fertile land east and west of the home lots between the ocean and the inner dunes or sand hills: the Little Plain, from Georgica Pond to Lily Pond; the Great Plain from Lily Pond to Hook Pond; and the Eastern Plain, east of Hook Pond.

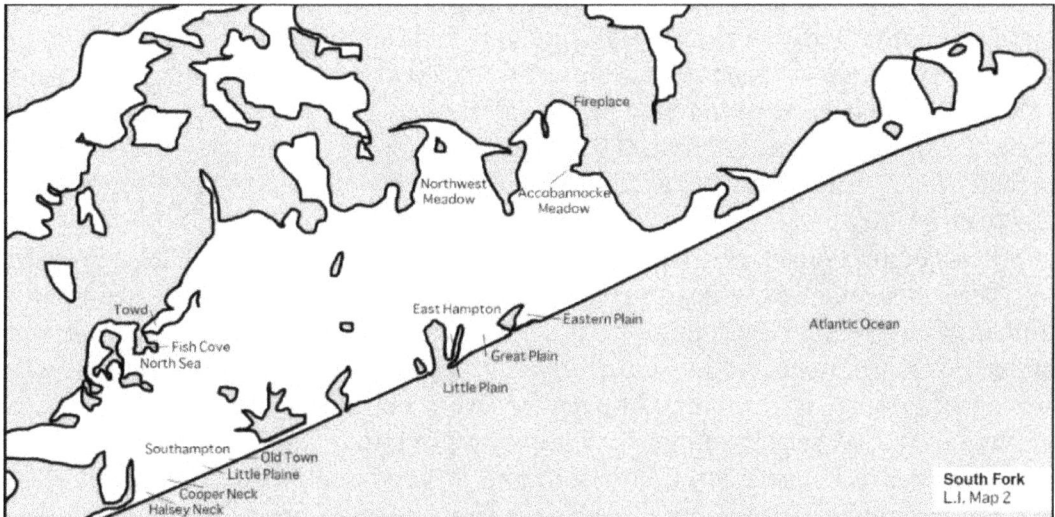

Figure 15. Long Island South Fork

The English settlers realized the value in the ancient Native American practice of maintaining grassland by annually burning the brush and other unwanted undergrowth. In doing so, great caution was exercised to control it, that the fire may not spread outside the burn fields (or woodlands) to properties such as fencing and dwellings. If ever a home caught fire, it would be consumed in very little time and

---

[369] (P. Shillingburg n.d.)
[370] (H. Hedges 1887)

would become a danger to the entire town. Very early into the settlement, the court mandated that every man own a ladder to enable him to extinguish cinders should they land in his thatched roof. The October 7, 1651 East Hampton record says,

> It is ordered that the three men shall haue power after the 10th of March to call forth men to burne the woods. It is ordered that every man that hath a house shal within 6 weekes gett a lader that may reach so hie that a man may goe to the top of his house and those that shalbe falty herein shalbe liable to pay 5s.

In the early days, the Puritans used thatch as a cover or roofing, skillfully woven of reeds they gathered along the coastline. When a roof was renewed, the new thatch was applied up to a foot thick, on top of the old thatch, sometimes building up to be a few feet thick on a substantial structure. This constant need demanded very large quantities of thatch for both original construction and regular renewal of existing structures. Each man was to take his turn gathering and delivering thatch to the town, regulated by fine. The November 17, 1651 record states, "It is ordered that William Edwards, William ffithian, Richard Brookes, William Simmons, Samuel Parsons shall get Sixe loade of thach within these fowerteene Dayes and if anie shall neglect to Doe his share he shal be liable to pay ten shillings." Probably at the same court, "it is orderd that Raphe Daiton Thomas Chatfild and Thomas Osbourne Senior shal fetch the thatch in the order before menconed vpon two dayes warninge vpon the fine fore menconed."[371]

Proceeding sequentially through the town records, it doesn't take long to realize how very important whaling was to the town, just as it was at neighboring Southampton. Next to farming, gardening and tending livestock and barnyard animals, which were necessities for nearly everyone, whaling was crucial to the town for its profitability. By this time, the settlers were not only harvesting drift whales, but were now also venturing out, by small boat, to strike whale close to shore. The November 6, 1651 record says, "It is ordered yt goodman Mulford shal call ont ye towne by succession to loke out for whale." These spotters were strategically posted near the beach, some climbing poles in order to get a better view. In December of 1652, the court ordered Thomas Talmadge to, "call out the towne by turnes to looke after whales this present yeare."

At the same November 6, 1651 meeting, the town recognized the necessity that each man be in possession of arms, both gun and sword, and that these be fitted with all the accompanying equipment and that they be in good working order. This is nearly the same as New Haven had done. Although the settlers of East Hampton had relatively peaceful relations with the local tribes, there occasionally was fear of attack. To make sure the arms could be utilized competently, it was also mandated

---

[371] Ibid.

138

that each able male, sixteen and older, attend at least six training and practice sessions per year. These mandates were enforced by fine and were recorded: "It is ordered yt all that are fit to beare armes shalbe sufficiently prouided with a good gunne powder shott sword worme and scourer shotbagg rest bolt and a fitt thinge to carrie powder in." and "It is ordered yt ye towne shall traine six tymes in a yeare and this is begin ye next March."

In the early 17th century, firearms were either matchlocks or wheel locks. A matchlock held a slow burning match, which was touched to the powder when the trigger was pulled. With a wheel lock a metal wheel spun against iron pyrites making sparks. During the 17th century both of these were gradually replaced by the flintlock which worked by hitting a piece of flint and steel making sparks.[372]

From May 17, 1652, "It is ordered that all men shal bringe thir armes to meetinge on the lords Dayes and whosoever shal be Defective herein shal pay twelve pence." Just as it had been in Connecticut, the men went armed to meeting where their weapons were stacked for easy access, should they be needed during service. Later, in January of 1653/54, it was ordered that half of the town must carry arms every Lord's Day.

Dangerous Work

There was also some continuing drama in East Hampton between two ladies, Goodys Price and Edwards. In what appears to be a "coded" or euphemistic message on January 5, 1651/52, the record says:

Beniamine Price hath entered an accon of suite with William Edwards for the forbearance of £3 7s and Damage thereby 20s. Beniamin Price hath entered an accon of suite with William Edwards for the deareness of the Comodities Damage 20s. an accon examined and Determined vpon by vs John Mulford Robert Bond & Thomas Baker betweene Beniaimine Price ptf and William Edwards Def touchinge the value of £3 18s in Commonityes…

We are not provided detail beyond the words above, and we are not given the particulars of the warrant, as if the entry was best withheld. Goody's response to the warrant resulted in the entry and judgment of February 2, 1651/52,

Goody Edwards shal pay £3 or have her tonge in a cleft sticke for the Contempt of a warrent in sainge she would not come... [She had asked for

---

[372] (T. Lambert, A World History Encyclopedia n.d.)

the magistrate's warrant to be delivered so her house so that she could burn it].

A cleft stick was simply a stick, used in a variety of lengths, that has been cleft, or split at one end, commonly used to carry or hold strung candles or other small items. In the American colonies, the cleft stick was a cheap alternative to the 'branks' used in Medieval Europe, an iron cage that was fastened around the offenders head, with a piece that projected into the mouth to prevent speech of women who used abusive language, especially against their husbands. One would expect that Goody Edwards probably paid the fine rather than enduring the humiliation of the cleft stick.

This wasn't the first time Goody Edwards was in trouble for her lack of self-control. Perhaps this record at Lynn, Massachusetts in 1643 gives us some idea of the subject of the 1651/52 action. At Lynn, she was...

admonished for striking a man and scoffing at his membership. [Wit:] John Wood and Boniface Burton. "She is conceaved to be a very ignorant fottish & Imperious woman.[373]

On June 13, 1653, more than a year after her recorded dispute with Goody Price, they were at it again. This time, William Edwards, as plaintiff, entered action of defamation on behalf of his wife, against Benjamin Price, for his wife's words. Goodwife Price had publically said that Goodwife Edwards was a base liar. When the jury found for the defendant, Goodman Edwards pleaded with the court, claiming that the accusation was a deep wound for his wife and a blemish for his children. Apparently Goody Price accused Goody Edwards of lying when she said she brought a petticoat out of England which she hadn't yet worn. When witness Goody Simons heard Goody Edwards say this, she replied that it was strange she never wore it at Lynn. Then when questioned, Goodman Edwards said the petticoat was brought out of England but later changed his story and said the money that bought it came out of England. Thomas Baker then testified that, when the constable was about to lay hands on her, Goody Edwards said that, "whosoever should lay hould on her she would kill them if she could." Goody Edwards kicked the constable [probably Ralph] and when others came to assist him, she kicked backward and broke the shin of Thomas Talmage. Edwards, her husband, told her to cooperate and take her punishment so she threatened him also. She angrily said her husband brought her "to live among the heathen" and she said she would hang him when she came home. Unfortunately, the story ends in the record, so what became of Goody Edwards and her company among the "heathen" has no conclusion. There was no mention of injury to Ralph.

---

[373] (Ackley 1997)

Quiet Enjoyment

The lands along with the home lots provided the base for the agricultural economy of the settlers. This area was roughly what is now the Incorporated Village of East Hampton. Other valuable lands were divided among the proprietors within the first years of the town. These included the meadows adjacent to Georgica Pond, Northwest creek, Three Mile Harbor, Accabonac Harbor and Napeague Harbor. Roads were laid out from Main Street to the nearby farmland and to outlying meadows and woodlots. The first mention of Northwest in the Town Records is in 1652, three to four years after the first settler arrived. It speaks of a "cartway to ye Northwest meddow." East Hamptoners went to the meadows after salt hay, a very valuable "crop" in those days. Northwest Harbor later became the port for East Hampton, the point of all trade and communication with the outside world.[374]

Inevitably, not all were satisfied with their allotments. Our interpretation of the May 4, 1652 entry that says, "It is ordered that those men Ralph Daiton Thomas Osbourne senior William Edwards should quietly enjoy their land that they now possesse with out any more Questioning." may be a little different from interpretations found elsewhere. Upon first reading, the entry may sound as if the men who are named were not happy with their allotments, but further study brings to light a legal phrase that has its origin in old English common law, the *Right to Quiet Enjoyment*. This covenant became a remedy for nuisance and was defined as the right to the undisturbed use and enjoyment of real property by a tenant or landowner.[375] Therefore, it appears that this order by the court was a warning to those having a difference with these three men, before the three might seek a remedy for nuisance. In her book, Rattray does not address this possibility. Her comment, "Sometimes a settler would be dissatisfied with his allotment" [376] is not directed at either party and ends there without opinion in the matter. Since the town record does not provide enough information to understand or determine the particulars or context, this order may have resulted from a proposal containing eminent domain or these men were perceived as being favored.

After the Great Plain, Eastern Plain and the "litell plaine" were divided, Thomas Baker, Thomas Chatfield and John Hand were called on June 29, 1652 to lay out the meadow at Accobanoke, the west side of Northwest meadow, and the meadow at the harbor, proportioned into 34 lots and 3 divisions. Once received into the community, inhabitants received distributed land in three phases; a house lot, then meadow or salt marsh when it was laid out, and last, a part of woodland divisions. Subsequent divisions followed as need was realized. The ETR Vol. IV says that Acabonach is a,

---

[374] (Hefner, A Brief History of the Village of East Hampton, NY 2002)
[375] (Lehman 2008)
[376] (Rattray 2001)

"neck of land, meadow and harbor in the northern part of the town, adjoining Gardiner's bay...now known as the 'Springs,' P.O."

The first division was to begin at the east end of "Accobannocke medow" and the second division was to begin at the west end of the same meadow. The middle 30 acres of Northwest were left unalloted, probably because they were inaccessible for harvesting and removing hay. Drawing carts through the meadow was challenging, yet so important that the men were granted liberty by the court to cart over other men's property without risk of trespassing. This was probably in effect until access to highways could be trenched. Further, the court ordered that if any man was not able to bring his hay out without a highway, the town would build the highway and sufficient cart ways "into several places" at the Northwest meadow. The order to build cart ways to several places at Northwest meadow was carried forward, with work to begin December 20. The need for trenching to drain the swamp at Accobannocke was recognized and the town ruled that every man was responsible for his own trenching.

For an idea of what trenching may have looked like, refer to the modern system of trenching at Northwest Harbor County Park that can be seen on Google© maps in 2013. It is believed that almost no current trenching systems on Long Island follow seventeenth century land boundaries.

On July 7 1652, "It is alsoe ordered that those 2 lots that are not it taken vpp namly the house lot by the metinge house for the one & the other house lot between Goodman Daitons & Goodman Price that thease 2 lotts shall have 45 ackers reserved vpon the plaine for them & to have meadow acordinge to their pportion laid out for them."

The order of business at the October 5, 1652 meeting included granting liberty to appeal decisions of the court. These appeals were to be heard at General Court held on the first Tuesdays of April and October. Apparently there was some ensuing discussion at the time of the recording because, at a General Court the same day, the previous order was appended to afford relief for those "agreived" [sic] not only at the next General Court, but also, "when the ffremen are Assembled together for their publike occasions."

On the same day, it was time to choose a new constable for East Hampton. One year had passed since Ralph was last elected and his term was nearing its end. Those first terms had exposed shortcomings in the design of the office which, no doubt, hindered its performance and the town set about to fix these deficiencies. The first problem to address was expenses incurred by the constable that were either not sufficiently reimbursed or maybe not at all reimbursed. The duties assigned must have created a hardship for the officer, in loss of time alone. "It is ordered that the Cunstabell shall haue six pence for the serving of every warrant in mater of suit and whatever travill or assistance is more shalbe judged by the Cort for his satisfaccon and the sum 6d for writing a warrant" and, "It is ordered that the Cunstabell shall always Doe execution as a pte of his office, and also moderat the Court." There is little doubt that these costs prevented or delayed execution or completion of various tasks. To remedy delays in the issuance of warrants, "It is ordered that any one of the 3 men that are Chosen for Towne affaiers shall have power to grant warrants if the other 2 bee out of Towne And to give an oath."

Even with all the problems that emerged, Ralph, by now in his mid-sixties, was chosen constable for the next year. But to get the first year in order, the court appointed an assistant to review the year's business and to make accounts up to date. "It is ordered yt Thomas Baker shalbe an assistant to the Cunstable for the making vp of the Towne accounts for time past and for this present yeare." Perhaps Ralph accepted a piece of land or other goods or considerations as compensation for the past year's work. It is affirmed that Ralph again accepted the position as the November 1652 record says, "Ralph Dayton, as constable, afixed his signature to two orders of the court,"[377] both holding cattle belonging to Daniel Howe, in bond, on behalf of Robert Bond and a trespass against a Connecticut man.

About four years after the little town of East Hampton was first gathered around the common, it was determined that the area on the south end, swamped by a spring, should be transformed into a watering pond. On June 24, 1653 the town record relates the order to dig the pond.

> It is ordered that there shalbe a wateringe pond diged at the Spring Eastward and the charge to bee borne by the heads of cowes and to bee begun the next second Day and Ralph Dayton and Thomas Baker are to oversee the worke and see that men bringe good sufficient tooles to worke with all, and all that have cowes are to apeare at the beat of the Drum.[378]

The properties of Ralph and Thomas, almost directly across the green, one from the other, were well within view of the pond. As overseer of the digging project, the job was probably well suited for Ralph, who was now advancing in years (and probably had a sore leg). At an October 1653 general court, Ralph was no longer town constable but had been made instead an assistant to the magistrates. In Book 2, the record says, "John Mulford Ralfe Dayton Ananias Coneline and Luke Lillie are Chosen by the towne to be assistance to the 3 townes men for the Caring on of towne affaiers according to an Order in yeare 1653." Ralph was replaced as Constable by his friend Thomas Osburne Senior, who had been with or near Ralph since Ashford, Kent: "At the Generall Court houlden the first tusday in october the three men that are Chosen for the orderinge of Towne afayers for this present yeare are John Mulford Thomas Baker and John Hand. Benjamine Price Secretary and Thomas Osburne Senior Cunstabell."

---

[377] (H. Hedges 1887)
[378] (Dexter 1917)

It is very likely that the owners of cows who were charged with the strenuous and formidable job of digging the pond carted the putrid mud out to their gardens and fields and spread the slime as fertilizer. Today, the Town Pond in combination with adjacent South End Cemetery and iconic windmills are notable landmarks for all who enter town, traveling east and north on NY-27.

Figure 16. Town Pond, East Hampton (2010)

Allotments of 34 divisions of the meadow at Northwest, as well as another 34 divisions of the meadow at Accabanock were listed on July 5, 1653, including every lot size with owner and neighbors. Of the 34 in each list, Ralph was listed 29th with about five acres and thirty two "poole" at Northwest, his division bounded by Thomas Tallmage Senior and William Edwards and two acres and ninety six "poole" at Accabanock, bounded by Samuel Parsons and Thomas Talmage on the other. Northwest is an area north and west of East Hampton, with Sag Harbor to its west and Springs to its east, and was the site of East Hampton's Northwest Harbor. According to Rattray, before the establishment of their harbor at Northwest, people living in East Hampton carted their produce more than fifteen miles, to Southampton's port at North Sea. Northwest harbor continued to serve East Hampton

144

and became a major whaling port in the 17th century but it was replaced by Sag Harbor, just a few miles west, when larger vessels could not enter its shallow water.[379]

Ralph's assistance to "the Three Men" embodied a variety of tasks, from dividing the town into work groups, to supervising tasks of digging and building. For example, a record from Dec 9, 1653 gives instructions for the disposal of a whale that was perhaps beached on the property of a Widow Talmadge. The town's people were ordered,

> …that the whale beinge Divided every Lott that the Towne gives out from thirteene ackers and vpwards shall have his share beinge possessed and Inhabited: the Division of the towne for this worke is betweene Thomas Chatfilds and Ralph Daytons and Tho: Tomsons and Tho: Bakers the oversears for the South end are John Hand and Robert Bond and for the North end Thomas Baker and Beniamine Price.

Apparently someone had been cutting trees, or had intentions to cut trees at the rear of the additions to the home lots so the town announced that anyone doing so would pay a penalty. Often these public pathways followed along common boundary lines, in order to provide easy access to multiple lots but, in doing so, also provided convenient access to trees deemed to be in the common area. Town officials used the occasion to proclaim and expand such regulations to other common lands. The town records of Jan 13, 1653/54,

> ordered that noe man shall fall any tree from Ralph Daytons Addition vpon the Common Ground all alonge to William Hedges corner and alonge to the westee end of Goodman Osburnes Addition vpon penalty of 5s a tree. nor vpon any of the comon land between the hook pond and the mill gate nor vpon any of the comon land betweene the towne and the plaines vpon same penalty.

A doubly important town record, at least to the Dayton family, is the entry of February 13, 1653/54 in which Ralph and his wife transfer a significant portion of his East Hampton property to son Robert, whose wife Elizabeth had recently delivered their first child, daughter Elizabeth. Robert received part of his father's property in East Hampton including home lot, meadow and woodland with house and barn and use of his team of horses or oxen and farm equipment. While all this gives the appearance of Robert being the "favored son," this might not be the case since Ralph would not remain at East Hampton long, but would soon join his son Samuel at North Sea. The second significance of this record is Ralph's use of the words "my wife," this being the very first time, as far as can be determined, Ralph's wife was mentioned since Ashford, Kent.

---

[379] (Hefner, A Brief History of the Village of East Hampton, NY 2002)

Perhaps Ralph's wife, presumably Alice, was ill at this time and Ralph was thinking about what would happen to his belongings with the changing of life circumstances. Transferring ownership to Robert would help relieve his tax burden but instead of transferring ownership of many of his belongings, Ralph granted the use of much of it, perhaps as a trial period or to signal his eventual intentions for distribution upon his death. Robert would gain from the use of the lands, animals and equipment while relieving his father of the burden of laborious maintenance and improvement.

> Know all Men whom it May Concerne that I Ralph Dayton of Easthampton vpon Long Island doe give vnto my son Robert Dayton at the prest Halfe my land that is vpon the great plaine and one third part of my hom lott and one third part of the Addition ajoyning to it to pay all such rate & taxes as shall arise on the land that I now give him. he is to have the us [use] of my teame & cart & plow and others provided he bear half the Charges in the Maintaining of them. I give to my son Robert half My Housing as namly my hous & barne he beinge to bere half the repaireing of them & to bere halfe the charge in Repaireing the fences the vse of them to be Improved one the whole land and wt prest it comes more by the vs of teame is to be devided betweene vs: and after the decrease of Me Ralph Dayton and My wife I Doe give all of the other parts of my lands meadows and housing that be above mentioned to him and his heires Lawfully begotten of his body forever in witnes hereof I set my hand.
>
> RALPH DAYTON L.S.
>
> witness
> Thomas Baker
> William Hiyd

The initials L.S. by Ralph's signature are Latin and mean "place of the seal." Their use sometimes, but not always, indicates that someone else actually wrote the document, and this symbol was placed where the document was to be signed. If Ralph did not write the document himself, it is not difficult to imagine possible reasons why, one being as simple as his eyesight may have been weakening.

In November of 1654, Ralph was overseer of the bridge project and was ordered to help select land for Ffulk Davis.

> It is ordered yt theare shalbe a Cart way made over the swamp to the plaines: and yt Mr Gardner and Goodman Dayton shall Over see the worke and shall Call men att a weekes warning to the worke: & this to be Done betweene this & the Last of ffebeuary. It is ordered the 5 of febeuary that the aforesd Order shalbe Crost.

It is Ordered Ralph Dayton John Mulford and John Hand ffor the towne
as Comite shall with ffluke Davis apoynt the place whear the said ffulk
Davis shall have his Land according to A fformer grant of 1653.

It was probably about this time, between the summer of 1654 and winter of
1655/56, that Ralph and the Dayton family lost his dear wife, Alice. If Alice was the
"wife" mentioned in Feb 13, 1653/54, they had been married about 37 years and
produced at least five children—Ralfe Junior, Alice, Samuel, Robert and Ellen, all
having been married by this time. It appears that Ellen married John Linley, lived at
Guilford, and died giving birth to her second daughter Hannah on April 6, 1654 and
was buried a day or so later. Hannah's sister Mary had been born Feb 11, 1651/52
according to Jacobus,[380] In *Barnes Families of Long Island and Branford, Conn*,
Jacobus suggests that Mary and Hannah were taken in and cared for by relatives in
East Hampton, probably either the Bakers or Robert, and less likely, Ralph.

Charge of the Meeting House

At first glance, the January 1654 assessment table entitled, "the charge of the
meetinge house" in the *Records of the Town of East Hampton Vol 1* seems to indicate
that Ralph owned an astonishing amount of acreage, almost six times the acreage of
the second-highest figure. Each landowner was listed, along with their contribution
in pounds (£), shillings (s), and pence (d). In the English system, they counted 20
shillings per pound and 12 pence per shilling. The fourth column contains the number
of acres that belonged to him in the yet undivided lands of the town; then his obligated
contribution in proportion to his share, and the last columns contain the balance due
to or from him in future divisions, depending on the amount of land received. An
explanation of the table is found on page 10 of our edition of ETR Vol 1,[381] using
Thomas Baker as an example.

In only minutes our initial astonishment became suspicion. No research, to this
point, had revealed that Ralph Dayton had wealth of any significance, not enough to
explain how he could come to own 126 taxable acres, nearly one-fourth of all acreage,
while others held 13 to 22 taxable acres.

After applying systematic analysis, creating our own assessment table from the
devised formula, it was concluded that Ralph did not own 126 acres, but instead, he
actually owned 26. Other discrepancies were revealed as well, some of which are
obvious transcription errors and are corroborated by Pelletreau on page 358 of our
edition of *History of Long Island*.

---

[380] (D. L. Jacobus, Barnes Families of Eastern Long Island and Branford, Conneticut 1969)
[381] (Osborne 1887)

On both the published table and on our adjusted table, Thomas Baker appeared to have contributed the greatest amount of prepaid taxes, in fact he contributed more than double that for which was due according to his acreage. His overpayment was so great that it exceeded the assessed tax of all but his father-in-law. Ralph's contribution of prepaid tax, on the other hand, appeared to be relatively little, considering his taxed acreage which was more than anyone in East Hampton at the time. Thomas owned the third greatest amount of assessed acreage, tied with Chatfield, at 21 acres.

Much to our surprise, the most significant finding in the "corrected" table was that Ralph was still reported to possess the most taxable acreage at this time, even more than his son-in-law. In our opinion, this is significant since Thomas was a principle, in place of Captain Howe. One explanation could be that Thomas had less land when the table was created than he had at the original acquisition, or when the tax was pre-paid. In other words, he had paid taxes proportional to the acreage he had previously owned. Perhaps after he paid the tax, he returned some land to the town for credit, and/or he might have sold acreage to another inhabitant, possibly to Ralph. To test the feasibility of this theory, the number of acres belonging to Thomas was calculated from his pre-paid taxes by dividing the tax rate into the pre-paid tax (£1 8s 6d/7.5d) or converted to pence (342d/7.5d)=45.6 acres.

So, our theory is that Thomas owned or at least paid taxes on approximately 45.6 acres at the time taxes were paid. After paying the tax, at the time the table *Charge of the Meetinge House* was finally recorded, Thomas had reduced his acreage by 24.6, leaving him with 21 taxable acres. It is possible Ralph and Thomas had arranged a deal, while they were living in Connecticut, whereby Ralph agreed to assist Thomas in financing the buyout of Captain Howe's estate and holdings from Alexander Bryan, in return for land that had taxes pre-paid. So Ralph would have purchased his share (about 13 acres) and gained more from Baker. Thomas also returned some of the land back to the town, probably for either tax credits or future considerations. This is known from a land record dated May 24, 1655, where part of the Ralph Dayton property was described as payment owed Thomas Baker by the town's men for property given to the town by Baker.

Ralph's acquisitions of land at East Hampton continued in May of 1655 as he received, "…eluen akers & halfe on the great plaine be it more or less bounded with the hie way South and Thomas Baker West and the hie way north and the hie way through the plaine east." A month and a half later, he received more land in the July division:

> July 6, 1655 It is voted by the major part of the towne that Thomas Osborne Senior and his son Thomas Osborne Junior shall have all yt Medow about the place Cald the Hogg Creek...It is also ordered by the Major part that Jeremiah Mecham & Richard Brookes shall have all yt medow allong by the beach calld the ffire place that is undevidad...that

148

Ralph Dayton shall have yt medow at the upper end of the bushes at the Swamp near the towne pvided yt it be not above 5 ackers west: towards the cart way...It is ordered by maior prt yt Mr. James shall have yt medow on the ffurthest side of Hooke pond Between the thickett of trees & the Beach & so along the Plaine side according to a row of Bushes by the medow side.

This Fire Place in East Hampton should not be confused with the Fire Place on the Great South Bay at Brookhaven. Hogg Creek and East Hampton's Fire Place are located at Springs, where it is said fires were built to signal to the ferry at Gardiner's Island. Fire Place in Brookhaven will be discussed in chapters to come as an important part of our story.

Alice, the matriarch of the Dayton family in the New World, might have been in failing health in February of 1655/56 when Ralph "set up" their youngest son Robert, then about twenty-six, in East Hampton. Robert received one half of Ralph's land on the "great plaine," and on the "Eastern plaine," and one third of the home lot and the addition to it, and one-third of his meadow, and the "use of teame, cart and plow..." The addition of the provision "...after the death of said Ralph and his wife he was to have the rest of the land"[382] makes it clear that Robert was receiving some or all of his inheritance. The provision also tells us that Alice was still alive, and perhaps it was she who convinced Ralph to see that Robert received some or all of his inheritance. In Ralph's mind, his action insured that both his wife and Robert would receive their shares, as he and Alice desired them. In addition, we think this was Ralph's level-headed way to accomplish other objectives as well. Ralph would further establish his son prominently in East Hampton, insuring he stay close by to take care of Alice, and he would begin handing over management of an estate whose maintenance and taxes were continuing to grow.

Ralph and Alice were still residing in East Hampton when Alice died, probably between February and May of 1656 N.S., at roughly sixty-nine years of age. Of course, this assumes that Alice was the wife Ralph referred to when he wrote, "after the death of said Ralph and his wife" in February of 1655/56. Alice had probably provided much of the strength and stability in the family for the roughly thirty-nine years of their marriage. Their many years of marriage is noteworthy in the first half of the seventeenth century, especially surviving the plague and the birth of at least five children. By 1656, Alice's children were married and had children of their own. She was able to see at least eight grandchildren before her death.

No gravesite has been identified for Alice but it should be safe to assume she was buried at East Hampton, perhaps one of the first at South End Cemetery. The cemetery is located just south, on the other side of James Lane, where the first

---

[382] (W. Pelletreau 1915)

meeting house stood since 1651, within view from her home. Very few first-generation Puritan immigrant grave identifiers survive.

Chapter 10

Ralph joins Sam at Southampton

By 1648, the center of Southampton town was moving about one mile west to form on both sides of a main street. Newcomers to Towne Street (now Main Street) were settled beginning near the ocean northward, in the direction of Little Peconic Bay and North Sea. By the time Sam arrived in 1648, he would have probably been placed more than a mile north of the coast, somewhere near where North Sea Road later connected to Main Street. Sam could have first lived on the home lot granted to him on arrival, but there is no record for him at the first home lot.

Containing enough land for substantial expansion, land divisions began near the village, at the Great Plains and the Necks, with systematic additions planned. Expanding to its east, west and north, it seems that Sam arrived at Southampton at a very opportune time, so much so that after just a few years at Southampton, his land holdings increased with each division. As was custom, almost immediately after land divisions, there was much buying, selling and trading, each man shuffling lots to his best advantage. For example, by February 10, 1653/54, Sam had sold 5 acres in the plain to George Wood, who was then exchanging the land with Thomas Burnet for his 4 acres already laid out at Scuttle Hole. Where the exchange included a house lot, we did not always assume that it was Sam's dwelling for a time, as it is clear some properties were acquired for different purposes. This makes it a challenge to trace his movements, as many records, especially those of early North Sea have become lost. Altogether, from 1648 to 1665, the Sam Dayton family was in at least two Southampton dwellings with the possibility of an additional three, and records account for the sale of five houses before it is finally determined that Sam had fully departed Southampton town and North Sea. Pinpointing that move is also made difficult because Brookhaven and Oyster Bay records suggest Sam was already involved with land ventures further west beginning before the time Ralph died and into the following decade while Southampton records refer to him as "of

Southampton" as late as 1665. One author wrote that it was supposed that Sam went to Brookhaven about 1658.[383]

The settlement of Southampton expanded eastward toward the boundary with East Hampton, as the land at Sagabonack (Sagg) was divided in January 1653/54, laid out approximately between Mecox Road, Fairfield Lane and Bridge Lane and the ocean on the south. The Sagabonack division lay generally south of the mill path which led west to east from Water Mill to East Hampton, the route of today's Montauk Highway.[384] The town cast lots for 41 allotments at a town meeting in February, some being £100 and some being £50. Lot #2 fell to Sam, but it is difficult to ascertain where lot #2 is. Lots #1 and #2 included, "24 acres at the wigwam & pond lying neare the extent of the towne boundes toward East Hampton and to be laid out by them yt they shall belong to."[385] This description leads us to believe that Sam drew a lot that placed him very close to the wigwam but there is no mention if the wigwam was occupied. Again, the following year, in the second Seaponnack Division Feb 1654/55, Sam was identified #32.

Although the harbor at North Sea (first called Feversham, then Northampton) had been the port for Southampton from the beginning, there were probably no more than a few dwellings and maybe a small "warehouse" or shelter located there by 1648, as settlers ventured the few miles south to the village upon arrival. Men came from Massachusetts, Connecticut and, "an important group…from Hempstead, probably following the Rev. Robert Fordham upon his removal hither from that place of which he had been one of the founders. Among those who came with him or subsequently were Jonas Wood, Capt. Thomas Topping and John Ogden, the last of whom was the founder of North Sea…"[386] We introduced the likelihood of Sam's relationship with Ogden in chapter 8 of this book. Ogden was granted the Necks before 1650, provided he would place six families there. "This settlement differed from others in the Town in that a separate set of proprietors was created."[387]

In June of 1654, Sam was already living in the house when he purchased it from Robert Marven [sic] in Southampton. Might this arrangement have resulted from the 1652 lien against John Hubby's property where, "Robert Mervin attached a paper in the hand of Samuel Dayton"? Whatever the stipulations had been, it seems clear that there had been some arrangement for exchange of services between Marven and Sam that allowed Sam to manage the house belonging to Marven.

---

[383] (T. A. Bayles 1882)
[384] (Henry 2000)
[385] (H. Hedges 1874). 98
[386] (Adams 1918)
[387] Ibid.

These Presents doe witness that Robert Mervin doth acknowledge to have received in full payment for his house and land with the privileges thereof in Southampton, of Samuel Dayton in whose possession the said house and land is in at present, And that there is a full and final end of all debts, dues and demands whatsoever for any cavse what soeuer, from first to this present date, that hath or might have been from either of the said parties to the other, and they doe hereby free each other from all dues or demands what soever that may bee made by any in the name of either the said parties unto the other.

Witnes their hands the seconde of Iune 1654.
In presence of   ROBERT MARVEN
Ralf Dayton   SAMUEL DAYTON
Henry Pierson Sec.

It is interesting, and we think revealing, that Ralph was there to sign the document as a witness. It is likely that Ralph was present because he was helping Sam with the purchase of his home. This acquisition occurred almost two years before Ralph gave much of his East Hampton property to Samuel's younger brother Robert. It is possible that since Samuel's younger sister Ellen had died in childbirth just two months before the Mervin transaction, Ralph might have been thinking more of his own mortality and wished to begin distribution of inheritance. Besides, it is likely Sam and Medlin needed more room for their growing family, as the three boys, Ralph, Samuel and Abraham, all under 6 years old, would soon be joined by a fourth brother, Issac.

As far as can be determined, the move to the Mervin house presumed to be on Main Street is the first recorded move for Sam's family since arriving at Southampton, although he probably lived for a time at the home lot on Towne (Main) Street and also at North Sea, among the Ogden recruits. Because of Sam's continued association with John Ogden, the probability that the growing family had already been at North Sea before 1654 is high and, by June of 1655, court records identified Sam back at North Sea again, as a resident.

Life after Alice

Among records during the decade 1655 to 1665, there occurred a variety of events involving Sam that appear to be disconnected because we are not able to sequence them or contextually understand how they fit together. Consequently, much of the underlying dynamic of the official record is not detectable.

Judging from both East Hampton and Southampton records, Ralph left East Hampton shortly after Alice died. Keeping in mind that our theory suggests Alice died sometime after February of 1655/56, it was not long before Ralph married the widow of James Haines, Mary [Knight] Haynes, who was more than 20 years younger than Ralph. The marriage occurred about June of 1656, probably at Southold. Although the quickness might seem insensitive to some, it certainly happened that widows and widowers remarried in very short course. This was not unusual, especially if the dying spouse had been ill with a disease that required nearly constant care and nursing, like dementia. For a single woman, there was a strong imperative to marry and for widows, as well as for widowers, to join families for mutual benefit.

By necessity to tell our story, we include some detail of James Haines below. James, a cooper by trade, and Mary had removed from Salem, Massachusetts to Southold, L.I. just a year or two before James died.

The Southold Town Records contain the will and inventory of James Haines or Hindes, March 1652/53, and these are also communicated in The New England Historical and Genealogical Register.[388]

I James Haynes being weake in bodie, but by divine Providence in p'fect memorie doe make this my last will and testam^t:

Inpris. I doe give and bequeath that small estate the Lord hath been pleased to lend me to my loveing wife Mary Haynes my children being smale, for to bring them upp with all, Only my tooles that belong to my calling, I give them all to my oldest son John Haynes.

2^d: My will is that my children continue with my wife till they bee twenty one yeares of age, th' older laboring to bee a helpe to bring upp the younger, unleste providence order it otherwise that shee shall dispose of herselfe in marriage and then shall see or have cause to put any of them forth to some honest trade or cauleinge.

I leave it to her & my loveing ffriends Mr John Youngs, Senr: & John Herbert my overseers to dispose of, or in case shee should not dispose of herselfe in marriage, that shee finde not herselfe able to govern them, or that it bee not advantageous to the family to keepe them all at whom, then I leave it to her and my aforesaid Overseers to dispose of them.—In testimony hereof I have sett my hand the 1 March 1652 [o.s.] Southold.
JAMES HINDES.

Signed and delivered in the p'sence of us.
Jo. Yongs   John Herbert.

The inventory seems to have been recorded[389] on December 5, 1655 and is also reported on page 161 of the NEHGR.[390] Note that John Youngs Senior was the

---

[388] (Haines 1883). 161
[389] Note: See *Southold Town Records*, liber B, page 91
[390] (Haines 1883). 161

minister in Southold, and grandfather of Reverend David Youngs of the Setauket Presbyterian Church in the 1740's. There was also a John Youngs Junior, who in 1654 was commissioned as privateer to patrol the waters of Long Island Sound, to prevent mainland Native Americans from crossing to exploit the quarrel between England and Holland.[391]

An Inventorie of the goods & chattels whereof James Haynes lately dyed possessed taken uppon oath according to order in that behalfe the 18th of 9 m 1655.

		£
Inpris.	houses and lands wth appurten'nces, 3 Cowes & 2 steeres	50.00.00
It.	1 Calfe, 2 hafers, and 1 Steere	08.04.00
It.	14 goats & Kidds & 7 Swyne younge and old	10.12.00
It.	1 debt £7. --11 yds of Searge, 2 yrds ½ more of Searge	12.02.00
It.	his wear'g cloathes, hatt, 5 pr Sheets, 12 Pillow cases	11.14.00
It.	2 Shirts—7 table napkins, 3 table Cloths & lynin cloths	03.08.10
It.	Fustian—pewter. warming pann & frying pann	03.02.00
It.	a bedstead--feather bed & curtains	08.00.00
It.	a chest & bedstead & all other household goods	09.17.00
It.	10 bushells of Indean corne & 7 bushells of Wheate	03.01.06
It.	6 bushells of Pease--3 loads of hay	03.04.00
		123.08.04

Apprais[rs] Barnabas Horton Thomas Moore

When James died, he left eight children of Mary, with John the oldest at about 14 or 15 and the remaining seven children, from about 12 down to 2 years of age. What happened to all of them is unknown, but apparently some were "put out to trades" as James had recognized would occur if his wife would remarry. The Southold Town Records Vol 1 indicates all members of the family left Southold.

The records of the First Congregational Church of Salem, Mass., show that James Haines was a member as early as December 25, 1637, and the baptism of his eight children are recorded:

John,	so[n] of	Broth Haines	28.	6.	1639.
James	"	Bro. "	2.	6.	1641.
Benj.	"	" "	26.	6.	1643.
Mary	d	" "	19.	2.	1646.
James	s	" "	27.	12.	1647.
Jona		" "			
Sarah	child	" "	11.	4.	1648
Thos	s	of James Haynes	4.	3.	1651

Again, more details of Mary's interactions with the court and with Ralph are included because they are important to the remainder of the story. Mindful of context,

---

[391] (Mowrer 1960)

a lengthy passage from the *Records of the Colony or Jurisdiction of New Haven* by Charles Hoadly is provided:

> [no date] Mr. Herbert of Southold informed the court that James Hindes, of their towne deceased, made a will (wch was now presented to ye court), wherin he giues away his estate to his wife, but none to his chilldren, and he being one of the ouerseers appointed by the said will, hearing that his widdow was aboute to dispose of herselfe in marriage, went to her and desired her to giue something to the children before, she said no, not till she dyed, but at last yielded to giue them twenty pound a peece, but would not confirme it till goodman Dayton came, whom she was to marrie, and though he at first dissented, yet after yeilded to it, but when writings should haue bine confirmed she refused.
>
> Being now asked the reason thereof, she said her husband gaue it her and she would keepe it while she liued, she was wished to consider if her husband had giuen all away to the children and nothing to her would not she haue considered and releiued, men may not make wills as they will themselues, but must attend the minde of God in doeing the same, who doth pvide that children, (vnless weightie reason be to the contrary,) shall haue portions, and the eldest a double portion, therfor the rest must have a part, and the Apostle saith it is the duty of parents to lay vp for their children, therfore if they will consider and agree among themselues, it will well satisfye the court, but if not then the court must issue it.
>
> After some debate amonge themselues, they desired the court to issue it, who were informed by goodman Dayton that a cow and calfe is lost sinc the goods were prised, and three or foure goates, and ye house and land is prised very much too deare, also that the eldest sonn had his fathers tooles giuen him, all wch the court tooke into consideration, and by way of sentenc did order, that the loss of ye cow and calfe wth the goates, be borne both by mother and chilldren, and also what loss shall appeare to be in the house and land, and that the tooles be reckoned as pt of the estate, wch were not before prised, & then the estate as it appears to be, be equally deuided, one halfe to the mother, the other halfe to the chilldren, out of wch the eldest is to have a double portion of wch the tooles to be a part, and if the chilldren be put out to trades, wch shall be done wth the consent of ye ouerseers, what shall bee necessary in point of charge to put y^m forth shall come out of their owne portions, and till this be pformed by Ralph Dayton, his bond whereby he was bound to appeare at this court, is to stand in force, wch bond was now deliuered to Leiutenant Budd, wth order that when ye sentenc is fulfilled he haue his bond in, and also a further

discharge from the ouerseers for so much as they receive to improve for ye childrens vse.

After w^{c}h, goodman Dayton informed the court that what was done in the case betwixt his wife and chilldren doth well satisfye them, onely he further declared that before James Hindes dyed, he desired that M^r. Herbert might be put out from being one of the ouerseers and M^r. Wells put in his roome. The court told him that they can doe nothing wthout proofe, but if M^r. Herbert desires to be free, and if it be proved that it was the mans minde before he dyed, they are willing vpon goodman Daytons desire, that the two deputies now present, Barnabas Horton & William Purrier, should joyne with M^r. Younge the other ouerseer, to take care of the chilldren and their estates, that they may be put out to trades and their estates improuved to their advantage.[392]

This was truly a tragic tale for all who were involved and still is, even for the reader. The record remains, and worse it doesn't require much effort to form unfavorable judgments of Mary, assuming all the pertinent facts are provided and circumstances understood. But the fact was, for whatever reason, Mary wanted what was given to her from her husband, even though it appears that it could come at some detriment to her children. She would have the children put out to trades and the assets would soon be transferred from James to Ralph upon marriage. It was not until a form of reprimand from the judge and "debate" with husband-to-be Ralph, she then yielded to "the mind of God" and she agreed that the children would each receive a portion from the estate. How could Mary object to what seems to be her duty to her children? We cannot say.

Once the couple agreed to give portions to Mary's children, Ralph made it known that the estate was now less than inventoried and appraised, and the court took this into consideration. Ralph then announced that just before James died, he desired that one of the overseers, Mr. Herbert, the man James had called a "loving friend," be replaced by another. Since Mr. Herbert was the person who objected to the unjust will in the first place, it is clear there had been tension between Mr. Herbert and Mary.

It is likely that Ralph and Mary were married within days of the court record. Ralph did not make Southold his home after assuming ownership of the Haines property there, but instead rented the property to Reverend Young while he and Mary probably lived in the vicinity of Towd,[393] just north of Sam. Towd (also spelled

---

[392] (C. J. Hoadly, Records of the Colony or Jurisdiction of New Haven, From May 1653, to the Union Together with the New Haven Code of 1656 1858) 159
[393] (W. Pelletreau 1915)

Towde and Toude),[394] supposedly an Indian name for the Fish Grove area, was located along the northern or eastern edge of the harbor at North Sea.

It was just a few months later, Sam's wife Medlin sold a few acres of their land in Sam's absence. Southampton town records state,

> John Howell hath bought of Medlin Dayton ye wife of Samuel Dayton with his consent 4 acres of ground in the great plaines being next to the 4 acres commonly called by the name of Haracres lot and the meadow belonging to it.

This sale was recorded on December 12, 1656 when Sam and Medlin were probably still living in the house they had bought from Marvin. It is possible Sam's attention was turning to investments in Brookhaven to the west, making the land down by the ocean in Southampton less attractive to maintain. These 4 acres were probably in the vicinity of Cooper's Neck. Being such an unusual record begs the question, where was Sam and why couldn't the sale wait for him to return? Should this provide clues to Sam's occupation?

It is interesting to note that Thompson places Sam about 45 miles away, north and west of North Sea, in his list of settlers at Setauket, "within two years after 1655,"[395] but Winans dismisses Thompson's list as do we. Still, the fact that neither Sam nor Ralph can be found on two 1657 lists of inhabitants of Southampton, namely the powder list[396] and the full list of Southampton inhabitants[397] seems to be problematic. Sam was found in the whale squadrons list for Southampton in 1657, but in *Early Southampton*, Winans said the preceding entry from 1657 is deceiving and the reader should not assume the squadron list was also from 1657. Furthermore, Winans claimed the list, "belongs to the year 1666 or 1668, and is not earlier." If Winans was correct, the Samuel on a 1668 list would probably be the son of our ancestor Sam, as it is not believed Sam Senior was still living in Southampton after 1665. Samuel Junior was the second son, born about 1651, making him between the ages of fifteen to seventeen at the time the list was created. His age does not disqualify him since it is known that minors were sometimes included on these lists, as stated in S.T.R., Vol 1, on page 32 of our edition: "The earliest complete list of male inhabitants at Southampton is the whale squads list of March 1644, forty–two names. It is especially to be noted that this list includes several landless servants, and also minors above 16 years."

---

[394] (Wallace n.d.). 229
[395] (B. F. Thompson, History of Long Island 1839). 262
[396] (H. Hedges 1874)
[397] Note: In his 1887 *Early History of Southampton*Howell listed Southampton men by their location on the Main Street and he then includes "Eastern men," and "North Sea men."

A June 5, 1657 STR says, "Iohn Ogden hath bought of Samuel Dayton his house and home lot and five acres in the ten acre lotts, and 4 in coopers neck, and two acres more in another place also he bouyht the meddow belonging to it." Could these 4 acres at Cooper's Neck be the same Medlin supposedly sold? At this point, Sam and John Ogden appear to be parting ways and it may sound as if Sam was leaving the remainder of his holdings in Southampton town until the very next record in the STR reveals that, just two weeks later, on the 20th, "Samuel Dayton doth acknowledge y thee hath boght of Mr Edward Joanes, three acres that was formerly Mr Stamboroughs with a house upon it." It is not assumed this is the same home lot found on Pelletreau's map of Main Street. This house was probably next to Howell's March 8, 1648/49 three acre home lot between, "Farrington's lot and Josiah Stanborough's house,"[398] on Towne Street in the village of Southampton. Whether Samuel ever lived there or if he just saw an investment opportunity is unknown.

In 1657, Medlin probably gave birth to the couple's fifth son, Jacob.

Troubles with John Cooper

Many authors have observed that bickering, name calling, boundary disputes, accusations and all manner of trespass are common in the town records. This is partially explained by the simple fact that Puritans made record of so many "minor" occurrences that seem trivial today. However, allegations of battery are not often found in early town records, so it is interesting to note the March 26, 1654/55 "action of battery entered by Thomas Burnet against John Cooper to be tried at a purchased court April 2." No conclusion was found to this case, but it introduces us to John Cooper Senior and John Cooper Junior.

James Truslow Adams says of John Cooper Senior, in *History of the Town of Southampton*,

> [he was] of strong character and will, with a somewhat choleric temper and a hasty tougue, a born fighter, bluff, honest and courageous, he could ill have been spared from the colony in the days of struggle. He may, with others, have been occasionally fined for passionate expression or hasty imprecation but the unrecorded occasions which called them forth may possibly have justified them, and as for his numerous law suits it must be granted that they were not seldom settled in his favor.

---

[398] (Seversmith, Colonial Families of Long Island, New York and Connecticut, Being the Ancestry & Kindred of Herbert Furman Seversmith 1939-1958)

"His main business apparently, which he carried on for a while at least with Thomas Cooper, was raising and selling horses, then one of the principal articles of export to the Barbadoes"[399] and many of the disputes between the Coopers and the Daytons involved horses. Ralph, and particularly Sam, seemed to have had frequent disputes with John Cooper Senior and Junior, usually pertaining to some type of trespass. The number of recorded differences imply frequent interactions, possibly even a working relationship or as a rival business. Naturally, when two "strong" characters have an exchange, things can easily escalate.

In September of 1655 and on December 3, 1656, John Cooper Junior was plaintiff against Sam for acts of trespass. In colonial America, the word *trespass* was used for legal action when it was felt one person had infringed upon another's rights, person or property. An example of *trespass*, as it was often used, was in reference to cattle or hogs straying into a neighbor's garden or creating other mischief. Sam lost the decision and appealed.

The following year, Ralph won his trespass case in a jury trial against John Cooper Junior, involving a horse.

> an action of tresspass vpon the case entered by Ralf Dayton plaintiff against John Cooper defendant... At a particular court december 1, 1657
> A jury impanelled to try the case depending betweene Ralph Dayton and John Cooper Junr... The Iury findeth for the plaintif ye horse and 2s 6d damage with increase of Court charges, Iudgment is given by the magistrates acording to the verdict of the jury.

The December 1 verdict fits nicely into a scenario that may help to explain an entry recorded just two weeks earlier. On November 13, 1657 Thomas Baker of East Hampton, gave in deposition, a detailed description of his father-in-law's missing colt, after a horse that looked very much like it was discovered among other horses in the pound and in possession of a Mr. Foster. The deposition reads:

> This Depont testifieth yt to his knowledge his father in law Ralph Daiton had a coulte come of his mare wch had white feete & white about the face & walle eyes the most part of his couler beinge a light sorrel wch coulte he put in my whome lott to kepe sum time to weane: afterward I saw such A coulte in the pound wth both his eares cropt allsoe I saw him severall times and had it not bene yt he had another eare marke yn my fathers I should have tooke him to bee my fathers & I should have taken my oath yt it was his & Goodman foster came to our towne on him and I looked on his eares and it made me further to thinke it was my fathers horse.

---

[399] (Adams 1918). 58

160

Seven months after the deposition of Thomas Baker, on June 24, 1658, William Simons also testified in what appears to be a similar, if not the same, case.

Willm Simons Deposed Declareth yt one time goeinge from my house to Mr Gardiners and as I was goeinge alonge I met Ralph Daiton wch was lokinge over into the pound vppon horses yt were yn there soe I cominge by at the same time saith to Goodman Daiton how doe you what are you a loking vppon yt ball faced Coult and Goodman Daiton tould me he should have taken yt coult to have bene his but only his mark he thought was sumthing Defaced but hee thought yt his mark might be sumthing Deserned yet; and this I Testifie yt Coult wch was yn in ye pound was very like unto yt coult yt suckt Ralph Daytons Mare for yt Coult yt did suck this mare before spoken of was a reddish couler as I call it and a ball face and wall eyes[400] and 4 white feete and white vnder the belly and farther this Depont saith not taken before me John Mullford. A true transcript compared by Thomas Talmage Secr.

Might this be the same reddish horse in Ralph's will, described as the, "sorill horse which I had of Jonas Wood"?

There are even more entries from 1658 involving Sam and John Cooper Junior that could either be a continuation or a similar case occurring September of 1655 and on December 3, 1656. In the 1658 case, Cooper was also victorious and Sam appealed to the court at Hartford.

Sept 21, 1658 An action of the case entered by Iohn Cooper Iun plaintif against Samuel Dayton defendant. The jury find for Iohn Cooper plaintif the horse and court charges with all damages, the court granted judgement according to the verdict, The defendant viz Samuel Dayton appeales to the court at Hartford.[401]

Sept 22, 1658 Bee it known unto all men by these presents yt I Samuel Dayton of the north sea, and Thomas Barker of East Hampton and Robert dayton of the same, doe by these presents engage ourselues mutually in the sum of thirty pounds for to prosecute the appeale with effect the next quarter Court at Hartford. Per me JOHN HOWELL Sec.

Bee it known unto all men by these presents that I Iohn Cooper Iun. of Southampton do by these presents bind myself with my father Iohn Cooper Sen in the some of thirty pounds to answer Samuel Dayton

---

[400] Note: "Baldfaced" means a very wide blaze, with white extending to or past the eyes. "Wall eye" is used in different ways but most often refers to more than one color in the eye or white around the eye. Being just a couple of months before Ralph's death, no conclusion to the matter is found.
[401] (H. Hedges 1874)

according to his recognisance in his appeale to the quarter court at Hartford.

It would be thoughtless not to point out that once again, as occurs throughout his life, Sam's brother-in-law Thomas Baker proves his valuable good will to the Dayton family by supporting Sam, along with Sam's brother Robert.

Ralph's Death

It was in that very same court that notice was brought of the death of Ralph Dayton. The Southampton record of Sept 22, 1658 stated that Ralph had died, most likely just a few days earlier.

> At a quarter court the will of the late deceased Ralph Dayton was brought into the Court and aproued of by the magistrates, and the £10 that Robert Dayton owed to his father hee hath put it into the estate.

When Ralph wrote his will in July of 1658, he was about 70 years old. In September, he left behind his wife Mary Haines Dayton and four grown children of his first wife—three sons and one daughter, having been predeceased by another daughter. His children were, in order of age, Ralfe who remained in England, Alice of East Hampton with her husband Thomas Baker, Samuel and wife Medlin whose residence was still officially in the Township of Southampton, Ellen who married John Linley but had died in childbirth, and Robert and wife Elizabeth who lived on the Town Green at East Hampton, across from his sister Alice. Ralph Senior had been married at least twice.

The original will of Ralph Dayton is an impressive and significant artifact of Dayton heritage that provides a glimpse of our family in the mid-seventeenth century. Ralph's will is preserved at the East Hampton Public Library, Long Island Collection archives, and at just over 350 years old, it is an amazing piece of paper to hold in one's hands.

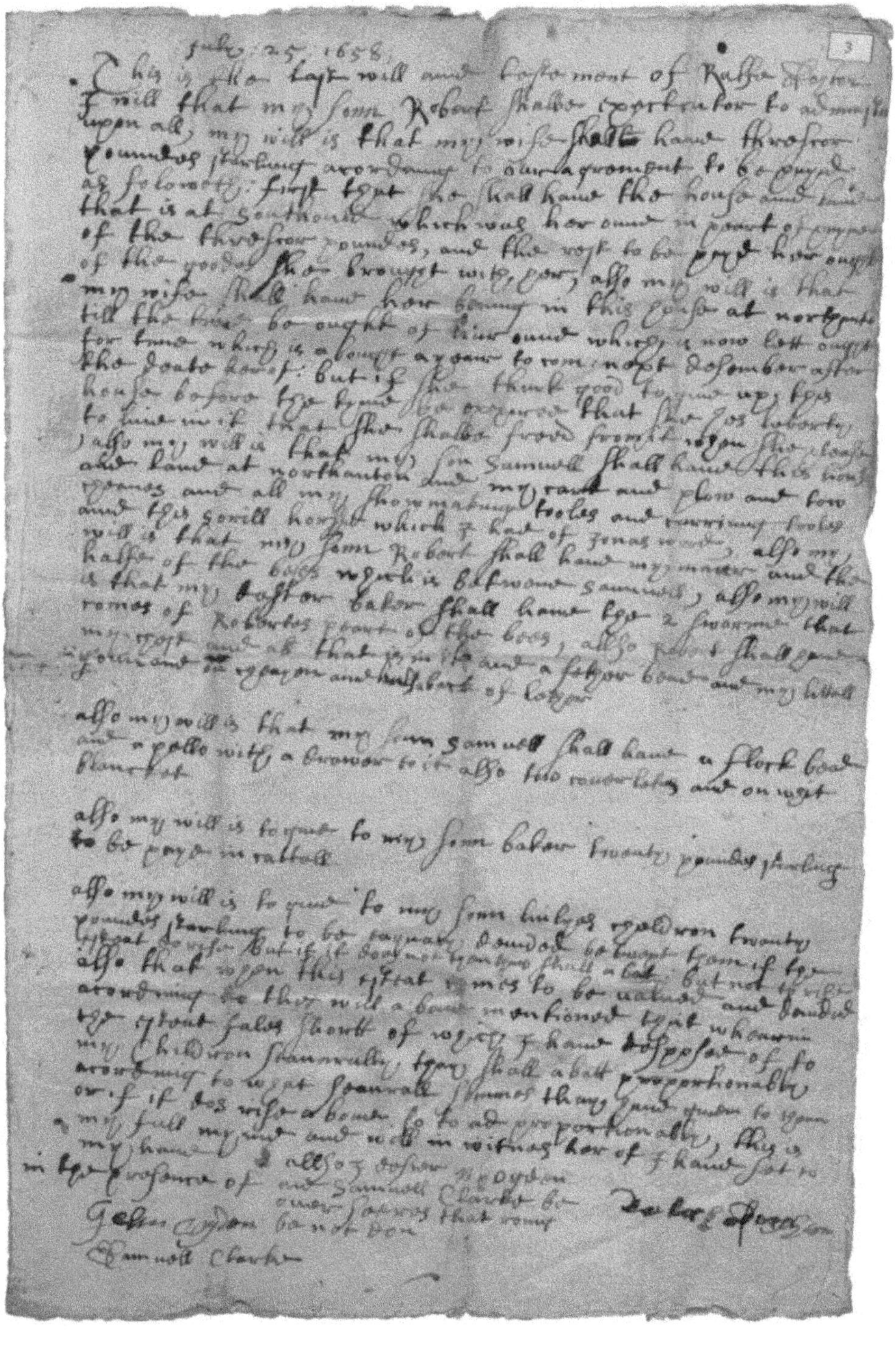

Figure 17. Ralph Dayton will, 1658

Photo courtesy of East Hampton Public Library, Long Island Collection. Used with permission.

163

Ralph's will, broken into numbered segments for analysis of delineated stipulations, reads:

July 25 1658

1. *This is the last will and testament of Ralfe Dayton. I will that my sonn Robert shall be executor to administer upon all.*
2. *My will is that my wife shall have three score pounds sterling according to our agreement to be paid as followeth:*

1st that she shall have the house and land that is at Southold which was her owne in part of payment of the three scor poundes and the rest paide her out of the goodes she brought with her.
Also my will is that my wife shall have her living in this house at Northampton till the time be ought for her owne which is now lett ought for a term which is about a year to come next December after the date hereof. But if she think good to give up this house before the tyme be expired that she have liberty to live in it that she shal be fried from it when she please.

3. *Also my will is that my sonn Samuell shall have this house and land at Northampton and my cart and plow and two chanes and all my showmaking tooles and cumeing tooles and the sorill horse which I had of Jonas Wood.*
4. *Also my sonn Robert shall have my mortar and the half of the bees which is between Samuell.*
5. *Also my will is that my daughter baker the two swarms that comes of Roberts peart of the bees.*
6. *Also Robert shall have my chest and all that is in It and a feather bead and my littel gunn and the cheayn and half a beck of lether.*
7. *Also my will is that my sonn Samuell shall have a flock bead[402] and a pello with a drawer to it. Also two coverlets and one white blanket.*
8. *Also my will is to give my sonn baker twenty pounds starling to be payd in cattel.*
9. *Also my will is to give to my son brinlyes children twenty poundes starling to be equally devided betwext them if the groat[403] do rise but if it does not, then they shall abate but not to rise. Also that when this groat comes to be valued and devided according to that will above mentioned that whearin the groat fales short of which I have desposed of to my children seavarally they shall abate proportionally according to what seavrall summs they have given to them or if it does rise above so to add proportionally.*
This is my full mynd and will -- in witness hereof I have set to my hand.
allso I desire Mr. Ogdon and Samuell Clarke for overseeres that rong be not don.

---

[402] Note: A flock bed was a bag stuffed with bits of cloth, wool or tow serving in place of feathers
[403] Note: 4d= 1 groat

The will is signed by Ralph and witnesses John Ogden and Samuel Clark, and it contains some curiosities. For example, why was Robert named executor when this responsibility is normally the duty of the "eldest" son? How does one interpret the addition of the sentence "allso I desire Mr. Ogdon and Samuell Clarke for overseers that wrong be not don" that appears to have been added to the bottom of the page? How does one account for the appearance of Ralph's autograph—did he attempt to sign the document weeks after it was written, when he was ill and weak?

Our inclination is to think of Ralph as being strong and independent, but less aggressive and boisterous than many in New England, "probably overstocked with men of strong minds and assertive dispositions."[404] In some ways, Ralph seems less comfortable with uncertainty or conflict, especially after the age of 55 when a natural mellowing often occurs. Or, perhaps he was just more humble and quicker to "forgive those who trespass" as stated in the Lord's Prayer, reminding us of our own father who, when a victim of significant theft or vandalism would not prosecute, but instead would just say, "That's between he and the Lord." Of course there is at least one glaring exception to the characterization of Ralph as subdued, one that might indicate a more venturesome energy in his youth; the fact that Ralph abandoned his beloved homeland and took upon himself and his family great risk in the perilous voyage to a foreign land that was not all that attractive or forgiving.

Ralph became one of the first of the early male settlers of East Hampton to die. As was the case with Alice, the site of Ralph's grave is unknown but it is probably either at North Sea or at East Hampton, near Alice's grave—both long ago unrecognizable and then vanished. It is believed that the first generation of Puritans rarely used processed markers, instead many used simple wood or undressed rock allowing deterioration and were lost rather quickly with the passing of time. However, many of the sons and grandsons of that first generation of Puritans saw to it that their fathers received more refined grave markers months or years after their passing. Ralph died before the sixth son of Sam and Medlin, Caleb, was born sometime in 1659. Caleb was to be Medlin's youngest child.

Executor to administer upon all

In his will, Ralph provided that Mary receive the house, "she brought with her" at Southold. But, since the Southold house was being rented, Ralph also stipulated she must wait for the current lease with [Reverend Young] to expire in December of 1659 before taking possession. With the lease on her Southold house continuing for more than a year, Ralph favored Mary to live in the house at Northampton meaning that Sam could not take possession of his inherited house until it was vacant. From

---

[404] (C. M. Andrews 1919)

what is known of Sam, he was not a patient sort of person, so the plan was destined to be a troublesome affair. Perhaps Ralph assumed that his widow would remarry rather quickly after his death, she being much younger than he.

When Mary is found next, she was already the wife of Ffulk Davis in March of 1660/61, though it is not known how long they had been married. Since Davis had been a neighbor in Northampton (North Sea), the marriage could have occurred in very short course. In this March 1660/61 record, Robert Dayton, the executor of his father's will, and Thomas Baker entered suite against the Davises that was addressed in both Southampton and East Hampton courts, in an action of trespass accusing Mary of interfering with the estate at Southold before the lease was expired. Apparently, the Davises had violated the terms of the inheritance and the court had placed them under bond for the purpose of keeping them from further interference with the Southold estate.

The Southampton court granted the Davises an additional period of time to answer the charges: "Fflulk Davis & his wife have liberty granted by the Court to anser next cort, & in ye meane time to [word gone] the bond to Mr Bakr & Robt. Dayton with such charges as they are [words gone] this court." This entry was not dated.

As more details of the case are provided in the March 21, 1660/61 East Hampton court,[405] it is learned that the Davises had entered into some kind of a business deal with two East Hampton men, in violation of their bond.

> Robert Dayton plt entreth an accon of trespas on the Case against Mary Davis wife of ffulke Davis of Northampton for molestinge of some pte of his estate lieinge in the hands of the Revrend Pastor Younge of Southould, and in soe doeinge hath forfeter or at lest violated abond wherein she was bound to stand to the arbitracon of five men, wch later clase Mr Thomas Baker Joyneth wth the other as plts. The Magistrates have entred an accon against William Edwards Nathaniell ffoster in an accon of the case for makeinge a bargaine contrary to an order of the towne by wch cause great damage may redowne to this litle comon welth or towne in wch we are...whereas there hath beene a difference betweene Mr Thomas Baker and Robert Dayton the one party, and Mary Davis the wife of ffulke Davis the other party, about an estate that was left by James Haynes the former husband, or Ralph Dayton her second husband doe by these prsence remise release and for ever quit claime each other of and from all and all manner of suits accon executions bonds bills and specially debts and demands what soever and doe herby bind our selves our heyers

---

[405] (H. Hedges 1887)

and all our children executors and assignes in the pen all sum of one hundred pounds never to molest or trouble each other for in or about any matter or thinge that is past from the begininge of the world to this prsent date and the sd Mary Davis doe by these engage that her husband and her sonn John Haynes shall the first opertunity that there are prsented subscribe hereunto: In witnese whereof we the above named have interchangably sett to our hands the one and twentieth Day of March, 1660.[o.s.]

THO: BACKER
ROBERT R. D DAYTONS marke

MARY I DAVIS marke

Once again, there may be importance to pointing out that Sam does not seem to be involved even though these actions should be of concern to him. It would not come as a surprise to learn that Thomas and Robert were acting in behalf of Sam.

Sam sold a large portion of what he had inherited from his father at North Sea to John Scott in June of 1659, except Samuel kept for himself Ralph's house and house lot (presumed to be at Towd). Medlin and the boys could have been living in that house by March 6 of 1659/60[406] according to court record on that date, since it was said of Sam in both 1658 and in 1659 that he was "of North Sea." Cox believed that Sam had accompanied Underhill to Setauket in that year.[407]

In October of 2010, I asked Richard Barons about the diversification of land. His insightful reply may very well be applied to Sam and his father Ralph, as there is the possibility that Ralph had actually purchased all the land where Sam and he had their dwellings.

Much of it [acreage] would be left, the next generation would buy acres and they would want to buy another ten acres, they would ask Dad or uncle or somebody, 'This is a great place, can you buy this? We'll tend it for you,' they then end up selling it and they would move somewhere else...[408]

More than eight months after the sale of North Sea land to John Scott, the March 6, 1659/60 STR says,

Samuel Dayton acknowledgeth to have sold unto John Scott about the 20th of June last past ffor the use of Anthony Waters, all that accommodations at ye North Sea belonging to Southampton, which said

---

[406] Ibid.
[407] (Cox 1912)
[408] (Barons 2010)

accommodations did belong unto the said Samuel his father Ralph Dayton, except only ye home lot whereupon the said Samuel dwelleth. Allsoe in like manner at the same time hee the Said Samuell sold and acknowledgeth to have sold vnto the said Mr John Scott for the vse of him the Said Mr Anthony Waters a home lott lying on that side of the creek (at ye North Sea aforesaid) on which ffulk Davis Dwelleth, with all the fenceing to the Said home lot belonging. All which Said parcells of land the Said Samuel affirmeth makes £100 lotment, and acknowledgeth to have Sold as abovesaid with all the comodities Immunities and privileges vnto the said land belonging, and for the only proper use of him the Said Waters as aforesaid. Witness Henry Pierson Sec. March 6, 1659 Mr John Scott acknowledgeth that about the 20th of June last hee ptd with and put off a pt of his home lott at the North Sea belonging to Southampton, of the quantity of about 2 acres, unto Mr Anthony Waters, and the Said Mr Anthony Waters acknowledgeth that in liew of ye Said land, and in regard of the remoteness of his home lott which hee had by vertue of purchase ffrom Samuel Dayton on that Side the creek wheras ffulk Davis Dwelleth, hee ye said Mr Anthony Waters then imptd and put off vnto him the Said Mr Iohn Scott the Said home lot with the fenceing therevnto belonging.

Pelletreau claimed that Fulk Davis lived on the east side of the Fish Cove, perhaps where land near that area is still called Davis Cove.[409] There is no reason to doubt Pelletreau's claims but we are not able to affirm these statements by referring to modern maps. Perhaps the place called Fish Cove today is different than the Fish Cove of old. Modern Davis Creek, if the same one, is still visible on maps, as is a road leading to Towd Point aptly named Towd Point Road.

It sounds as if Scott, who had acquired Ralph's former property on the other side of the creek, close to Ffulk Davis, complained that the land had poor accessibility and so refused to take possession of it after planning to acquire it for use by Anthony Waters.

Meantime, Anthony Waters recorded the purchase of Ralph's former house and lot from Sam "of North Sea" on March 6, 1659/60. No attempt was made to unravel Scott's many transactions except to say that he was still involved with home lots involving Waters in August of 1660. According to Mary Cummings in *North Sea, the First Step*, Scott was in the process of buying up much of North Sea.

Strong tells us that in the summer of 1659, Waters, who was a Southampton resident, had purchased the exclusive rights from Unkechaug sachems to drift whales

---

[409] (H. P. Hedges 1877). 204

on the barrier beach along the south shore of meadowland which Setauket men had already purchased from Wenecoheage.[410] It may be possible that Waters' involvement with the salvage of whale carcasses south of Brookhaven somehow entered into the exchange for Sam's inherited house since Sam was probably already involved in some way with Raynor's whaling company in that same general area, as he would be a few years later.

It appears that it was Scott's intention to buy the land in order to profit from its rent or sale to Anthony Waters. After he refused the land from Scott, Waters dealt directly with Sam. Another interpretation of the March 1659/60 record might be that Scott claimed that his purchase included the house where Sam was living, the house that he had inherited from Ralph. It could be that Sam wanted to clarify the earlier agreement out of fear that Scott might try to renege on some portion of the agreement or even claim more than he was entitled to. According to Mary Cummings,

> One of North Sea's most notorious early residents was Captain John Scott, an entrepreneur or, as East Hampton historian Sherrill Foster prefers to describe him, 'a wheeler and dealer.' Wherever he went, Scott left a trail of the swindled and cheated. He even traveled to London, where he tried to con King Charles II. Actually, Scott began life in England, but was banished for bad behavior as a youth, landing in Salem where he became a bound boy to a Quaker family. In 1654, he went to sea, became a buccaneer, accumulated a fortune and began acquiring huge tracts of land, including considerable acreage in North Sea. North Sea, at the time, was arguably something of a wheeler-dealer's paradise with land ripe for acquisition and a port that promised excellent opportunities for trade. Also on site and available was Deborah Raynor, the granddaughter of wealthy Thurston Raynor,[411] whom Scott wooed and wed in 1658. While she raised their two children on their "manor" at North Sea, the captain himself was rarely at home. He was too busy selling land he didn't own, appropriating land owned by others, making dubious deals and promoting himself as president of Long Island.[412]

Even while Captain Scott was away, his dealings still created problems for his wife (who was also sister of Joseph Raynor). At a purchased court January 17, 1661/62, George Miller entered action against Deborah Scott and Samuel "Dayten" for a horse he claimed Sam was to appraise and receive, according to Miller's previous agreement with Scott. Although the complexities and scope of the jury's

---

[410] (J. A. Strong 2011)

[411] Note: Thurston Raynor, along with John Scott, John Biggs and Ralph Dayton, all of Long Island, appear in the parish records, at St. Mary's, Ashford, Kent, England.

[412] (Cummings 2007)

"special verdict" are not disclosed, Miller and Mrs. Scott agreed that Miller pay Scott with bushels of wheat and in return and she pay Miller, "20 shillings in wampum and he can keep his house." Apparently, the potential implications were great, more than were stated in the record.

Aspersing the Towne

If Sam had accompanied Underhill to Setauket in 1659 as Cox believed, there is a chance that Sam, as a seaman, would assist Underhill at Oyster Bay and get a share of the profit from disturbing Dutch West Indies trade, as was Underhill's self-imposed vocation.

Within a year after Ralph's death, on June 8, 1659,[413] thirty-five year old Sam and at least two other men were attending Southampton court[414] and heard charges that they removed cargo from a Dutch vessel docked at Northampton. In their defense, the men said the vessel had prohibited goods aboard (liquor). As strange and inadequate as that defense sounds, at the time, seizure of Dutch assets (including the vessel itself) was considered justified in some instances, in East End waters. In addition to the Dutch carrying other prohibited goods, the English were of the opinion that the Dutch were supplying the Native Americans with muskets and urging them to use them against the English.[415] As a result, many were encouraged to drive the Dutch from Long Island. We take no pleasure in concluding from the court's action that it was probably not Sam's intention to serve the greater cause, but instead it appears to have been for his own indulgence.

> June 8, 59 an acompt taken of the goods that were taken from the dutchman £12, 10s, and an ancre of liquors. The men viz Ioseph Raynor and Samuel Dayton and Iohn Woodruff [probably should be Wendall] doe acknowledge that they proseeded to take the vesell without any comition or power from any, only from information as they say the dutchman sould prohibeted goods,

> June 8, 59 bee it knowne vnto all men that wee Ioseph Rayner Samuel Dayton and Iohn Wendall, doe acknowledge ourselues to bee indebted to the authority of this towne the sum of thirty pounds sterling, vnder this

---

[413] Note: Some sources report the date June 1655 but this date is believed to be given in error. Among them are *History of Long Island: From Its Earliest Settlement to the…*Vol 2 by Peter Ross page 352 talking about Thomas Diament and "unlawful seizure."

[414] Note: At times, attendance was mandatory for those in the community

[415] (Ross 1905)

condition that wee doe personally apeare at the next court to be holden for Southamptonwhich is adjourned until the 24 day of this present month, then and there to answer to such matters, as shall be brought in against us, Ioseph Raynor and Samuel Dayton and Iohn Wendal subscribed to these recognisances.[416]

On June 21 the court fined five men in the case; three of them 20s each, but Sam and John Wendal 50s each for arguing with the court. Had Sam not been so stubborn and quarrelsome, the original fine seems to have been relatively small, despite the verbal reprimand and description of particularly offensive and egregious acts. Instead, Sam was fined a third time, an additional 50s for saying to the Court, "What should we yield for to have a trial in this towne that never did good." The events are recorded in the Southampton Town Records.

> At a court Iune ye 21, 1655 [59] The Court having considered and weighed the miscariage of the men who wer Same bound over to this court, viz, Ioseph Raynor Samuel Dayton and their associates viz, Thomas Diament, Iohn Wendal Edmond Shaw they finde them deeply guilty in the maner of acting in or about taking the vessell, in seueral particulars, first for contem of authority, manifest breach of the peace in many mutinous expressions, whereby some were afrighted, and many grieved, at such vile expressions, and actions, for which miscariages and others the court doth sentence them to pay 20s apeace, viz Edmond Shaw Ioseph Rayner and Thomas Diament, the other two viz Samuel Dayton and Iohn Wendal 50s apiece for their presumption preceedings 2 times after they had covenanted and engaged to the contrary, making further molestation and disturbance in the place, further the courte sees just cause to fine Samuel Dayton 50s for aspersing the towne with an unjust accusation in saying, what should we yield for to have a triall in this towne that never did good.

The reader should note that the last digit of "June 21, 1659" was incorrectly copied from the original STR book as June 21, 1655 which calls into question the selection of the last digit of all three records. Nonetheless, we accept 1659 for all three segments of the case.

From court accounts, it is evident that Sam was strong willed, rebellious and defiant to authority. In addition to the theft, the record says that the men were foul enough that some were in fear of being harmed and so offensive, even at meeting, that the court ignored their own decree from Jan 10, 1658/59 that, "whosoever shall speeke disorderly in the time of the meeting, or if any shall interupt another whilst

---

[416] (H. Hedges 1874)

hee is speeking for evey such default shall pay 6d." Sam's fine amounted to 100s, the equivalent of 1200d or £5. As a disclaimer, it is recognized that there is a possibility that the description of Sam's actions are "overstated" when compared to standards of behavior in the modern world, as some of what was considered vile then might be accepted behavior today.

As mentioned, it was not unusual for Dutch vessels to be stopped, cargo searched and papers examined when in English waters, especially on the east end. Another claimed confiscation that began at Northampton was described by Benjamin Thompson as an "extraordinary instance" that involved Lion Gardiner and the seizure of a Dutch vessel and cargo, taken to the Isle of Wight (Gardiners Island, part of East Hampton). The compelling similarities recorded in East Hampton would convince us that the second action was actually a continuation of the first action, but it is concluded upon closer examination that the two cases likely occurred at least five months apart. However, there is a strong possibility that the same Dutch vessel was involved in both episodes because, in his deposition, John Ogden related that he had [helped] them twice already and he, "wondered why they would come again and stay so long this time."[417]

The second case included a series of depositions from John Scott, John Griggs and Humphrie Hughes, Nathan Birdsall, David Gardiner and Richard Bennett, Commander John Peny and George Lee, Philemon Dicason, Andrew Miller, John Cooper, Robert Dayton and John Ogden. The depositions began in mid-November 1659 and extended into the following year and they provide more detail to this entangled affair. The East Hampton case also involved a Dutchman carrying freight (including liquor) from Manhattan to East Hampton, making a stop at Northampton (North Sea) where the vessel and cargo were first seized and then taken again by John Scott and Lion Gardiner from those who seized it.

Thompson summarized the events and we have added additional information, in brackets, provided from various sources in the hope of clarifying it.

> [Lion Gardiner] was prosecuted in this court for a claim of five hundred pounds sterling. The case was this: A Southampton man had hired a Dutchman [Renek Garrison, son of Garret DeVries] to bring him a freight from the Manhadoes [New York: Manhattan] to Easthampton. The vessel was taken by the English [Humphrey Hughes and John Griggs at Northampton], and brought to that island [Gardiner's Island], when Captain Gardiner retook her in behalf of the Dutch owners.[418]

---

[417] Ibid.
[418] (B. F. Thompson, History of Long Island 1839). 187

In this entangled case, it is not clear who had actually hired the Dutch men, although both John Scott and John Cooper had been negotiating with them at Manhattan. The original English captors of the Dutch vessel wanted Gardiner prosecuted for £500 damages for retaking the vessel while at Gardiner's Island. In his book, Benjamin Thompson provides an account of Sam as one of two witnesses February 21, 1659/60 to, "John Peny Comander of the Rowbuck ridinge in New haven harbor," appointing George Lee to be his attorney in this action of trespass against Gardiner. Apparently Peny did not travel to East Hampton, but instead sent Miller to represent him. Did Sam ferry Miller to Long Island? The fact that Sam was there with another witness, Caleb Carwithen/Carwithey, is particularly interesting because Carwithen was reported to have been a mariner, with regular routes between New Haven and Boston prior to 1654, and later had routes from Long Island when he moved to Southampton.[419] This may be only circumstantial evidence, but this once again adds support to the theory that Sam traveled often between various ports.

In these depositions, both the associates Griggs and Humphrey as well as John Scott talked about taking the boat at Northampton and then involving Gardiner at his Isle of Wight. Benjamin Thompson goes on to say,

> Being prosecuted by the original captors to recover from him the value of the vessel and cargo, as well as damages which had been sustained, and the subject matter being not only of great importance, but involving principles of law beyond the learning of the town magistrates, it was very properly determined to refer the case to the court at Hartford. The plantiff having probably little confidence in the justice of his cause, failed to appear, and the matter was dropped.[420]

But the matter was not dropped by Gardiner. Gardiner had made the crossing to appear at Hartford, but was not satisfied that Scott was there to answer for George Lee, in Lee's absence. Gardiner's March 1660 letter of complaint to his friend, Governor Winthrop of Connecticut, provides other details of the event.[421]

Through the years, agitations between the Coopers and the Daytons continued, many arising from the horse trade, just as they had with others who dealt with John Senior and John Junior on a regular basis. It is reasonable to assume that many more conflicts went unrecorded because there are the occasional town records that provide glimpses of additional disputes. For example, "Mar 11, 1661/62 John Cooper declaringe that he was sumoned here to appear to answer Samuell Dayton he Declared himselfe ready to answer and the plt not there to psecute,"[422] and on the

---

[419] (Curtis 1955)
[420] (B. F. Thompson, History of Long Island 1839)
[421] (C. C. Gardiner 1890)
[422] (H. Hedges 1887) 189

very same date, in Easthampton, Book 2, page 131 of our edition has, "Jonn Copper iunior hath entred an accon of trespass of the case agt John Howell Concerning wronge donne to him by Rateinge."

In another action, this time recorded at Southampton, Cooper acted to defend his right to a drift whale against Joseph Raynor and his whaling company.

> In the purchased Cort Jan 15, 1662/63 Iohn Cooper plf in an action of trespass vpon the case against Ioseph Raynor Richard Howell Thomas Cooper and Samuel Dayton defendts concerneing theire takeing away whale off from the beach...The verdict of the jury concerning Iohn Cooper plf and Ioseph Raynor and his co partners is the jury find for the plf all that peece of whale that was cast vp against that neck commonly called Mr Ogden's neck with increase of Cort charges.[423]

Ogden's Neck was south and east of today's Francis Gabreski Airport, Westhampton Beach and just east of Quogue. This means that the case of Cooper v Joseph Raynor and associates places Sam at Southampton, indicating that Sam had not fully evacuated, even though he also appears at Setauket.

When the court found for the plaintiff, the group appealed to the court at Hartford as recorded in *Connecticut Early Probate Records*:

> John Cooper, 6 May, 1663, makes appearance at this Court to answer the Appeal of Joseph Reiner, Richard Howell, Thomas Cooper & Samuel Dayton, according to his bond. The Pltf. Appeare not to prosecute accorind to their Bond of 20.[424]

The Connecticut Colony imposed an arson fine on the Shinnecock Indians who were suspected of attacking Southampton and burning homes but Southampton officials were unsuccessful in forcing payment. Ogden purchased the debt from the Southampton officials and acquired the lands of the Quogue Purchase as part payment of the fire money. Wyandanch had assumed the debt of 400 pounds and was paying in land.[425] Ogden sold the lands of the Quogue Purchase to John Scott and Scott sold them to the proprietors of Southampton on February 2, 1663/64. On this

---

[423] (H. P. Hedges 1877) 27

[424] (Manwaring 1904) 61

[425] Note: State of NY, NYS Racing and Wagering Board, NYS Department of Environmental Conservation, and Town of Southampton, Platiffs, Versus the Shinnecock Indian Nation, Frederick C. Bess, Lance A. Gums, Randall King, and Karen Hunter, Defendants. Town of Southampton, Plaintiff, Versus the Shinnecock Tribe AKA the Shinnecock Indian Nation, Frederick C. Bess, Lance A. Gumbs and Randall King, Defendants. United States District Court for the Eastern District of New York, 2007.

date, Ogden confirmed that he had purchased the land from Wyandanch and Sam, along with John Woodruff, gave deposition as witnesses to his purchase that had taken place in 1659.

> The Deposition of John Woodruff Jun[r] & Samuel Dayton this 2nd of February 1663 these Deponents say they were present when Wiacombowne delivered unto Mr John Ogden quiet seizen and possession of all the Lands above recited with the premises mentioned and for the end mentioned in Mr Ogden his subscription above written. This taken before me the day & year above written. Thirston Raynor.[426]

The decade of the 1660's was a particularly difficult time for Sam and his family. Sam was away much of the time, occasionally recorded near a harbor, at port with cargo at settlements on Long Island's ocean coast and on the sound including Setauket and Oyster Bay and at port in Connecticut. If none of Sam's six boys were apprenticed, Medlin was left to care for them all. Considering that he was often associated with others who frequented the port, it seems likely that Sam's profession had close connections to ports and harbors. One such example, from September 1665 at East Hampton, causes the reader to imagine that Sam was a "regular" at the port and it is possible he is referred to as a "ffraiter" (one who hauls freight).

> The Deposition of mr John Blackleech Mr John Osburne & Samuell Dayton Taken before me Testifieth as ffollowest That on the twenty third Day of this Instant Moneth there was a debate betwixt the Master of the Catch "Triall" Of Boston and the Merchant & ffraiters of the sd Catch she then Ridinge in the Roade of Easthampton at Ancor and she then not beinge very well fitted with masts sailes provisions and water whether she should goe to sea in the condition that then she was in or that she should land her goods at the port without Confiscation of goods or vessell [Book 2, page 132.] and in order there unto Answer was made by the Cunstable of the sd place by name Thomas Chatfield, that they might if they would willingly come a shore without being forced ashore she might as well come a shore at the sd place and Land her goods wth as much freedome as the whalemen might strike a whale, and bringe her ashore at the sd place and this to our best Remembrance he spoke at the prsent Instant., And afterwards we doe attest that on the twenty ffowerth of this prsent Moneth he did affirme the same in our hearinge whereupon this beinge an encoragement to the Merchant & ffraiters they under their hands gave

---

[426] (Howell 1887). 453

the Master of the sd Catch an order to acte as they have Donne: Taken before me John Mulford.[427]

For only the second time in American records, Sam referred to himself as a cordwainer on December 28, 1663 when he "sold" his house and home lot in North Sea to Jonathan King of Boston, the sale to be void if Sam paid King £17 2s 7d before the first of the next December. This exchange was probably either a loan or mortgage, and it was probably advantageous for Sam to declare the more "reliable" and solid means of income, like that of a skilled cordwainer. Perhaps Sam was acquainted with the craft from making shoes during the winter, but we have never seen evidence to suggest it other than these instances where he self-disclosed it. As will be discussed later, Sam was negotiating risky land purchases at Oyster Bay or Matinecock and perhaps also at Setauket and required help to fund his venture.

Records as late as 1665 provide evidence that Sam had not yet fully removed from Southampton, for in November of that year it was said he was "of Southampton" (see purchase of a horse from Richard Brooks at East Hampton). Perhaps he was labeled "of Southampton" because he was renting one of his properties there. In September of the same year, he was found in an East Hampton business deal but in December, Sam acquired the use of land just west of Setauket after having already purchased land at Oyster Bay (The distance between Oyster Bay and East Hampton is about 100 miles by water).

By July 1666 and March of 1666/67, he was described as "of Oyster Bay," and by age 40, the wanderer had experienced a couple of very challenging years. He was confronted with the first of a series of life-changing situations and losses and, as a result, there would be noticeable development in his dependability and self discipline, as he eventually anchors himself in Brookhaven. For a third time, Sam referred to himself as a cordwinder, as he sold his house [or tenement] and accommodations at North Sea to John Cooper.[428] He had earlier sold two parcels of meadow measuring three quarters of a hundred pound allotment to Henry Pierson. "The greater part of which accommodations Iyeth in the Neck commonly called Cow Neck lying at the east end thereof with a pond and spring in it, and Mr. John Scotts land lying at the west end thereof and Mr. John Jennings land to the Southwest thereof," witnessed by Henry Pierson and Humphrey Hughes (Recorded 1682). From the description, assuming the pond has not been drained, it might be possible to identify this property on a modern map.

It is also interesting to note that in the Fifth Volume of Records, there is mention of 80 acres of land and meadow on Cow Neck, "and about tenn ackers of beach as it is now fensed, which is commonly called Daytons beach, a pond and spring within

---

[427] (H. Hedges 1887)
[428] (W. &. Post 1910)

said land." In 1717, the Southampton Town Records (Vol 6) still made reference to the old Dayton property: "…and the Proprietors of North Sea, and their children and heirs shall have liberty to gather Bay berries and plums on Dayton's Beach."

Chapter 11

Goe a-whalin

Any story of colonial eastern Long Island would not be complete if it excluded the prominence of whaling, "the second most important industry after farming."[429] Contrary to popular belief that whaling started in Massachusetts, "It is likely that the first organized prosecution of the whale fishery in America [other than by aborigines and Basques] was made along the shores of Long Island."[430]

Some of the earliest accounts of Long Island whaling refer to the unpleasant and mundane chore of salvaging carcasses that deposited onto the ocean shores of the East end. There was nothing romantic about this winter harvest, drift whaling. The unwieldy endeavor was glutinous and bloody, the labor made more difficult in the piercing winds and freezing water. However, as menial, gruesome and miserable as the tasks were, the whales were valued bounty and were viewed as an unanticipated gift, "in the providence of God." Just as the Native People so treasured the fins and tails, the English devised many commercial uses for whale products, especially for the precious oil extracted from the blubber of the right whale through a process called, "trying out." Blubber was cut into large strips and once peeled and transported, was boiled in giant trying pots, producing odors offensive to anyone in close proximity or downwind.

The whale that frequented these waters was called the *right* whale. Legend has it that these whales got their name because they would not sink like the sperm whale, but instead would float after the kill, and this characteristic also enabled their floating to shore.

> But 'dead right whales do not invariably float.' A North Pacific whaling captain wrote that…right whales sink more than bowheads. He reported that in a season on the Kodiak Ground 28 right whales were killed, of

---

[429] (P. Shillingburg n.d.)
[430] (R. E. Reeves n.d.)

which 11 sank. The frequency with which whales were struck but lost in the Long Island fishery was substantial.[431]

Great measures were taken to retrieve many sunken whales. Often, buoys would be fastened to the whale, and it would be watched, waiting for eventual surfacing or in preparation of techniques for raising a sunken whale.[432] The right whale species is a type of baleen whale. Hairy baleen plates work as comb-like strainers to entrap and filter plankton and very small prey as they swim. Strong but flexible baleen (often mistakenly referred to as whale bone) was harvested for an incredibly large number of applications such as women's garments and accessories like corset stays, parasols and hair brushes, but also for buggy whips, chair springs and even fishnet material. The average right whale would yield about 30 to 50 barrels of oil and 650 pounds of baleen.

While the native islanders used whale oil mainly in cooking and as a treatment for animal hides, the English set up trying stations and processed much of the oil for export or for barter and used "oyle" as currency. On Long Island, even the minister's and schoolmaster's salaries were paid in oil.[433] Once schools were established, many of them would be closed during whaling season, December to April, because the entire family would be involved in the work.

Whale oil was the choice fuel for oil lamps, burning cleaner and more efficiently as illumination than lard or reed lamps. Whale oil produced less smoke and was also used for soaps, candle wax, as various lubricants and even for margarine. The harvesting and production of these and other whale products provided Southampton and East Hampton early contact and connection not only to markets in New England, but also to foreign markets.

Drift Whaling

Most of the early whale-related references to Ralph and Sam refer to their involvement in compulsory actions, in fulfillment of community responsibilities, such as squadron duty that resulted in their share of oil and bone. From the very establishment of the settlement at Southampton, collective concerns for security and economic interests were taken into consideration for planning the arrangement of buildings in the village, and for accomplishing necessary tasks for the benefit of all.

---

[431] Ibid.
[432] (Long Island Whale Hunt, Amagansett Village Headquarters for the Sport 1894)
[433] (Rattray 2001)

180

Collective participation was especially critical for the swift and efficient processing and disposal of drift or beached whales.

"Drift whales," as they were called, washed ashore regularly after storms, some having died at sea, while others might have become disoriented or stranded on sand bars. As late as 1702, thirteen whales were counted on a single day, on the shore between East Hampton and Bridgehampton.[434]

Europeans knew of whaling opportunities in New England very early on, being made aware of them from earlier explorers. English Captain George Waymouth reported that he observed Native Americans pursuing and killing whales along the coast in 1620.[435]

It has been claimed that even before they settled on Long Island, English colonists from New Haven traveled to Southern New Jersey to engage in whaling.[436] Cape May included a number of New Haven people, the first of whom came there as early as 1640 under the leadership of George Lamberton and Captain Turner, seeking profit in whale fishing.[437]

In 1640, the Lynn Massachusetts Company that had been turned back from their attempt to settle in western Long Island, landed somewhere near or in North Sea Harbor. Upon arrival, they were quick to journey the few miles across the lower fork to settle on the ocean and establish the town of Southampton. Could the farmers from Kent have already been focused on harvesting whale? Although claimed by some to be the case, Breen argues that the discovery of beached whales and their profitability was an unexpected winter harvest, "a fortunate accident."[438] Perhaps so, but whaling was one of the first industries in this seafaring town. In fact, Southampton Town Records are, "the first record of [American] colonists' attempts to organize community efforts to hunt drift whales…in March of 1644."[439] It also appears from the record that Southampton men established the neighboring town of East Hampton, less than 15 miles east, and soon followed in the lucrative practice. In East Hampton's original deed of 1648, Native Americans were promised, "to have fynnes and tayles of all such whales as shall be cast upp, and desire that they may be friendly dealt with in other parts."

On Feb. 9, 1645/46, the Southampton Town Record says,

> Yt is ordered by the General Court that yf by the prouince of God, there shall bee hence forth cast vp within the limitts of this towne of Southampton any whale or whales,…whosoever shal finde or espie eyther

---

[434] (H. Hedges 1897)
[435] (Gish 1998)
[436] (Heston 1924)
[437] (Planters and Traders of Southern Jersey 2006-2013)
[438] (Breen 1996)
[439] (American Whaling 2014)

whale or whales or any part or peece of a whale, cast vp, vpon notice giuen unto the Magistrate or Magistrates, shall have for his paynes allowed vnto him fiue shillings, but yf yt shall be by the Magistrate or whom he shall appoynt, adjudged not to be worth fiue shillings, Then the sayd partie which shall giue information, shall haue it for his paynes. And that from yeare to yeare the Marshall giue notice after any storme or according to his discretion, unto two persons in whose ward by turne yt shall belong or appertaine. And yt is further ordered that yf any shall finde a whale or any peece there of vpon the Lords daye then the aforesayd fiue shillings shall not be due or payable.[440]

Soon after commencing the salvage of drift whales, whale-related regulation and court records began to appear and were scattered throughout the Town Record, even before whaling became a competitive commercial enterprise. Early regulation provided for the harvest and distribution of shares, processing of claims and licensing of whale companies. Disputes over shares of whale are recorded very early also. For example, in 1653, "It is ordered that the share of whale nowe in controversie betweene the Widow Talmage and Thomas Talmage shalbe devided betwene them according as the lott is."[441]

Harvesting drift whales became known as drift whaling, the first known type of whaling found in the Town Records of eastern Long Island. One of the earliest records of East Hampton states the shared responsibility, penalties and benefits to each householder and to Native Americans—

It is ordered yt if any whales be cast up within our bounds that every househoulder shall do his part of ye worke about cutting of them out according as his turn shal cum the towne being for this worke devided into two parts ye one halfe to goe at one time & the other at an other, and everie one upon warning given is to take his turne to look out to find them and whosoever shall be found to be a delinquent in doing his part in cutting or looking out when his turn is shal pay a fine to ye value of 5s. [Crossed in original.]

It is also ordered yt if any Indean find a whale and do forthwth tiding of it he shal have 5s for his pains, and if any Inglish man of ye Town doe accedentally find a whale & doe bring ye first tidings of it he shal have a peece of whale 3 foot broad.

---

[440] (Howell 1887)
[441] (Talmadge 1909)

The first record of our Dayton ancestors having to do with whaling was found in The First Book of Records of the Town of Southampton.[442] On March 8, 1653/54, Sam, then about age 29 or 30, was on the list of four "squadrons" of men, in the second squadron, with fourteen other men. The town had actually begun the practice of establishing whale watchers and dividing all the capable men and older boys into squadrons in the mid-1640s. As all whales belonged to the town, it was an orderly method to divide the work of cutting up the whales found on the beach and to distribute the prize. Each man got one third part of what he cut, in addition to his share from the town as parts were marketable.

As greater profits were realized, townsmen (and outsiders) began to organize to pursue whales offshore and the activity quickly yielded to the formation of partnerships and chartered companies to "goe a-whalin," replacing squadron duty.

Shore Whaling

The second type of whaling was shore whaling, and also involved, "looking out for whale" but this time included spotters, placed strategically near the shore, whose job it was to watch for whales just off shore. Sometimes men would climb atop a long pole, positioning themselves to see farther. In early East Hampton records, is it difficult to tell if the task of "looking out" includes only the search for drift whales or includes also whales that are close to shore. On November 6, 1651, it was ordered that each man was to take his turn as the lookout: "Goodman Mulford shall call out ye Town by succession to loke out for whale."[443] Early settlers also paid Native Americans to spot whales for them, probably as their replacements.

The boats were left staged and were ready for service should the lookout wave his shirt or yell something like, "whale off" or "there she blows!" In reply, whatever they were doing was dropped to man to boats and paddle towards the spout. An experienced spotter could even tell the species of whale by its spout. The whale was pursued in small whale boats, each about 20 feet long, containing the harpooner, tiller and rowers, struggling to get close enough to strike. Once engaged and fatally struck, a chase usually ensued until the whale could no longer pull the line. Once ended, the whale was towed toward shore where it was beached and the blubber was dragged above the seasonal high water line to be processed.

Since whaling was a seasonal activity, hunting was necessarily intense during the peak of whale migration December to May, and seemed to be the perfect

---

[442] (H. Hedges 1874)
[443] (Starbuck 1876)

complement to farming for young men, with determination to meet the task, especially since long voyages were not necessary and investment was minimal.[444]

"Inexperienced as they were, these hardy Kentish and Yorkshire yeomen plunged into the whaling venture without delay…"[445] This was very much a young man's endeavor, demanding strength, and a good share of enthusiasm and determination. For many young men, the threat of danger was compensated with excitement and the prospects of quick money. The dangers or inappropriateness of the profession are conspicuous in the 1665 will of William Beardsley where he stipulates that his son Joseph must be, "married and give up the sea" in order to acquire his inheritance. There are frequent but disputed claims that this particular Beardsley son married a Dayton from Brookhaven, but that has not been pursued in this compilation.

We've already stated our belief that Sam worked for John Ogden, at least at some point, before Ogden was granted permission to organize his whaling company at North Sea. This makes the likelihood of Sam continuing to work for Ogden and his whaling company quite high, especially since Sam's was one of the original families recruited by Ogden, to live at North Sea when Ogden agreed to establish a settlement there. When Mr. Odell [Woodhull] was added to Ogden's company in 1654, he brought with him permission to kill whales in the south sea also. Perhaps Sam's occupation took him out to sea, and if so, that would help explain his frequent absences. In 1659, Ogden purchased from the Shinnecock tribe the land from Canoe Place to Beaver Creek Dam (currently in Westhampton). This very large tract of land offered access to the beach but conflict would be brewing because John Cooper had bought rights to the beach for whaling.

Drift whaling and shore whaling alone were probably not enough to provide steady employment in the winter months for the Long Island farmer, but the lure and demands of a profitable off shore whaling enterprise added more possibilities for regular employment. Besides going out to sea, successful off shore whaling required the regular processing of whale, warehousing at the harbor, ship maintenance and supply, transporting to markets, and exporting of whale products. These opportunities were enough to entice many farmers away from home and their lackluster winter chores.

Off-Shore Whaling

As the whales off Long Island and New Jersey became more scarce and wary of the shoreline, the whalers had no choice but to adapt. Several small companies

---

[444] (R. E. Reeves 1987)
[445] (Rattray 2001)

184

were soon formed on the east end, some with ocean-going boats that permitted ventures lasting weeks and hunts further from shore.

The earliest whaling companies, if they did participate in any off-shore whaling excursions, probably ventured out to sea for only a few days at most. Since John Ogden's whaling company operated upon the south sea (the ocean),[446] one cannot help but wonder if Sam ventured out to sea on occasion, as a seaman or whaler, or as a transporter of goods, either working for himself, for John Ogden or for Joseph Raynor. The demands and rewards seem to fit Sam's disposition at age 26, given his restless nature and inclinations toward impulsiveness and independence. As has been noted repeatedly in this compilation, Sam seemed to be "absent" even at significant times where you would expect his name to be prominently recorded. The idea of Sam being "out to sea" with a whaling company is certainly more attractive than other possibilities of incarceration or incapacitation, and probably more likely.

Sam's whale-related accounts in the 1660s and 1670s placed him more prominently among his peers as he assumed the position of Setauket squadron leader and representative to the governor, "to treat about the whale." On April 2, 1670, he received the favor of whale-rent and he supervised all four Brookhaven squadrons beginning July of 1673.

In the late 1670's, Sam's son Abraham was enticed to stay on land during a whaling season because the need for laborers in the steadily growing settlement meant he could insist on strong compensation without engaging in a lengthy adventure at sea. In order to avoid paying high wages, many Long Island farmers developed a variety of skills themselves. Even with the demand for higher wages both on land and sea, there was much work to be done and whaling was an opportunity for investors in these small companies, so long as they were able to hire enough skilled men and others to perform the more menial tasks for little investment. It is said that the severe shortage of labor contributed to dependence on Native American labor on the farm and for skilled Native Americans among the whaling companies on the south shore. According to T.H. Breen,

> The problem with the economy of colonial America, as contemporaries never failed to observe, was that no one was willing to serve as a common laborer. The prospect of working for wages held no appeal for the ambitious immigrant. Even men who had been common laborers in England or Holland became independent yeomen in the New World, or, at least, they tried to do so.[447]

Breen continues,

---

[446] (Adams 1918)
[447] (Breen 1996).

As one New Yorker explained to uncomprehending royal officials in London, 'North America containing a vast Tract of Land, everyone is able to procure a piece of land at an inconsiderable rate and therefore is fond to set up for himself rather than work for hire. This makes labor continue very dear, a common laborer usually earning 3 shillings by the day & consequently any undertaking which requires many hands must be undertaken at a far greater expense than in Europe.'

In *Leviathan*, Dolin argues,

> ...many of the authors who claim that the Indians were America's first whalemen also indicate that the Indians taught the colonists how to whale, but there is no evidence for this. What is far more likely is that the colonists employed Indians not as teachers, but because they were cheap labor.[448]

In short time, some of these stronger Native Americans did become so skilled as steersmen and at harpooning that their services were bid between companies, driving up the demanded wage. Dolin states, "Although many Indians willingly engaged in shore whaling, and some even bargained for better wages, the relationship between the Indians and their employers was hardly simple."

So why did Sam's son Abraham (who was a whaler) stay home for some of the whaling season? It may have been that Abraham could not compete with the current wages being offered by rival whaling companies or demanded by skilled whaleboat men, both English and Native American. As noted, some of these competitor companies had agents with "deep pockets" and stores of liquor. It is possible that Abraham had men under contract but these men were snatched by more attractive wages elsewhere. This problem became so serious and widespread that some whalemen had complained to the governor for assistance.

As Native American labor became so essential to the success or even survival of some of these whaling companies, and the competition between companies to gain the services of the Native American became so crucial,

> ...special laws were passed to ensure that Indians were available for the hunt. In 1708, for example, New York passed an act for 'Encouragement of Whaling' which said that any Indian who was signed on to go whaling should not 'at any time or times between the First Day of November and the Fifteenth Day of April following, yearly, be sued, arrested, molested, detained, or kept out of that Imployment by any person or persons whatsoever.'[449]

---

[448] (Dolon 2007)
[449] Ibid.

186

The shortage of labor increased pay, "to a point where the white community as a whole deemed it necessary to enact a law for the regulation of the matter." The act declared that, "whosoever shall hire an Indyan to go-a-Whaling, shall not give him for his Hire above one Trucking Cloath[450] Coat, for each whale, hee and his Company shall Kill, or halfe the Blubber without the Whale Bone."[451]

The Unkechaug of Eastern Long Island had taken notice how the whaling companies exploited the Native Americans who agreed to work for them. In his book, John A. Strong said that they complained so much when the first Setauket company was formed, that the Brookhaven officials complained to the governor that "the Indians were demanding the unreasonable amount of one barrel of oil for every whale taken, as well as compensation for cutting the wood required for the trying process."[452] Native Americans then tried to set up their own company after receiving permission from the governor who decreed that they, "are at liberty and may freely whale or fish for or with Christians or by themselves and dispose of their effects as they think good according to law and custom…without any manner of let, hinderance or molestation." Some Native Americans were successful in setting up their own companies, according to Strong.

Whaler Yeomen and Cape May Settlers

There are a few histories that suggest that English whalers from Long Island and New England were fishing at the Cape in New Jersey prior to the English takeover, as early as 1640 in Cape May, but proof is difficult, if not impossible to find. In 1640, Nathaniel Turner, agent of New Haven Colony, was mentioned as a purchaser and in 1641 George Lamberton also secured lands from Native Americans. A part of the English purchase extended from Cape May to Raccoon Creek.[453]

The records of the whaling industry largely begin when Dr. Daniel Coxe set up a whalery in 1687. The history of the whaling industry before the arrival of whalers from Long Island in the 1680s is almost nonexistent.[454] *In History of Long Island From Its Earliest Vol 2*, Ross and Pelletreau talk about the 1663 group of Long

---

[450] Note: Trucking cloth was made in pieces about 30 Yards long X 1 Yard ¾ broad, usually dyed red or blue because Native Americans preferred these colors. –from Clothing Through American History: The British Colonial Era by Kathleen A. Staples, Madelyn C. Shaw, 2013

[451] (Spears 1910). 6

[452] (J. A. Strong 2011)

[453] (Lee 1902)

[454] (Romm May 2010)

Islanders who formed a company for the exploration and occupation of South New Jersey.[455] No Daytons were listed. On the other hand, Richard Romm writes:

> Although whalers from Connecticut and Long Island may have had a temporary shelter or camp at the Cape as early as 1638, Burlington Court Book records show that there was not a permanent removal to Cape May until 1685…The whaling industry was so profitable that in October 1693, the West Jersey Assembly approved a tax of ten percent of the value of oil and bone extracted from every whale caught by non-residents [whalers from Long Island]…Whereas the whalery in Delaware Bay has been in so great a Measure invaded by Strangers and Foreigners, that the greatest Part of Oyl and Bone, recovered and got by that imploy hath been Exported out of the Province, to the great detriment thereof; to obviate which mischief, BE IT ENACTED….that all Persons not residing within the Precincts of this Province, or the Province of Pennsylvania, who shall kill or bring on shore any whale, or whales within Delaware Bay, or elsewhere within the Boundaries of this Government, shall pay one full and entire Tenth of all the Oyl and Bone made out of the said whale or whales, unto the present Governor of this Province for the Time being.

Romm adds,

> The 'Strangers and Foreigners' that the act addressed were interloping whalers from New England and Long Island who came to Cape May during the winter months to hunt whales. There were early whaling expeditions from the Hamptons in Long Island to Cape May. Offshore whalers would arrive in December and stay until the migrating right whales left the bay in February. The Southampton and East Hampton offshore whalers made mass relocations to the Cape in the 1680s and 1690s.

Jeffrey M. Dorwart says,

> One third of the family names that appeared in the first Cape May County records of the 1680s and 1690s were identical to those of the New Haven families of the 1640s. Some of those names—most notably Osborne, Mason, Badcock and Godfrey—were involved in the Delaware River settlement. "Other families listed in the New Haven records whose names

---

[455] (W. S. Pelletreau, A History of Long Island From Its Earliest Settlement to the Present Time 1905)

188

were similar to the first Cape May settlers included Dayton, Davis, Parsons, Raynor, Johnson, Smith, Swain, Willets, and Peck.[456]

Our ancestors Henry Dayton and/or his son David may have had some loose connection to whaling in New Jersey because Henry's estate, later inherited by David, was located at the whaling town of Great Egg Harbor, NJ in the 1750s. It is also possible that the connection had been no more than Henry taking advantage of the opportunity to invest in an estate at the time the market was saturated and prices were low.

Perhaps Dowart's reference to the Dayton name was invoking Sam's son, Jacob whom Sam disposed to the child's aunt and uncle, the Bakers, in 1664, when he was about 7 years old. In his early life, Jacob lived in Easthampton with his wife Ruth Diament whom he had married in 1682. In 1693, Jacob moved to New Jersey from East Hampton but the following year, Jacob published a declaration that his wife Ruth, "doth prove extravagant and refuseth to he ruled by her husband or to go with him to the place that he hath provided for their habitation," and he therefore will not be responsible for her debts.[457] However, Ruth is found with the family at Cape May in August of 1702. In his 1867 *Sketch of the Early History of Cape May,* Maurice Beesley wrote that,

> Whaler yeomen were hardy men who braved the frigid temperatures, rough winds, and the risky business of hunting and catching whales. They followed the whales to Cape May and profited from them. These men owned hundreds, in some cases even a thousand acres of land in Cape May and often owned additional property in Long Island. In some cases, second and third generation whaler yeomen prospered as farmers and large landholders, and some of them owned slaves.[458]

The revered historian and genealogist Donald Lines Jacobus said he was certain that Daytons in New Jersey did not descend from Robert in East Hampton, no doubt in response to someone's reference to Jacob. It would have been an understandable assumption that Jacob was a descendant of Robert because Sam's son, Jacob lived with the Bakers in East Hampton until adulthood and Robert must have appeared to some to be the only possibility for Jacob's father.

---

[456] (Dowart 1992)
[457] (H. Hedges 1887)
[458] (Beesley 1857)

Chapter 12

Setauket, by Way of Oyster Bay

After Ralph, the next five generations of our ancestral line would remain on Long Island, residing almost entirely within the town of Brookhaven, until the rebellion of the American colonies. It was probably at some point during the British occupation of Long Island that our ancestor David Junior finally left. Our family's one hundred and twenty five year written history in Brookhaven relies considerably on Brookhaven Town Records and on the works of Belle Barstow. To the many people involved—Brookhaven Town Clerks and committees, especially Osborn Shaw, gratefulness is due for the magnitude of time and care dedicated to the volumes of early town records.

Attempting to follow Sam through the records from about 1658 to 1667, the trail quickly becomes muddled, as documentation suggests his dwelling intermittently at North Sea and Main Street Southampton, Setauket and Oyster Bay/Matinecock. If one did not know differently, it would appear there was more than one adult Samuel Dayton at this time.[459] To help clarify Sam's many movements, we have included a table as an Appendix listing some locations where he was reported to be.

Sam's next significant venture was in land speculation, as western lands opened up near the north shore at Cromwell Bay [Setauket] and further west, at Oyster Bay or Matinecock, 70 miles west of Southampton. Sam's prospecting probably began just before his father died, when he sold the former Marvin house. Was his impulsive nature driving him to spend his inheritance even before his father's death?

While in East Hampton, the compiler asked Richard Barons why the English moved so often. How could Sam be in Southampton, Setauket and Oyster Bay simultaneously? His reply was illuminating, when applied to Southampton:

> The second generation made a point of leaving the area and they saw great riches in the west; they didn't see great riches in the east. Remember that

---

[459] Note: The only other *Samuel Daytons* near this time are Sam's son, born about 1651, and Sam's nephew, son of Robert who was not born until about 1666.

the majority of settlers arrived here [speaking of East Hampton] because they were focusing on one particular aspect which was raising cattle and sheep. There is no pasture land in Boston. No pasture land in Lynn. There are lots of these areas where the first generation arrived which is one of the reasons why that first generation got out as fast as possible…You've got this first and second generation with this wanderlust who really don't make roots…a lot of them leave part of their family here, often to take care of the land they have there, because that's an investment, they don't want to lose that…[460]

So, in our attempt to order records of Sam somewhat sequentially, at least for a while, random documentation gets entangled, creating a challenge for the reader to maneuver.

Setauket, a settlement begun on the north shore bay in the town of Brookhaven, got its name from Setalcott, the once prominent Native American tribe living there. When the English arrived from Southold, Southampton and New England in 1655, with intentions to establish the original settlement, the inhabitants were persuaded to sell their land in exchange for protection against their enemy from across the sound. Their enemy, the Pequots, had been raiding and plundering them repeatedly so many of the Setalcott's fields where crops once grew were laid waste and some were abandoned. The English—John Swezey, Roger Cheston, Thomas Harlow, John Scudder, Thomas Mapes and Jonathan Porter acting in behalf of others, purchased an area of 32 square miles from Warawakmy, and fourteen next kindred.[461]

Beverly Tyler of Three Village Historical Society said, "The settlers built crude shelters along the run or creek (today the Setauket Mill Pond). This area had probably been cleared by the Setalcotts." By 1659, the area was called Cromwell Bay in honor of Oliver Cromwell who had died in 1658, but the name was dropped in 1660 when exiled King Charles II was restored to the English throne.[462] The settlement was first referred to as Brookhaven around 1664, and then was temporarily renamed Ashford by John Scott, for his hometown in Kent, the same town where the Ralph Dayton family hailed. After Scott's arrest in 1665, the town reverted back to the name Setauket.[463] Adkins[464] cites Shaw who said,

The exact number of settlers who came to Setauket in 1655 is not known. Tradition long fixed the number at fifty-five, but more recent research has shown that the original number was much smaller, probably not more than

[460] (Barons 2010)
[461] (J. A. Strong 2011)
[462] (Tyler, History Close at Hand-Three Village/Brookhaven-Chronology 2014)
[463] (Town of Brookhaven, Brookhaven's Comprehensive Plan, Existing Conditions and Trends Report n.d.)
[464] (Adkins 1955)

twelve to twenty during the first few years. The records indicate that there were but thirty-five home lots occupied in 1668.

John J. Innes described the early years at Setauket:

> Of these, one extensive tract occupied nearly the entire northern part of Crane Neck, from the modern light house to the so-called 'Flax Pond.' Another of these cleared tracts extended from the town brook of Setauket on the west to the later Floyds Swamp and the small brook forming its outlet on the east, and stretching north to the isthmus connecting the tract with the present Strongs Neck. The bulk of this cleared land appears to have been cultivated by the first settlers as 'common fields' for the production of wheat, oats, Indian corn and peas from about 1658 to 1661. For this purpose the settlers were divided in June, 1659, into 'squadrons' to work together on appointed days in the more or less distant fields, while the village itself by this arrangement was always assured of the presence of one of these squadrons as an armed guard. (Records, 126,127). In 1661 the plan of working on the main crops in common seems to have been abandoned. Large portions of the 'Old Field' were then distributed by lot in parcels of 3, 4 and 6 acres to the individual settlers. Each man received his individual ground to cultivate, but the system of working in squadrons seem to have continued (Records, 145). Finally, the purchase of most of the Little Neck (now Strongs Neck), and the removal of the Indians therefrom in 1662 to their planting grounds at the modern Mount Sinai, together with the increase of new settlers led to the laying out of 'New Town' (along the modern South Street) in 1667; the allotments of land radiating out from the town in all directions into the forests were made in large and larger parcels, and the system of cultivation by squadrons disappeared.[465]

Building off the work of Thompson and others, Fredrick Kinsman Smith believed Richard Smith migrated directly from Southampton to Setauket within the first two years, joining planter Richard Woodhull from Southampton whom some say was already there. He adds,

> The name of one other of the early Brookhaven proprietors is also found on the early Southampton records, that of Samuel Dayton. With these and doubtless other acquaintances and friends already located there, it would appear as a logical sequence that Richard Smith, in leaving Southampton, should turn his steps toward Setauket.[466]

---

[465] (Innes 1935)
[466] (F. K. Smith 1967)

The second purchase, occurring in 1657, was for the meadow at Mastic. This was very significant because it gave Setauket access to the ocean at Great South Bay, connecting it with the 1655 purchase. This time, the purchase was agreed between sachems Wyandance and Wenecoheage and Richard Woodhull, "for himself and the Rest of his Neighbours of Setauket." Woodhull may still have been living at Southampton where he was a respected leader, but about to make the move to Setauket, being keenly aware of the opportunities from harvesting whale. This deed transferred ownership of two great necks of meadow, lying east from the Connecticut River to the Wegonthotak River, to Richard Woodhull and the Rest of his Neighbors, of Seatuck. If the Connecticut River was the western boundary, these necks also bordered Fire Place Neck on the west side of the Connecticut River. The necks in the 1657 purchase should not be confused with the necks just west of the Connecticut [Carmans] River that were later named east to west, Fire Place Neck, Tarmen's Neck and Dayton's Neck, bordering modern Bellport (see figure 20).

> In 1658, the small Brookhaven Settlement expanded from the area of the original settlement around the run that empties into Conscience Bay to Stony Brook on the west, Mount Sinai (then Old Mans) on the east and Mastic on the south... By 1659, the settlement at Setauket became more self-sustaining with a few more families arriving and with the orchards and fields taking hold.[467]

Strong said that the Setauket settlers, "opened negotiations with Mahue, a Setalcott who was joined by Wyandanch and Wyandanch's advisors, Checonow (aka Cockenoe) and Sasarataicko (aka Sassakataka), sometime in 1659, shortly before Wyandanch's death." The goal was to attain more land around the village which was advanced by receiving the deed that transferred the neck called "Old Field," a piece of land, just north of the settlement, that protrudes into the sound. Strong said,

> Setauket settlers did not need an intermediary to help in negotiating with Mahue, but they may have wanted to strengthen their title against possible challenges. At the time the Setauket settlement had no patent, nor was it under the protective jurisdiction of the Colony of Connecticut. The settlers were, in fact, nothing more than a squatter community, and thus their land claims were vulnerable.[468]

---

[467] (Tyler, Setauket becoming Self-sufficent: 1657-1662 2010)
[468] (J. A. Strong 2011)

194

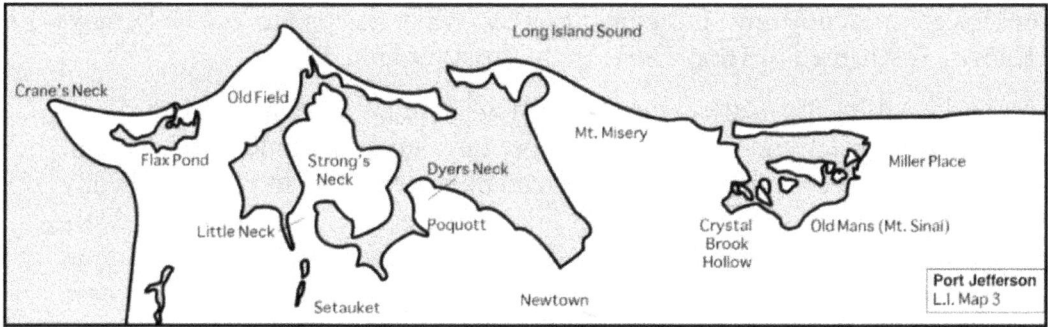

Figure 18. Setauket and Old Mans

According to Cox, "Our ancestor [referring to the ancestor of Rev Henry Miller Cox] next appears at Ashford on Cromwell Bay... He was accompanied thither by Capt. John Underhill, William Frost, Thomas Mapes, John Bayles, and probably William Simson and Samuel Dayton. With his neighbors at Setauket he joined in the following petition to the General Court at Hartford"[469] that asked to be admitted under the jurisdiction and protection of Connecticut and to receive similar benefits as those realized by Southampton and East Hampton, worded as follows:

> Cromwell Bay alias Setauke Aug. ye 6, 1659 It having pleased God to dispose the harts of us the inhabitants of the place aforesaid, to subject our plantation, persons and estats under the protection and government of the Coloney of conetocoke, for the full accomplishment of the premises, wee the said inhabitance doe request the faviour of our trusty and beloved associates Ensign Alexander Brian and Samuel Sherman to solicit our union with the said Colloney, that we may be accepted a member of the sayd body politick.

According to Bayles, "The town placed itself under the protection of Connecticut in 1659 and in 1662 became part of that colony. This connection was broken off by the conquest of 1664, after which it came under the Duke's government with the other towns of Long Island."[470]

It is likely that Sam had explored residency somewhere in or around Setauket between 1658-64, perhaps to establish himself there in order to be a recipient in their land divisions or perhaps using it as his base while dealing in properties further west, at Killington upon Matinecock (or Oyster Bay), as early as 1662. This is believed despite the fact that there is a general scarcity of records to firmly establish his

---

[469] (Cox 1912)
[470] (R. M. Bayles 1874)

195

Brookhaven residency until December of 1665 when he appears on the Setauket List of Known Townsmen in 1666-1667. Belle Barstow said,

> Those taking up settlement in the new plantation shared all the land divisions in common. No one had more than any other unless they bought up another accommodation. It was a man's prerogative to purchase in any town, though at times they had to first secure permission from the town's overseers or had to seek a town vote for approval. Once purchasing an accommodation, they could expect to be rated equally as the other townsmen, whether actually living in the town or not.[471]

The scenario for Sam might have looked something like what was said of James Cock: "Cock seems to have had several allotments of land at Setauket in 1661 which were assigned to Henry Perrin, and early in 1662 he appears in Oyster bay as purchasing a House and house lot."[472]

Adkins tells us that the growing settlement had, "divided into squadrons for the purpose of more efficiently cultivating the fields" but this collective system may not have been agreeable to the independent spirit and stubbornness of New England pioneers, so by 1662 was largely rejected. In 1661, the settlement was expanded to the area of Old Field [west of Conscience Bay], where Adkins says much of it was parceled out in lots of from three to six acres and, "with the purchase of the land on what is now Strong's Neck, the practice of giving larger and larger portions of land to the settlers became common."[473] Setauket's Setalcotts were living mainly on Little Neck (Strong's Neck) and their proximity to the constant influx of "foreign" people exposed them to the outbreak of smallpox that nearly decimating the small population.

Like Setauket, Oyster Bay was situated on the north shore, but was 30 miles west, about half-way to Flushing (Refer to the map of Long Island, figure 13 in Chapter 8). According to Cox, [Oyster Bay] "is an arm of the Sound running in Southerly between two headlands, Lloyd's Neck on the East and Hog (now Centre) Island on the West." Near Oyster Bay, just a couple of miles west, was Matinecock, Native American for "high country." Today, Matinecock is inside the town of Oyster Bay. If our theory that Sam (and later, some of his sons) were sometimes involved in a shipping enterprise is accurate, Sam probably would have been quite familiar with the ports and harbors of the north shore and the prospects of greater profits might have attracted him to Setauket and Oyster Bay.

---

[471] (Barstow, Setauket, Alias Brookhaven 2004) 133
[472] (Cocks 1914)
[473] (Adkins 1955)

Southold, with Setauket, Huntington and Oyster Bay had a very considerable trade with West India Islands, sending thither salted meats and pipe-staves with which to construct barrels, hogsheads and pipes to contain sugar, molasses, rum and sack for the return cargo, with then being transshipped to smaller vessels, was delivered in New Amsterdam without payment of customs duties to the Dutch.[474]

Had Sam been present at Setauket or Oyster Bay by 1659, he would have found an abundance of work to keep him occupied. According to Frost, it was to break up smuggling in north shore harbors, especially at Oyster Bay and Musketa Cove that brought, "Captain John Underhill to Matinecock as Deputy Sheriff and Surveyor of the Customs."[475] Merwick said, "In 1653, [Captain John Underhill] turned against the Dutch, gathering soldiers and seamen to seize Dutch vessels and drive the Netherlanders from Long Island."[476] This scenario presents the very real possibility that Sam had been employed as a privateer back at North Sea and had moved efforts to the north shore.

Meanwhile, Southampton Town Records still referred to Sam "of North Sea" in both 1659 and 1660 records and then they contain the sale of Sam's North Sea house to Waters in 1660. The STR also implies that Sam not only had cattle at North Sea in 1662, but it also indicates he still retained lots in Southampton, for in November, "An action entered by Christopher Lupton & Henry Pierson plf against Samuel Dayton deft to bee tryed at ye adjourned Cort December 9th 1662, the said Action being of trespass vpon the case, concerning a calfe."[477] Apparently, the house at North Sea that Sam mortgaged to Jonathan King in 1663 was not the same house sold to Waters because Sam, along with Samuel Clark, witnessed the sale of Anthony Water's house to George Harris on September 27, 1663.

To help understand why Sam seems to be in both places, we are reminded of what Barons said, "…a lot of them leave part of their family here, often to take care of the land they have there, because that's an investment, they don't want to lose that." Perhaps Medlin and the boys stayed behind at North Sea for a few years,[478] tending the farm, while Sam was trading or delivering goods far from home, or he could have been attempting to establish sufficient connection with Setauket by 1664, in order to be included in the distribution of land "Drawers of Lot of Meadow" at South-Fire Place.[479]

---

[474] (Cox 1912)
[475] (Frost 1912)
[476] (Merwick 2006)
[477] (H. P. Hedges 1877)
[478] Note: Sam would have occasion to visit often, as he traveled harbor to harbor
[479] (Redboat Design 2012)

In 1664, the significant purchases and general expansion of Brookhaven properties, as well as potential possession at both shores must have been quite an inducement for Sam to relocate there. Not only did Mayhew, Sachem of Setauket, surrender the, "Feede and timber of all the lands from the ould manes to the wadeing river," but Massetewse and the Sunke squaw sold Old Mans to Setauket. The purchase at the Great South Bay from Tobaccus, Sachem of the Unkechaugs, became known as the Old Purchase. The acquisition of the vast property would have hastened Sam's final uprooting from Southampton, it seems to us, motivating him to sell his remaining assets at North Sea, in order to invest in Brookhaven (at the time, settled at Setauket). Much of the 1664 purchase of about 750 acres was meadow containing rich salt hay meadow, an important and valued commodity at the time. The purchase connected the north shore community of Setauket to the south shore, with 20 miles between, and allowed access to whales that were so often stranded there by ocean tides.

In 1664, immediately following the purchase…the land along the Great South Bay was divided into forty-nine lots of about fifteen acres each. These lots were numbered from east to west, starting at the Connecticut River (now known as Carmans River)… Lots 1-32 were in Fire Place (now known as Brookhaven Hamlet), and lots 33-49 were in what is now know as the Village of Bellport. These lots were all low-lying, usually marshy, and contained little if any upland. They would have been generally not especially suitable for settlement.

While Samuel was recorded in the Town of Brookhaven records as one of those who acquired a lot, Osborne Shaw, Brookhaven Town Historian (1933), suggests that he did not actually take possession of it. An explanation may be that he had not yet been accepted as an inhabitant of Brookhaven or otherwise did not meet the requirements for a share. However, he must have had some connection with the Town to have been included in the drawing,[480] but perhaps not enough at this time to receive accompanying meadow.[481] It is also believed that lot 13 was too far east to have been on what later became known as Dayton's Neck or West Fire Place.

A list of the men, called, "Drawers of Lots of Meadow Old Purchase, South-Fireplace, Bought 1664," appears in *Records of the Town of Brookhaven up to 1800*.

If Sam did not take possession of the lot as Shaw suggests, one might find an explanation in Oyster Bay Town Records. He seems to have been occupying his lot at Matinecock at about the same time he is also recorded at Brookhaven and Southampton. His acquiring the use of 4 acres that belonged to Akerly near Setauket at Old Field in 1665 might be an indication that he was either living nearby or was in

---

[480] (Deitz, Brookhaven/South Haven Hamlets & Their People 2006-2015)
[481] (Shaw, History of Brookhaven Village October 5, 1933)

the process of acquiring a dwelling close by. If that was the case, perhaps the purchase had not been complete by the time of the 1664 division of lands in the Old Purchase at South.

Even before Brookhaven's 1664 purchase at South, Sam was already involved as a planter and perhaps agent, along with others, in a June 1663 covenant with inhabitants of Hempstead in New Netherlands, enabling a broader settlement of Matinecock. The deal was probably negotiated in that period between 1661 and 1663, as some writers suggest that Sam proceeded directly to Oyster Bay or Matinecock from North Sea and settled there. In Josephine C. Frost, page 5 states: "The first attempt at a settlement of Matinecock appears to have been made in 1661." In 1663, when Capt. John Underhill purchased the land from the Native Americans, Hempstead and its neighboring land were still under Dutch jurisdiction and, as part of the agreement, the settler families of Matinecock were to be subject to the laws of Hempstead.[482]

The agreement between inhabitants of Hempstead and the planters was included in the early Hempstead records and reads as follows:

> This Indenture or Covenant made between the Inhabitants of ye Towne of Hempsted upon Long Island in ye New Netherlands on the one part, and Thomas Terry and Samuel Deering, [or Dayton, according to other researchers] Planters, on ye other part, Witnessing, the ye foresaid Inhabitants of Hempsted, upon ye sute and request of the afforesaid planters for granting them Liberty to setle themselves upon a parcell of ground on the North side of ye Iland, on the East side of our harboure, Bounded on ye West side by that Bay Commonly Called Hempsted Harbour, and one ye South side by ye harboure hill, And so by an east line to run as far as their boundes goe, and so downe to ye North Sea. The said Inhabitants of Hempsted do grant their request, and freely give leave to the aforesaid Planters to setle themselves, and some of their friends on that tract of land above Described, to have and hold it and Injoy the priviledges thereof by our Patent. With these Conditions, that ye aforesaid Planters shall engage themselves and any that they shall bring with them, or any of their successours, not to trespas against ye towne of Hempsted, by letting any of their Cattell Come upon ye great plaines and spoyle their corne or do the like harme, and if they shall, to make satisfaction to any person or persons so wronged. Also the abovesaid Planters do Ingage themselves, and those they bring, and their successors to bring in no Quakers, or any like opinionists to bee inhabitants amongst them, but such as shall be approved by the Inhabitants of Hempsted, And Furthermore

---

[482] (Frost 1912). 5

they binde themselves and their Company that shall settle with them and Inhabit in ye aforesaid plantation, or trackt of Land granted by the Town of Hempsted, to bee subject to ye Laws of Hempsted according to their Patent, Accounting themselves to bee and being members of ye said Towne of Hempsted...and whereas there being not any Limytation of what number of persons or ffamilies should be settled thereon: Therefore it is now further hereby confirmed, and likewise agreed and concluded upon by certaine Men formerly Chosen and appointed by the Towne for that purpose, and Mr. Thomas Terry, that hee ye said Mr. Thomas Terry shall settle seven families there-upon forthwith (as soon as Convenience will suffer) And that the towne shall have liberty (if they see good) for to make them up to ten families at the least. In witness whereof both parties do hereunto subscribe their hands this 23d Day of June 1663.[483]

Cox sums it up, "Planters Thomas Terry and Samuel Dayton were made indenture or covenant with inhabitants of Hempsted, New Netherlands—parcel of ground for themselves, their company and cattle. They were to allow no Quakers." Apparently, the settlement of Hempstead was not as lenient toward religion as Setauket, according to Barstow, "their broadmindedness encouraged the outcasts from other plantations to seek residency in Setauket."[484]

Life is Hard

However, very soon after the agreement was signed in June of 1663, the sale was challenged by previous Native American owners, claiming that the land of Matinecock had not been included in the Dutch patent executed by Governor Kieft to the Wethersfield and Stamford Company and the Native People claimed they were never adequately compensated for it.

If the Native American challenge wasn't enough concern, it turned out that the timing of the indenture between planters and inhabitants of Hempstead was very unfortunate for investors because, about August 1664, the Dutch finally lost control of Long Island to the English. The Duke of York claimed Long Island as part of New York and subjected the towns to "Duke's Laws" which meant they could no longer govern themselves. New Amsterdam was renamed New York and Long Island became Yorkshire, east and west ridings. The Dutch patent was now open to reevaluation by the English governor and, considering the Native American claims to the land, he was well aware that his ruling on the matter would impact relations between the new rulers and the Native Americans.

---

[483] (Cox 1912). 7
[484] (Barstow, Setauket's Religious Beginnings 1984)

But the rulings of New York on Dutch patents wouldn't impact only Native American relations, but also the investments made by the settlers and agents in territories that had earlier been claimed by the Dutch. By this time, Sam had already dug his cellar on one of his lots, no doubt preparing for a more permanent dwelling to settle his family there. Frost says, "No record appears showing the date of settlement of the "Seven Families," but it must have been by 1664, at which date Tackapousha and other Native Americans brought complaints before Governor Nichols, that they had not sold Matinecock to Hempstead."[485]

"In the fall of 1665, the Unkechaug sachems had the opportunity to meet face to face with Governor Nicolls. The governor invited the Unkechaug, Shinnecock and Montaukett sachems to meet with him in New York for a three-day conference to formally establish diplomatic relations."[486] Apparently, between the fall of 1665 and April of 1667, the patent was dissolved and a new agreement was established. Sam had been forced to give up the venture and relocate as indicated in the following letter from Governor Nicholls to Underhill.[487] The reference to Sam in this letter indicates that Underhill inquired of the governor what should be done with the vacated lots Sam had purchased. Consistent with the Governor's statement that anyone already settled there should not be disturbed, "its thought fit hee should have one" but he would lose the other three. The letter reads:

Capt. Vnderhill New Yorke Aprill 19, 1667

The Generall having received yo[r] letter & with the inclosed from those at Matinicocke hath given mee Order to write this in answer both to you & to them: That hee is very glad to heare of the friendly & quiet Agreement & Complyance of those Indyans for the continuance of those familyes already settled upon their land, wherefore hee thinkes it very reasonable that the persons concerned should joyne together in makeing the Indyans some Guift or Gratuity by way of Requitall, since they never rec[d] any pay for their Land That if (as they alleadge) they have already paid their Neighbo[rs] at Hempsteed for the Sd Land Its right the moneys or goods should bee returned backe to the End the Indyans may be satisfied.[488]

He continues:

That as to the buisnesse of Samuell Daytons having of foure Lotts & his exposing them to sale upon his Removall, Its thought fitt hee should have

---

[485] (Frost 1912) 6

[486] (J. A. Strong 2011)

[487] Note: According to Frost, Capt John Underhill had come to Matinecock as Deputy Sheriff and Surveyor of the Customs to break up smuggling in north shore harbors, especially at Oyster Bay and Musketa Cove.

[488] (Cox Jr. 1916)

one either to enjoy or otherwise to dispose thereof, but no more the other three may bee reserved for the Encouragement of other familyes to come & settle upon them. And for the proposall of the Inhabitants of giving a Name to the place, The Governo^r doth approve of what they shall doe therein as well that no person shall bee forced upon them without his Approbation. What the Indyans have given to Robert Williams may bee confirmed to him as likewise the severall Lotts to the Inhabitants when the Bounds shall bee layd out & certainly knowne, to prevent future Cavill about it. This is all I have in charge to deliver to you at present, which you'l please to impart to the Rest, So I conclude being Yo^r loving ffriend Matthias Nicolls.

The town records at Oyster Bay contain a letter, taken from the original document, from the patronizing Secretary of the Province in reply to the Matinecock settlers.

It was adjudged by the Council that Hempstead's title to all of Matinecock was defective, but that the English that were then seated on said Matinecock lands were under no pretence to be be molested or disturbed.

The Governor wrote to Capt. John Underhill It is not that I give very much credit to what they [the Indians] say but for quietness sake and to prevent further contests...they say they have never received any pay for the land. Pursuant to this recommendation, negotiations were concluded by which at Kelenworth on 22d day of June, 1667, the Indian Proprietors Aseton, Arumpas, Seahor, Nothe, Soometamok, Shoskeene and Matares executed deeds conveying to Robert Williams, William Hudson, William Simson, Henry Reddock, Christopher Hawxhurst, Matthew Priar and Nathan Reddock, Christopher Hawxhurst, Matthew Priar and Nathan Birdsall each a specified tract of upland and an undivided one-seventh interest in the adjacent salt meadows, together with the right of commonage of grassing and timber in the unallotted part of the whole tract.[489]

The Frost Genealogy said,

Contemporaneous with the Seven Purchasers on Killingworth upon Matinecock...were Richard and Josias Latten, William Frost, John Coles, Samuel Dayton, Edmund Wright, John Dyer, John Robins, John Davis,

---

[489] (Cox 1912). **8**

202

Joseph Eastland, Samuel Tillear, Auron Forman Junior, Henry Bell and Lawrence Mott, but with the exception of the Lattens, Frost and Forman all had removed from hence before the close of the century.[490]

At this juncture, it might be appropriate to comment on a statement that is found in some of the popular internet communities and is repeated several times elsewhere. The statement reads, "He [Samuel] apparently contemplated going to Killingworth, Connecticut where four lots had been assigned him before April 19, 1667." Of course, this date refers to the April 19, 1667 Underhill letter where Kelenworth is named as the location of negotiations, and might be the proposed name for that particular area inside Matinecock. Without question, Killingworth upon Matinecock was on Long Island and no record can be located of Sam's intention to buy land or settle in Connecticut. Frost says that the origin of the name Killingworth upon Matinecock is unknown.

It appears that, even though Sam still owned a residence at North Sea in 1665, he rented and perhaps owned lots in Brookhaven by the end of that year, but not in time to possess the land that fell to him in the Brookhaven drawing of lots. In addition, he had also dug a cellar (referred to as "Doyton's sellar" in the *Oyster Bay Town Record*) sometime between late 1663 and 1666, but was already vacated. It had been Sam's intention to construct a house there because it was quite common to dig a cellar as a temporary shelter until a more permanent structure was ready for dwelling (this procedure was also noted at New Haven, CT). It sounds as if Sam never got beyond early preparation for settlement at Oyster Bay, and probably retreated sometime after the council announced judgment that Hempstead's title to Matinecock was defective.

Having "lost" his long lot at South and then this investment at Matinecock, Sam had to be discouraged. Already "beaten back," sometime between 1663 and 1665, Sam and the boys lost Medlin, Sam's wife of about fifteen years. Medlin could have died at either Setauket or Matinecock, or less likely, back at North Sea. As is the case with most women of her day, no record of Medlin's death has been found. If her death came while at Matinecock, we can't help but wonder if the ancient burial place of the Frost family became established where William Simson found Medlin's grave upon his arrival, on higher ground, not far from Sam's cellar. It is believed Medlin was Sam's first wife and the couple had at least six sons, Caleb being the youngest.[491]

---

[490] (Frost 1912)

[491] Note: There are a few claims of two additional sons, Robert and Daniel, but no evidence has been found for them.

The approximate location of Sam's lots can be determined from reading the description of William Simson's property. In 1667 (after Sam forfeited at least three lots), William Simson purchased from the native Matinecock people a tract of forty acres with rights in the, "undisposed medows, fresh and salt, with crik, thatch, with ye benefits of ye cricks and coves, with fre hunting, fishing, fouling with ye benefit of all minerals according to law." Here he erected a house and lived until 1674 when he conveyed it with all improvements to William Frost described as of Setauket or Brookhaven.[492] This William Simson had built his house by the side of Samuel Dayton's Swamp, northeast of what would later become the Frost family burial place, and another lot on which the house and outbuildings of the late Valentine Frost stood, both of which were assigned to William Frost in 1674.

More is learned about what had been Sam's land in November 1677 Oyster Bay records. The "suskaneman of mantenecocke in ye parish of oyster baye" sold land to William Frost, shipwright, "…being bounded by the Cartt path on ye west side, on ye East side by A swomp side Called doytons swomp, on the south side bounded by ye sayde william ffrost, ten rods southwards of doytons sellar, on ye north side by the medowes…"[493] William Frost was probably a, "ship or boat builder and perhaps was influenced to come to Matinecock by his quondam Setauket neighbor William Simson, who was captain or master of a merchandise boat plying on the Sound." Cox also tells us that William Simson had his house lot by the side of Samuel Dayton's Swamp, located just northeast of the Frost family burial place.[494] This might place Sam's cellar somewhere in the vicinity of the current Creek Club golf course in Lattingtown, where the old Frost Family Cemetery is near the 16th hole.[495]

Figure 19. Frost Family Cemetery, Lattingtown, NY

---

[492] (Frost 1912) 18-19
[493] (Cox Jr. 1916)
[494] (Cocks 1914)
[495] (Wyckoff 1978)

In figure 19, the Creek Club Golf Course, Lattingtown, NY contains the Frost Family Cemetery. Viewed from another angle, the small knoll and rows of grave markers in the center of this Pictometry Bird's Eye© image on Bing© are discernable. The cemetery is directly north (left, in the photo) of the circular green, near the end of Danton Lane South. Also to the north, just outside the photo frame sit two small ponds that may have been formed by what was "Dayton's Swamp."

Jacob and Caleb Disposed

With so many young children and no wife to care for them, Sam determined he could not provide adequate care for his family. It was a somber time for Sam, first losing his investments, then losing his wife, and now facing the difficult task of raising the boys while his work called him away for periods of time. Sam decided to stay near Setauket and would eventually sell his North Sea farm at Cow Neck to John Cooper. The realities of that day meant that the boys who could work and somewhat attend to themselves could remain, but the two youngest boys, Jacob at 7, and Caleb at 5, would not be able to contribute adequately to the work. Since Jacob and Caleb would themselves require care and instruction, Sam drew up two articles of indenture on December 24, 1664, in East Hampton, to place them in the care of his remaining family until their majority. Where else could he go for help but to East Hampton, to his family—brother Robert and sister Alice? How his heart must have been aching.

Sam "disposed" his son Jacob as an indentured servant to his sister Alice and her husband, Thomas Baker of East Hampton. This was to last for fourteen years unless Jacob's aunt and uncle died, which would then make Jacob a free person. It was only natural for Sam to turn to the Bakers, as Thomas proved time and again a dependable and trusted friend to all of the Dayton family. Jacob would be living with relatives who were solid and respected in the community, and likely to see to it that he received kindness and at least a rudimentary education. There is little doubt the boy already knew the Bakers and, as another benefit of his residence there, Jacob's uncle Robert lived right across the green. It was probably the best situation for him.

No doubt Sam wanted to keep the young boys together but that was not possible. Sam then indentured his youngest son Caleb, on the same date, to Joshua and Elizabeth Garlick of Setauket for sixteen years. With the Garlicks, Caleb would remain close by his father. Like Sam and Medlin, the Garlicks had moved from Southampton but were in East Hampton before that, so the families had known each other for some time. Joshua had been identified as a gardening hand for Lion Gardiner and Southold Town Records would later identify Garlick as a carpenter in 1674.

How difficult these separations among Sam's children must have been, not only for the "disposed," but for all of the brothers, made especially painful following the death of their mother. Ralph, the oldest son, was probably about 15, followed by Samuel and Abraham, and also Isaac would have been about 9 years old at this time.

The brothers were probably quite willing to accompany their father on trips to East Hampton in order to see their brother Jacob. He is the same Jacob of East Hampton who became the whaler at New Jersey, identified in the whaling chapter.

Accusations of Witchery

Before the Garlicks arrived at Southampton, Elizabeth was the subject of East Hampton's only witch trial, six or seven years earlier. Goody Garlick was first accused of bewitching Lion Gardiner's daughter on her deathbed, then she was suspected of causing strange occurrences that could be explained by the presence of a witch. Not feeling adequate to try such a case, the East Hampton court charged Thomas Baker and John Hand to transport her to Hartford for the trial, a round-trip excursion lasting quite a few days, depending on the weather. One would assume that Thomas and John did not take part in accusations against Elizabeth and had little or no fear of her supposed powers. One wonders what kinds of conversations could have unfolded during the journey.

A descriptive account of the death of Elizabeth Howell (Gardiner's teenage daughter) can be found in the Town Records of East Hampton and in many books and articles about Long Island's famed first witch trial. Young Elizabeth had recently given birth to a daughter and became stricken with a piercing headache shortly before her death. Ultimately, on her death bed, fever brought hallucinations and, unfortunately for Goody Garlicke, she was one of those present, and it was she who became the personification of the witch Elizabeth struggled with just before her death. As rumors spread, people around East Hampton began contemplating imaginary relationships between Goody Garlick and some rather unexceptional activity, accidents or coincidence propelled by gossiping ladies who were jealous of Goody's standing with the Gardiners or were challenged by her personality. Various testimonies are spread across the record. Goody Garlick was apparently a well favored servant of Mr. Gardiner, the most prominent man on Long Island. Joshua Garlick did bring an action of defamation in behalf of his wife, "against the wife of fulk Davis" whom he had singled out as one of the most difficult of the troublemakers. Goody Davis had even implied that Goody Garlick was somehow responsible for the death of her own child. When the East Hampton court decided they should refer the case to Hartford, they produced the following order and indictment on March 19, 1657/58:

> It is ordered and by a Major vote of the Inhabitants of this Towne agreed upon, that Thomas Baker & John Hand is to go into Kenitcut for to bring us under their government according to the terms as Southampton is, and alsoe to carry Goodwife Garlick that she may be delivered up unto the authorities there for the triall of the cause of Witchcraft, which she is suspected for.

The indictment read as follows:

> Elizabeth Garlick, thou art indicted by the name of Elizabeth Garlick the wife of Joshua Garlick of East Hampton, that not having the fear of God before thine eyes thou hast entertained familiarity with Satan the great enemy of God and mankind, and, by his help, since the year 1650 hath done works above the course of nature to the loss of lives of several persons (with several other sorceries), and, in particular, the wife of Arthur Howell of East Hampton, for which both according to the laws of God and the established law of this Commonwealth thou deversest to die.[496]

The trial ended with an acquittal and she was sent back home with instructions for the town to carry on neighborly and peaceably with no unjust offense. Remarkably, the Garlicks returned to East Hampton and lived in relative peace with their neighbors. Books that feature the events and accusations that resulted in the Garlick witchcraft trial are easily accessible, as even to this day, interest in the case doesn't seem to wane. Despite much testimony, no records were found to suggest that, at any time, the Daytons and Bakers took part in the accusations. Both Ffulk Davis and the Garlicks will be revisited later in this chapter.

There was another Long Island witchcraft trial in 1665, this time in Setauket. It occurred shortly after Caleb was taken in by the Garlicks, when he was five years old. Ralph and Mary Hall of Setauket were tried for witchcraft after the death of George Wood. It is clear from the indictment that the constable was not Sam because he was not elected to that office until 1667. Wood had been the proprietor of the ordinary, at the harbor. The trial, at the court of Assizes in New York, acquitted Ralph and placed Mary on probation for three years.[497]

Mary Dingle/Dingee

One year after "disposing" his youngest boys, Sam acquired the use of lands just west of Setauket, December 18, 1665. With the help of the remaining four boys, Sam would have all the crops he could use, with surplus to sell or barter.

> Samuell Daiton haue taken 4 akers of land in the ould feeld of Robart Akerly; 2 akers in his six aker lott and 2 akers in his 5 aker lott and in consideration of the same, the sayd Samuell is to pay vnto the sayd Robert

---

[496] (Tomlinson 1978)
[497] (Tyler, History Close at Hand-Three Village/Brookhaven-Chronology 2014)

or his asings, 3 bushels of Indien corn for that which is (stuble a aker and 3 bushell of wheat a aker of the Indien stubble) [498]

Although Sam has been placed in Brookhaven (probably Setauket) by various authors in 1657 (Thompson), 1658, and 1659 (Cox), he probably was not able to fully establish residency at Setauket as a freeholder until 1667 and proprietor in 1668.

With the passage of a town regulation on March 28, 1664 which limited formal additions of newcomers to desirables only, Sam probably had to show himself worthy of admission by successfully completing a trial period in lieu of presenting a letter of recommendation to town officials. Not yet a freeholder of Setauket, he would still have to pass examination at the Town Meeting. Perhaps working the rented land from Ackerly may have served the purpose of demonstrating his competence to buy land there. The regulation read,

> To the end that the towne be not spoyled or impoverished, it is ordered that noe Acomadations shall bee sowld by peece meeles, but Intire, without the consent of the Overseeres and Constable, and that noe person bee admitted to be an Inhabbetant in this towne without the consent of Constable and Overseers or the maior parte thereof.[499]

Once prospective members of the community were accepted and received the privilege to own land there, they were under promise to, "…not sell, let, nor give his accommodations, nor any part of it to any but whom the major part of the town shall assent to and willing to take in as inhabitants." If the regulation was violated, all the land the offender owned was forfeited to the town.

By spring of 1666, Sam was courting Mary Dingle of Brookhaven and the couple obtained a license to marry May 14, 1666. Sam was about 42 years of age and Mary's age is not known. There was a family in Hempstead with a similar last name, but it seems more likely that Mary was the widow of Mathias Dingle of Brookhaven, Setauket's blacksmith who had replaced Robert Bloomer. No record of the actual marriage between Sam and Mary was found but the union presumably took place in the same month they obtained the license to marry.[500]

At this point, several problems for the researcher arise that cannot be resolved with certainty. The first question is why Barstow says Mary Dingle died May 1666, the same month and year Sam and she applied for their marriage license. Nothing can be found to support Barstow's hypothesis and, although it is possible, in our view her premature death probably occurred after May 1666 but before 1669.

---

[498] (W. J. Weeks 1930)
[499] (Brookhaven Town Clerk, BTR 1880)
[500] (Tucker 1860)

In addition, Barstow claims Mathias Dingle died June 1667, but that date was actually from an inventory of his estate. If Mathias died in June of 1667, who was his widow mentioned in ensuing proceedings? Barstow was probably not constrained by the belief that Mathias was the husband of Mary, so, for her, the date is not of consequence. While it is logical to assume that an inventory would immediately follow death, it is also possible that either the date of the marriage application with Sam was copied incorrectly or the June 1667 inventory was not the first inventory taken. Our proposition says that Mary was still alive when Mathias died. It is not unusual that more than one inventory might have been ordered, just as was the case when Ralph protested that the inventory of James Haynes' belongings was no longer accurate. Ralph's protest made a second inventory necessary. The probability of more than one inventory would especially be true in a case of bankruptcy, it seems. Perhaps something similar happened to items that would be distributed to those to whom Mathias was indebted at the time of his death. Of course, if Mary was his widow, a Mathias death based on the time of inventory in 1667 does not align with Mary's 1666 application for marriage to Sam. There might have been a delay in bankruptcy settlements, as is not uncommon, where protection (seizure) of assets and the work of distribution to creditors have to be determined by the courts. Therefore, it is our humble opinion that Barstow would have been more accurate to say something like, "Mathias died sometime before June 1667." Barstow records the events this way:

> It was then ordered by the court that Capt. Tooker and Thomas Biggs both of Brookhaven, alias Setauket, shall upon oath take an exact inventory of all such goods as Mathias Dingle died seized of, left in [with?] his relict widow in Brookhaven aforesaid. And then to price [appraise] the same [without prejudice] upon the oath above said. And then cause proclamation hereof to be made that all his creditors may come in at a certain day and to share the goods among them; according to their just proportions in law after the nature of the Statue of Bankruptcy that the said widow may legally be discharged from all her late husband's creditors; herin fail not.

Because this inventory of the Mathias Dingle estate took place in June 1667, some family historians are more comfortable pushing Mary's marriage to Sam to 1667 or 1668, instead of in 1666, when the license was obtained. Of course, the simplest explanation might be that the handwritten record for a 1668 application for marriage license had been copied incorrectly as 1666.

At a town meeting held on December 16, 1667, it was ordered that Edward Avery should have the home lot that was Mathias Dingle's and that he was to do the blacksmith work of the town as cheap as other smiths did.[501]

Land Juggling

If the 1666 marriage year is accepted, Sam was already remarried and was described in Oyster Bay Records as being "of Oyster Bay" in July when he bought lot 52 in Matinecock from Abraham Smith of Hempstead. The area included 74 acres of timber, pastures, marshes, mines and a stone quarry. But, on the very same page, Samuel of Oyster Bay, in November 1666, sold same to William Simson and John Dyar. On the following page, "Samuel of Montinacock" Dec 7, 1666 sold lot 59 (28 acres to Henry Ruddick) and on Dec 31, 1666 sold lot 58 (38 acres).

Today, the neighboring communities of Matinecock and Oyster Bay are within the township of Oyster Bay. The distance between ponds in Matinecock and Oyster Bay, for example, is just over a mile which explains why the two names were sometimes used interchangeably. Hempstead, another settlement in the area, is about 14 miles SW from present-day Matinecock, and it is Hempstead town records that were consulted for context and insight into early settlements. Beginning with page 22 of our edition of *Oyster Bay Town Records, Book A* says,

> Know all men whome, this p[r]sent may cunsern, yt I Abraham Smith of Hemstead on Long Island, in ye North Rideing, of New Yorke, sheare have for a valuable sum moving mee thare unto, aliniated, & sold from mee my heires Executors administrators, or assines, all yt my divadant of land lying at Matinacock in lot 52 & quantie of Ackers, three Score, & forteene more or less as it was laid out, to Samuell Dayten, of OysterBay of ye same Riding, to him ye Sd Dayten his heires excut[es] Administrators or assines, to have & to hold free Land, as a for Said with all previlleges & appertenances, of timber pasters or pastareges, ferem Marshes en Mashes Mines Minerals Quarells [obsolete term for stone quarry] or any other prevellige, yt is or hereafter shall arise... Seale this 10th of July: Anno: 1666 and in ye 18th yeare of his Magesties Raine, Charels ye Scecond, by ye Grace of God, King of England, ffrance Ireland defender of ye faith, King—
>
> Witness, Thomas Hickes   Abraham Smith O
> Jeremiah (J) Wood, his marke:

---

[501] (T. R. Bayles, List Notes on Town Meetings that Date Back to the 1600's 1963)

The assinement of this abovesd: bill of Sale, to Wm Simson, from Dayten

From Cox Family, page 291:[502]

> Simson had first taken in 1666 an assignment from Samuel Dayton of the title of Lot 52 as laid out by the Town of Hempstead, then having jurisdiction over this territory, but subsequently repudiated. On the north end of this lot was his residence as shown by the description of the adjoining lot on the west as being bounded "east by William Sinson's House Lot." In 1667, as one of the "Seven Purchasers" of Matinecock Lands William Simson received title from the Indians to 40 acres of woodland "as by us bounded" and one-seventh interest in all their undisposed meadows, with commonage right of grassing and timber.

Sam sold his land in Matinecock:

> Know all men, by this p^{r}sants, yt I Samuell Dayten, doe wholy & truly assine all my right & intrest, of this within written, premises to William Simsson and John Dyar of Hemstead, in Matinacock, as writtness my hand, this November ye — 1666

> Wittness, Mosis Mudg   Samuell Dayton
> Nathan Birdsall

Oyster Bay Town Records p22 Book A:

> Bee it Knowen unto all men, whome this, p^{r}sent writting may any wayes conseren yt I Samuell Dayten of Montinacock, in ye North Rideing, in ye Colloney of New Yorke, have bargened Sold and delivered unto Hennery Rudick of Oyster Bay, of ye above-said Rideing & Colloney, a Sertaine percell of Land, lying and being at Muntinacock, in Num: 58 and Quantytie of ackers 38: be it more or less, I say I ye above said Samuell Dayten have sold ye above percell of Land, being my Lawfull right unto ye said Henery Rudick, to him his heires & assines forever, to have & to hold as his or theire proper right, and doe by these p^{r}sents, Ingaige myselfe, my heires, & assines, to defend ye abovesaid Hennery Ruddick, his heires or assines, in his or theare, quiet or peaceable possestion, of ye above Spracefied Lands, from any person or persons, whatsomever, Laying Claime theare unto, or Molesting ye aforesaid Hennery Ruddick or any of his Substitutes in his or theare peaceable possestions, ye abovesaid Lands I doe owne to be sold, wth all previlliges whatsomever, doeith now belong unto it, or shall any waye here after belong unto it, and

---

[502] (Cocks 1914)

full Sattisfaction, in hand allredie received, by mee ye abovesaid Samuell Dayten, from ye aboveside Hennery Ruddick, & this as my lawfull act, doe pass & make over, my right of all ye abovesaid Lands, & all prevelliges thereunto belonging, from mee my heires & assines, forever to have & to hold at his or theare proper right & Lawfull Interest, & to all true intents, & for ye faithfull performance heereof I have heere beneath sett, set to my hand & Seale, this last December, in ye yeare of our Lord, 1666 and in ye 18th Yeare, of ye Raine of our Sufiferraine Kinge Charles ye Seacond

Signed Sealed and   Samuell Dayton O[503]
Delivered in p^rsents of us
Matthias Harvy
Nathanyell Coles:

Was there another reason Sam had been attracted to lands in Matinecock? It might be interesting to research the possibility that Sam had once worked on that very same land, for John Ogden, when the Ogden brothers were hired by William Kieft to build the large stone church at Fort Amsterdam. When Sam "of Oyster Bay" sold land with timber, pastures and marshes to William Simson in July of 1666,[504] it is also discovered that the land contained a stone quarry. Could he have worked there over twenty years earlier, mining and transporting stone by boat to New Amsterdam? One source claims that the stone Ogden used had been quarried, under the Ogdens' supervision, on western Long Island, which had not yet been settled by Europeans.[505] The stone church called St. Nicholas, was completed in 1645, about the time Sam appears at New Haven CT, joining his father for a short time before striking out on his own. In 1645, Sam was 21 years old. Could this have been when Sam first met Medlin so many years before?

John Scott

In the middle of all the changes occurring on Long Island in the 1660s entered a primary character, John Scott who had recently returned from London after earlier rumors had spread that the King had appointed Scott governor (or president) of Long Island. Barstow says,

---

[503] Note: According to the Oyster Bay Town Records, Vol 1, page IX, the "O" after Sam's name is a seal, not a mark.
[504] (Cox Jr. 1916). 21
[505] (Langner n.d.)

212

…not that any of it was true but that didn't stop Scott from acting as if it were true, as he claimed power given him from the crown over of the people of Brookhaven. This caused great anxiety as inhabitants were unclear of Scott's authority, questioning whether they might present any defense to his threats and wondering what recourse might be available.

Beverly Tyler adds, "John Scott became a thorn in the side of Brookhaven residents with his land claims, lies and schemes to bring all of Long Island under his influence." As Scott planned to settle there, he soon was pronouncing Native American deeds invalid and began buying (swindling) these lands for himself. He announced that deeds for town lands were void and that he was the majority landowner in the town. In 1663, Scott renamed the town of Setauket "Kent: Ashford"[506] for his hometown in Kent and he even advised people that they would have to move away to make room for his "great manor."[507]

One would wonder how Capt. Scott was so bold and able to get so far before his arrest and imprisonment.

> Scott had stolen the town of Setauket from her originators…Setauket's townsmen were no doubt impressed, and when coupled with the perpetuity signifying royal approval of land ownership, felt completely intimidated by this ambitious man…if they hadn't signed the agreement to exchange their twenty-square-miles for another of similar size—he signed for them.[508]

Eventually, Connecticut Governor John Winthrop Junior arrested Scott, put him on trial in May of 1664 and Scott was sentenced for, "villainous and seditious practices." He was imprisoned and all of his property was sequestered.

Coming from the same town and church in England, the Daytons knew of the Scott family, but probably not young John. Had he been familiar to townsmen, he would not have been able to make such grandiose and provocative claims of impressive pedigree with immunity, says Barstow. She goes on to say, "No doubt this is the reason some men disappeared from the town records about this time, not willing to wait out, or fight for their chances against this seemingly most powerful man." It is likely Sam and his associates did not have knowledge of Scott in England because Scott was probably between ten and fifteen years younger, born just before Sam left England. The estimation of his age is based on the first New England mention of Captain John Scott in Hartford just before he was made Freeman in Southampton in 1657 and the birth of his son is 1663. But Sam had dealt with John Scott back at North Sea, before Scott's arrival at Setauket, when Sam sold his

---

[506] Note: The change of name was brief. "Ashford" disappears from town records after 1664
[507] (J. A. Strong 2011)
[508] (Barstow, Setauket, Alias Brookhaven 2004)

inherited house and land to Scott sometime before March 1659/60. Sam was not about to be bullied. A year later, he felt the need to clarify that the lot of his own dwelling, as well as the lot where Ffulk Davis lived, had not been included in the sale to Scott. Perhaps Scott had been trying to claim them. On the other hand, since this occurred shortly after Sam's stepmother Mary Haynes Dayton married Ffulk Davis, the clarification could have been associated with the attempted eviction of the Davises, an action brought by Thomas Baker and Robert Dayton. A few years later, Sam had another association with Scott as he was to appraise and receive a horse for John Scott's wife, Deborah.

By the time of Scott's trial in May of 1664, Thomas Baker renounced his former oath in support of John Scott's claim to Smithtown. Apparently, he and Sam had come to realize that they had been deceived into believing Scott's legitimate claim to a sale and could no longer verify its authenticity.

These are to sidggify (Hono) court or aney whom it may Concearn, that I Tho Backer doe declare that whereas John Scott declared in the Court that he hath vnder my and my Brother Samuell Daitone hands, whoe are witnesses to that, that mr David Gardener hath taken his othe agaynst him and has given vnder his heand that he has recanted from his oath, which thing I am not prevy tow; nor haue seene to my knowledge, nor sett my heand vnto any such thing, to this I am redy to testefy.

    Witness   Thomas Backer
    John Mulford
    Rob. Bond

Chapter 13

Starting Over at Setauket

The township of Brookhaven received its patent, about 1666, from Governor Nicholls and the newly established Colony of New York. The naming of the large area, stretching from Long Island Sound to the Great South Bay, distinguished the settlement of Setauket from other holdings and the Nicholls patent recognized title to, "all that tract of land, which already hath been or that hereafter shall be purchased, for and on behalf of the said town." Now, not only could the inhabitants of Brookhaven be secure that previous purchases were protected from future claims on them, but the patent also allowed for additional purchases.

Ironically, one of the very last entries of Sam in Southampton was actually recorded in East Hampton on November 17, 1665 when, "Richard Brooks sould unto Samuell Daiton of Southampton one browne horse about 6 yere ould cropt in the right eare & a halfe peny in the fore part of the same eare & A on the right buttuk."[509] It is evident that, from early 1666, Sam was no longer living at North Sea, though he did retain a dwelling there for a short time.

In an effort to help clarify the sequence of some significant events, a summary is provided in this paragraph and is also listed in the Appendix. In December of 1665, Sam had rented lots just west or north of Setauket, at Old Field and then obtained a license to marry Mary Dingle in May of 1666. By July, Sam was described as "Samuel Dayton of Oyster Bay" and "Samuell Dayten of Montinacock" at the time he bought lot 52 in Matinecock. Based on these records, Sam and the family could have lived briefly (though not necessarily) in their cellar at Oyster Bay before their move back to Setauket. Sam also sold Matinecock lots 52, 58 and 59 only to have the sales retracted and three of his lots forfeited, as declared by the governor in 1667, as a result of former Dutch patents not being honored by the English. In 1666/67, Sam sold the house at North Sea with land at Cow Neck to John Cooper, probably it having

---

[509] (H. Hedges 1887)

215

been Sam's partial income from rent. The record said Sam sold, "my house or tenement and accommodations at North Sea." By early 1667, Sam had established residency at Setauket as he was included on the Setauket List of Known Townsmen and, according to Deitz,[510] he was accepted as full proprietor of the town about 1668.

Assuming Sam and Mary married, she died within three years after May of 1666, leaving Sam alone again with the four oldest sons, none younger than 11. There is no suggestion as to her cause of death, but it is assumed that if she was still in childbearing years, death in childbirth is a possibility.

With the youngest of the sons living at home now becoming a young man, it seems that Sam had begun to settle down a bit from his wanderlust. Not that his traveling ended completely, but he would at least confine himself to land ownership in one Long Island town (not counting land gained through marriage) and Brookhaven would become his home for the remainder of his life. Perhaps he accepted responsibility to provide stability for his family, something that had always fallen to his wife, or maybe the loss and hardships of the previous five years wore him down, but either way, Sam was attempting to establish roots at Setauket now that his sons were old enough to work the land with him.

In Setauket, Sam was voted constable in April of 1667, just as his father had been back in East Hampton, and one year later he was elected to a two year term as overseer, along with Mr. Woodhull. Sam's elections seem to mark a change of direction and may indicate his desire to remain planted. One of the chief duties of the constable was to collect the town's taxes for the High Sheriff and, according to Barstow, the number of responsibilities attributed to the overseer grew over the years, so just how many of the responsibilities were applicable to Sam in these early years is questionable. Barstow tells us that later overseers were, "separate from the fence viewing and demonstrated more power…the overseers were now making decisions about the town's laws, overseeing obedience to those laws, overseeing the maintenance of the minister, distributing land to newcomers, deciding on land divisions, working up the tables and methods for the tax rate…"[511] So, a few of these duties probably did fall to Sam in this capacity.

On the occasion of becoming a proprietor at Setauket at such a momentous time in the history of Brookhaven and its villages, he would receive the significant benefits that accompanied his habitation. For example, in 1667, a new division of land called Newtown was created near modern-day East Setauket, to become the commercial

---

[510] (Deitz, Brookhaven/South Haven Hamlets & Their People 2006-2015)
[511] (Barstow, Setauket, Alias Brookhaven 2004)

216

center of the plantation, and consisted of lots drawn by 39 proprietors and 9 new purchasers.

DRAWERS OF LOTS IN NEWTOWN 1667[512]

Thomas Thorp	1	Robert Smith	20
Zachariah Hawkins	2	Zakery Hawkins	21
Mr. Woodhull	3	Richard Waring	22
Mr. Woodhull	4	John Roe	23
Henry Rogers	5	Mr. Smith	24
William Fancy	6	John Gennors	25
Weavens	7	William Satterly	26
Jacob Longbottom	8	Francis Money	27
Mr. Briant	9	Thomas Biggs, Jr.	28
Henry Rogers	10	John Tooker	29
Mr. Lane	11	**Samuel Dayton**	**30**
Edward Avery	12	John Tooker	31
Obed Seward	13	Joshua Garlick	32
Mr. Briant	14	Robert Akerly	33
Arthur Smith	15	Samuel Akerly	34
Capt. Platt	16	Mr. Lane	35
Mr. Brewster	17	Henry Rogers	36
Zachr. Hawkins	18	Henry Pering	37
Mr. Lane	19	Richard Woodhule	38
		Thomas Smith	39

The ten acre Lots that were laid to the new Purchasers:

Joshua Garlick	1	Obed Seward	6
Thomas Biggs	2	Jacob Longbottom	7
Francis Money	3	Edward Avery	8
Richard Waring	4	Samuel Akerly	9
John Roe	5		

With the arrival of Joshua and Elizabeth Garlick to Newtown, a couple of years after receiving Caleb, the boy would again be close to his father and brothers.

Almost immediately after the distribution at Newtown, Brookhaven once again was focused on the lucrative south shore, for all of its resources, and in order to secure rights to whales at Great South Bay. For many of the farmers of Brookhaven's north shore, the potential for supplemental income in their off-season held an irresistible allure. The March 23, 1667/68 BTR says that Tobaccus, Sachem of Unkechauge, sold all the rights to the whales that either beached or came near to shore within the boundaries of the agreement. The sachem would receive 5 pounds of wampum for each whale plus the fins and tails, to use at their ceremonial feasts. Barstow said:

---

[512] (Brookhaven Town Clerk, BTR 1880)

Competition on the south coast was heating up and soon whaling companies, as well as other patents were claiming rights to the whales. Obviously, Setauket was disadvantaged by their distance so spotting fees were paid and Indian runners would be employed to run the distance to Setauket, to bring word of a beached whale. For additional payment, the Indians would deliver the whale to a specified location suitable for processing.

According to Strong, the South Bay was coveted for more reasons beyond whaling.

> They were drawn to this area by the rich oyster beds in Great South Bay, by the salt grass meadows on both banks of the Carmans River, which provided nutritious feed for their livestock, and by the stands of pitch pine trees, a rich source of tar and turpentine. In the late 1660's, a cart path linked Setauket with the Great South Bay, providing access to these resources.[513]

In the fall of 2012, local historians Marty Van Lith and John Deitz, took the compilers to Squassux Landing on Carmans River (in colonial times it was called the Connecticut River), and they explained the importance of this piece of high ground. Today, it is owned by the Brookhaven Village Association, a gift from the Post family, for use by residents of the area. This location on the west side of the river was significant in the seventeenth century as it was the first high ground as travelers came up the river from the bay, and so it was the natural landing for boats, possibly even for the smallest whaling ships. Much of the once-valuable salt hay that dominated the area has now been replaced by phragmite, an invasive Asian plant. Van Lith, who is also Brookhaven Village Historian, told us that the whole shoreline would have been salt hay, all the way up to the tree line, what the English settlers called "uplands." These meadow lots follow all along the bay, and were originally the 49 lots that stretched all the way to Bellport, about three miles away, along the shore. Later, Bellport Bay, east from Carmans River and Fire Place Neck, to Bellport on the west would become important for the Dayton family and meaningful for Dayton descendants because Sam probably holds the distinction of being the first White man to live in that area he named "West Hampton,"[514] and that section settled by Sam would later become known as "Dayton's Run" or "Dayton's Neck."

Rattray continues, "The men of Setauket were benefiting so much from whaling that they began to pay Indians to drive whales away from neighboring waters toward their own, or so it was probably claimed by their competition, namely Joseph Raynor's Southampton whaling company."[515] It didn't take long for the town of

---

[513] (J. A. Strong 2011)
[514] (Shaw, History of Brookhaven Village October 5, 1933)
[515] (Rattray 2001)

218

Brookhaven to send Mr. Wodhull and Sam Dayton to, "treat about the whale" with the governor of New York. Their mission proved successful for the people of Brookhaven, as the Governor granted the right to whales within their patent on April 1, 1668. But the achievement was short-lived because just six months later the Nicholls grant was suspended when Francis Lovelace replaced him as governor.

Again, in October of 1668, Brookhaven voted to send Mr. Woodhull and Sam Dayton back, "to go to the Governor to treat about the whale." This time, they found that the governor had already considered Joseph Raynor's appeal for relief including complaints against the men of Brookhaven. In the following letter, Governor Lovelace granted rights to Brookhaven's beach at The South[516] to Raynor's whaling company and in return, Raynor was to pay rent to Brookhaven. This condition was to hold until after whaling season, when the governor could make the journey to the East End to hear and issue judgment on the case. By December, the governor responded with the following letter:

A Letter from the Gouerno[r] to y[e] Constable & Overseers of Seatalcott. Dec 15, 1668

Loving friends
I have rec'd an Adresse from yo[u] by the hands of Mr Woodhull & Mr Dayton full of dutifull & kind expressions wch I take very well at yor hands & hope yor expectation shall not be frustrated as to my Endeavors in the Encouragement of all good people & dispensaçon of Impartial Justice throughout the Governmen[t] his R. Highnes hath intrusted me w[th] all. The persons yo[u] sent did also make a Complaint against Joseph Raynor & Richard Howell as if they had surprised yo[u] by obtaining an order from me about the Whales cast upon the beach to the south of the Island wi[th]n yo[r] p[r]cincts, w[ch] yo[u] had a former order to injoy from my p[r]decesso[r] I doe thinke it conuenient to respite my judgm[t] therein untill the beginning of March next when I doe intend (God willing) to goe downe to the East End of the Island & shall then heare what both of you & they have to say to the matter & accordingly will giue my judgmt there upon. In the meane tyme if any Whales shall be cast vp You or they who first haue notice may take care to preserve them & where the right shall be adjudged those who shall take them without a good title shall bee accountable to the other for them I have no more but to recomend yo[u] to Gods protection & rest.
Yo[r] assured loving friend
Fran: Louelave[517]

---

[516] Note: Lands along the south shore of Brookhaven became known as "South."
[517] (Fernow 1883) 614

Samuel bought a home lot at Setauket from Richard Smith and the transaction was entered into the record on May 8, 1668. According to BTRs, "Richard Smith have given up his right of the home lot that he sold to Capt Scott to Samuel Dayton from him and his heirs forever to him the said Dayton with all the housings and fencings that doth belong to it."[518] The statement is made more interesting when the background and context is added by turning to another of Belle Barstow's books called *Setauket's Religious Beginnings*, and to the Smithtown Historical Society to learn more about the story of Richard Smith. Barstow said:

> Long Island came under New York's supervision in 1665, a time when Setauket was in its infancy. Already this settlement had exhibited a rather lenient attitude towards religion–perhaps even modeled on Roger William's Rhode Island plantation. Their broadmindedness encouraged the outcasts from other plantations to seek residency in Setauket. When Richard Woodhull purchased land for himself and his neighbors in 1657, one of his neighbors and friends was Richard 'Bull' Smith. In 1657 Richard Smith was ordered out of Southampton because he became a Quaker.[519]

Then, a few years later, John Scott enters the story.

> The earliest record connecting Richard Smith with the purchase is that found in the Southampton Records, of an agreement date 22 Nov 1663, by which he deeds half the land west of the Nissequoque to Captain John Scott, of Setauket, who claimed to have previously purchased the land from Gardiner.[520]

Scott was afterward shown to be an impostor and he was arrested at Setauket and tried before the Hartford Court, which ordered, 12 May, 1664, a sequestration of his estate. At Setauket, June 9, 1664, Mr. Smith was appointed, with the constable and Will Crumwell, to sell some of Scott's goods for the relief of his victims.

The house and home lot that Sam bought from Richard Smith, entered into the Town of Brookhaven record on May 8, 1668, had apparently been sold to John Scott but had gone back to Smith when Scott's schemes were exposed. The following explanation appears in the footnotes of Pelletreau:

> Capt. John Scott was a notorious adventurer, whose scandalous escapades kept the western towns in an uproar for many years. His principal scheme was to pretend to be the owner of large tracts of land on Long Island, and then to sell them to some credulous purchaser who found out too late that

---

[518] (W. J. Weeks 1930)29
[519] (Barstow, Setauket's Religious Beginnings 1984)
[520] (F. K. Smith 1967)

this title was baseless. There can be no doubt but that the pretended agreement with Lyon Gardiner was entirely imaginary, but it is equally plain that Richard Smith thought it advisable to conciliate his good will. The original papers from which these copies are made are now in the possession of Robert E. Smith, Esq. The exposure and flight of Capt. John Scott seem to have rendered the whole agreement void.—W.S.P.[521]

The ETR reveals that on August 26, 1668, Sam's son Caleb, who had been with the Garlicks since 1664, was placed with John and Mary Jessup of Southampton. Sam's brother Robert and Sam's brother-in-law Thomas Baker, both of East Hampton, acted under Sam's direction. Caleb may have been released from the Garlicks sometime earlier, but what remains unclear to us is why Sam wasn't there to facilitate the process. Perhaps Elizabeth's rumored "difficult personality" had something to do with the alteration of their previous agreement. Caleb was by then about eight years old and was to remain with the Jessups for twelve years and four months with the provision that the Jessups sufficiently feed him meat and drink, provide clothing for Caleb and, "doe for him duering the time as for his owne."

According to the agreement, if both Jessups died before the duration, Caleb should have been free. But Caleb likely served the full term because 1681 STRs have John Jessup Senior selling his homestead there to James Herrick in the very same year of Caleb's freedom. The name of John Jessup also appeared in the February 1663/64[522] list of men representing the town in an agreement with John Scott "of Ashford" to purchase the land he had acquired from John Ogden called Quogue. John Ogden Junior had a whaling company at Southampton in 1687, appearing on the list of fourteen known whaling companies in Southampton in that year who reported estimates of oil in their possession.[523] According to Howell, each of these companies were made up of twelve men.

One week previous to the record of Sam's purchasing the Richard Smith property (May 1668), Sam had bought a house from John Budd of Southold. This house was probably in Brookhaven because the sale was recorded there and it is known that Budd had land holdings at Brookhaven. Barstow says,

> The continual movement of Alexander Briant and John Budd on and off the list of accommodations in Setauket demonstrates there were no restrictions at this time. These men provided a service to the townsmen

---

[521] (W. S. Pelletreau, Records of the Town of Smithtown, Long Island, NY , with other Ancient Documents of Historic Value 1898)

[522] Note: Howell gives the year 1653, but this is believed to be copy error and should read 1663.

[523] (Howell 1887)

by purchasing land from whom ever wanted to leave town before they had a buyer for their property.[524]

In 1668, there were 35 occupied home lots in an area around the mill pond, and as far away as East Setauket and Stony Brook. The Village Green extended from the area where the Presbyterian Church now stands to the mill stream.[525]

Six months after Sam entered into the agreement with John Budd to purchase his house, John Bayley of Jamaica took over Sam's mortgage on the house, with payments to John Budd. Upon receiving compensation from Bayley for the first payment of the mortgage already paid by Sam, Bayley was allowed to occupy the house.

> These pressents testifies that I John bayly of Jemeca on long Iland doth ingage to pay or cause to be payd vnto John Bud of South hould, the som of eleven pounds fiue shillens pr yere for three yeres following according to the bill menchond that is betwixt samuell daiton and John bud and the whole som being thirty three pounds fiffteene shillens and to the true performenc of the same I doe here sett my hand.

> These tesstifyeth that I John bayly doe ingage to deliver vnto samuell daiton a mare wich I bought of edward Rouse within a month where vnto I sett my hand.[526]

The record for December 2, 1668 says,

> Recd then from Mr John bayly of Jamica A gray mayr as satisfaction for his first payment in Referanc to the house & land bought of me, & doe giue the aboue said bayly full position of the aforesayd acomadacions acorden to agrement formerly mad betwne vs as witness my hand the day & yeare aboue writen.[527]

Barstow believes that Sam was unable to afford the payments, but that is not necessarily the only explanation. It appears to us that Sam was continually calculating, obtaining properties by taking opportunities as they presented themselves. After all, not many days passed before Sam is on record purchasing part of the Richard Smith estate. The record continues:

---

[524] (Barstow, Setauket, Alias Brookhaven 2004)
[525] (Tyler, History Close at Hand-Three Village/Brookhaven-Chronology 2014)
[526] (A. C. Weeks 1924)
[527] Ibid. 101

Three days after Bayley assumed Sam's mortgage, on December 5, 1668, John Bayley of Jamaica was taken in as townsman by a free vote. This indicates that the house Sam had purchased from John Budd was probably in Brookhaven and not in Southold, as some authors have assumed. Barstow believes that Sam likely was granted a new purchasers accommodation, a meadow at the south, paying, "the full purchase money as others do and have done."[528]

According to Barstow, the transcriber of the town record in 1924 commented that a very old piece of paper was fastened to the record which said, "the list of the first lotments [allotments] that was in the towne" and she adds that this was probably just a simple updating of the record.

It was then recorded that Sam, presumably as part of his responsibilities, appraised the Joseph Raynor property in Brookhaven. This was the same Joseph Raynor whose whaling company had been in dispute with the town of Brookhaven whose representatives, Mr. Woodhull and Sam, were sent to argue their case before the Governor.

Entered into the record on November 20, 1668, Sam acted as a witness for enumeration of the Richard Floyd house and accommodations in Brookhaven, purchased from Alexander Briant of Milford (to be in two payments).

Then, on January 9, 1668/69, the town divided the hollows:

It is further agred upon and voeted that the towne haue giuen to John geners a share of the hollowes that is from the towne southward, Runing eastwards ouer against the ould mans the town haue alsoe giuen henery pering a share and samull dayton and william fancy and Robart smith... [plus 9 more names] –all these Reqested of the towne to haue a share of (them) hollowes and granted to euery one in pertickler and it is further agred upon that those that haue more then one llotment, thay ar to haue it made up where they can find it next to them that is laye dout.[529]

On July 10, 1669, Sam was counted among those in a list of, "Them that are freely willing and do engage to give to the smith freely for his encouragement..." William Brinkly was given these contributions, in addition to a home lot and new purchaser's accommodations, with stipulations, to serve as the town blacksmith. Apparently, Edward Avery who was to begin the duties of blacksmith after December 1667, did not provide the needed service. The town had been having problems keeping a satisfactory smith since Mathias Dingle died sometime before May of 1666, that date approximated according to Mary's (his theoretical widow) record.

---

[528] (Barstow, Setauket, Alias Brookhaven 2004)
[529] (A. C. Weeks 1924), 157

With Sam's apparent interest in horses and his need for the services of a blacksmith, it was certainly prudent to donate to the cause. His contribution was £0-10s-0d.

Elizabeth Harvey Beardsley

The next time Sam is found, he is in Connecticut records, February 1669/70, and he was already married to his third wife. In *Entries in the old Brand Book of Stratford, 1640-1720,* the implication is that Sam had taken Elizabeth back with him to Long Island and he was caring for horses that have belonged to her children. The record did not state where Elizabeth's children were living.

> Goodman Daiton, of Long Island, has the care and use of some horses for widow Elizabeth Beardsley, or good wife Daiton, for her children. Ye 26th February 1669, hath a sorrel mare colt, year old this spring, with a streaked hoof, sorrel mane and tayle. For ye children aforesaid a kinde of a dunnish black horse colt a year old this spring.

Elizabeth Beardsley (born between 1633 and 1636), daughter of Josiah Harvey, was the widow of Thomas Beardsley who had died at Stratford March 29, 1667. It appears that she had remained there after his death so courting likely took place in Connecticut. When Sam and Elizabeth married, he was about 45 years of age while she was about 34. Whether Elizabeth's daughters remained with her after her marriage to Sam is not known, but it is possible that, while Sam was courting her, she made it a stipulation that the girls would not be, "put out." Neither was there a will stating permission or the desire to do so. For reasons that will be later developed, it is possible to believe if the girls were not living with Sam and their mother, they were close by. In addition to Elizabeth's daughters, it is believed that Sam and Elizabeth had two daughters born to them, Sarah and Elizabeth, both provided for in Sam's will.

Sam was no doubt envisioning the futures of his sons and their families spread across Brookhaven, from Setauket to South, when he brought his bride back to Long Island and eventually located near the same area where Thomas Beardsley and Elizabeth had lived previous to their relocation to Connecticut in 1661. Records suggest, "Thomas Beardsley of Stratford" had sold property at, "Newfield, being on Carman's Neck" and meadow in Great Meadow to Richard Cowls in November of 1661, as well as twenty acres in the New-field on Stony Brook, to Hugh Griffin.[530] Moving to Connecticut, Thomas had purchased a house and a ten acre lot of land in

---

[530] (Beardsley 1902)

Stratford[531] in February 1661/62 and, in the same volume, Elizabeth later appears on the, 'First Inhabitants and their Home Lots' as "Wid. Elizabeth Beardsley."

"Thomas Beardsley, deceased, hath five ½ acres lying in the New field on ye near side of Nessingpaws Creek, south with highway west Mrs. David Mitchell."[532] The Fairfield Probate Record says that Thomas died February 13, 1668 (new style calendar). The inventory of his estate amounted to £78 5s, as reported March 29, 1668, by the selectmen. No heirs were mentioned.

In April of 1670, with at least three teenage boys at home to help work the land, Sam rented more land from Robert Ackerly. This time, he rented seven acres of field. In addition to any servants Sam might have had, it is possible that Sam may have had four sons at home, if Ralph had not yet gone out on his own.

> These [presented] testify that Robert Ackerly has let to Samuel Dayton 3 acres in his 3 acre lot and 4 acres in his 6 acre lot lying in the old field. And in consideration, the said Samuel is to pay three bushels per acre; paid in ears when it is husked, two bushels for one to him or his assigns.

By June 15, 1670, "Samuel Dayton has agreed with Robert Ackerly to pay him 3 bushels of (sugar corn) [per] acre for 4 acre and a half according to a former bargain and the other is satisfied for."

---

[531] (Orcutt 1886). 104
[532] (Abstract of Probate Records Feb 13, 1668)

Chapter 14

At South

The search for whales, dead or alive, intensified along the ocean shore, and East Hampton, Southampton and Brookhaven men, and their whaling companies continued to negotiate with Native Americans and dispute among themselves to acquire rights to whales beached on the south shore or to hunt in coastal waters.

In 1659 Southampton entrepreneurs had pushed their control of whaling rights on the south beach westward into Unkechaug territory. In 1662 Ogden met with sachems Tobacus and Winecroscum to negotiate a contract for the rights to drift whales on the south beach lying to the west of the lease held by Anthony Waters. This area of the barrier beach was probably between Enaughquamuck at the mouth of the Carman's River and Namkee Creek on the west.[533]

The inhabitants of Brookhaven at Setauket made their purchase of meadow at South in 1664, part of the approximate area on the bay that would later become known as the Fire Place. One of the first references to Fire Place was in early 1675 when it was recorded that Sam made a land exchange there with Francis Muncy. The area was roughly bounded by the Connecticut (Carmans) River on the east and Bellport on the west. There are various theories of how Fire Place got its name but the most prevalent, made famous by Osborn Shaw,[534] seems to involve signal fires set either to guide ships across the bay to the mouth of the Connecticut River or to communicate with shore whalers working on the outer barrier island. But, since there was no inlet in 1675 when the name Fire Place first appears in the record, Marty Van Lith argued that this is not a credible explanation.[535] He also views the ideas that the name derived from the site being used for whale processing or for tar manufacturing with suspicion

---

[533] (J. A. Strong 2011)
[534] (Shaw, History of Brookhaven Village October 5, 1933)
[535] (Van Lith, Fire Place Name Origin Jul 3 2012)

as well, but rather he favors the theory that the name originated from the work of a Native American pot-maker named Wessquassucks who lived and worked on the neck. The area was called Fire Place until 1871, when this name was dropped and it officially became the hamlet of Brookhaven. Because the hamlet is in the Town of Brookhaven, there is regular confusion between them.

Settling at South: The Fire Place

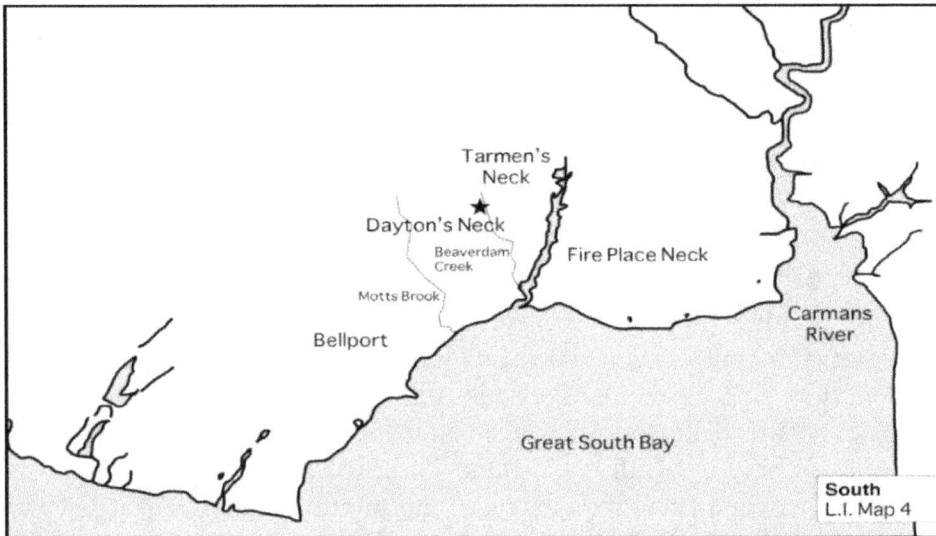

Figure 20. The Necks at South

"The Necks at South" are drawn, roughly following an illustrated John Deitz map.

By 1666 and 1667, the men of Brookhaven had become quite successful at striking whales close to shore, but they became frustrated when some of the whales finally drifted to their shores (Howell says a considerable number) and the Native Americans would seize them, as was their right. Finally, in March of 1667/68, the settlers of Brookhaven town negotiated with Tobacus, the Sachem of Unkachaug for the right to whales coming onto the beach. Within a couple of weeks, the town had provided for four squadrons of men to process whales and then make the long transport by cart from the south (ocean shore of Brookhaven) across to the northern settlements. Samuel Dayton was leader of the first squadron:

> at a full towne meeting it was fully agred vpon concerning the cutting out and bringing whome of the whales that comes up at the south as followeth the towne is devided in to fower sqadrens and they draed lotte wich shuld goe ferst wich fell out samuell daitons squadren ferest mr whodhull 2

228

henery perings 3 Josua garlick 4 for to cutt it out and gett it fitt for cartting every pertickler sqadern ther whall sucksesfully and every sqaderan to find a cart to goe vnto euery whale and what ther wants more to hire in generall every cart that is suffissient to be allowed 20s a turn to be brought to the midle of towne and then to be devided equally acording to there lottmente and if there be any man that canot or will nott goe to the cutting out nor gett suffuissent man in there Roome thay are to loose there part of that whale to the resst of the sqadern.[536]

Sam must have possessed a logical mind with knowledge and good communication skills because, once again, he was called upon to negotiate a resolution to a dispute between the town of Brookhaven and a neighboring whaling company. The entry was recorded only one day after the, "Goodman Daiton, of Long Island" Stratford entry (Feb 27, 1669/70), confirming that Sam and Elizabeth were living at Brookhaven. Sam was probably in attendance at the meeting.

> Inhabitants of the town, wee the Cunstable and overseers of the same doe by these presents authorize and appoint Samuel Daiton to make a final Ishue with Ioseph Rainer and Richard Howell about the drift whales that come on the beach within our bounds for the terme of years they claim, by virtue of their purchase which is about seven or eight years, and then to bee returued to the Inhabitants of Brookhaven, without any further molestation from them or any in their name always provided, that this our attorney doe obtaine some acknowledgement for this for each whale, and what this our agent shall doe in this matter wee give him due satisfaction provided hee exceed not the bounds of moderation, Inhabitants of the whole towne have subscribed their hands.[537]
>
> DANIEL LANE,
> RICHARD WOODELL.

It appears that Sam's mission was successful and a resolution was secured, as on April 2, 1670, "At a town meeting it is voted and agreed upon that Samuel Dayton is to have the rent of the first two whales that come up upon the beach that is due to the town from Joseph Raynor and his associates and a gallon of cider." The meaning and benefits of, "having the rent" have been lost in this case but it does sound like Sam liked his refreshment. In the colonies, hard cider was extremely popular and, being "hard," it would keep through the winter, without spoilage.

According to Barstow, when John Tooker was Brookhaven recorder and Sam was overseer of the south lands, the pair began to accumulate land holdings at South, beginning with purchases of several necks of land near the end of the 1660's. Just a

---

[536] (A. C. Weeks 1924). 150
[537] (W. J. Post 1877)

few weeks after Sam received the first two whales above, the following entry was recorded in the STR, containing a few words that cannot be deciphered, but might involve Mahue the Setalcott. Perhaps a small piece of the document was torn.

> John Tooker and Samuel Dayton have bought a neck of land and meadow at the south of [mehuni...It foswas sonn] the 22 of April, 1670 as by a deed of sale it does appear.

If Sam liked his cider as most Puritans did, his friend John Tooker was probably ready to supply it, for on July 12, 1670, the record says,

> The hy shrefe, Capt, Salsbery, with Mr. Woodhull, have granted liberty to John Tooker, Senyer, for to sell Strong drink by Retaile, soe long as he entertaines people for there monys, untell there be a suttled ordnery in this towne.[538]

Cider would remain a very popular drink even into the 1800's, until replaced by beer with the influx of German immigrants.

Also in July of 1670, Brookhaven town again voted to divide themselves into four squadrons under the direction of Sam, for the purpose of harvesting whale at South. Leaders of the four squadrons for the first year were Samuel Dayton, Francis Muncy, Andrew Miller and Obed Seward.

In August of 1671, Sam had granted and laid out twelve acres lying east of the Newtown lots. In addition, the Brookhaven men continued to enlarge their South holdings as there were yet additional south meadows to secure. These would be divided among the proprietors according to their allotments earlier that year.

> At a towne meeting, it was vueted and agreed upon, that John Tooker, henery pering, Mr. Bayles and Samuell daiton to goe and vew the medoes at Unkechaege and treete with sachem about the purchas of the medows, thay caring some likers with them to the Indiens upon the towne's acount.[539]

One more time, the Dutch recaptured New York in the summer of 1673, after a swift and successful invasion, while Governor Lovelace was in Connecticut, on official business. Dutch control was brief however, and only one year after the Dutch recaptured New York, the English recaptured it from the Dutch and installed a new governor, Edmund Andros, in the fall. Before Andros could take office, on Sept 17, 1674, "Tobakes" decided he was ready to sell the south meadows. In response, the town of Brookhaven voted and agreed to send Henry Perrine and Samuel Daighton to the South, to meet with the Sachem and other Unkechaug leaders to sign a bill of

---

[538] (Brookhaven Town Clerk, BTR 1880)
[539] Ibid.

sale, finally settling the long standing question of the south meadows. In *The Unkechaug Indians of Eastern Long Island,* author John Strong states,

> Tobacus gathered seven men…to meet with Perring and Dayton. The presence of Massetuse among the signatories again indicates that kinship networks linked families across tribal lines. He was apparently a member of an extended family that had authority over lands on both the northern and the southern shores of Brookhaven. These men, perhaps village headmen, had authority over the meadows between the Wegonthotak (aka Mastic, Forge) River on the east and the Carmans River on the west.

Strong continues,

> The status of this tract of meadowland had been the subject of controversy and contention since 1657…Apparently the question of who owned the land had been settled among the Brookhaven proprietors during the negotiations. Perring and Dayton met with Tobacus and the Unkechaug delegation and negotiated the sale to Brookhaven of 'all the mowable meadowland' between the Forge and the Carmans rivers. The Unkechaugs gave the Brookhaven farmers permission to build houses and clear yards, 'for the convenience of their meadows,' and granted them unmolested access to the meadows. The deed, however, does not mention woodlands, bays, or river banks where Unkechaug villages were usually located, nor did it include the lands on the southern half of the Mastic Peninsula.[540]

This was at least the third time Sam was appointed to negotiate with the Native People, again carrying liquor to assist in the exchange. In an article by Thomas Morton published in *The American Journal of Sociology*, he spoke of trading with the Indians, with the help of liquor:

> Liquor was, indeed the Indians' undoing. Their savage days had been passed in ignorance of 'the refreshing of beer and wine, which God hath vouchsafed Europe.' But like so many Calibans, they liked liquor, once they learned its potencies, and in the words of one who had large experience in consuming and dispensing it, 'They will pawn their wits to purchase the acquaintance of it.' The earliest temperance legislation in America was an effort to check the resulting demoralization. It forbade the sale of 'strong liquors' to Indians, and conditioned the sale of all

---

[540] (J. A. Strong 2011)

Indian lands upon the sanction of the General Court, an important restriction in light of the Indian indifference to the relative values of acres and ale.[541]

It's nearly impossible to determine what special qualities or abilities Sam possessed for the favored role and responsibility in these exchanges. What ability suited him to be chosen for the assigned task—his skill in negotiation, his camaraderie with the Native People, or was it simply his ability to hold his liquor? The evidence suggests that he must have possessed some skill in the art of persuasion because, in addition to treating with the Native Americans, he was twice selected to meet with the governor about whales and at least two additional times acting as attorney on behalf of the town. There were other instances too, where he was called upon to meet with someone from the town.

As payment to Sam for his work and possibly for other services, in February of 1671/72, it was, "voted and agreed upon that Samuel Dayton is to have laid out a quantity of upland lying on the westward where Capt. Tooker wintered his cattle between two creeks that is to say 2 acres for one which is due to him from the town."[542] From this entry, it is fair to assume that Sam might also have intended to use the run as a pen for his cattle and horses, especially in the winter, during whaling season when Sam was to receive a double portion.

Setauket was forever trying to secure a long-term blacksmith and one after the other, attempts failed. At a town meeting in July 15, 1672, it was recorded that Henry Brooks met with a constable and overseers and gave up one of two smith's lots which had been his accommodation granted by the town. Brooks was allowed to keep a share of West Meadow, upland and meadow at South. In turn, the smith's accommodation was given to John Tomson, along with payment to Brooks for what he had laid out, in consideration that Tomson become the town's blacksmith. In September, the transaction was confirmed and recorded by the town, as was the vote to have Mr. Woodhull and Samuel Dayton lay out Henry Brook's land. At the same meeting, "It was Voted and agreed upon that there Shall be no more Land given out to Strangers…"[543]

The meaning of the following Brookhaven entry has not been deciphered, but it is interesting enough to mention. Apparently Sam and neighbor[544] Andrew Miller, who had moved to Brookhaven from East Hampton in 1671 and from whom Miller Place takes its name, were in conflict. Because payment to Ebenezer Hook was part

---

[541] (Morton 1916)
[542] (W. J. Weeks 1930)
[543] Ibid.
[544] Note: Andrew Miller is neighbor to Sam according to a 1675 document

232

of its resolution, it is not understood if the dispute occurred in performance of Sam's official capacity or responsibilities as overseer, or if the dispute was of a more personal nature. Miller was a cooper who could have been a supplier of casks[545] to the whalers and tar men. The entry is worded,

> June 5, 1673 Sam Dayton and Andrew Miller have come to reckoning. Andrew must give Ebenezer Hook 25 shillings…and Sam Dayton and Ebenezer Hook have come to reckoning.

Again, this time on September 17, 1674, it was, "Voted Henry Perring and Sam Dayton to go to the south and to get Sachem Tobaccus to get him to set his hand to a bill of sale for the south meadows." The record does not make it clear if these meadows were the same as treeted in August 1671, merely a clarification of the original, or if these are additional meadows. Henry Perring and Sam had negotiated the 1671 agreement. Nonetheless, divisions of land at, "The Old Purchase of Meadow at the South" had been recorded on June 20, 1674. According to Osborne Shaw, these 49 lots were numbered east to west, starting in Brookhaven and proceeding to Bellport, with lots 1-32 being in Brookhaven, bounded on the west by Dayton's River and lots 33 to 49 were situated in Bellport.[546]

At what is now the hamlet of Brookhaven and was then Fire Place, Lots of the New Purchase at South were drawn in 1675. The meadow was divided into 50 lots, with one being a town lot, Sam receiving lot #38. After at least two large land divisions there,

> Some men found that land so far away from their home was worthless and were quite willing to sell, while others sought land in the south for their own purposes: whaling and the exploitation of the pine barrens. In time the settlers developed new commodities from the bountiful pines: tar, turpentine and pipestavers…The south shore also provided excellent pasturage for horses. The necks a natural holding pen when the open end was fenced and the animals could be left to roam with minimal attention from man, providing there are kettle holes or fresh water streams available; all valid reasons for this new move of some men of Setauket to the south.[547]

It appears that Sam was still living in Setauket in 1675 where he referred to himself as husbandman (typically, overseer of a farm). He received a loan from Benjamin Gibbs, merchant of Boston, using his house and land as collateral. The mortgage was quitclaim (a quitclaim transfers the interest to the recipient but contains

[545] (Gass 1971)
[546] (W. J. Weeks 1930)
[547] (Barstow, Setauket, Alias Brookhaven 2004)

no title covenant, offering no warranty as to the status of the property). The loan was to be repaid by March, near the end of whaling season. Payment was to be in whale oil or bone, at Boston market prices, delivered to the landing at Brookhaven. As part of the agreement, Gibbs assured Sam that he was not in danger of losing his house to Gibbs unless Sam could make payment in March of 1676. Was Gibbs betting on nonpayment, should Sam have an unprofitable season? The agreement was copied in both BTR Book 1 and in Book A, but because the Book A copy is more complete, it is given below:

Brookhaven (July 30, 1675)

To all Christian people unto whom these presents Shall or may come know ye that I Samuel Dayton husbandman living in the Town of Brookhaven or Seatauket on Long Island in the County of York Shire Send Greeting know ye that I the Said Samuel Dayton for divers good causes and Vallueable Considerations me thereunto mouing but more especyally for the Sum of twenty and four pounds Sixteen Shilings and three pence paid in hand do by these presents give grant bargain Sell or Mortgage and hereby have given granted bargained Sold Mortgaged Alienated infeofed a ceartain Dweeling House with a home Lot thereunto adjoyning of which ten acres properly belongeth unto me the Said Samuel Dayton the whole Containing to twelve acres being buted and bounded by or not far from the Side of a brook between the house of Andrew Miller and the house of Nath. Norton with all the fence found Standing or any way belonging to the Same unto Benjamin Gibbs Merchant in boston his Heirs Executors Administrators or Assigns Moreover that I the Said Samuel Dayton do by these presents for my Heirs Executors Administrators forever quitclaim any Right Title chalenge or pretence unto the aforesaid house and Land and that I the Said Samuel Dayton Shall and will warrent this my bill of Sale or Mortgage to be good in Law or in any Court from any person or persons that Shall Claim any Right or title to the Same and Shall and will defend the Said Benjamin Gibbs his heirs Executors Administrators from any that Shall So pretend any Right to the Same provided that the Said Dayton have the Vse of the Said House and Land untill the month of March in the year one Thousand Six hundred Seventy and Six being the begining of the Next year provided the Said House be in the Same Repair if not better than now it is furthermore that Benjamin Allen Servant and factor unto Mr Benjamin Gibbs aforesaid in his behalf doth promise and grant that always provided that the Said Samuel Dayton Shall and doth faithfully and truly pay unto the Said Benjamin Gibbs of his Assigns the Sum of twenty four pounds Sixteen Shillings and three pence at or before March aforesaid either in good Merchantable Whale oyl after the Rate of twenty five Shillings for every

234

Barrel in good Staunch Cask or whale bone at the rate at Seven pence for every pound or good Merchantable provisions at the common Money price in Boston or what else the Said Benjamin Gibbs or his Assigns Shall except all which or either of the abovesaid Commodities to be delivered at the landing place in Brookhaven the which being done and performed the Said Benjamin Gibbs or Assigns Shall and will make Void the premises and Surrender the Same and forever quit Claim any title to the land by Vertue of this bill of Sale and Absolutely to exonerate aquit and discharge the Said Dayton from any demands but in Case of Nonpayment according to the Month appointed in commodities as aforesaid I the Said Samuel Dayton for my Heirs Executors and Administrators do covenant and grant to and with the Said Benjamin Gibbs his heirs Executors Administrators or Assigns that free and legall possession Shall be given without any Molestation to have and to hold the Said house and Land in Consideration of all and every the premises have unto Set unto my hand and Seal this 23, day of May 1675_ being the twenty Seventh year of the Reign of our Sovereign Lord Charles the Second Signed Sealed and Delivered in the presence of us_ Richard Woodhull Samuel Dayton with a Seal John Tomson

The exact purpose for the loan has not been determined, but there is little doubt it had something to do with Sam's intentions at Great South Bay, for by 1675 he was beginning to accumulate land at Fire Place. At this time, other men also took out similar loans from Benjamin Gibbs. Just a few months earlier, Sam had traded his property on the east side of the Connecticut River for property at Fire Place. A record of March 30, 1675 says:

francis muncy, before he died, exchanged his medow at the fire place, in the ould purchas, with Samuel daiton, for his lott of medow at Seabamuck, in the nue purchas; and at this time, the widow muncy is willing to the same and gives her assent.[548]

According to William Wallace Tooker, the place called Seabamuck was, "one of the lesser necks of land into which the Manor of St.George, Mastic, Brookhaven town, is divided. The first neck east of the Connecticut or Carman's River, at its mouth."[549]

Perhaps in addition to accumulating land at Fireplace, Sam needed the loan to set himself up for business, establishing a trying station,[550] or buying a vessel and irons. There are statements repeated on the internet that Samuel's move from

---

[548] (Brookhaven Town Clerk, BTR 1880)
[549] (Tooker 1911)
[550] Note: A trying station consists of giant pots in which to boil whale blubber, in order to extract oil.

Setauket was due to "his interest in the whale fishery," and that is not disputed for it is known that competition was still fierce as whaling was beginning to move men from the beach to off-shore opportunities.

Someone has made the claim that, "he [Sam] was identified as being the first to establish an offshore whaling business...the place where the business originated was at Dayton Run." Although we would very much prefer to echo this claim, no basis can be found to agree. However, it can be stated with reasonable confidence that Sam was one of the early settlers to engage in whaling and to establish an off-shore whaling interest at Brookhaven.

At that time, Sam had three, possibly four sons twenty-one years of age and older. Our ancestor, Abraham, his third oldest, would have been about twenty-two or twenty-three when Sam's attention seems to turn in earnest to the south. In addition, there is little doubt that Sam was employing the skill of Native Americans to work his whaleboats because it made good business sense, especially considering their abilities. Brookhaven men had been employing Native Americans for some time to direct whales to their shore.

But, in 1675, Sam would have faced much competition for whales and Native American whalemen. One can only imagine the potential for clashes at sea as rival companies competed in "crowded" waters, and on land as bidding wars for Native American labor cut into profits. Eleven English settlers from the East Hampton area,

> adventurers upon the whale designe, engaged a double crew of Montauk Indians to go to sea for them, promising them one-half in blubber and bone secured. The colonists were Thomas James, first minister at Easthampton: William, John and Thomas Edwards: Thomas Chatfield, Robert Dayton (Sam's younger brother), Richard Stratton, John Hopping, John and Benjamin Osborne and Richard Shaw.[551]

There are also abundant records of Sam's son Jacob (1657-1705) involved in whaling at East Hampton and New Jersey. By 1678, Jacob was twenty-one and finally free of his bond to his uncle, Thomas Baker, which had begun that heart wrenching day back in December of 1664. Jeannette Rattray tells us that Philip Leek and others in 1678-79 engaged Native Americans to man two boats to, "kill whales and other great fish" and for, "cutting ashore according to custom." Within the next few years the Montauks entered such agreements with Benjamin Conkling, John Wheeler, Samuel Mulford, John Kirle, Robert Keddy, John Miller Junior and Jacob Dayton, all of East Hampton.[552]

Fortunately, the deterioration of Native American relations on the mainland had not spread to Long Island. Adventures on its south shore and out in the ocean were

---

[551] (Rattray 2001)
[552] Ibid.

further distant from King Philip's War in New England, "which began in Massachusetts in June of 1675 as retaliation for the execution of three Wampanoag Indians by the Plimouth colony. The war continued through 1676 and spread to Maine, Rhode Island, and Connecticut before ending in August 1676, after hundreds of settlers and Indians were killed."[553]

In a May 24, 1676 Brookhaven town document, Sam continued to refer to himself as "of Setauket," at the time he transferred, "a parcel of meadow lying on east side of a brook by the fireplace at the south side that meadow I had of Francis Muncy unto William Rogers of Southampton."[554] This Muncy parcel previously acquired by Sam was probably lot 22 of the Brookhaven distribution. Why Sam would give up this parcel at fireplace is a mystery since, at the time, he seems to have intended to increase his holdings there. Perhaps this agreement was in trade for a loan or some transferable right held by Rogers. It is likely that William Rogers was a long-time acquaintance of the Dayton family because he was at Wethersfield, CT with Prudden and, according to some Rogers family research, was living in the Flushing/Hemp-stead area before 1649, about the time he lived in Southampton. Some of these movements bear a strong resemblance to the movements of Daytons.

Barstow also reports a badly torn page of record from 1676, in whose fragments are seen Samuel Dayton acquiring at least one unknown person's rights in the Old Purchase, at South.

Sam was official witness to a multitude of land transactions, many of which are not included in this compilation but, as examples, two from July of 1676 are given, taken from Barstow's *Setauket, Alias Brookhaven*:

> July 5, 1676 These [presented] testify that I, Samuel Dayton of Setauket, do engage to give Benjamin Gould quiet possession of fifteen acres of upland of John Roe's of this town, lying between the Old Mans and the going down of the * * with two acres of meadow at the south, having his choice of John Roe's meadow at the south according to (bill) upon consideration that the said John Roe be satisfied his money or monies worth, according to agreement * * and to the truth of this I do here to set my hand this 5 day of July 1676. Samuel Dayton

> July 13, 1676 Know all men by these presented, that I, John Thomas of Setauket, alias Brookhaven, for valuable causes and considerations, me moving, have given granted bargained and sold, all that piece and parcel of land that lies by the harbor side next to Nathaniel Norten's lower part of his lot, that was given me by the town with my house that is on the said land, to William Jayne of the above said town. I say John Thomas, does

---

[553] (Tyler, History Close at Hand-Three Village/Brookhaven-Chronology 2014)
[554] (W. J. Weeks 1930)

for myself my heirs and assigns, give grant bargain and sell, the above said parcel of land and house to the said William Jayne, his heirs executors administrators or assigns forever to have and to hold. Only I, the said John Thomas, am to live in the house and to have the herbage of the above said land until the first day of March next ensuing. And to the true and thorough confirmation of all the above said premises, I do here to set my hand and seal this 13th day of July, 1676.

> Witness
> John Thomas
> John Tooker
> Samuel Dayton.

Dayton's Neck

Barstow claimed, "Samuel Dayton moved permanently from the town of Setauket to the south in 1675."[555] From the body of evidence, it can be concluded that the move was probably 1676 or early 1677, although before September 13th of 1678, when it was recorded that, "Sam had 40 acres laid out at the south in the neck called Dayton's Neck, running from river to river excepting the meadows that is laid out by Mr. Woodhul as also another addition of land adjoining to it of the Northeast Corner from a lot that was part Muncys where the tarr mens house stood."[556]

The website "Brookhaven South Haven Hamlets & Their People," maintained by local historian John Deitz, expands on this and provides a sound explanation:

> Most historians, including former Brookhaven Town historian Osborne Shaw, have interpreted this entry in the Brookhaven Town records to mean that Samuel Dayton acquired from the Town forty acres on the necks (Dayton's and Tar Men's necks) defined by the creek now known as Motts creek on the west (essentially the eastern boundary of the Village of Bellport) to Beaver Dam creek on the east, excepting out the meadow lots and their upland portions along the Great South Bay that had been previously granted to other Town proprietors. Since the meadow/upland lots would have stretched from the Great South Bay to approximately modern South Country road, Dayton's grant was likely north of South Country road.[557]

On February 6, 1676/77,

---

[555] (Barstow, Setauket, Alias Brookhaven 2004)
[556] (W. J. Weeks 1930)
[557] (Deitz, Brookhaven/South Haven Hamlets & Their People 2006-2015)

At a meeting of the deputy constable and overseers [they] have agreed with Thomas Ward and William Salliyer to make a sufficient highway for carting over that place that they call Dayton's Run, to make it of both wood and stone, 13 feet wide from firm ground to firm ground on both sides as agreed...[558]

Since a primitive cart way no doubt existed along the north boundary of the distributed meadow lots, giving access to each, this improved cart way might have been the beginnings of some of the southernmost portions of either Beaver Dam Road or South Country Road, bisecting the Neck. The longest sections of these two roads are too far north today and run a far different course. When Sam chose a location for his dwelling, he chose a very desirable spot just north of the nearby cart way that followed along the boundary of the meadow lots. Nothing of the original road can be detected today, as 250 years has wiped away any trace of the path.

The planting of Sam at Fire Place did spawn controversy however, especially after he built his house there. Strong says:

For the Unkechaugs and the other Indians on Long Island, the only chance for survival was to continue employing the diplomatic strategies they had already been using with some degree of success. They had come to understand, for example, that they could take their complaints about the local town officials directly to the governor. This is what they did on November 4, 1677. The Unkechaug sachems and several other Long Island Indians joined in a protest to Governor Andros, led by the Massapequa sachem Tackapousha. Most of the complaints were about whites who settled on Indian lands without purchasing them.[559]

Strong continues,

One of the complaints concerned the land that Tobacus had given to Governor Winthrop in 1664. Winthrop, who died in 1676, had never made any use of the tract. The Unkechaug sachem said that when 'Governor Winthrop came over upon the island, they gave him a piece of meadow, he being a very good man; but now he is dead,' and he complained that Samuel Dayton, who had represented Brookhaven in the negotiations for the meadowland east of the Winthrop tract three years earlier, had built a house on the land without paying the Indians. Tobacus had given Winthrop the land as a gift, but anyone else who wanted to farm on the land, the sachem argued, must pay Tobacus for that right. The governor, who had apparently already investigated the complaint, told the

---

[558] (Barstow, Setauket, Alias Brookhaven 2004)
[559] (J. A. Strong 2011)

Unkechaugs that Dayton claimed that his farm, which he had been occupying for some time, was actually not on the Winthrop tract. The complaint, said Andros, was still under investigation and if Woodhull and the Unkechaugs 'cannot accommodate the matter betwixt them,' they should return the next summer 'when care shall be taken in the matter.'

Since no further reference to the complaint is found, it appears that Woodhull and the Unkechaugs resolved the conflict over Sam's farm. In fact, on December 2, 1679, "It was voetted and agread vpon that Samuell daiton shall haue a hundred akers of land for his fifty aker lott layd out aJoyning to his land at the south from his home land towards the bever brook."[560] In his "Three Village Chronology 2005-2014," Beverly Tyler says, "Samuel Dayton received an additional 100 acres to add to the 50 acre home lot he already owned near Beaver Brook. The area is now Brookhaven hamlet."

Sam may have lived his remaining years at this farm, becoming the homestead on Dayton's Neck. The best authority available to locate the homestead is from the official Town of Brookhaven historian, in, "A paper written by Mr. Osborn Shaw of Bellport for the Fireplace Literary Club, and read by him at the Brookhaven Free Library, October 5th, 1933." Shaw entitled this paper, 'History of Brookhaven Village"[561] from which is quoted:

Dayton's Neck is the next neck to the west. It lies between the Head-of-the Neck and the Bay and from Fire Place Creek on the east to Dayton's or Osborn's Brook on the west. It was in later years sometimes called West Fire Place. The neck was named after Samuel Dayton who on 13 Sept. 1678, had 40 acres laid out to him by the Town in lieu of some other land he did not get in a former allotment. At the same time he received 'another adition of land aloyning to it of the nor est corner from a lot that was part munces where the tarr mens hous stoode,' hence it is evident that Samuel Dayton owned a part of both Tar-men's Neck and the neck that bore his name. However, he did not own the fifteen acre lots with their adjoining meadow shares which extended also along the south of his neck as they did along the south of fire Place Neck as I have previously told you. Dayton came from Southampton to Setauket and finally removed to his neck here on the South Side, probably about 1678 and from an entry in Book B of the town records, it appears that he gave the name of 'West Hampton' to some part of the section…He was probably the first white man to live in this section. Just where his house stood is not known, but it probably was somewhere in the vicinity of Clam Hollow, (which some

---

[560] (Shaw, Records of the Town of Brookhaven 1679-1756 Book B 1932)
[561] (Shaw, History of Brookhaven Village October 5, 1933)

240

of you may not know is the name of the hollow east of the George Washington property), possibly even nearer to Bellport and he may thus properly be claimed by both villages. As the Bellport School District and Fire District boundary line is at Arter's or the Hollow Road, the western part of Dayton's Neck is consequently in Bellport.

The compilers were privileged to be hosted by local historians Marty Van Lith and John Deitz as the men led my brother and I on a tour of key locations on the neck that included the George Washington Lodge Estate purchased jointly by Suffolk County and the Town of Brookhaven. Exactly where Sam built his house is not known, but, according to Shaw, Sam's house and farm were probably somewhere in the vicinity of Clam Hollow, perhaps about 269-299 South Country Road.

The men explained to us that this particular ground has a long and colorful history, and it seems to have been inhabited very early and experienced fairly consistent habitation—it seems there has been enough activity to fill a book dedicated exclusively to its history. Most recently, in 2012-2013, the property was purchased by Isabella Rossellini, "donating a conservation easement to the Peconic Land Trust, to preserve the property and create a six acre working organic farm."[562]

After studying the early Daytons on Long Island for decades, visiting the site was truly a noteworthy and somewhat emotional event for us. Just to stand in that place where learned historians and researchers consider the probable location for Samuel Dayton's dwelling provided a connection that inexplicably made it feel like "home" to both my brother and I. As my brother and I viewed the ground and listened to Marty Van Lith and John Deitz tell the history (and story) of the property, we sensed an ability to relate with our ancestor and his dream on this beautiful neck.

> In 1678, nearly 100 years before the signing of the Declaration of Independence, Samuel Dayton, the first English settler in this area between Bellport and Brookhaven, built his house on this very piece of land. Then, as now, it was a choice piece of land. [563]

The estate of George Washington Lodge is located in the modern hamlet of Brookhaven, near the Bellport town line, on a stretch of South Country Road (Route 36) that bends east-west, and, drawing a straight line north and south, is situated approximately halfway between Montauk Hwy to the north and the bay to the south, in the vicinity of where Woodland Avenue meets South Country Road.

---

[562] (Allegrezza 2015)
[563] (Van Lith, Purchase of Washington Lodge Estate Approved by Suffolk County 2010)

There would be little wonder why this prominent location was selected, and the fact that both Shaw and Barstow consider the Dayton family probable founders of the town of Bellport[564] makes it all the more special since Sam chose this spot from all other possibilities.

It is good, high ground and once possessed a natural fresh water spring sufficient for family and farm. Today Clam Hollow is "dry" as the ground water fed stream that emptied into Beaver Dam Creek is no longer active, Van Lith says probably due to, "the development and other disturbance that took place since the 1940s." Where a garden and swimming pool were once located, the large oval of broken concrete is now almost unrecognizable without assistance to point them out. Some satellite photos show what remains of the large concrete pool among the trees, obscured from view in the spring and summer. The pool was situated at the edge of Clam Hollow where George Constant Washington kept his private zoological garden. Mr. Washington, of New York City, owned his country home from about 1915 to 1926.[565]

Moving over to the easterly boundary of Sam's property, we stopped along Beaver Dam Road, on a bridge crossing Fireplace Creek, as it was sometimes called. Again, the choice of location in the proximity of Sam's dwelling to Beaverdam Creek was no accident. A couple of hundred years ago, the creek provided wider and deeper passage to the bay than what can be observed today. Deitz adds, "This was a convenient place since most whaling was done over on Fire Island, across the bay." Of course, proximity to the early road was no accident either, probably originating to enable passage along the northern boundaries of the meadow lots. At this point, Van Lith reminded us that there would have been no bridge for travelers on the cart way. Instead, the dip in the road where the creek crosses would have been called a wash over and required a fording of the water. "At high tides, they would have had a problem." According to our hosts, Sam probably kept his boat near the location of the current bridge, with the Great South Bay no more than about 100 to 200 yards to the south. In the 1600's, there were so few people in this area, Sam could have kept his sailboat just south of the road without objection from others.

---

[564] (Barstow, Setauket, Alias Brookhaven 2004) 237
[565] (Deitz, History Volume: Building Structure Inventory Form for Washington Lodge 2014)

Figure 21. Pool at George Washington Lodge

The "Swimming Pool Washington Estate" post card is owned by John Deitz and is posted on the website *Brookhaven/South Haven Hamlets & their People*, maintained by Deitz.

Van Lith also spoke of the western-most boundary of Sam's property, Dayton Creek, today known as Motts Creek. Mott was the person who had the playhouse in Bellport.

> …Dayton Creek used to be a beautiful little creek going out into the bay…and the western most boundary of his property. So he would probably have the advantage of getting a boat out into the bay because this runs right out…it's quite a large creek. This would eventually become a wetlands area by itself.

Sam as Attorney for the Town's Right

Brookhaven was, once again, without the services of a blacksmith, judging from a BTR dated April 3, 1678. The record reads,

> At a town meeting, it was voted and agreed by the town to sue John Thompson the next [Court of] Sessions at Southold for non-performance of his agreement with the Town and Town's rights. As likewise it was

243

voted and agreed upon that Sam Dayton and Peter Whitehair shall manage the case and be the Town's attorneys against the said John Thompson for the Town's right.

In May of 2014, on a return visit to Long Island, we asked Barbara Russell, Brookhaven Town Historian, what it meant to act as an "attorney" back in those days? She replied,

> …it would be someone who had a level of education to understand the deeds, the patents that they were required to get; probably could read and write, and not everybody could.

When asked if there were any town occupations of full-time attorney or attorney offices. She replied,

> No. I don't think any of those occupations were full-time because, remember, they were carpenters and farmers, shoemakers and blacksmiths and then they served the town in different positions. I don't even remember that far back ever seeing appointment for an official town attorney, not as you would have a clerk or overseer of the poor…

In other business, Mr. John Lemmings and John Laughton were chosen by the town to visit a property at its western boundaries and, "to procure the Assistance of Sm'll Dayton of Brookhaven to effect the same."[566] The purpose of the mission was, "for setting of county rate" and what assistance or expertise Sam was to share is unknown—whether in official capacity or because of some other knowledge or skill.

On September 13, 1678, after Sam's fourth son Isaac had gained his majority, the record states, "Samuel Dayton has given to his son Isaac Dayton a piece of land that is at the rear of his home lot, lying eastward as it is staked out by Andrew Miller and Walter Man(ven) and the land is given for part of his portion lying in the town." As Barstow points out, this apportionment was given outright, not dependent on Samuel's death.

Drowning of Sam Junior

Sam lost his second oldest son, Samuel Junior, to accidental drowning when the younger Samuel was between twenty six and twenty nine. Werner says:

> Among the original proprietors of Brookhaven in 1656 was William Satterly, who with John Moger and Samuel [Dayton] was drowned in the Long Island Sound sometime between 1677 and 1680, in returning from Milford Conn., where they had been for the purpose of having their

---

[566] (H. P. Hedges 1877)

244

own and their neighbor's grain ground into flour as was the practice of that day before the erection of a mill in Brookhaven. Their hats were found washed ashore on the beach but their bodies were never recovered. William Satterly was a man of considerable wealth and possessed silver household utensils which were exceedingly rare in those days.[567]

Mildred Gillie said that the settlers took turns sailing across the sound, on the dangerous trip transporting grain. Gillie states that the men made it all the way back to Port Jefferson Harbor when the heavily laden boat was upset by a sudden squall.[568]

According to Barstow, the early mills built in Setauket, in the first 25 years after the beginning of the settlement in 1655, were constantly breaking down and the water source (mill pond) behind the mills often failed, leaving the mill without water power. Finally, shortly after the drowning, the mill was built where Old Field Road crosses the stream that is now the mill pond, and it remained at the same location for almost a century. Isaac Satterly later became the miller in Setauket. The mill is no longer there but the home of the Satterly family, built circa 1680, remains at the west entrance to the Frank Melville Memorial Park.

If he had walked in the footsteps of his father, Samuel Junior may have been a shipper or may have run a ferry or freighter, even as his brother Isaac did a few years later. In a Brookhaven record dated May 24, 1683, Sam's 28 year old son Isaac became legally employed by Abram Smith of Long Island (probably Brookhaven or Jamaica), partnering with Smith to operate and be responsible for freighting with Smith's boat. It is apparent by the language and nature of the agreement that Isaac must have earned Smith's confidence in his ability, so perhaps Isaac had been working for Smith previously. Isaac's familiarity with boats and the transportation of freight could have been skills Isaac attained from Sam's many years doing the same. Book B says:

> Iseck Daiton [of Brookhaven] is to goe in the boete of the above said Abram Smiths and to doe his labor to the best he can doe for freighting and the lieke and they or both of them to goe equall shares I what they shall get by the boate onlly they ar to allow the boate a therd part of what thay both getteth and it is to be noeted that the saide Iseck daiton is to go in her as long as he pleaseth.

---

[567] (Werner 1919) 77
[568] (Gillie 1955)

James Hook says: "One could think that Abram Smith, because of his advancing age, was employing a younger man to operate his vessel for him. What supposition, therefore, is more reasonable than that Adam Smith's boat with Isaac Dayton as captain, plied the waters around Cape May and influenced the Smiths and Daytons to settle there…"[569]

Tar as Currency

A difference had existed between Sam Dayton and John Budd concerning cattle that was still not settled in June of 1678. Budd had been the person who owned Sam's house ten years earlier, when Sam transferred his mortgage to John Bayley. The town records of December 4, 1679 said Sam was to pay the debt with 22 1/2 barrels of tar and 5 barrels within a year. The record says:

> These pressents showeth wheareas there a vardett of John Tooker senyer of a difference bettwene liftenant John bud and samuell daiton that was putt to the sayd Tooker to end the differens bearing date the 11 day of June 1678 and there aRiesing some difference aRiese betwene them Therefore these presents testifieth that samu(ell) daiton doth ingaege to pay forthwith to the sayd mr John bude twenty two barells and a halue of marchantable tarr full gaege and flue barells of marchentable tarr this time twelfmonth to be delivered to the sayde John bud or his order and then the saide dai(ton) to be cleared from all former debts that is to say all former debts or whatsoever is els aboute cattle and whatever cattle was formerly in the sayd daitons hands of m^r buds it is now whoelly the sayd daitons only some nue debts of aboute £4 or (what) the saide daiton ownes to pay.[570]

Since no misconduct was mentioned and there had been transactions between the two men, it is assumed Sam had Mr. Budd's cattle as a result of doing business with him.

The reference to barrels of tar as a commodity is interesting also. Both tar and turpentine were processed from pine trees, an abundant resource at South. An area between Carmans River and Beaver Dam Creek was called "Tar man's Neck" supposedly because the tar man's house stood there, no doubt with processing close by. In his 1914 book, Armbruster claimed, "The house erected by Dayton stood on Dayton's Neck, about present Brookhaven village and was occupied by men engaged in the making of tar."[571] Tar Kilns were constructed close to a harbor or landing for

---

[569] (Hook 1955)
[570] (Shaw, Records of the Town of Brookhaven 1679-1756 Book B 1932)
[571] (Armbruster 1914) 36

246

convenience, and very often, the tar and pine products were traded or used as currency. The commodity was in high demand in Europe, but because it was also sought after in the colonies and the work was so labor intensive, very little was exported from New England. The resins that protect the tree can be processed into a form of tar, used to protect other wood, especially wooden ships and riggings, from the weather. Tar can be extracted from pine logs and branches during the process of slowly burning them.

The compilers of this book are very familiar with pine pitch, having both worked at the family sawmill owned by our father and uncle. Passers-by the mill were observed at times scraping and collecting the pitch that oozed from the bark or from the ends of piled logs into jars so they might later convert the gooey mass into salves. This was a Native American practice, according to lore, for use on both human and livestock wounds. After handling pine lumber and edgings, it became a ritual at the end of the day to peal the accumulated layers of pitch from our hands, arms and clothing.

Some of the more popular uses of tar on Long Island were probably as a component of axle grease and preservatives for wooden pipes, foundations and for fence posts. Despite the many uses for these products, because New England experienced a shortage of manpower and a limited number of the trees containing adequate resin, the difficult and demanding "industry" became dominated by the "turpentine farms" of North Carolina, where labor was cheaper and pine trees were more abundant.

With the expansion of his property and his enterprises that required manpower, there is little doubt Sam hired workers. One such occasion was on July 19, 1680, when the BTR says,

> These pressents testifieth that simon hallefax doth ingaege to sarue samuell daiton duly and truly six months with such work as the saide daiton shall sett him aboute the saide simons tieme to begin when his time is oute with John Tooker seny(er) which will be aboute the begining november or thereabouts and in concideration of the aboue saide samuell daiton doth ingag(e) to pay or cause to be paide the full and Just some of forty shille(n) pr month tell the full terme be oute to be paide in marchents pay or as thay shall agre.[572]

Nothing more can be found of Mr. Hallifax. Perhaps Sam may have found a possible source of cheap labor for these laborious tasks in men working to pay off debts. This is not to suggest anything negative in regard to Mr. Hallifax because he

---

[572] (Shaw, Records of the Town of Brookhaven 1679-1756 Book B 1932). 45

might also have been a manager for a crew of unfortunate men paying off their fines, having been sold as servants until earning the necessary funds. All of this is simply the compiler's conjecture. Theft was punishable firstly by fine, paying to the victim double damages for some items, or other penalty as the court saw fit for cattle and swine.[573]

Sam made an agreement with the same fellow, Simon Hallefax on February 22, 1680/81, to trade horses. Apparently neither of the men had physical possession of the horses since they were wandering loose. The record says, "Samuell daiton haue exchaing his mare he had of Ri(chard) hulse for a mare and a coult of Simon hallefax that (he) had of Johnathan horten that was John Roe both of the(m) to take them ReSeued as thay Run in the woods."

Samuel continued to buy land and expand his holding at South, west of Fire Place. On May 27, 1681, two acquisitions are recorded in the Brookhaven record,

> These pressents testifieth that andrew miller haue sould given grantted and allinated from him his hairer and asaigns a allottment of medow at the south at the west sied of the fire place creeke nomber 31 unto samuell daiton to his hairers and asaigns to haue and to hould for ever being part of allotment

> These pressents testifieth that Joeseph daves haue for himselue his haires and asaings given gratted bargened and sould unto samuell daiton of west hapton a pece of medow lying of the west siede of the Run or creke being the west sied of the fire place so comanly called the aboue saide Joseph daves doth sell allinate and make over to the aboue said samuell daiton to him his haires and asaigns for ever to haue and to hould for ever the medow being nomber 24[574]

In another purchase of land, on November 14 of that year, Sam again traded tar as currency.

> know all men by these pressents that I henery Rogers of brookhaven haue sould unto samuell daiton my fifteene aker lott and share of medow at the end of the saide lott both aJoyneing to mr wodhulls two lotts nomb 3 I say I the saide henery Rogers haue sould from me my haires eckseckators adminestrator or asaignes to him the saide samuell daiton his haires or asaigns to haue and to hould for ever with all prevedges that doe or ever hereafter shall belong to the saide lott or medow I doe alsoe ingage to make this my saele good in law against any parson or parsons that shall claime any Right or interest in the same and for the true parformence of

---

573 (Yale 1997)
574 (Shaw, Records of the Town of Brookhaven 1679-1756 Book B 1932). 74

the same I haue here unto sett to my hand the day and dat aboue written mark

        wittnes John Thomas John Roe   henery *M* Rogers

This bill biendeth me samull daiton to pay or cause to be paide to henery Rogers the Just some of 14 pound which some is to be paide in tarr at marchants price to be payd at or before this day twelfmonth and to be delivered at the fire place and to the true performens of the same I doe here vnto sett my hand" samuell daiton wittnes John Thomas John Roe

James Askum received land from Sam, providing Askum would remain there three years and improve the land. Our search for additional information on James Askum has been unsuccessful, leading us to believe he might have been somewhat transient, perhaps a worker for one of Sam's businesses, the trading, extraction or production of oil or tar. Since he is not found again, Askum probably did not satisfy the requirement, if indeed he ever accepted it. The July 5, 1681 entry says,

Samuell daiton haue frely given unto James Askum seven akers of land lying and beeing upon the left hand of bever pond goeing to Samuell daitons being over the brook I say that Samuell daiton haue for him selue his haires and asaignes frely given and allinated unto the aboue saide James Askum the aboue saide seven akers to him his haires and asaigs to haue and to hould for ever upon the condition that the saide James Askum shall forth with buld and Improue the saide land and liue upon it three yeares or othe wayes the land to Return to the fore said daiton[575]

Samuel dealt in tar again, as he bought additional acreage at South from Benjamin Smith for 15 barrels on June 2, 1682. Since Sam was buying "upland," it is assumed he was buying land to keep his horses or wooded acreage, perhaps pines from which to extract pitch to produce tar.

These pressents testifieth that benJemen smith haue for himselue his haires and asaigns haue given grantted bargened and sould his 15 aker lott and share of medow in the ould purchas at the south nomb 26 unto samuell daiton to him his haires and asaigns to haue and to hould for ever with out lett mollestation and in concideration of the aboue saide 15 akers of upland and share of medow the aboue saide samuell daiton doth ingaege to pay or cause to be paide the Just some of fifteene pounds to be paide in tarr being 15 barells to be paide at or before the 29 of sept next ensueing

---

[575] (Shaw, Records of the Town of Brookhaven 1679-1756 Book B 1932)

the date here of what tarr canot be Redy to send by the boets when thay come to the south the aboue said daiton is ingaeged to bring it to this to towne.[576]

In Defense of Honor

When reading the records of any of the early east end settlements on Long Island, the reader can find many accounts that allude to the value placed in defense of one's name. If a person perceived his or her reputation had been harmed, the town meeting or court was the venue equipped to clear one's name in front of all since attendance was often mandatory. Edson Dayton says, "The standards and the courts of that day were more strict and reached down into the daily conduct in a more exacting way than earlier on. Human nature was the same then as now. We of this day probably go further in condoning its lapses and excesses."[577] In a July 6, 1681 entry, Nathaniel Norton, once Sam's neighbor, claims to have been defamed by Hannah Hulse, one of the daughters of Elizabeth Beardsley, and sister of Mary, one of the two hiers to Joseph Beardsley's estate. One cannot help but wonder if an offense was actually meant or even implied, but an offense was perceived just the same, despite there being no witnesses. Whether or not the supposed offense was real, the view of Mr. Norton would negate Hannah's, and Mr. Norton would be satisfied with nothing less than a public apology. No other punishment resulted. It is interesting that the admission of defamation written for her referred to Sam as her father, even though she was already married. Does this indicate that the girls had lived with Sam and Elizabeth?

> whereas I Hannah Huls through inadvertanc and pasion defamed Nathaniell Norten of this Towne by saying he had stollen Indian Corn out of my fatther daiton's corn cribb these may surtifie all whome it may concern that I the saide hannah Huls never had any cause soe to say and that I never knew that the sayd nathaniel had ever stoele any Indian Corn from theare and, am hartely sory for my defaming of him nott knowing any cause soe to doe___As witness my hand in brookhaven this 5th day of June 1681[578]

---

[576] Ibid.

[577] (E. C. Dayton, The Record of a Family Descent from Ralph Dayton and Alice (Goldhatch) Tritton, Married June 1617, Ashford, County Kent, England 1931)

[578] (Shaw, Records of the Town of Brookhaven 1679-1756 Book B 1932)

250

Witness   Hannah Hulse
Richard Wodhull

The Dress

An entry from 1682 gives us a rather unusual glimpse into the culture and particularly the laws and legal system concerning property rights of women. William Williams, a merchant probably from Wenham, Massachusetts[579] who first appeared in the Setauket records April 2, 1677, had died and his widow Jane had married Jonathan Roe (Rose). Apparently someone had questioned whether the dress Jane wore for her wedding had belonged to her former husband's estate. The argument was that she, as wife, did not own her own clothes but instead, her clothing belonged to her husband. So, when her husband died, the clothing she "possessed" while married, was not hers but belonged to the estate, to be disposed of as the court ordered.

Sam, Joshua Snell and John Beswick were witnesses for Jane and Jonathan, testifying that the dress Jane wore for her wedding was furnished by her fiancé Jonathan Ro(s)e. In addition, two ladies that helped dress the bride also said Jonathan Roe provided the apparel.

> 28 maij 1682 the day aboue written Johnathan Roese was maried to the widow Jane williams by m[r] nathanell Bruster in brookehaven and by the wittnes of Severall parSons concerning the way of there mareg as followeth the wittnes of Samuel' daiton that he knew the cloething that the aboue Saide widow was maried in was of Johnathan Roese owne bying and finishing and that they was maried in the kings hy way and the said Rose denie medling of her astate John besweek doth wittnes the same that Samuel daiton doth wittnes m[r] Josua Snell doth wittnes that the aboue Saide two doth wittnes sarah the wife of John houltem and marae the wif of John wood doth wittnes that thay help to dress the aboue saide bried the widow Jane williams and thay wittnes thay se Johnath Rose giue her all her aparell she then putt on and saide moreover that he would not medle with anything that was formerly m[r] william williams nott aboute any goods.[580]

It is assumed that that was the end of the matter, but it does leave one to wonder if such a situation was a regular occurrence. Did the widow legally own any of her clothes or was this occasion an isolated incident?

---

[579] (W. &. Post 1910)
[580] (Shaw, Records of the Town of Brookhaven 1679-1756 Book B 1932)

251

Sam's acquisitions of meadow (and upland) in January 1685/86 helped to "fill in" and push his boundaries on the west side.

> 25 of Jenuery 1685 Joseph daves haue exchanged his medo at the South in the ould purchas nomber 27 which was formerly Robart Smiths with Samuell daiton for a lott of medow nomber 26 which was formerly benjemens Smiths and further the saide Joseph daves haue sould to samuell daiton two peesses of medow of the west siede of the brook nomber 25 and nomber 26 to each of them and there haire(s) for ever to haue and to hould with the uplan belonging to (it)

By 1686, the same year when the settlers received a patent from the Governor that fixed the name of the town of Brookhaven and established a representative form of government, Tashanisk appealed, "on behalfe of himselfe and other Indians," to Governor Thomas Dongan for proper and just compensation for those lands they called Unkechalk. In the 1670's, Samuel Dayton had moved there and was followed soon by others. The Native Americans had complained about Samuel's farm back in 1677 but this time, Tachanick had objected that the inhabitants of Brookhaven had built houses and broken up land without any satisfaction to him. On July 7, 1686 Samuel Terrell, along with Samuel Dayton, Jonathan Rose and Walter Jones, had to appear before the Governor General's Council regarding Tachanick's petition. Strong says that no record of the council's decision can be found after Richard Cornell, John Jackson and Daniel Whitehead were called to view the land, "but Brookhaven must have made things right with the Indians as Samuel and Samuel Dayton were undoubtedly still neighbours on 15 May 1688 when Samuel Terrill and his wife 'Abigaill' witnessed a deed in south Brookhaven for Samuel Dayton and his wife Elizabeth."[581] This would make one wonder if Brookhaven acted on behalf of Sam and, in return, Sam contributed a few of the 39 barrels of whale oil required as Brookhaven's payment for their new patent they were forced to buy, issued December 27, 1686.

It appears that Sam made efforts, just as his father had done, to lend support to his children in his lifetime, providing them with land and partial inheritances before his will was engaged. In this way, each would be set up with his or her own household and Samuel would insure that the younger sons/brothers would receive what he felt was just. Samuel also cared for his married daughter Sarah and her husband William Weatherby by giving them land at Occumbamacke, on the bay. BTR Book B says,

> Know all men by these presents that I Samuell Dayton dwelling within the bounds of Brookhaven in the County of Sullffolke doe by thes

---

[581] (Theodore, Samuel Terrill and Yamphank Neck 1686 Forward 2010)

252

presents give grant alienate & make over unto my son in law William Weatherby all my Right and Jnterest which J have in a Certaine parcell of land at Occumbamacke bounded westardly by John Munseys land Eastward by Zachary Hawkings Northerly by the Commons & southwardly by the sound or the bay Also a Piece of Meadow lying within the sd land which J bought of Jonathan Rose The which upland & meadow with all timber trees Jmmunities and appurtenances any ways belonging to the same J ye abovesd Samuell Dayton doe by thes presents freely & firmely Give grante alienate & make over unto the sd William Weatherby To him his Heires Executors Administrators and Assignes to Have and to Hold for ever Without any let hinderance or Molestation by me or mine laying any Claime to any parte of the same but to be to him & to his use for ever which J doe freely give unto him for parte of his Portion with my Daughter Sarah further if need require J doe promise to Asigne any ffirmer Deeds of Conveyance for the Ratifying & Confirming this my Deed of Gift To the true Confirmation hereof J doe set to my hand & fix my seale at Brookhaven south this 15th of May 1688

Signed sealed & Delivered

In presence of   Sam   } Dayton hands & Seales
                                        Elizabeth
                                                               O

          Sam   } Terrill
          Abigaill
Registered by me Tho: Helme

By this record, Sarah was already married to William Weatherby in May 1688 and because she is not mentioned in the document, she was not yet 21 and the land may have been a wedding present from her parents, as the couple began their new household. It would not be totally out of the question that Sam and Elizabeth, wanting to assure that Sarah and husband received her inheritance, encouraged the wedding before Sarah became 21.

Looking backward, this 1688 record contributes to the pool of circumstances that help to unravel the order of events in the complicated years between 1664 and 1670. To approximate Sarah's age, it is known that Thomas Beardsley had died March 29, 1667, so her mother Elizabeth was available for marriage in 1667. Sam and Mary Dingle applied for a marriage license in May 1666, and assuming they married, Mary may have died in childbirth as soon as the following year. If true, Mary and Thomas died roughly the same time. The fact that Elizabeth was already referred to as "good wife Daiton," in February of 1669/70 and Sam had legally assumed use of Elizabeth's daughters' horses implies that she and Sam were only recently married. This means that Elizabeth probably did not give birth to Sarah before fall of 1670.

So, because Sarah Dayton and William Weatherby were already married in May 1688, it is reasonable to say that Sarah was probably not yet 19.

Weatherby would hold the land for ten years before selling it to his father-in-law's friend and neighbor.

> William Weatherby sells to Jonathan Rose, A lot of meadow on the east side of the land of Jonathan Rose at a place called Occumbomack, and a piece of land near the same, formerly in possession of Samuel Dayton, my father-in-law, late of Brookhaven…April 11, 1699.

According to Jacobus, "There are several conveyances from Samuel's son-in-law William Weatherby for what may be pieces of the Neck, but the Town later re-granted a large part of the Neck to Elias Bayles."[582] While giving land to his married daughter and son-in-law would not have been unusual in the day, it may not have been the norm either, considering that Sam had so many sons. But Samuel did seem to be softening, as his health was probably failing with age. Less than a year before his death, Sam seems to express public sentiments unlike what has previously been found. From the following entry, it is also learned that Sam still owned beach land at Old Man's (modern Mt. Sinai). Records of this land will again be visited with subsequent generations.

> Know all men by thease presents that I Samuel Dayton of Brookehaven in the County of Suffolk on Long Island for and in regard of the fatherly love and naturall affection I have and beare to my son Isack Dayton of the sd Towne and County have given granted and by these presents doe frely fully and absolutely give and grant to my sd son Isack and his Heires for Ever halfe a right of Comonage for free feed for Creatures and for any DeVision that shall from time to time bee laide out to Have and to Hold the sd Comonage wth all the preVeledges proffits and Emoluments thereunto belonging Except what Jnterest I have or may have to any meadow or Crickthatch lying or adjoyning to the old mans beach or with in the Harbor on the Islands lying at the sd old mans: to the use and behoofe of the sd Isack & his Heires for Ever and I Doe heareby rattefy and Confirme the premises in as full and ample manner as if this writing weare made wth all the terms of law and art whatsoever Jn Confirmation wheareof I doe hereunto Set my hand and Seale this fivth day of September Anno Dom 1689

> Witnessed by Moses Owen and Thomas Helme   Samuel Dayton O

---

[582] (E. C. Dayton, The Record of a Family Descent from Ralph Dayton and Alice (Goldhatch) Tritton, Married June 1617, Ashford, County Kent, England 1931)

pr Tim Brewter Clerk

Isaac received additional acreage at Old Man's, after he was to pay his share of patent money to the town.

> Vpon a training day on May ye 27th 1690 Jt was agreed on by the majority of Votes that Jsack Dayton should have twenty acres of land layd out to him of unapropriated land wheare hee shall see convenient provided it bee not neerer the towne then ye old mans meddow and noe predgadice to high ways nor watering places this being the first grant to ye halfe lott men: it is alsoe thought convenient that 20 acres more which was the latter grant to ye halfe lot men apearing to bee his due provided hee pay the patent mony to ye towne: that ye abovesd lands bee laide out to ye abovesd Jsack Dayton at his request: pr Timothy Brewster[583]

Sam's Death and Will

Sam's will was written the day before he died, witnessed by Jonathan and Jane Rose, leaving his house and land on Dayton's Neck to his wife and daughters. Sam had wisely made it a point to set up each son while he was still alive, and then sought to provide for his wife and daughters, his "second family," who were both probably still under the age of 21. A portion of Sam's will is shown in figure 22, in the town record which is held at the Office of the Brookhaven Town Historian.

> To all Christian people whom thease may Concerne Samuel Dayton sendeth greeting Know yee that for the love good will & affection which I have and doe beare unto my wife Elizabeth and my two daughters web God gath given mee by her Viz Sarah and Elizabeth: I doe give unto them my now dwelling house wth all ye land & meddow thearunto belonging that is all that I have here upon this Neck which was layd out to mee wth the Swamp as also severall parcells web I have purchased all the abovesaide land & meddow know yee that I doe freely & absolutely give unto my wife Elizabeth wth all priveliges & apertenancyes any waise belonging to it to bee for her use for her maintenance Dureing her naturall life alsoe know yee that my Daughter Sarah and my Daughter Elizabeth that they may bee encouraged to bee loveing and helpfull to theire Mother after my decease I doe give unto them all the abovesaide land & meddow with all the priviliges and apurtenances any wayes belonging to the Same to them theire Heirs Executors administrators or asigns for Ever tto have and to hold without any hinderance or molestation from mee or any of

---

[583] (Shaw, Records of the Town of Brookhaven 1679-1756 Book B 1932)

mine but are to bee quietly posesed wth it after theire mothers decease and then it is to bee equally devided between them *two** and that is to bee theire portion to the Confirmation hereof I doe hereunto Set my hand and fix my Seale at my Now dwelling house in Brookhaven South this 4th of July in the yeare of owr lord God 1690

Jn presence of:

Jonathun (mark) Rose   Samuel ^M Dayton his
Jane (mark) Rose   mark and Seale   O

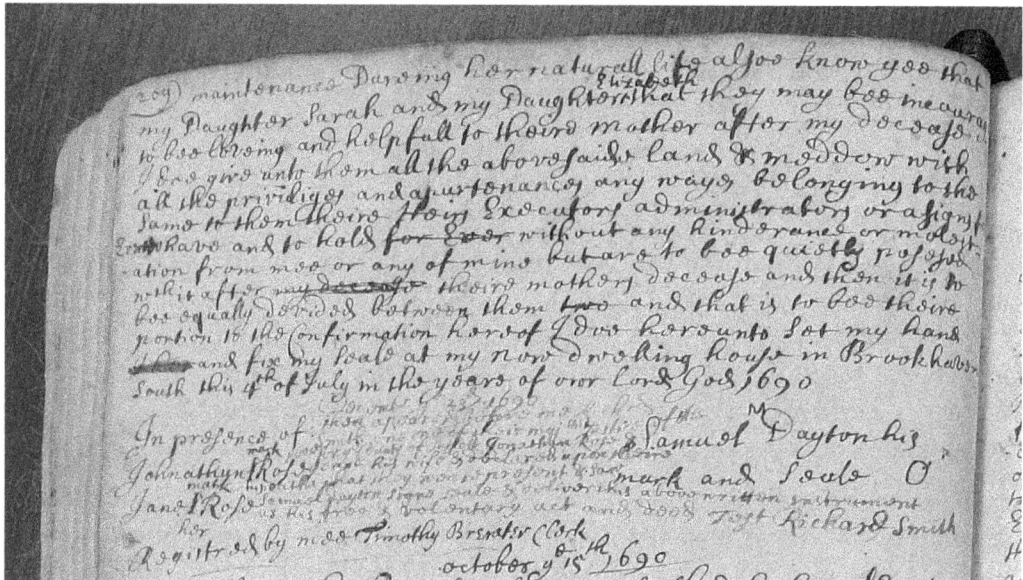

Figure 22. A portion of Sam's will

Brookhaven Town Historian's Office, Brookhaven Township Municipal Building

Sam died the very next day, on July 5, 1690 in Brookhaven, on his Neck at South, at age 66. He named no executor. Samuel Dayton had had at least three wives and at least eight biological children plus stepchildren. At the time of his death, his eldest child Ralph was about 41, followed by Abraham at about 37, and Isaac and Jacob, all by his first wife Medlin. In addition, he left two daughters, Sarah and Elizabeth, by his third wife, Elizabeth. Second son Samuel and sixth son Caleb had predeceased their father. Although Edson Carr Dayton[584] claims, without citation, "at

---

[584] (E. C. Dayton, The Record of a Family Descent from Ralph Dayton and Alice (Goldhatch) Tritton, Married June 1617, Ashford, County Kent, England 1931)

least ten: Samuel Jr., Ralph, Abraham, Isaac, Jacob, Caleb, Daniel, Robert, Sarah and Elizabeth," we, like Jacobus, found no evidence for Daniel and Robert as sons of Samuel. However, both of these names are contemporary to East Hampton. Robert, Sam's younger brother, had sons named Robert and Daniel. If Sam also had Robert and Daniel, they probably died in childhood.

December ye 23d-1690

...then apeared before me Richrd Smith one of their mgj^{stice} Justice of the Peace for ye County of Suffolk Jonathan Rose & Jeane his wife & declared upon theire oaths that they weare present & Saw Samuel dayton signe seale & deliver this above written instrument as his free & volentary act and deed Test Richard Smith[585]

With no executor named, Samuel's eldest son Ralph appealed to the Court to receive the power to administer the estate and this was granted to him:

By the Hono^{ble} *Col. William Smith* Judge of their Mat^{yes} Perogative Court within the County of Suffolk on Long Island in ye Province of N. York in America. To all whom these presents shall come Greeting Know ye that whereas *Samuel Dayton* late of *Brookhaven i*n ye County of Suffolk aboves^d Husbandman departed this life the fifth day of July Anno Dom 1690 leaving no Executor & *Ralph Dayton* ye eldest son of the deceased for certain causes him thereunto justly moving hath prayed that ye administration of the goods & chattels of ye s^d deceased may be granted unto him ye s^d *Ralph Dayton*—I therefore by virtue of ye power & authority to me given reposing special trust and confidence in you *Ralph Dayton* aboves^d have nominated constituted & appointed & and be these presents do constitute & appoint you *Ralph Dayton* aboves^d administrator of all and singular goods & chattels & credits of s^d *Samuel Dayton* deceased with full power to ask receive demand & recover all & singular ye goods chattels & credits whatsoever to ye deceased afores^d belonging or in anywise appertaining by all lawful ways and means whatsoever in the first place paying those debts whereby s^d deceased stood obliged in ye time of his death as far as ye lawful goods & credits of ye s^d deceased may to this Extend, you taking your oath truly to administer the same and to make or Cause to be made a true & perfect inventory of all & singular the goods & chattels debts rights & credits to ye s^d deceased belonging which shall or may come to your hands possession or knowledge & further to

---

[585] (Shaw, Records of the Town of Brookhaven 1679-1756 Book B 1932)

give a just & true account in & concerning the s^d administration before me or such Judge or Judges as may be thereunto appointed at or before the first day of June next ensuing the date hereof. Witness my hand & seal at Brookhaven this nineteen day of November Anno Dom 1691[586]

The location of Sam's grave is unknown but it was most certainly somewhere on or near Dayton's Neck, probably not far from the George Washington Lodge property. Though it is believed that none of Sam's sons settled at South after his death, three more generations in our direct line remained in Brookhaven Township.

It seems a little unfortunate that none of Sam's sons remained at Dayton's Neck after Sam's death but it can only be assumed that none of the sons shared Sam's love for the area or, at least, they saw more promise in the north. The sons must have made it known that they preferred to live north of the Great South Bay. The only exception may have been Isaac, but only for a time. In September of 1678, Sam gave Isaac a portion of land at the rear of his home lot, perhaps as a wedding present, but it is not certain to which home lot Sam was referring. On two occasions in 1684, Isaac bought property at Little Neck (near Seatuket) from John Weade, near his father.[587] Then, in April of 1688, Isaac's house was mentioned as being in New Town (near modern day East Setauket) and the following year, in September, just months before his father's death, Sam gave Isaac property at Old Man's beach. A bi-fold map illustrating "Isaac Dayton's land" on the extreme left-hand side in its "Long Chestnuts" section is found in Evelyn Meier's *The Wading River Pauguaconsuk* (Riverhead: Wading River Historical Society, 1955).

In February of 1676/77, when he was 22 years old, Abraham was granted land which was adjacent to his father and included road frontage. Since Abraham's brother, Samuel, was still alive in early 1677, it is not certain to which Samuel this entry refers. Brookhaven Book A, on January 24, says,

> Abraham Dayton had by Vote granted a Small piece of Swamp lying between the highway over against Samuel Daytons and So to Run as Thomas Ward Shall Stake it out leaving the whole bredth of the highway that comes from Mr. Norton that goeth over to Henry Rogers.

On November 3, 1680, Abraham recorded the purchase of a parcel of land, "at the poynt of gorges neck." Seventeen days later, his father gave him a house lot in New Town. These two transactions, in tandem, seem to indicate that Abraham has made a declaration that he was going to be a "northerner." All subsequent acquisitions were in the north, at Old Field, Old Mans and at West Meadow Beach (north of Stony Brook). His father gave Abraham his home in the north end of town

---

[586] (W. S. Pelletreau, Early Long Island Wills of Suffolk County, 1691-1703 With Genealogical and Historical Notes 1897)
[587] (W. J. Weeks 1930)

and it appears that Abraham stayed in the northern end and was active in the acquisition of land in the north.

Not much was said about eldest son Ralph's land dealings in the Brookhaven books. He drew many lots in the Town drawings, but appears to have lived somewhere near Old Field. According to Beverly Tyler, the first recorded deed to a house in Old Field was not until in 1725. In 1683, Ralph sold fifteen acres in Georges Neck and in 1684, Ralph rented a five acre lot in little neck for 3 years.

As an adult, Jacob, who had lived with the Bakers, appeared several times in East Hampton records and then apparently removed to Cape May, New Jersey. Likewise, Caleb who had also been bound out, had little to do with Brookhaven as an adult, despite his father's gift of twenty acres there, from Sam's last allotment. Instead, he took up residence in Southampton.

When Sam gave the 20 acres of land to his youngest son Caleb, and recorded it on November 5, 1685,[588] Caleb was about 26 years old, five years free of the Jessups. It is supposed that, even before 1681, Sam referred to his neck as "West Hampton," but the name largely disappeared after just a few years.

> These pressents testifieth that Samuell daiton of west hampton in the bounds of brookhaven haue freely given and bequethed unto his sonn Calleb daiton the twenty akers of land that did belong to his a lottment the last devission this he haue given to the Said Calleb daiton to him his haires and aSaigns to haue and to hould for ever to his owne disposing.

Caleb's removal to Southampton and his early passing of unknown cause, at about 29, came two years before his father's death. An inventory of Caleb's estate was taken Oct 8, 1688, appraised by John Howell Junior and Joseph Peirson [sp], with Jacob as his executor. The inventory, valued at just £15-14d-2s, includes a writing book and irons (presumed to be whaling irons) and can be found in the Suffolk County Deed Book A-33. One wonders if there was a special bond between Caleb and Jacob, even though they had been separated as children.

In Sam's later life, it seems he was able to find greater peace and contentment within himself and he may have attempted to bring his family back together as adults. One gets the impression that Sam desired the best for all his boys, but he respected their independence. Perhaps he saw some of his own restless soul in them.

By February 24, 1714, the land at South, from Dayton's Neck all the way to the east side of Tarmen's Neck that had been granted by the town to Samuel Dayton, was possessed by Elias Bayles, upon his request.[589] Even as late as 1733, when more

---

[588] Ibid.
[589] (Brookhaven Town Clerk, BTR 1880)

divisions were laid out at South, town records still referred to Dayton's Crick (later called Osbornes's Creek)[590] and Dayton's swamp.

---

[590] (W. S. Pelletreau, A History of Long Island From Its Earliest Settlement to the Present Time 1905)

Chapter 15

Abraham, Dealer in Oyl

Abraham, our sixth great-grandfather, was born to Samuel and Medlin before 1655, while the family lived at North Sea (Southampton), and he died sometime after June of 1726 and was probably laid to rest somewhere near Setauket, Long Island. Abraham was the third of six sons and his naming began the patriarchal order of brothers Isaac and Jacob. Abraham was only the third Dayton male to be born in America, after his brothers Ralph and Samuel, for Abraham's uncle Robert had not yet had a son.

The first reference to Abraham is found in 1675, shortly after he reached majority and just before his father moved permanently from Setauket to "South," to be close to the Great South Bay. During much of Abraham's youth, it seems his father was traveling between harbors around Long Island and beyond, while his family called North Sea, Oyster Bay and Setauket home. Before Abraham was twelve years old, his mother had died and his younger brothers were "given" to apprenticeships outside the home. Probably by the time Abraham was thirteen or fourteen, his father had married again and then his stepmother had died. It wasn't until Abraham was about eighteen years of age, after his father had married for at least the third time, that Sam was establishing roots that would ground him in Brookhaven. Abraham probably worked alongside his older brothers and father farming their properties around Setauket and dealing in whale products and perhaps tar at South.

As a legal adult in 1675, Abraham appeared on the Brookhaven rate list on May 18th. The town record also had Abraham Dayton and Thomas Beardsley selling 16 (or 18, depending on the translation) barrels of whale oil, "lying on the South Side of the Island at a place commonly called the fire place." One version of the record says,

> Know all men by these presents that we *** and Abraham daiton for divers good causses *** mouing but more aspessially for a sartain *** hand doe here by bargen sell and haue her by *** sould and allinatedall our Right ti(tle) and * in sixteene barrels of oyle on the Sou** Island at a place comanly called the fi(re)* due by these pressents for ever quit claime (any) title or interest in aforesaid oyle but shall warrent that our bill of sale to stand good against a(ny) in law that shall pretend any Right

to the same in Confermation of which have here vnto set our hands this aighteene of may 1675.[591]

brookhaven   Thomas Beardsley
Signed sealed and delivered   Abra daiton
In the pressens of vs   with two seals
Nickoles chatwell
Richard Southcutt

Nicholas Chatwell and Richard Southcotte appear to be the other party in the transaction. They were both mariners, from Salem and Boston, trading in the West Indies in the same year as the great slave insurrection occurring there. The presumption is the two men paid in currency, already in hand, but because the tattered receipt is incomplete, other theories also exist. Most realistically, the words "haue her by" were actually meant to be "have hereby." There exist various records for descendants of both captains and their vessels, a Richard Southcott leaving for Antigua in 1723 and yet probably a third generation of Richard Southcotts, captain of the William and Mary sailing to Barbados in 1763.

Less than two weeks before Beardsley and Dayton's exchange with Chatwell and Southcott, the town voted to grant the Massachusetts traders each some upland and five acres of meadow in the "Great Fly" at Fire Place on the condition they occupy the land before Christmas. This proposal occurred or was recorded on May 5, 1675. Shaw says they probably didn't accept the land under these conditions, as their names do not appear again.[592] It is possible the town was interested in fully occupying and developing their interests at South and suggested that the mariners establish an active coastal trade there.

The use of the word "Fly," as it appears in the land grant, is an English adaptation of Vlaie, an Old Dutch word, according to Osborne Shaw. The term, meaning *a low marsh piece of ground*, still survives today and the compilers have heard it used among woodsmen and "old timers" in the Adirondacks, usually referring to low swampy areas, often between mountains. The reference to Fire Place in the exchange of whale oil (one of the partial words contained in the Beardsley/Dayton document), was perhaps only the second time it was used in town records, the first time being a few months earlier, when Sam acquired the meadow share of Francis Muncy.

A short time later, both Sam and Abraham appear on the Brookhaven tax list of 1675, and again both are present in the 1683 rates.[593] The Samuel listed on both tables was Abraham's father because he already had 11 lots in 1675 and Samuel Junior had drowned before the 1683 assessment. The tables also contain other curiosities. Might

---

[591] (A. C. Weeks 1924)
[592] (Shaw, History of Brookhaven Village October 5, 1933)
[593] (O'Callaghan, The Documentary History of the State of New-York : arranged under direction of the Hon. Christopher Morgan, secretary of State 1849)

262

it be surmised that Abraham's interest in horses was acquired from his father? Perhaps they were using the horses to haul goods across the island or the men might have been small-time breeders or renters of horses, since there was always great demand for the suitably bred in the colonies and at Barbados.

Methodical analyses of relative wealth, based on livestock valuations for 1675 and 1683, were undertaken in an attempt to gain comparisons to fellow townsmen. In 1701, Brookhaven County Rates were devised by a different method causing those to be less comparable to the previous two rates, but relatively comparable to others in that same year.

On September 22, 1675, Suffolk County established a tax valuation for each species of livestock. For example, a four year old or older horse had the highest value of the livestock, worth £12 and by contrast, an ox or bull was worth £6, and a sheep at one-third of a pound. At the young age of 21, Abraham may have already had a livery service, horse rental business or he might have even been a breeder of horses. If that was the case, his father most likely set him up in the business. Like most farmers in Brookhaven, Abraham also had a team of oxen, which very often were purchased together to learn the yoke.

A valuation for the contry parte of Brookhaven in the yere of our Lord God 1675[594]

	Heads	Oxen	Cows	1 yere	2 yere	3 yere	Horses	Swine	Meadow lands	Val
Saml Daiton	2		5	2		3	2	5	11	1-17-0
Abr Daiton	1	2	2				5	1	3	1-04-0

By 1683 valuations, Sam had moved up slightly from a ranking of 14th (of about 30 townsmen) to 11th place or £111 total value by livestock for tax purposes. Some adjustment had taken place with Abraham as it appears he was shifting assets, dropping to 23rd out of 52 or £66 at the 56th percentile of all. He retained his team but had gone from five to three horses. It appears that by 1681 Abraham was either investing elsewhere or he had experienced some difficulty in his business and had defaulted to whaling for a season, in an attempt to supplement or recover.

Valuacon of the Ratable Estate Belonging to Brookhaven Anno 1683[595]

	Heads	Lands and Meadow	Horses	Oxen and Bulls	Cowes	3 yeres old	Yearlings	Sheep	Swine
Samll Dayton	1	6	5	2	4	1	1	0	8
Abra Dayton	2	4	3	2	2				4

Our belief is that Sam had been continuing to transfer lots and livestock to his sons, beginning with eldest son Ralph in about 1670, as each consecutive son reached legal age. This belief is not disproven by the reduction in the number of "lands and

---

[594] Ibid., 1675: 468-9, 1683: 532-4
[595] (Christoph 1993). 286-7

meadows" reported for Sam between 1675 and 1683, while at the same time, he was acquiring additional lots. Few of these supposed transfers have been identified until fourth son Isaac received, "a piece of land that is at the rear of his home lot" in September of 1678. Whether or not the transfer records ever existed, the lack of records may indicate that Samuel felt that the transfers were secure as he did not see the need to confirm them in his will as his grandson Henry would do in his will more than seventy years later. In addition, this could also indicate that Samuel didn't feel the need to "control" his sons with the promise of land, as was so common in that day (see the Joseph Beardsley example).

Living on Long Island had assured Sam and his family's involvement in whaling since lookout, squadron duty and other whale processing tasks were compulsory. Whaling and whaling products touched most everyone in some way, exposing the boys at a young age. At the time of his mother's death, Abraham's age meant he could take care of himself without being a burden in addition to doing chores around the farm and in the house garden, and was big enough to help his father much like an apprentice, and it is assumed that is what he did. Abraham could also have apprenticed somewhere close by, perhaps as a carpenter, or overland hauler and transporter, perhaps preventing benefits from any formal or informal education.

But, as was true with the majority of men, women and children living in East Hampton, Southampton, and in Brookhaven, particularly from 1640 to the 1680s, Dayton families were both interested and involved with whaling. So, in that context, the statement found many places on the internet that Abraham *continued the family interest* in whaling is true. "Small groups of men partnered with one another, pooled their resources, and launched whaling companies."[596] If Abraham was possessed with sufficient courage and endurance in his later teen years, he would have opportunities to earn appreciable amounts of money on a whaleboat. To quote Rattray, "Most of the whalemen were young, and they needed to be." The companion statement of proof that is usually offered to support the idea of Abraham's continuing the family business is the reference to the sixteen or eighteen barrels of whale oil sold at "the fire place." But is that passage really sufficient proof?

It is interesting to note that Samuel[597] and Abraham not only sold and bartered oil, but also received oil in barter with bone and tar, as trading was common in those days since currency was scare. We asked Barbara Russell, Brookhaven Town Historian, if it would be safe to assume anything about Abraham's occupation from

---

[596] (Dolon 2007)

[597] Note: Another Samuel Dayton appears quite often in the East Hampton and Brookhaven records, born in 1666, the grandson of Ralph, Robert's son. Generally speaking, the early Daytons are known for repeated use of names generationally. Other Ralphs, Henrys and Davids also begin to appear around Brookhaven at this time. The compilers focused on direct ancestors in our published research. Relatives are mentioned occassionally, but where this occurred, appropriate relation of the kinsman were given.

the fact that he traded large quantities of oil. She indicated the amount would imply that the trader was a, "professional—a handler of oil and not a layperson. Such a large quantity of oil supply would have been from a commercial enterprise—not from a farmer or other non-tradesman. Commercial, meaning someone who probably employed others to engage in the whaling business, where the bone and oil were lucrative."[598] Not stopping there, we suggest that it is reasonable to conclude that such quantities of oil and whale products would require a storage facility in close proximity to the water.

The following entry in the record at Brookhaven is but one of many references that connect Daytons to whaling on Long Island. Included in the passages that contain evidence, perhaps the most explicit archive taken from Brookhaven Book B is the statement by a Native American who was committing to go to sea in Abraham's company:

> These pressents ingaegeth me sequenankquos otherwayes knowne by the name Roben Indgen doth ingaege to goe to sea the next season for William Tomson in Abrams daitons company to goe a half share[599] man the aboue saide william Tomson fiending boets and craft for the de Saigne to begin this seasson when they see cause and the saide Roben to begin and end at the same time as others doe and to be liab'le to all orders that shall be made and to the truth of the same I sett to my hand ths 12 of Agust 1685.

There are a variety of ways to interpret what is meant by, "goe to sea the next season for William Tomson." We are inclined to favor the interpretation that William Tomson, who was bound to go the next season, was buying a substitute to "go a-whaling" in his place. Typically, this might cost him his share of oil as well as possible penalties (many times dependent on the worth of his craft or occupation), but the record does provide an example of other means for Abraham and Thomas Beardsley's acquisition of quantities of oil or bone.

In addition to the "Abrams daitons company" reference above, there exists an abundance of related and circumstantial evidence scattered throughout Town Records, particularly in Southampton and Brookhaven, where Daytons strategically positioned themselves near the coast. Despite initial skepticism to the contrary, there is sufficient evidence found to warrant the claim of an Abraham Dayton company, and we conclude that Dayton commercial whaling, although probably not sustained beyond Abraham, need not be questioned. In addition, it is very possible that Sam had built a small storage facility slightly upriver, near where he docked his boats, on Dayton's Creek (or Beaverdam Creek).

---

[598] (Russell 2014)
[599] (Breen 1996). 171

The Thomas Beardsley who, with Abraham, sold the quantity of whale oil in 1675, should not be confused with the first husband of Abraham's step-mother, Thomas Beardsley who died in 1667 or 1668. It is likely he was a son of Elizabeth and Thomas Beardsley, but this is not certain as there are other Thomas Beardsleys (with various spellings) and there seems to be no consensus about various Beardsley family members at this time, even among their descendants.[600]

Whatever Abraham's marital status was at the time, it is observed by way of the August 1679 sale of Robert Goulsberry's house and home lot, that twenty-four or twenty-five year old Abraham had a newly-constructed house. As part of the agreement between Richard Hulse and Robert Goulsberry, BTR Book B says Hulse was to build a house for Goulsberry that would be a duplicate of his own, except it was to be a foot longer and wider. Materials for the house were to be delivered near "Abraham Dayton's new house."

> BenJemen gould haue Sould unto Richard hulse his hous and land that is with in fence that he had of Thomas highum with the orchard. and fences belonging to it and this for concideration him moueing this is for and in concideration of twenty flue pounds to be paide as followeth that the sayd Richard hulse doth deliver him a frame of a house with clapbords and shingles that is to say one thossand shingles and flue hundred clapbords with 25$^£$ waight of nailes to Reckon them as the said hulse pay for them onely the say(d) hulse is to haue fifty nailes out of them for doeing of the end of his chimny and the clapbords and shingle to be delivered by the 10 day of Sept next hard by abram daitons nue house and the Sayd gould is to alow 12^S for bringing them there the pay to be pay for the aboue sayde house and land as followeth

In the course of our study, we had become conditioned to believe that men married almost as soon as they turned 21. But with the lack of any record to the contrary, it appears that Abraham may not have married until he was in his mid to late 20's.

If Abraham hadn't been married earlier, we may have discovered why.

Mary Beardsley

When Abraham's father married Elizabeth Harvey Beardsley by 1669, she already had two daughters, Hannah and Mary. Elizabeth was about 34 years of age and it is likely she had given birth to Hannah about 1658 and Mary about 1660. If Sam allowed the girls to remain under the care of their mother, fifteen year old Abraham had a few years to become well acquainted with his nine year old stepsister

---

[600] (Beardsley 1902)

Mary before he moved out of the house. Sometime between eight to thirteen years later she would become his wife. It is easy to let the imagination create the way the events played out. If Mary was Abraham's first wife,[601] and she likely was, his waiting for her to "grow up" might explain why Abraham was as old as 28 before marriage, an age quite unlike any other Dayton male in our study, excepting Ralph back in Ashford, England. In this scenario, the estimate for setting a marriage date comes from a record of an inheritance received by the couple in 1684. Since they had probably developed an interest in each other, Abraham had prepared his new house by the time he was 25, still waiting for Mary. Of course, this is the romantic view that some cynics might scoff at, if they take the view that Abraham had lost his first wife and had married Mary when he learned that she could gain an inheritance when their benefactor died unexpectedly.

If Mary was Abraham's first wife, he was far from idle in the years leading up to their marriage. The assumption that Abraham would be at sea every whaling season, it turns out, was not true. It was surprising and a bit puzzling to find the town record of January 10, 1676/77 conveying Abraham's agreement to take on a large fencing project at such a time of profit and adventure for young men in the seasonal peak for Long Island whaling. This was one or two years after Abraham had sold the quantity of whale oil. The fence was to surround William Jayne's 6 acre home lot that was probably the one laid out to him July 14, 1676, after moving to Long Island from Connecticut and then marrying Ann Biggs. The record says:

> Abraham Dayton does engage to fence William Jayne's 6 acre lot that was given to him by the town with a sufficient 5-rail fence around about it, and to stub it, clear the brush fit for plowing, trees all excepted. This to be done by this and the last day of April next ensuing the date hereof. And in consideration of the same, the said William Jayne does pay him for the money in hand, the whole being 8 pounds in the whole; four pounds in hand in trucking cloth, being four yards, and the other four pounds ** by the last of April next ensuing (current pay to the merchant).

Though vertical plank fences were preferred by Pilgrims, the Puritans on Long Island often constructed split rail fences, in this case consisting of five-rail sections.

---

[601] Note: There exists a theory that Abraham was married previously and already had two sons named Abraham and Jacob but conclusive evidence of neither son can be found. Jacobus mentions the possibility that "Abraham and Jacob Dayton of Salem County, NJ, may have been older sons of Abraham Dayton of Brookhaven." There is ample time for this theory to work as Abraham could have married the unknown wife after 1674 and had the two sons between 1676 and 1684. According to Jacobus, Jacob died intestate in 1742 leaving Widow Ann while Abraham died testate in 1745, leaving his property to Hannah Graves.

Split rail fences did not keep small animals out but restricted the movements of larger animals which could otherwise cause damage and consume pasture. Actually, splitting logs in winter is preferable, as the frost inside the log made splitting quicker by requiring less effort. Once the rails were split and piled, the actual construction and any digging would occur after snow and frost melted.

Perhaps Abraham hadn't gone to sea for the winter because he had just married or, if he was waiting for Mary, she could have been uncomfortable with Abraham going to sea, due to the inherent danger of off-shore whaling, as injury to life and limb was not uncommon. Could it be that Abraham's partner Thomas Beardsley was injured or even killed while whaling and Abraham had already cheated death?

One such concern was recorded in the 1660/61 will of a William Beardsley of Stratford to his son Joseph:[602]

> If Joseph, my sone, please to be an assistant to my wife, for the carrying on of her b--- while she lives, or marries and leaves the sea, I give to him the halfe of my acomodations in Stratford; if not I give him twenty pounds of my share of y--- bark, to add to his part.[603]

According to Isaac Beardsley in *Genealogy Beardsley-Lee Family in America*, William's son Joseph not only left the sea but he resided in Brookhaven and married Abigail Dayton there in 1665. The author provided no citation for this claim and no record of an Abigail Dayton at this time and place has been located, much less on Long Island. In order to be of marriageable age, this Abigail would have had to belong to Samuel's generation, another daughter of Ralph the immigrant, born to the Daytons when Ralph was at New Haven. This claim supports the theory that Ralph had an additional wife between Alice Goldhatch Tritton and Mary Haines, a Dorothy Brewster, who bore this child in 1650. However, no basis has been found for the existence of anyone named Abigail Dayton in the 1650s or 1660s, much less the existence of a wife Dorothy Brewster for Ralph. It is believed Ralph named all his children who were in America in his will and Abigail does not appear.

Another enticement for Abraham to stay on land might have been the continued need for both skilled workers and common laborers on Long Island, as the towns grew and new settlements developed, workers could demand a respectable wage without wandering off on adventures. In order to combat the lack of laborers, New Englanders (most Long Islanders on the east end still identified with New England) were forced to develop a range of skills to protect themselves from hiring others to perform assorted tasks at these high wages. The resulting sense of independence and self-sufficiency became a way of life for generations and New England ingenuity became a celebrated attribute in family legend and a source of pride well into the twentieth century.

---

[602] Note: Joseph's relationship to Elizabeth and Mary was not researched and is unknown.
[603] (Beardsley 1902)

But, for whatever reason, Abraham was developing his interests near the sound, preferring to set up his house there and away from the ocean, at the same time his father was moving his interests from the north to the south, toward the ocean. As discussed at the end of Chapter 14, Abraham was granted land in early 1676/77 which was adjacent to Samuel's and included road frontage. It is not difficult to assume, from the wording of this BTR entry, that Abraham had been earlier living on land that legally was still in his father's name but was intended to become his own. Perhaps attaining this "piece of swamp" was to compliment properties acquired by him close by.

On September 22, 1678, it was recorded that, "William Williams has exchanged that two acres and a quarter that he had of Joseph Davis and two acres and a half that he had of Abraham Dayton that is in the Old Field—the Scotch man on the east side and Thomas Biggs on the west—for land of Joseph Davis."[604] Perhaps Abraham had also acquired parts of his property at Old Field from his father, Sam having earlier rented multiple lots there beginning around 1665. Williams had once been Samuel Dayton's neighbor, so Abraham's land had probably once belonged to his father.

On March 1, 1679/80, Abraham and his oldest brother Ralph both received lots when 15 acre divisions were laid out by the town at George's Neck. The location of George's Neck was given to us by John H. Innes who said, "down at the harbor in 1662 George Wood builds his 'ordinary' apart from the village, and on a special grant of land from the town which doubtless gave rise to the term of Georges Neck."[605] Beverly Tyler says, "This neck of land sticking out into Setauket Harbor was mentioned in Town records numerous times including March 9, 1685 when town records defined Georges Neck, the area that is now Poquott, as bordering Dyers Neck, on the west side of Georges Neck, from Scott's Creek south."[606] Abraham received Lot #4 and Ralph Lot #2 as recorded.

> the lotts that was layde out in gorges neck or there abouts march 1 (1679) Thomas generss was the 1 lott 15 akers mor or less Ralfe daiton the 2 John Smith the 3 Abram daito 4 John benett 5 anthony Tom Son the : 6 : John bigs the 7 nathanell norten the 8 John mosure the 9 Richard hulse 10 william williams 11 John geners 12 the all aboue layd out for 15 akers more or lese a pece then there was layd out twenty akers for mr bruster by the siede number 13 there was layde oute to Robart kellam fifteen akers more or les the front butting vpon the hy way that Runs by floyds swamp est ward as by marks it doth apeare and soe Runs to the siede of mr brusters cloese home to that liene there was layd out to benJemen gould

---

[604] (Barstow, Setauket, Alias Brookhaven 2004)
[605] (Innes 1935)
[606] (Tyler, History Close at Hand-Three Village/Brookhaven-Chronology 2014)

15 akers buting vpon the foresiede hyway and soe Runing to mr busters liene as doth apeare by the bounds.[607]

In another BTR,

June 14, 1680 Abram daiton haue Sould the part of that which Robart Smith six aker lott unto Robart gouldsbery all that is below the path or hy way all that planting land and the medow at the end of it for and in concideration the said Robart goulsbery doth pay unto abram daiton the two steers that he had of beJemen Smith and a thre aker lott that he had of samuell fancy that Joyned to good man daitons swamp lott at nue towne.

In a July 30, 1680 transaction between Thomas Biggs and Robert Goulsberry, Abraham's former property at Old Field was again mentioned.

Thomas Bigs senyer haue exchanged his fifty aker lott that lyeth at the ould mans number 11 with Robart goulsbery lese or more for fower akers in the ould feeld that was Robart smiths that is to say lying the lower siede of the path that Runs in the ould feeld lying nor(th) est from the by way and soe to the watter siede with medow and all that he bought of Abram daiton

Judging from the record, it is apparent that Robert Kellam really wanted what must have been a special horse belonging to Abraham, perhaps to use for breeding. Kellam was a cordwinder of Huntington, NY, a former resident of Brookhaven, who was quite active buying and selling land at this time. The town recorded a transaction on September 16, 1680 after Abraham traded his horse with Robert Kellam for another horse, two barrels of whale oil, a pair of good shoes (to fit Abraham), a horse bridle and reins—all "delivered to the beach" on or before May 5th.

Abram daiton haue exchanged his horse that he haid of IoeSeph Tooker branded of the neere butteck with I[J] T with Robert kellam for a horse that was william Sallyers and the-saids Robart kellam is to pay to boote[608] two barells of good marchantab(le) barells of oyle at the beacH and a paire of good frech full shoose that shall fitt the Sayd abraham and a paire (of bri)dle Raines: withe a hed staele* to be delivered all the bea(ch) att or before the feit of may next ensueing the date h(ereof)[609]

Huntington, NY is about 30 miles by boat from Old Mans, so the referenced beach was the convenient location for the exchange. Assuming all elements of the

---

[607] (Shaw, Records of the Town of Brookhaven 1679-1756 Book B 1932)
[608] Note: "To boot" in Old English meant "a making better." Today, it is used much as "moreover" or "on top of that."
[609] (Shaw, Records of the Town of Brookhaven 1679-1756 Book B 1932)

lop-sided trade were disclosed in the record, it is deduced from the details that Abraham's horse was of much higher value than Kellam's horse.

This exchange marks only the second time in our study that we have come across our Dayton ancestors transferring shoes or boots in trade. In both instances, Dayton's were receiving the shoes. This is significant because the initial expectation was to find many transactions that included bartered shoes since it is generally claimed that Dayton shoemaking, in our line, extended forward to Abraham's father. It is amusing to ponder the possibility that these new shoes could have been intended for Abraham's wedding to Mary because it reminds us of the story told about our great grandfather Charles Dayton who hurried barefoot "crosslots" to church, carrying his new shoes, so they wouldn't get scuffed in his rush to get there. According to the story, he stubbed his toe on something like a tree root and it was bleeding a bit by the time he arrived at church. His bloody foot being quite obvious, he said "boy, am I lucky." Somebody asked, "what do you mean, lucky?" He responded "Well, it's a good thing I didn't have my new shoes on."[610]

About 1681, John Inians, a wealthy landowner with interests along the northern shore of Long Island, was moving to purchase large tracts of land along the Raritan River, west of New York City, approximately where the city of New Brunswick, New Jersey would later be built. In conjunction with the New Jersey purchases, Inians, referred to as a merchant of New York City, began buying deeds around Setauket through agents on Long Island, providing loans to many men in that area, Richard Hulse and Abraham Dayton among them. Abraham, who called himself a Brookhaven planter, may have had problems repaying the original loan and still owed £6 8s to Inians so he granted his 15 acre lot at George's Neck (lot #1 that was formerly Thomas Jenners) to Inians in mortgage against the debt. In return, Inians agreed that if Abraham repaid in whale oil and whale bone at his terms, delivered at the common landing place at South before April 15, the deed would be void (if it means anything, there was no wife mentioned in the agreement).

> whereas there is a somm of six pounds aight shillens due unto John Inians of the sitty of new yourk marcht which saide some by these pressents I doe acknoledg doth yett Remaine unpaide Therefore Know all men by these pressents that I Abraham daiton of brookhaven in the est Rieding of yourkshere upon long Island planter haue bargened and sould and doe by these pressents grant bargen and sell allien asaigne and Sett over unto the afore saide John Inians all my fifteen aker lott of land lying upon gorg his neck being nomber one and which formerly belonging to Thomas Jeners to haue and to hould the afore saide lott of land together with all the preveldges and apurtenanses there unto belonging or in any wayes apertaining to him the saide John Inians his haires eckseckators administrators or asaigns for ever without the lest hinderence of me the

---

[610] (C. Dayton 1999)

saide Abraham daiton my haires exseckators Adminestrators provided and it is Herby agreed that if I the saide Abram daiton my haires eckseckators adminestrators or asaigns shall well and truly pay or cause to be paide unto the saide John Inians his haires eckseckators Adminestrators or asaigns the full and Just aforesaide sum of six pounds aight shillens at or before the fifteene day of Aperell next ensueing the date here of in good marchentable whale oyle in nue thiete cask at therty flue shillens par barell and good marchentable whalebone at aight pence Pr pound and delivered at the coman landing place upon the south beach without fraud or delay: that then this deede to be voyde and of no efeck other wayes to stand in full forse and vertue as full and as ferm and cleare as if this deed had bene maede with all the terms of art and law as deede or morgege whatsoever in wittnes whereof I the saide Abraham daiton haue here unto sett my hand and scale at brookhaven the 26th day of maij in the 34th yeare of his magestys[611]

the mark of

Raigne anno domie 1682   Abraham A daiton with a seale
saigned sealled and delivered in the
presens of Thomas Bigs Junior Andrew gibb
know all men by these pressents that within menchoned Abraham daiton doe confese a Judgment for the within written morgege as witnes my hand at brookhaven 26th of may 1682

wittnes Thomas bigs Junor Andrew gibb   Abraham A daiton

Abraham and Inians agreed to set the value of whale oil at 35s per barrel and whale bone at 8p per pound, delivered at the common landing place. Even though prices of oil and bone fluctuated, the agreement suggests that Abraham's whale oil and bone were deeply discounted. In a manner of speaking, Inians had Abraham, "over a barrel."

As stated, the oil and bone were to be delivered to the common landing place at the south beach. Of course this was the likely location for storage of oil upon rendering and was possibly the place where Abraham's father was operating a small "warehouse." Is it possible that Samuel might provide the balance of the promised goods, should Abraham fall short on production or acquisition that year? With this agreement, it is surmised that Abraham became more active with whaling again.

---

[611] (Shaw, Records of the Town of Brookhaven 1679-1756 Book B 1932)

Competition among whaling companies was fierce, for both whales and good whaleboat crews. In 1682, Andrew Gibb, who had organized a whaling company in Brookhaven, was then competing with companies at Southampton and East Hampton for the seasonal services of skilled Unkechaug whalers. Gibb hired a crew that included John Indian, Jeremy (aka Washaram, Waseramus), Goodger, Chesen, Patiqua, Gover, Wopsha (Miller), and Jacob Indian (STR, book D; BTR Book B).[612]

As with many competitive whaling enterprises on Long Island, Abraham also hired Native Americans, perhaps as harpooners or steermen, as some became especially skillful at the work. Two such records were listed together, on the same date, August 7, 1684. Both Samuel Seward and Abraham hired Native Americans in anticipation of the upcoming whaling season.

> Jacob Ingen doth ingaege to sea to kill whale fish this next seson after the date here of for samuell seward being a halfe share man and the saide samuell is to fiend all boets and craft and the saide Jacob to begin and continue the season tell his master freess him.

> Japhat Ingen doth ingaege to goe to sea the next season after the date herof for Abram daiton being a half share man and to begin and end as the major part doth the saide Abram fiending all tackling fitt for the desaigne[613]

Both Jacob and Japhat Ingen were contracted half-share men, indicating that they were quite valuable crewmen. In order to recruit such men, it was common to, "promise higher pay through shares of profits." As this practice continued into the eighteenth century, "whalemen were capped at a half-share, around a thirty-second part of the voyage's yield," a full-share being one sixteenth.[614] Abraham also agreed to provide "all tackling" for the venture, which probably included long, sturdy ropes and harpoons, and possibly pulleys, blocks and even chains. The next year, Roben Indgen was engaged in Abraham's company, as has already been mentioned.

Not only were the prospects of wealth tempting for whale fishing on the ocean coast of Long Island, but increasingly for New Jersey, as this was about the time the great exodus of eastern Long Island men to Cape May and the Egg Harbors began. Long Island whalers had long been making seasonal trips to New Jersey but it is said that whaling was particularly productive at this time, even after towing their catch back to Long Island for processing. No evidence of Abraham's involvement has been found but his younger brother Jacob, who was brought up in East Hampton with the Bakers, was very much involved with whaling in New Jersey and even registered his cattle mark in Cape May County in 1694.[615] Other men besides whalers were also following the trade to New Jersey, in part-time or ancillary seasonal occupations that surrounded and followed the whaling industry. Eventually, New Jersey taxes on the

---

[612] (J. A. Strong 2011)
[613] (W. J. Weeks 1930)
[614] (Stewart 2010)
[615] (Stevens 1897)

profitable venture for Long Islanders not living there made it necessary for seasonal Long Island whalers to buy land in New Jersey. These "degrees" of involvement in whaling included farming and providing of cattle, cutting timber (big business in N.J. early on) and provision of tar to mend and maintain boats. About 1688, there was an organized attempt of Southamptoners to set up a colony of six or seven families at Cape May, under the leadership of Humphry Hughs and Chistopher Leeming, with their principle object being that of whaling off the Delaware Bay.

At some point, Daytons in our direct line of ancestry probably became involved in some New Jersey venture. There exists irrefutable proofs, coming to us through will and inventory they were there, but when the involvement began remains unknown. For now, there is no workable theory that suggests Abraham was in New Jersey,[616] although his son Henry owned an estate at Great Egg Harbor in Gloucester County.

Many sons left Long Island in the late 1600's, especially the second or third born because quite often much of the inheritance went to the eldest son, and what was the younger son going to do on Long Island? He might help take care of his mother and get a little money for that, and be allowed to stay in a third of the house until she passed. If he's moved once, it wouldn't be as difficult to move a second time.[617]

In Brookhaven records, Abraham and Mary were already married by 1684, when they inherited part of the Joseph Beardsley estate, along with Hannah and her husband, Richard Hulse. Since Abraham was about 30 in 1684 and Mary was in her early 20's, it is possible that the wedding occurred up to a few years before the inheritance. Hannah and Richard (the same Richard who bought Benjamin Gould's house) had been married sometime before June 6, 1681.[618] Joseph Beardsley, we believe, had been either uncle to the sisters or, as Jacobus believed, their unmarried brother.[619]

The 1684 record of Abraham and Mary can be found in the old *Brand Book of Stratford, 1640-1720*, on page 23 of our edition, on the occasion of Joseph Beardsley's death. According to Isaac Haight Beardsley,

> Joseph Beardsley, of Brookhaven, Long Island, must also have been another son of the first Thomas. He, July 4, 1684, conveyed divers tracts of land in Stratford, Conn., which no doubt had fallen to him by heirship, to Andrew Gibbs, a merchant of the same place, who, on the above date, conveyed to Joseph Beardsley, 'yeoman,' lands and meadows in

---

[616] Note: A group of Rogerenes (discussed in chapter 17) did move to Southern New Jersey, along with Quakers.

[617] Richard Barons

[618] Note: Hannah married Sam Swayze after Richard's death in the summer of 1698.

[619] (D. Jacobus 1959) 19

Brookhaven. In December, 1684, Joseph Beardsley died, and his estate was divided between Abraham Dayton and Mary, his wife, and Richard Huke [Hulse] and Hannah, his wife. From which it seems that these two women were his only heirs, probably his sisters, for on Oct.16, 1686, they submitted to the court a document, showing that they were 'co-heirs' to the estate of Joseph Beardsley, and they were admitted as joint administrators of the same.[620]

By the information in the *Brand Book of Stratford*, it seems that this Joseph, Abraham's supposed brother-in-law, traded his land in Stratford, CT with Andrew Gibb for his lands and meadows at Brookhaven. This information is disputed however, as the trade has also been attributed to another Joseph, son of William. Only five months later, in December of 1684, Joseph died without a will and later his sisters, one being Abraham's wife Mary, became administrators of his estate. Especially because of their ages, there is little doubt that just as Abraham had known of Mary for many years, he probably knew of Joseph also, even before Abraham married Mary. As was the case with Thomas Beardsley, there are also divergent and conflicting histories concerning Joseph, probably in part because there was more than one Joseph Beardsley around Brookhaven and Stratford at the time.

As a result of the Articles of Agreement for the estate of Joseph Beardsley, divided between Abraham and Richard Hulse, Abraham and Mary gained a substantial number of lots and properties close to today's Stony Brook, Old Field, Port Jefferson, Mt. Sinai, Brookhaven hamlet and Great South Bay. Among these,

- 9 acres at Old Field (6 acre lot that was William Fancys & 3 acre lot formerly Robert Goulsberry)
- 5 acres at Little Neck
- 10 acres in the South West Division
- 3 acres adjoining William Sayer (formerly Richard Hulse)
- 50 acres at Old Mans
- Half the 20 acre lot over against Old Mans
- 15 acres at Fire Place and a share of meadow belonging to it
- Share of Meadow at Sebameck in the New Purchase and all the upland belonging to the meadow
- Share of Meadow here at home in the West Meadow

The town records say:

Artickls of agrement made and conclueded this 11 day of desemb 1684 betweene Abram daiton of the one party and Richard huls the other party as followeth that the aboue saide parttes haue devieded all the astate that was Joseph Bearsles late deseassed the aboue saide Abram daiton is to

---

[620] (Beardsley 1902) 396

haue niene akers in the ould feeld the six aker lott that was william fances and a thre aker lott that was formerly Robart goulsbery as alsoe flue akers in the litle neck as alsoe tenn akers in the south west devission and alsoe three akers aJoyning to william salyer that was formerly Richard hulses and alsoe a fiffty aker lott at the ould mans and alsoe half the twenty aker lott over against the ould mans as alsoe fifteen akers of land at the fire place and a share of medowe belonging to it and alsoe a share of medow at sebameck in the nue purchass with all the upland that shall here after belong to the saide medow and alsoe a share of medow here at home in the west medow and what land shall falle to the acomadations hereafter shall be devieded betwene the aboue saide partes besiedes that at sebamack Richard huls devident is as followeth that is to say therty aker(s) of land and a smale house upon it neare to floyds swamp and fifteene akers of upland and the share of medow which was formerly Richard stars and a fifty aker lott at the ould mans and the half of the twenty aker lott over against the ould mans and a share of medow in the ould purchas at the south wich is to be layd out these aboue diffedents the aboue saide partes haue fully agread to that the aboue saide lands and medowe shall be to them and there haires to haue and to hould for ever[621]

The relative locations of some of these parcels can be identified because they occupy well defined areas, but in the expanse of Old Mans, it is not so easy. "Although the exact boundary of Old Mans is not known, it is said to have reached from what is now Port Jefferson to Rocky Point."[622] As the area contains abundant artifacts, it is evident that it was inhabited for many centuries, by Native Peoples. Once acquired, the English had farmed the land since the 1660's and before long the surplus crop was shipped, supplementing other portions of the colony and beyond in trade.

Occupations relating to the harbor and shipping also kept varying numbers of residents busy. Many young men preferred to pursue careers at sea rather than stay on the farm. Some families of Mt. Sinai (Old Mans) had sons engaged in worldwide shipping while others were engaged in shipping throughout Long Island Sound and along the east coast… Grist mills were located somewhere along Pipe Stave Hollow and Crystal Brook Hollow Roads. Records indicate that a number of windmills were located on the hills overlooking the harbor.[623]

---

[621] (Shaw, Records of the Town of Brookhaven 1679-1756 Book B 1932)
[622] (Mt. Sinai Hamlet Study Committee 2013)
[623] Ibid.

It might be that Abraham, like his father, was somehow involved in breeding or trading horses and shipping grain, produce, livestock, oil, wood and all manner of cargo, trading around Long Island and New England and possibly New Jersey.

With all the scattered pieces of land, probably desirable to the neighbors of each, Abraham and Mary received much with which to trade or sell. In less than two years, the couple sold the five acres at Little Neck back to Andrew Gibb (Gibb had sold to Joseph) for £9. The following is found in BTR Book B,

To All Christian People to whom this present writing shall come Wee Abraham Dayton & Mary his wife living in Brookhaven in Comit. suffolc. upon Long Island yeoman sendeth Greeting, Know Y^e That wheras Andrew Gibb of Brookhaven aforesd Mercht. did on the ffifteenth day of July 1684 by his certaine Jndented deed under the hand & seale of the sd Gibb Sell Bargaine Alien Asigne & set over unto Joseph Bearsly late of Brookhaven aforsd Deceased a Certaine five Acre lotte of land lying & Scituate in the little Necke soe called within the Towneship of Brookhaven aforesd And wheras the sd Abraham and Mary Dayton being not only with Richd Hulse & Hannah his wife Coheires of ye Estate of ye sd Joseph Bearsly but also at a Court of Oyer & Terminer holden at South Hampton in ye year aforesd were admitted Joynt-Administratours of ye Estate of ye sd Joseph Bearsly And wheras by a deed of Partition of ye Estate of the sd Joseph Bearsly the sd five Acre lot of land did fall unto the sd Abraham & Mary Dayton & wheras the sd Abraham & Mary Dayton have Recd of the sd Andrew Gibb the sum of Nine pounds currant pay of this Country the receite wherof they doe herby ackowledge & themselves to be fully satisfyed & contented & therof & of every parte & parcell doe freely & fully clearly acquit & discharge the sd Andrew Gibb his Heires Executors Administrators & Assignes for ever and by thes presents doth remise release & for ever quit Claime from them their heires & Assignes from & for the sd five Acre lot of land in ye little Necke aforesd in as full & ample manner as if this Release were drawn with all the Tearmes of law & Art whatsoever Jn Witnesse wherof we the sd Abraham & Mary his wife have Here unto set their hands & seales this 16th of Oct. 1686

Sealed & delivered in presence of   Abraham A Dayton

Tho: Helme: Wm White   Mary M hands & Seales

In the 1686 document, it was stated that Abraham and Mary were of [Comit], which it is supposed could actually be Coram because Coram is said to be the oldest settlement in the middle of the Town of Brookhaven, taking its name from Wincoram. Interestingly, there developed a settlement less than two miles north and east of

Coram referred to as Sweezytown, Stephen Swezey given credit for its founding in 1745 (The Swezey name will become important to us in just a few years). As the name Old Field implies, this valuable tract of land was settled very early, so is also a likely location for Abraham and Mary as they had already acquired nine acres there from Joseph Beardsley.

After at least three years of marriage, Caleb was born to Abraham and Mary in December of 1687 (counting back from May 1696 when he was 8 yrs 8 mths), less than one year before the baby's uncle Caleb died. Perhaps Abraham named his son after his little brother Caleb who, with Jacob, had been "taken" from them and disposed by their father Samuel.

Because there is no record to indicate births or deaths of siblings before Caleb, history sets Caleb as the eldest of Abraham's six children. It is interesting to note that Abraham did not follow the tradition of his father and grandfather, that of naming his oldest son Ralph. Nor did Abraham name any of his sons after himself or his father Samuel which were also tradition. Perhaps this fact might suggest there had been an older son born to Abraham and Mary who had lived long enough to keep the name Ralph, Samuel, or Abraham? Caleb's birth also occurred three years before the death of his grandfather Samuel, so if Caleb had had memories of his grandfather, they would soon be lost.

There is no mention again of Mary after the birth of Caleb so presumably she died sometime between 1687 and 1692. Perhaps Mary had difficulty carrying the baby or birthing Caleb which could have led to her death at between 25 to 32 years of age.

In a deed dated April 16, 1691, 'Abram Dayton' sold to Col. Smith two acres on Ye Little Neck for, "divers good causes and considerations and fourtie and two pounds tenn shillings in good and merchantable Countrie pay." According to *Merriam-Webster's Dictionary*, "country pay" refers to rural commodities used in lieu of money in transactions. Kate Wheeler Strong wrote in the *Long Island Forum*,

> It is a curious thing that although it was dated April 16, the deed states that Dayton had bought the land on April 23rd from John Biggs. Dayton also states that he 'encloses the deed' from John Biggs and Elizabeth his wife, but it is dated April 25, 1691. I would like to know how much Abram Dayton made on this deal which certainly was a quick turnover.[624]

Because the exchange with Col. Smith carried such significant monetary value, the land almost certainly had to contain other unstated assets, improvements, considerations or perhaps it was in a strategic location. However, it seems unlikely that a large building or resource would occupy that property without reference to it in the sale. Other questions to consider are the possibility that Abraham was profiting by "flipping" the land, as Strong suggests, or did this record contain copy errors, especially considering the order of the dates given?

---

[624] (K. W. Strong, Land Deals on Ye Little Neck 1953)

There exists another interesting study that presents itself when viewing deeds with the seals and marks of Abraham and wives. Unless one has been overlooked, the reader will notice that every document signed by Abraham contains his mark, an "A," and nowhere did these deeds refer to his signature. But, in every case, the word "seal" was also used. According to colonial and legal dictionaries, a mark was the sign of an illiterate person while a seal was a mark of authenticity used mainly by the literate.

Mary used her mark "M" in 1686, although the word "seal" was used in the body of the document and we were inclined to believe both of Elizabeth's children from her prior marriage were literate. It is much the same for Catherine, as the words seal and mark are used almost interchangeably.

Because at least seven seals and five marks are referred to in the case of Abraham, and he actually used six marks in this collection of documents, it cannot be stated definitively that Abraham was literate.

Catherine [Sweezey]

According to July 22, 1693 land transfer records, Abraham was already married to his next wife Catherine so Torrey's wedding date on the same day is probably mistaken.[625] The marriage likely occurred sometime between early 1688 and 1693 when Catherine was in her 20's (her birth is estimated between 1663 and 1671). The dominant theory assigns her the last name Sweezey, a name which is well known around the area of Coram and Middle Island, having many variants in spelling as does Catherine's first name. Many of those who adhere to the idea of Sweezey believe that Catherine was either daughter or widow of a John Sweezey. An older John and Catherine Sweezey[626] are found in Southold, when this John wrote his will in May of 1692, naming his sons and daughters, but he made no mention of a daughter Catherine. However, the same will does have a son John who, at one time, lived at Brookhaven. The will of John Swesey of Southold (born about 1619) follows.

> In the name of God, Amen: I John S. of Southold, in Long Island, in county of Suffolk and in ye Province of New York, being of good and sound memory and calling to mind ye uncertainty of this life, and that I must yield to death when it shall please God, do make, constitute and ordain this my last Will and Testament, hereby revoking and annulling any other or forms of wills by me made either by word or writing.
>
> Imprimis: I give my soul unto God who gave it and my body being dead to be buried, and my worldly, estate (my just debts being paid) - first I give and bestow in name and form following:

---

[625] (Torrey 1985)
[626] (Lythgoe 2001)

Item: I give and bequeath unto my son John my dwelling house and orchard together with the buildings, fencings and other improvements on my home stall and all ye land by me improved southward of ye land which my son John hath fenced in containing ye whole breadth of ye land as far as the South Bay-ye other lot westward of it being a second lot with half ye share of ye meadow commonly called "Horton's Meadow", and being another share of meadow at a place called ye "Great Meadow" and also ally my implements of husbandry and other tools.

Item: I give and bequeath to my son Joseph S. one hundred acres of land upon which he is settled lying westward of my son John's land and northward of my son Joseph's home lot, and half of ye above of the great meadow lying on the other side of the river which was formerly John Younge's and also ye other half of ye lot westward of it and my horses in ye woods to be equally divided between my three sons.

Item: I give and bequeath to my son Samuel ye land now in the occupation of my son John lying between my son Joseph's and the house stall which by these presents I have given to my son John and ye other half of ye above of ye meadow called "Horton's Meadow", with this condition or limitation that my son Samuel shall not have power to sell or dispose of any part or parcel of ye land hereby granted to him, so that if he shall decease without issue ye right of inheritance of ye land shall be to the next proper heir. Also I give to him half of my cattle and the bed and furniture he lyeth on.

Item: I give to my daughter Aldridge and to the heirs of Peter Aldridge deceased one hundred acres of land lying on the north side or the land given to my son Joseph, if there be so much land there, be it more or less.

Item: I give to my youngest daughters Sarah and Mary Swesey ye other half of my cattle to be equally divided between them.

Item: I give and bequeath to my four daughters, Abagail, Mehitable, Sarah and Mary, all my household goods to be equally divided between them.

Item: My will is that consideration of ye lands given to my sons John and Joseph they shall pay to my two youngest daughters Sarah and Mary ye sum of 20 pounds current pay of the country; that is to say, 10 pounds apiece to each of my youngest daughters within two years after my decease.

Item: My will is that Bessie my servant shall be free and set at liberty at my decease and she shall have the bed she lyeth on.

Lastly: I do hereby nominate and appoint John Tuthill of Southold and John Hallett to be the Executors of this Will and Testament.

In witness whereof I do hereunto set my hand and seal ye 20 of May, 1692.

John Swesey (Seal)
　　Witnessed by us Thomas Hulse Joseph Tooker
He died 1706 in Aquebogue, a few miles from Southold.[627]

At present, no other noteworthy theories concerning the origin of Catherine have been found.

In May of 1693 "Ralf"[628] and Abraham Dayton were both elected trustees of the town and appear again at actions and duties of their office. On July 22, 1693, an agreement was written up and it was recorded two days later for "Abram" and wife "Katharine" at the occasion of the very substantial sale – their estate for £140 to David Eddowes! The description of the property in 1693 named Isaac Norton as a neighbor and when Isaac inherited his land from his father Nathaniel in 1684, Abraham was already described as his neighbor, so is it possible that Abraham lived there, on at least part of the estate, before his father gave him the home lot?

Not much is found in the Brookhaven record for Eddowes (also Edowes and Edwards) except that he served as collector and he once had a difficult time paying his taxes. More can be found in Southold Town Records, but the BTR says:

This Indenture made the 22 day of July in ye fifth year of ye reign of William and Mary by ye grace of God of England & e king & Queen Defenders of ye faith & c. anno Dui 1693 Between Abram Daiton of Brookhaven in ye County of Suffolke on Nasaw Island of ye Province of N yorke ye _____ of ye one parte & David Eddowes of Southold in ye said County of ye other parts. Witnesseth

That I said Abram Dayton & Katharine his Wife for ye sum of one hundred & forty pounds of good & lawfull money of this Province to them by ye said David Eddowes well & truly paid at ye ensealing hereof when with ye said Abram Dayton & Katharine his wife doe acknowledge themselves to be satisfied contented & paid & thereof & of every parte & parcel thereof do clearly acquit & discharge ye said David Eddowes his heires & Executors by the present. Have bargained sould given & granted & by thes present doe fully freely clearly & absolutely bargain sell give & grant unto ye said David Eddowes a certein house and home lott being free-hold scituate lying & being in ye said Province of Brookhaven near ye land of Isaac Norton on ye north ye land of Ralph Dayton on ye East & on ye South & ye Creeke on ye west saving the highway by Computation two or three acres together with a clofe(?) at a place called New towne scituate & lying on ye southeast side of ye land of Peter Whitier on ye south _____ computation twenty acres or therabouts as it was layd out & bounded. To Have & to Hold ye said house land barne

---

[627] (Swezey 1997)
[628] Note: This Ralf was probably Abraham's older brother, born about 1649.

orchard garden fencing & other ye improvem's thereunto belonging or in any wise appertaining unto ye said David Eddowes his heires & assignes for ever to ye one ___ use & behoofe of ye said David Eddowes his heires & Assignes for ever And ye said Abram Dayton for him selfe his heires Executors or Administrators doth hereby Covenant promise & grant to & with ye said David Eddowes his heires or Assignes mentioned ___ be bargained & sould & hath power to sell & that ever parte & parcel thereof now be & soe shall Continue clearly Discharged & Exonerated of & from all of her fformer bargaines sales tax & mortgages or other incumberances whatsoever and that he shall warrant ye sale hereof against any laying claime thereunto and the said Abram & Katharine his wife at ye reasonable request of ye said David Eddowes shall & will doe make & knowledge & exceed all & every reasonable act & acts thing & things, Conveyance & Conveyances, assurance & assurances in ye __ for ye good assurance and lawfull Conveyance of ye premises in Confirmation whereof the said Abram Dayton & Katharine my wife doe hereunto set their hands & seales the day & year above named

Sealed & Delivered in presence of   Abram Dayton   [seale]

Tho: Helme John Hallueke Tho Jenner   his **A** marke

          Katharine Dayton

          [seale] her **C** marke[629]

Brookhaven July ye 24th 1693 did personally appear Before me William Smith Judge & Chiefe Justice of their Ma___ Province of N yorke Abram Dayton & Katharine his wife Parties to the _____ & acknowledge the same to------(bottom of copied page missing)[630]

A few months after Eddowes bought Abraham's estate, at a meeting of the Trustees, with Woodull, Jeane, Brewster, Ralfe and Abraham on November 27, 1693, the high way, at a place called "the going over" by David Edors was identified for repair.

In the same meeting, Col. William Smith had his patent read before the trustees and the document was signed by all and includes the marks of Ralf and Abram Daiton. The original November 1693 document was salvaged from the great fire of 1911 at Albany and was then bound and archived at the NYS Archives at Albany, where the compilers viewed it in May of 2015.

---

[629] Note: Despite spelling her name "Katharine" throughout the document, the mark she uses is a "C."
[630] (New York Land Records 1630-1975, Suffolk Deeds 1660-1719 Vol A 2015)

The following year after selling the farm, Abraham and Catherine had been living on another choice piece of land at Old Mans. Abraham was described as a yeoman when the purchase was made final in 1694. There may not be significance to the fact that Catherine's name is not on the deed.

Selling his estate at New Towne, where his father had helped to establish him in 1680, represents a mile post in Abraham's life. Sam had died just a few years before the sale. What could have prompted him to leave his farm, all he had worked for with Mary—his house and barn, with garden, his orchard and other fenced lands to move to Old Mans?

On the first day of the year on the Old Style (Julian) calendar, March 25, 1694, Abraham consummated what earlier agreement he had probably made for land at Old Mans from Smith, Wodhull and Floyd Jr. for it appears that Abraham and Katharine had been living there and had already made payment of £90. BTR Book B says:

This Jndenture made ye 25th day of March in ye Sixth yeare of the Reigne of William & mary by the grace of God of England Scotland France & Jreland King & Queene Defenders of the ffaith &c Annoqe Domini : 1694 Between William Smith Esqre Richard Wodhull & Richard Floyd Gent" of the Towne of BrookhaVen in the County of Suffolk on Nassaw Jsland of the Province of New yorke of the one parte & Abraham Dayton of the saide Towne & County Yeoman of the other parte Wittnesseth that the saide William Smith Richard Wodhull Esqe and Rich Floyd Iunior gentl" of the saide Towne & county for and in concosideration of ninety pounds good & Lawfull mony already in hand received before the insealing & delevery of these [of these] presents hath bargained & Sould given & granted & by these prsents doe fully & clearely & absolutely bargaine & sell give & grant unto the said Abraham Dayton a Certaine Tract of Land Scituate lying & being within the Towneship of Brookhaven aboved at a place comonly Knowne by the name of the old mans on the East side of the Land of Joseph Davis being bounded by a beech Tree at the head of the Spring & from thence Southward to a marked tree in the hallow joyning to ye said Joseph Davis his land & from thence bounded by the Marked trees neer the high way on the southsid & Eastward bounded by a marked tree Neare the heade of the hallow leading to Andrew Millers & Soe to the clefts on the North Side as alsoe all theire Rights of the Comon Meddow as it shall become due To have & to hold the sd land & meddow with all & Singuler the apurtinances benifitts & profits thereof Vnto the Same abraham Dayton his heires & assigns for Ever to ye only use & behoofe of the sd Abraham his heires & assignes for Ever_and the saide William Smith: Richard Wodhull & Richard Floyd Either of them theire Heires Executors or Administrators doe covenant promise & grant to & with the saide Abraham his heirs or asign(s) that the premises & Every part therof Now are & soe shall continue clerely discharged & aquitted from all other former. Bargaines Sales Morgages or incumberances whatsoever on theire parts & that the saide William Smith Richard Wodhull & Richard Floyd shall warant & Defend the Same against any laying claime thereunto Moreover to performe & Execute any act or act thing or things needful to bee done for the better conVeyainc assureance or confirmation of the Same In Wittness whereof the saide William Smith Richard Wodhull & Richard Floyd have hereunto Set theire hands and Seales the day above Named

Sealed and Delivered in presence of: *(Signed)*   *Wm* Smith   O
Sarah Hanmer   Richard Wodhull O
John Tompson   Richard Floyd   O
pr Timothy Brewster Clerk

The First-born

Catherine's first-born was Abraham's second known son Jonathan, born about 1694. Catherine would have at least four additional children before about 1704, at which time Abraham was fifty and she was probably in her late thirties. Although Jonathan is believed to be Catherine's first, there exists the theory that she had been widowed, meaning she could have had children unknown to us.

On May 12, 1696, Abraham bequeathed his son Caleb "Daighton," then aged 8 years and 5 months, to William and Jane Rawlinson, of Stratford, CT. Some knowledge of the Rawlinsons might be gained from the Stratford Episcopal Church where Rawlinson was a member and was probably warden. We don't understand why Abraham sent his son away two or three years after his marriage to Catherine. If older children did not exist, it seems unlikely that Abraham would willingly lose his only son (of Mary) to another couple. For an introduction to the arguments for and against two additional sons before Caleb, see *The American Genealogist*, Number 87, Volume XXII, no. 3, January 1946, *The Daytons of South Jersey* by Walter Lee Sheppard, Jr.

Why would Abraham do this? The cynic would wonder if Catherine prompted Abraham to formalize the arrangement with the Rawlinson's so that her son Jonathan would "become" the eldest and heir, thereby securing for herself a safety net should something happen to Abraham. With Abraham's eldest brother as her neighbor at New Towne, he might naturally be in place to determine Catherine's future.

On the other hand, is it possible that Caleb had never lived with his father, if Caleb's mother died in childbirth? If that was the case, it is not out of the question that he was sent, even as an infant, to live in Connecticut, where he might be close to his mother's relatives. The Rawlinsons, no doubt, were acquaintances of Caleb's mother's family or were relatives themselves.[631]

Whatever the scenario and whenever the decision was made, arrangements were formalized in 1696 for Caleb to remain with the Rawlinson's until he arrived at the age of 21. They were to treat him in all respects, "as if ye said Caleb was there own natural child" (Stratford Land Records, 2:497). At some point after taking him in, the Rawlinsons unmistakably thought of Caleb as their own and adopted him. They provided Caleb with a fine upbringing and, although he retained the Daighton name, he probably identified more with the Rawlinsons. If Caleb had ever been viewed as Abraham's first-born, that privilege was probably lost, especially when Catherine gave birth to Jonathan. When Mr. Rawlinson died in 1712, he left his estate to his "loving adopted son Caleb Daighton."[632] William Rawlinson's death was recorded under the name William Rollins on February 12, 1712.[633] Caleb's would become the line leading to George Draper Dayton,[634] born 1857, businessman and philanthropist, and is remembered as founder of Dayton's department store (origin of Target Discount Stores).

After Jonathan was born to Abraham and Catherine between 1691 and 1695, the births of Ephraim and Deborah followed, probably both before 1700. Next, it is believed Abraham's sons, David and Henry were born between 1696 and 1706, with Henry being the youngest. Deborah could have been named after Catherine's mother, just as it is assumed Jonathan was named after Catherine's father since these names do not appear on Abraham's side of the family. These may be good clues to Catherine's identity. Through the years, researchers have often confused Abraham's son David with his brother Henry's son, (David's nephew) also named David. Both Henry and his son David are our ancestors coming down in the direct line.

On Becoming Presbyterian

Regrettably, as is the case for his father, very little can be found of Abraham's relationship to the church, although in 1697 Abraham voluntarily subscribed to payment for the call of a pastor at Setauket. We believe Abraham's first wife, Mary, his own stepsister, had Godly influences from her parents and his second wife, Catherine Swayze/Katharine Sweezy, was also of strong character and saw to it that

---

[631] Note: In light of the Rawlinson's love and adoption of Caleb, the theory arose that the Rawlinsons were actually Caleb's step-grandparents. See History and Geneology of the Families of Old Fairfield compiled and edited by Donald Lines JacobusVol I for the listing of Rawlinson, William and possible relation to Elizabeth Beardsley.

[632] (D. L. Jacobus, History and Genealogy of the Families of Old Fairfield 1991). 204

[633] (Cothren 1872)

[634] (Dayton, Peterson and et al, The Known Ancestors of George Draper Dayton I in England and the United States of America 1987)

the children received education. The identity of Catherine continues to be in dispute, but it is commonly believed she might have been widow of John Swasey, member of a prominent Long Island family, or the daughter of another John Swasey. This John Swasey, it is said, refused to take "The New Haven Colony Oath of Fidelity" in 1659 because he belonged to the Quaker movement.[635] However, we conclude, along with Darrin Lythgoe of *Sweezey.com*,[636] that no proof has been found that the family was Quaker and that John's motivation for refusal may have been more political than religious since he was the owner of significant lands. It is evident that Abraham and Catherine's children were educated and, in that day, being educated meant you had the ability to read the bible, as the bible was the text used.

It is not known if Abraham participated in the 1719 protest against the dissenting church[637] (Presbyterian) in Brookhaven, when thirty-one men resigned their seats. If so, he may have later attended the Episcopal (later, Caroline) church or returned, as many did, to the Presbyterian Church since it is known that his son Henry attended there many years later.[638]

Note: This small section of our compilation borrows profusely from Belle Barstow's *Setauket's Religious Beginnings* in combination with some town records. In effect, the section is a summary of her work as it relates to the story of our ancestors and we should accept little credit for most of its content. We apologize that some context is lost in our summary and direct the reader to her book for a more complete understanding.

By 1666, the settlement of Setauket had both a minister and a meeting house. Almost upon the arrival of Reverend Nathaniel Brewster, the town acquired the large house that had belonged to John Scott before he fled imprisonment in Connecticut to Barbados. The building was situated beside the harbor, on Scott's Cove, so it was dismantled and reassembled at the common in Setauket. Already by 1669, the town was again involved in discussions about a new building. Nathaniel Norton, the grandfather of Henry Dayton's wife, was named carpenter for the job, but after a few years without much progress, it was awarded to another.

Reverend Brewster served as minister of Setauket for almost twenty years, beginning about 1666 until about 1685 when he likely became physically debilitated. Brewster died about 1690 and was buried in the "usual" burying place, "as was the

---

[635] (Swasey 1910)
[636] (Lythgoe 2001)
[637] Note: After the Meeting House became Presbyterian, and the Episcopal Church was established, the Presbyterian became know as the "dissenting" church to those outside of the denomination. The Puritans had recognized one true church while all others were "dissenters."
[638] (Caulkins 1895)

custom ever since the first need arose in Setauket-alias-Brookhaven." The Town Burying Place, "was in today's Setauket Presbyterian churchyard. There is no gravesite to mark this first minister's mortal remains, but he no doubt was buried as directed, his stone marker being destroyed as so many others were during the British occupation of Setauket in 1777."[639]

After a string of interim ministers and some difficulties in convincing a minister to stay, Mr. George Phillips was invited to consider the charge, and after much wooing, Mr. Phillips decided to accept the offer on a trial basis.

On April 30, 1697 Abraham Dayton joined with 32 others of the town of Brookhaven to sign a voluntary subscription of payment (instead of by a tax) for a call to Mr. George Phillips of Jamaica to minister among them, at what would become the Setauket Presbyterian Church.[640] The BTR says,

> Wee ye Trustes & ffreeholders & Inhabitants of ye Towne of Brook-havi(n) ye County of suffolk in ye provinc of new yourk:out of a Due senc of ure Duty to Almi(e)ty god. & being Desierus to haue his word preached a mongest uss & haveing had sume good Experienc of M^E: Gorge Phillips both of his a billites :&: good Inclination to uss Do unanimous a gree to giue ye sayd M^E Phillips a full call to settel among uss and for his incorragement to Continue With uss in the Work^e. of ye ministy wee Doe agree with him ye sayd M^E Phillips & ye sayd mister Phillip with ye Towne in maner & form as followeth ffirst ye Towne of Brook havens & smith Towne. wth sume liver in ye Maner of saint Gorges Do agree & oblidge oure selues by volintary subcription to paye unto M^E Phillips ye sume of forty poundes currunt mony of this provinc paranam & to giue him that house & home lot y^t was thommas Jeners aJoyning to ye parsonage ass. allso ahundered akers of Land Nere to Nasakeg swamp: all which sd tracks of Lande a fore mentioned With ye improuements thereof shall bee Confermed to the sayd M^E Phillips & his heire forever provayded & allwayes Exseped that ye sayd M^E Phillips shall perform and Discharg faithfully ye Duty of a minester of ye Gospel in everry Respect as farr ass maye become ye minestry of ye Gospell Dueeing ye time of his Naterall Life a moungst: us further yt ye Charg of Remoueing M^E Phillips with his family from Jemeca to this Towne & Repaireing ye hous to make it Desently habitable for his family subsistanc and beeing among uss shall bee Equally bourne by ye publick ass a foresayd[641]

> The Condishon of this a boue Writen a grement is such that if y^o aboue sd: M^E Phillips & ye towne after Mutuall triall of Each other for ye space of one yeare shall haue no Just cause or grounds to obIect a gainst Each

[639] (Barstow, Setauket's Religious Beginnings 1984)
[640] (Brookhaven Town Clerk, BTR 1880)
[641] (Shaw, Records of the Town of Brookhaven 1679-1756 Book B 1932)

other then the a boue sayd is in full force and vertue to all intents and purposes otherwise of none Efect any further than for yᵉ yeares sayllery : to yᵉ true performanc of all & Every of yᵉ a boue-sayd premises both partys haue hereunto sett oure hands this 30ᵗʰ Daye of Aprill 1697*

Mr. Phillips evidently recognized the possibilities within the town, perhaps expressed his concern about the current parsonage (or lack of one), and inquired about the opportunities of a new accommodation. The repairs on the meeting house encouraged the prospective minister in regard to the sincerity of the people in obtaining religious leadership, and he agreed to a "mutual trial" between himself and the town. [642]

Sometime around 1711 the people of Brookhaven, once again, considered building a new meeting house. This in itself is not startling, but what does catch our attention is the fact that it was to be approved for, "Publique Worship of God in such manner as the majority of contributors shall mutually agree." In *Setauket's Religious Beginnings*, Barstow said the building was no longer to be simply a "meeting house," but was to be instead a church, affiliated with an organized denomination. "As recently as 1705, those people subscribing to Mr. Phillips' annual maintenance had titled Mr. Phillips a "protestant Minister of the Gospel," as he was also called in his 1702 ordination, with no specific church mentioned. By August 9, 1714, in a town meeting, the congregation and church building were declared Presbyterian.

…with all ye inhibits above mentioned, out of a due senc of thaire indispenable Duty, Do Humbly dedicate, constitute, Establish & apint the aforesayd building to bee a house to promote & propagate the Honour of Almity God, in yᵉ purity of holy Relegion & in quallyte of a Presbeterian Meeteing House forever, and no other use or uses what soever… [643]

In so many New England towns, as meeting houses became churches, steeples were attached to the front of the buildings that identified their use. But in Setauket, the original Meeting House that had been the focus of the town as the gathering place, was replaced with a new Presbyterian Meeting House, constructed on the Village Green. Many in its congregation, being of Puritan heritage, still harbored deep prejudice toward England and her established church, so the Presbyterian Church there became known as the dissenter's church. At this time, the eastern half of Long Island was increasingly going Presbyterian with Brookhaven following Southampton and Bridgehampton. Barstow says, "Southampton's records in 1710 declared their new church would be in 'stile Presbiterian' and Bridgehampton in 1712 declared certain land was set aside 'for the use of a Presbyterian Ministry and noe other.'"[644]

---

[642] (Barstow, Setauket's Religious Beginnings 1984)
[643] (Brookhaven Town Clerk, BTR 1880)
[644] (Barstow, Setauket's Religious Beginnings 1984)

In 1719, two prominent members of the church at Setauket, Richard Floyd and William Smith, did not approve of the pastor or what he was proclaiming (along with Richard Woodhull, these were the gentlemen who sold Abraham Dayton acreage at Old Mans in 1694). As large land owners, Smith and Floyd would be paying large amounts of the taxes, with some going to the church. They petitioned the President of the Council of the Province of New York to investigate the wrongful levying of taxes by the trustees of the church for "private uses," specifically for the use of the minister. Mr. Phillips had ordered repairs to his own house, at "taxpayer's expense."

> When the Trustees of Brookhaven became aware of the accusations of Justice William Smith and Richard Floyd, the repercussions were immediate and powerful. In a remarkably short time for the early eighteeth century, a counter-petition was written, signed by sixty-seven men and sent to Peter Schuyler, President of the Council. This petition refuted the charges as false and declared the monies collected had been…judiciously appropriated…[645]

Examination of the documents, including the petition of Mess[rs] Ffloyd and Smith, the counter petition and the Order in Council produced no record of Daytons.[646] Barstow says:

> The two men who protested the cost of repairs to the home of the dissenting minister caused a canker in the town that grew to such proportions that it threatened to rend the town apart. For this town, choosing a particular denomination had brought such confusion and arguments, for and against its practices. Many people refused to attend church, while others objected when certain members went to the communion table.

In December of 1719, preferring that God's worship "be united in Love," a group of thirty-one men formally resigned their seats "in the publick meeteing house" as long as that house was to remain Presbyterian and to end accusations that they were preventing others to take ordinances. Again, no Daytons were found on this list. History does not record how long these men remained separated but, according to membership lists, many of them did eventually return.

The last record of Abraham, or anyone in the Dayton family during Abraham's lifetime, in membership of the Setauket congregation was April 1697, well before the meeting house was replaced by the Presbyterian Church.

Near the time of separation in 1719, some of the discontented contacted the *Society for the Propagation of the Gospel in Foreign Parts* requesting a Church of England missionary be sent to Setauket and in 1723, Reverend Wetmore was sent to the town of Brookhaven. It is known that this manner of worship had been practiced

---

[645] Ibid.
[646] (O'Callaghan, The Documentary History of the State of New York 1850)

in the town before 1719, but it is not known if the Anglicans (Episcopals) had some kind of building of their own before they formally organized in 1723.

What is apparent however, is the view of officials toward the "State of Religion in the Province 1657-1712" in Suffolk County:

ACCOUNT OF SUFFOLK COUNTY

In Suffolk county in the East end of Long Island, there is neither a church of England minister, nor any provision made for one by law, the people generally being Independents, and upheld in their separation by New-England Emissaries. But there are several already well affected to the Church, and if one or two ministers were sent among them, supported at first by the society, it would be an excellent means of reconciling the people to the Church, and of introducing an Establishment for a Minister by Law. Wm Vesey[647]

It wasn't long before the Episcopals argued for town privileges as accorded to the Presbyterians. By July of 1729, Reverend Alexander Campbell was minister and, under his leadership, Christ Church was built on the same Village Green, within view of the Presbyterian Church. Christ Church was consecrated in January of 1730, and on the same date, the small and impoverished congregation, being firmly loyalist, voted to change its name to Caroline Church in honor of Queen Wilhelmina Karoline who had presented the church with cherished gifts of embroidered alter cloths and a silver communion service.[648]

The conversion of the Meeting House at Setauket to the Presbyterian Church meant that the community burying ground, established in the 1660's, was now in the Presbyterian churchyard. Not long after the Episcopal Church was erected, the town, still a Presbyterian majority, voted to give them some adjacent ground for their own cemetery. It was the later church built in 1766 and the expanded burying ground that was desecrated by the loyalist and British occupation and fortification on church grounds in 1777.

---

[647] (O'Callaghan, The Documentary History of the State of New York 1850)
[648] (Ross 1905)

Chapter 16

An Unfinished Story

Forming the stories of our ancestors and revising them will never be finished, as gathering bits of history and piecing them together will be an ongoing labor of love for whomever is stricken. But a resolute characterization of Abraham Dayton continues to be particularly challenging, especially given the mysteries spanning what are thought to be his last twenty years. What can be found of that yet-to-be-told story seems disconnected from the first fifty years of his life. In a very short period of time, Abraham appears to go "from riches to rags" in some disturbing and baffling passages. These lead the anxious researcher to follow his or her own "hunches" which aren't always fruitful. Nonetheless, it's a place to start and it is our hope that someone who follows us will be inspired to either reject or confirm and build on our analysis, and provide the family a truer picture.

Big Money

Maybe there is no connection, but it seems a bit curious that our introduction to Catherine occurs with the momentous sale of what had been Abraham and Mary's estate at New Towne. What could have prompted Abraham to leave his farm and the investment of at least thirteen years? Was it to free a broken man's heart from reminders of his dreams with Mary? Maybe the reason was to acquire another choice piece of land and to start a new life with Catherine. Their New Towne farm must have been situated on very good ground in order to fetch £140. Would we dare suggest it was Catherine's desire or could Abraham not bear to stay, even when his farm was developed and orchard matured to the point of productivity? Apparently, the couple had their eyes on attractive land at Old Mans, for it is discovered that when they finally did complete the purchase at Old Mans, they had already been living there.

Only four years after purchasing the Old Mans property for £90, Abraham and Catherine sold it (assuming it was the same acreage) to Thomas Clarke of New York City for £152. In those four years, Abraham had improved the land significantly with a house and garden, out buildings and fences. The June 20, 1698 document said,

This indenture made ye twenty eth day of June in the tenth year of ye Raigne of William ye third by ye grace of od of England Scotland ſ france & Ireland King defend of y^e ſ faith are in ye year of our Lord one thouſ and six hundred ninety and eight Between Abram Dayton of Brookhaven in ye county of Suffolk on y^e jsLand of Nasaw yeoman of y^e one part & Thomas Clarke of y^e city of New York merchant of y^e other part witneſ eth that y^e said Abram Dayton & Katherine his wife for & in Consideration of y^e sum of one hundred fifty and two pounds currant money by those already received y^e receipt ___ is hereby acknowledged have aliened granted bargained & sold by thos y^e have defully clearly & absolutely give grant bargain sold and confirm to said Thomas Clarke a certain tract of land situate lying & being within y^e township of Brookhaven at a place commonly called the Old Mans on y^e east of y^e land lots in y^e ___ of Benjamin Davies being bounded by a beach tree at ye head of a spring & from thence southward to a marked tree in ye hollow joyning to ye land of ye said Benjamin Davies & from thence bounded by ye marked tree ___ ___ ye highway on ye south side as on ye east by a mark tree near ye head of ye hallow leading to Andrew Miller's & so to ye cliff on ye north side as also of rights of common meadow at ye said old man's as it shall become due which said land & right of meadow ye said Abram Dayton purchased of Col. William Smith, Richard Woodhull, & Richard Floyd Jr. as also ye edifices fencing & other Improvements therein made to have & to hold ye said house land & meadow with all & singular appurtenances benefits & profits there of as ye ___ & ___ of ye said Thomas Clarke his heires & assigned forever & ye said Abram Dayton & Katharine, his wife their heires executers or administrators do hereby covenant, promise & grant to & with ye said Thomas Clarke his heires or assignes __ __ __ & every parte thereof now are & ___ shall continue already discharged and acquitted from all other former bargains sales Mortgages or Incumberences ___ forever on their parts or to Warrant & Defend ye same against any laying claime thereunto Moreover to performe and execute any act or act thing or things needful to be done for ye better conveyance assurance or Confirmation of ye Same In Witness whomof ye said Abram Dayton & Katharine his Wife have ___ set their hand & seales ye day & year above named.

Sealed & Delivered in the presence of	Abram Dayton
Thomas Helme William Jayne	His Marke
Daniel Smith his WE marke	Catharine Dayton
The Deed above written ___	Her marke
Ye 20th Day of June 1698 Tho Helme & ___	

The following year, BTR Book B has Sam Swazy[649] & Hannah (Beardsley Hulse), Thomas Hulse,[650] Abraham & Catherine selling 120 acres, being in three lots at Old Mans, to Isaac Norton for only £24. Two of the lots were fifty acres each and were numbers 6 & 7. There may have been more to this lopsided exchange than what was included in this record but possibly the agreement included some provision for Abraham to farm or otherwise use the land. This is only supposition for lack of a better explanation.

> This Indenture made ye twenty sixth day of Aprill in ye Eleventh yeare of the Reigne of William ye third by the grace of God of Jngland Scotland ffrance & Jreland King Defender of the faith &c anno Domin 1699 between Samuel Swazy & hannah his wife Thomas Hulse Abraham Dayton & Catharine his *wife** of Brookhaven in the County of Suffolk on Nasaw JsLand in the ProVince of Newyork on the one partie and Jsaac Norton of the same place of the other parte Witnesseth that the saide Samuel Swazy Hannah his wife Thomas Hulse Abraham Dayton & Catharine his wife for & in consideration of twenty four—pounds currant money of New york to them in hand paide before the Ensealing & delivering of thease p^{E}sents the receite whereof is by them and all of them acknowledged and therewith to bee—fully satisfied contented & paide Have bargaind sould given—granted & by these pEsents doe freely clearly and absolutely Bargain Sell give and grant unto the saide Isaac Norton one twenty acre lott & two fivety acre lotts by number six & seven att a place—called the old mans within the Township of Brookhaven aforesd as it was. Laide out & bounded To have & to hold the sd land with ye benefitts proffitts and apurtenances therunto belonging or any wayes apertaining to the saide Jsack norton his heires or assignes for ever to the use & behoofe of the saide Isaac Norton his heires & assignes for ever and the saide Samuel Swasy & Hannah his wife Thomas Hulse Abraham Dayton & catharine his wife for themselves theire heires & Executors and—administrators & Either of them doe hereby covenant promise and—grant to & with ye saide Isaack norton his heires & assignes shall & may at—all times hereafter use possess & Enjoy the abovgranted pEmises free from incumberances without the lett hinderance or molestation of the saide samuel Swasy Hannah his wife Thomas hulse Abraham Dayton & Catharine theire heirs Executors or administrators or Either of them & the saide land hereby granted & sould to ye saide Jsaac Norton his heires & asignes The—saide samuel swasy Hannah his wife Thomas Hulse Abraham Dayton & Katharine his wife theire heires

---

[649] Note: Son of John and Catherine Kinge Sweezey, according to B.F. Sweezey. This is disputed. See "Swezey History" by Richard Bayles.

[650] Note: Presumably a relative of Richard Hulse, Hannah's first husband.

Executorsv or Administrators shall & will warrant & defend all persons as alsoe to doe performe & execute any act or thing devise or devices in the law needfull to bee done for ye sure-making or better Conveyance of the premises Jn testimony whereof ye saide Samuel Swasy Hannah his wife & Abraham Dayton and—Catherina his wife parties to thes presents have set to theire hands & Seales ye day above written—

Samuel Swasy seale—O

Sealed & delivered in presence of   hannah Swasy—Seale-O
Tho Clarke   his

Arthur ffuthy   Tho T Hulse Seale-O
Elizabeth Clarke mark   his mark

                                                        Abraham A Dayton Seale-O
                                                                mark &

Entered pr Timothy Brewster Clerk   Catharine [C] Dayton Seale O

Mysterious Quarter Century

There are many missing pieces to the puzzle of Abraham's life after the turn of the century. If our estimations are correct, he and Catherine had four or five young children by this time and they had just sold a significant portion of their land in two important transactions totaling £176. Although the records after 1700 are important in subject matter, they are insufficient to join together in order to make sense of the larger picture. What pieces can be discovered suggest a turn of events or tragedy that is bound to disappoint those descendants of Abraham who anticipated celebrations of accomplishment and glory.

For now, the circumstantial evidence points to some unknown events that led to his devastating loss of material wealth and may have caused separation from some in his family. Could these be explained by some debilitating progressive disease like dementia or disability like blindness?

In the BTR, on September 11, 1701, there appears an odd entry of Abraham protesting the subpoena to appear before Justice Smith of Smithtown by Justice Helme of Old Mans to answer the complaint of mowing in a common meadow belonging to Old Mans. The record makes little sense to us.

Whearas Complaint hath been made by Abraham Dayton that hee is Sumomed before Justice Jonathan Smith of Smith Toune by Justice Helme to answer the Complaint of the saide Justice Helme for mowing the common medow of this Towne within the old mans harbour_ Ordered that Capt. Thomas Clark & William Jeane bee a comittee to apaere before the said Justice Jonathun & thear to defend the right of this Towne &c Adjornd till further order.[651]

Perhaps because the complaint was initiated by Justice Helme, he therefore had to recuse himself, the incident having happened in his jurisdiction. The summons was entered into the record to reflect his vested share of the common meadow "violated" by Abraham. Other than this explanation, how may it be interpreted?

In the October 22, 1701 Brookhaven County Rate for 4-17-6 ¾ (figure 23), "Abram" Dayton was listed for 0-02-02 ¼. So, in 1701, our analysis of wealth based on land value places Abraham at about the 72nd percentile of townsmen.

One common thread, woven throughout most of the transactions beginning in 1698 is the presence of Capt. Thomas Clarke, who lived at Brookhaven until 1704, when he moved to New York City. It appears from the records that follow, Clarke had purchased the Old Mans property in 1698 from Abraham and Katharine and sold it to John Roberson Junior. The sale to Roberson occurred sometime between 1698 and 1706. The arrangement and components of the sale from Clarke to Roberson Junior were not disclosed but it must have contained or allowed some kind of agreement for the first large payments from John Roberson Senior while the remainder was to be paid off with interest. As part of the deal with Clarke and the Robersons, Abraham was to retain a certain seven acres for his use, with stipulations. It was also not disclosed what composed the seven acres, except it was called a farm so it probably included Abraham's house. It is possible Roberson Junior had intended to partner with Abraham in whatever he was doing with the seven acres, to help pay his debt.

In 1706, Thomas Clarke wrote a receipt upon payment of £152 received from Roberson's parents which said he had received partial payment of the £200 owed him. This £200 may have included some interest also, if the agreement had been made previous to that date. Three years later, Roberson Junior had still not contributed payments toward the total owed. Since Clarke made the agreement with Abraham and Roberson, Abraham may have felt threatened enough that he thought it was prudent to meet with Clarke, perhaps in NYC, to show good faith (or to avoid legal action or punishment), and to get the exact amount now owed, as interest on the loan was added. Probably while Abraham was still with Clarke, one of them composed the note to Roberson. The 1709 note addressed to John Roberson Junior said that the amount owed to Clarke as of that date was just over £70, after subtracting the £152 received from Roberson's parents. The additional £22 could have been either very high interest added or payment due in the place of whatever labor or product he was

---

[651] (Brookhaven Town Clerk, BTR 1880)

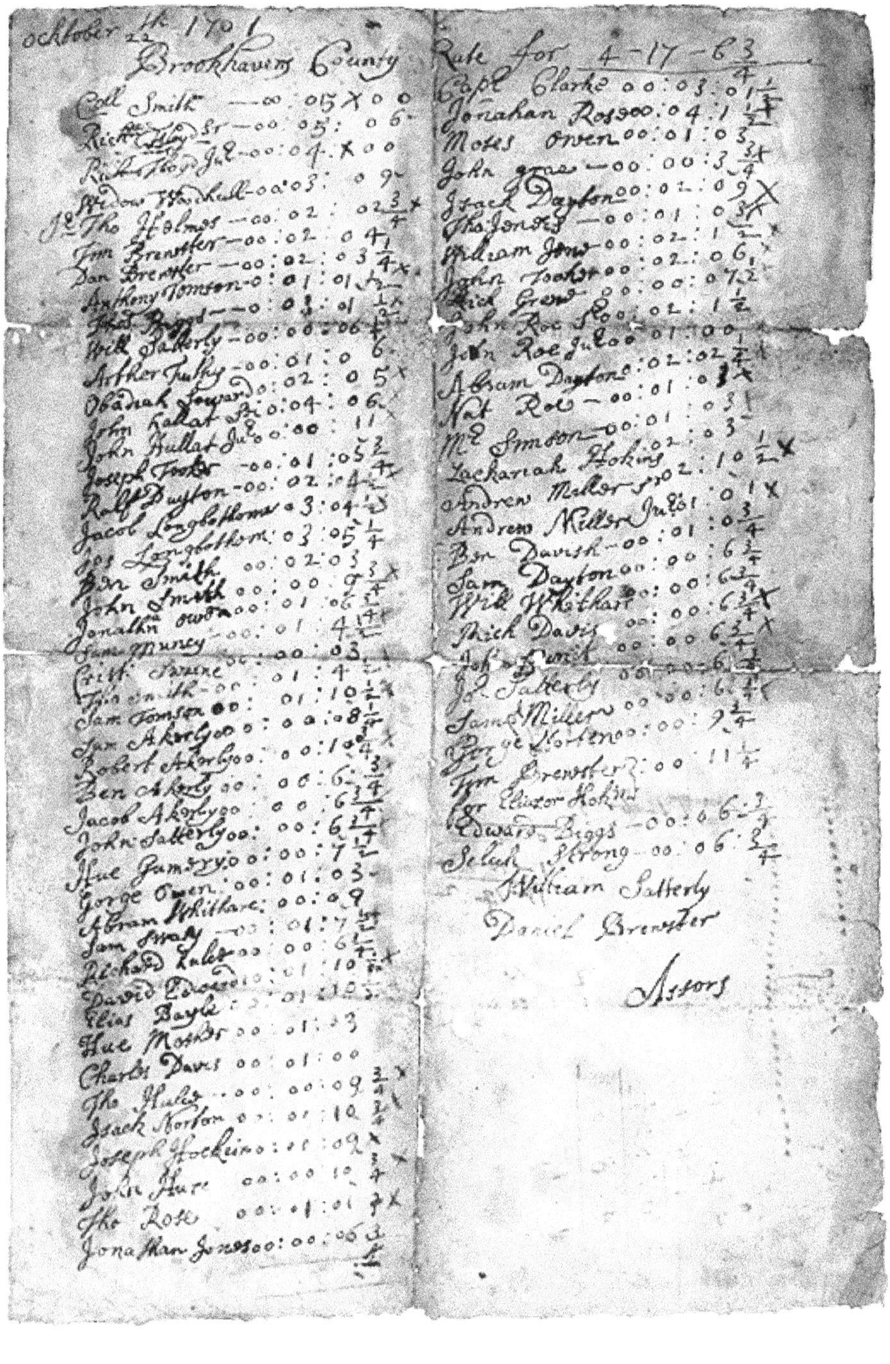

Figure 23. October 1701 Brookhaven County rate

Brookhaven Town Historian's Office, Brookhaven Township Municipal Building

to have received from Roberson Junior as part of the deal. BTR Book B reads:

> New York June the 13, 1706: Received then of John Roberson the sum of 100 pounds; and June the 21, 1706 received 52 pounds which makes 152 pounds which I received in part of 200 pounds sum (from) John Roberson is to pay me in consideration of my assignment of my right title and interest to all my lands except 7 acres bought of Abraham Dayton & now in his and John Roberson Junior's possession I say received by me

> Daniel Brewster Clark (clerk)   Thomas Clarke

Abraham then told Roberson that he needed to comply with his own agreement and Abraham needed to see the receipt from Clarke upon any payment. Was Abraham in danger of forfeiting his holdings?

> Mr. John Roberson according to your order I have been with Captain Thomas Clark and have made up accounts and there is due to him 222 pounds 17 shilling an 2 pence in all where of he owns to have received from your father & mother 152 pound in part so that there is now due to him said Clarke the just sum of 70 pounds 17 shillings and 2 pence which said sum I do here by order you to pay him or order and in case you do not pay said sum which is for the rent of the farm. When you pay said money bring me Captain Thomas Clarke's receipt for all you have paid as you are bound by bond to do & in complying with this my order you obligate your friend and servant to command.
>   Abram

> New York the 23rd July 1709   The mark of A Dayton

From the NYGBR, it is discovered that John Roberson Senior deeded a large tract of land in Brookhaven over to his son John Junior of Oyster Bay in 1712.[652] It is not known if it is the same piece of land.

Perhaps John Roberson Senior rescued his son from indebtedness, but it was too late for Abraham. Less than a year after the July 1709 letter to Roberson, on May 15, 1710, Abraham considered himself destitute and appealed to the New York State Senate for a license to collect charity. Abraham's request was recorded in the *Executive Minutes of the New York Colonial Council*, found in Volume 8, and reads simply:

"Orders on petitions: by Abr'm Daiton of Brookhaven for a brief for charity."[653]

---

[652] (Robinson 1921)
[653] (New York 1903)

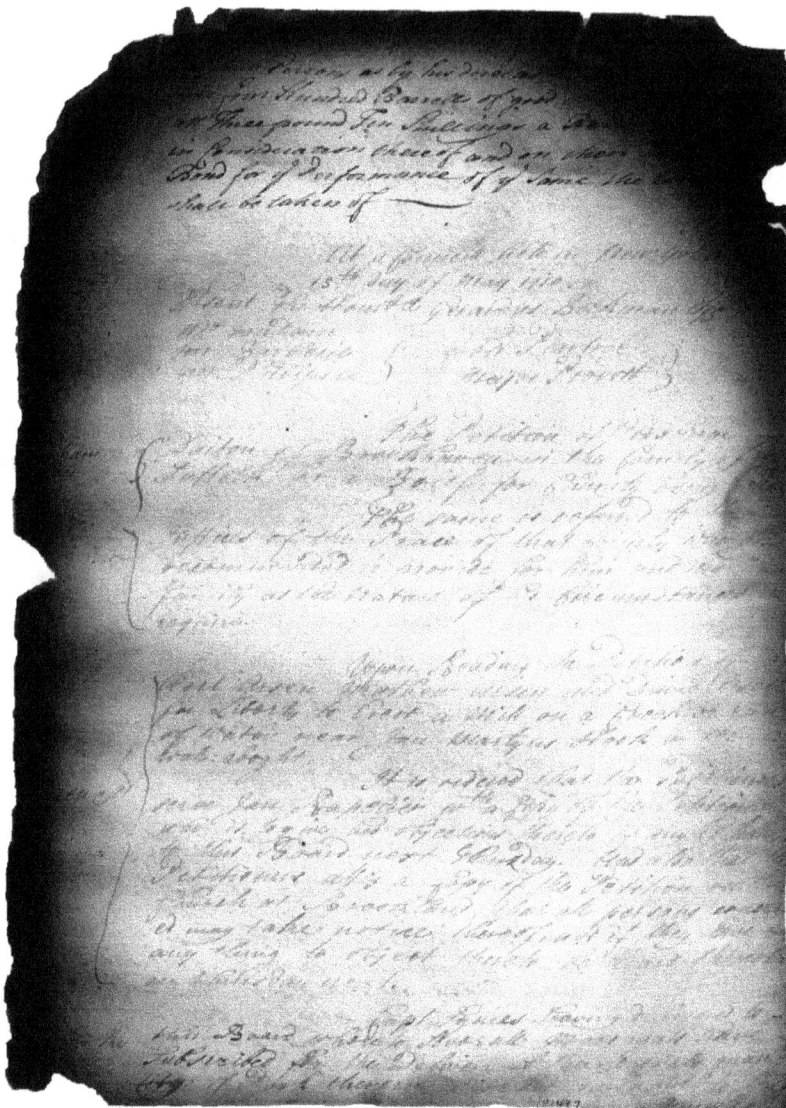

Figure 24. Orders on Petitions: Reply to Abraham's brief for charity

New York Council Minutes Volume 10, 1706-11, pages 473-603, New York State Library, Bound March 1919.

More often than not, at least in Volume 8, licenses to collect charity were granted to refugees, victims of disaster or extreme hardship like those who had lost their houses or farms by fire, their livelihoods by injury, or in the case of widows whose husbands were killed in service to their country. Briefs for charity were also granted to collect funds for building or repairing churches or parsonages. In the case of Abraham, it is assumed he appealed in the interest of his family since the Council Minutes refer to Abraham's family, but it is revealed that his license to appeal for charity was not immediately granted, but instead the request was referred back to Suffolk County.

A charred survivor of the March 1911 fire,[654] the original document (figure 24) is dated May 15, 1710, and in the middle of the page, the Council Minutes state,

> The Petition of Abraham Daiton of Brookhaven in the County of Suffolk for a brief for Charity being [read][655] The same is referred to the Justices of the Peace of that County who are recommended to provide for him and his family as the nature of his circumstances require.

May 5, 1712 was the last time "Katherine" was mentioned in any known record, when she and son Jonathan were granted use of town land where they were presently living. It is estimated that Catherine was about 44 years of age. The town of Brookhaven acknowledged their need, whether or not a result of Abraham's appeal. Mysteriously, the same record did not recognize Abraham,

> Jt was Likewise granted that Katherine Dayton & her Eldest Son Jonathun shall have free Liberty to Jmprove twenty acres of Land at a small pond where they have began to Jmprove already being about three quarters of a mile westward from ye flaxpond and that they shall & may peceably & quiately Jnjoy the same during theire naturall Lifes & at theire Decease that it shall returne to ye Towne againe[656]

What is to be made of the deliberate exclusion of Abraham in the grant? In response to its reading, Donald Lines Jacobus said,

> Mr. Edson C. Dayton in his excellent book naturally assumed that Abraham Dayton 'expired before 1712' because of the fact that the Town in that year granted the improvement of a certain acreage to Katharine Dayton and her eldest son Jonathan, but the fact is that Abraham was still living in 1726. Hence a more probable interpretation of this record is that Abraham was considered improvident and that the grant was made on these terms for the protection of his family. [657]

Jacobus continued, "the record indicates that Abraham was either unwilling or unable to represent himself or the town judged him feeble or incompetent to participate."[658]

---

[654] Note: The devastating fire in 1911 at the New York Capitol Building in Albany, destroyed about 450,000 books and 270,000 manuscripts.
[655] Note: "read" is a very questionable interpretation of the word that is nearly obliterated.
[656] (Brookhaven Town Clerk, BTR 1880)
[657] (D. Jacobus 1959)
[658] Ibid.

In this single town action are found a few possible allusions to the family's situation. First, it seems that Abraham was no longer recognized as "the man of the house." Instead, the town perceived eighteen year old Jonathan had assumed that role, and along with his mother and his siblings, had been working the land they already occupied "on loan" from the town. However, this does not necessarily mean that Abraham was not still living with his family. Jacobus said Abraham may have been "improvident" but the fact that Abraham was not included in the town entry indicates that they may not have been pursuing Abraham to take responsibility for his family, as if they understood something unknown to us. The "nature of his circumstances" could indicate that he had become disabled either physically by accident or mentally from illness, as many did, from smallpox.

The selection of that particular plot of land the town lent to Catherine and Jonathan is very interesting because of its remote location, with its high bluffs along the Long Island Sound. Three-quarters of a mile west of Flax Pond places the Dayton family on Crane Neck, near to the edge of the steep banks. Just east of Flax Pond was Old Field, another remote grazing area with natural boundaries, which would have required little supervision or fencing to control movements of livestock. Old Field remained undeveloped, with almost no population or commerce for an extended period. In fact, it was probably because of its isolation that the site would be chosen for a hospital at the time of the 1770 eruption of smallpox, for patients of a Dr. Muirson were ordered to remove to the place, "most safe and least dangres to ye inhabitants of this Town of Brookhaven." For precisely the same geographical features, it is considered prime real estate today.

If Abraham was disabled by blindness or some other ailment, or considered infectious, or if he was not around at all, how might that affect his standing with the church and town? The local church was in great upheaval at this time, after having just announced that the church was joining the Presbyterian denomination. Even with divisions forming between some of its members, attendance at church was still expected, but was more difficult to regulate. No record or even evidence has been found to indicate where this Dayton family attended church in Brookhaven after 1697.

Ironically, it is because of the virtual absence of Abraham that some things may be learned about he and his family that might otherwise have not been known.

First, from the 1724 BTR, it is learned that Jonathan's family was very ill, no doubt with smallpox. The epidemic had struck Boston in 1721 and had spread from there to Connecticut and Long Island. If Catherine was still alive, there was no specific mention of her but she may have been included in Jonathan Dayton's "famyle" since Jonathan was now of age. Jonathan was about thirty and probably was married, with a few children.

Second, if not for the notation concerning the care and provision for "Abram Daytons Negro Woman," it might never have been known that Abraham had legally owned another human being. This fact introduces all kinds of questions, but for the purposes of this book, they are limited to: Who was she? When and how did Abraham acquire her? Was the 1675 trade of sixteen barrels of whale oil with Chatwell and

Southcutt for a slave? Were there others? Had she lived with the family, as many did in those days?

In April of 1724, the first records of both the illness of the Dayton family and the existence of the woman appeared. Thomas Bayles said,

> In 1723, a very severe epidemic of smallpox swept over Brookhaven town, and many were the deaths among the Indians and the Negro slaves…Masters were required to keep their servants in at night. Fences were erected around houses in which a case of smallpox occurred, to quarantine the family, and one regulation stated that 'all persons are hereby strictly forbid pulling down any fences made to prevent the danger of spreading the smallpox.'[659]

The April 1724 town record said,

> Att ye same time voteed that Josefh Phillips shall bee payd for his Charg & truble in Doeing & prouayding for Jonathan Dayton & his famyle the sume of thurty shillings att ye same time that John Smith shall bee payd for his goeing to ye flax pon to Looke after Abram Daytons Negro Woman ye sume of fower shillings AJornd untill further order[660]

Again, the following year,

> Att a meteing of the Trustes on the: 7: Daye of aprill 1725 present Me Woodhull Justis Strong Justis Brewster Samuel Tom[son] Ensine Satterly John Wood: & Josef: Plillip: ordered that John Smith of Cor[um] Shall haue twelue shillings for Lookeing after abram Daytons Negro W[oman]

Also in 1725,

> …pertickerlerly for Keepin Ionathan daytons famely In there Sickness payd to John Smith at Corum for goeing to Look After a Negro wench

From these entries, it is learned that Jonathan was alive in 1724, as were some members of his family, living in an undisclosed location in Brookhaven. The woman was at Flax Pond. It is assumed that many, if not all were suffering with smallpox and were in isolation.

There is almost a ring of finality in the 1725 records, as if the family and the woman have either recovered or they have succumbed, and the woman was no longer referred to as belonging to Abraham. Catherine may have died and perhaps the woman also, but some of the family did escape the scourge, or at least they escaped death from the smallpox epidemic of 1723. Jacobus believed that the Jonathan Dayton who married Mary (Buttis) at Greenwich, CT on August 13, 1718 and later removed to New London, CT may have been Catherine's son.[661] If that is indeed the

---

[659] (T. R. Bayles, The Doctor in Colonial Days 1947)
[660] (Brookhaven Town Clerk, BTR 1880)
[661] (D. Jacobus 1959)

301

case, he likely married at Greenwich and returned to the land "borrowed" from the town of Brookhaven to care for the remainder of his family until about 1724. The youngest of the siblings, Henry, was probably about 16-18 years of age when Jonathan returned.

It is known that the four youngest children of Abraham and Catherine—Ephraim, Deborah, David and Henry did survive and probably Jonathan did also, but not as much is known about Jonathan's young family. At least two of Abraham's children had already removed 70 miles to New London, Connecticut years earlier, as found in Hempstead's diary. Deborah was in New London upon her marriage to John Rogers on Sunday, January 11, 1718/19, about five months after Jonathan married at Greenwich. One year after his sister Deborah married, the marriage of Ephraim was also recorded in Hempstead's diary in New London, where Ephraim remained until his death in 1748.[662] Had their mother taken the children to Connecticut? Two separate records exist for the appeals of Administratrix Deliverance Dayton to enable her to sell her husband, Ephraim's real estate, to pay quite sizable debts.[663] There are no records found for youngest son Henry in Connecticut.

Hempstead also talked about a Jonathan Dayton at New London but it is yet unclear which Jonathan Dayton that is. In a New London Probate index, this Jonathan was noted, "1760 No Town Listed."

One of the ongoing mysteries is the answer to the question—how did the children of Abraham and Catherine come to settle at New London? Formative questions are: Were Abraham or Catherine followers of the Rogerene sect? Did Catherine choose the name Deborah in honor of Deborah Moody? How involved was John Rogers, husband of Deborah Dayton, in the group?

From Anabaptists to Rogerenes

There is the possibility that the Rogerene movement, an offshoot of the Anabaptists, had somehow been a factor in the marriage of Catherine and Abraham, but to what degree it influenced or determined the course of unexplained events and circumstances is not known. Evidence seems to suggest a strong attraction to New London.

As stated, Abraham's daughter Deborah married John Rogers, son of Joseph Rogers and Sarah Haughton, grandson of James Rogers, the patriarch of the Rogers family,[664] and Elizabeth Rowland. Deborah was probably about 21 at the time and John nearly 25 years her elder. Joshua Hempstead, in his famous diary, noted the event simply as, "Jno & Deb Daton published."

The genealogies of the Rogers become quite challenging because names are repeated—of particular note is the name John. In fact, it has been claimed that John

---

[662] (Manwaring 1904)
[663] (C. J. Hoadly 1876). 495-6
[664] (Hempstead 1901)

and Deborah even gave the same name to two of their sons—their children were named John, Joseph, John, Rowland, Deborah, Catherine and Lucy. Deborah's husband was born March 20, 1675/76 and died July 13, 1739 at the age of 63 due to the effects of what Joshua Hempstead called the, "measles, fever and the flux."

An unusual story about how the town of Southold acquired a valued piece of land in Wading River from Brookhaven is told in BTR Book C and involves a John Rogers, described as a poor, lame indigent of Southold. No relationship between this John Rogers and Deborah's John Rogers has been established, but this account is provided because it is contemporary with our story and might be of some unforeseen value. In about 1707, after Rogers was cheated out of his land, he was delivered across town lines into Brookhaven, in order that he be the responsibility of that town for his support. A few days later, Brookhaven Trustees ordered him carried back to Southold, but they did not carry through on their threat. Neither town wanted to assume support for Rogers until finally in 1709 Southold proposed an exchange of land from Brookhaven plus money to absolve or clear Brookhaven from any responsibility for Rogers.

Nor should Deborah's husband be confused with his uncle John Rogers, the third son of James, the founder of the religious sect, the Rogerenes.[665] The emergence of the sect from Anabaptist has been described this way:

> The first Connecticut Anabaptist ministry began in New London County in 1674, and by 1678 the congregation could count about ten members… Among the first converts to Anabaptism in Connecticut were family members of James Rogers Sr., a man who arrived in America in 1635 at the age of twenty on the *Increase*…Rogers had a family of five boys and two girls, and most of the family would leave its mark on New London radical religious history…In 1674, two of his sons, John and James Jr., embraced Sabbatarian principles professed by the Newport Seventh Day Anabaptist congregation, and in 1675 a third son, Jonathan, was also baptized; he was followed in 1676 by James Sr., James's wife Elizabeth, and one of their daughters, Bathsheba. They formed the core of a New London branch. Connections with the Newport Seventh Day Anabaptists in Rhode Island were cemented…[through marriage, with] multiple connections between various families.[666]

In 1677, when elders from the Newport Seventh Day Anabaptist branch were to baptize the wife of Joseph Rogers at New London, they were asked by town

---

[665] (Bolles 1904)
[666] (Rust 2004)

officials to perform the ceremony outside town to avoid confrontation. The Newport elders agreed, but John did not. So began John's, "unhappiness with the Seventh Day Anabaptist leaders" and his eventual separation to form his own movement.[667] John was not one to shy away from provocation. In fact,

> He maintained that true believers ought to disrupt normal religious activities of the Puritan congregations and invite persecution on the part of the Puritans. The movement inspired by John Rogers eventuated in the formation of a separate religious organization, known generally as the Rogerenes, a radical religious group that emphasized spiritual gifts, particularly divine healing…Many Rogerenes were ancestors of early LDS converts…[including] Joseph Smith Sr.'s wife, and her grandfather, Ebenezer Mack, had belonged to the Open-Communion Baptist Church in Lyme, Connecticut.[668]

Modern perspectives of the tactics used by Rogerenes and their confrontational and "obnoxious" leaders are probably much like they were at the time—they were seen by many as outcasts and trouble-makers, probably possessing a share of arrogance. But revolutionaries, as long as they remain in the minority, are usually seen this way.

> John Rogers maintained obedience to the civil government, except in matters of conscience and religion. A town or county rate the Rogerenese always considered themselves bound to pay; but the minister's rate they abhorred, denouncing as unspiritual all interference of the civil power in the worship of God. The Rogerenes were the first in this State to denounce the doctrine of taxation without representation, the injustice of which is now universally acknowledged. All their offences may be traced to a determination to withstand and oppose ecclesiastical tyranny.[669]

Bolles and Williams qualify that statement by saying, "the fact that certain sons of Capt. James and of Joseph inclined to, and finally united with, the Congregational Church readily accounts for the less prominent stand of their parents."[670] It should be of interest to the Dayton family that Bolles and Williams wrote,

> The family of Joseph Rogers, many of whose descendants were (and are) Baptists of the regular persuasion…nothing has been found to disprove the supposition that Capt. James Rogers and his wife and Joseph Rogers and his wife continued in the Rogerene faith to the end.

---

[667] Ibid.
[668] Ibid.
[669] (Bolles 1904)
[670] Ibid.

In the book *For Adam's Sake* (discussed in the next chapter), the author states that many in the Rogers family, including Deborah's father-in-law, joined the Rogerene movement.

> Despite the fact that James [grandfather or our John Rogers] had lived a life of success and conformity, he seemed to bathe in the bright light of his son's emergence as a spiritual force and leader. The elder Rogers avidly embraced his son's convictions and encouraged the rest of his family to unite and follow…Most of the Rogers family decided to follow the lead of their patriarch, James Rogers…Siblings joined—including the baker Samuel, the yeoman Joseph, the sailor-cooper James Junior, the yeoman Jonathan, and the youngest, Elizabeth.[671]

Deborah's in-laws, Joseph and Sarah, stayed in the New London area their entire lives, as did, it appears, their ten children.

> Vintson Ackley, writing in *The Rogerenes of Ledyard*, claims the people of Quakertown mingled comparatively little with those of other faiths, following a policy of isolation aimed at producing a people "firm in their faith and resolute in maintaining their convictions of righteousness.[672]

> [Quakertown] is in a sense a misnomer…as the settlers of Quakertown and Quakerhill in Waterford were followers of the teaching of John Rogers, who lived from 1648-1721 at Quakerhill…John Rogers was never in any way affiliated with the Quakers or Friends. He was in his youth a Congregationalist, but he withdrew from that church and joined the Seventh Day Baptists. He later drew away from that church as his own convictions became more established. Some of his beliefs were the same as those of the Quakers, and it was doubtless on this account that the name became attached to him and to his followers. But his teachings were as a whole more similar to those of the Baptists than to those of the Friends.[673]

Rogerenes believed in separation of church and state. "When Rogerenes refused to pay a minister's rate or tax in support of a corrupt ministry, authorities satisfied the rate through criminal prosecutions, fines and confiscations."[674] In Hempstead's diary can be found many documented accounts of the commotion. For example, in 1719, Hempstead wrote, "Jno Rogers & his crew made a disturbance…the midst of prayer time, they came in a Horse Cart Commited to prison at night."

It is evident that Abraham Dayton had formed a bond with his son-in-law John by 1726, as is proven by a record of conveyance in New Haven. But it can not be

---

[671] (di Bonaventura 2013)
[672] (Rogers 2012)
[673] (Ackley 1997)
[674] (Hempstead 1901)

determined how or when that friendship developed—as a result of Abraham following his son-in-law's uncle years earlier or as a result of his relationship through the marriage of his daughter. It has been noted that John was about 25 years older than Deborah, making either scenario possible. Abraham's support of Deborah's husband was expressed in the New Haven (CT) Town Records.

> June 21, 1726 Abraham Daten of Brookhaven on Long Island in the province of New York...in consideration of the love and good will which I have for my son in Law John Rogers of New London...[conveys to Rogers] all such Right Estate Title Interest Claim and demand which I now have or ought to have of in and unto any Housing fences Lands Commons or common Rights or any other Estate by any ways or means what so ever belonging to me in the Township of New Haven [*New Haven Land Records*, 7:281].

The conveyance is of great importance in proving that Abraham survived to 1726 and also in proving that he was the father of the Deborah Dayton whose marriage to John Rogers in 1718/19 was recorded in New London. It informs the reader that Abraham was still living in Brookhaven, which gives reason to believe that at least one son also remained with him on Long Island. As youngest son Henry was later a member of the Setauket Presbyterian Church, it is likely he stayed at Brookhaven also.

Because there was no description of the New Haven lands, their locations cannot be identified. In fact, Jacobus suggested that the nebulous nature of the wording indicates Abraham may not have owned any land at New Haven. A search of indexes in two films of a three part set titled "Colonial Land Records of Connecticut, 1640-1846: Including Patents, Deeds and Surveys of Land,"[675] yielded no Rogers or Daytons. Some records were searched to 1726 and only two or three New Haven Land transactions were found, none to help our research. Film specifically covering the county of New Haven might reveal some significant clue. The best guess is that Abraham was referring to his grandfather's lands obtained by Phillip Leeke when Abraham was a toddler. As stated in chapter 6 of this compilation, Leeke, upon hearing of Ralph's death at North Sea, registered his ten year old purchase, probably seeking protection from Ralph's heirs. This fact suggests that the terms of the sale may have been disputed, implying that one or more lands were believed not to be included in the sale. Abraham had ample opportunity to listen to his father's telling of this story as well as stories of the homeland from his Aunt Alice and Uncle Robert, the last two survivors of that generation of immigrants. It is difficult to imagine that Sam had many good things to say about his experience at the New Haven Colony. Perhaps the potential claim against Leeke was part of the story of the Daytons' move to East Hampton.

---

[675] (Colonial Land Records of Connecticut, 1640-1846:Including patents, deeds and Surveys of land 1954)

Figure 25. Alice's Gravestone, Amagansett

Abraham was almost sixty when his uncle Robert died in 1712. No original memorial stone has been found for him. In fact, it is possible that Robert's sister Alice's stone is the only **original** marker for the burial place of any one of the Daytons who came from Ashford, Kent and settled on Long Island. Alice probably died at the home of her son in Amagansett because she is buried in the cemetery at Amagansett on Montauk Highway (see figure 25). See *Chronicles of the Family Baker* by Lee C. Baker (no date) for more details. The inscription on her stone says:

Here Lie_h y Body of Alice Baker Formrli y Wife of Thomas Baker Who
Died February y 4: 1708:9 In y 88 year of Her Age

Judging from Abraham's gesture, his son-in-law John may have helped him when few others would or could. Abraham wanted to do something for him and this is all he could offer, probably more an expression of gratitude than repayment.

Jacobus also claimed, "the two witnesses [on the deed] were New London men, and Abraham personally acknowledged the deed there eight days later."[676] If Abraham did cross the sound, it is interesting that there is a record of a Dayton leaving New London, going back to Long Island that very week, as found in Hempstead's diary. Just four days after the "deed" was written, on June 25, 1726, an entry in Joshua Hempstead's diary says,

> Saturd 25 fair. In the Morn I went down to ye Lower End of Mr. Tinker farm with Brothr & Sister Salmon who are now gone home with Daton of Latoket.[677]

Of course, Hempstead meant "Dayton of Setauket," as an early eighteenth century S could look like an L since both letters often had "tails." Hempstead's friends, the Salmons, were from Long Island.

Who was this Dayton of Setauket? If he was a member of the Abraham Dayton family, the only possibilities are Henry, David, Jonathan or Abraham himself because there is no proof that any of them were yet living in New London. At the time, Henry was about 24, David was about 25-29, Jonathan about 32 and their father Abraham, was about 72. Could one of the boys possibly be running a ferry service or was Hempstead simply referring to Dayton as a fellow passenger with the Salmons?

So, is this possibly the last record of Abraham while he was living?

A Surprising Twist

The path through Abraham's life continues to be unpredictable. Once destitute, it is comforting to learn that he may have died neither alone nor penniless. To the contrary, an Abraham Dayton was included among only ten men on the Brookhaven plate tax list in 1726. But is it reasonable to conclude that this Abraham who qualified for a luxury tax in 1726 is the same man who was destitute in 1710? It would appear that our Abraham is the only candidate in Brookhaven who was of age in 1726. Of course, there is still that lingering theory that Abraham had a wife before Mary and this unknown wife gave birth to his oldest son, Abraham of Salem County New Jersey. This may be one of the more convincing evidences of his existence.

As "plate" meant silver, the plate tax was a luxury tax intended specifically for those wealthy enough to own silverware, a status symbol of the day. There appears an example of such a tax in 1726, to be assessed and collected in His Majesty's name. The warrant for £3,600 was issued in August and by act of the General Assembly, was proportioned to all towns, with Brookhaven's share calculated to be £16-6s-8d. Collection was required by October 1 of the same year.

The Brookhaven plate tax list appears in the record under the title, "Conserning ye five thousand pound Tax Warrant to Collector-1726." All but one man appears

---

[676] (D. Jacobus 1959)
[677] (Hempstead 1901)

twice, in what seems to be a second event. In comparative wealth, judged on the plate tax alone, this Abraham was placed fifth of ten townsmen. The first installment of Abraham's tax was 0-0-5 and the second tax was 0-0-3. The record of the original warrant is held among the Trustee's papers and documents in the Brookhaven Town Clerk's Office.

If this Abraham is indeed ours, how he came to own silverware, of course, is another mystery. Did Catherine and he again prosper, perhaps through inheritance? If Catherine had died, did Abraham gain such extravagance through remarriage?

It then appears that Abraham died sometime soon after these 1726 events, but without record of his death. He was the only one in this present study of six generations of direct descendancy for whom history has left neither mention nor reference to his time of death. Where he was laid to rest is not known.

In addition to Caleb, son of Mary, who had been living with the Rawlinson's,[678] Abraham's recorded family included his wife and five children, all from Catherine—Jonathan, Deborah, Ephraim, David and Henry. Of these five, Jonathan and Deborah are the only children positively proven by record, but as Jonathan was called eldest son of Catherine, the inference is that there were younger sons. There are abundant references to Ephraim in the Diary of Joshua Hempstead of New London, CT, along with his sister Deborah. David married Eunice Brewster in 1729[679] and the youngest, our ancestor Henry can be found throughout the BTR, including details in his will in 1760.

---

[678] Note: Caleb had just become sole heir to William Rawlinson's estate when Rawlinson's will was approved March 1711/12. It is interesting to note that, in the will, an Elizabeth Beardsley was thanked for her care of William in his sickness.

[679] (D. Jacobus 1959)

Chapter 17

Servitude and Slavery

"The Unresolvable Challenge"

The book *For Adam's Sake: A Family Saga in Colonial New England* by Allegra di Bonaventura tells the story of a slave and his owner, Joshua Hempstead of New London, CT by means of Hempstead's own diary. In her review of di Bonaventura's book, in *The Hartford Courant* of May 9, 2013, Susan Dunne expressed the author's dilemma, as explained by di Bonaventura herself. This problem is a common one for anyone who writes or speaks with historical accuracy and realizes his/her audience's sensitively about the subject.

> di Bonaventura said she knew that contemporary readers would be appalled at the casual acceptance of slavery by a person who is the hero of the story. As the book describes him, 'A kindhearted widower [who] could devote himself to motherless children but still enslave another man's boy without a whiff of remorse.'

> One of the challenges of the book is really an unresolvable challenge. He was such a good man, and yet he did something so evil.

> She said that readers must be able to look at people in different time periods and try to understand their world in their terms. 'Joshua Hempstead lived in a world where the people to whom he looked for guidance, such as his minister and members of the elite families, were some of the leading slave owners and people involved in the slave trade. They often invoked Biblical sanctions for owning slaves,' she said. 'This is a world where forms of servitude, slavery, indentured servitude, different kinds of domestic or other laboring service was much more common that it is now. Sometimes the distinctions for colonial people between servants and slaves were not as stark, in terms of the actual work they did. Joshua spent a period of life as a servant, as did most people.'

> …practical everyday distinctions between freedom and servitude, slaves and servants, could be subtle in early New England. The word 'servant'

itself was ambiguous and could mean indentured servant, wage laborer, or perpetual slave, depending on its usage.

Since many degrees of servitude, from apprenticeships to slavery played such an important part in the culture of the times, space must be dedicated to some of the institutions on Long Island, rather than ignoring them. These systems, in one way or another, involved the first five of our generations of lineage in the New World. One must believe only a very small portion of the subject has come to light and the portion that has been left to us is wholly inadequate to gain an understanding of its realities.

It reminds us once again of Hugh King's quote in the 2012 *Newsday* article[680] mentioned at the beginning of this compilation. It is appropriate to repeat it here. King promoted the idea of,

> seeing the reality of East Hampton's history as more than just attractive windmills and wooden houses. [Samuel Dayton] pledged to give his son, Jacob, to his brother Thomas Backer and his wife for 14 years of servitude, in exchange for a promise the boy would get 'sufficient meate Drink and apparell & to Doe for him as his owne …'

Apprenticeship

In colonial America, the typical route to making a living as a craftsman, such as a shoemaker, printer or cooper began with an apprenticeship. This meant learning your father's craft or living and working in the shop of a master craftsman for maybe four to six, or even ten years. The apprentice, almost always a young boy, normally worked under a contract to serve and obey the master, beginning with the performance of menial tasks, then gradually gaining responsibility, with the goal of attaining the skills of the trade. That way, the master had use of the labor until the contract had expired and the apprentice would be discharged to open his own shop. The master was also supposed to feed the boy, provide clothes and lodging, and sometimes even provide a workable education. Perhaps our own Ralph, American progenitor, learned his craft in this way.

Occasionally, a boy's father would pay for the master to take him, as an avenue to gain education and opportunity or, in the case of troublesome sons, to gain discipline. In other families who lost a mother or father, for widows with little support and those families who could no longer provide for their children, it was simply a way to cut household expenses.

"Discharged apprentices were bound out to other masters, in compliance with the law which required that all children not of independent estate be brought up in some 'honest lawful' calling. The same legislation made provision for 'Refusal of

---

[680] (Freedman 2012)

Necessaries' and 'after due proof made,' apprentices who were denied 'sufficient meat, drink and lodging,' were set free." A case in point appears in a Long Island record of Nov 2, 1738 for Joseph Dodge apprenticed to Jeremiah Dodge.[681]

The Duke of York's Laws contained orders that apprentices who ran away from their masters were obliged to serve, "double the time of such their absence." If necessary, in order to bring back runaways, "Every Justice of the Peace or any Constable with two Overseers where no Justice is at hand," had the "power to press Men, Horses, Boats or Pinnaces, at Publique Charge, to pursue such persons both by Sea and Land and to bring them back by force of Armes."[682] It is not known how often this provision was utilized.

Indentured Servitude

The availability of land and labor were essential and fundamental ingredients for the establishment and advancement of the colonies. As lands became available for the influx of settlers, adequate labor to support these endeavors, especially on Long Island, became scarce. To fill the need, an industry to provide labor was developed and was sometimes an effective means to provide opportunity for the poorer masses of Great Britain. Unfortunately, where there is opportunity to gain greater or faster money from exploitation, there are human beings who will degrade others beyond enterprise and self-preservation to base self-indulgence and to their own detestable nature.

"Once the English had settled in and established their homesteads, they began to employ Indians, poor whites, and free African Americans as indentured servants and as day laborers. These arrangements especially suited the small landholders who could not afford to buy slaves."[683] By signing indenture contracts, masters and servants agreed to specific terms and obligations. According to law, masters owned the labor of their indentured servant and therefore essentially had control of their lives. The indentured servant was not free to move or to marry, or to work outside of the contract without their master's approval. Of course, they could not work for themselves. Such contracts "bound" their lives for three to seven years, depending upon what was to be repaid.

It seems difficult to believe, but it has been claimed that after the Puritan migration of 1630-1640, not less than half of the Europeans who arrived in North America in the seventeenth and eighteenth centuries may have come as indentured servants,[684] with a higher percentage along some of the Atlantic coast, south of New England.

---

[681] (Seybolt 1917)
[682] Ibid.
[683] (J. A. Strong 2011)
[684] (Hofstadter 1972)

Just as was the case with apprentices, Richard Hofstadter tells us that runaway indentured servants often had years added to their contracts as punishment. But, unlike slaves, servants also had legal rights including the right to testify in court and to petition. Often a young person agreed to serve a master as an apprentice and be trained in a skill. In this way, apprenticeships are often confused or used indiscriminately with indentured servitude. According to Hofstadter,

> indentured servitude had its roots in the widespread poverty and human dislocation of seventeenth-century England. Still a largely backward economy with a great part of its population permanently unemployed …drifting men and women gathered in the cities, notably London, where they constituted a large mass of casual workers, lumpenproletarians, and criminals. The mass of the poverty-stricken was so large that Gregory King, the pioneer statistician, estimated in 1696 that more than half the population—cottagers and paupers, laborers and out-servants—were earning less than they spent. They diminished the wealth of the realm, he argued, since their annual expenses exceeded income and had to be made up by the poor rates, which ate up one-half of the revenue of the Crown. In the early seventeenth century, this situation made people believe the country was overpopulated and emigration to the colonies was welcomed.

Hofstadter continues,

> The English poor, lured, seduced, or forced into the emigrant stream, kept coming to America for the better part of two centuries. It is safe to guess that few of them, and indeed few persons from the other sources of emigration, knew very much about what they were doing when they committed themselves to life in America. Yet the poor were well aware that they lived in a heartless world. One of the horrendous figures in the folklore of lower-class London in the seventeenth and eighteenth centuries was the 'spirit'—the recruiting agent who waylaid, kidnapped, or induced adults to get aboard ships for America. The spirits, who worked for respectable merchants, were known to lure children with sweets, to seize upon the weak or the gin-sodden and take them aboard ship, and to bedazzle the credulous or weak-minded by fabulous promises of an easy life in the New World.

Some of the abducted English children were sold as plantation servants, "a thriving trade that Charles II and his Privy Council found very disturbing"[685] and so, it became necessary to create laws to counter the spiriting of children.

As mentioned earlier, there exists confusion in some ways caused by improper use of terminology. Some "contracts" referred to as apprenticeships were actually indentured servitude or even slavery. For example, "apprentices" could also be

---

[685] (Barstow, Setauket, Alias Brookhaven 2004). 294

acquired by other means which, upon application, degrades beneath that status. In 1644, in Southampton, two servants belonging to Edward Howell admitted to "carnal filthiness" together. As a result, the child of the white man and a Native American woman was made a servant of Mr. Howell's for thirty years, then, "shall be released of his aforesaid Apprenticeshippe." In return, Howell agreed to provide, "meat, drinke, and Apparel and necessaryes fit for such a servant dureing the sayd tyme."[686]

Like apprenticeships, indenture was also utilized by poor families who, under certain circumstances, could not or would not support a child or children. If you were fortunate to have a compassionate relative close by or an acquaintance who could use the labor from indenture, that was certainly preferable over sending your child to a master who was unknown to you. The former seems to be the case in some of our own Dayton family on Long Island. Belle Barstow says, "The use of children did go on in Setauket, as noted in the records when the two young sons of Samuel Dayton were indentured to serve until their coming of age; some fourteen to fifteen years."

It was fortunate for Jacob that his father convinced trusted relatives to care for Jacob and, though not ideal, Caleb was placed close to his family, with the Garlicks. Despite the lack of any sentiment expressed in the official record, these separations had to be an emotional time for all, even though our assumption is they were well-placed.

One generation later, on May 12, 1696, Sam's son Abraham of Brookhaven repeated the procedure when he gave his son Caleb "Daighton," then aged 8 years and 5 months, to the Rawlinsons of Stratford, CT. Caleb was to remain until age 21, with the agreement that they were to treat him in all respects, "as if ye said Caleb was there own natural child" (Stratford Land Records, 2:497). Actually, the extraordinary record indicates an affectionate bond resulted, enough so that the Rawlinsons referred to Caleb as their "loving adopted son."[687]

The earliest indication (on this side of the ocean) of a Dayton being an employer or master, occurred in the 1650s. The passage is a deposition concerning Ralph Dayton's missing horse given by Joshua Garlicke, where Garlick(e) testified that the last time he saw the horse, it was with "Goodman Daitons man" indicating that Ralph had some kind of employee or servant, as was most common (rather than slavery) at that time.

Slavery

Slavery, in some form, has no doubt existed almost since the beginning of mankind. In the compiler's own view, it is a result of man's natural bent toward depravity, and it can be argued that its existence has not been exempt from any culture. Despite the wishes of some revisionist historians, the reprehensible practice

---

[686] (H. Hedges 1874)
[687] (D. L. Jacobus, History and Genealogy of the Families of Old Fairfield 1991)

315

was not introduced to Long Island by the Europeans, but existed as an institution among Native American peoples for centuries before the white man arrived.

Of course, when talking about slavery in the early Americas, the horrendous treatment of Africans kidnapped from their native land first comes to mind. In school, history books told us about plantation slavery across the South and about heroic northerners (and southern sympathizers), many of them abolitionists of the Underground Railroad, who helped courageous escaped slaves find their way to Canada. Rightly so, but many history books failed to address or even mention slavery in a broader view and in other contexts, outside of the buildup to the war between the states. Bondage was not confined to the South and was not confined to African Americans, although after slave laws were passed in the 1660s, Africans quickly lost any freedoms they may have had as indentured servants. Slavery in northern states and New England in the colonial era also included Native Americans, Irish Catholics and multitudes of poor adult White persons and kidnapped English children.[688] Among these groups, the title of indentured servant or just "servant" has been assigned but, in reality, they were slaves—stripped of their humanity; they were sold, brutalized and never gained or regained their freedom.

"Indian slavery was recognized both in the Connecticut code of 1646 and by the United Colonies…In New York, nearly all laws relating to slavery between 1644 and 1788 recognized the existence of Indian slavery and treated it as an integral part of the slave system."[689] The regulations concerning these slaves generally applied to Black and Mulatto as well.

"Old documents and records also indicate that the Indians were bought and sold like other slaves."[690] Anne Hartell tells about the existence of a 1663 Dutch law that stated: "To encourage the settlers to assist in the war against the Esopus Indians, the Governor promises them all the plunder they could gain, and whatever Indians they might take prisoners to be their slaves." According to Lisa Cordani-Stevenson, "Legal Indian slavery started in 1636 with captives of the Pequot War in New England and continued with those captured in King Philip's War of 1675. Indians could be indentured due to debt or enslaved as a penalty for a crime. A small number of Indian slaves were also imported from the Carolinas and from Spanish colonies."[691] Ultimately, it is very difficult to delineate between Native American servants and Native American slaves on Long Island. Sometimes legal documents between employers and employees, though generous, had the effect of perpetual servanthood, while other times, it is argued, they were designed to degenerate into slavery especially if the Native Americans were paid in liquor.

Both the servant and slave were locked into submission and oppression, serving a master by some type of legal contract, but there were also some real differences. In

---

[688] (Jordan 2008)
[689] (Cordani-Stevenson 2011)
[690] (Hartell 1943)
[691] (Cordani-Stevenson 2011)

servitude, there were many who were not bound for life, but in slavery, not only was the slave bound but also children born to the slave were in bondage while children of servants were "free."

Many Long Island historians, among them Benjamin F. Thompson, agree that the importation of African slaves to Long Island began in 1626. These dozen or so slaves were brought to New Netherland and on the west end, and were made to labor for the Dutch West Indian Company. Just one generation later, African slaves began to appear on the east end, then "For almost two centuries, New York was a slave colony and Long Island was a slave island."[692] From about 1680 to 1740, as the population of Africans increased, New York State slavery law placed increasing restrictions and regulations not only on Native American and African American slaves but also on free African Americans, and gave owners of slaves more freedoms to punish and discipline them as they saw fit, short of death or loss of limb. In the process, enslaved persons became thought of as possessions or chattel, rather than human beings.

Generally speaking, on the east end, those who had any money owned slaves. A majority of the time, they didn't use the word "slave," but rather "servant." The word "slave" was used when dealing with Native Americans or African Americans.

Life for a slave in rural Long Island was lonely and isolated. In contrast to the gang-oriented plantations of the South, most Long Island slaveholders were yeomen (or free) farmers who usually owned one to three slaves to work their limited acreage.[693] In the rare occasion that a master owned more than a few slaves, he might house them in their own slave cabin. Slaves were scattered widely across the island, many without family, and with no one to socialize. Slaves usually labored alongside day laborers, indentured servants and their owners and lived in their houses.[694] Everyone labored from dawn to dusk in dozens of occupations. Long Island's African American slave population was highly multi-occupational. Besides agriculture, slaves also worked in secondary industries such as tailoring and whaling. African American females were often assigned roles as domestic servants with tasks ranging from cooking to caring for their owners' children. African American slaves, along with the occasional Native American slave, often worked alongside free African workers, European indentured servants, paid European workers, and even the slave owners themselves.[695]

After the land itself, the next most valuable asset to a yeoman farmer was his slaves.[696] Slaves were highly valued in the colonial period and sometimes received better treatment because they were regarded as lifetime investments, whereas the servant would be gone after a few years.[697] Anne Hartell wrote,

---

[692] (Dewan 2005)
[693] (Wagner 2006)
[694] (Shillingburg, The Disposition of Slaves on the East End of Long Island from 1680 to 1796 2003)
[695] (Wagner 2006)
[696] (Shillingburg, The Disposition of Slaves on the East End of Long Island from 1680 to 1796 2003)
[697] (Indentured Servitude In the Atlantic World n.d.)

317

On the farms on Long Island anyone who could do a good day's work was appreciated, and the family usually worked in field and kitchen along with the slave help. The farm hand might do such things, besides laboring in the fields, as caring for the horses and cows, working the dairy and mill of his owner. The women slaves were nurses, cooks and kitchen help. Farm workers who showed intelligence might rise to managing the plantation.[698]

Colonel William Brayne wrote to English authorities in 1656 urging the importation of Negro slaves on the grounds that, 'as the planters would have to pay much more for them, they would have an interest in preserving their lives, which was wanting in the case of (Irish) ...' many of whom, he charged, were killed by overwork and cruel treatment. Black males cost generally 20 to 50 pounds Sterling, compared to 900 pounds of cotton (about 5 pounds Sterling) for an Irish.[699]

In 1700 the high price was fifty pounds for a male and forty-five pounds for a female. Kings County records show that on December 16th, 1719, a Negro woman and her child were valued at sixty pounds while five milch cows, five calves, three young bulls and two heifers were collectively worth only twenty pounds.[700]

It is said that Black slavery reached the East End of Long Island when Nathaniel Sylvester[701] brought slaves from Barbados to his plantation on Shelter Island in the 1650's. From that point, it very slowly spread across Long Island. One of the first Blacks of Setauket was Anthony, brought to town by Richard Floyd in 1672 after purchasing him from John Ogden in Rye, New York (Note: In genealogical circles, the two Ogdens are differentiated by reference to "John Ogden the Pilgrim" and "John Ogden of Rye"). Floyd paid 48 pounds sterling for Anthony.[702] From that point on, slavery was spreading more quickly so that, "census and tax data from the late 17th century indicate[d] that approximately two out of five households in Queens and Suffolk Counties included one or more slaves."[703] "Blacks were 15 percent of the total population in Suffolk by 1723."[704]

The following excerpts are selected examples of references to slaves from the 2003 Shillingburg paper. These particular examples were chosen because they involve Europeans mentioned previously, from town records:

---

[698] (Hartell 1943)
[699] (Gjohnsit 2013)
[700] (Shillingburg, The Disposition of Slaves on the East End of Long Island from 1680 to 1796 2003)
[701] Note: Another Nathaniel Sylvester was the compiler of the book *History of Saratoga County New York with Illustrations and Biographical Sketches of Some of its Prominent Men and Pioneers,* Philadelphia: Everets & Ensign, 1878. He is quoted several times, usually pertaining to Hadley, NY.
[702] (Barstow, Setauket, Alias Brookhaven 2004) 293
[703] (Moss 1993)
[704] (Naylor, Women in Long Island's Past: A History of Eminent Ladies and Everyday Lives 2012)

In 1683, Ralf Dayton, probably Abraham's oldest brother, sold "negro Jack" for 3 acres in Newtown, beef and cash.

In his will in 1684, John Budd, a yeoman farmer in Southold gave his "negro woman Catherine and her child" to his wife Mary.

That same year, Thomas Jessup of Southampton decreed in his will that his "negro man" was to be "freed after four years."

In 1690, Benjamin Horton of Southold was of like mind: "I give to my man Joseph one sow one gun one sheep and his time to be out next May day..."

John Swazey of Southold in 1692 agreed: "My will is that Besse ye servant shall be free & set at liberty at my decease & she shall have the bed she lieth on." This John Swazey was possibly a relative of Catherine, Abraham Dayton's wife.

Stephen Hand of East Hampton, in 1693 gave his Indian boy to his eldest son Stephen with the admonition, "also ye Indian boy he paying five pounds to ye boy to ye end of his time if he shall have a full year to serve." Freedom in the end.

In Smithtown, Richard Smith to his son Job: 'we give and bequeath our negro Robin for ye term of twelve years...and at ye end of ye said twelve years, the said Robin shall be freed.'

Abraham's son in our direct line, Henry, owned at least five or six[705] African American slaves at the time he wrote his will. On October 7, 1759, Henry Dayton, of Brookhaven left to his wife Abigail a Negro named "Charity" and "a negro boy, aged 3 1/2 years" to his son David, who is also in our direct line of descent. The fate of this boy is unknown but we would like to believe that David freed him. Henry, "also value[d] a small negro girl at £60, and she is to go to my two daughters at that value." Henry also had three slaves listed in the inventory of his Egg Harbor, New Jersey estate. Anne Hartell tells us that,

slavery spread throughout the [Long] Island among all types of people. Even ministers and Quakers held them as personal servants or as laborers on their farms. The number of slaves a man owned was indicative of his wealth. The poorer families held one or two, and the more prosperous as many as eight.

A slave in colonial Suffolk County was among the farmer's most costly investments, and because the farmer was so dependent on his labor, slavery, "had a long and complicated death." It appears that to David, who inherited a slave child on Long Island and probably three more slaves in New Jersey in the early 1760's, his slaves may have been viewed with less utility and therefore the 1776 census lists no Black persons in David's household.

---

[705] Note: There are six mentioned in the will, but one may be double-counted.

In 1785, the New York Legislature set in place a policy for the gradual abolition of slavery and by 1826 trade in Black persons ceased altogether on Long Island, and by the next year, it was no longer legal to hold slaves.

Chapter 18

What did Henry Gain?

While contextual references are gathered from a variety of sources, the primary source for Henry continues to be the Brookhaven Town Records. Proceeding forward from Ralph to Sam, to Abraham, and now to Henry, the quantity of available historical records and information specifically pertaining to our line of descendancy becomes proportionally less. Regrettably, the same will be true proceeding through the eighteenth century, from Henry to David and to his son David. There remains much work to be done as accessibility to documents and information is expected to increase.

Henry Dayton, our 5th-great-grandfather, was almost certainly the youngest of Abraham and Catherine's children, born about 1702-1706 (estimate varies sharply from 1700 to 1712 among scholars),[706] into that period of time of great mystery surrounding his father. His birth preceded his father's appeal to collect charity. Henry had at least four brothers—Caleb, Jonathan, Ephraim and David, and one sister named Deborah. There is some speculation that another brother or brothers named Abraham Junior and Jacob were born of Abraham's unknown wife before Mary and the birth of Caleb, but there is no proof. Supposedly, it is these two men who were found in Salem County, New Jersey, possibly through disposition with the unknown wife's relatives. We recognize that provision for the oldest, unproven brothers is convenient for answering questions, but judge their existence not likely. Henry's father, Abraham, was roughly fifty at the time of his youngest son's birth and Catherine was probably in her mid-forties. Most likely, Henry was in this twenties when his father died. With Henry being the youngest of at least five boys, it would be reasonable to conclude he received a very small inheritance, if he received anything at all.

It is observed that Samuel's third son Abraham was about four years old when his grandfather Ralph died in 1658. It turns out that this overlapping of three generations is rare in our direct line of ancestry because this is the only time in ten

---

[706] Note: Jacobus, on page 29, appears to be the source of the 1700 estimate for Henry's birth year, but a later date is preferred with reasoning found in the Vital Statistics table in this compilation.

generations where the grandson was born before the death of his grandfather. So, Henry never knew his grandfather. Without vital statistics of Ralph's ancestry, we cannot know how long this pattern continued backward. It is common for families to enjoy the benefits of generational continuity which affords shared communication between three and sometimes four generations. In our own Dayton line, for various reasons, this has not been the case. It is not known what this cascading effect has had upon contributions to our collective family experience (legacy) and oral tradition.

In figure 26 below, a few ages are approximated for display purposes.

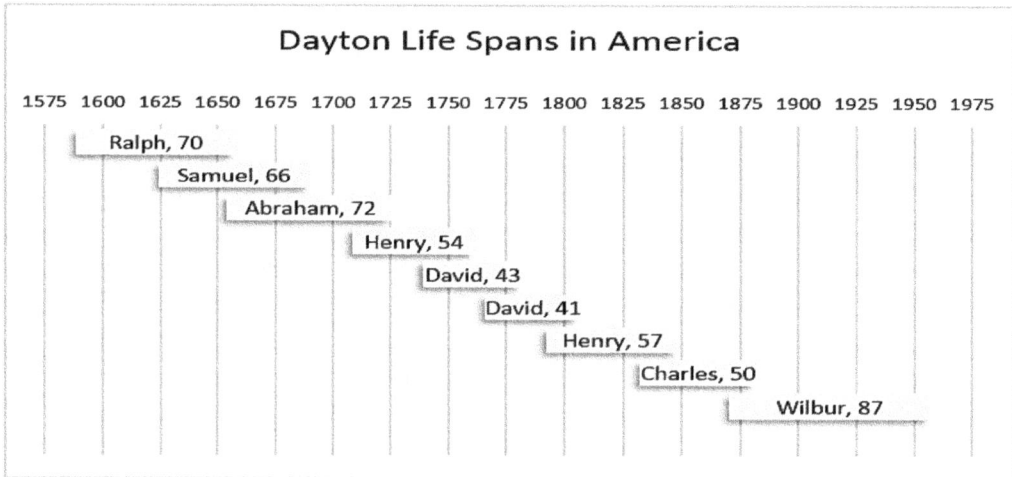

Dayton Life Spans in America

1575 1600 1625 1650 1675 1700 1725 1750 1775 1800 1825 1850 1875 1900 1925 1950 1975

Ralph, 70
Samuel, 66
Abraham, 72
Henry, 54
David, 43
David, 41
Henry, 57
Charles, 50
Wilbur, 87

Figure 26. Generational chart spanning nine generations

Perhaps the economic hardships of the time—rampant smallpox and uncertain income from Abraham—nourished a desire in Henry for material wealth, as he grew. Certainly, a residual effect of this loss of generational contact is the loss of material wealth in the form of gifts or inheritance. But someone in the family valued education and a strong work ethic, and saw to it that Henry received instruction in both. Most likely, Henry received an education from whomever his caretakers were. Whatever the impetus, Henry Dayton grew into relative prosperity, considering the economic modesty of his youth.

Henry married Abigail Norton, daughter of Jonathan Norton,[707] between 1725 and 1728, within a short time after both reached legal age.[708] Henry and Abigail had

---

[707] (Seversmith, George Norton of Salem, Massachusetts, and His Supposed Connection with the Norton Family of Sharpenhoe, Bedfordshire 1939)

[708] Note: As Henry and Abigail are very common names in the Dayton and Norton families, there are an abundance of birth dates for Henry in early publications and on the internet. No attempt has been made to sort them all out since we are reasonably confident that our estimate is appropriate for our line.

probably not lived far apart because Jonathan's father Nathaniel's homelot and Henry's father Abraham's house had neighboring lands in Brookhaven for many years.[709] Abigail's family was established, Jonathan being a surveyor of highways, fence viewer and commissioner at Old Man's.[710] Norton was a very common surname around the area of Old Mans and Middle Island. Like the Daytons, the Nortons had also come from Southampton to Brookhaven, moving at about the same time, depending on how Sam's gradual move is dated. Abigail's father was three generations removed from George Norton, a merchant (probably from London) who sailed from Gravesend, Kent to America in 1629. Nathaniel Norton, the carpenter hired to build the meeting house at Setauket in 1669, was the grandfather of our Abigail. Another Nathaniel Norton, Abigail's nephew, was a minister of the Baptist Church,[711] presumably at Coram or one of the neighboring communities. Unlike the previous three generations of Dayton men whose first wives predeceased them, only one wife has been identified for Henry and she survived him, so it is assumed that Abigail was the biological mother to the six identified children.[712]

Sometime within the first three years of marriage, Henry and Abigail had their first child, a son they named Henry (Junior). He is one of the Henrys often confused by early authors for his father. It seems that for many years, the existence of father and son, both named Henry, was not known so each has been attributed "facts" belonging to the other.

Three more sons and two daughters followed the birth of Henry Junior—Norton, born about 1730-1734, David about 1737-39, Abraham about 1739, and at least two daughters—Abigail born about 1734 and Katherine about 1740. Each is mentioned by name in their father's will, beginning with the sons and following them the daughters, establishing birth order.

According to one theory, Henry and Abigail were living in Connecticut the first few years of their married life together, but they were probably already residing at their farm at Comesewoge, where in June of 1734, Henry had both cattle and sheep. Henry retained this property for the remainder of his life, although he did not spend all his time there. In William Tooker's book, *The Indian Place-Names of Long Island,* the author gives the original spelling as "Cumsewogue" and describes it as, "a farming district upon the high level plain, about a mile south of Port Jefferson."[713] Author Eugene Armbruster says, "The place now occupied by Cedar Hill Cemetery was named by the Indians Cumsewogue."[714] Judging from the post card (figure 27),

---

[709] Note: See Nathaniel Norton's will, 1684 Brookhaven, NY—from *Early Long Island Wills of Suffolk County 1691-1703*)
[710] (Seversmith, George Norton of Salem, Massachusetts, and His Supposed Connection with the Norton Family of Sharpenhoe, Bedfordshire 1939)
[711] Ibid.
[712] Note: some years ago, there was confusion between Henry Senior and Henry Junior. Herbert F. Seversmith's citing of Henry Junior instead of Henry Senior on page 199 is an example.
[713] (Tooker 1911)
[714] (Armbruster 1914)

if this location was included in the land Henry owned, it was quite desirable and picturesque when the view of the harbor was unobstructed.

Figure 27. Cumsewogue, before Cedar Hill Cemetery

Post card from private collection of G. Moraitis, used with permission

Pelletreau says there is another piece of land known as Copsowoge, near Southampton, "on the north side of the South Beach, being on the east side of a certain house which Stephen Boyer and Company made when they made a Whaling Company near to a place called Copsowoge about a mile and a half from ye gut near a place called ye Green pines."[715]

Earmarks

When animals grazed in common meadows, earmarks often helped avoid disputes over individual ownership of cattle identified by unique patterns cut into their ears. For the genealogist, earmarks can be invaluable for establishing linkage between generations, as earmarks were very often transferred from father to son.

There is an abundance of Dayton earmarks registered in Brookhaven, through the generations, a sufficient quantity to develop an interesting and involved study.

---

[715] (W. Pelletreau 1915) 144.

324

On March 6, 1733/34, Henry registered his cattle earmark with the town clerk and it was recorded in the BTR, using both description and diagram. The Dayton family had been using earmarks on Long Island for eighty years, since the first generation at East Hampton. In fact, we believe that the very first mention of a cattle mark in East Hampton was for our own Ralph Dayton,[716] when his son Robert testified that his father had ear marked his colt that had been missing and then was found in the possession of another man. Ralph's earmark has never been located. In 1944, author Frank Overton M.D. described the purpose of the earmark.

> Pasturing cattle on unoccupied lands, especially the salt-water meadows and town properties, was a common practice throughout Long Island during Colonial days and even as late as 1880. The cattle were driven to the public lands in the spring, and were taken home in the fall. During the pasturing months the cattle were left in charge of a keeper who watched over them and received a fee for his services. Each owner identified his cattle by means of earmarks which had the same legal significance as the brands on the flanks of cattle on the Western prairies. These earmarks were registered in the offices of the town clerks as evidence of private ownership.[717]

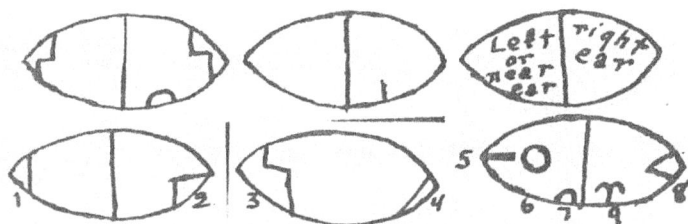

Figure 28. Overton's nine fundamental earmarks

In the same *Long Island Forum* article, Overton provided drawings of six forms of earmarks, followed by descriptions of nine fundamental earmarks.

Overton's descriptions of earmarks
    1. A Crop — The end of the ear was cut off squarely.
    2. A Latch — A right-angle piece was cut out from the end of the ear.
    3. A Crop-Latch — Numbers one and two combined into a single unit.
    4. A Slope — The end of the ear trimmed with a slanting cut, in distinction, which is square.
    5. A Slit — A short straight cut into the end or side of the ear

---

[716] (Springs Man Revives Cattle Ear Marks Used by Ancestors 1963)
[717] Frank Overton, "Cattle Ear Marks of Long Ago," *Long Island Forum*, April 1944.

6. A Penny — A round hole punched through the ear.
7. A Half-Penny — A half circle punched on the edge of the ear.
8. A Wedge[718] — An acute angle cut out of the end of the ear.
9. A Fleur-de-lis — A crude imitation of a lily or tree. It was seldom used, for it was hard either to make or recognize.

Numbers 1, 2, 3, 4, and 8 may be placed at the outer end of either ear, or both ears. Numbers, 2, 4 and 7 may be placed on either the upper side or the lower side of either ear or both ears: Number 5 may be placed on the end or the top edge or the lower edge of either ear, or two slits may be made side by side.

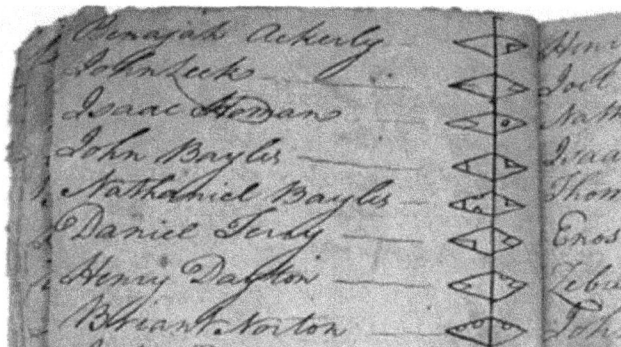
Figure 29. Henry Dayton's earmark in registry

Henry's earmark can be found in the "Brookhaven Earmark Registry"[719] where he registered on March 6, 1733, and a diagram of his earmark is found in the seventh row of figure 29. "Henery Dayton Eare marke is a forke in Each Eare and a hapeny on the uper: sid of the Rite Earr"[720]

Brookhaven Town Historian, Brookhaven Township Municipal Building

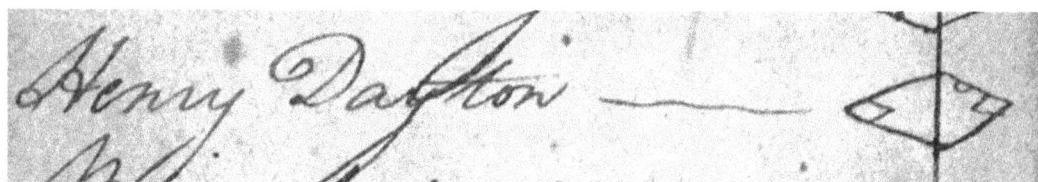
Figure 30. Closer view of Henry's earmark

It is significant for the genealogist that there is a record of Henry's former earmark being transferred to his son David (figure 31). The record is held at the Office of the Town Historian at Brookhaven Township Municipal Bldg, Farmington. Considering that David was the third of Henry's four sons, it seemed at first curious

---

[718] Note: It is believed that another name for wedge is fork.
[719] Brookhaven Municpal Buildings's Town Historian's Office, Cabinet III, Drawer E.
[720] (Shaw, Records of the Town of Brookhaven 1679-1756 Book B 1932)

that David received his father's earmark in 1766, after his father's death. The image of the town record that follows says:

> June 6th 1766: David Dayton's Ear Mark is a shallow fork in each ear and a half penny in upper side of right ear which mark was his father Henry Datens mark formerly.[721]

> At the Same time: Entered to Abraham Dayton for his Ear mark a crop on the Right Ear and a half penny in the upper Side of Same and a [notch] the under Side of the Left Ear.

Figure 31. Record of David receiving his father's earmark

What can be learned of the family and what are the implications of David registering Henry's earmark as his own? Since David had two older brothers, they probably required their own ear marks before their father died. David's younger brother Abraham, about twenty-five in 1766, may have already received other cattle and would register another of Henry's earmarks. David was already in possession of inherited cattle in New Jersey (cows, calves and oxen listed in the inventory) and the earmark may have required registration in Suffolk County. It is assumed that the Abraham who accompanied Henry to the town clerk's office was his oldest brother.

Yet another variation of the same earmark belonging to Abraham above is shared by a David Dayton (identity not yet determined) in the list below. In another list, a Samuel Dayton has what seems to be a variant (not shown), further removed from the original.

---

[721] (Brookhaven Town Clerk, Brookhaven Earmark Registry circa 1750)

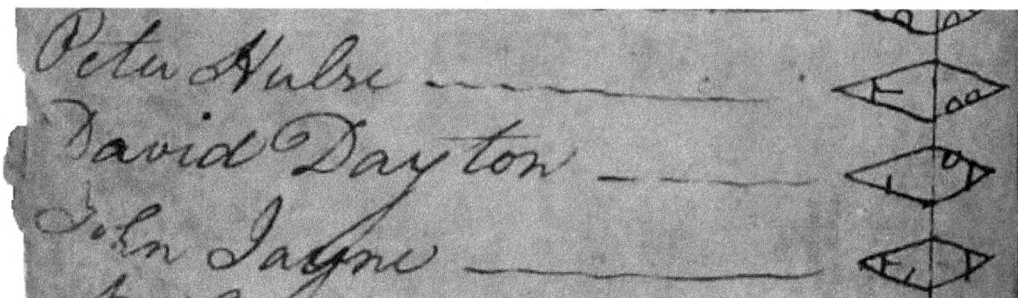

Figure 32. Earmark of a David Dayton

The description of our Abraham's (son of Samuel and father of Henry) earmark in November of 1680 was given, "Abram daiton Eare mark is a slit downe the eare and a hole through the far Eare with a halfe peny under ye slitt of the neer eare." Another earmark registered to Abraham's son John Dayton (born about 1694), seems to be a slight variation on his father Abraham's earmark.

Overton stated that, although the system of earmarks made possible thousands of combinations, the system was not perfect. Men didn't always keep the same earmarks when they moved, but they often did. What had probably worked well in the beginning eventually became unmanageable, as men moved, traded, bought and sold cattle, and sons inherited livestock and with them, their earmarks. In Brookhaven, an attempt was made to deal with the confusion, by force of law, in April of 1770.[722]

As stated, many more Dayton earmarks are worthy of examination, and a thorough study has the potential to contribute greatly to the knowledge of extended family. Just one example is the existence of an earmark for an Oren Dayton (figure 33). Pertinent Earmark books can be found at both the Office of the Town Historian, Brookhaven Town Hall in Farmingville, NY and at the Emma S. Clark Memorial Library at Setauket.

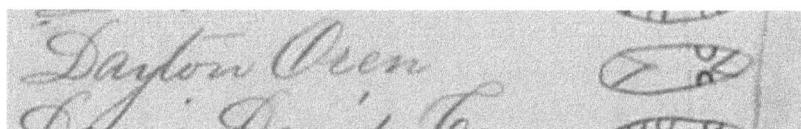

Figure 33. Example of additional Dayton earmarks

Crystal Brook Neck

Back in 1674, the division or allotment of 50-acre lots was made and extended into Old Mans. In that drawing, John Tooker is listed with lot 35 at

---

[722] (Brookhaven Town Clerk, BTR 1880)

Crystal Brook Neck, in the general vicinity of "Indian Ground" set aside for Native Americans as part of the purchase. It was probably on this neck that Tooker settled and kept the "ordinary" or roadhouse-tavern, authorized by the town. John Tooker also acted somewhat as a Town Recorder, performing a few duties for what would become the office of the Town Clerk in 1686.

Presumably the land stayed in the Tooker family, for on April 13, 1734, Henry Dayton Senior and a Jacob Dayton[723] agreed to court appointed third-party assistance in resolution of a boundary dispute with John Tooker Junior, after Tooker complained.[724] The boundary in question was to determine how large a cross-section of Crystal Brook Neck, a neck extending into the Old Man's Harbor, the Daytons owned. The town record says:

> Memmorandom that ye Plaintiue John Tooker Junier and ye Defend. Iacob Dayton & Henry Dayton a pered according to ye sumons mutally agred that all Defferences Relateing to ye bounds & property of land in Dispute John Tooker Iacob Dayton & henry Dayton also the Charge that is Relateing to ye same should bee absolutely & finally Determened by samuel Tomson Richard Woodhull & william Jeane or any two of [of] them on or before ye thurtenet Daye of maye Next insueing & if either of ye parties Refuse to Comeply with ye a ward hee is to forfit to the other ye sume of flue poundes Currant Monny to bee Recovered by a Due cores of Law in Witnes hereof thaye haue set thire hands in Brookhaven the 13 Daye of Aprill Anno Domini 1734
>
> Hy Smith   John Tooker
>   Jacob Dayton
>   Henry Dayton

As decreed by the court, resolution was reached within a month, with judgment in favor of Tooker for the boundary dispute and the Daytons ordered to pay a fine for a related but unspecified charge.

> Whareass thare is a referenc to uss by an instrement bareing Date the 13 Daye of aprill 1734 Concerning ye boundes and Land in Dispute betwene John Tooker Jacob Dayton & henry Dayton allso ye Charg __ that is accrued Relateing to ye same in persuat thare of wee haueing heard ye Evidences & alligation of Eachparty Do Judg a ward & Determine the sayd Deferanc & Dispute in maner following viz that the bounds betwen ye Lande of Henry Dayton & Christal Brookneck [neck] shall begin att a cartaine stake. standing nere the head of Christial brook marked with two

---

[723] Note: The identity of this Jacob Dayton has not yet been determined. Henry's uncle Jacob had died about 1705. The record is one of the instances cited to support an older brother of Henry born to Abraham and an undetermined wife, before Caleb was born to Mary.

[724] (Shaw, Records of the Town of Brookhaven 1679-1756 Book B 1932)

noches & so Runing Esterly a cross ye sd neck untill it cumes to ye High Waye that goes a cross ye neck in a Derect line from ye sayd stacke marked With tow noches unto a nother stake standing on ye East side of saide Neck at ye head of the spring: nere the house of Josef Tooker and ass Concerning the Charg being: £1—s8—d6 Wee Do Judg & order it to bee payd by Jacob Dayton & Herry Dayton ass Wittness oure hands this 13: Daye of maye 1734

Samuel Tomson
Richard Woodhull
William Jayne

It should be noted that Henry later acquired land from both George and Charles Tucker (Tooker) as mentioned in his will.

It is with great interest that the 1735 signature of witness Henry Dayton is noted, found in the BTR, on an agreement to trade lots, one bordering Henry's land (figure 34). This example of Henry's distinctive signature, as seen on other documents as well, combined with the fact that books are found in his inventory of possessions upon his death, give no reason to question Henry's literacy. The account reads,

Maye the sixth 1735: Then John Smith att Corom Exchanged a qorter of [the] lot Drawne on fancys Rite noumber: 20: in the skirt Divishon for the one halfe of a lot Drawne on Thomas Jeners Rite on ye East Devishon Nomber: 27: begining att ye Contry Rode & soe Runing half a mile North With Henery Daytons for ye lande afore mentioned so to Remaine for them & theire Eaires for ever Ass wittnes oure hands the Date and Daye aboue Written

Entered by mee Daniel Brewster Clarke_John Smith **8** his mark:

Henry Dayton[725]

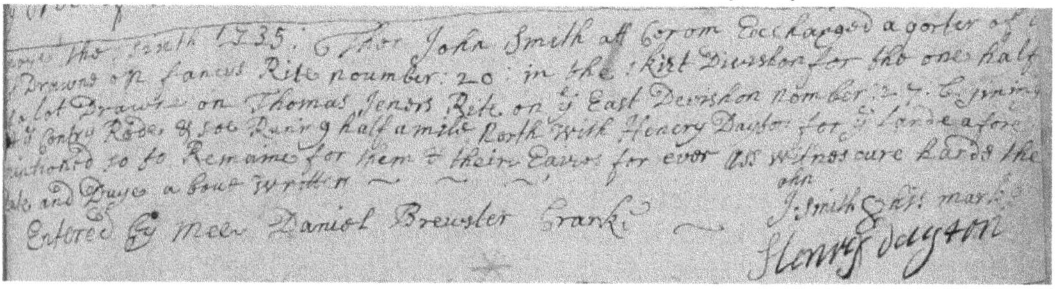

Figure 34. Henry's signature on 1735 land transaction.
Brookhaven Town Historian's Office, Brookhaven Township Municipal Building

---

[725] (Brookhaven Town Clerk, BTR 1880)

330

The March 1735 "skirt division" record in Book C was a division of common lands, referenced more than once in Henry's will, 55 lots which lay around Mount Misery. At the south end of Mount Misery, a steep hill sloping down to the area of Crystal Brook and mill pond (no longer distinguishable), was called Mount Ararat. It should be noted that near the bottom of the hill in lot no. 24, Crystal Brook was dammed to form a pond for Moses Burnett's grist mill. Daytons would continue to own land on Mount Misery and would have land dealings with the "Burnit" family.

Shaw's List of Freeholders

In 1938, Osborn Shaw compiled a list of sixty-two Brookhaven men he had taken from a 1737 Suffolk County list that had been filed in Albany and printed in 1851 in *The Documentary History of the State of New-York*, Vol. IV. Shaw noted on the bottom of his list,

> The list is not grouped under the various Town headings. The Brookhaven names occur near the end of the list and are somewhat mixed with those of other towns in the County.

Shaw added, "…the list is not complete and is confined strictly to Freeholders"– a term which is defined in Bellamy and Gordon's *English Dictionary* as ones holding lands for life. Although Shaw's "List of Freeholders" was incomplete, it did include Daytons—Henry, Hezekiah and Nathaniel.

Henry and Setauket Presbyterian

The maintenance of the meeting house and minister of the church at Brookhaven, from the beginning, had been almost entirely the responsibility of the town through taxation and generosity of its people. The earliest churches of eastern Long Island, including the Setauket Meeting House, were Puritan and so were independent of denominations. Jere C. Austin said, "the Puritans recognized only one true or 'pure' church, all other sects being 'dissenters.'"[726]

Both the Dayton family and the Norton family had attended the church at Setauket before it became Presbyterian. Henry's father Abraham had attended even before a new Meeting House was built in 1714 while the names of Henry Dayton and Jonathan Norton are both attached to its early documents. Abraham had signed the subscription of payment to call Reverend Phillips to serve as minister at Setauket back in 1697.

With the controversial declaration of Presbyterian affiliation in 1710 not being supported by all in the Old Town Church, divisions had quickly emerged and differences led to disheartening strife among its people. The Presbyterian church then became "the dissenters church," as loyalist-minded congregants called it. This group broke from it and appealed to the Church of England for a missionary. Their request was answered and within a few years, the Episcopal Church, first called Christ

---

[726] (Austin 1967)

Church, was established and its building consecrated about 1730. The fracture in community worship was now formalized as the two churches sat at the Village Green, within view of each other, at the town's gathering place. "This disagreement held ominous undertones for the coming struggle over independence which would soon rage over Long Island, as well as all of the British colonies."[727] The original congregation of Christ Church demonstrated its strong loyalist leanings when its members decided to honor Queen Wilhelmina Karoline, Queen of George II of England, by renaming their Setauket church after Caroline.

By 1741, under the ministry of Reverend Isaac Brown, the congregation of Christ Church had grown persuasive enough to cause the town to appoint a committee that successfully organized divisions of property that the town had set aside for use by its church between the Presbyterian and Episcopal Churches. What had been the community burying ground was now in the Setauket Presbyterian churchyard and Christ Church (now Caroline Church) was given their own ground. Even though the resolution to the problem of parsonage lots was peaceful, it marked the further separation of the community's churches. It also marked the "completed" separation of town government from its church and helped to provide shelter for the strong opposing convictions of its congregations toward the mother country, for years to come.

Even though Mr. Phillips had served as minister at Setauket, satisfying his side of the agreement, he had not received what was promised to him so he appealed to the congregation for fair treatment in a petition written in 1738. The petition can be found in the *Records of the Town of Brookhaven up to 1800*. The townsmen of Brookhaven readily agreed with Mr. Phillips' assessment of his accomplishments and voted to award him the land he desired with over 95 signatures appearing on the quit-claim, including townsmen from Wading River, the Old Mans, Setauket and Southaven.[728] Included in the list of names on the Quitclaim to Mr. Phillips are Henry Dayton and his father-in-law, Jonathan Norton. There is also a signator David Dayton (spelled *Dateton*), who was probably Henry's brother but could be a cousin. There are also three other Daytons; a Hezekiah, Nathaniel and Samuel, probably all cousins of Henry, but their identities have not been researched.

Quitclaim to Mr. Phillips'

WE, ye subscribers, do hereby give to Mr, Phillips our right & title to ye acre & a half of land he desires, yt is joining to his now dwelling hous, to him & his heirs or assigns forever.

Reverend Phillips's burial stone was placed in his memory, in the minister's corner of the present Presbyterian churchyard by his grandson in 1797, after the original was destroyed in the war.

---

[727] (Atteberry n.d.)
[728] (Barstow, Setauket's Religious Beginnings 1984)

Even though Henry Dayton had attended Setauket Presbyterian, he was among those men in neighboring communities who supported the creation of a church closer to home, at Old Man's, perhaps occasioned by the death of Rev. Phillips in 1739. "Previous to that time preaching only took place in Setauket, in the Presbyterian Church and Caroline Church"[729] and residents of Miller Place had to travel up to twenty miles to Setauket for services.

Nathaniel Prime noted in his history of Long Island that no proof of early success at Old Mans has been found although tradition says a house of worship did exist "in the early part" of the eighteenth century. People at South could not go to Setauket on Sundays easily and as far back as 1695 a meeting was held at Coram, the half way point. Prime noted that the church at Setauket was slow to release its members in a subsequent attempt to form the church at Old Mans.[730]

Evidence of attempts to sustain a church at Old Man's appeared in an undated newspaper clipping, and a typewritten transcription of that newspaper article can be found on file in the "Church Papers" folder at the Brookhaven Town Historian's office.[731] According to the transcription, four lists of men attempting to begin church services at Old Man's existed, including—(1) a 1740 list of pledges for a new building and (2) a 1743 promise to pay beyond what was pledged in the first subscription, and (3) an undated invitation to Rev. Potter, and (4) an undated record of receipt, naming those who had paid toward what was promised to Mr. Potter.

Also found in the same file at the office of the Brookhaven Town Historian is a note, in Osborn Shaw's own hand, attached to the typewritten transcription of the newspaper clipping. In his note, Shaw compared the transcription to the original newspaper clipping, correcting or clarifying some misspellings with ink pen on the actual transcription. Shaw later referred to the subscription lists in his writing and it is possible this very newspaper article was his source for some of his references to early subscription lists.

Our interest in the undated lists also lies with their potential support for our Dayton family living near Old Mans, and this cannot be accomplished without proper date approximations. If there really was a church at Old Mans in 1720, it is reasonable to believe that Abraham, Henry's father, may have attended that church.

The first undated promise includes two Daytons, Abraham and Norton (the bold used below is ours). Since there may have been Abraham Daytons in at least four consecutive generations in our direct line alone, attention must be given to the name Norton first, to determine the approximate date of the list. Henry Dayton married Abigail Norton about 1727 and she gave birth to son Norton about 1730-1733, making Norton 21 years of age no earlier than 1751.

---

[729] (Old Man's Had [A] House of Worship in 1740 1915)
[730] (Prime 1845) 227
[731] Note: Paper entitled Mount Sinai Congregational Church (copy of an old undated newspaper clipping owned by Mr. Ralph B. Dayton, Port Jefferson, L.I.), archived at Brookhaven Town Historian's Office

We the inhabitants of the old mans together with the wading river and the middle of the Island people do agree to call or invite Mr. Potter or Some other minister of the gospel to preach amongst us for the space of six months one third of the time att the old mans one third att the Wading River and one third att at the middle of the Island for his So doing we the Subscribers do promise to give or pay the Several Sums annext to our names: **Abraham Dayton 0-5-0**, Nathaniel Tooker 0-5-0, William Kinner 0-2-0, Gillam Davis 0-2-0, Elnathan Davis 0-4-0, Samuel Hopkins 0-8-0, John Woodhull 1-5-0, Andrew Miller Sr. 1-6-0, William Miller 0-10-0, Richard Miller 1-0-0, Thomas Helmes 1-0-0, Ebenezer Miller 1-0-0, James Davis 1-0-0, Timothy Miller 1-10-0, Isaak Dauis 0-2-0, Samuel Hopkins 0-4-0, Jacob Eaton 0-3-0, Timothy Norten 0-12-0, Theos Phillips 0-2-0, Samuel Phillips 0-3-0, Azel Carrard 0-4-0, Joseph Brown 0-8-0, Joseph Davis 0-5-0, Noah Hallock 1-0-0, Iasiah Hallock 1-10-0, Eliphelet Tooker 0-4-0, **Norton Dayton 0-10-0**, Thomas Bayles 0-4-0.

On the reverse side of the original list above is found the record of who paid. Neither Abraham nor Norton appear on the list indicating that either they had not yet contributed, but more likely, were attending elsewhere, as will be discussed.

Payd to Mr Potter 6-13-0, more payd A-M 1-05-0, Timothy Miller 0-10-0, Theophilus Phillips 0-02-0, Hopkinses 0-12-0, Timothy Norton 0-12-0, Nathaniel Tooker 0-5-0, Eliphelet Tooker 0-04-0, Azel Carrard 0-04-0, Samuel Phillips 0-08-0, Widow Phillips 0-02-0, Isaac Davis 0-02-0, Gillom Dauis 0-02-0. what we promist him was 11-15-4 it being the third of 35 pounds. Elam Poter acompts mot all payd to us and I should be glad if we could git the Remainder.

Closer examination of Mr. Potter and the list of men inviting him, "or some other minister of the gospel"[732] reveals it is not contemporary with the building-related lists as many of the signers were still children in 1751, when Norton may have reached legal age. Reverend Elam Potter was born to Daniel Potter in East Haven, CT in January of 1741/42 and his known ministry locations began in the southern colonies in 1767-68.[733] Although the transcript doesn't specify, he could have served at Brookhaven no earlier than 1765, his year of graduation from Yale. Either date would have positioned him to arrive in Brookhaven more than 20 year after the proposed building of the meeting house. Thomas Bayles said:

---

[732] Note: Paper entitled Mount Sinai Congregational Church (copy of an old undated newspaper clipping owned by Mr. Ralph B. Dayton, Port Jefferson, L.I.), archived at Brookhaven Town Historian's Office
[733] (Mallmann 1899) .54-55.

This was the Rev. Elam Potter, who afterward became a missionary to the Indians. Who followed him at Old Man's is not known, but according to Prime's history of Long Island a Presbyterian church was regularly organized there on Sept. 3, 1760. This was short lived and after 1763 nothing is known of it, so apparently the community was without church services[734] According to the The Encyclopedia of The Presbyterian Church in the United States of America, Elam Potter was ordained at Shelter Island in June of 1766.

As for the Daytons on *The Call to Reverend Potter,* it is concluded that both Norton and Abraham were probably sons of our Henry Senior and brothers of our David Senior. Norton died in his mid-thirties, sometime before August 15, 1768 according to Jacobus in *Early Daytons* which might explain why his name did not appear on the list who had paid. The estimated birth year of Norton makes his age the mid-thirties in 1765 or 1766, the estimated time of Potter's calling. Norton's father Henry died in late 1759, and was therefore not on the mid-1760's subscription list. Henry's son David and his wife Anne (from whom we are descended) had probably returned to Long Island from Great Egg Harbor, NJ by 1763 but may have lived in another community with its own church.

As significant as these lists are, more important is the fact that Henry appears on the 1740 subscription list to contribute £3 to the construction of a meeting house at Old Mans. This Henry is believed to be ours, the youngest son of Abraham, and father of our David who was probably born between 1737 and 1739. Bennet Dayton was probably either Henry's nephew or cousin. The 1740 subscription list is copied below:

> We whose names are hereunto subscribed do promise and oblige ourselves to disburse and pay the respective sums of money as we shall set to our names for the use of building of a meeting house to Thomas Strong, Andrew Miller and Joseph Davis when the call for it for that use fore sd to be for promised sum in a case of Law and the to improve ye money to the best advantage for that use.
>
> in witness whereof we hereunto set our names to ye sums.
> April ye 4 day 1740.

Thomas Strong 5-0-0, **Henry Dayton 3-0-0**, Daniel Davis 2-0-0, Timothy Norton 1-10-0, James Meger 1-0-0, Samuel Davis 3-0-0, Joseph Davis juner 3-10-0, Benjamin Davis 3-0-0, Joseph Phillips 1-10-0, James Tuthill 1-0-0, William Miller 3-0-0, Andrew Miller 3-0-0, Benjamin Brown 2-0-0, Thomas Green 3-0-0, Noah Hallock 3-0-0, John Tooker junyr 1-10-0, Thomas Robinson 3-0-0, Nathaniel Norton 0-12-0, David Davies 2-0-0, **Bennet Dayton 1-0-0**, George Tooker 0-12-0, Justus Barto 0-10-0

---

[734] (T. R. Bayles, Footnotes to Long Island History "Old Congregational Church" 1949)

It appears that the group was having much difficulty in their endeavor as insufficient funds and perhaps an insufficient number of those committed to the project delayed the building of a church thereby prompting the attachment of an addendum three years later where members of the Phillips, Miller and Davis families, along with Timothy Norton and Thomas Strong, pledged beyond their first promise to see that the church was built. In his work, Bayles simply says the subscription was circulated again but church organization that was there did not last long.[735]

> June ye 5day 1743.
> We whose names are hereunto subscribed do promis to pay towards the meeting house if not payd all redy beyond our furst subscription what we sine to below to pay. Joseph Phillips 1-00-0, William Miller 1-10-0, Timothy Norton 0-15-0, Joseph Davis 1-10-0, Andrew Miller 1-10-0, Benjamin Davis 1-00-0, David Davis 1-00-0, Joseph Phillips Jun 1-10-0, Thomas Strong 2-00-0, Samuel Davis 1-00-0.

No Daytons appeared on this list of "core" supporters who pledged over and above their 1740 promises in 1743. Probably many men at Wading River, Old Mans (now Mt. Sinai) and Middle Island attended church at Setauket when no minister was present at Old Mans, though the Presbyterian Church was also without a pastor for a time. It would normally be expected of them to attend the church of their tradition but these were not ordinary times, as a tidal wave of religious passion altered the status quo. The 1740s was the time of the "Great Awakening" that swept Protestant Europe and the colonies. In England, after preaching to ever-increasing open air crowds, John Wesley laid the foundation stone for the first Methodist meeting house in 1739 at Broadmead in Bristol, a place he referred to as "the Horsefair."

It is conceivable that, to some degree, the New Light revivals played a role in the demise of the first church at Old Mans or the infusion of new members at Setauket, as Evangelical itinerate preachers were in competition with the regular town ministers.

The Reverend Isaac Browne became the Anglican rector of the Brookhaven mission, and,

> ...ushered in a new period of growth between 1733 and 1747...[It] became home to a substantial number of worshippers, many of them former dissenters...The religious revival worked to the advantage of the church as some dissenters, displeased by the excesses of the Awakening, attended the Caroline Church and sometimes converted...[In 1741, Browne] listed 125 adherents to the church that year...part of Browne's success can be attributed to the death of the Reverend George Phillips,

---

[735] (R. M. Bayles 1874)

the Puritan parson, in 1739, which left the dissenters without a shepherd until 1745.[736]

Jere C. Austin wrote:

The old Puritan spirit, however, did not become extinct. Attempts at reform by formal bodies were paralleled by efforts of others who emphasized "experimental religion," the "quickening" of individual experience, the "washing of regeneration." ...revivals were developed into recognized means of gaining church members or arousing and sustaining religious enthusiasm. ...During the Great Awakening, prayers for a revival were answered, but in a spectacular manner that filled many ministers with dismay and almost destroyed many churches. ...itinerate preachers, notably, Gilbert Tennent of New Jersey and James Davenport of Southold, awakened a widespread religious enthusiasm in 1740. It extended to practically all places in New England and Long Island, among all kinds of persons and affected religious life for fifty years. ...those awakened became "the New Lights." ...The Old Lights associated the movement with the insidious work of the devil and denounced it as destructive to true religion and public welfare. To Old Lights it was a time of wild enthusiasm, hysteria, and violations "of Scripture and Reason."[737]

Author George Nicholson said:

Organisation was impossible to hold or contain the unpredictable outbursts of God propelled men. As often happens it was accompanied by some distasteful excesses of zeal. Lack of Presbyterial control on Long Island resulted in the fierce rivalries of the Great Revival having no forum.[738]

Jere C. Austin continued:

Old churches were violently shaken by these differences between their Old and New Light members. Many of the latter refused to remain in the same church with the "unconverted" and split off to form Separatist churches. Where a majority of a congregation became "New Lighted," it generally forced a secession of the Old Light minority.[739]

According to Barstow, David Youngs, the third ordained minister of the Setauket Presbyterian Church was probably the 'Methodist or New Light' minister

---

[736] (Cray 1990)
[737] (Austin 1967)
[738] (Nicholson 1956)
[739] (Austin 1967)

protested by church members in the foregoing subscription…To further confirm Mr. Youngs' connection with the revivalists, we find that he and a Miss Bethiah Parshall were married on February 21st, 1743, by the Southold leader of the revivalist movement, Mr. James Davenport.[740]

Barstow also noted that a majority of Setauket Presbyterian members on Reverend Youngs' *Later Members in My Time* list are also on the 1740 pledge list for the church at Old Mans. Indeed, Henry Dayton is first found on the subscription list at Old Mans and then on Mr. Young's *later members* of Setauket Presbyterian. So, with this knowledge, what can be assumed of Henry and his leanings? The title of Mr. Young's *later members* list implies that perhaps these men either were not earlier members or were members who returned to the church at Setauket, having attended before Mr. Youngs arrived. Apparently Henry wanted a more local church but sometime after Mr. Youngs was ordained at Setauket, he became a member of that church. Checking with the Brookhaven Town Historian, no evidence was found of any Daytons in attendance at Caroline Church under the leadership of Isaac Brown.

It is our hope that discoveries in the quest to determine which churches our line of Daytons attended might, by extension, indicate their inclinations in the coming rebellion against British rule.

It is known that both Abraham and Henry had attended the Presbyterian Church at Setauket and the failure to locate their grave markers on adjacent properties does not indicate that neither had been buried there. In fact, there is a good chance that either or both Abraham and Henry were laid there and the possibility also exists that their memorial stones and their graves met the same fate as Reverend Young's during the British occupation in the Revolution.[741] Barstow adds, "Very few of those named (in Reverend Youngs' list of later members) can be found in the Presbyterian churchyard in Setauket," perhaps an indication of the degree of destruction and plunder inflicted on the premises. Because Henry's son David died during the occupation and after the initial fortification and gutting of the dissenters' church building and destruction of the grave yard, it is questionable whether his burial there would have been preferred or even possible.

As suggested earlier, a result of the Great Awakening was the establishment of many new evangelical[742] churches after separating from the established churches, so the possibility also exists that David Dayton attended one of these churches upon his return from New Jersey and was buried at another location outside Setauket. One such location was Coram, where a Baptist congregation[743] was organized and a church building was erected about 1747. According to Beverly Tyler, "the old Baptist Cemetery is now a historic site just east of the intersection of Middle Country Road

---

[740] (Barstow, Setauket's Religious Beginnings 1984)

[741] Ibid. 63

[742] Note: See Donald W. Dayton's *Discovering an Evangelical Heritage*, Baker Academic, 1976 for a discussion of Evangelicalism

[743] Note: No attempt is made to relate the more recent burial sites of Henry and Susanna Dayton, Baptist Cemetery, Coram.

and Route 112." Torn down after one hundred years, the Baptist church at Coram was believed to be the first church of that denomination in Suffolk County but not much is known of its history. Tyler continues, "In 1766, the Middle Island Presbyterian Church was built and the Union Cemetery in Middle Island was established and opened for burials in 1767." According to Thomas Bayles, "there seems to be no record of what happened to the Middle Island church during those long, dark years when Long Island was in the hands of the British soldiers…Any record of the first thirty-four years of the history of our church has been forever lost, and the first record appears under the date of June 1, 1800…"

But if Henry had earlier joined another such church, it is likely, although not certain, that he had returned to the Presbyterian Church at Setauket by May of 1756 as he is found objecting profoundly to the sale of "parsonage land" still in possession of the Presbyterians. His motivations cannot be known, but he was one of only three on record who protested the sale. Since Henry probably was raised in this church and he was there again just a few years before his death, his children probably also attended the dissenting church and so came under its influence. Henry's opposition to the sale is recorded below.

To ye. Constable of Brook haven. Greeting
These are to Will and Require you to Summon and warne all the prisbyterien or Dessenting party of ye. Jnhabetents of your Said Town to be and Appear on ye meeting house Green* in your Said Town on Thirsday ye. Twentith Day of this Jnstent May at one of ye Clock in ye-afternoon to Consider of and Regulate Some afares Relating to ye sale of their parsonage Lands here of fail not Given under our hands and Seales at Brook haven this 11th- Day of May-1756

Richard Woodhull
Jos:Brewster Justices

WHEREAS. there is an Award Given up in writing under ye hands and seals of Mr- Jsaac Browne William Smith James Tuthill and Richard Woodhull Arbitrators and Entred in oure Town record wherein there is asigned to the prisbyterian or Dissenting party of ye Jnhabetents of this Town and their Sucessors forever Seuerall Tracts or Lotts of land and Meadow to and for the use of any Such presbytearen or Desenting MiniSter or teacher as they or the Major part of them shall think at any time for ever hereafter to call in order to afficoatt in that quality Amongst them and whereas ye several lots of land and Meadow Assigned in ye said award to ye sd- Desenting party of sd- Jnhabetents of sd- Town Lye so Catred as to be of little searvics to their Minister Nor of Much advantage to his Congeration intheir suport of him, AND Therefore at a Town Meeting of yesd- Desenting Jnhabetents on y^e. 20th- Day of May- 1756: warned by y^e. ConStable of sd- Town by virtue of a Warrent under ye hands and seals of two of his Majestys Justices of ye- peace: Jt was voted and Agreed by ye said Jnhabetents that all ye lands and Meadows specefied and Assigned to ye said prisbyteren or Desenting party of sd- Jnhabetents of sd- Town; shall be sold: and ye Moneys arising from said sales to be put out and keept at Jnterest thereby to Jnable them the better to Suport Such a priesbyteren or Desenting MiniSter of ye Gospel as shall be called from time to time in Manner as above said - At this Meeting were voted in John Roe Benajah Strong and Benjamin Brewster TruStees to act in Behalf of ye- presbyteran or DeSenting society in Brook haven in ye- temporalities pertaining to said society acording to reseding vote;

At this Meeting were voted in John Roe Benajah Strong and Benjamin Brewster TruStees to act in Behalf of ye- presbyteran or DeSenting society in Brook haven in ye- temporalities pertaining to said society acording to preseding vote;

Att This meeting Nathaniel Biggs Henry Dayton and Capt George owen protested against ye- sale of any parsonage lands heretofore Set apart and laid Down by our fore fathers for a parsonage in this Town and that to be and remain parsonage lands forever[744]

Entred by me Daniel Smith Clerk

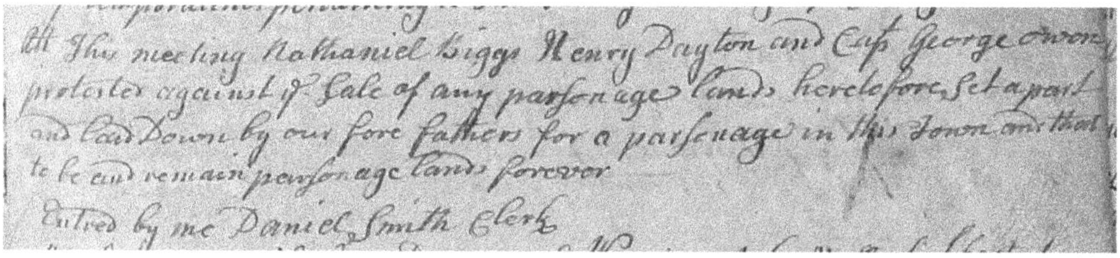
Att This meeting Nathaniel Biggs Henry Dayton and Capt George owen
protested against ye sale of any parsonage lands heretofore set apart
and laid Down by our fore fathers for a parsonage in this Town and that
to be and remain parsonage lands forever
Entred by me Daniel Smith Clerk

Figure 35. Henry's protest against sale of parsonage recorded
Brookhaven Town Historian's Office, Brookhaven Township Municipal Building

What was Henry's motivation for such a protest? Was it a sentimental attachment or could he have been nursing a grudge having to do with the church's or minister's treatment of his father? Or, was he taking a position as a large land owner who had paid more than his share of taxes toward the maintenance of that property?

Five Generations at Brookhaven

The Town of Brookhaven, the only Long Island town that stretches from the north shore to the south shore, was home to five generations in our Dayton lineage, from Samuel to David Junior, spanning about 125 years, from about 1656 to 1782.

Brookhaven had begun with the settlement at Cromwell's Bay (Setauket) and most of the early building took place within a mile of the harbor at Setauket. After common lands were distributed, other settlements were established near Setauket,

[744] (Shaw, Records of the Town of Brookhaven 1679-1756 Book B 1932)

spreading east and west but slowly spread southward, as much of the immediate surroundings were used for farmland, pasture or for their woodlands.

East of the Setaukets (Setauket and East Setauket), the Old Mans area was large, probably stretching from today's Port Jefferson to Rocky Point, including today's Miller Place. Like Setauket, windmills sat above Old Mans Harbor and the salt marsh in the area contained valuable salt hay which was harvested for multiple purposes, and the harbor itself provided fish, clams and shellfish. The shipbuilding trades in Port Jefferson that grew so quickly after the Revolution were supplied logs and planks from the woodlands at Old Mans. Shipbuilding was known at Setauket as early as the 1660s and later the Hand family was prominent and Benjamin Floyd was in the business about the time of the Revolution.[745] Because the harbor at Old Mans was not suited for larger vessels, it could not support a shipyard so ship carpenters and other tradesmen at Old Mans traveled back and forth to Port Jefferson for work.

Author Thomas Bayles says, "In the early years of the eighteenth century tradition tells us the younger men established homes upon the southern half of the long lots of their fathers which extended from the north side to the middle of the island."[746] Still, relatively, "few houses were built south of North Country Road until the late 19th century. Much of the land south of North Country Road was owned and cultivated by farmers."[747] Bayles tells us that there was probably no settlement made in the interior for half a century.[748]

Osborn Shaw claimed that, "Coram is the oldest settlement in the middle of the Town of Brookhaven." Its early name was Wincoram, and legend says it was named after a Native American who lived there as late as 1703. Shaw says:

> In 1728, 1731, 1735, and 1739 the whole central section of the Town was laid out into four divisions with each division subdivided into 55 lots. These lots were given to the heirs and assignes of the original town proprietors and it was from that period that Coram and Middle Island began to develop into scattered settlements. By Dec. 10, 1749 Coram had grown enough to be called a "village of the Town" and the large families of Smiths, Hulses and Overtons made up the population, followed later by the Hammonds, Stills, Davises, Nortons, Yaringtons, Wallaces, Bishops and Daytons and probably others.[749]

In *Setauket's Religious Beginnings*, Barstow says "Once the population of the town moved east and south, new villages of eight or ten families were created and

---

[745] (Ross 1905)
[746] (T. R. Bayles 1946)
[747] (Committee 2012)
[748] (T. R. Bayles 1946)
[749] (Shaw, History of Coram 1947)

the amount of land owned by an individual increased. This altered the economic picture of Brookhaven forever."

Henry Dayton was elected fence viewer in February 1741[750] and again, in May of 1747, he was elected by the Freeholders of the town of Brookhaven. The presence of livestock in close proximity to the planting fields made elaborate regulations regarding fences essential and, although it might seem a little odd today, regulating fence repair was one of the more important functions of the town meetings early on. They decided when cattle and swine should enter particular meadows, ordered pounds and fences built and repaired.[751]

From a June 29, 1754 record, it is learned that Henry owned an orchard when the Commissioners requested a road be built running along the north side of it[752] and Henry's brother Norton also had his own orchard closeby. Henry's orchard might have been apple and peach which were popular on Long Island at the time as well as cherry and plum, which had been dispersed throughout New England. Some of the largest pear orchards could also be found on Long Island. Once the supply of an orchard farmer grew beyond family and the needs of the locality, he found profits in the ever-increasing New York City market. Susan A. Dolan wrote in her book that, "the first commercial orchards in the United States were planted in the Hudson Valley and on Long Island, New York."[753] It is possible also that Henry's estate at Great Egg Harbor, New Jersey was an orchard as well.

Examination of three Brookhaven Town Assessments indicate Henry's taxable wealth between 1741 and 1758 was significantly above average, tied with a number of others, at 17th highest of 250 tax payers in 1741. Henry's assessment was £3 4s 0d against an average £1 0s 3d per tax payer. Other Daytons on the list are Widdow Dayton, Nathaniel, Samuel and Hezaciah.

By the 1749 Brookhaven Town Assessment, when Henry was investing in out-of-state properties, he had slipped to about 26th highest as others he had previously tied crept ahead. The 1749 Brookhaven Town Assessment is found in a folder entitled "Early Tax Assessment and other Lists of Brookhaven Town from 1665 to 1799 Inclusive, July 3, 1944 (Andrew Havens, town clerk)." A handwritten note in the folder says, "...the original list is preserved among the Trustees' papers and documents in Envelope No. XVI, paper No. 23, in the Brookhaven Town Clerk's Office. The list is all in one person's handwriting..."

By the 1758 assessment, Henry was a man of considerable wealth, tied with others for 9th highest assessment for his properties in Brookhaven alone. Henry, no doubt, was dedicated to hard work and had good business sense trading livestock and land. He could have been involved with the sea in his youth, whaling or even privateering, but forever conscious of his father's economic roller coaster.

---

[750] (Brookhaven Town Clerk, BTR 1880)
[751] (Calder 1934) 153
[752] (Shaw, Records of the Town of Brookhaven 1679-1756 Book B 1932)
[753] (Dolan 2009)

342

We do not know how the process of special care for the poor in the Brookhaven community initiated, either by volunteer or by assignment, but it wasn't long before the community developed a more efficient system that would ensure care on a regular schedule. "Even during the colonial period in Brookhaven Town, attempts were made to help the less fortunate within the Town. Before the Revolution money in the Town was collected and the poor were placed with those who bid the least for care."[754] Henry was probably appreciative of the process as he remembered his youth, when his mother Catherine and his siblings had benefitted from the town's charity beginning about 1712 and then attended to his brother Jonathan's family, kept, "in their sickness."

At meetings of trustees on May 10, 1739 and October 1742, a few men were recognized and received payment for care of widows and for performing other civic responsibilities. Henry was paid on the account of William Jarad 14 shillings and 3 pence[755] and again in 1742, Henry Senior received payment on the William Jarad account 13 shillings and 9 pence for the costs of unspecified tasks and/or services. Also, at this meeting, "The Trustees paid to Doe [Doctor] Gilbert Smith the Sum of Eight pounds and three pence for his Searvice in tending Bennet Daytons famely in ye Small pox."[756]

Henry's Death and Will

1759 was a pivotal year in England's effort to drive the French out of North America. In the Seven Years War, Suffolk County men enlisted as "provincials" in the king's army and engaged in the Niagara Campaign. Meanwhile, in the township of Brookhaven, in October of the same year, Henry's health was failing and he wrote his will. Much of what is known about him today has been passed to us by means of what was stated in his will. Henry was probably still in his fifties when he died and he was still blessed with the wife of his youth. Henry referred to himself as a yeoman and named each of his six children in order of their birth, first his sons and then his daughters. After thanking God and accepting his own mortality, he disposed of his many earthly possessions, distributing them among his family. There is no doubt Henry accumulated wealth for, in his will, Henry mentions 3 dwellings (houses with land), an orchard, 3 slaves,[757] multiple lots and long lots, 3 upland and meadows (1 with beach), 4 acreages of varying size with woodland and adjoining skirts, as well as livestock and household items including silver spoons. The dwellings he left were a farm at Colchester in Connecticut, a farm or plantation at Great Egg Harbor in New

---

[754] (Torreblanca 2015)
[755] (Brookhaven Town Clerk, BTR 1880)
[756] Ibid.
[757] Note: As well as 3 additional slaves in the New Jersey inventory.

Jersey, and he specified that another farm on Long Island and many other lands and meadows were to be sold to pay debts, with the remainder to go to his children.

Below is a transcription of Henry's will in its entirety. The inventory of the Egg Harbor, NJ estate took place in January of 1760, so it is believed that Henry died late fall of 1759, probably in November or December.

Jacobus says the copy by Pelletreau is more detailed than the copy by Petty in NYGBR 12:48. The copy chosen below comes from the "Record of Wills, Office of the Surrogate Court."[758]

> In the name of God Amen the seventh day of October ano Domi 1759 I Henry Daten of Brook Haven in the County of Suffolk Provance of New York on Nassau Island Yeoman being low in helth by [but] sound in mind and memory thinks [thanks] be to God for the same calling in mind my own mortality and knowing it is appointed for all men once to Die do make and ordain this my last Will and Testament in manner as followeth. Inprimas and first of all I recommend my Soule to Allmighty God that gave it, and my body to the Earth to be buried in as Desint & Christian like manner at the Descresion of my Executors hereafter mentioned and touching any Wordly Estate Wherewith it hath plasd God to bless with I dispose as followeth First I give to my Well beloved Wife Abigail Dayten besides her Lawful Dower the half of my dwelling house that I formerly lived in now in the tennure of Justus Burnit during the time of her remaining my Widow and also I give to her the Negro Wench named Charity and half the use of the Orchard where my son Norten Daten lives during her widowhood. Item I give and bequeath to my Eldest Son Henry Dayton all that farm or tract of Land in New England that he now lives on with every part & parcel of the same to him his heirs and assigns forever I likewise give and bequeath to my Son Henry aforesaid five of my long Lotts on Long Island beginning at the most Eastermost Lott and taking them together, to him and his heirs and asigns for ever, Item I give and bequeath to my second son Norten Daten the house and homestead of Land I had of George Tucker during his natural Life also I give and bequeath to him one third Part of my Meadows lying in the old mans Meadow, being the Eastermost part during his Life likewise my uper land I give and bequeath to my Son Norten Daten, the Western acre Lott together allso with two long Lotts Lying near ajoyning to the same all the above Premises during his natural Life,
>
> Item I give to my Well beloved Son David Daten my tract of Land in Egg Harbour in the County of Gloucester that I bought of Jeremiah Addoms to him his heirs and assigns for their own proper use for ever, Item I give and bequeath to my youngest Son Abraham Daton the Dwelling house and all

---

[758] (Court Recorder n.d.)

the building together with all the land I bought of Charles Tucker except the Eastward Lott which I have given to Norten Daten also I give to my Son Abraham one nine acre and two ten acre Lotts and all my wood Lands Joyning thereto that lyeth Westward of Couram Path and one twenty Acre Lott also one twelve Acre Lott and a Scurte ajoining to it and a quarter of a Lott of Land Joining with Lisua Tucker, I Likewise give and bequeath to him the said Abraham Daten the <u>Pikele</u> with all the meadows Joining to it commonly known by the name of the long hallow likewise all my Meadows in the Old mans meadows with two shears on the Beacthe to him his heirs and assigns for ever, Item I give and bequeath to my Eldest Dafter Abigal Satters fifty Pounds besides what she has gott which is one Mair two Cows and Calves two potts two beds and furniture six silver Spoons to her heirs and assigns for ever, Item I give and bequeath to my Daughter Cathrine Daten Six Silver spoons and two feather Beds and furniture worth fifteen pounds and as much other Household goods as to make the two above Articles fifty pounds and fifty pounds in Cash to her and her heirs and assigns for ever, I likewise Value a small negro Girl Dosh at sixty pounds and order that she go to my two Dafters at that Value to pay part of their Portions which I have given to them as Cash for the same Each one to have equal value, Item I likewise give to my son David Daten a small negro Boy named Ishmall now about three years & an half old to him and his heirs and assigns for ever, likewise I ordain and appoint Collonet William Smith, Timothy Norton and my loving wife Abigal Daton and my Son Norton Datton, David Daton and Abraham Datton to be the sole Executors of this my last Will and Testament. I do hereby or and appointt my Executors to Sell and dispose all such Lands and Meadows as shall be found belonging to me on Long Island as is not hereby given away In particular one piece of Land and Meadows at South allso a certain farm known by the name of Comsewoog, also a certain Tract of Land that I had of Moses Burnit together with all my lands lying betwixt Samuel Datens and Drownded Meadow laid out in Scort Lotts, likewise all to the Southward of Samuel Datens, likewise a ten acre Lott lying in the Town I bought of Benjamin Jones the said money arising therefrom to pay my Just debts and defray such charges as shall arise on the same and the residue if any be to be Equely divided amongst my Children and I do hereby Utterly disallow revoke and Disanull all and every other former Will and Testament heretofore by me given allowing this to be last Will and Testament In Witness whereof I have hereunto set my hand & seale the day and year above written.

Henry Daton   (LS)

Signed Sealed and Declared to be his last Will and Testament in presence of William Oatman, Henry Junery, Robert Morss.

Be it Remembered that on the sixteenth day of March one thousand seven hundred and sixty two Personally came and appeared before me Henry Smith Surrogate of the said County Abigail Dayton Widow, Norton Dayton and Timothy Norton being the Persons named Executors in the within Instrument and being duly sworn on their Oaths did Declare that the within Instrument Contained the true last Will and Testament of Henry Dayton Deceased as far as they know or believe and that they would well and truly perform the same by paying first his Just debts and then the Legacies Contained in the said Will as far as his Goods Chattles and Credits would thereunto Extend and the Law Charge them and that they would make a true and perfect Inventory of all and singular the said Goods Chattles and Credits as also a Just account and Exhibit the same when they should be thereunto Required.

Henry Smith Surrogate

A year and a half before Henry's will was written, and less than a month before his marriage, Henry Dayton Junior, "of Long Island," bought a farm of 89 acres in Colchester, CT, the section which in 1803 became part of the town of Marlborough, with a dwelling house and sawmill.[759] Although bought in his own name, his father's will the following year gave him this farm, from which is inferred that the father aided in the purchase and retained some interest. However, no mortgage or agreement has been found, so this might have been a private family arrangement. Upon marriage, Henry and his wife settled on this farm and remained there until they died. The deed of purchase reads in part:

Jacob Root of Middletown...for 2.180...to Henry Dayton Junr of Long Island in ye County of Suffolk and province of New York...one Certain Tract or parsell of Land Lying and being in ye Township of Colchester in the County and Colony aforesaid Containing Eighty Nine Acres bounded as followeth Viz beginning first at a white oak Stump at ye South East Corner of Land that ye sd An Root bought of Saml Kimberly thence running West 30: g1 56 Mint southardly about 152 Rods to a white oak tree with stones about it thence running Northwardly 30:sec 56:minutes Rods West about 106 Rods to a Stake and stones about it thence Easterly about 152 Rods to ye first Mentioned bounds and tis to be understood Said Land is to Extend So far North and a proportionable Width as is mentioned in ye East and West Line as to Contain 83: and Extending ye Highway which bares North Near acrost said Land & No more together with a Dwelling House and Sawmill Standing thereon... Witnessed by Samuel Gilbert Junr and Samuel Gilbert 3rd; dated 8 June 1758 and recorded 31 June 1759.

---

[759] Colchester Deeds, 7:161

Henry Junery [Junior] was present as a witness when his father signed his will but he was the only one of the four sons not named an executor, probably because he was living in Connecticut. The circumstances which first brought Henry Junior across Long Island Sound to Connecticut are not disclosed but perhaps Henry Senior had lived at the Colchester farm for a time because it has been claimed that his daughter Abigail was born there. No evidence has been found to prove the claim but Abigail and her husband, Stallworthy Waters, were buried in nearby Marlborough, CT. Since Henry Junior was already thirty when he married at Lyme, it is possible that he had been engaged as a mariner or trader in the coastal trade. On the other hand, he may have met his future bride, a Lyme girl of good family (she is called "Mrs." Marvin in the record of her marriage at the First Congregational Church of Lyme, now Old Lyme), while visiting Dayton relatives in nearby New London. Also, the Jeremiah Adams family that had sold the Egg Harbor property to Henry Senior seemed to also have some connection to Colchester but it is yet to be determined if the members of the family had some connection to the sale of the Colchester farm.

Many records concerning Henry Junior are retained at the Connecticut State Library at Hartford including a copy of what appears to be the original receipt from Henry Junior's estate. The bill of sale states:

Marlborough 9 January 1804

Received of Abraham Dayton Administration of the Estate of Mr. Henry Dayton deceased sixty one dollars and forty nine cents in full of all demands except the demand on deceased Dayton Sawmill for me. John Custis [Curtis]

Of interest to a few in the compiler's extended family is Junior's sawmill which he owned for over fifty years, named in both the purchase and the bill of sale. Our own father and uncle together owned and operated Dayton Brothers Lumber Company, a sawmill, in Corinth, NY for fifty years, beginning one year after the end of WWII.

By the time Henry acquired the sawmill, the days of pit sawing were nearing their end in America as there was a shortage of labor and an abundance of streams to drive water-powered sawmills by water wheel. By 1840 there were about 5,500 sawmills in New England, with nearly 700 in Connecticut alone. Most of these sawmills were on small scale with a single saw, and were part of the local economy.[760]

Another curiosity in the will of Henry Dayton Senior is the "Pikele" (with all its meadows), which Abraham received from his father. It is believed that the Pikele was the hill behind the house of Thomas Strong, who built in a hollow at Mt. Misery.

---

[760] (Sawmills in New England 1600-1900: A Brief Overview n.d.)

His father came to Setauket in 1699 when "Drowned Meadow" was the name for Port Jefferson. High up on the hill was a slave burying ground.[761] Another explanation or definition for "Pikele" is found in an article written by Philip Marshall:

> …the initial purpose of fencing in the colonial period was not the containment of livestock in fields, but rather the exclusion of free-ranging stock from the small area of improved land, the "home lots" or "pightles." The latter term, variously spelled "pichtel," "pikel," or "pikell," (from the Middle English pigtel, a small field or enclosure) persisted in common usage on Long Island through the end of the nineteenth-century as a designation for the outdoor portion of the domestic space (roughly synonymous with the modern suburban "yard") long after it had become a forgotten archaism in the rest of the English-speaking world.[762]

In 1765, Henry Junior was in Hartford, CT accompanied by his brother-in-law Stallworthy Waters, to appoint his good friend Tim Norton of Brookhaven to be his attorney to facilitate the disposal of his inheritance on Long Island. Brookhaven Book C, page 334 of our edition says,

> Know all men by these presents that I Henry Dayton of Colchester in Hartford County in ye Colony of Connecticut Do make Constitute ordain and appoint My Trusty and well beloved Frind Mr Timothy Norton of Brook haven in ye County of Suffolk on Long Island in ye Province of New York, to be my Lawfull Attorny; Jn my Room and Stead to tranSact any affair Relating to ye Estate of my Howl Father Henry Dayton Late of said Brook haven Deceased to Settle and adjust any Debts or Demands Due from sd Estate to me or any other person and I Do hereby in Special; Jmpower and order my Said attorney to sell that Land on Long Jsland which my sd Father gave to me by his Last Will and Testament Described in sd Will by ye Denomination of ye five Long Lotts, to ye best advantage and to Dispose ye Money so Much as shall Be Necessary for my part or Proportion towards the Discharging my Sd Fathers Just Debts and to account with me for ye overplus, and I Do hereby Jmpower my Sd Attorney to Make and Execute a good Deed or Deeds of sd Lands which shall operate in Law to conclude and bind me and my heirs forever to all Jntents as fully and absolutely as if Sd Deed, or Deeds was Executed by my own hand; and Do hereby promise and bind my Self and heirs to be concluded and abide by what my said attorney shall Lawfully Do in ye premises: And in Witness hereof I have hereunto set my hand and seal this: 12th Day of June; Anno Dom, 1765;

---

[761] (K. W. Strong, Tales of Mount Misery 1952)
[762] (Marshall 2005)

Henry Dayton (Seal)

Signed Sealed and Delivered
In presence of us
Ricd Miller
Worthy Waters

NB: ye Land not to be sold untill account is Rendered for: 13: head of Cattel which I Left with my Father and ye money Disposed toward my part of S^d Debts (Execpt what of sd Cattle Died that spring I came away_Henry Dayton, Hartford County: ss: Colchester June ye 12th 1765; then Henry Dayton ye signer and sealer to ye above written Instrument personaly appeared and acknowledged ye same to be his free act and Deed Before me____

Dan" Foot Justice peace

There is little doubt Henry Senior's accumulated wealth exceeded that of his forefathers. In addition to this difference, in comparison to his forefathers, Henry held his material wealth closer and longer than his grandfather or great grandfather had. Sam and Ralph both were in possession of valuable properties but they periodically lightened the burden of their acquisitions, gifting their children. Without adequate record, so much of Abraham is speculation, but he may have been shrewd enough to divest before the circumstances and mystery of his later years.

One difference between Henry and his forefathers appears to be that Henry waited until death before transferring legal ownership of what had already been distributed. This is the case with Henry Junior's farm, Norton's orchard and perhaps David's estate at Egg Harbor. Henry's daughter Abigail was apparently given some of her inheritance at marriage while younger daughter Katherine had not yet married. This is not to find fault with Henry, for he had seen how quickly his father's wealth was lost and he may have feared his children might make poor business decisions in their younger adulthood should they have real estate with which to deal.

Chapter 19

"We will behave ourselves, Peaceably and Quietly"

David Senior

David was born between 1737 and 1739, a century after his great-great grandfather left England, the fourth of six known children, as named in his father's will. David and his wife were the fifth generation in our line of ancestry to live on Long Island. His brother, the first-born, was Henry Junior, born about 1728 or 1729, followed by Norton and then Abigail who was probably a few years older than David. Of course Norton and Abigail received their names from their mother, Abigail Norton Dayton. David also had a younger brother Abraham and sister Katherine, named after Henry Senior's parents, Abraham and Catherine. David might have been named after his father's older brother David.

As was also true for the four generations preceding him, almost nothing is known of David until he reached legal status as an adult. Although his father also owned properties in Connecticut and New Jersey, it should be safe to assume most of David's childhood was spent on Long Island. Henry had a few houses in the Town of Brookhaven also, but it is not known which was favored as the homestead when David was growing up. Like his father, it is obvious from David's writing and signature that he received some education, and possibly some formal schooling, as schools were becoming established even in some smaller communities in the first half of the eighteenth century. The high value the community placed on education was evident in the town of Brookhaven long before state legislatures created taxation to fund schooling.

On June 5, 1760, David applied for a license to marry Anne Frances "of Great Egg Harbour" in what was then Gloucester County, New Jersey. Just a few months earlier, David had begun the process of taking possession of his father's Great Egg Harbor estate as stipulated in his will: "I give to my well beloved son David Daten my tract of land in Eggharbour in the County of Gloucester that I bought of Jeremiah Addoms [Adams]." David had probably been in New Jersey before 1760 but it has never been determined where and when he met Anne. Her family was likely from either Brookhaven or from a community in Gloucester County, but both he and Anne were described as being of "Great Egg Harbor" in the application.

The entry in *New Jersey Colonial Documents*, lists the application for marriage this way: "Francis, Anne, Gt Egg Harbor, and David Patton, Gt Egg Harbour 1760 June 5…"[763] Of course, on first reading, David Patton does not appear to be our

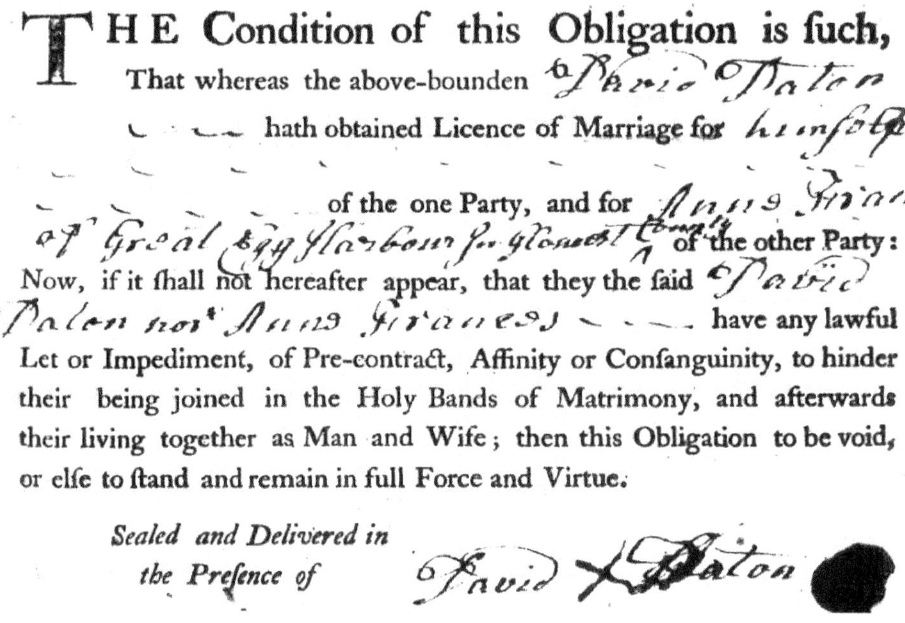

THE Condition of this Obligation is ſuch, That whereas the above-bounden David Daton hath obtained Licence of Marriage for himself of the one Party, and for Anne Frances of Great Egg Harbour in Gloucester County of the other Party: Now, if it ſhall not hereafter appear, that they the ſaid David Daton and Anne Frances have any lawful Let or Impediment, of Pre-contract, Affinity or Conſanguinity, to hinder their being joined in the Holy Bands of Matrimony, and afterwards their living together as Man and Wife; then this Obligation to be void, or elſe to ſtand and remain in full Force and Virtue.

Sealed and Delivered in the Preſence of David Daton

Figure 36. David and Anne Dayton's marriage license

David, but when another copy of the same record was located that has "David Paton," it became apparent how closely the spelling resembles "Daton," the spelling often found in New Jersey records. Once an image of the original document was located,[764] it became evident that the document clearly says "David Daton" a total of four times and "Anne Frances" appears two times—with no variations in spelling.
Transcribed New Jersey marriage records state:

> #129; David Paton and Richard Wescot, both of Great Egg Harbour in the County of Gloucester, Gentlemen...[bound to]...Francis Bernard, Governor...500 pounds...5 June 1760. ...David Paton...obtained a License

---

[763] (Nelson, Marriage Records 1665-1800, First Series Vol XXII 1909)
[764] (New Jersey Secretary of State 2015)

of Marriage for himself...and for Anne Frances of Great Egg Harbour in Gloucester County.

Should anything be made of the use of "Gentlemen," as it refers to both David and Richard Wescot/Wescoat?[765] It is somewhat puzzling to find the title of gentleman applied to David because, before this time, "gentleman" was a title given to someone just below nobility, a man of wealth and leisure. The use of "gentleman" might be an appropriate title for Richard Wescott (born 1733) who owned a large quantity of land along the Great Egg Harbor River and who would later become a Revolutionary War officer. The title also seems appropriate to Henry Dayton, David's father, who was no doubt known in the area.

What is most interesting to us is the fact that Wescott was a ship builder, because our David was later identified as a carpenter and, in those days, carpenters were very often ship builders. "Wescott was an active ship builder and major timber exporter, and was one of the few slaveholders who owned more than one slave. He served numerous public offices, mainly at the local level"[766] and gave land for the Methodist Church and graveyard.[767] Could David have been apprenticed in New Jersey before 1760?

The identity and heritage of Anne Frances has always been a mystery to researchers and has yet to be solved. Perhaps it is convenient that Joel, son of David and Anne, named his son David Francis Dayton,[768] possibly following a colonial tradition of parents naming a son with the paternal grandfather's name and his middle name being his mother's maiden name. For a long time, there has been speculation that Anne was of French descent and that is not impossible because there were Huguenot refugees fleeing France to England, and then to New York and New Jersey before, during and after this period.

We asked Richard Barons if it is possible that Anne could have been French. This question was predicated with the statement that Henry Dayton, David's father, seemed to be relatively well off. He replied:

> These communities were small. If you were a certain stature in life, that is something the family would want you to maintain. So the Gardiners go off to Boston, or go off to New Haven to find appropriate sons or daughters for their family to marry. There's not a big pool here...The

---

[765] Note: There are various spellings (Westcott, Wescott) but his signature indicates he preferred "Wescot" at this time

[766] (Hack 1971)

[767] (Barber 1846)

[768] (C. N. Dayton 196?)

French seem to have a little more respect here than the Dutch, particularly in the 18th century or the 17th century. Many of the French who migrated were well-to-do. They were merchants. Remember that in the 18th century, France was the seat of culture and that would have been readily recognizable to these people. [769]

If Anne really was French, perhaps Henry was concerned enough with appearance and self-image that he wanted to influence the selection of his children's spouses. Perhaps whatever the struggle Henry's father Abraham endured in the last few decades of his life ignited Henry's drive for success and respect, not only sought through his collection of possessions, but by restoring family honor. This is merely the compiler's musing. Or, maybe Henry just wanted the best for his sons and Anne met with his approval (assuming he was aware of her or her family before his time of death). Henry might have thought that his son was interested in possessing the estate at Egg Harbor, but if she was from New Jersey, perhaps David's main interest there was with Anne.

There are also allusions to the theory that Anne's family migrated to New Jersey from Long Island just prior to 1760 but, to our knowledge, convincing evidence to support the theory has never been found, and basis for the conjecture has never made its way to formal publication.

Few references to surnames Francis or Frances are found around Brookhaven before 1760 and none suggest any relation to Anne, except possibly one. Weak circumstantial evidence that there might have been a Francis family in the area of Patchogue many years before is found in records of Winthrop's Patent, the early name for Patchogue. One of the nine necks of land contained in the 1680 purchase was called Francis' Neck, the easternmost neck, described as adjoining a place called Acombamock. No trace of the origin of the name has been found.

It is known that David and Anne's daughters lived at Patchogue or married Patchogue men after their father died so it is assumed Anne lived there also. This raises a few questions—were David and Anne living in East Patchogue at the time of his death or did Anne move there after David died? If she moved the family there, what drew her there? It would be logical to assume Anne had family at Patchogue. With much of Long Island laid waste and dangers ever present, a retreat in order to be close to friends or family would have been in order.

The search to learn more about David was extensive, but not exhaustive, and the search continues. During the search, many references to other David Daytons led us along unproductive detours. For this reason, the existence of other contemporary David Daytons is noted, especially the often-mentioned David of New Castle in Westchester County, New York and another David and Ann Dayton of Fairfield, New

---

[769] (Barons 2010)

354

Jersey. The researcher may even find documents from more than one David Dayton mistakenly placed in the same file or microfiche. The Fairfield couple can be found as early as 1744, when our David was only 5 years old, and they also had a son named David. Perhaps some of the assumptions for our Anne should rather be attributed or applied to this Ann Dayton of New Jersey. The first record discovered for the "other" Dayton couple was the tombstone inscription that reads "In memory of an Infant Dau'tr of David & Ann Dateu who died April 3d 1760."[770] Of course this date was at first a little troublesome since our David and Anne obtained their marriage license two months after the death of the infant daughter recorded in the tombstone inscription.

In order to assist family and fellow researchers, and perhaps to alleviate some of their potential frustration, a few "rabbit trails" are given for your consideration.

David Daton of Brookhaven and Eunice Chancey July 21, 1729:[771] He is assumed to be the younger brother of Henry and Ephraim at Hempstead, born about 1704. No further research was done to determine his identity.

A 1744 record, mentioned earlier, has Peter Dayton of Cohansey, Salem Co. naming cousin David Dayton to possess the lands if his daughter Lucey should die. Our David would have been about 5 years old in 1744.

The 1761 marriage bond between Jacob Ireland and Barbara Tyce has been sometimes construed as a marriage record for our David. The record reads: #151; David Daten (Dayton) and John Doe (no signature), both of Egg Harbour and County of Gloucester...[bound to]...Thomas Boone, Governor...500 pounds...9 Sept 1761...David Daten...obtained license of marriage for Jacob Ireland of the same place...and for Barbara Tyce of the same place, spinster...[w] Gab: Blond, Sam'l Allinson [affidavit] Burlington, Sept 9, 1761...appeared before me Abraham Hewlings...Justice of the Peace for the County of Burlington David Daten...saith that Barbara Tyce...is of the age of 21 years or more...[772]

According to Walter Lee Sheppard Jr.,

The David Dayton who obtained the marriage license for Jacob Ireland can only be David, son of Ephraim...David would be brother-in-law of

---

[770] (F. Andrews 1909)
[771] (Klett 2008).135
[772] FHLC 0888703; Vol. D (1736 - 1791) [total of 421 bonds] #151 - #200

Silas Ireland [Junior]. David Dayton's wife has not been positively identified but was probably Ann, daughter of David Sayre Jr.[773]

We do not share Mr. Sheppard's view. While it is agreed that it is not David who is getting married in this record, it is believed that the David who signed the marriage bond for Jacob Ireland to marry Tyce in 1761 was probably our David, of Great Egg Harbor, as the record states. As Jacobus points out, the other David was of Fairfield, Cumberland County before and after this record.[774] Modern-day Fairfield is only about 30 miles from Great Egg Harbor so, at first, it seemed likely that our David and Anne had moved to Fairfield but it soon became apparent that this was not the case as this David died in 1770 and his widow remarried that same year. It is now believed that many of the Dayton clan in New Jersey were probably descended from Ephraim, our David's uncle.

> Stratton, John, of Cumberland Co. Ward. Son of Benjamin Stratton, of Fairfield, said Co. Guardian—Joseph Daten. Fellowbondsman—David Datten; both of said Fairfield.[775]

> The February 6, 1770 will of David Datten of Fairfield, Cumberland Co; My lands to be sold, except my homestead. Wife, Ann Daton, moveables. Son David, my homestead. Daughters, Hannah Datten and Ruth Datten, rest of estate, when 18... Witnesses—Joseph Daten Jr., Ephraim Datten and George Ferebe. Proved Feb. 28, 1770. 1770, Feb. 13. Inventory, £314.7.10, made by Theophilus Elmer and Joseph Dayten. 1772, July 13. Account by Executor. Lib. 14, p. 437; Lib. 15, p. 22.[776]

> The same year David Datten of Fairfield died, Ann Dayton of Cumberland married Daniel Dixson, Cumberland 1770 Oct 30.[777]

> An Ephraim Dayton, son of another David Dayton, owned slaves at Egg Harbor in 1750.[778]

Lastly, a record of an insolvent David Dayton can be found in *The New York Gazette; and The Weekly Mercury* No. 1085, August 10, 1772. No further research was carried out on this record.

These are but some examples to illustrate once "promising" diversions that, in the end, proved unproductive.

---

[773] (Sheppard 1960).171-174
[774] (D. L. Jacobus, Recent Books 1960)
[775] (Calendar of Wills 1761-1770: 1762, May 3 n.d.). 239
[776] (Administration First Series 1928)
[777] (Nelson, Marriage Records 1665-1800, First Series Vol XXII 1909)
[778] (Amorosi 2011)

In contrast to these side-excursions, it was truly an exciting day when the inventory of Henry's New Jersey estate was located. Finally, some idea of what David inherited could be revealed and that might lead to the reason for Henry's investment in the property. The record in Microfilm by Geneaological Society of Utah, January 1968, Gloucester County, NJ Record of Wills 1694-1900 IH-5909H___ appears to be a poor photocopy of the original document. Written at the bottom of the inventory itself was, "A trow inventory of the Goods and Chattles of Henry Daten late of Long Island but since of Eggharbour desest."[779] Despite the indication in the title that Henry was "of Eggharbour," at its writing, Henry's residence was most likely Brookhaven, NY. Perhaps "of Eggharbour" indicates that one of his sons was a caretaker there.

The inventory was dated January 24, 1760 (Julian calendar ended in 1752) and the actual list contained about 49 lines, beginning with Henry's house and ending with three slaves. Of the more than £185 total, the value of the Negro man accounted for £55 while the house, the next highest value, was only £11. Surely, with high value placed on the slaves, the man was skillful or perhaps educated in management of the farm/orchard and the children must have been judged to possess good potential. Valued labor would demand care, so it could have been David's intention to sell them with the estate, although we would very much like to believe that he granted them freedom. At the bottom of the inventory document, two witnesses added their signatures and on page 4 is found the signature "David Dayton" that matches his signature on other documents years later. The witness Robert Moris (he may also be Robert Hunter Morris Esq.)[780] was probably the same Robert Morss who was executor, along with David Adams' wife in 1754, for the will of David Adams of Great Egg Harbor. David Adams was no doubt a relative of Jeremiah Addoms.

It seems that the closest we have come to determining the possible location of the Dayton land, "my part of the land at Egg Harbor," was to find in the John Covenover will of May 19, 1762, proved March 26, 1771 at Great Egg Harbor, that son, Peter, inherited land between David Addoms and Nehemiah Leeds, being the half of the plantation, formerly belonging to Jeremiah Addoms.[781] This leads us to believe that the land inherited by David Dayton from his father Henry was also half

---

[779] (Records of Wills 1694-1900, Gloucester n.d.)

[780] Note from the Cape May County Historical and Genealogical Society: An historic Robert Morris Holmes House stands as a museum today. We have not researched its relationship to the Robert Morris who witnessed David's inventory, but there probably is a relationship. The post and beam house is a fine example of a method of building that was brought to New Jersey from Long Island when whalers settled at New Jersey, lured by the thriving whaling industry in the last quarter of the 17th century. Some were also drawn by the availability of large tracts of land which could be purchased relatively cheaply. http://cmcmuseum.org/about.html

[781] (New Jersey Historical Society 1931). 112-3.

of Jeremiah Addoms' plantation. The other witness was John Smith, probably the son of John Smith of Long Island and Egg Harbor who had just died fourteen days earlier.

Even in possession of the inventory, the function or intended purpose of the estate still is not apparent as nothing distinctive to a single-purposed craft or venture can be identified. Nearly all the items in the inventory are of "common" nature for a family farm except for silver and the existence of the two Africans and a child (race/ethnicity unknown). However, the unusually large number of tablecloths, chairs,[782] plates, kitchen pots and pans and utensils indicate that there were more than just a family to feed. The bell probably called workers from their work at dinner time.

The books and looking glass indicate that someone in the house was educated. This new information introduces a few questions. If Henry was in fact living at Brookhaven, 150 miles distant by water, had David's brother Norton or another family member been supervising the "farm" at Great Egg Harbor, with David, in the manner that Henry Junior was supervising the farm in Connecticut?

INVENTORY OF HENRY DAYTON ESTATE AT EGG HARBOR, NJ

			£	s	d				£	s	d
To	his	housing appraisal	11	0	0	To	3	small silver tea spoons	3	3	0
To	8	yards of new cloath	1	10	0			at 3/shillings apeace			
To	3	pewter platers 3 basons 9 plates	1	5	0	To	1	saddle	1	0	0
		with som others of pewter				To	1	dito	0	7	6
To	one	iron cettle	0	4	0	To	2	pair rope hook ??	0	6	0
To	one	iron pott	0	6	0	To	1	ox ****	0	9	0
To	one	brass cettel	2	5	0	To	1	old *** hock	0	2	6
To	one	frying pan	0	3	0	To	2	old S ??	0	6	0
To	one	warming pan	0	5	0	To	1	old *** and 1 broken ?? Hook		1	9
To	4	large pair of *****ard 12/ and	0	16	0	To	1	falling ax 4/6 each and hewing ax		1	5
		on small pan				To	2	forks		3	0
To	1	gun	2	0	0	To	1	horse cart	1	8	2
To	1	tea cettles	0	12	0	To	1	ox chane	0	18	0
To	1	lantorn	0	3	0	To	2	old plows	1	18	0
To	1	Churn 2/ and one café & bottles	0	14	0	To	1	yoak of oxen	9	0	0
To	1	looking glass	0	2	6	To	1	yoak of oxen	8	0	0
To	4	small chairs and 1 large one	0	16	0	To	3	cows of fifty shillings apeace	7	10	0
To	7	Du***	2	0	0	To	2	calves at 20/apeace	2	0	0
To	5	Ch***	0	7	6	To	1	small ox chane	0	7	6
To	1	pair fire tongues	0	4	0	To	1	bell	0	5	0
To	1	board table	0	12	0	To	1	Negro man	55	0	0
To	3	old books	0	3	0	To	1	Negro Boy Named Harpo	35	0	0
To	1	feather bed and bedhead with	6	10	0	To	1	child	10	0	0
		?? Furniture belongs to it				To	1	Note	10	0	0
To	1	dito and short bedhead	3	10	0						
To	1	dito and short bedhead	2	10	0	A Trow Inventory Taken January the twenty fourth 1760					
To	2	old candle sticks	0	1	0			John Smith			
To	3	large silver spoons at 8/shilling									
		of a peace						Robert Moris			

Figure 37. Inventory of estate at Great Egg Harbor, NJ
The total value of the items inventoried was £185 5s 10d.

---

[782] Note: The seventeenth item which is not discernable could be more "chairs"

358

After inheriting the entire New Jersey estate, David and Anne did not remain there but sold the estate relatively soon after obtaining it. The last record found of David still in New Jersey was in 1761 when he was described "of Great Egg Harbor" at the time he obtained the marriage license for Jacob Ireland and Barbara Tyce. Perhaps Jacob worked for David or was the potential purchaser of the estate? After 1761, David appears exclusively in the Town of Brookhaven until his death in or before 1782. The first of David and Anne's nine children was probably born late in 1761, meaning that they returned to Brookhaven to start and raise their family there.

While it is true that some Long Islanders were living in New Jersey during whale season (winter), it is not believed that David conforms to this pattern as every remaining record finds him in New York and there is nothing to indicate his involvement with whaling which might remove him seasonally. Rattray says there was an exodus from Eastern Long Island in the late seventeenth and early eighteenth century partly due to whaling around Cape May, NJ, and partly for the desire for large land-holdings. She says, "Many pioneer settlers of New Jersey bore old LI names—Barnes, Bennett, Chatfield, Davis, Edwards, Fithian, Garlick, Hand, Hughes, Jones, King, Loper, Ludlam, Miller, Mulford, Osborne, Parsons, Schellinger, Stratton and Vail."[783] Jacob Dayton, Henry's uncle (younger brother of David's grandfather), was already at Cape May County around 1694. It is interesting to ponder the possibility that whaling, ship-building, or lumbering may have influenced Henry's decision to acquire land there.

If David and Anne returned to Long Island with a slave, their attendance at the Setauket Presbyterian Church might have become quite difficult after just a couple of years. The arrival of Reverend Elam Potter about 1765 had to make many local farmers uncomfortable because the reverend was very much opposed to slavery and was consumed with the subject, explicitly declaring the institution evil and its participants evil-doers. It's little wonder his stay there was shortlived. On the other hand, it is not known what possessed the hearts of David and Anne; perhaps the couple freed their slaves, if David was not of the same mind as his father.

The first records of David back on Long Island can be found in the Denton Account Book belonging to Setauket saddler Joseph Denton (kept by Joseph 1762-1776). After Joseph's death at age 44, his wife Betsy and his brother Samuel continued the business and extended entries in the book (1776-1793). Today, this account book is held by the Three Village Historical Society at the Emma S. Clark Memorial Library, East Setauket. Generally speaking, colonial account books were used mainly to record debt. For this reason, the researcher has an incomplete view of transactions with particular individuals. There are records of David beginning in June of 1763 and ending 1771, as well as accounts between David's brothers, Abraham and Norton, and the saddler.

---

[783] (Rattray 2001)

Since the colonies were not allowed to mint currency, and Britain provided no substitute or supply of her coins, the colonies were without any official currency. To compensate for lack of currency, they traded in foreign coin at the ports while the common folk bartered and traded goods as substitutes for money and these substitutes were even referred to as "cash" on a regular basis. As a high percentage of the business done in shops took place with local customers on credit, store-keepers' books kept record of debts due to the merchant, while most "cash" transactions or balanced (even) exchanges were often not recorded. Therefore, when studying accounts, it is crucial to keep in mind that, when coin was exchanged, it sometimes accompanied goods, so that the record utilized a mix of means that can construe what appears to be the account of an item's value. Thus, much business was taking place in addition to those recorded in the Account books[784] so the recorded exchange could be representative of a small portion of the total.

Thompson's *History of Long Island*[785] contains the following record about another Joseph Denton of Brookhaven in 1775. This Joseph, according to Denton Family Genealogy,[786] was a loyalist who fled to Digby, Nova Scotia, and lived until 1835. Still another Joseph died August of 1775 and his will was witnessed by Benjamin Floyd (mentioned below). No further research of Joseph, the yeoman,[787] has been performed to establish relationship to the saddler Joseph, but the passage is useful because it expresses some of the strife and agitation among family and friends on Long Island during the armed rebellion of the colonies.

> August 11th, 1775—Congress are informed by letter, dated the 3d, from Thomas Helme of Brookhaven, Chairman of the committee of safety of that town, than Parson James Lyon, Benjamin Floyd, Doctor Gilbert Smith, Joseph Denton, Richard Floyd and John Baylis, Inn-keeper, had, from the beginning, taken every method in their power to seduce the ignorant, and counteract every measure recommended for the redress of grievances; damning all congresses and committees, and wishing them in hell. They had also been suspected of furnishing the vessels of the enemy with provisions.[788]

As a saddler and harness maker, Joseph Denton did repair work, and estimates have about 60% of a saddler's time spent "mending" saddles, collars, bridles and harnesses, as new ones were very expensive for the average person. Some saddlers

---

[784] (Baxter 2004)
[785] (B. F. Thompson, History of Long Island Containing an Account of the Discovery and Settlement to the Present Time 1839)
[786] (Denton 1943)
[787] (Hicks 1882) 141
[788] (B. F. Thompson 1843)

had their own tanneries while others also sold imported goods or ran other side businesses.

The first record of David Dayton in Denton's book, in June of 1763, was for a horse bridal and 60 nails. Next was an exchange dated February of 1765, when Denton noted that he, "bargained for a cow of David Dayton's, to take her when cattle can live by grass in the spring and am to give £4, 5d, 0s for her if she has a calf with her or £3, 5d, 0 if she has no calf." In April, the earlier note was crossed out and the notation was added, "brought home the cow." Many times, when ownership of cattle transferred, there was mention of an earmark, but there was no mention in this exchange. Perhaps David already had his own earmark registered with the town but it is likely that he did not because, as mentioned earlier, David registered his mark "formerly of his father Henry Daton" in June of 1766. What David received in February, for the promise of the cow, was not specified. On the same page, it is noted in June of 1766 that David paid the balance of his account with Denton.

David was not found again in the ledger until March of 1768 when he became indebted for 100 nails and in May settled his account again, paying the balance, probably when he was paid for completing a job. After other transactions between Denton and David's brothers Abraham and Norton, David purchased a hammer in October of 1768.

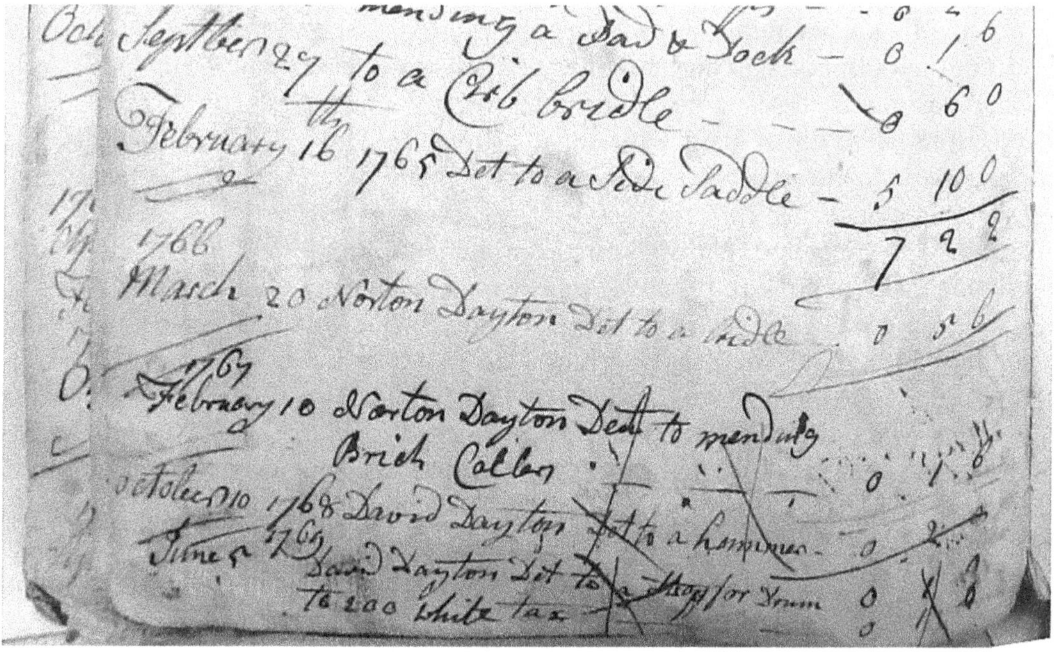

Figure 38. David Dayton's purchases in ledger belonging to Joseph Denton

But a curious transaction, at the very bottom of the page, occurs in June of 1769 when he appears to purchase "straps for drum" as well as 200 white tasc (tacs). This makes us wonder if the drum was an instrument or if the drum refers to a shipping or storage container, both of which use straps.

The last records of David in Denton's ledger have David buying on credit (Det) in October of 1771 and the next record (figure 39) says, "1771 December 16 Paid in Cash by David Dayton – 0 1 6." David and Norton were neighbors at this time, probably situated at Old Mans[789] or Coram, so it is concluded that the saddler's shop might have been located in that general vicinity.

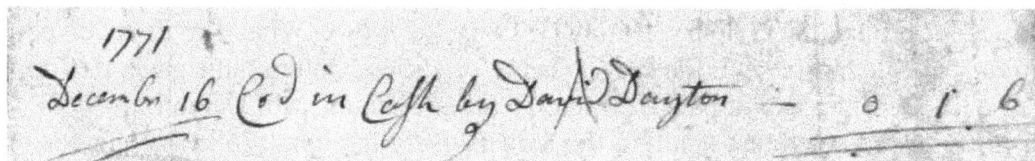

Figure 39. Last David Dayton record in Denton's ledger

Photo used with permission from Three Village Historical Society,
Emma S. Clark Memorial Library, Setauket

David's six accounts, spread over about eight years, should not be interpreted as being the only purchases of supplies at Denton's shop and store. If David was a regular customer, the half-dozen accounts might indicate that a majority of his transactions were either paid with some official coin, were joint purchases under another name (contract work as a carpenter), or were "even trades."

When pondering the meaning of ledger entry "white tacs," a Brookhaven historian was consulted and suggested another interpretation—that these may not have been tacks, as we know the word. Instead, white tack may have been white cedar peg because cedar trees that grew here provided wood that was sought after for its strength. A less likely explanation might be found in the occupation of the white cooper who used both staves and tacks. The white cooper made straight staved containers which did not require shipping of liquids or bending of the wood. These strips he rolled into cylindrical drums and riveted in shape with tacks. Bottoms for boxes and measures were thin wooden disks tacked into place and lids were similarly made. White coopers were known to make military drums and small fireplace

---

[789] Note: At a May 6, 1766 meeting, Norton is named Trustee "at ye old mans"

bellows, he shaped thick wooden soles for clogs, produced buckets, washtubs, and butter churns.[790]

David had become well-established in the Town of Brookhaven by 1766 when, on May 6th he was one of eight men elected fence viewer,[791] one month before registering his cattle earmark, formerly belonging to his father. David was elected fence viewer again in 1767 and that year was on a list of 23 subscribers to the schoolhouse, along with his brother Norton, and relatives Brit and Samuel Dayton. The list was preserved for a while in an account book kept by Isaac Overton, of Coram, eventually in the possession of his great, great grandson Frank Overton of East Patchogue, who submitted the *Forum* article. David contributed 16 shillings,[792] a relatively large amount as the schoolhouse would benefit his family greatly, with at least four children and maybe five and an additional four that would be born in less than ten years.

On June 19, 1769, David sold and may have written[793] a deed to, "Elnathan Davies for Lot #32 in Coram, Brookhaven Towne, NY on New Rhode." The transaction was for the sum of 40 Pounds. The original document had been in possession of the Davis family[794] and is reproduced in figure 40. If it can be proved that David did write the document, as some believe, he must have possessed a level of education made possible by determined parents. A small portion of the deed is translated here:

> In the township of Brookhaven near the place called or known by the name of Corom upon the south side of the new road that leads southwestwardly from the old Country Road ___ ___ ___ (tear in paper) from the said Corom. And being the east ~~and south end of the~~ (crossed in the original and per memorandum at bottom of deed) side and south end of the lot number thirty two butted and as it was laid out as followeth bounded southward to Wintreps line at the middle of the island and bounded westwardly to the mid del of the said thirty second lot and bounded northernly to the highway or road called the New Road to and with the fence as the fence now stands and bounded eastwardly to the thirty third lot to have and to the hold the said granted.

---

[790] (Wright n.d.)
[791] (Brookhaven Town Clerk, BTR 1880)
[792] (A School of 1767 1947)
[793] (A. H. Davis n.d.)
[794] Ibid.

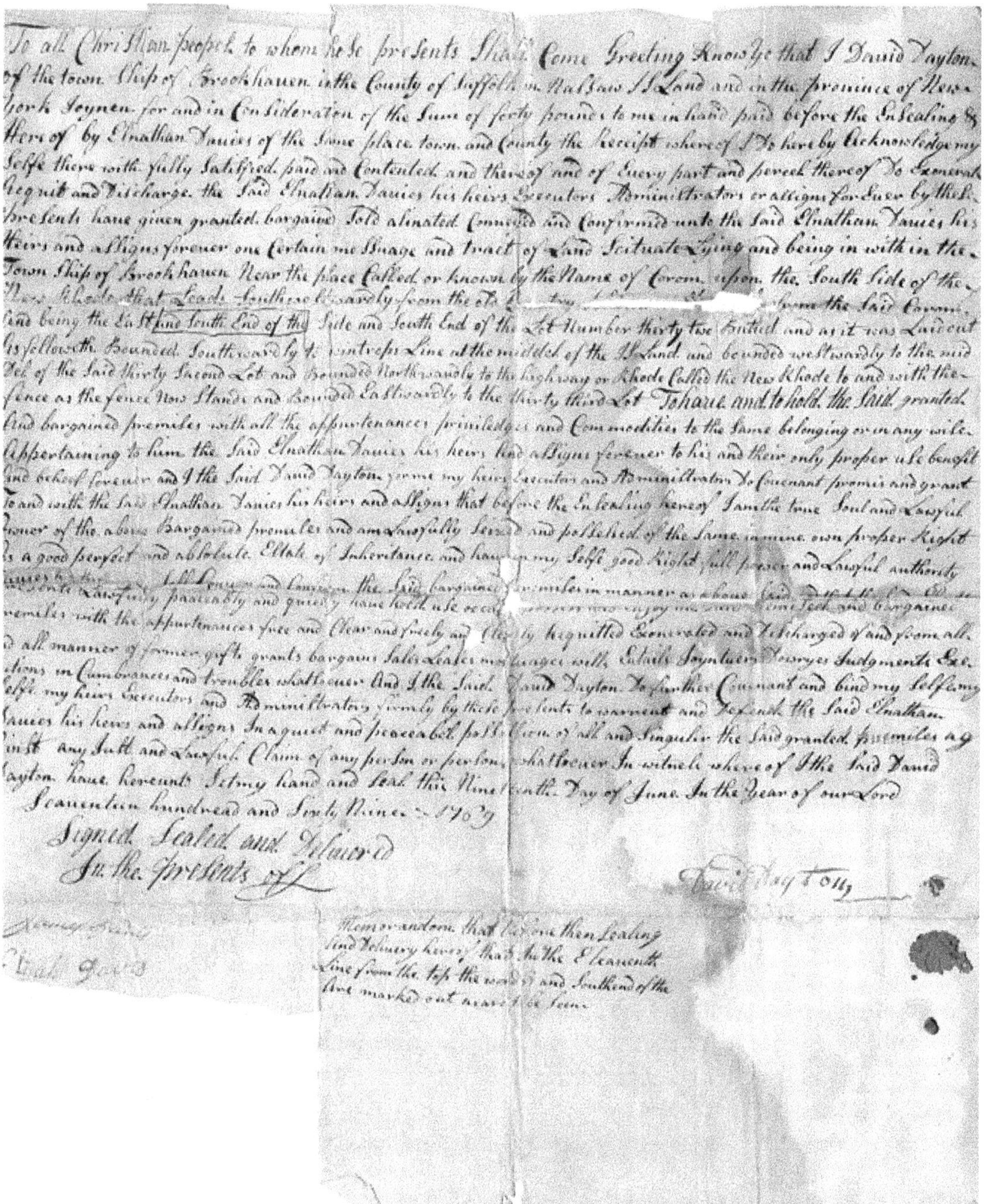

To all Christian people to whom these presents Shall Come Greeting Know Ye that I David Dayton of the town Ship of Brookhaven in the County of Suffolk on Nassau Island and in the province of New York Joyner for and in Consideration of the Sum of forty pounds to me in hand paid before the Ensealing & hereof by Elnathan Davies of the Same place town and County the Receipt whereof I Do here by Acknowledge my Selfe there with fully Satisfied paid and Contented and thereof and of Every part and parcel thereof Do Exonerate Acquit and Discharge the Said Elnathan Davies his heirs Executors Administrators or assigns for Ever by these presents have given granted bargained Sold alinated Conveyed and Confirmed unto the Said Elnathan Davies his Heirs and assigns forever one Certain messuage and tract of Land Situate Lying and being in with in the Town Ship of Brookhaven Near the place Called or known by the Name of Coram upon the South Side of the New Rhode that Leads Southeastwardly from the [illegible] from the Said Coram Land being the East line South End of the Side and South End of the Lot Number thirty two Butted and as it was Laid out as followeth Bounded Southwardly to the [illegible] Line at the middle of the Island and bounded westwardly to the middel of the Said thirty Second Lot and bounded Northwardly to the highway or Rhode Called the New Rhode to and with the fence as the fence Now Stands and bounded Eastwardly to the thirty third Lot To have and to hold the Said granted and bargained premises with all the appurtenances priviledges and Commodities to the Same belonging or in any wise Appertaining to him the Said Elnathan Davies his heirs and assigns forever to his and their only proper use benefit and behoof forever and I the Said David Dayton for me my heirs Executors and Administrators Do Covenant promise and grant to and with the Said Elnathan Davies his heirs and assigns that before the Ensealing hereof I am the true Soul and Lawful owner of the above Bargained premises and am Lawfully Seized and possessed of the Same in mine own proper Right as a good perfect and absolute Estate of Inheritance and have in my Selfe good Right full power and Lawful authority [illegible] Sell [illegible] the Said bargained premises in manner as above Said [illegible] Lawfully peaceably and quietly have hold use occupy possess and enjoy the above granted and bargained premises with the appurtenances free and Clear and freely and Clearly Acquitted Exonerated and Discharged of and from all and all manner of former gifts grants bargains Sales Leases mortgages wills Entails Joyntures Dowryes Judgments Executions in Cumbrances and troubles whatsoever And I the Said David Dayton Do further Covenant and bind my Selfe my Selfe my heirs Executors and Administrators firmly by these presents to warrant and Defend the Said Elnathan Davies his heirs and assigns In a quiet and peaceable possession of all and Singular the Said granted premises against any Just and Lawful Claim of any person or persons whatsoever In witness whereof I the Said David Dayton have hereunto Set my hand and Seal this Nineteenth Day of June In the Year of our Lord Seaventeen hundred and Sixty Nine — 1769

Signed Sealed and Delivered
In the presents of

David Dayton

[illegible]
[illegible]

Memorandom that before the Ensealing and Delivery hereof that In the Eleaventh Line from the top the words and Southend of the Are marked out as [illegible]

Figure 40. David's signature on Davis deed, possibly written by David

Photo image courtesy Long Island Genealogy (longislandgenealogy.com). Used with permission.

David's signature on the 1760 inventory of his father's Great Egg Harbor estate bears a strong resemblance to his signature on the Davis deed, 1769.

Figure 41. David Dayton's signatures from 1760 and 1769

Rising Tensions

It was during these years, while the Daytons were living in the area of Coram, Britain's pressure and control on the colonies were visibly increased through a series of actions and events.

As a result of the poor economy in England coupled with the debt incurred from fighting the Seven Years War (also known as the French and Indian War), Britain needed to raise revenues. In order to contain the costs of protecting its territories, and to help Native American relations, King George proclaimed in 1763 that the colonists could not expand their boundaries west of the Appalachian Mountains. Of course, this did not set well with many colonists, particularly with the revolutionaries influenced by "republican" ideology and John Locke's individual rights.

Following in sequence, the Navigation Acts & Writs of Assistance (already in effect, but now enforced), the Quartering Act, Stamp Act and the Townshend Act (1765) each contributed to tension and hostility, as colonists questioned the authority of Parliament to tax them because the colonies had agents only, but no member in Parliament.

In the 1770's, there was further escalation as more colonists rejected the authority of Britain and considered her taxes to be oppressive. The decade started with the "Boston Massacre," as it was called by the revolutionaries, that proved to be especially useful, being advertised to its full advantage, even though it was not clear who fired the first shot. In 1772, colonists attacked and burned the British revenue schooner HMS Gaspee, having run aground while pursuing a packet boat in to Warwick, RI. The Tea Act gave rise to the "Boston Tea Party" of 1773, followed by the "Coercive" and "Intolerable" Acts of 1774. Finally, the First Continental Congress convened in Philadelphia. In 1775 there was an attempt to disarm colonial militias which met with resistance at Concord.

As late as spring 1775, when anxiety had become violence at Concord and Lexington, and Massachusetts was resisting King George and parliament's efforts of intimidation, parts of Long Island remained deceptively tranquil. "Suffolk inhabitants remained aloof and more concerned with farming and the weather than with political strife."[795] In comparison to New England, a significant portion of Long Islanders were orderly, law-abiding subjects of the British Empire, and content to remain so. As prosperous as many Long Islanders were, it would seem they had little reason for discontentment and were probably confident that the New England agitators, with their misplaced passions, would be brought back into line.[796]

Even as preparations for war got underway, most colonists retained their loyalty to the king, somehow separating him from confrontation and hostilities with His Majesty's troops. In a general sense, across the colonies, both patriots and loyalists still possessed some loyalty to the king and couldn't conceive of a government without a king. The King was considered the protector of their liberties. His name was inscribed on flags placed on liberty poles, and there was no intentional irony in the playing of "God Save the King" when these poles were raised.[797]

Though a minority on Long Island were passionate to choose a side between America and Britain, the contest did translate to two main camps among the colonists—the patriot party and the tory party. There were varying degrees of commitment in both so trying to pinpoint the date or occasion when the sides formed to oppose each other is difficult.

With a majority of Long Islanders basically neutral or leaning toward the status quo, "they wanted to get on with their lives, take care of their families and avoid trouble as much as possible. [To this group], the choices weren't only patriot or tory."[798] Before the war, the combined groups of loyalists (or tories) and neutrals in the colonies probably accounted for between 45-55% of the population, but in the British stronghold of Long Island, this percentage was higher. Going back almost as far as the second generation of British settlers on the East End, Islanders enjoyed better health than their relatives in Great Britain (excepting disruptions of smallpox) and by the eighteenth century, they also enjoyed high levels of literacy and lower taxes than anywhere else in the British Empire.[799] Why would they risk disturbing the existing state of affairs by taking sides in what they viewed as an unprovoked war? Many loyalists didn't view Britain's taxes with the same amount of contempt felt by the patriots, but instead considered taxes right and proper obligations in return for the benefits of protection by the mother land to her people. Besides, many Suffolk County men had bravely and faithfully volunteered to serve their king as New York Provincial Troops from 1756 to 1763, during the "French and Indian War." They served two hundred miles up the Hudson River in such places as Lake George and

---

[795] (Tiedmann, Joseph S 2005)
[796] Author unknown
[797] (Mann 2013)
[798] (N. Smith 2012)
[799] (Batten 1999)

Bolton, NY, very near where David Dayton Junior and family would call home forty years later.

The remaining population consisted of rebels (patriots), some who were ready to defend "their country" against the control and oppression of Parliament, and their unfair taxes. These pockets of patriots thought of themselves as Americans, and viewed the English throne as an authority America had outgrown. Though still a minority, these men believed it was time for America to declare its self-dependency, no longer subject to an imperialistic mother country that had little respect for its subjects.

The Presbyterian Church also aided the patriot's cause. In his book *The Story of Long Island Presbytery and Churches*, George Nicholson says that no less than 385,000 predominately Presbyterian Ulster Scots came to America in the 1700's. According to Nicholson, they "formed the hard core" of the Revolution... Most were absorbed in the frontier area of Pennsylvania. Driven from their homeland by harsh treatment they had no love for the Crown and were ripe for independence. The Presbyterians became identified with the Revolutionary cause, as their democratic structure and bedrock principle of "constitutional republicanism" possessed at the time of the Revolution, "the most powerful inter-colonial organization on the continent." Eleven of the fifty-five members of the Continental Congress who signed the Declaration of Independence have been identified as Presbyterians. Walpole, Prime minister of England, called it a "Presbyterian rebellion."[800]

> In harmony with the country's political leaders, local Presbyterian ministers led public opinion in favor of colonial resistance. From their pulpits they extolled the actions of the Continental and Provincial congresses and the righteousness of the American cause. In 1776, Charles Inglis, the Anglican rector of Trinity Church in New York City, wrote that he knew of no Presbyterian minister on Long Island 'who did not, by preaching and every effort in their power, promote all the measures of Congress, however extravagant.' ...Presbyterian support of the Revolution was fostered by the fear that the British government was plotting to increase the authority of the Church of England by creating an Anglican Episcopate, the jurisdiction of an Anglican Bishop, in America. Presbyterians saw the supposed establishment of an American episcopate as being part of an effort to create an exclusive and monopolistic Anglican establishment. Even though no such course had been planned by the Church of England at that time, the fear of such a possibility was enough to compel Suffolk's Presbyterian ministers to believe that their religious liberties were at stake and that their only defense was to make a clean

---

[800] (Nicholson 1956)

break from England. Anglican Loyalism gave the rebel cause an additional religious sanction. In the minds of most residents, Whig triumph ensured religious freedom while a Loyalist victory would lead to the establishment of the Church of England throughout the colonies. By 1776 the drift toward Revolution in Suffolk County was charged with religious passions on both sides.[801]

The Association and Military Census

In April of 1775, without the knowledge of what had occurred the day before at Lexington, the "Freemen, Freeholders, and Inhabitants of the City and County of New York" met at convention and adopted a "General Association." In May, the New York Provincial Congress was convened and, as a result of the recent bloodshed in Massachusetts Bay, resolved "never to become slaves" (of the British Parliament).[802] The Association sent documents to every county in New York, aimed to compel every man, by his signature, to reveal and proclaim himself either for or against the statement and design of the rebels. Those who did not sign were treated with contempt. A facsimile of the actual Form of Association to support Congress is provided by Mather in his *Refugees of 1776* book and the wording is given below.

Persuaded, that the Salvation of the Rights and Liberties of America, depends, under GOD, on the firm Union of its Inhabitants, in a vigorous Prosecution of the Measures necessary for its Safety; and convinced of preventing the Anarchy and Confusion, which attend a Dissolution of the Powers of Government; We, the Freeholders, and Inhabitants, of _____, being greatly alarmed at the avowed Design of the Ministry, to raise a Revenue in America; and shocked, by the bloody Scene, now acting in the Massachusetts Bay, DO, in the most solemn Manner resolve, never to become Slaves; and do Associate under all the Ties of Religion, Honour, and Love to our Country, to adopt and endeavor to carry into Execution, whatever Measures may be recommended by the Continental Congress; or resolved upon by our Provincial Convention, for the Purpose of preserving our Constitution, and opposing the Execution of the several arbitrary, and oppressive Acts of the British Parliament; until a Reconciliation between Great-Britain and America, on Constitutional Principles, (which we most ardently Desire) can be obtained; And that we

---

[801] (Dept. of History, SUNY Stony Brook 2011)
[802] (Calendar of Historical Manuscripts Relating to the War of the Revolution 1868)

368

will, in all Things follow the Advice of our General Committee, respecting the Purposes aforesaid, the Preservation of Peace and good Order, and the Safety of Individuals, and private property. Dated in _____ May, 1775.[803]

A majority of Brookhaven men, mostly from Setauket and Stony Brook, signed the "Association" calling for a preservation of the, "rights and liberties of America."[804] David Dayton of Suffolk Country (our David) can not be found on the lists but the David Dayton of Westchester County is listed. In fact, it is a very curious thing that our David is not found on any list—those of delegates, of deputies, of those in the first, second, third and fourth companies for Brookhaven, lists of representatives, of signers, as well as in those lists of men who didn't sign, those who refused to sign, or those who chose more time for consideration. We are at a loss to explain his complete absence.

Any hope of reconciliation between the factions on Long Island was shattered by the events of summer and fall of 1775. Desperate for arms to equip New York's troops, the Provincial Congress ordered the 3rd New York Regiment to disarm the people of Queens County, using force if necessary. Lasher's men met with little success, however. One subordinate, William Williams wrote, 'The people concealed all their arms that are of any value; many declare that they know nothing about the Congress, would sooner lose their lives than give up their arms; and that they would blow any man's brains out that should attempt to take them.' Not only were the Loyalists of Long Island unwilling to give up their arms, but they were actively soliciting additional weaponry from the British. On November 30, the warship Asia landed a large quantity of gunpowder, bullets, small arms, and even a cannon to bolster the Loyalist forces in Queen's County.[805]

By January 1776, the situation became even worse. Andrew Batten continued:

With passage of 'Black Listing' and the 'Tory Act,' many Long Islanders were now pursued like criminals because of their loyalist beliefs, and some were compelled to take refuge in the swamps along the South Shore.

Loyalists were singled out by neighbors almost right away. Some escaped and found refuge on Western Long Island with loyalist friends. E. F. Denton, speaking of "Non-Associate" Joseph Denton, said,

---

[803] (F. G. Mather 1913)
[804] (Tyler, History Close at Hand-Three Village/Brookhaven-Chronology 2014)
[805] (Batten 1999)

[he] was soon to find himself held in great disfavor by his neighbors in the little town of Brookhaven. Finally feelings became so bad that he and members of his family were openly attacked on the street by some of the more fanatical patriots, and as no sympathy was forthcoming from the authorities, it became clear that there was only one thing to do—to join the exodus to Nova Scotia. It was a heartbreaking departure in many ways—to have one's best friends turn out to be one's enemies, and to be forced to leave the country which one had grown to love and which now was so hostile, was more than ample justification for heavy hearts.[806]

On July 2, 1776, the colonies declared independence from the British rule, and a few days later, after debate and revision, the Continental Congress approved a formal declaration that would "dissolve the political bands" which had connected the colonies to the mother country. The document was a call to arms against British rule and was largely responsible for turning the rebellion into a fight for freedom. The action was a calamity for those who supported the crown. "Their own countrymen had turned against them; many were arrested and charged with treason and the remainder were made to feel so uncomfortable that abandonment of their homes for life in their native England, or in nearby Nova Scotia, seemed the only way out."[807]

Later in July of 1776, Justus Roe conducted a census of military-aged white men in Brookhaven and found:

> …that of the 424 men available, fifty were known Tories and of the rest, only 280 were physically able to bear arms. From the 280 however, the Town of Brookhaven supplied three regular companies to the Continental Army and proudly sent more commissioned officers (who were obliged to serve for at least fifteen years) into service than any other Long Island town.[808]

The *Census of Suffolk County* in 1776 listed the Names of the heads of Families by Township. The Dayton family was well represented in the census for the Township of Brookhaven, although it is interesting to note that the extended Dayton family seems to have been moving southward, as none appear on the list of Heads of Families living North of Middle Country Road but at least seven families are represented on the list for Heads of Families living South of Middle Country Road. Found south are Samuel, John, Willem, Bennet, another Samuel younger than the first, Ebenezer and David. According to the census, none of the Daytons appear to

---

[806] (Denton 1943)
[807] Ibid.
[808] (Barstow, Setauket's Religious Beginnings 1984) 69

own slaves at this time. Ned Smith, librarian of Suffolk County Historical Society at Riverhead, pointed out that the original copy of the 1776 *Census of Suffolk County* orders its list of heads of families in the Town of Brookhaven by location, rather than by alphabetic order of name. Mr. Smith examined the names on the list and determined that their order probably places David in or near Coram at the time of the census.[809] This ordered list can be found in *War of the Revolution, in the Office of the Secretary of State, Albany, N.Y. Vol I*, Weed, Parsons and Company, Printers, 1868.

In response to our query about the location of David according to the census, Smith explained:

> When they took the census of 1776 in Brookhaven, they divided the town in half and one person did land north of the county road which is currently State Route 25 and the other did south, so that immediately helps us locate where David Dayton was—he was in the southern half. Looking at the people right before him, John Holts, David Monroe, Isaac Overton, Ebenezer Dayton, Nathanial Longbothom, William Yarrington are all Coram people. Right after David Dayton is Brewster Tarry…I'm not sure where he lived but Alexander Wicks, Nathanial Smith,[810] Andrew Pagchen, Seth Scribner, Joseph Scribner, those were all Patchogue people. At that time it was called Winthrop's Patent.

So, where was David?

> I would tend more toward Coram than Patchogue because all those people right before him were from Coram. Brewster Tarry, I'm not sure. Alexander Wicks, I know he was later in Patchogue but I don't know where he was in 1776. Nathanial Smith was later in Coram, but he could have been in Patchogue at that time or if he was a different Nathanial Smith he might not have been in Patchogue at all. I'm not 100% sure, but then when you get to Andrew Pagchen, Seth Scribner, and Joseph Scribner, I know they were in Patchogue at that time.

In the 1776 census, David's household consisted of 1 male between 16 and 50 (David), 2 males under age 16 (2 boys of 5 total, were probably toddler Telem and infant Joel), 1 female over 16 (Anne), and 3 females under age 16 (Abigal, Annie and Deborah). Anne was probably pregnant at this time with Rhoda. According to C. Nathan Dayton, Abraham had already gone to Connecticut by 1770 and it is possible that 14 year old Henry and 10 year old David had also been put out in apprenticeships or were not at home at the time. Again, it is observed that no slaves were counted among David's household.

---

[809] (N. Smith 2012)
[810] Note: A Nathaniel Smith later married David's daughter, Abigail Dayton.

One reason we are so quick to suggest apprenticeships for the boys is because the 1775 tax list for the Town of Brookhaven shows David with only 0 pounds-0 shillings-10 pence. If this tax is representative of wealth, David was not well off and may have had challenges supporting his family. Of the 369 Brookhaven households on the 1775 Tax List totaling £154-1-1, there were only about 54 households that were taxed the same or less than David, so he was in the 15th percentile in terms of taxable assets. David was relatively poor, but in the same economic status as many others in the town.[811]

Occupied Long Island

Everything was about to change on Long Island, as the British army turned its attention to New York. "It was a sad day for the Associators when the enemy left Boston and advanced upon New York. The Battle of Long Island (August 1776), and the occupation by the enemy, brought good fortune to the Tories."[812] Andrew Batten continued:

> Then, when the fortunes of Queens County's loyal majority looked almost hopeless, the tide turned. Now it was the Rebels who were pursued, and Long Island became a haven for displaced Loyalists from other colonies.

Following the British victory at the Battle of Brooklyn in August 1776, all of Long Island quickly came under British control, being complete by November, and remained under British control until November of 1783, when the last of them left New York City.

Two days after the battle, the Convention recommended to the Inhabitants of Long Island, "to remove as many of their women, children and slaves, and as much of their livestock and grain, to the main, as they can; and that this Convention will pay the expense of removing the same…This was the general permission for the removal."[813] Many patriots and their families became refugees as they acted on the recommendation of the Convention and "removed" to exile across the Sound to Connecticut. In total, about five thousand fled to Connecticut and upstate New York.

> All the towns and counties on the Island were now at the mercy of the invaders. The few companies of regular troops withdrew to Connecticut along with the leading Whigs and others. The militia disbanded and went to their homes. Civil government was almost completely dissolved.[814]

---

[811] (Haven July 3, 1944)
[812] (F. G. Mather 1913)
[813] Ibid.
[814] (T. R. Bayles, During the Revolution in Brookhaven 1985)

Considering the dangers involved in announcing one's allegiance, it is impossible to know the proportions of civilian supporters enjoyed by either side but Setauket Spy Abraham Woodhull later estimated that, at the time the British took control of Long Island in 1776, more than half of the residents were loyalist.

With New York City as its headquarters, the British used Long Island as a major source of supplies, ransacking farms and businesses, and appropriating what they wanted. Bayles said the army, "drew its supplies from the farmers on the Island, who were ordered to furnish whatever was required, with the threat of, "laying waste the farms and homes of the disobedient."[815] "Over the next five years, many of the remaining stands of trees on Long Island were cut down to supply cordwood and building materials for the British Army in New York City. Long Island was basically devoid of trees."[816]

Suffolk and all of Long Island was under martial law longer than any other part of any colony during the Revolutionary War.[817] Courts did not operate and the British quickly lost the ability to control and protect residents from raiding parties. On Long Island, loyalist families were frequently no better off than patriot families as both were subjected to all manner of depravity, plunder and kidnapping. Families were divided and neighbors turned on each other. There are many examples of father against son, brother against brother and friends and neighbors against one another. The situation resembled a civil war.

Both sides made prisoners of many non-combatants whose convictions did not suit their captors. Hence, each side had an array of political prisoners; while the Americans had small chance of securing enough military prisoners to offset the large numbers taken after the Battle of Long Island and as late as the disasters in the Highlands of the Hudson, in the fall of 1777.[818]

Much of the activity of this nature on Long Island Sound was for the purpose of securing prisoners. The object was two-fold: first, to make the tories less harmful by capturing some of them; and, second, to provide for an exchange of American prisoners held by the enemy. The constantly growing number of captive Americans made the second object of greater importance than the first.

Early in the occupation, the British identified Loyalists by a piece of red cloth in their hats. Faced with military occupation, almost all the men

---

[815] (T. A. Bayles 1882)
[816] (Tyler, History Close at Hand-Three Village/Brookhaven-Chronology 2014)
[817] (Staudt 2007)
[818] (F. G. Mather 1913)

wore red in their hats, even those who might not have taken the oath of allegiance. Women tore up their petticoats for these...[819]

Oath of Allegiance

Residents were required to swear allegiance to the crown. In order to avoid taking the Oath, many became refugees to Connecticut. Others, too indigent or too infirm to leave, took the Oath perfunctorily, in order to escape insult, imprisonment and confiscation.[820] Frederic Gregory Mather continues:

> What should they do? Take the oath and live? Refuse and die? They took the oath but in heart were as devoted to their country and as hostile to their oppressors as before. This is a subject avoided by writers, but fidelity to historic truth demands expression. When residents in Sag-Harbor and the Hamptons took this oath, as they in fact did, they reasoned thus: Refusing, I die with no benefit or help to my family, friends or country's cause; living, I may be a help to all, ministering to aged parents, to sick and dying of family and friends, protector of wives, sisters and children from brutal assaults on their purity and honor. In law and morals, fraud or force annuls a deed or contract, and undue influence voids a will and why not an oath? To hold an oath procured by force, valid, is to hold force the law and above the right. When Col. Gardiner as commissioner, with a company, surrounded the house of Col. Jonathan Hedges, of Sagg, and at the point of a bayonet compelled the old hero to take the oath, what else could he do? What else could Col. Hedges do? It was this or death. They were both known as patriots then and after. If Col. Gardiner did not compel Col. Hedges and others to take the oath he was liable to all the penalties of Martial Law just as Col. Hedges was if he did not take it. At this very time Nathaniel Gardiner, son of Col. Gardiner was a Surgeon in the American Army and served as such until the end of the war. Who can doubt the patriotism of the father?

Reverend Charles Craven wrote in *A History of Mattituck*:

> To flee was to leave all and go out empty-handed. For the aged, the sick, those encumbered with dependent families, flight was impossible...The few who had ready money might flee with some hope, young men or unattached men might flee, but the majority had no choice but to remain and give up their arms and take the oath of allegiance. Many who had

---

[819] (Naylor, Surviving the Ordeal: Long Island Women During the Revolutionary War 2007/2008)
[820] (F. G. Mather 1913). 117

374

fought in the disastrous Battle of Long Island had nothing for it, when once the invaders were established in the Island, but to return to their homes and families and submit to the inevitable. There were no other people in all the bounds of the colonies so helpless as the Long Islanders, utterly cut off from their fellow Americans. And there were no people of the colonies who suffered more.[821]

Craven also wrote:

Those who remained on the Island were compelled to swear allegiance to King George. Some did this with good grace, and some of necessity. To none was it so distasteful as we are disposed to imagine. The men of that day had all the inveterate respect and affection for the sovereign that British have today. The revolution began in protest against injustice, but with Loyalty to the king unimpaired, and with no thought of ultimate separation. Washington, when he took command of the continental army, desired to right the wrongs of the colonies but "abhorred the idea of independence."

Together Royal Governor William Tryon and others such as Lt. Governor Andrew Elliott, with a force of 1,000 provincials, visited every village green to secure the peaceable behavior of the disaffected inhabitants and to, "assist the Commissary in obtaining about 1,000 fat cattle for the army. Peaceable behavior was encouraged by demanding that male inhabitants swear their allegiance or remove with their families and furniture to Connecticut."[822] The oath read:

We whose Name are hereunto
Subscribed, do Promise and Swear, to bear Faith
and true Allegiance, to his Majesty King George
the Third, and that we will not directly or
indirectly, openly or secretly, aid, abet, counsel,
Shelter or Conceal, any of His Majesty's Enemies
or those of His Government, or Molest or betray
the friends of Government, - but that we will
behave ourselves, Peaceably and Quietly
as faithfull Subjects to His Majesty and his
Government
So help us God.

---

[821] (Cravens 1906)
[822] (Kearney 2011)

According to *The New York Genealogical and Biographical Record* of April 2011, over 2,700 male inhabitants aged 15 and over, from all towns in Suffolk, signed the oath. Our David Dayton is among the signers of the Oath of Allegiance to the crown. These individuals had remained on the island under two years of martial law and may represent, "72% to 82% of the corresponding male population of Suffolk County in 1771."

From the entry of David Dayton on the Oath, the birth year of 1739 is provided,[823] and so is the confidence to believe that David did remain on Long Island during the occupation while others left. The entry "David Deaton, [age 39], farmer," is found in *A List of Persons in Suffolk County, on Long Island Who Took the Oath of Allegiance and Peaceable behavior before Governor Tryon, 1778* Town of Brookhaven.[824]

David called himself a farmer in the entry as most did, not only because nearly all were farmers, but it was also expedient not to disclose ones' craft or skill for fear of being drafted into some occupation in the British forces wherever needed. Early historians interpreted the presence of a person's name on the oath to indicate his true allegiance, so David would have been included on the side of the loyalist, but this thinking changed as more historians could not defend the presence of many known patriots, including patriot leaders. Since no other record of David can be found on either side of the conflict, he probably chose to be evasive, but staying close to his family.

During the whole war the inhabitants of the Island, especially those of Suffolk Co. were perpetually exposed to the grossest insult and abuse. They were oftentimes deprived of the stock necessary to work the soil. The best rooms in their houses; the stores of fuel, provisions and clothing for bed and person were ruthlessly seized without ceremony and without compensation. Besides violating the rights of person and property, British officers committed many acts of barbarity for which there could be no apology.[825] Again, as is sometimes the case at times when selfish man has few boundaries, he is left to degenerate, giving in to his natural bent. This was the case when even some patriots became pirates,[826] working in gangs mostly for themselves, or for sale to the highest bidder. Silas Wood, writing in 1824, summarized the impact of the occupation. "The army was a sanctuary for crimes, and robbery, and the

---

[823] Note: It is believed that David could have actually been about 41 by this time and his actual birth year was probably closer to 1737. The wrong birth year was not unusual for this listing.
[824] Ibid.
[825] (Littell 1876)
[826] Note: see some accounts of Ebenezer Dayton as privateer

grossest offences [by civilians] were atoned by enlistment" which "shielded them from punishment."

> The war so devastated the communities in the region of the Long Island Sound that the necessities of survival sapped many citizens their ideals and virtue and led them to commit atrocities against their former friends and neighbors. As a result, by the end of the war Long Island was a chaotic no man's land of lawlessness, mayhem and violence as the brutality of the British army was often outdone by the viciousness of American plunderers from New England.[827]

These American raiding parties from Connecticut, "compounded the war's viciousness by looting and killing loyalists, whigs and neutrals alike…Many residents buried their silver and valuables, even if they remained in their homes, fearful of being robbed because the British did not maintain law and order during the occupation." [828] According to author Frederic Gregory Mather, the favorite points of attack by refugee raiders in Connecticut were Setauket and Huntington. Thompson ("Long Island," I.120) quotes the *New York Gazette*, of July 17, 1780, as saying:

> We hear from Setauket, that last Friday night a party of rebels surrounded the dwelling house of Doctor Punderson, took him prisoner, and carried him to Connecticut; and on that night the same party took Mr. William Jayne, Jun. The rebels told Mrs. Punderson that they had taken the doctor to exchange for John Smith, and Mr. Jayne for William Phillips, who were taken at Smithtown, at the widow Blydenburgh's, on a trading party.

On the other hand, the British often made raids of this sort from Long Island to Connecticut. The captures of Rev. Moses Mather and Gen Silliman are described in chapter 22 of Mather's book. From many instances of the taking of civil, or political prisoners, two are noted among others in the biographical sketches of the *Refugees of Long Island*—Ebenezer Dayton and Jonas Youngs. If interested in learning more about these accounts and others, the reader should consult the diverse works and research of historian Henry Onderdonk (1804-1886) and the American Loyalist and historian, Thomas Jones.

[British soldiers] made garrisons, storehouses and stables of the houses of public worship in several towns, and particularly of such as belonged to Presbyterians.[829] The Presbyterian Church at Setauket, the church of both Abraham and Henry Dayton, was not exempt from desecration, as told by *The History Trekker*:

---

[827] (Naylor, Surviving the Ordeal: Long Island Women During the Revolutionary War 2007/2008)
[828] (Naylor, The Other New Yorker n.d.)
[829] (Littell 1876)

Loyalists tended to attend the newer Caroline church, and as elsewhere, the British occupied the church which they didn't use, in this case the First Presbyterian Church of Brookhaven. The militarization of the church was done under the command of Colonel Richard Hewlett, a notable loyalist from a loyalist family from Hempstead, Long Island. He had about 150 men under his command, mainly other loyalists from around Long Island. And they set about fortifying the Presbyterian Church.[830]

The cemetery next to the Presbyterian Church at Setauket was desecrated as remains of forebearers were unearthed and discarded, thrown about as defense works were dug. Tombstones were removed and piled up in breastworks six feet tall and five feet thick on which swivel guns were mounted. Pews and pulpit were removed from the church and destroyed and the building was used to stable horses and house soldiers.[831] No church services were held for seven years. It has been said that pieces of tombstones from the cemetery have been discovered all over central Long Island, in building foundations and under roadways, for a century following the occupation.

In August of 1777, The Battle of Setauket took place when about 150 patriots came across the sound from Connecticut in whale boats with the purpose of taking on the Tory force in and around the fortified church.

They landed before day break the next morning at Crane Neck, where they left their boats with a sufficient guard and marched as quickly as possible to the village. A flag of truce was sent to the church demanding a surrender which was refused, and firing commenced on both sides. In a short time word was brought from the boats that some British ships were preceding down the Sound, and fearing that their return might be intercepted, Col. Parsons ordered a retreat to the boat [and withdrew].[832]

Around 1778, the infamous, "Setauket Spy Ring or Culper Spy Ring was organized by Major Benjamin Tallmadge with Abraham Woodhull (Samuel Culper) as operations chief. All the main figures, except one, were Setauket men. The ring operated secretly during the remainder of the war carrying messages to General Washington on the activities of the British in New York City."[833]

In 1779, the Culper spy ring gained this other member in New York City when Robert Townsend, a merchant and a Quaker from Oyster Bay, allowing Woodhull to remain in Setauket. Then, in 1780,

---

[830] (Concerning the Battle of Setauket: A Tale of Two Churches, a Minor Battle in the American Revolution and the Village Green Today n.d.)
[831] (T. R. Bayles, During the Revolution in Brookhaven 1985)
[832] (W. J. Post 1877)
[833] (Tyler, History Close at Hand-Three Village/Brookhaven-Chronology 2014)

The Culper Spy Ring performed its greatest service, notifying General Washington that the British were sending ships and men down Long Island Sound to attack the French fleet and troops at Newport, RI. Washington's successful ruse that he was going to attack the British in New York City, caused the British to return to protect the city. General Benedict Arnold failed in his attempt to turn West Point over to the British as Major Benjamin Tallmadge uncovered the plot, arrested British intelligence chief Major John Andre, and almost succeeded in capturing the traitor Arnold.[834]

Because of the treatment of its people by British transgressors, the majority of Long Island were now patriots, most having been swayed from indifference. This is conceivably the case for David Dayton, though no indication of passion or even preference for either side has been found. As attention shifted away from the Northeast to the southern colonies, the British withdrew most of their troops from the East End and more refugees sought permission to return to Long Island. The head of the town of Brookhaven up to 1780 were either loyalists or leaned in that direction but in 1780 Selah Strong (husband of spy Anna Smith Strong) was elected head of the town government. In 1781, with the decisive victory, the outcome of hostilities was becoming evident—Selah Strong's election was the precursor of things to come.[835]

> Almost all the refugees found their property in shambles, wasted and often destroyed altogether. Fields were overgrown and orchards trampled. It is arguable that Long Island suffered more than anywhere—certainly longer...[836]

Once again, the tables were turned so that those who had remained faithful to the crown were at risk. Their land was confiscated. Just as before the British occupation of Long Island, loyalists feared for their futures and determined that their best choice was to flee. Across the United States, "Some 60,000 loyalists—one in 40 members of the American population—decided to leave their homes and become refugees elsewhere in the British Empire."[837] In his *Refugees of 1776* book, Frederic Gregory Mather says:

> The situation [on Long Island] was a tragedy. Nearly all of the Refugees were men of small means. They returned one by one; not in large groups as was the case in New York. They found their properties wasted, and

---

[834] Ibid.
[835] (Naylor, Women in Long Island's Past: A History of Eminent Ladies and Everyday Lives 2012)
[836] (Naylor, Surviving the Ordeal: Long Island Women During the Revolutionary War 2007/2008)
[837] (Jasanoff 2011)

often destroyed altogether. Their average age was older than that of the Refugees from the City; and, in discouragement and poverty, they must begin life anew. And while New York suffered beyond the fate of any other City; yet Long Island more than any other rural district, save perhaps the Valley of the Mohawk. The records of mortgages for the years immediately following the War show that many men who had been wealthy were forced to borrow money on their lands…Many fine properties that had been handed down from father to son for more than a hundred years passed to other families.[838]

It is not known where and how David died in 1782, but it is assumed, from what little is known, that he was still on Long Island, not only because documents say David was "late of Suffolk County," but because there is no indication he was elsewhere. The following record of David as witness on a will between December 31, 1779 and June of 1782 comes from Coram and could be the latest record of David before his death.

Benjamin, Jonathan, of Coromm, Brookhaven Township, Suffolk Co., yeoman. Wife Elisabeth, daughters Phebe, Hannah, Behia, Sarah and Rachel. Real and personal estate. Executors the wife, son-in-law Benjamin Ovirton, and John Bellos. Witnesses Elijah Davis, David Dayton, John Leek. Recorded in Wills and Probates, vol I, p.20[839]

David's Administration

David Senior did not witness the formal end of the war as he died one year before the end of the occupation. It is known that he had already died because Anne received a Letter of Administration, dated June 26, 1782, from General James Robertson, who had been appointed governor of the province of New York in 1780. The general's placement in New York City was an effort to show Britain's desire that civilian government be restored, in contrast to the tyranny and chaos experienced the previous four years. Unfortunately, distance and danger and expense of travel and stay in NYC prevented most Long Island inhabitants from seeking justice there.

According to a legal dictionary, Letters of Administration were formal documents issued by a court of probate appointing a manager of the assets and liabilities of the deceased person's estate where property will pass under Intestacy

---

[838] (F. G. Mather 1913)
[839] (Fernow 1883)

Rules. Very often, the Letters were utilized where there was no will, no executors have been named in the will, or where no executors were living.

Anne, along with witnesses Joseph Ruland and Elisha Hammond appeared before Justice Nathan Woodhull in Setauket to initiate the procedure to obtain management of David's estate. Two documents were prepared in her behalf. The first was a certificate filled out by Judge Woodhull, dated June 17, 1782, which confirmed that Anne was David's widow, and she had agreed to bond.

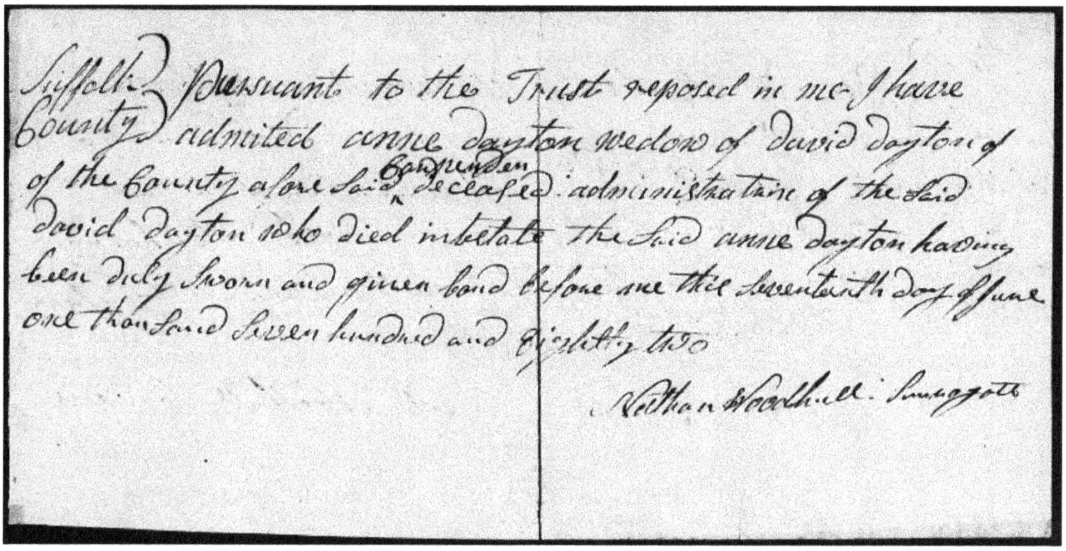

Suffolk County } Pursuant to the Trust reposed in me I have admited anne dayton widow of david dayton of the County afore Said Carpenter deceased administratrix of the Said david dayton who died intetate the Said anne dayton having been duly Sworn and given bond before me this Seventeenth day of June one thousand Seven hundred and Eighty two

Nathan Woodhull Surrogate

Figure 42. Nathan Woodhull's admission of administration to Anne

The certificate (figure 42) says:

Suffolk County. Pursuant to the Trust reposed in me I have admitted anne Dayton widow of David Dayton *of the County afore Said Carpenter deceased administration of the Said David Dayton who died intestate the Said anne Dayton having been duly Sworn and given bond before me the Seventeenth Day of June one thousand Seven hundred and Eighty two*

Nathan Woodall Surrogate

The second document is the Intestate Letter of Bond (figures 43 & 44) that Woodhull and Anne completed together with the document above. The Bond was the obligation that Anne agreed to if she would become administrator of her husband's estate. Both documents were sent to New York City, where Britain still had her seat of authority in civil government.

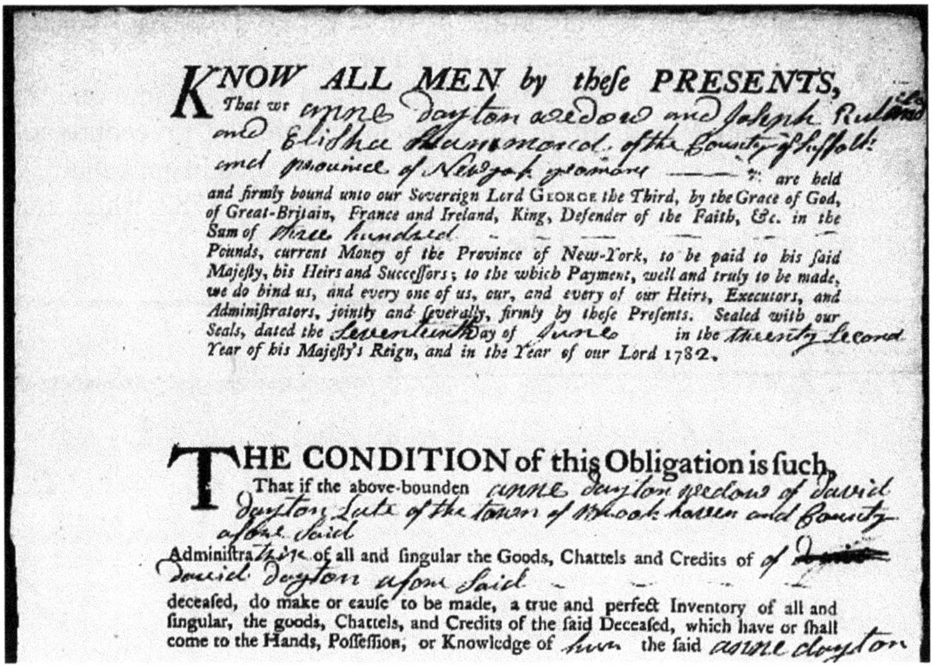

KNOW ALL MEN by these PRESENTS, That we anne dayton widow and Joseph Ruland and Elisha Hammond of the County of Suffolk and province of New york yeomans ——— are held and firmly bound unto our Sovereign Lord GEORGE the Third, by the Grace of God, of Great-Britain, France and Ireland, King, Defender of the Faith, &c. in the Sum of three hundred — — — Pounds, current Money of the Province of New-York, to be paid to his said Majesty, his Heirs and Successors; to the which Payment, well and truly to be made, we do bind us, and every one of us, our, and every of our Heirs, Executors, and Administrators, jointly and severally, firmly by these Presents. Sealed with our Seals, dated the seventeenth Day of June in the twenty second Year of his Majesty's Reign, and in the Year of our Lord 1782.

THE CONDITION of this Obligation is such, That if the above-bounden anne dayton widow of david dayton late of the town of Brook haven and County afore said Administratrix of all and singular the Goods, Chattels and Credits of david dayton afore said — — — deceased, do make or cause to be made, a true and perfect Inventory of all and singular, the goods, Chattels, and Credits of the said Deceased, which have or shall come to the Hands, Possession, or Knowledge of her the said anne dayton

Figure 43. Intestate Letter of Bond, Anne Dayton (top of document)

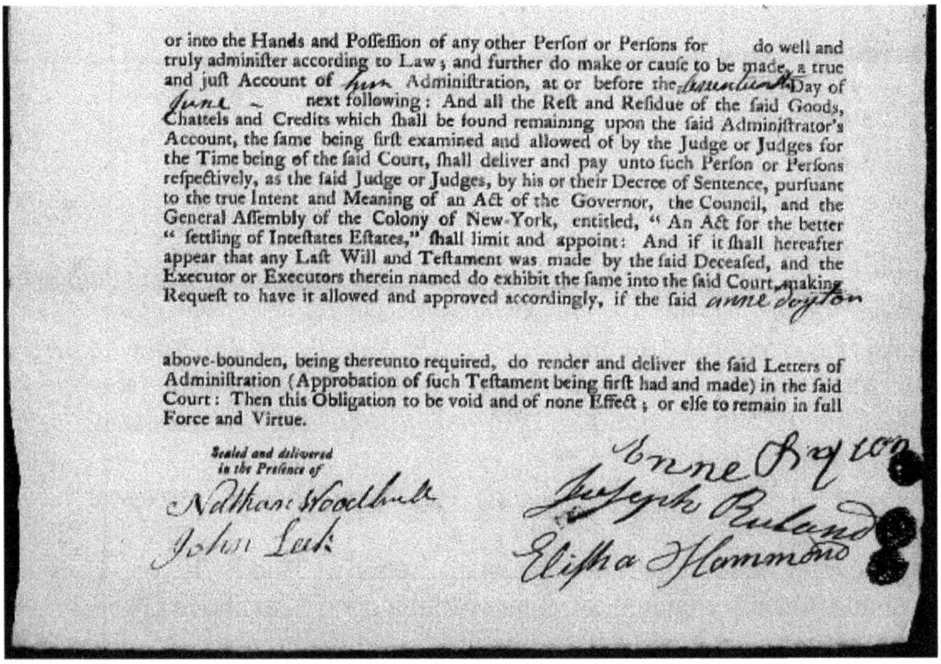

or into the Hands and Possession of any other Person or Persons for do well and truly administer according to Law; and further do make or cause to be made, a true and just Account of her Administration, at or before the seventeenth Day of June — next following: And all the Rest and Residue of the said Goods, Chattels and Credits which shall be found remaining upon the said Administrator's Account, the same being first examined and allowed of by the Judge or Judges for the Time being of the said Court, shall deliver and pay unto such Person or Persons respectively, as the said Judge or Judges, by his or their Decree of Sentence, pursuant to the true Intent and Meaning of an Act of the Governor, the Council, and the General Assembly of the Colony of New-York, entitled, "An Act for the better "settling of Intestates Estates," shall limit and appoint: And if it shall hereafter appear that any Last Will and Testament was made by the said Deceased, and the Executor or Executors therein named do exhibit the same into the said Court, making Request to have it allowed and approved accordingly, if the said anne dayton above-bounden, being thereunto required, do render and deliver the said Letters of Administration (Approbation of such Testament being first had and made) in the said Court: Then this Obligation to be void and of none Effect; or else to remain in full Force and Virtue.

Sealed and delivered in the Presence of

Nathan Woodhull
John Leek

Anne Dayton
Joseph Ruland
Elisha Hammond

Figure 44. Intestate Letter of Bond, Anne Dayton (bottom of document)

Nine days later, the Letter of Administration (figure 45) was granted to Anne, filled out on the governor's letterhead, with the information that was provided by

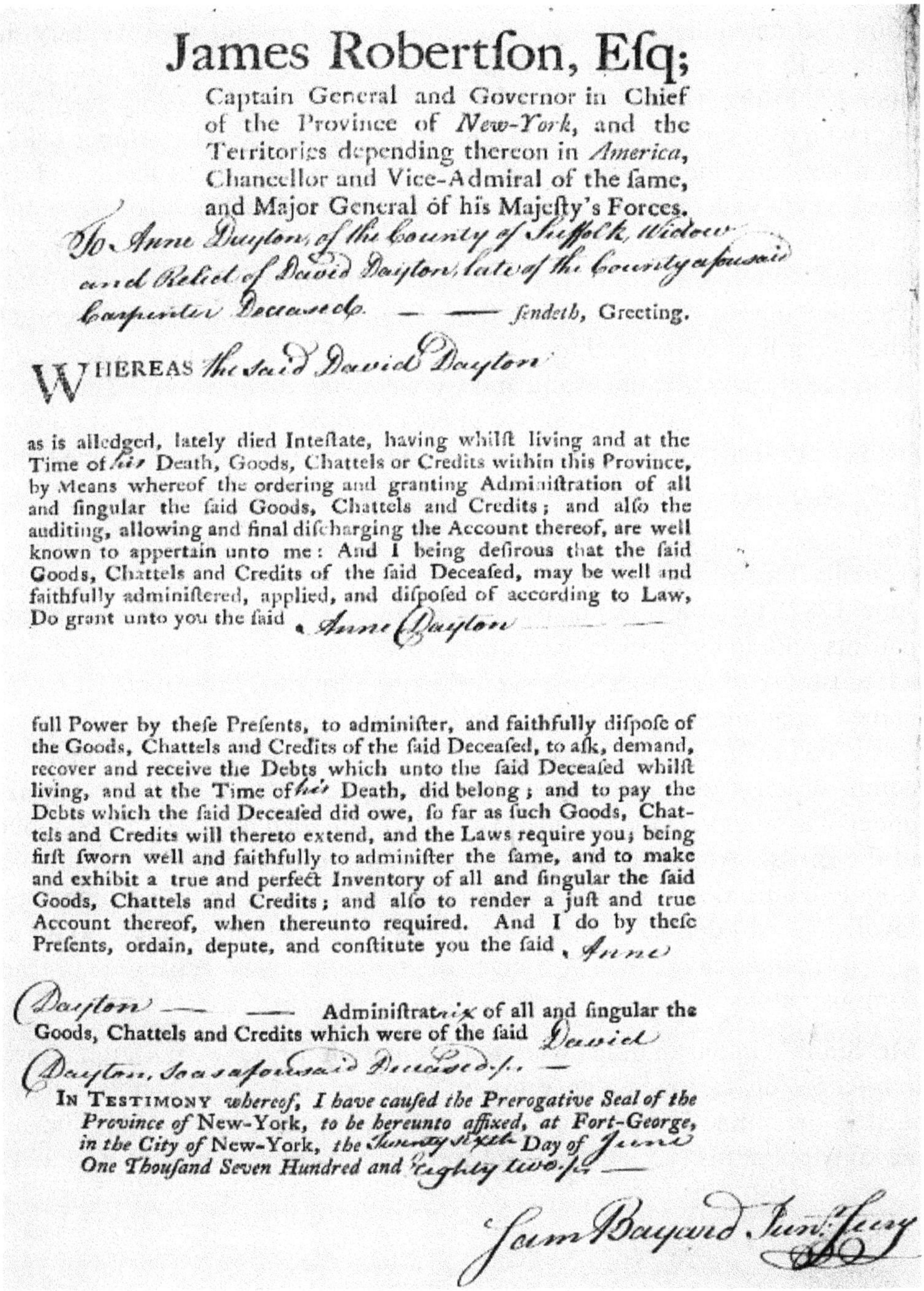

James Robertson, Esq;

Captain General and Governor in Chief of the Province of *New-York*, and the Territories depending thereon in *America*, Chancellor and Vice-Admiral of the same, and Major General of his Majesty's Forces.

To Anne Dayton, of the County of Suffolk, Widow and Relict of David Dayton, late of the County aforesaid Carpenter Deceased. — *sendeth,* Greeting.

WHEREAS *the said David Dayton*

as is alledged, lately died Inteftate, having whilft living and at the Time of *his* Death, Goods, Chattels or Credits within this Province, by Means whereof the ordering and granting Adminiftration of all and fingular the faid Goods, Chattels and Credits; and alfo the auditing, allowing and final difcharging the Account thereof, are well known to appertain unto me: And I being defirous that the faid Goods, Chattels and Credits of the faid Deceafed, may be well and faithfully adminiftered, applied, and difpofed of according to Law, Do grant unto you the faid *Anne Dayton*

full Power by thefe Prefents, to adminifter, and faithfully difpofe of the Goods, Chattels and Credits of the faid Deceafed, to afk, demand, recover and receive the Debts which unto the faid Deceafed whilft living, and at the Time of *his* Death, did belong; and to pay the Debts which the faid Deceafed did owe, fo far as fuch Goods, Chattels and Credits will thereto extend, and the Laws require you; being firft fworn well and faithfully to adminifter the fame, and to make and exhibit a true and perfect Inventory of all and fingular the faid Goods, Chattels and Credits; and alfo to render a juft and true Account thereof, when thereunto required. And I do by thefe Prefents, ordain, depute, and conftitute you the faid *Anne*

Dayton — — Adminiftrat*rix* of all and fingular the Goods, Chattels and Credits which were of the faid *David*

Dayton, fo as aforesaid Deceased fc. —

IN TESTIMONY *whereof, I have caufed the Prerogative Seal of the Province of* New-York, *to be hereunto affixed, at* Fort-George, *in the City of* New-York, *the Twenty sixth Day of June One Thoufand Seven Hundred and eighty two fc* —

Sam Bayard Jun Secy

Figure 45. Letter of Administration on Governor's Letterhead

Woodhull. Anne was granted permission to dispose of David's estate, on the condition that she pay all debts and that she make an inventory and submit it to the court at New York within the next six months (by December 17, 1782). The Obligation also stated that if the task of creating and submitting the inventory should fall to others, they were to receive an additional year to present the inventory (by December 17, 1783). The letter is dated June 26, 1782 and probably went back to Woodhull who then saw to it that the inventory was done before December 1782. The Obligation contains the signatures of Anne Dayton, Joseph Ruland and Elisha Hammond, each with a seal. In order to get an idea of the requirements and restrictions on who received Letters of Administration during this time of occupation and war, Ned Smith was contacted once again and he confirmed that Letters of Administration during Britain's occupation of Long Island could have been granted to families regardless of sympathies.

While those who fled the island and were actively involved in the patriot cause probably wouldn't show up in such documents, families who do appear could have been loyalists, neutrals, or even pro-American but coerced into outward obedience.[840]

Very early into our inquiry Smith wrote of his cursory findings:

> For instance, letters of administration on the estate of Jonathan 'Yainton' (actually Yarrington) of Suffolk County, were granted 2 weeks earlier (14 June 1782) to Uriah Smith, brother-in-law. I know that both men were patriots prior to the British occupation. Additionally Smith was also named administrator of another estate the following year. In 1780 Austin Roe was named an administrator; at the time he was one of Washington's leading spies on Long Island. And in 1781 Josiah Smith was named an administrator; earlier he had been commander of the Suffolk County troops under Washington at the Battle of Brooklyn, and then for a while a prisoner of the British. Altogether I found 22 letters of administtion with a Suffolk County connection issued between 1779 and 1783. A few I recognize as loyalist. Most I don't know, and many may have not taken sides. So all in all, it seems clear that a range of opinions was reflected in the administrations.[841]

Mr. Smith's initial findings were the inspiration for our own search. A sample of thirty letters appearing in the registry[842] before and after Anne's letter were examined to determine if there were any visible patterns of geographic location or wartime conviction; instead the deceased were well dispersed in New York City and

---

[840] (N. Smith 2012)
[841] Ibid.
[842] (New York Probate Records, 1629-1971 n.d.)

Long Island and an almost even number appeared to lean loyalist and patriot, six or seven each, while the remaining sixteen or more were not apparent.

It may have been that, by the summer of 1782, much had changed to embolden the patriots and weaken the British resolve. By that time, Abraham Woodhull had already reported that the end was in sight. The patriot victory at Yorktown in October of 1781 had pushed the British Prime Minister to seek immediate negotiations with the American peace commissioners in February of 1782. The fact that all four of the men whose signatures appear on the bottom of Anne's Obligation: Joseph Ruland, Elisha Hammond, Nathan Woodhull and John Leek appear to be patriots may not only implicate the leaning of Anne or David, but also the relative speed of the process indicates that civilities were greater after Yorktown. That fall, Americans would sign preliminary articles of peace with the British, in Paris.

Faithful to the information provided him in Anne's Certificate from Woodhull, Junior Secretary Sam Bayard repeated in the Letter of Administration that David was a carpenter. It is interesting to note that Anne identified her husband as carpenter in 1782 after David himself claimed to be a farmer just a few years earlier, when he signed the oath of allegiance. A carpenter would certainly have been an occupation needed in 1778 but there were at least three other carpenters in Brookhaven, as shown on the 1778 loyalty oath extracted by Gov. Tryon. There might have been even more since many craftsmen doubled as farmers and might have listed that as their primary occupation.[843]

Beverly Tyler, Three Village Historical Society Historian and writer, was asked what it meant to be a carpenter in those days. Tyler said:

> A carpenter is also a builder such as a shipwright or housewright. He could have been either. A carpenter in old English is also a carriage maker.[844]

William Minuse said:

> From the days of Richard Bullick[845] to the 19th century, there is very little known about the ship building industry in this area. That it went on, however, we may be sure. The descendants of the first settlers were actively engaged in whaling, and must have built their own whale boats. During the Revolutionary War, these same boats were used by patriots such as Caleb Brewster, associate of the master spy Abraham Woodhull..."[846]

---

[843] (N. Smith 2012)

[844] (B. Tyler 2013)

[845] Note: About 1662, Richard Bullick [Bullock] was given four months to build a boat and leave town.

[846] (Minuse 1955)

What would it mean to be a carpenter in the Setauket-Coram area of Brookhaven, in the period leading up to the American Revolution? We asked Barbara Russell, Brookhaven Town Historian, about carpenters and carpentry and what that occupation would entail in the mid 1700's. She indicated that the job of carpenter often varied with the season.

> …ship carpenters here were sought out for the ship-building industry, but if there wasn't a ship under construction or it was a particularly cold winter and you couldn't work outside, they often became house builders and we see that a lot more even, going into the 19th century where, for instance in Port Jefferson, which was Suffolk County's largest ship-building center, houses have magnificent woodwork, all done by the ship-builders.[847]

The Episcopal Church in Setauket was possibly built by ship-carpenters also. Russell continues:

> When they did the restoration of the church in 1937 and they basically stripped out most of the interior, they realized that the basic 1729 frame was built with ship-building style…ship's knees, which is a brace in the corners, and the barrel ceiling which you think of a ship, upside down... So, we do know that, or we do feel that, in 1729, ship-builders were here in Brookhaven, to have that style of building.

Anne was in her early 40s when she lost David. Their nine children ranged in age from about twenty one to six. It is not known where the grave of David Senior is, but it is probably located somewhere in Brookhaven, near Coram or Patchogue.

---

[847] (Russell 2014)

Chapter 20

The Wilds of New York

Out of Necessity

David Junior was the sixth generation in our line of Daytons to live in America. He was also the sixth and last generation to live on Long Island, one of three generations born in the eighteenth century.[848] Like his father and grandfather, he was born and spent some of his childhood in the town of Brookhaven, but his childhood there would be quite different as he was born at the beginning of America's "road to war" with Great Britain. The mother country had just been victorious over France in the Seven Years War, and in the Treaty of Paris in 1763, she gained new dominance in the Americas. The prolonged struggle and victory came at great expense to Great Britain and the American colonies were taxed to help pay for the war. The colonists endured a series of new taxes (what would be considered small by today's standard), but the Acts which also contained other restrictions created unrest. In a show of power, British troops were sent to occupy Boston in 1768 when David was just two years of age. Following the Battles of Lexington and Concord and of Bunker Hill, the conflict was brought to New York as British forces were victorious at the Battles of Long Island and White Plains and then controlled and occupied New York City and Long Island beginning in 1776, by the time David was ten years old.

David was likely born at the home of his parents near Coram in 1766, when David Senior was almost thirty years of age and Anne was probably about twenty seven. It is supposed that David Junior spent at least his first ten years at Coram, near Patchogue. In the months before the occupation, though not at war, parts of Long Island were becoming less comfortable, as neighbors, friends and relatives were

---

[848] Note: David Junior's son Henry, next in our line, was also born in the eighteenth century, but is not included because he never lived on Long Island.

pushed to choose sides in the conflict and so many others were trying to remain neutral and live their lives, taking care of family and farm, without drawing attention to themselves. Somehow David Senior had avoided declaring his convictions and commitment to the rebellion in the General Association but he could not avoid the census that followed. When the war was brought to Long Island and the British occupation began, David's nine children were all under the age of seventeen and Anne had either just delivered or was still pregnant with the youngest, Rhoda. The birth order of the children has not been firmly established but it is believed that David Junior's 1766 birth should be placed about fourth in the line of nine that stretched from about 1761 to 1776. The children's names were Abigail, Henry, Annie, David, Abraham, Deborah, Telem, Joel and Rhoda.

As Long Island was taken by Britain and held with the aid of local loyalists, it must have been increasingly difficult to elude judgment and the consequences that resulted from whatever position one would take, even if not appearing to side with either combatant. The appearance of neutrality would certainly not exempt one from the hardships or evils of the time and was probably a difficult stance to maintain, given the relentless provocations from both sides. In fact, Quakers who tried to remain neutral because of their pacifist views were accused by both sides of aiding the other;[849] therefore it is certain that David's family also suffered.

Marking David Senior with the convictions of either group seems nearly impossible, as circumstantial evidence is examined and weighed. For every recognizable association that would favor one side, another conflicting connection refutes or cancels the first, leading the modern-day observer with no compelling defense that David belonged to either side in the conflict. Neither has any conclusive evidence been found to suggest that the family joined thousands of Long Island refugees who fled to Connecticut at any time during the seven-year occupation, yet since some children appear to be absent, they may have gone, possibly staying with relatives. After they had lost their father, the children's leaving out of necessity is easily understood. For the purposes of this book, it is assumed that most of the family remained on Long Island during the occupation, near their farm in Coram or Patchogue because both David and oldest son Henry (aged about 16) were present to sign the Oath of Allegiance in 1778. Sadly, most Long Island records from the occupation, especially around Patchogue, are lost and believed to be destroyed.

It is believed that David Senior and his family (including Senior's brothers) were most certainly under duress, and some of their farms, if not seized for quartering troops, probably were laid barren of anything of value and then fell into states of disrepair. Whatever their initial convictions—patriot, tory or neutral, the farmers of Coram were defenseless, as that community was occupied and became the British collection point for 300 tons of hay, in storage to get the horses of their cavalry

---

[849] (Naylor, Women in Long Island's Past: A History of Eminent Ladies and Everyday Lives 2012)

through the winter. With so much attention on the effort, surrounding fields of the local farmers must have been taken early on. In November of 1780, Major Benjamin Tallmadge with about eighty men in eight whaleboats left Connecticut and executed a raid on Fort St. George, at present-day Mastic Beach on the south shore, capturing it. With the blessing of General Washington, twelve hand-picked men digressed from the company's return to their hidden boats at Old Man's (present-day Mt. Sinai), overtook the guards at Coram and burned the giant storage of hay.

This celebrated undertaking must also have come at great cost to the small number of farmers that remained (assuming a few farmers still had milking cows or other livestock), as the ready supply of hay on central Long Island was destroyed. It is easy to imagine that David Senior tried to maintain his farm for a while, enduring intensifying hardships, but if he and his family had endured to this point, still at Coram, this event surely must have had an impact. Whether David was involved in any way, for either side, will probably never be known, but the blazing inferno was probably visible from the Dayton's house.

Over time, with mounting misconduct by British officers against civilians, many Long Islanders who had been neutral or even loyalist at the beginning of the occupation were turning patriot[850] and it is believed the same could be true for David Dayton before 1782. If David had been leaning toward loyalism or neutrality at the beginning, it appears that he may have favored the idea of a new nation by the time of his death. It should be noted that even though David and Anne were still living on Long Island in 1782, Anne emerges in good standing with remaining or returning patriots in the Town of Brookhaven, and in Patchogue particularly. It is interesting to consider that in 1790, President George Washington personally thanked his supporters on Long Island by selecting a route through Patchogue, Coram and Setauket (according to his personal diary), stopping along the way presumably to meet with members of his secret spy ring.

We are not suggesting that David was in any way involved with the network of spies, but at the same time, it is recognized that his involvement was not impossible. No cause of death has been established for David and not a shred of evidence has been located that points to a specific time or place or even circumstance for his death. But, by his mid-forties, David was gone, leaving no will and leaving Anne with a large family and probably no means of support other than by her oldest son Henry who would inherit anything left of his father's estate. Within a few years, and with Anne's blessing, the four younger boys—David, Abraham, Telem and Joel left Long Island and headed north, probably with others from Brookhaven, through Connecticut and Massachusetts to Vermont and extreme eastern New York, to be in position for opportunities as forfeited loyalist lands would become available. Dayton

---

[850] Note: see the many publications of Joseph S. Tiedermann, Loyola Marymount University Department of History

relatives in Connecticut, descendants of Samuel's son Isaac, also made their way to that rapidly growing area.

Parting Ways

David Junior must have been about fifteen when his father died[851] but, as was the case for his forefathers, no record was found for him until after he reached legal age. At age twenty three in 1790, David is found in the first Census of the United States with wife and child, over 200 miles away from Long Island, in Cambridge, New York. His wife Chloe was about twenty two. At that time, Cambridge included what are today the towns of Cambridge, Jackson and White Creek, all in Washington County. Researching by geographical reference becomes quite complicated around the time of the 1790 census because this large area was in great political transition. Cambridge was part of Albany County, Bennington County in Vermont and part of Charlotte County, but became part of Washington County the following year, bordering Rensselaer County. Modern-day Cambridge is situated almost halfway between Bennington, Vermont and Saratoga Springs, New York.

Three of the five brothers—David, Telem (also spelled Telim and Telam) and Joel begin to appear in records in the same general area of extreme eastern New York and western Vermont as each becomes of age. Interestingly, more than one person named Abraham Dayton can be found in the Cambridge/Granville area so it is uncertain which one (if either one) was David's younger brother. Rattray says that the Abraham who died in Granville in 1825 was a descendant of Nathan. At the same time the brothers are found in upstate New York, it is apparent that three of the four sisters—Abigal, Annie and Deborah remained on Long Island as it is believed that each of their marriages occur near Patchogue. If all of these marriages can be proven, it may also be fair to assume that their mother remained on the island, near the girls, after all the boys except Henry left.

Though no one seems to know why, Donald Lines Jacobus chose to give David's marriage date December 29, 1789, without providing his sources.[852] Considering the stature of Jacobus, it is understandable that those who followed also used the date he provided, and this date has persisted these many years without published investigation of the source Jacobus used. We are aware of only one

---

[851] Note: Junior's age can be calculated from the year of birth given on his gravestone which is in Lake Luzerne, NY Cemetery on Lake Avenue (Route 9N).
[852] Note: The 1959 Donald Lines Jacobus publication *The Early Daytons and Descendants of Henry Jr* contains the wedding date without citation. Normally it is not a good idea to question Mr. Jacobus but the wedding date is suspect.

publication that precedes Jacobus and it is part of an 1896 collection of purchased "biographies" entitled *A Memorial and Biographical Record of Iowa Vol II*, created for the pleasure of the purchaser.[853] In the book, a short biography of "Honorable Henry Dayton" appears and, while his ancestry is sprinkled with truths, it is replete with erroneous information presented as fact and should be viewed as family folklore.

Our respect for Jacobus leads us to believe that he did not use the *Record of Iowa* publication but instead might have discovered the same source used in that publication. It is a possibility that both Lewis Publishing and Jacobus used Charles Nathan Dayton's personal notes, many of which were later edited by James W. Dayton and released in 1963. In a 1902 handwritten letter to an unknown descendant of David Dayton, Charles relates that the marriage date came from "Chloe Dayton's Bible," suggesting the possibility that Charles might have shared this information before the *Record of Iowa* was published. In his letter, Charles does not mention if he actually saw Chloe's bible or if he received the information secondhand.

If the bible can be located, perhaps it might be determined if the date actually referred to the couples' wedding or if it was simply the first reference found of their married life. Similar errors are frequent in genealogy and occur much the same way as baptism dates are often construed as birth dates. It is just as likely that David and Chloe were wed sometime late in 1788 or early in 1789.

How David Dayton of Long Island and Chloe Skiff of Massachusetts met continues to be a mystery. Chloe, born January 2, 1768, was the oldest of three daughters of John and Eunice Skiff of Worthington, all three being baptized on September 1 of 1773 at Worthington,[854] the same year her father was received by the church. As soldiers in the revolution, John Skiff and his father were patriots and were taken prisoner in 1778 at New Bedford, MA, but had escaped.[855] Like many who migrated west across the state of Massachusetts and settled in the Lake George and Saratoga region, Chloe's family was old-line Yankee with Mayflower ancestry,[856] but John's family may have detoured by way of Preston, CT.

---

[853] (Lewis Publishing Staff 1896) The Iowa book is an example from the turn-of-the-century genealogy craze, when it became popular for many well-to-do families to purchase space in memorial or biographical publications from certain traveling salesmen, in order to register their pedigrees. Once purchased, the buyer would submit information about himself and provide genealogies of his choosing. The publisher would gather many of these genealogies into a book after proper editing and maybe some embellishment. In other words, a single book of this kind could have hundreds of contributing authors.

[854] (Vital Records of Worthington, Massachusetts, to the Year 1850 1911) 61

[855] (Pease 1918)

[856] Note: Chloe's great grandfather Nathan Skiffe (Nathan, Samuel, John) married Mercy Chipman, the daughter of John Chipman, born in Brinspittle Eng., and Hope Howland of Plymouth Colony.

Chloe's father was still at Worthington, MA in 1790[857] after David and Chloe's marriage, indicating that Chloe was probably in or near Worthington when she and David met. Worthington and Middlefield, just a few miles over the hill from one another, were in a period of great growth and prosperity between 1775 and 1830. The prominent colonial model of farming for a family's own household sustenance was changed with the introduction of cattle, and especially sheep, which were perfectly matched with the area's abundant rocky pastures and plentiful water sources. Nearly three-quarters of Middlefield's forestland was eventually cleared for sheep grazing.[858] Considering that some of David's descendants would become sheep farmers of precious Merino wool, perhaps it might be safe to assume that David had

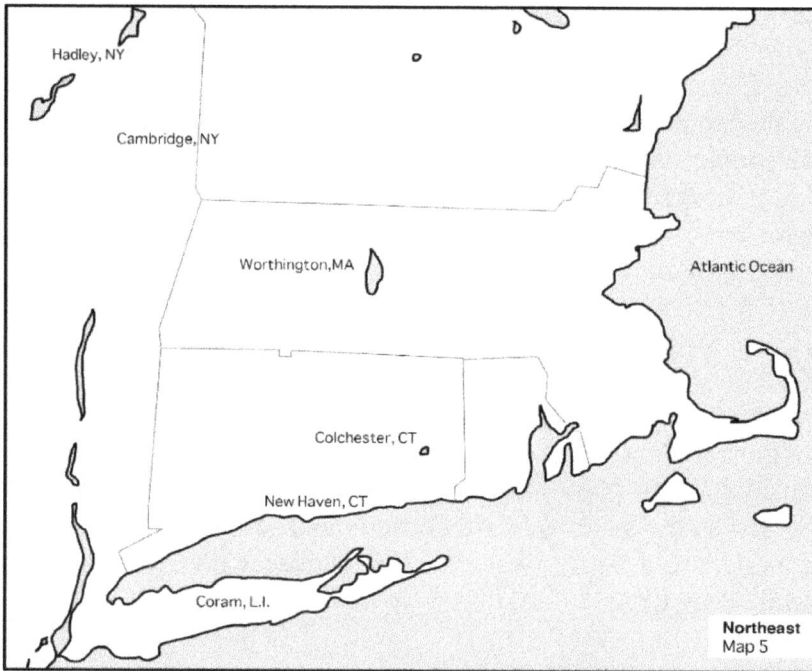

Figure 46. The route to Hadley

Hope was the daughter of famed Mayflower passengers John Howland and Elizabeth Tilley about whom much is written. Elizabeth's parents, John Tilley and Joan Rogers, were also Mayflower passengers but died that first winter upon arrival leaving fourteen year old Elizabeth without guardian. Her husband was a servant aboard the Mayflower and will always be known as the passenger who fell off the ship during the voyage and was rescued.
[857] (Lee 1902) 1274
[858] (E. P. Smith 1924)

been tending flocks in the Worthington/Chesterfield area, then also known for its Merino sheep. No earmarks have been found for David Junior.

By the 1790 Census, David and Chloe had moved to Cambridge, NY (then in Albany County) and were already a family of three, with first child Joel born August 29, 1790.[859] Cambridge was transferred to Washington County (named Charlotte County before 1784) the following year, the same year the boundary dispute between Vermont and New York was settled, establishing what is now Washington County as a border county with Vermont. With the removal of the threat from Native American raids and the construction of good roads converging at Cambridge, the patent of fertile land there was attractive to many New Englanders, as well as to immigrants from the lower Hudson valley.

Today's Cambridge is about sixty-five miles northwest from Worthington. But, if the road was not yet completed, the sixty-five miles would have been no ordinary journey to be undertaken in the winter or early spring. Circumventing natural impediments all along the way, any sections of still uncompleted highway would have been difficult and dangerous. The Cambridge area, about 10 miles from Vermont, was also known for its sheep farming and still has Skiff families living there, as of 2015. Since no other record of David is found in the Cambridge area, it is wondered if perhaps the family was squatting there,[860] waiting for the anticipated availability of forfeited loyalist land just to the west, in or near the Hudson valley.

Dartmouth Patent, Hadley

Sometime between 1790 and 1796, David and Chloe relocated again, this time moving about forty miles northwest of Cambridge to Hadley, NY (today in Saratoga County). At the time David settled in Hadley it is possible that the settlement was still in the town of Greenfield.

There can be no doubt that David and Chloe were among the first settlers of Hadley which claims its first inhabitants about 1788 with Richard Hilton and 1790 with Alexander Stewart settling in the Dartmouth Patent. In 1772, the Dartmouth Patent was described as about 47,000 acres divided into two parts called the Great Tract and the Small Tract, bordering the Hudson River on its east and the Sacandaga

---

[859] Note: According to his gravestone also located at Lake Luzerne Cemetery, Route 9N.
[860] Note: There is occasional inference that squatters inhabited some "unclaimed" regions in eastern upstate New York, but little has been recorded about their existence. It is also possible that David and Chloe were hosted by relatives, or even by Abraham or Telam Dayton, residing in Granville NY at the time of the 1790 census. Or perhaps the squatting referred to a first Hadley dwelling, just before moving upriver to establish their farm.

branch of the river on its south. The Patent was in Albany and Charlotte Counties, later becoming Warren and Saratoga Counties. The Small Tract, about 18,000 acres, contained the lots distributed along the Hudson, one of which was Alexander Stewart's lot 9.

Oral tradition claimed that David briefly lived "near the Post Office" (established long after David's death) before moving upriver to start his farm on the Dartmouth Patent. This Post Office, it is said, was close to the current Luzerne-Hadley bridge, at a narrow gorge, separating Saratoga and Warren Counties. This is the very spot where local legend says the Jessup brothers jumped across to escape their pursuers, and joined other loyalists fleeing to Canada. The gap has since been widened to accommodate needs of a factory or mill a few hundred feet downstream.

David is said to be the second recorded settler of the Dartmouth patent, after Alexander Stewart. Stewart's son Daniel and grandson Daniel (son of Charles) are credited by Sylvester for providing much of the knowledge about the settlement of Hadley and another of Alexander's sons, David, was said to have surveyed much of Hadley.

Hadley remains a very small town today, with most of its population scattered across a large space, 200 miles directly north from Manhattan, where the Sacandaga River empties into the Hudson. Just above this point, the Hudson River provides a source of rapid flow below what is now called Rockwell Falls. Hadley is also about 200 miles from New Haven, CT, depending upon the route taken; sometimes around the Green and Taconic Mountains that extend along the boundary of Massachusetts and New York and into Connecticut.

A descendant of our David, and contemporary of Nathaniel Bartlett Sylvester, contributed some family legends published in the Iowa book;[861] he added that David was a surveyor of land, despite the absence of anything to substantiate the claims. In the author's defense, it should be pointed out that he was probably speaking of his grandfather, just seventy years removed, so it could have been that David was an assistant to the surveyor in multiple capacities, perhaps clearing heavy brush and small trees from lines of sight, in order to set boundary lines.

Sylvester probably was the source for so many authors who claimed that David Dayton settled on lot 10 of the Dartmouth Patent in 1796.[862] Figure 47, the 1895 Julius Bien & Co. map identifies Lot 10 in the Little Dartmouth Patent (nearest center) and Henry's Lot 1 on Hadley Hill purchased in 1828. David and Edythe Haskell, highly respected tri-county genealogists from Stony Creek, NY said, "David and Chloe moved to Hadley in 1796 where they lived just south of the intersection of the Hadley-Stony Creek Road and the Hadley Hill Road."[863] The intersection they

---

[861] (Lewis Publishing Staff 1896)
[862] (Sylvester 1878)
[863] (Haskell 1991)

referred to was obviously in the middle of lot 10 and nineteenth century maps clearly indicate the existence of converging primitive roads even then. Considering a few strong pieces of evidence that will be discussed in this chapter, there is little reason to doubt that David settled lot 10 of the Dartmouth patent, but proof that specifically states "David settled lot 10" is yet to be found. Sylvester had access to the New York State Library at Albany, the largest genealogical and town and state record repository in America, before Dartmouth patent records were lost to fire at Albany in the early 1900's. Sylvester also said that Alexander Stewart's farm, lot 9, "consisted of 150 acres of fine river bottom lands, and was densely covered with a heavy growth of extremely fine white pine timber,"[864] and he added, "from May to December he cleared up fifteen acres without the aid of horses, cattle or men." This observation and description gives us an idea of the work David faced on his neighboring lot.

The outline of Dartmouth Patent Lot 10 can be seen on the 1895 Bien map, following the labeled lots northward—with labels *4, 6* and *8* which are clearly visible, with the label for *10* partially obstructed at the intersection. These lots extended down to the river on their east, and were bisected by the Hadley-Stony Creek Road. At this intersection is the site believed to be the Dayton farm, about three miles north of the present village, on the west side of Hadley-Stony Creek Road, traveling along the west side of the Hudson River. Just southwest of the intersection sit the current buildings and pond, while the lower end extends from the road down to the river bank. Being one of the first settlers of Hadley, David may have selected this choice plot of land at the bottom of the Hadley Hill Road, next to Alexander Stewart, because there was a natural spring that even today feeds a small pond situated near the house, standing in 2015.

New York State imposed a war tax to pay down debt, collected annually from 1799 to 1804. This additional tax was assessed on the value of real estate and the personal estate of each property owner. The personal tax would be representative of the value of the contents of the home and farming tools, implements, livestock and any other "valuables" that the resident owned. Analysis of these tax lists provides a glimpse into the relative worth of individuals in the community. In 1800, David Dayton is found in the town of Greenfield because Hadley was not to be formed until 1801 from parts of Greenfield and Northumberland. In 1800, David's real estate was worth $800 and his personal estate was worth $68 which translated to $1.50 tax (annual rate). In order to understand the relative impact of the tax on the family budget, consider that there were 556 tax payers in the town of Greenfield and the "poorest" landowner in town paid one cent in taxes ($15 real estate and $15 personal property). The largest holding of value was $292 real property and $1494 personal property and he paid $9.59 in taxes. Based on assessed value of his estate, David ranked 105th most wealthy person in Greenfield, with 451 taxpayers below him. Most

---

[864] (Sylvester 1878)

of David's wealth was in real estate, placing him in the top 20% for the area. Since David had moved to Greenfield from Cambridge within the previous 4 to 7 years, he

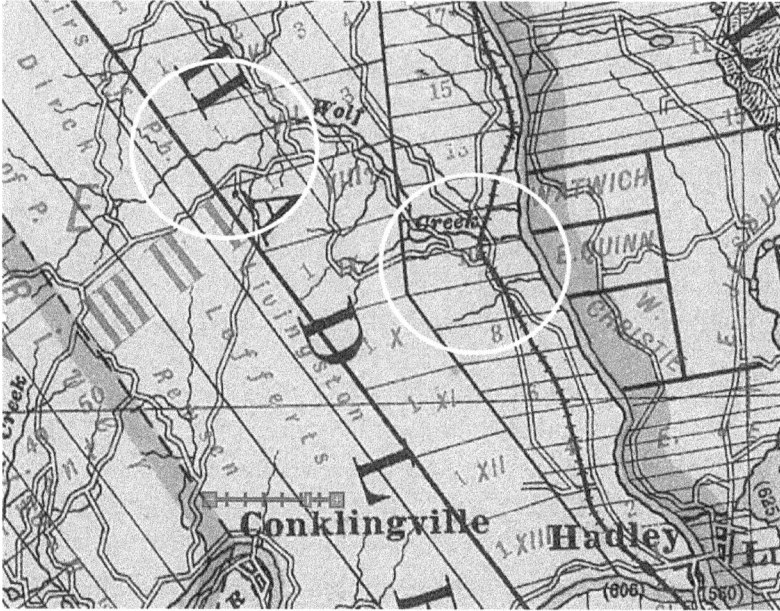

Figure 47. Little Dartmouth Patent

probably had little in the way of personal possessions. He was probably limited to moving one wagonload of essential tools and utensils and he had little time to acquire the personal assets of longstanding taxpayers.

Accounting for the 1800 Census

It is very likely that David and Chloe had four children in their first six years of marriage. After Joel, born about 1790, came Henry about 1792, Chloe about 1794, and Eunice about 1796. We are not prepared to defend a birth place for Joel or Henry or even Chloe, but Eunice was probably born at Hadley.

An account of the Dayton family appeared in the census of 1800 at Greenfield, Saratoga County. Hadley was formed from Greenfield in 1801, but then comprised the present towns of Hadley, Corinth and a part of Day. By 1800, the family of David "Daton" was a family of eight, consisting of four males and four females. The first three girls were named after Chloe and her sisters, Eunice and Irinda. The census however reported six males (2 boys under 10, 2 boys 10-16, 1 man 26-45, 1 man over 45) and three females (2 girls under 10, 1 woman 26-45). The 1800 census was taken starting August 4, 1800 and lasted for 9 months, extending into 1801. The applicable page is represented below.

Heads of Families	FREE WHITE MALES					FREE WHITE FEMALES				
	to 10	10 to 16	16 to 26	26 to 45	45 & c.	to 10	10 to 16	16 to 26	26 to 45	45 & c.
David Daton	2	2		1	1	2			1	

Census miscounts were not uncommon. Classroom instructors of genealogy are quick to say, "don't believe everything you read." In particular, discrepancies are expected and will be found in census data, but they should not be ignored.

Comparison of Numbers of Reported Family Members and Number of Actual Family Members:

Census Males- total 6	Actual Males- total 4	Difference
Under 10 (2)	Henry, Telem	No difference
10-16 (2)	Joel	Reported one too many
26-45 (1)	David	No difference
Over 44 (1)	No record of this person	Reported one too many

Census Females- total 3	Actual Females- total 4	Notes
Under 10 (2)	Chloe, Eunice, Irinda	Reported only 2 of 3 girls
26-44 (1)	Chloe	No difference

Some differences can be reconciled with simple application of circumstances of everyday life. In some cases, the census taker had many square miles to cover in a relatively short period of time. Maybe the census taker couldn't cross a stream so he asked the neighbor for the information. Perhaps the parents were in the field, so he asked one of the children. Sometimes the parents made errors in the count, the census taker was tired or careless and counted inaccurately or maybe the transcriber copied in error. However, the big one, and we think the one that can easily explain most of our situation is this. The census taker was REQUIRED to count everyone in the household ON THAT DAY; otherwise it wouldn't be a census. In our present day, the count would be describe as a "snapshot." That presents a dilemma because, if the individual was visiting family from the next town for the day, he or she would be counted in the other's household. Then, next week, if the census taker went to the next town and the family was back home from the visitation, he would be counted again. Something like that may have happened here. A man (over 44) and his son (aged 10-15) were helping for a couple of days with the haying or other work and were counted in David's household. The same problems exist to this day, even with the aid of modern technology.

On the 1803 Assessment Roll of Hadley are David and Abraham Dayton, who appears to be David's brother, but who could also be David's uncle, the younger brother of David Senior. If so, at sixty in 1800, he could have been the "over 44" in the 1800 census.

Between 1799 and 1807, the couple had at least five more children—Irinda, Anna, Orrin, Orange and Erastus plus the youngest, Louisa, who was born after her father's death.

Chapter 21

Memorials

According to his cemetery marker at Luzerne Town Cemetery, David was only 41 years old when he died on February 8, 1807 at Hadley but he and Chloe had already had ten children. David was predeceased by one child, Orrin, who died during infancy so Chloe was left with nine children and she would give birth to the youngest child more than six months later, in August of 1807.

This coupled with the fact that no will has been found for David, it is likely there may not have been a long illness before his death. In fact, no probate records have been located for either David or Chloe.

David was buried near the south property line of his lot, adjacent to the Stewart lot,[865] where a small Dayton family cemetery was formed as others were buried around him. His infant son Orrin was probably the first buried there, but his grave was not identified. This cemetery was located on what later became the Jay Smead farm, on the east side of the Hadley-Stony Creek Road, just before the railroad tracks cross the road, as you are heading north. To this day, the owner of the property has respectfully not plowed where the cemetery was once located and a small square of trees grow in the field there.

"On the 1804[866] Assessment Roll of Hadley are David and Abraham Dayton. On the 1807 Roll, the only Dayton is Chloe"[867] because her oldest child Joel was still under legal age.[868] Chloe remained in Hadley with her ten children, all under age 18, and never remarried.

It is comforting to learn that Chloe's father was living nearby at Bolton, NY, on the west side of Lake George, by the time the 1800 Census was taken and was probably still there during the difficult time when David died. David and Chloe may

---

[865] It is assumed the Dayton Cemetery was on David's property, but because Stewarts were also buried there, it is possible it was actually just across the boundary of the lot, on property owned by Stewart.
[866] Note: It has since been determined that it was the 1803 Assessment roll that contained the names of both David and his brother Abraham.
[867] (J. Dayton, The Descendants of Ralph Dayton 1998)
[868] Note: There are no Dayton wills found in the Saratoga County, New York Probate Records, Index 1799-1893 vol 1-31.

have moved with Chloe's father from Worthington to Cambridge, although no record of John Skiff can be found in the Cambridge area. However, it is known that John's daughter Eunice lived at Cambridge with her husband William Hough in 1791. William had come from Wallingford, Connecticut. Although we have not been successful in our attempts to uncover the story, we believe Joel and his brother David had some significant early connection with Hough for William and Eunice named their eighth of ten children Joel Dayton Hough. Later, there is a Eunice with John Skiff at the Warrensburgh Baptist Church.

Figure 48. David Dayton's Gravestone, Lake Luzerne Cemetery

The Skiff family (spelled Sciff in the census), had probably moved to Bolton, a very large area that included Hague (then called Rochester), Horicon and North

Caldwell (now the town of Lake George) about the same time David and Chloe chose to go to Hadley. The distance between modern-day Bolton and Hadley is just over 20 miles, but could have been closer depending in which modern-day township John resided. John was listed with sixteen others including his wife Delight and daughter Eunice Hough, as first members of the Warrensburgh, NY Baptist Church in 1807. A frame building owned by Nathaniel Smith was used for the school and church.[869] This may be significant because Nathaniel Smith was also the name of the husband of David Dayton Junior's sister Abigail, who had lived at Patchogue, Long Island about 1782. The possibility that they are the same Nathaniel Smith was not pursued. The date on John Skiff's will is May 21, 1813.

Family of David and Chloe

Most of the children of David and Chloe stayed in the general area after marriage, although Orange and Erastus did go west and settled in Oneida County, in central New York State.

David and Chloe's eldest son Joel, born August 29, 1790, married Jane Cameron of Thurman about 1814 and the couple lived at Hadley, Athol and Stony Creek. They had five children who were Warren, James, Christy Ann, Chloe Jane and Charlotte. Joel was 78 when he died May 21, 1869.

Their second son was our ancestor Henry, born April 18, 1792. In about 1815, Henry married Christie Ann Cameron of Thurman, the niece of Joel's wife Jane. Christie Ann was the daughter of immigrants and the eldest of eight children of William Cameron and Mary Hodgson. Christie Anne's father was born in Scotland and her mother was born in England. In the 1820 census, and again in the 1830 census, Henry and Christie Ann are listed among Hadley Hill neighbors (Laughton, Gilberts, Flanders, Kennedys) with Henry as head of household, but not as land owner. As implied in Henry's 1830 deed for the property, Henry bought the land they had been living on, so apparently they had some kind of rental agreement for at least some years. These 200 acres were roughly three miles away, up the hill from his parent's homestead at the base of the hill, at the intersection.

David and Chloe' first daughter was named Chloe, born May 29, 1794. It is believed, but not proven, that she married a man named Palmer from Vermont, but she died shortly after, on Aug 20 1813 at Hadley. Almost nothing is known of this daughter or her husband, but he was included in the distribution of his father-in-law's estate which would occur many years later. It is suspected Chloe died in childbirth, but there is no direct knowledge to support it.

It should be noted that there have been many Chloe Daytons closeby and they are often confused in various genealogical records. Following is a sample of just some of these women present in local histories.

---

[869] (H. P. Smith 1885)

Name	Husband	Born	Died	Father
Chloe Skiff Dayton	David Dayton Jr.	1768	1848	John Skiff
Chloe Dayton	-------- Palmer	1793	1812 or 13	David Dayton Jr.
Chloe Ann Dayton	George Hillman	1816	1904	Henry Dayton
Chloe Jane Dayton	Rev T E Pomeroy	1830	1872	Joel Dayton
Chloe Dayton	William Stone	1831	------	Telem Dayton

Second daughter Eunice was born Feb 5, 1796. She married David Palmer of Northumberland before 1817. They had 9 children named Eunice Elizabeth, Henry, Asa, David, Harriet, Chloe Jane, Rebecca, Emeline and Iranda. Since the first and the last were born in Northumberland, it is assumed that all were born there. She lived 70 years and died Oct 13, 1866 and was buried at Edwardsville Cemetery, Morristown, St. Lawrence Co, NY.

The third son Telem was born Aug 21, 1797 and married Lucinda Fletcher. His name is found spelled Telem, Telam and Telim but his gravestone provides the spelling and also an interesting spelling for his wife; the stone says, "Telem Dayton, Husband of Lucindia Fletcher Dayton." Telem and his wife lived on the old Dayton Homestead that had been his father's and had eight children there. They were Simon Nelson, Lucinda, Sarah Ann, David, Chloe, Lewis Telem, Henry and Erastus. After waiting for all the males in the family to come of age (Erastus had just turned 21), Telem and Joel bought out the inherited shares of the other siblings in 1827, leaving mother Chloe, Joel and Telem in sole possession of the farm. With all the other land transactions Joel was involved in, including others along the lower water division, it is difficult to say when or how his portion was later released to Telem. In May of 1837, Telem acquired land from the Stewart's and then on June 21, 1837, Chloe deeded the remainder of her share of "David Dayton's lot" to Telem and, on the same day, Telem acquired many more acres along the Hudson from his brother Joel. Telem would live on his farm for another fifty years, dying Nov 16, 1887 at the age of 90.

Third daughter Irinda was born June 12, 1799 and she married Robert Van Duesen, farmer, about 1820. Robert and Irinda had nine children. They were Hiram, Abner, Archibald, Halsey, Lydia, Harriet, Sidney, Ransom and Mary. They were living in Queensbury from the time of the 1850 census to the 1880 census. Irinda was also 90 when she died Jan 5, 1890 and was buried in Mount Hermon Cemetery, Queensbury, NY.

Fourth daughter Anna was born March 2, 1801 and married John Hillman (born Feb 28, 1800) about 1825 in Cambridge. They had four children named Irinda, Chloe A, Mary Ann and Erastus D. John had two children by his previous marriage to Hannah Potter. They were Sarah and Leroy. John was listed as farmer in each of the 1850, 1860 and 1870 Census and they lived in Jackson and then Easton. She died in Greenwich March 26, 1889 at the age of 89 and she and John are buried in the Greenwich Cemetery, Greenwich, NY.

Fourth son, Orrin was born Oct 18, 1802 and he died as an infant, on Jul 8, 1803.

Their fifth son, Orange was born about Sept 5, 1804 and married Mary Ann Phinney on March 20, 1828. In 1830 he was Hadley Town Clerk and by 1850, he was living in Camden, Oneida County, NY as a shoemaker. Orange and Mary had six children named Samuel James, Lois Amelia, Melville Emory, Wilber Fiske, Oscar Milton and Orange. Orange died before his 78th birthday on Jul 5, 1882 and he was buried at Sunset Cemetery, Kirkland, NY.

Sixth son, Erastus was born about Jan 26, 1806 and married Adaline Lucinda Brown of Willimantic, CT on Sept 3, 1828. They had six children named Walter B, George B, Ellen Amelia, George Erastus, Cecelia Evaline and Josephine Marie. In the 1850 census, he was listed as farmer in Vernon, Oneida County, NY. He was reported to be a tanner, shoemaker and farmer. Erastus died at just 48 years old, on Oct 25, 1854 and he was buried in Columbus, WI.

David and Chloe's fifth daughter, Louisa was probably born Aug 22, 1807, after her father died in February. Very little is known about Louisa and no reliable reference is found for a husband and children. She is included here as a child of David and Chloe based on Donald Lines Jacobus' reference to her.[870]

It seems a gross understatement to simply say that things were difficult. It must have taken all of Chloe's strength to raise and care for ten children (most not yet teenagers) and to run the working farm, without her husband. But she was up to the task. The death of their father would demand the advance of the two teenage boys, Joel and Henry, beyond doing only chores to a place of immense responsibility, learning the disciplines and economies of the business while the girls did their share of the chores and helped with the toddlers and baby.

The Unpopular War

Added to the concerns at home, there were rumors of war once again as Britain continued to violate U.S. sovereignty, treating the new nation as if it was still a collection of British colonies. Perhaps families in Hadley at first felt a world away from the trouble, but the war would move closer to home before it ended.

The American government had taken a neutral stance in the Napoleonic War between France and England so neither country was content with U.S. merchants trading with their enemy. Both countries were harassing American vessels, confiscating cargo and kidnapping their sailors, but in 1807, anger toward Britain was particularly strong, at least with the Jeffersonians in power. Because New England's economy was dependent on trade, President Jefferson saw the opportunity to exact his revenge on New England, his political opposition, and he punished them with a self-imposed embargo, blocking U.S. ships from doing any business with

---

[870] (D. Jacobus 1959)

foreign lands, thereby removing them from all danger, or so he claimed. It decimated the economy of New England but Jefferson's Democratic-Republican Party was based in southern agricultural states, where the embargo wasn't as painful.[871]

While New England continued to oppose war and some officials openly discussed secession, communities in eastern New York, on the outskirts of New England, were not necessarily in lockstep with either political party, yet they were eventually vulnerable to the agitations of the "war hawks" of western New York. In response, many communities in Albany, Saratoga and Washington Counties raised militias and even a few men from Hadley joined the ranks in soldiering. As President Madison was another Virginian and a Francophile, he foolishly sent the nation to war without preparation, banking on England's preoccupation with Napoleon. Madison and the war hawks nearly cost the nation its very existence, despite the fact that Britain had considered the conflict as only a side issue of the Napoleonic Wars. Once free of military conflict with France, however, the British army went from a defensive posture to an offensive posture in North America and quickly marched into Washington DC and burned the White House in 1814. The Dayton family must have felt dread and then relief when the war was brought to Lake Champlain and then turned by Macdonough's miraculous victory that would end the invasions of the northern states.

In 1848, forty-one years after her husband died, Chloe died and was placed next to her husband and her daughter (also named Chloe) who had died thirty six years earlier. Chloe had lived long enough to see all of her surviving children reach forty so she must have known many of her grandchildren. Some of the neighboring Stewart family had also been buried at the Dayton Cemetery which is logical since it bordered the Stewart lot. Cornelius Durkee called the Dayton Cemetery, "a small private enclosure located about two and one half miles north of Hadley between the highway and the Hudson River." Durkee is remembered for his book entitled, *Some of Ye Epitaphs in Saratoga County, NY.* Chloe's memorial stone appears to be contemporary with the time so it was probably placed shortly after her death, perhaps by her son Henry who died just a few months after his mother. Several of the early Daytons were buried around David and Orrin, including wife Chloe, daughter Chloe, Jane, Joel and Telem.

By the time burials ceased, there were at least 45 bodies in that cemetery, including many from the Stewart family, and also surnames Allen, Bovard, Chandler, Chesney, Dingman, Dubois, Eldridge, Gilbert, McMillen, Plunkett, Reynolds, Scofield and Van Auken. In some records, it is believed that Chloe Dayton was mistakenly listed as "Chloe Pomeroy," who actually died about twenty-five years later.

According to Dave Bixby, compiler of *Town of Hadley Cemeteries*, all forty five identified remains in the Dayton Cemetery were removed between 1926 and 1928, and were reinterred at the Luzerne Town Cemetery located just north of the

---

[871] (Ellis 2012)

village of Lake Luzerne. Many of these markers are located in two rows on the left of the left road, entering the cemetery from Route 9N, and are about three-quarters of the way back, as the cemetery is currently arranged in 2015. The relocation occurred as preparations were underway to create a reservoir by building the dam at Conklingville and, flooding the Sacandaga Valley.

Figure 49. Chloe Dayton's Gravestone, Lake Luzerne Cemetery

The Hudson River Regulating District consummated the plan by private commercial interests[872] to build the Conklingville dam, in order to control annual flooding in the Hudson valley. In the process, the valley hamlets of Osborn Bridge, Edinburg, Munsonville, Day, West Day, and parts of the communities of Benedict,

---

[872] (Hart 1967)

405

Northampton, Cranberry Creek, Mayfield, Sacandaga Park, Northville, Bachelorville and Conklingville would be covered by the waters, according to Hart. The plan made necessary, "the transburial of 3,872 bodies from 22 cemeteries in the peaceful valley to plots in various outlying districts." If the body count provided in the report included only those cemeteries in the "valley of the Sacondag," the actual count was probably much greater than reported because there were plots like the Dayton Cemetery along the Hudson that were also moved. The Dayton Cemetery on the Hadley-Stony Creek Road would have been just a few miles away from the new dam, over the mountain, above where the two rivers converge.

Our line from David

The second son of David and Chloe was Henry, our ancestor. Henry was about twenty-two when he married Christie Ann in late 1815 or early 1816 and the couple worked on the Hadley Hill farm they eventually purchased in 1830. Henry is our earliest ancestor for which a cause of death is known with certainty, as it is recorded in the United States Census of 1850. A few of the early series of forms included a mortality schedule for all persons who had died within one year of the census and since Henry died in 1849, his death was recorded. The ledger reports Henry, farmer, died in September at age 57 after being ill with "summer complaint" for about 14 days. According to a variety of sources, summer complaint was an acute diarrhea that often occurred during the hot summer months, caused by bacterial contamination of food.

On their Hadley Hill farm, Henry and Christie Ann had nine children—five sons and four daughters.

Henry and Christie Ann's first child was a daughter, Chloe, born November 12, 1816 and she married George Hillman, a farmer. Chloe died May 10, 1904. They lived and were buried in Greenwich, NY.

Second was another daughter, Mary, born 1819 and she married Hiram Creal. Mary died and was buried in Colton, CA. Hiram had died in 1886 in Wilton, NY where he was a farmer on 185 acres.

The eldest son was Silas, born 1820, and he married Rhoda Wells August 1850 in Luzerne. He died October 18, 1889 in Preston, Minnesota. He and Rhoda lived most of their married life in Decorah, Iowa and they are both buried there. Silas was a successful merchant while in Iowa.

Joel was the second son, born 1824 in Hadley. He married Martha Cameron in December of 1861, and he died 1906 in Iowa City, Iowa. Joel was a businessman. At varying times he was a farmer, schoolteacher, surveyor and owner/operater of a nursery.

George Nelson was the third son, was born December 4, 1826 in Hadley NY, and he died January 17, 1910 in Lyle, Washington. He married Anna Liza Sawyer 1861 in Moanoa, Iowa. They are both buried at Lyle. George was a farmer.

406

Their third daughter, named Irinda, was born Jun 9, 1830 in Hadley, and she married Benjamin Roberson. He was a farmer. They lived and are buried in Greenwich, NY.

Henry and Christie Ann's fourth son was our ancestor Charles Erastus, born 1832 and he married Nancy Goodnow after 1855. Nancy was born 1838 in Hadley, the daughter of Thomas Goodnow and Lucy Harris. On November 29, 1856 his brother George Nelson of Hardin, Clayton County, Iowa, sold Charles 220 acres (this appears to be part of their father Henry's farm) for $800 described as Lot 1 in the 7th Range of Little Dartmouth Patent plus a lot just north. In an interesting map of Hadley by Beers, 1866, the farms belonging to "Mrs. Dayton" and Telam Dayton are labeled. This implies that at the time Christie Ann died in 1865, she was still identified as one of the land's owners. In a newspaper article from *The Saratogian* dated June 28, 1881, a correspondent for Conklingville said, "In sheep husbandry, Charles Dayton of Hadley Hill excels. He reports 57 sheep and 30 lambs."

Charles died 1882 and was buried in Dean Cemetery, Stony Creek. Nancy died March 17, 1883 in Hadley and was also buried in Dean Cemetery. Children of Charles and Nancy were Delbert born 1858, James born 1862, Jenny born 1866, Wilber Thomas born October 30, 1870 and Carrie born 1872. Wilber died in 1957. Wilber was orphaned at the age of 13, and was left to run the farm with his older brother James.

The fifth son was Henry Oren, born Nov 10, 1834 in Hadley. He married Maria Aldrich Aug 27, 1866 in Hadley. They spent their married life in Hardin and Waukon, Iowa and died there. Henry Oren was a surveyor and teacher.

The fourth daughter Christina Ann, born February 23, 1837 was the youngest child. She married Joel Dean and died March 2, 1874. Joel and Christina remained in Hadley. They are buried in Dean Cemetery, the same cemetery that now holds the remains of her parents.

Their parents, Henry and Christie, were reinterred at Dean Cemetery in 2005 because their private family plot on the Hadley Hill farm had been encroached upon by a housing development. Paul Dayton was the Dayton patriarch who ceremonially oversaw the reinterment project.[873] All nine of the children grew up on the Hadley Hill farm. Henry and family developed some of the fields for plowing, clearing them of trees, brush and rock for planting corn while others were thinned for pasturing cows and sheep in the meadow. These field rocks were piled neatly at the boundary lines, establishing orderly walls as was the custom around so much of the area. Although many walls have been subject to pilphering and sections have disappeared over the past century, some walls still stand, stretching through now forested lands as a testimony to what once was there. Still other fields were planted with fruit trees, especially apple, whose early blossoms fed his honey bees and pollinators before the

---

[873] Note: Jim Dayton and Ramon Orton accomplished all of the tasks that made the reinterment possible. Jim witnessed and recorded every step of the process. He has the brass corners from the casket and a small button from Christie Ann's burial dress.

spring flowers arrived. Henry's beekeeping produced over 100 pounds of marketable honey and wax annually. His wax was very desirable at market and was used to form foundations for the frames in his hive. Henry lived at the farm until his death in 1849, at which time five of his nine children had reached majority and the four youngest—Irinda, Charles, Orren and Christy were teenagers.

For more information about Christie Ann's family after Henry died, see the Census of 1855, and for farm inventory and data, refer to the tables for Christie Ann, Silas and Telam in the *Agriculture and Domestic Manufactures, Agricultural Statistics from Hadley*, June 12, 1855.

Though our first six generations in America lived on Long Island, David Junior moved from Long Island and redirected our line to settle Hadley Hill. Counting David in Hadley, we are part of the sixth generation to have lived in Saratoga County and it will forever hold our fondest memories.

Appendix I
Sequence for Some of Sam's Locations

A Supplement to Assist Following Sam in Chapters 8-14

1645-46	New Haven	New Haven Town Records
1646-48	Unknown	Possibly Flushing
1648 May	Southampton (SH)	Arrival, granted £50 lot, "last lived at Flushing"
1649/50	North Sea	Believed to be among the original settlers
1653/54 Feb	SH or N Sea	Took part in first lot drawing at Sagabonack (east of SH)
1654 June	Southampton	Prob. already in Marvin house when purchased from Marvin
1654/55 Feb	SH or N Sea	Took part in second Sagabonack division
1655 Sept	North Sea	Identified as resident in Southampton court records
1657 June	Southampton	Sold house (Marvin's?) plus Coopers Neck land to John Ogden
1657 June	Southampton	Bought Edward Jones house, probably on Main Street
1657 June	Setauket	Unsubstantiated Thompson claim
1657	Unknown	Neither Sam nor Ralph appear on inhabitants list or Powder list at Southampton or North Sea
1658	North Sea	Sam inherited his father's house next to his at North Sea
1658	Brookhaven (BR)	*History of Suffolk County* claims he went to Brookhaven 1658
1658 Sept	BR & N Sea	Southampton Court entry said Samuel Dayton of the North Sea
1659 June	Unknown	Dutchman case at North Sea Harbor
1659 Aug	Setauket	Cox says Sam accompanied Underhill to Setauket
1659/60 Mar	North Sea	"Sam of North Sea" sold inherited house to Waters
1662	SH or N Sea	STR indicates Sam still had cattle there
1663	North Sea	Sam "sells" (mortgage) North Sea home to Jonathan King
1663 June	Matinecock	Possible planter and agent for Hempstead (Matinecock)
1664 Aug	Matinecock	Lost his land when Dutch retook the island. He had already dug a cellar and vacated it sometime between 1664 and 1667
1664	Brookhaven	Sam must have been in Brookhaven to be included in Drawer of Lots, Old Purchase, but may not have fulfilled the requirements
1665 Nov	Southampton	Richard Brooks says Sam was living at Southampton
1665 Dec	Brookhaven	Bought 3 lots just west of Setauket (Old Field and New Towne)
1666 May	Brookhaven	Obtained license to marry Mary Dingle
1666 July	Oyster Bay/Matinecock	Sam was "of Oyster Bay" when he bought lot 52 and he was "of Matinecock" when dealing with Abraham Smith of Hempstead
1666 July	Unknown	Sold Matinecock lot with quarry to William Simson
1666	Unknown	Sold house at North Sea to John Cooper
1667	Setauket	Established residency at Setauket, on list of known townsmen
1668	Setauket	Accepted as full proprietor at Setauket
1669/70 Feb	Brookhaven	Had married Mrs. Beardsley of CT
1670-72	Brookhaven	Multiple town records in Brookhaven
1676 May	Setauket	Self-identified "of Setauket" at time of a land exchange
1676 July	Setauket	Self-identified "of Setauket" in exchange with Benjamin Gould
1676 or 77	South	Implication taken from Brookhaven Record
1678 Sept	Dayton's Neck	Brookhaven Record

Appendix II

Concerning Vital Statistics

Life Expectancy

It is imagined that two of the first Daytons recorded to be in New World, Ralph and his son Samuel, were in relatively good health throughout their lives, judging by lifespan and the absence of noted illness. Ralph, Samuel and Abraham, representing the first three generations in our study, had lifespans of about sixty-five to seventy-five years, which was longer than the regional average for the time.

In contrast to Virginia Colonies, New Englanders had average life expectancies of 45 additional years for those reaching age 20, so average age at death was mid-to-late 60s, not so different [from] today.[874]

Probably related in part to their longevity, the first three generations of Dayton men in America outlived at least one wife and fathered an average of at least seven children, while the second three generations had shorter lifespans with an average of forty-six years. The fourth, fifth and sixth generations of our line of Dayton men had an average of nine children, born to them by one wife each.

The lifespans of all known wives who were still of child-bearing age at the time of marriage to our six subjects average about fifty-six years, or about ten years below the expected lifespan for time and place. Of course, this assumes all deaths are recorded, which it is known they are not. For the six generations, nine of ten wives were included in the calculation and accounts for Mary Dingle, whose marriage to Samuel is assumed because they obtained a marriage license, and excludes Mary Haines who was almost forty when she married Ralph.

Mortality Due To Childbirth

Mortality due to complications of childbirth was more common three hundred years ago than today although some believe the mortality rate in colonial New England is often overestimated.[875] We had been under the impression that the mortality rate for these Dayton wives might have been higher than average, but it could not be determined if any pregnancies or childbirth resulted in the death of the mother or child, so there is no definitive conclusion on the matter.

It was not uncommon for the death of very young babies to go unrecorded, whether before or after birth. Richard Wertz goes on to say:

---

[874] (Centolanza 2009)
[875] (Wertz 1989)

...people often did not record infants of stillborn, miscarried, and short-lived infants. The greater concern in the colonial period was for the life of the mother. Some historians have estimated infants' deaths in early months to be as high as 10 percent. Many infants died, however, because of infectious diseases rather than birth damage.

Regretfully, the deaths of women in general; wives, mothers and daughters were very often not recorded unless the event was included in regard to some other matter. Many of these women were recognized with only a passing acknowledgement that leaves history with a sense of incompleteness. It is our obligation to support a history that invests in their memory, but doing so was discouraged by the lack of information which forced us toward so much conjecture. It is difficult to overstate the importance and influence of wives, mothers and daughters in the lives researched and their inclusion adds a share of humanness that is otherwise missing.

Of the nine known women who were married to our subjects during child-bearing years, at least three deaths occurred at less than age forty-five, and two of the three deaths might indicate that death was due to complications involving childbirth.

Colonists infrequently recorded the exact causes of death, so rates for maternal mortality must be inferred from gross statistics. A summary of the evidence, at least from New England...seriously distorts the dangers of childbirth. In the seventeenth century men did live longer than women, but in the eighteenth century women began to live longer than men. [876]

The curious and unrecorded, yet conspicuous death of Mary Dingle was most probably the result of pregnancy or childbirth, assuming she did marry Samuel after they obtained a marriage license in May of 1666. Mary, the likely widow of Mathias Dingle, appears to have been married to Samuel less than three years and died some time before Sam's marriage to his third wife, widow Elizabeth Beardsley. Since procreation very often began at about one year after marriage, it seems reasonable to attribute her early death to complications involving pregnancy or childbirth, rather than to serious illness such as smallpox or tragic accident.

The second instance of early death to consider involved another Mary, Mary Beardsley, who was both the wife and stepsister of Abraham. It appears that Abraham married her after Samuel, his father, married Mary's mother, Elizabeth Beardsley. Best estimates place Mary's death as early as 1693 or 1694, which would result in her calculated age at her time of death to be the mid-thirties.

There are also theories to support the existence of a previous wife for Ralph (in England) before Alice and a previous wife for Abraham before Mary, but these will not be addressed here.

---

[876] Ibid.

Samuel's first known wife, Medlin, gave birth to at least six children during their estimated nineteen years of marriage, but she probably died at about 40 years of age. Her early death is less likely due to childbirth, but is still noteworthy here because of her age.

> Births usually occurred about fifteen to twenty months apart because conception was biologically unlikely as long as a woman was still nursing an infant...Where births occurred at shorter intervals than fifteen months, examination of the family records shows that the baby died before the period of nursing would normally have ended...frequent childbearing taxed their energies and made performing household chores immediately before and after birth nearly impossible. Managing a household was simply so difficult and exhausting that the last state of pregnancy, delivery itself, and the postpartum period would weaken and even kill a woman if she also had to continue her chores without help. The practices of social childbirth permitted the mother to *lie-in*, to keep to her bed for three to four weeks, sometimes longer, while others took over the responsibility of the household. The mother was able to rest, to regain her strength, and to initiate her nursing and care for the new child without interruption.[877]

Other Observations from Vital Statistics

Primogeniture, the practice of passing inheritance to the eldest son, was the form of succession utilized by the gentry in England throughout the period of our study. In much of Kent however, gavelkind was practiced, where,

> ...the land inherited was divided among all the sons. This meant as the land was divided among several sons, it was barely able to support a good sized family. The practice was doubly harmful when the lots were in turn passed on to their sons and divided even more. In truth, the greatest lure of America to the English yeoman was the promise of land, especially enough land to pass down to all his sons.[878]

The practice of gavelkind in Kent was transferred to America. Even though our Puritan ancestors might have favored the eldest son, and in some cases he might receive a "double portion," the land to be inherited was divided among all the sons. Of the first six generations in the Americas, no one in our direct line was an eldest son so, even if an eldest son could be found favored over his brothers, it would not have enriched our line.

The Vital Statistics also illustrate another consequence of the birth order and father's age at the time of the next generation: there was very little or no opportunity

---

[877] Ibid.
[878] (Barstow, Setauket, Alias Brookhaven 2004)

for generational connectedness with grandparents. In nearly every case, the younger sons did not have contact with their grandfather, often because the grandfather had already passed away by the time of their birth. In just one case, Abraham was about four years old when his grandfather Ralph died and because they did not live distant, they were probably able to enjoy some interaction, although it may not have been remembered.

Appendix III

Vital Statistics
With spouse, marriage year and number of identified children

(A) refers to all children under legal guardianship, but does not include children of prior marriages

Daytons with Maiden and Widow Name	Birth Year	Marriage Year	Children Of Bond (A)	Death Year
RALPH	s 1588[1]			1658[2]
Alice Goldhatch Tritton	Bap Sep 24, 1587[3]	Jun 16, 1617[4]	5	Btw 1654 & 1656[5]
Mary (Knight?) Haines	Btw 1617 & 1620[6]	1656[7]	0	Aft 1660/1661[8]
SAMUEL	Bap 1623/24[9]			1690[10]
Medlin (?)	s 1627[11]	Bef 1649[12]	prob. 6	c. 1664[13]
Mary (?) Dingle[14]	Bef 1645[15]	Lic 1666[16]	0	Btw 1666 & 69[17]
Elizabeth Harvey Beardsley	Btw 1633 & 1636[18]	Btw 1668 & 1669[19]	prob. 2	Aft 1690[20]
ABRAHAM	c.1654[21]			Aft Jun 1726[22]
Mary Beardsley	s 1660[23]	Bef 1684[24]	prob. 1	Bef 1693[25]
Catherine (?) Swazey	Btw 1663 & 1671[26]	Btw 1690 & 1693[27]	prob. 5	Aft 1712[28]
HENRY	Btw 1702 & 1706[29]			1759[30]
Abigail Norton	s 1702[31]	s 1727[32]	6	Aft 1765[33]
DAVID SR	Btw 1737 & 1739[34]			1782[35]
Ann Frances	s 1739[36]	1760[37]	9	Aft 1782[38]
DAVID JR	1766[39]			1807[40]
Chloe Skiff	1768[41]	1789[42]	11	1848[43]

1. Based on wife's baptismal date. They are assumed to be quite close in age. Date was first suggested by Donald Lines Jacobus in 1959.
2. Will was written July 25, 1658; was proved September 22, 1658. He died beween those dates.
3. Parish records St Mary the Virgin, Ashford, Kent, England.
4. Parish records St Mary the Virgin, Ashford, Kent, England
5. Although Alice is not mentioned by name when Ralph says "my wife" at the time he is giving land to Robert in 1654, we believe he is referring to Alice. Ralph married Mary Haines in June 1656, therefore Alice died between these two dates.
6. First child bapt at First Congregational Church Salem, MA 1639.
7. Inventory of the estate of James Haines tallied September 18, 1655 [TAG] which made her eligible for remarriage.

8. Mary married Ffulke Davis after Ralph died. Robert Dayton and Thomas Baker, her son-in-law, sued the Davises in 1660/61 for interfering with Ralph's estate after he died (her former house).

9. Parish records St Mary the Virgin, Ashford, Kent, England.

10. The probate record lists his death date of July 5, 1690 in the court case dated May 22, 1691.

11. Samuel and Medlin's oldest son was born in 1649.

12. Jacobus, [in his *Early Daytons and Descendants of Henry Dayton*, Jr, page 22], places the birth of eldest son Ralph in Southampton Plantation about 1649.

13. Sam disposed sons Jacob and Caleb December 24, 1664 probably shortly after Medlin died and he probably remarried in 1666.

14. Dingle could have been a surname from a prior marriage, linking her to Mathias Dingle whose inventory can be found in Brookhaven records June 5, 1667. His date of death is not known but this may not have been the first inventory since his estate was in bankruptcy.

15. It is assumed that Mary was available for remarriage to Samuel in 1666. Her birth is estimated based on the common age of marriage being 21 making her birth before 1645.

16. License issued by the province of New York as filed in Orders Warrants and Letters vol. II p.134

17. Stratford, CT town record suggests marriage of Samuel to Elizabeth Harvey Beardsley before February 26, 1669. Mary must have died prior to this event.

18. If Elizabeth's birth were in 1636, she would have been 19 at the time of her marriage to Beardsley.

19. Stratford town records show Samuel Daiton, of Long Island, registering horses for "widow Elizabeth Beardsley, or good wife Daiton," February 26, 1669.

20. In July 1690, Samuel gave land and house to Elizabeth, Brookhaven Town Records, Book B, p.20 of original book.

21. Abraham was assessed taxes 1675 (Brookhaven Historical Society), therefore he was at least 21 years of age.

22. New Haven township land record 7-281 mentions Abraham Dayton of Brookhaven. The record is dated June 21, 1726 when Abraham is 72 years of age. Abraham mentions "son-in-law John Rogers." There is no further record of Abraham, except for the Brookhaven Plate Tax in August, but no record is found indicating the tax was collected from him.

23. Mary was Hannah's younger sister, both of Elizabeth and Thomas Beardsley. Hannah was born about 1658, roughly 2 years after the marriage of her parents. There are claims of one older brother and our dates allow for that possibility.

24. Abraham and Mary were already married in 1684, when they inherited land.

25. Abraham was already married to Catherine in July 1693, therefore Mary died before then.

26. Estimated birth based on age at marriage and age of husband Abraham.

27. Torrey's Marriages shows July 22, 1693. That date is a land transfer record for the couple. It is not known how long they had actually been married before that date. The estimate for the birth of her first child is 1692.

28. The last mention of Catherine is found in 1712 when she and son Jonathan were given the use of town land. It is possible that she was part of the Jonathan Dayton family who were ill in 1724, but she is not mentioned by name.

29. The first town record found of Henry was in 1734 making him at least 21 by then. Henry may have been Abraham's six or seventh child, not taking into account the theory of sons before his marriage to Mary Beardsley. Since Henry's first child, also named Henry, was born 1728, it would follow that Henry Sr. was born in or before 1706. The approximation of 1702-1706 is likely, in order to fit the births of at least five more children of Catherine after the birth of Jonathan about 1692.

416

30. Henry's will was dated October 7, 1759. His Egg Harbor estate inventory was dated 24 Jan 1760.

31. Abigail's father, Jonathan, was born in 1678. This would have made him 24 when Abigail was born say 1702.

32. Oldest child, Henry Junior, was born April 3, 1728. It is estimated that Henry and Abigail were married the year prior.

33. Abigail was recorded in a merchants account book on February 7, 1765/66.

34. The 1778 Oath of Allegiance lists his age as 39, making his birth year 1739. Marriage Banns in 1760 would make him at least 21 when he was married. However, his father named David's brother Abraham as his youngest son. If it is accepted that Abraham is "of age" to inherit in 1759, he would have to be born by 1738 so David would be at least one year older, making his birth about 1737.

35. Death was before June 26, 1782 because that is the date of his letter of administration. It is highly unlikely that a Letter of Administration would take longer than 6 months.

36. Marriage Banns filed with state of NJ in 1760.

37. Marriage Banns filed with state of NJ in 1760.

38. Anne named as heir in David's Letter of Administration.

39. Gravestone marker.

40. Gravestone marker.

41. Gravestone marker.

42. According to the 1790 census, David's family includes one child. Since Joel's Gravestone marker gives his birth year as 1790, it is concluded the child is Joel. It is therefore likely that David and Chloe were married by 1789. Jacobus gave a wedding date of December 29, 1789 but he did not provide his source. The December date was likely a first mention of the married couple, found in a record that is now lost.

43. Gravestone marker.

Appendix IV

Children of Six Generations

	Born	Birth Reference	Died	Death Reference
Children of Ralph & Alice Goldhatch				
Ralph	Bap June 28, 1618	Parish record-Ashford, Kent, England	Feb 10, 1705	Parish record-Ashford, Kent, England
Alice	Bap May 1620	Parish record-Ashford, Kent, England and record in the Baker bible	Feb 4, 1708	Cemetery marker "Here Lieth Ye Body of Alice formerly Ye Wife of Thomas Baker Who Died February ye 4 1708 In ye 88 year of her Age"
Samuel	Bap Feb 1, 1623/24	Parish record-Ashford, Kent, England	Jul, 1690	Court judgement dated Nov 19, 1691 est Samuel's death at Brookhaven Jul 5, 1690.
Ellen	Bap Dec 3, 1626	Parish record-Ashford, Kent, England	1654	NEHGS, *Identity of Ellen ____ Lindley* Vol 128 pp.147-8
Robert	Bap Jan 5, 1628/29	Parish record-Ashford, Kent, England	1712	Will dated Feb. 11, 1710/11, codicil Apr. 14, 1714, probated Nov. 1, 1712 [NY Wills, 2:98-100, with correction, 16:67]
Children of Ralph & Mary Haines				
No Issue				
Children of Samuel & Medlen				
Ralph	c. 1649	Estimate: Oldest child; born about 1 year after marriage of parents	After 1739	1739 Land record Brookhaven Book C p.213 [original document p.146]
Samuel	c. 1651	Estimate: 2nd oldest child born perhaps 2 years after Ralph	Btw 1677 and 1680	...three of the first planters, William Satterly, Samuel Dayton, and John Moger, were drowned. From *The History of Long Island from its Discovery and settlement to the Present Time*, Vol I, Benjamin F Thompson, 1843.
Abraham	c. 1654	Abraham was assessed taxes 1675 [BTR], therefore he was at least 21 YOA. 1675-21= 1654. BTR Book A has Jan 10, 1675/76 record has Abraham building a fence under contract. Therefore, 1676-21= 1655	After June 1726	New Haven Township Land record 7-281 dated June 21, 1726. From *The History of Long Island from its Discovery and settlement to the Present Time*, Vol I, Benjamin F Thompson, 1843. A few weeks later, Abraham was to be taxed in Brookhaven, but no record was found that he participated

Isaac	s 1657	Typically, names of children sequenced following the Biblical pattern: Abraham, Isaac and Jacob. Isaac was given land 1678 at the rear of his father's home lot making it likely that he was establishing his household after "coming of age. [1678-21= 1657]"	After Nov 1716	*Brookhaven Town Records Book B* p355; [Original book p.261] is a land transaction involving Isaac on November 13, 1716.
Jacob	c. 1658	He was disposed by his father in 1664 for 14 years [until he became "of age"]; so 1664+14 -21= 1658. He purchased 6 acres of land in 1681, so he was "of age" 1681-21= 1660.	1705	The inventory of his estate was taken in Cape May NJ June 7, 1705. *The American Genealogist, The Dayton's of New Jersey*, Jan 1946, Vol XXII, NO.3
Caleb	1659	Samuel disposed his son Caleb in 1664 for 16 years until he became "of age."	1688	[*Southampton Town Records*, Vol 2: page 283].
Children of Samuel & Mary Dingle				
No Issue				
Children of Samuel & Elizabeth Beardsley				
Sarah	Btw 1669 & 1672	In May 1688, Sarah was already married to William Weatherby.	After 1690	Samuel conveyed property to wife Elizabeth and daughter Sarah in July 1690.
Elizabeth	Prob before 1680	Samuel conveyed property to wife Elizabeth and daughter Elizabeth in July 1690.	After 1690	Nothing was found of Elizabeth after 1690
Children of Abraham & Mary Beardsley				
Caleb	Dec 1687	On May 1696, Abraham gave son Caleb "Daighton" then aged 8 y 5 m, to Rawlinsons of Stratford, until Caleb arrived at age 21. [*Stratford Land Records*, 2:497].	1730	His will was written Nov 12, 1730 and was probated Jan 18, 1730/1; [Fairfield Probate District, File]. Jacobus, p.26
Children of Abraham & Catherine Swazey				
Jonathan	c. 1692-1695	If Mary died 1687 (Caleb's birth), Abraham married Catherine btw 1690 & 1693 and Jonathan's birth estimated 2 yrs after wedding	After Apr 1724	Apr 23, 1724, he was mentioned in the BTR
Ephraim	c. 1693-1696	He was already married in 1720.	May 26, 1748	Jacobus p.28 (without reference)
Deborah	c. 1694-1698	Estimate based on wedding to John Rogers Feb 1, 1719, New London CT	After 1739	Survived husband John Rogers and is mentioned in his will of Jul 9, 1739.

David	c. 1695-1701	Estimate based on knowledge that wife Eunice Brewster was born 1701.	1742	Jacobus p.28
Henry	c. 1702-1706	His first town record was 1734 making him "of age." Henry Jun. born 1728-(21+1 yr)= no later than 1706	1759	Henry's will dated Oct 7, 1759. His Brookhaven will was probated in 1760.
Children of Henry & Abigail Norton				
Henry	1728	Cemetery Marker; Century Cemetery, Marlborough, CT	1803	Cemetery Marker; Century Cemetery, Marlborough, CT
Norton	Btw 1730 & 1734	Norton's father referred to him as the second son in his will Oct 7, 1759. Since Henry's eldest son Henry was born in April 1728, it seems reasonable that Norton could be born two years later.	c. 1768	He died of small pox. His will was dated Aug 25, 1768
Abigail	1734	Cemetery Marker; Century Cemetery, Marlborough, Hartford Co., CT	1806	Cemetery Marker; Century Cemetery, Marlborough, Hartford Co., CT
David	Btw 1737 & 1739	1778 Oath of Allegiance lists his age as 39, making his birth year 1739, but Abraham was the youngest son, as stated in Henry's will. Marriage Banns in 1760.	Bef 1782	It was before Jun 26, 1782 because that is the date of his Letter of Admin. It is unlikely that a Letter of Admin. would take longer than 6 months
Katherine	c. 1738-1742	Estimated based on her being the next to youngest child in her fathers will. She was not yet married when the will was written.	Unkn	Unknown
Abraham	s 1738	Henry calls Abraham "his youngest son" in his will. It is believed he was of age at the time the will, 1759.	After 1776	Listed on Brookhaven Tax List of 1776
Children of David Senior & Anne Francis				
Abigail	c. 1761	Based on age of parents' marriage; oldest child	Unkn	m. Nathan Smith, Patchogue
Henry	c. 1762	Year of birth according to Oath of Allegiance	May 18 1815	As recorded from Coram Cemetery records
Anne	c. 1764	Estimate based on birth sequence	Unkn	m. Davis (possibly David) Rose; Patchogue
David	1766	Gravestone Marker; Lake Luzerne, NY	1807	Gravestone Marker, Lake Luzerne, NY
Abraham	1773	Age 77 in Phoenix, Oswego Co., NY 1850 census.	After 1850	Listed in the 1850 census in Phoenix, Oswego Co., NY

	Born	Birth Reference	Died	Death Reference
Deborah	Btw 1762 - 1782	Unknown. It is reasonable that birth occurred between the parents age 23 and 43	Unkn	Prob. Patchogue
Telem	1778	Age 77 in Palermo NY, 1855 Census	After 1855	Listed in Palermo, NY in 1855 NYS census.
Joel	1776	Death Record; Town of Middletown Springs, Rutland Co, VT	1845	Vital Records of Middletown Springs, Rutland Co., VT
Rhoda	1776	Based on 1776 Brookhaven census of David's household	Unkn	Unknown
Children of David Jr & Chloe Skiff				
Joel	1790	Gravestone; Luzerne, NY Cemetery	1869	Same as Birth Reference
Henry	1792	Gravestone; Stony Creek, NY Dean Cemetery	1849	Same as Birth Reference
Chloe	1793	Gravestone; Luzerne, NY Cemetery	1812	Same as Birth Reference
Eunice	1796	Gravestone, Luzerne, NY Cemetery	1866	Same as Birth Reference
Telem	1797	*Biographies and Portraits of the Progressive Men of Iowa: Leaders in Business*, p.521	1887	NYS Death Certificate #36474
Irinda	1799	Gravestone; Mt Hermon Cemetery, Queensbury, NY	1890	NYS Death Certificate #761
Anna	1801	Gravestone; Luzerne, NY Cemetery	Unkn	unknown
Orrin	1802	Jacobus, p.34; no family record found; unknown to family	1803	Same as Birth Reference
Orange	1804	Year taken from Gravestone; Clinton, NY; Sunset Hill Cemetery	1882	Clinton NY Courier Obituary;
Erastus	1806	1850 Census; Vernon, NY (44 YOA)	After 1850	1850 Census, Vernon, NY
Louisa	1807	Jacobus: p.34; unknown to Dayton family	Unkn	Unknown to Dayton family

Works Cited

Abbot, Susan Woodruff. 1979. *Families of Early Milford, Connecticut.* Baltimore: Genealogical Publishing Co.

Ackley, Vintson A. 1997. "The Rogerenes of Ledyard." *Quakertown Online.* November. Accessed May 2015. http://home.comcast.net/~schultz3025/vackley.htm.

Adams, James Truslow. 1918. *History of the Town of Southampton East of Canoe Place.* Bridgehampton, NY: Hampton Press.

Adkins, Edwin P. 1955. *Setauket: The First Three Hundred Years, 1655-1955.* New York: David McKay Co., Inc.

Allegrezza, Nicole. 2015. "Camp Explore Visits Farm." *The Long Island Advance,* August 13.

Amorosi, Francis. 2011. *Index to Slaves and Servants in the New Jersey Calendar of Wills 1670-1817.* Woodbury, NJ: Gloucester County Historical Society.

Andrews, Charles McLean. 1919. *The Fathers of New England: A Chronicle of the Puritan Commonwealths.* New Haven: Yale University Press.

Andrews, Frank. 1909. *Inscriptions On the Grave Stones in the Old New England Town Burying Ground Fairton, Fairfield Township, Cumberland Co, NJ.* Vineland, NJ: Vineland Historical Society.

Armbruster, Eugene L. 1914. *Long Island Its Early Days and Development.* Brooklyn, NY: The Brooklyn Daily Eagle.

Armstrong, William C. and Michael Armstrong. 2009. *Pioneer Families of Northwestern New Jersey.* Baltimore: Genealogical Publishing Company .

Atteberry, Todd. n.d. "Concerning the Battle of Setauket: a Tale of Two Churches, a Minor Battle in the American Revolution and Village Green Today." *History and Haunts.* Accessed August 12, 2014. http://www.thehistorytrekker.com/travel-photographer/long-island/revolutionary-war-battles-concerning-the-battle-of-setauket-and-the-village-green-churches.

Atwater, Edward E. 1902. *History of the Colony of New Haven to its Absorption into Connecticut with Supplementary History and Personnel of the Towns of Branford, Guilford, Milford, Stratford, Norwalk, Southold, etc.* Edited by Robert Atwater Smith. Meriden, Connecticut: The Journal Publishing Company.

Austin, Jere C. 1967. "Long Islanders in the Great Awakening." *Long Island Forum,* March.

Baggs, A.P., G. H. R. Kent and J. D. Purdy. 1976. *A History of the County of York East Riding: Ouse and Derwent Wapentake and part of Harthill Wapentake.* Vol. 3. London: Victoria County History.

Baker, Frank. 1914. *Baker Ancestry,The Ancestry of Samuel Baker of Pleasant Valley, Steuben County, New York, With Some of His Descendants.* Chicago: Privately Printed.

Baker, Lee C. n.d. *Chronicles of Family Baker.* Accessed July 23, 2015. http://www.mikebaker.com/chronicles/Chronicles_of_the_Family_Baker.pdf.

Barber, John and Henry Howe. 1846. *Historical Collections of the State of New Jersey.* New York: S. Tuttle.

Barons, Richard, interview by Stephen Dayton. 2010. *Executive Director of the East Hampton Historical Society* (October).

Barstow, Belle. 2004. *Setauket, Alias Brookhaven.* Bloomington, Indiana: Authorhouse.

—. 1984. *Setauket's Religious Beginnings.* Smithtown, NY: Rost Associates Inc.

Batten, Andrew C. 1999. "Long Island's Loyalists: The Misunderstood Americans." *The Freeholder,* Spring. http://www.oysterbayhistory.org.

Baxter, William T. 2004. "Accounting in Colonial America: Observations on Money, Barter and Bookkeeping." *Accounting Historians Journal* 31 (1).

Bayles, Richard Mather. 1874. *Historical and Descriptive Sketches of Suffolk County and Its Towns.* Boston: Harvard University.

Bayles, Thomas and WIlliam Pelletreau. 1882. *History of Suffolk County, New York with Illustrations, Portraits & Sketches of Prominent Families and Individuals.* New York: W. W. Munsell and Co.

Bayles, Thomas R. 1946. "The Historic Coram Church." *Long Island Forum*, January.

Bayles, Thomas R. 1985. *During the Revolution in Brookhaven.* Town of Brookhaven Historical Advisory Committee.

Bayles, Thomas R. 1949. "Footnotes to Long Island History 'Old Congregational Church'." *Longwood's Journey.*

—. 1963. "List Notes on Town Meetings that Date Back to the 1600's." December 19. Accessed Dec 2014. http://170.161.70.116/history/midisl/bayles%20stories/ town%20 notes.htm.

—. 1947. "The Doctor in Colonial Days." *Patchogue Advance*, September 22.

Beale Jr., Joseph Henry. 1906. *The Law of Innkeepers and Hotels.* Boston: William J Nagel.

Beardsley, Isaac Haight. 1902. *Genealogical History of the Beardsley-Lee Family in America.* Denver, Colorado: John Dove Press.

Beesley, Maurice. 1857. *Sketch of the Early History of Cape May.* Trenton: Office of the True American.

Bolles, John Rogers and Anna Bolles. 1904. *The Rogerenes: Some Hitherto Unpublished Annals Belonging to the Colonial History of Connecticut.* Boston: Williams, Stanhope Press, F. H. Gilsson Co.

Bolton, Robert. 1848. *A History of the County of Westchester, From its First Settlement to the Present Time.* Vol. II. New York.

Bouron, Hannah M. 1900. "The Dayton Family." *The American Monthly Magazine, DAR Volume 17*, July-December.

Breen, T. H. 1996. *Imagining the Past: East Hampton Histories.* Athens, GA: University of Georgia Press.

Brooke, Bob. 2004. "Coming to 'Terms' with Genealogy." *Genealogy Today.* Accessed March 1, 2013. http://www.genealogytoday.com/columns/everyday/040607.html.

Brookhaven Town Clerk. circa 1750. *Brookhaven Earmark Registry.* Setauket: Three Village Historical Association.

Brookhaven Town Clerk. 1880. *Records Town of Brookhaven up to 1800.* Patchogue, NY: Printed at the office of the Advance. Accessed 2014.

Brown, David C. 1994. "The Key to the Kingdom: Excommunication in Colonial Massachusetts." *The New England Quarterly* 67 (4).

Burrage, Champlin. 1912. *The Early English Dissenters in the Light of Recent Research (1550-1641).* London: Cambridge University Press.

Calder, Isabel MacBeath. 1934. *The New Haven Colony.* New Haven, Connecticut: Yale University Press.

n.d. "Calendar of Wills 1761-1770: 1762, May 3." In *New Jersey Colonial Documents.*

Carpenter, Laurie, webmaster. 2005. "The Rev. Henry Whitfield and Guilford, Connecticut." *Stone Family Association.* Accessed February 6, 2013. http://stonefamilyassociation.org/ index.php?pr=Rev._Henry_Whitfield.

Center for Hearth Tax Research, Roehampton Uniiversity. 2010. "Percent of Households With Between Five and Nine Hearths." *Hearth Tax Online.* Accessed 2013. http://www. hearthtax.org.uk/.

Christian, John T. 1926. *A History of the Baptists, Vol II.* Texarkana, TX: Bogard Press.

Christoph, Peter R. 1993. *The Dongan Papers, 1683-1688: Files of the Provincial Secretary of New York During the Administration of Governor Thomas Dongan.* Syracuse: Syracuse University Press.

Clay, Charles Travis. 1911. *Three Yorkshire Assize Rolls for the Reigns of King John and King Henry III.* Vol. XLIV. Leeds: The Yorkshire Archaeological Society.

Cocks, George William & John Cox. 1914. *History and Genealogy of the Cock, Cocks, Cox Family:Descended from James and Sarah Cock, of Killingworth Upon Matinecock, in the Township of Oyster Bay, Long Island, NY,.* New York: Privately Published.

Coffey, John. 2006. *John Goodwin and the Puritan Revolution: Religion and Intellectual Change in 17th Century England.* Woodbridge, Suffolk: Boydell Press.

Cohen, David S. 1992. *Dutch-American Farm.* New York: New York University.

Collins, Francis. 2002. "Admissions to the Freemen of York-Temp. Edward I (1272-1307): Register of the Freemen of the City of York: Vol. 1, 1272-1558." *British History Online.* Accessed April 2013. http://www.british-history.ac.uk/source.aspx?pubid=378.

Collins, Francis. 1897. *Register of the Freemen of the City of York: Vol 96.* Vol. 96. Surtees Publication.

Committee, Mt. Sinai Hamlet Study. 2012. "The History of Mt. Sinai." *Mount Sinai School District.* Accessed July 3, 2014. http://www.mtsinai.k12.ny.us/community/history/index.hm.

Compiled by Staff. 1896. *A Memorial and Biographical Record of Iowa Volume II.* Chicago: The Lewis Publishing Company.

n.d. "Concerning the Battle of Setauket: A Tale of Two Churches, a Minor Battle in the American Revolution and the Village Green Today." *The History Trekker.* Accessed August 2015. http://www.gothichorrorstories.com/category/the-history-trekker/.

Cordani-Stevenson, Lisa. 2011. "Slavery on Long Island Part 3." *Examiner.com.* February 12. Accessed Oct 2014. http://examiner.com/artile/slavery-on-long-island-part-3.

Cothren, William. 1872. *History of Ancient Woodbury Connecticut From the First Indian Deed in 1659 to 1872.* Woodbury.

Court Recorder. n.d. *Record of WIlls, Office of the Surrogate Court; Lieber 23, entry 291.* New York: Surrogate Court.

Coventry, Thomas. 1832. *On Conveyancer's Evidence.* London: J. & W. T. Clarke.

Cowper, Joseph Meadows. 1894. *Canterbury Marriage Licences 1568-1618 and Canterbury Marriage Licences Second Series 1619-1660.* Canterbury: Cross & Jackman.

Cox Jr., John. 1916. *Oyster Bay Town Records 1653-1690.* Vol. I. New York: Tobias A Wright.

Cox, Rev, Henry Miller. 1912. *The Cox Family in America: A History and Genealogy of the Older Branches of Family from the Appearance of its First Representative in This Country in 1610.* Somerville, NJ: Unionist Gazette Association.

Cravens, Charles E. 1906. *A History of Mattituck, Long Island, NY.* Published for the Author.

Cray, E. Robert. 1990. "Anglicans in the Puritan Domain: Clergy and Laity in Eastern Long Island, 1693-1776." *The Long Island Historical Journal* 2 (1).

Culbertson, Judi & Tom Randall. 1987. *Permanent New Yorkers: A Biographical Guide to the Cemeteries of New York.* Chelsea: Chelsea Green Publishing Company.

Cummings, Mary. 2007. "North Sea: The First Step." January 17. Accessed November 2013. http://www.hamptons.com/Lifestyle/East-End-Heirlooms/1336/North-sea-The-First-Atep.html.

Curtis, Harlow Dunham. 1955. *Richard Curtice, Master Mariner.* Manlius, NY: Curtis Society of Stratford, CT.

Cutter, William Richard. 1922. *American Biography: A New Cyclopedia.* New York: The American Historical Society.

Database. 2012. *Kent Archaelogical Society.* Accessed 2013. http://www.kentarchaeology.org.uk/contact-us/.

Davis, Albert H. n.d. "The Davis Family of Long Island, Descendants of Ffulke (Foulk) Davis." *Long Island Genealogy.* hhtp://longislandgenealogy.com/surname_Pages/davis.htm.

Davis, Albert Henry. 1888. *History of the Davis Family.* New York: T.A. Wright.

Dayton, Charles Nathan. 196? *A Dayton Record.* New Haven: New Haven Historical Society.

Dayton, Chester, Interview by James P. Dayton. 1999. (January).

Dayton, Cornelia Hughes. 1999. *Excommunicating the Governor's Wife: Religious Dissent in the Puritan Colonies Before the Era of Rights Consciousness.* Albany: SUNY University Press.

Dayton, Edson Carr. 1931. *Genealogical and Biographical Account of One Branch of the Dayton Family in America.* Privately Printed.

Dayton, Edson Carr. 1931. *The Record of a Family Descent from Ralph Dayton and Alice (Goldhatch) Tritton, Married June 1617, Ashford, County Kent, England.* Case, Lockwood & Brainard Company.

Dayton, Edson Carr, A. H. Peterson, and et al. 1987. *The Known Ancestors of George Draper Dayton I in England and the United States of America.* Wayzata, Minnesota: A.H. Peterson.

Dayton, Eldorous Lyon. 1978. *The Eldorous Daytons of Ulster Co, NY.* Madison, Wisconsin: University of Wisconsin.

Dayton, Jim. 2012. *Some of Ralph Dayton's Descendants Through Eight Generations 1588-1900.* Byron Center, MI: Self-Published.

Dayton, Lewis Scott. 1949. *Ancestors of Chauncey Lemon Dayton (1810-1897).* Unknown Binding.

De Kirby, John. 1867. *1862 Edit of Names from Domesday, Kirby's Inquiry: The Survey of the Colony of York.* London: Whittaker and Co for the Surtees Society.

Deaton, Lawson Alexander. 2000. *Sons and Daughters of Thomas Deaton.* Vol. 1. Annapolis, Maryland: Deaton Genealogical Publishing Co.

Deering, Mary. 2003. "Women in Puritan Society." *Education Portal.* Accessed January 14, 2014. http://study.com/academy/lesson/women-in-puritan-society-roles-rights.html.

Deighton, H. 1938. *Dyghtons of West Riding and Their Descendants.* Brooklyn, New York: Self Published.

Deitz, John. 2006-2015. *Brookhaven/South Haven Hamlets & Their People.* http://brookhaven southhaven.org/hamletpeople/ tng/index.php.

Deitz, John. 2014. "History Volume: Building Structure Inventory Form for Washington Lodge." *Brookhaven/South Haven Hamlets.* May 16. http://brookhavensouthhaven.org/history/ BuildingInventoryForm.aspx?InventoryCode=Br10.11-S.

Denton, E. F. 1943. "Descendants of Joseph Denton, Loyalist 1752-1835." *Denton Family Genealogy.* Accessed July 1, 2014. http://www.dentongenealogy.org/Joseph%20Denton%20Loyalist. htm.

Dept. of History, SUNY Stony Brook. 2011. "Suffolk County in the American Revolution." *The Long Island Historical Journal*, September 7.

Devlin, Jane. 2012. "The Story of Thomas Bakers Bid to Serve as Constable." *Lee Family History.* May 8. Accessed June 2014. http://vanarsdaleleefamilyhistory.blogspot.com/2012/05/ story-of-thomas-bakers-bid-to-serve-as.html.

Dewan, George. 2005. "The Rise of Slavery." *Newsday*, September 3.

Dexter, Franklin Bowditch. 1917. *Ancient Town Records: New Haven Town Records 1649-1662.* Vol. I. New Haven, Connecticut: New Haven Colony Historical Society.

di Bonaventura, Allegra. 2013. *For Adam's Sake.* New York: Liveright Publishing Corporation.

Dolan, Susan A. 2009. *Fruitful Legacy: A Historic Context of Orchards in the United States, With Technical Information for Registering Orchards in the National Register of Historic Places.* Washington, DC: National Park Service.

Dolon, Eric Jay. 2007. *The History of Whaling in America.* New York: Norton & Company.

Dossena, Marina & Roger Lass. n.d. *Studies in English and European Historical Dialectology.* Germany: International Academic Publishers.

Doude, Rev. W. W. 1885. *The Descendants of Henry Doude Who Came From England in 1639.* Hartford, Connecticut: Press of the Case, Lockwood & Brainard Company.

Dowart, Jeffrey M. 1992. *Cape May County, New Jersey: The Making of a Resort Community.* Cape May: Rutgers University Press.

Earle, Alice Morse. 1891. *The Sabbath in Puritan New England.* New York: Charles Scribner's Sons.

Editorial Staff. 2015. *Merriam-Webster Dictionary.* Encyclopedia Britanica. Accessed Sep 1, 2015. http://www.merriam-webster.com Education IT Services. 2015. *Here's History Kent.* Accessed Oct 13, 2013. www.hereshistorykent.org.uk/choosearticle.cfm.

Emery, Samuel Hopkins. 1893. *History of Taunton, Massachusetts From Its Settlement to the Present Time.* Syracuse: D Mason .

Felt, Joseph Barlow. 1855. *The Ecclesiastical History of New England.* Vol. I. Boston: Congregational Library Association.

Fernow, B,. 1883. *Documents Relating to the History of the Colonial Settlements Principally on Long Island.* Vol. XIV. Albany: Weed, Parsons and Co.

Fessenden, Laura Dayton. 1902. *Chronicle of a Branch of the Dayton Family.* Cooperstown, NY: Crist, Scott & Parshall.

Fischer, David Hackett. 1989. *Albion's Seed: Four British Folkways in America.* Oxford: Oxford University Press.

Fisher, Sydney George. 1920. *The Quaker Colonies: A Chronicle of the Proprietors of the Delaware.* Vol. 8. New Haven: Yale University Press.

Flagg, Ernest. 1990. *Genealogical Notes on the Founding of New England : My Ancestors Part in That Undertaking.* Baltimore, MD: Clearfield Publishing Co.

Flagg, Ernest. 1926. "Parish Register Ashford, Kent." In *Genealogical Notes on the Founding of New England: My Ancestors Part in that Undertaking.* Baltimore: Clearfield Publishing Co.

Flower, C.T. 1947. *Calendar of Close Rolls, Henry VI, 1454-1461, Index C.* Vol. VI. London: His Majesty's Stationery Office.

Fogg, John S. H. . 1892. "Will of Henry Poole 1643." *The New England Historical and Genealogical Register* 46: 244-246.

Ford, George Hare. 1914. *Historical Sketches of the Town of Milford.* New Haven, Connecticut: Press of the Tuttle, Morehouse & Taylor Co., Limited Edition.

Foster, Joseph, ed. 1887. *London Marriage Licences, 1521-1869.* London: Bernard Quaritch.

Foster, Sherrill. 2001. "Merchants and Early East Hampton." Lecture, East Hampton.

Fowler, John W. 1887. *An Historical Sketch and Genealogical Record of the Fowlers of Milford Conn.* New Haven: The Stafford Printing Co.

Fowler, F. (editor) 1911. *Vital Records of Worthington, Massachusetts to the Year 1850.* Boston: New England Historic and Genealogical Society.

Freedman, Mitchell. 2012. "His Longtime Job as East Hampton Town Crier." *Newsday.* December 16. Accessed April 2013. http://www.newsday.com/long-island/towns/his-longtime-job-as-east-hampton-town-crier-1.4340660.

Frost, Josephine C. 1912. *The Frost Genealogy: Descendants of William Frost of Oyster Bay.* New York: Frederick H. Hitchcock Genealogical Publisher.

Gardener, Henry. 1660. "New England's Vindication." *Jouurnal of the Privy Council.*

Gardiner, Curtiss C. 1890. *Lion Gardiner and His Descendants.* St. Louis: A. Whipple Publisher.

Gardiner, David. 1871. *Chronicles of the Town of Easthampton.* New York: Browne and Co.

Gass, Margaret Davis. 1971. *History of Miller's Place.* St. Gerard Print.

Geree, John. 1646. *The Character of an Old English Puritan, or Non-Conformist, Tewksbury, but now at St.Albons.* London: W.Wilson for Christopher Meredith at the Crane in Paul's Church-yard.

Gillie, Mildred Hanson. 1955. *Historical Sketches of Settlements and Villages of North Brookhaven Town, 1655-1955.* Brookhaven: Privately Printed.

Gish, Noel J,. 1998. "Pirate, Whales Wrecks and Salvage." Transcript. http://longislandgenealogy.com/PiratesWhales.html.

Gjohnsit. 2013. "The Slaves that Time Forgot." *Daily KOS.* December 27. http://www.dailykos.com/story/2013/12/27/1265498/-The-slaves-that-time-forgot#.

Goddard, David. 2011. *Colonizing Southampton: The Transformation of a Long Island Community, 1870-1900.* Albany: State University of New York Press.

Greene, M. Louise. 1899. "Early Milford." *The Connecticut Magazine* Vol V (No. 3).

Hack, Timothy. 1971. *Richard Wescott.* Newark, Delaware: University of Delaware, Department of History.

Haines, A.M. 1883. "Will of James Haines of Hindes, of Southold, Long Island, N. Y., 1652." *New England Historical and Genealogical Register* CCCVII.

Hallam, Elizabeth. n.d. "Domesday Book...." *Addison Publications Ltd.* Accessed October 29, 2013. http://www.addisonpublications.com/domesday_book.html.

Hammond, John E. 2003. *The Early Settlement of Oyster Bay.* Oyster Bay: The Oyster Bay Historical Society.

Hanley, H.A. and C. W. Chalkin. 1961, rev. 2008. *The Kent Lay Subsidy Roll of 1334/5.* County Kent, England: Kent Archealogical Society.

Harpster, Jack. 2006. *John Ogden, the Pilgrim (1609-1682):A Man of More Than Ordinary Mark.* Fairleigh Dickinson University Press.

Harrington, Duncan. 2000. *Kent Hearth Tax Assessment Lady Day 1664.* Vol. XXIX, in *Kent Records*, London: The British Record Society Limited.

Harrington, F. C. , Admin. 1939. *History of Milford, Connecticut, 1639-1939.* Bridgeport, Connecticut: Press of Braunworth & Co.

Harrogate Borough Council. 2011. "Conservation Area Character Appraisal." North Deighton. https://www.harrogate.gov.uk/plan/Documents/Heritage%20and%20Design/Conservation %20Areas/DS-P-CAA_Ripon_240609.pdf.

Hartell, Anne. 1943. "Slavery on Long Island." *The Long Island Historical Journal*, Fall.

Hartford Courant. 2013. May 9.

Haskell, David and Edythe. 1991. *A History of Stony Creek, NY-The First Hundred Years.* Stony Creek: Self Published.

Hasted, Edward. 1798. *The Town and Parish of Ashford.* Vol. 7, in *The History and Topographical Survey of the County of Kent*, 526-545. Canterbury: W. Bristow. Accessed October 30, 2013. http://www.british-history.ac.uk/survey-kent/vol7.

Hatcher, Patricia Law. 2006. *Researching Your Colonial New England Ancestors Ancestry.* Provo, Utah: MyFamily.com.

Hatfield, Edwin. 1868. *History of Elizabeth, New Jersey: Including the Early History of Union County.* New York: Carlton & Lanahan.

Haven, Andrew. July 3, 1944. *Early Tax Assessment and Other Lists of Brookhaven Town from 1665 to 1799 Inclusive.* Folder, Brookhaven: Brookhaven Town Historian.

Hedges, H. P. 1887. *Records of the Town of East Hampton, Long Island, Suffolk Co., NY, With Other Ancient Documents of Historical Value.* Sag Harbor, New York: John H. Hunt, Printer.

Hedges, Henry et al. 1874. *The First Book of Records of the Town of Southampton With Other Ancient Documents of Historic Value.* Sag Harbor, New York: John H. Hunt Book and Job Printer.

Hedges, Henry P. 1897. *A History of the Town of East-Hampton.* Sag Harbor, New York: J. H. Hunt.

Hedges, Henry P. et al. 1877. *The Second Book of Records of The Town of Southhampton with Other Ancient Documents of Historic Value.* Sag Harbor: John H. Hunt, Printer.

Hedges, Henry P. 2001. *Tracing the Past: Writings of Henry P. Hedges 1817-1911, Related to the History of the East End.* Newmarket Press.

Hefner, Robert. 2002. "A Brief History of the Village of East Hampton, NY." *Village of East Hampton.* Accessed May 2014. http://www.easthamptonvillage.org/villagehistory.htm.

Heinsohn, Robert Jennings. 1998. "Pilgrims and Puritans in 17th Century New England." *Sail 1620.* Accessed July 22, 2015. http://www.sail1620.org/ Articles/pilgrims-and-puritans-in-17th-century-new-england.

Hempstead, Joshua. 1901. *Diary of Joshua Hempstead 1711-1758.* Providence, Rhode Island: Journal of Commerce Co.

Henry, Geoffrey B. 2000. "Cultural Resources Survey of the Town of Southampton New York." http://www.southamptontownny.gov/DocumentCenter/Home/View/1238.

Heston, Alfred Miller. 1924. *History of Cape May County New Jersey; South Jersey, A History, 1664-1923.* New York: Lewis Historical Publishing Company.

Hicks, Benjamin D. 1882. "Records of the St. George's Church, Hempstead, L.I. from June 5, 1725." *The New York Genealogial and Biographical Record*, 141.

Hinkemeyer, Arlene. 2001. *A History of the Incorporated Village of Plandome Heights.* Manhasset, NY: Village of Plandome Heights.

n.d. "History." *The Delaware Bay Company LLC.* Accessed January 24, 2015. http://www. delawarebayllc.com/history.html.

n.d. "History and Heritge." *Ashford Borough Council.* Accessed Jun 2014. http://www.ashford .gov.uk/history-and-heritage.

Hoadly, Charles J. 1857. *Records of the Colony and Plantation of New Haven From 1638 to 1649.* Hartford: Case, Tiffany & Co.

Hoadly, Charles J. 1858. *Records of the Colony or Jurisdiction of New Haven, From May 1653, to the Union Together with the New Haven Code of 1656.* Hartford: Case, Lockwood and Company.

Hoadly, Charles J. State Librarian. 1876. *The Public Records of the Colony of Connecticut from May 1744 to November 1750 Inclusive.* Hartford: Case, Lockwood and Brainard.

Hofstadter, Richard. 1972. "America in 1750, A Social Portrait." *The Journal of American History,* September: 407-409.

Honeyman, A. Van Doren. 1928. "Administration First Series." *In Calendar of New Jersey Wills 1761 - 1770, Vol. IV.* Somerville, NJ: The Union-Gazette Association Printers.

Hook, James W. 1955. *Smith, Grant, and Irons Families of New Jersey's Shore Counties : Including the Related Families of Willets and Birdsall.* New Haven: J.W. Hook.

Hotchkiss, Stuart. 2001. "Ffulke (Foulk, Fulk Davies) C.Davis." *Lucius Family Genealogy.* Accessed Oct 2014. http://www.lucius.us/getperson.php?personID=I7450&tree=Lucius.

Howe, Paul Sturtevant. 1921. *Mayflower Pilgrim Descendants in Cape May County, New Jersey.* Cape May, New Jersey: Albert R. Hand.

Howell, George Rogers. 1887. *The Early History of Southampton, L.I. New York with Genealogies, Second Edition.* Albany: Weed, Parsons and Co.

Hussey, R, C,. 1858. "On Caesar's Landing-Place in Britain,." *Archaelogian Cantana* (Kent Archaelogical Society) Vol. I.

Hutchinson, Thomas. 1865. "A Letter from Captain Israel Stoughton to the Governor of Massachusetts." In *The Hutchinson Papers, Vol I.* Albany, New York: Joel Munsell.

Hutchinson, Thomas. 1795. *History of Massachusetts.* Salem: Thomas Cushing printer.

n.d. "Indentured Servitude In the Atlantic World." *Gettysburg College.* Accessed August 2015. http://public.gettysburg.edu/~tshannon/hist106web/site18/servitude.htm.

Innes, John H. 1935. *The Earliest Records of Brookhaven (Setauket) on Long Island.* New York State Historical Association.

Jacobus, Donald Lines and Arthur Bliss Dayton. 1959. *The Early Daytons and Descendents of Henry, Jr.* New Haven, Connecticut: New Haven Colony Historical Society.

Jacobus, Donald Lines. 1969. "Barnes Families of Eastern Long Island and Branford, Conneticut." *Genealogies of Connecticut Families.*

Jacobus, Donald Lines. 1991. *History and Genealogy of the Families of Old Fairfield.* Vol. I. Baltimore, Maryland: Genealogical Publishing Co., Inc., 1991.

Jacobus, Donald Lines. 1960. "Recent Books." *The American Genealogist* 36.

Jasanoff, Maya. 2011. *Liberty's Exiles: American Loyalists in the Revolutionary World.* Knopf: Doubleday.

Jones, Mary Jean Anderson. 1968. *Congregational Commonwealth: Connecticut, 1636-1662.* Middletown, Connecticut: Wesleyan University Press.

Jordan, Don and Michael Walsh. 2008. *White Cargo: The Forgotten History of Britain's White Slaves in America.* New York: NYU Press.

Kearney, Mitchell. 2011. "A List of Persons in Suffolk County, Long Island, NY, Who Took the Oath of Allegiance and Peaceable Behavior Before Governor Tryon." *New York Genealogical and Biographical Record* 142 (s).

Kelly, Franklin. 1987. *The Early Landscapes of Fredric Edwin Church, 1845-1854.* Arlington, TX: Amon Carter Museum.

Keltie, J. Scott. 1913. *The Statesman's Year-Book.* London: MacMillan and Co Klett, Joseph R. 2008. *Records of the East and West Jersey Proprietors.* Trenton: New Jersey State Archives.

Lambert, Edward R. 1838. *History of the Colony of New Haven.* New Haven: Hitchcock & Stafford.

Lambert, Tim. n.d. *A World History Encyclopedia.* Accessed September 2013. http://www.localhistories.org.

Lambert, Tim. 2013. "Society in 17th Century England." *Daily Life in England in the 1600s.* Accessed 2013. http://www.localhistories.org/stuart.html.

Langner, Roxanne. n.d. *Descendants of Robetus Okeden.* Accessed June 2013. http://familytreemaker.genealogy.com/users/l/a/n/Roxnne Langner/FILE/0002text.txt.

Lee, Francis Bazley. 1902. *New Jersey As a Colony and As a State.* New York: The Publishing Society of New Jersey .

Leggitt, Roy C. n.d. "Descendents of Richard Osborne." *royc.cts.com.* Accessed Jul 22, 2015. http://royc.cts.com/Genealogy/Descendants%20of%20Richard%20Osborne.pdf.

Lehman, Jeffery. 2008. *West's Encyclopedia of American Law.* Detroit: The Gale Group, Inc.

Littell, Rev. William H. 1876. *July 2nd and 16th, 1876 by the Rev.William H Littell, 9th Pastor of the First Presbyterian Church.* Brookhaven: self published.

Long Island Forum. 1947. "A School of 1767." January: 18.

Lythgoe, Darrin. 2001. "John Sweezy." *Welcome to Sweezey.com.* Accessed November 2014. http://sweezey.com/genealogy/getperson.php?personID=I00148&tree=sweez.

Mallmann, Jacob. 1899. *Historical Papers on Shelter Island and Its Presbyterian Church.* New York: A. M. Bustard Co.

Mann, Frank Paul. 2013. *The British Occupation of Southern New York During the American Revolution and the Failure to Restore Civilian Government.* Dissertation, Syracuse: Syracuse University.

Manwaring, Charles William. 1904. *A Digest of the Early Connecticut Probate Records.* Vol. I. Boston: Harvard University: R.S. Peck & Company.

Markham, Clements R. 2011. *Richard III: His Life and Character.* Project Gutenberg. http://www.gutenberg.org/files/36451/36451-h/36451-h.htm.

Marshall, Philip. 2005. "Lopped Trees: The Living Fences of Old Long Island." *Long Island Historical Journal*, Fall.

Mason, George. 2000. "How to Read 18th Century British-American Writing." *Do History.* Roy Rosenzweig Center for History and New Media. http://dohistory.org/on_your_own/toolkit/writing.html.

Mason, Thomas, ed. 1898. *A Register of Baptisms, Marriages and Burials in the Parish of St. Martin in the Fields, In the County of Middlesex from 1550 to 1619.* Vol. XXV. London: The Harleian Society.

Mather, Cotton. 1820. *Magnalia Christi Americana: Or, The Ecclesiastical History of New-England.* Vol. I. Hartford: Silas Andrus.

Mather, Frederic Gregory. 1913. *The Refugees of 1776 from Long Island to Connecticut.* Albany: J.B. Lyon Co.

McHardy, A. K. 1977. *Taxation of the Clergy, 1379-81: Poll Tax of 1381 in Cathedral and its Jurisdiction, in the Church of London, 1375-1392.* London: London Record Society.

McLaren, John & Harold Coward. 1999. *Religious Conscience, the State, and the Law: Historical Contexts and Contemporary Significance.* Albany: State University of New York.

Merwick, Donna. 2006. *The Shame and the Sorrow: Dutch-Amerindian Encounters in New Netherland.* Philadelphia: University of Pennsylvania.

Miller, Robert J. 2001. "Economic Development in Indian Country: Will Capitalism or Socialism Succeed?" *Oregon Law Review* 80 (3).

Minuse, William B. 1955. *Ship Building in the Setaukets.* Manuscript inside a folder, Setauket: folder entitled Ships and Shipbuilding located at the Three Village Historical Society.

Morse, Stephen P. 2011. "Coverting Between Julian and Gregorian Calendar in One Step." *Stevemorse.org.* Accessed Jun 16, 2014. http://www.stevemorse.org/jcal/julian.html.

Morton, Thomas. 1916. "The Puritan and His Indian Ward." *The American Journal of Sociology* 22 (1). http://www.jstor.org/stable/2763930?seq=3.

Moss, Richard Shannon. 1993. *Slavery on Long Island: A Study in Local Institutional and Early African-American Communal Life.* New York: Garland Publishing, Inc.

Mowrer, Lilian T. 1960. *The Indomitable John Scott: Citizen of Long Island 1632-1704.* New York: Farrar, Straus and Cudahy.

Murrin, M. John. 1998. "East Hampton in the 17th Century." Lecture, East Hampton. http:/longislandgenealogy.com/EastHamptonin17Century.html.

Nash, Rev. Sylvester. 1853. *The Nash Family, Records of the Descendants of Thomas Nash of New Haven, Connecticut 1640.* Hartford: Press of Case, Tiffany and Company.

Naylor, Natalie A. n.d. "The Other New Yorker." *Long Island Historic Journal*, 50-55.

Naylor, Natalie A. 2007/2008. "Surviving the Ordeal: Long Island Women During the Revolutionary War." *Long Island Historical Journal* 20 (N. 1-2): 114-134.

Naylor, Natalie A. 2012. *Women in Long Island's Past: A History of Eminent Ladies and Everyday Lives.* Charleston, SC: The History Press.

Nelson, William. 1900. *First Series, Documents Relating to the Colonial History of the State of New Jersey, Marriage Records, 1665-1800.* Vol. XXII. Paterson, New Jersey: Archives of the State of New Jersey.

Nelson, William. 1909. *Marriage Records 1665-1800, First Series Vol XXII.* Paterson, NJ: Archives of the State of New Jersey.

n.d. "New Haven Historic Resources Inventory Phase I: Central New Haven, City of New Haven Plan."." *City of New Haven.* Accessed February 25, 2013. http://www.cityofnewhaven.com/CityPlan/pdfs/HistoricInventory/NH%20HRI%201%20Hill.pdf.

New Jersey Historical Society. 1931. *Calendar of New Jersey Wills, Adminstrations, etc, 1931.* London: Forgotten Books.

n.d. *New York Probate Records, 1629-1971.* County Courthouses: New York State. https://familysearch.org/pal:/MM9.3.1/TH-1942-28640-30722-3?cc=1920234&wc=9V3Z-C68:213306101,220060101.

New York Times. 1894. "Long Island Whale Hunt, Amagansett Village Headquarters for the Sport." May 6.

New York, (State) Legislature. 1903. *Documents of the Senate of the State of New York, One Hundred and twenty-Sixth Session, Calendar of Council Minutes 1668-1783.* Vol. VIII. Albany, New York: The Argus Company, Printers.

n.d. *NGS Gardens Open For Charity.* http://www.ngs.org.uk/gardens/find-a-garden/garden.aspx?id=30626.

Nicholas. 1636/37. *Book of Rough Notes: a Calendar of State Papers of the Reign of Charles I.* London: Her Majesty's Public Record Office.

Nicholson, George. 1956. *The Long Island Presbytery and Churches.* Long Island Presbytery.

O'Callaghan, E. B. 1850. *The Documentary History of the State of New York.* Vol. III. Albany: Weed Parsons & Co.

O'Callaghan, E. B. 1849. *The Documentary History of the State of New-York : Arranged Under Direction of the Hon. Christopher Morgan, Secretary of State.* Vol. II. Albany: Weed, Parsons & Co.

O'Connor, Dr. Michael. n.d. "Unit Three: Pilgrims, Puritans, and Opponents." *DIgital American Literature Anthology.* Accessed December 7, 2013. http://www.digitalamlit.com/Unit3.html.

O'Donnell, Pearl Foster. 1976. *Medlin Clan and Kin In America.* Fort Worth, TX: Private Printing.

Ogilby, John. 1671. *History of America.* London.

n.d. "Old Calendar and Dating Information." *US GenWeb Project.* Accessed Jun 10, 2015. http://www.usgenweb.org/research/calendar.shtml.

Orcutt, Samuel. 1886. *A History of the Old Town of Stratford and the City of Bridgeport, Connecticut.* Vol. I. Fairfield County Historical Society.

Osborn, Andrew. 2014. "British Experts Say They Have Found London's Lost Black Death Graves." *Reuters*, March 30. Accessed June 25, 2014. http://www.reuters.com/article/2014/03/30/us-britain-history-blackdeath-idUSBREA2T09V20140330?feedType=RSS&feedName=top News.

Osborne, Joseph. 1887. *Records of the Town of East Hampton, Long Island, Suffolk Co., NY With Other Ancient Documents of Historic Value*. Sag Harbor: John H Hunt.

Page, William ed. 1914. *Parishes: Northallerton, A History of the County of York North Riding*. Vol. 1. London: Victoria County History. Accessed Oct 6, 2013. http://www.british-history.ac.uk/report.aspx?compid=64779.

Parish, W. D. 1888. *Old English Core Vocabulary and Dictionary of the Kentish Dialect*. University of St. Andrews: Farncombe & Co.

Pearman, Augustus John. 1868. *History of Ashford*. London: H. Igglesden publisher.

Pease, Zephaniah. 1918. *History of New Bedford*. New York: The Lewis Historical Publishing Co.

Pelletreau , William S. & James A. Early. 1915. *The Sixth Volume of Record of Southampton, Long Island, NY*. Sag Harbor: John H. Hunt, printer.

Pelletreau, William S. & William J. Post. 1910. *The Fifth Volume of Records of the Town of Southampton*. Sag Harbor: John H. Hunt.

Pelletreau, William S. 1905. *A History of Long Island From Its Earliest Settlement to the Present Time*. Vol. II. New York and Chicago: The Lewis Publishing Company.

Pelletreau, William S. 1878. *A Land Map of Main Street, Southampton, New York, from 1648-1878 Book of Records of the Town of Southampton*. Vol. III. Sag Harbor: John H Hunt.

Pelletreau, William S. 1897. *Early Long Island Wills of Suffolk County, 1691-1703 With Genealogical and Historical Notes*. New York: Francis P. Harper.

Pelletreau, William S. 1907. *Historic Homes and Institutions and Genealogical and Family History of New York*. Vol. III. New York and Chicago: The Lewis Publsihing Company.

Pelletreau, William S. 1898. *Records of the Town of Smithtown, Long Island, NY , with other Ancient Documents of Historic Value*. Huntington, NY: Published by Authority of Town.

Perry, Retta Bostwick. 1974. "Identity of Ellen (_____) Lindley." *NEHGR* 128 (2).

Phillimore, William and Watts. 1910. *Kent Parish Registers Marriages Index to Vol 1 & 2*. Phillimore & Company.

Pollick, Lindsay. n.d. "Warrenside: The Context, Deighton: Three Railway Lines, Two Stations and a Canal." *The Cricket History of Calderdale and Kirkless*. Accessed October 2014. http://www.ckcricketheritage.org.uk/southkirklees/bradley/docs/Context.pdf.

Poole, Margaret Ellen. 1902. *The Poole Family of Poole Hall, in Wirral: A Paper Read Before the Historic Society of Lancashire and Cheshire 16th March, 1899*. T.Brakell.

Pope, Charles Henry. 1900. *The Pioneers of Massachusetts, a Descriptive List, Drawn from Records of the Colonies, Towns and Churches and Other Contemporaneous Documents*. Boston: Published by Charles H. Pope.

Post, Marie Caroline De Trobriand. 1905. *The Post Family*. New York: Sterling Potter.

Post, William & William S. Pelletreau. 1910. *The Fifth Volume of Records of the Town of Southampton*. Sag Harbor: John H. Hunt printer.

Post, William J. 1877. *The second Book of Records of the Town of Southampton, Long Island*. Sag Harbor, NY: John H Hunter.

Powell, Sumner Chilton. 1963. *Puritan Village, The Formation of a New England Town*. Middletown: Wesleyan Universty Press.

Prime, Nathaniel S. 1845. *A History of Long Island, From Its First Settlement by Europeans, to the Year 1845*. New York: Robert Carter.

Rattray, Jeanette Edwards. 2001. *Discovering the Past: Writings of Jeanette Edwards Rattray*. East Hampton: Newmarket Press.

n.d. *Records of Wills 1694-1900, Gloucester*. Trenton: Division of the State Library and Archives.

Redboat Design. 2012. *Ashford, Kent - Index of All Known Births, Marriages and Burials from c.1570 - late 1800's*. http://www.kentarchaeology.org.uk/Research/01/ASH/01/00d.htm.

Reeves, Randall R. & Edward Mitchell. 1987. *Shore Whaling for Right Whales in the Northeast.* Ste-Anne-de-Bellevue, Quebec: Arctic Biological Station.

Reeves, Randall R. & Edward Mtchell. n.d. "Report of the International Whaling Commission." In *The Long Island, New York, Right Whale fishery: 1650-1924.* Ste-Anne-de-Bellevue, Quebec: Arctic Biological Station.

Reynolds, Cuyler. 1911. *Hudson-Mohawk Genealogical and Family Memoirs.* Vol. 4. New York: Lewis Historical Publshing Co.

Reynolds, Susan, Ed. 1962. "West Drayton: Mills." *British History Online.* Accessed July 21, 2015. http://www.british-history.ac.uk/vch/middx/vol3/p196.

Rivers, R. W. n.d. *From Hothfield and Ashford to New England, The Story of Thomas Baker and Ralph Dayton, 17th Century Emigrants to New England.*

Roberts, Gary Boyd. 2004. *The Royal Descendents of 600 Immigrants to the American Colonies of the United States.* Baltimore: Genealogical Publication Co.

Robinson, Doane. 1921. "John Roberson of Oyster Bay." *New York Genealogial and Biographical Society* LII (3): 201-213.

Rogers, Steve. 2012. "Sketches From the Lanthier-Rogers Family Tree." *Raking Leaves.* April. Accessed May 2015. http://raking-leaves.blogspot.com/2012/04/.

Romm, Richard M. May 2010. *America's First Whaling Industry and the Whaler Yeomen of Cape May 1630-1830.* Camden, New Jersey: Lambert Academic Publishing.

Rosenkrans, Allen. 1900. *The Rosenkrans Family in Europe and America.* Newton, New Jersey: New Jersey Herald Press.

Ross, Peter and William Smith Pelletreau. 1905. *A History of Long Island: From Its Earliest Settlement to the Present Time.* Vol. II. New York and Chicago: The Lewis Publishing.

Ruderman, Arthur. 2011. "Abstracts from Ashford, Kent Will." *Kent Archealogical Society.* http://www.kentarchaeology.org.uk/Research/01/ASH/04/00.htm.

Russell, Barbara, interview by Jim Dayton. 2014. *Brookhaven Town Historian* (May 14).

Rust, Val Dean. 2004. *Radical Origins: Early Mormon Converts and Their Colonial Ancestors.* Champaign, IL: University of Illinois Press.

Rutherford, Adam. 2015. "So You're Related to Charlemagne? You and Every Other Living European." *The Guardian,* May 24.

Sage, Henry J. 2012. "Colonial Life: Work, Family, Faith." *academicamerican.com.* Accessed October 2014. http://www.academicamerican.com.

Saguto, Al. 1984. *The Honourable Cordwainer's Company.* http://www.thehcc.org/.

Savage, James. 1860. *A Genealogical Dictionary of the First Settlers of New England, Showing Three Generations of Those Who Came Before May 1692.* 4 vols. Boston: Little, Brown and Co.

n.d. "Sawmills in New England 1600-1900: A Brief Overview." *Ledyard Up-Down Sawmill.* Accessed August 13, 2014. http://www.ledyardsawmill.org/history/early-sawmills-in-new-england.

n.d. *Seeley Genealogical Society.* Accessed March 18, 2013. http://www.seeley-society.net/nathaniel/sgs1.html.

Secretary of State, Connecticut. 1954. *Colonial Land Records of Connecticut, 1640-1846:Including Patents, Deeds and Surveys of Land.* Salt Lake City: Genealogical Society of Utah.

Secretary of State, New York. 2015. "New York Land Records 1630-1975, Suffolk Deeds 1660-1719 Vol A." *Family Search.* Accessed April 6, 2013. https:// familysearch.org/search/collection/2078654.

Seversmith, Herbert Furman. 1939-1958. *Colonial Families of Long Island, New York and Connecticut, Being the Ancestry & Kindred of Herbert Furman Seversmith.* 5 vols. Washington, DC: Self Published. http://catalog.hathitrust.org/Record/005756269.

Seversmith, Herbert Furman. 1939. "George Norton of Salem, Massachusetts, and His Supposed Connection with the Norton Family of Sharpen." *The American Genealogist,* April: 199.

Seybolt, Robert Francis. 1917. *Apprenticeship & Apprenticeship Education in Colonial New England & New York.* New York: Teachers College, Columbia University.

Shaw, Osborn. October 5, 1933. "History of Brookhaven Village." paper presented at Brookhaven Free Library, Brookhaven, NY.

Shaw, Osborn. 1947. "History of Coram." *Longwood's Journey.* Accessed May 24, 2014. http://www.long wood.k12.ny.us/cms/One.aspx?portalId=2549374&pageId=5434499.

Shaw, Osborn. 1932. *Records of the Town of Brookhaven Book B 1679-1756.* Edited by Osborn Shaw. New York, New York: The Derrydale Press.

Sheppard, Walter Lee. 1960. "Dayton and Ireland of South Jersey." *The American Genealogist*, 171-174.

Shillingburg, Patricia and Edward. 2003. "The Disposition of Slaves on the East End of Long Island from 1680 to 1796." Accessed 2014. www.shelter-island.org/disposition_slave.html.

Shillingburg, Patricia. n.d. "The Settlers of the East End." Accessed 2013. http://www.shelter-island.org/new_history.html.

Smith, Edward Church & Philip Mack Smith. 1924. *A History of Middlefield, Massachusetts.*

Smith, Frederick Kinsman. 1967. *The Family of Richard Smith of Smithtown, Long Island, New York.* New York: The Smithtown Historical Society.

Smith, Hon. Ralph D. 1877. *The History of Guilford, Connecticut, from its First Settlement in 1639.* Albany: J. Munsell, Printer.

Smith, Ned, Interview by Stephen Dayton and Jim Dayton. 2012. *Colonial Brookhaven and Long Island*

Smith, William ed. 1882. *Old Yorkshire.* London: Longmans, Green & Co.

Spears, John R. 1910. *Story of the New England Whalers.* New York: The MacMillan Company.

Speight, Harry. 1894. *Nidderdale and the Garden of the Nidd: A Yorkshire Rhineland.* London: Elliot Stock.

Speight, Harry. 1906. *Nidderdale, from Nun Monkton to Whernside: Being a Record of the History, Antiquities, Scenery, Old Homes, Families, & c., of the Beautiful Valley of the Nidd.* London: Elliot Stock.

Starbuck, B Alexander. 1876. *History of the American Whale Fishery From its Earliest Inception to the Year 1876.* Waltham, MA.

Starr, Burgis Pratt. 1879. *Starr Family of New England, From the Ancestor Dr. Comfort Starr of Ashford, County Kent England Who Emigrated to Boston, Mass in 1635.* Hartford, CT, Connecticut: The Case, Lockwood & Brainard Co.

Staudt, John G. 2007. "From Wretchedness to Independence: Suffolk County in the American Revolution." *Long Island Historical Journal* 20.

Stevens, Lewis Townsend. 1897. *History of Cape May County New Jersey From the. Aboriginal Times to the Present Day.* Cape May, NJ: L.T. Stevens.

Stewart, James. 2010. *Venture Smith and the Business of Slavery and Freedom.* Amherst: University of Massachusetts.

Stokes, Lori. 2013. "Puritans V. Pilgrims in Early America." *U.S. History Scene*, May 22. Accessed December 19, 2013. http://www.ushistoryscene.com/uncategorized/puritanspilgrims/.

Strong, John A, James VanTassel and Rick VanTassel. 2010. "In Search of Catoneras: Long Island's Pocahontas." *Long Island History Journal*, Spring.

Strong, John A. 2011. *The Unkeckaug Indians of Eastern Long Island: A History.* Normal, OK: University of Oklahoma Press.

Strong, John. 1992. "The Thirteen Tribes of Long Island: The History of a Myth." *The Hudson Valley Regional Review* 9: 39-73.

Strong, Kate Wheeler. 1953. "Land Deals on Ye Little Neck." *Long Island Forum.*

—. 1952. "Tales of Mount Misery." *Long Island Forum*, April.

Students, Longwood Middle School. 2004-2015. "1776 Brookhaven Town Census, Heads of Families Living North of Middle County Road, and Heads of Families Living South of Middle County Road." *Longwood's Journal.* Accessed August 16, 2014. http://www.longwood.k12.ny.us/cms/One.aspx?portalId=2549374&pageId=7008700.

Swasey, Benjamin Franklin. 1910. *Genealogy of the Swasey Family.* Cleveland, OH: Privately Printed.

Swezey, Thomas F. 1997. "Salem to Long Island." *John L. Swesey's History of his Line of the Swesey Family.* Accessed June 2015. http://www.winternet.com/~swezeyt/gene/Swesey2.htm.

Sylvester, Nathaniel Bartlett. 1878. *History of Saratoga County, New York.* Philadelphia: Everts & Ensign.

Talmadge, Arthur White. 1909. *The Talmadge, Tallmadge and Talmage Genealogy; Being the Descendants of Thomas Talmadge of Lynn Massachusetts, With an Appendix Including Other Families.* New York: The Grafton Press.

n.d. "The 1752 Calendar Change." *US GenWeb Project.* Accessed Jun 10, 2015. http://www.cslib.org/CalendarChange.htm.

The East Hampton Star. 1963. "Springs Man Revives Cattle Ear Marks Used by Ancestors." May 16:1.

n.d. *The National Gardens Scheme.* Accessed Oct 29, 2013. http://www.ngs.org.uk/.

The Port Jefferson Times. 1915. "Old Man's Had [A] House of Worship in 1740." October 9.

Terwilliger, James. 1868. *Calendar of Historical Manuscripts Relating to the War of the Revolution.* Vol. I. Albany, NY: Weed, Parsons and Company.

Themeweavers. 2015. *Ashford Kent.* Accessed Jun 10, 2015. http://www.ashford-kent.kentpoi.co.uk

Themeweavers. 2015. *Maidstone Kent.* Accessed Jun 10, 2015. http://www.maidstone-kent.kentpoi.co.uk/.

Theodore, Nancy Tyrrel. Jun 2009. *Milford First Congregational Church Records-1639-1837.* LDS Film #1012263.

—. 2010. "Samuel Terrill and Yamphank Neck 1686 Forward." *Descendents of Roger Terill of Milford, Connecticut.* January. Accessed February 2014. http://dorterrill.net/index. php?option=com _content &view= article&id=213&catid=43.

Thompson, Benjamin and Robert H Dodd. 1918. *History of Long Island.* Vol. III. New York.

Thompson, Benjamin Franklin. 1839. *History of Long Island Containing an Account of the Discovery and Settlement to the Present Time.* New York: E. French.

Thorpe, Francis Newton. 2008. "Fundemental Agreement, or Original Constitution of the Colony of New Haven, June 4, 1639." *Yale Law School:The Avalon Project.* Accessed July 24, 2015. http://avalon.law.yale.edu/17th_century/ct01.asp.

Threfall, John Brooks. 1970. *Ancestry of the Children of John Brooks Threfall.* Privately Printed.

Tiedmann, Joseph S, And Eugene R. Fingerhut. 2005. *The Other New York: The American Revolution Beyond New York City 1763-1787.* Albany: State University Press.

Tolkien, J. R. R. 1954. *Fellowship of the Ring.* London: George Allen & Unwin.

Tomlinson, R. G. 1978. *Witchcraft Trials of Connecticut: The First Comprehensive, Documented History of Witchcraft Trials in Colonial Connecticut.* Hartford: Bond Press.

Tooker, William Wallace. 1911. *The Indian Place-Names on Long Island and Islands Adjacent: With Their Probable Signification.* New York: G. P. Putnam.

Torrey, Clarence Almon. 1985. *New England Marriages Prior to 1700.* Baltimore: Genealogical Publishing Co.

n.d. "Town of Brookhaven, Brookhaven's Comprehensive Plan, Exisiting Conditions and Trends Report." *Brookhaven.org.* Accessed March 24, 2014. http://www.brookhaven.org/portals/ 12/documents/Chapter%202%20-%20Introduction%20.pdf.

Tucker, Gideon J. 1860. *Names of Persons for Whom Marriage Licenses Were Issued by the Secretary of State of the Provence of New York Previous to 1784.* Albany: Weed, Parsons and Company.

Twomey, Tom. 2001. *Exploring the Past: Writings from 1798 to 1896 Relating to the History of the Town of East Hampton.* New Market Press.

Tyler, Beverly C., Interview by Stephen B Dayton. 2012. Setauket, New York: Emma Clark Library, (October 23).

Tyler, Beverly C. 2010. *Setauket becoming Self-sufficent: 1657-1662.* Village Times Hearld.

Tyler, Beverly C. 2014. "History Close at Hand-Three Village/Brookhaven-Chronology." *Times Beacon Record.*

University of Connecticut. 2001. *Colonial Connecticut Records 1636-1776*. Accessed August 2015. http://www.colonialct.uconn.edu/.

Unknown Author. 2004. "Montauk Indian Heritage." *Montauk Life*. Accessed July 27, 2015. http://www.montauklife.com/ history /davidmc9.html.

Unknown Author. 2006-2013. "Planters and Traders of Southern Jersey." *Chronicles of America*. Accessed Jan 2014. http://www.chroniclesofamerica.com/ quakers/ planters_and_ traders_ of_southern_jersey.htm

Unknown Author. 2011. "Chronology of American Whaling." *New Bedford Whaling Museum*. Accessed August 2014. http://www.whalingmuseum.org/programs/whaling-history-symposium.

Unknown Author. 2014. "American Whaling." *New Bedford Whaling Museum*. August 22. Accessed September 2014. whalingmuseum.org/learn/research-topics/overview-of-north-american-whaling/american-whaling.

Unknown Author. 2014. "Bible Translation Magazine." *bible-translation.net*. October. Accessed January 2015. http://bible-translation.net/issue-printer/october-2014.

Unknown Compiler. 1855. "Ordinance Map-Deighton Hall." East Riding: Yorkshire Council.

Unknown Compiler. 2013. "Ancestors of Gregory Thomas Wirt." *Yumpu.com*. Accessed October 2014. https://www.yumpu.com/en/browse/user/swgdezign.com.

Unknown Compiler. Feb 13, 1668. *Abstract of Probate Records*. Fairfield, CT: B 1 87.

Van Lith, Martin. 3 Jul 2012. *Fire Place Name Origin*. Webpage, Brookhaven: Self published. http://brookhavensouthhaven.org/history/FirePlaceNameNote.htm.

Van Lith, Martin. 2010. "Purchase of Washington Lodge Estate Approved by Suffolk County." *Brookhaven/South Haven Hamlets*. December 13. http://brookhavensouthhaven.blogspot.com/2010/12/george-washington-lodge.html.

Vicar, Church. n.d. "St. Mary's Parish Registry." Ashford, Kent, UK.

Wagner, Stephen. 2006. "Slavery on Long Island." *Hofstra University Library Special Collections Department*. Accessed 2014. http://www.hofstra.edu/pdf/library/libspc_soli.pdf.

Wallace, William. n.d. *The Indian Place-Names on Long Island and Islands Adjacent: With Their Probable Significations*. Sag Harbor, N. Y.: Tooker.

Waller, Henry. 1889. *History of the Town of Flushing*. Flushing: J. H. Ridenour.

Weeks, Archibald C et al. 1924. *Brookhaven Town Records*. Vol. II. New York: Tobias A. Wright.

Weeks, William J. et al. 1930. *Records of the Town of Brookhaven Book A*. New York: Derrydale Press.

Weis, Frederick Lewis. 2004. *Ancestral Roots of Certain American Colonists Who Came to America Before 1700*. Baltimore: Genealogical Publishing.

Werner, Charles J. 1919. *Genealogies of Long Island Families*. New York: Charles J. Werner publisher.

Whitaker, Rev. Epher. 1881. *History of Southold, L.I. Its First Century*. Southold: Printed for the Author.

Whittemore, Henry. 1897. *The Heroes of the American Revolution and Their Descendants: Battle of Long Island*. Brooklyn: The Heroes of the Revolution Publishing Co.

Williams, Roger. 1973. *A Key to the Languages of America, (1643)*. Detroit: Wayne State University Press.

Williston, George C. 2001. "A Cape May, NJ Hand Lineage." *handfamily.org*. June. Accessed April 16, 2011. http://www.handfamily.org/.

Winans, S. R. 1911. "Early Southampton, Long Island, Inhabitant Lists." *New York Genealogical and Biographical Record* (NYBGS) XLII.

Wright, Byron. n.d. "The Cooper: Colonial Maker of Barrels and Casks." *Colonial Sense*. Accessed August 6, 2015. http://www.colonialsense.com/societylifestyle/signs_of_the_times/cooper.php.

Wyckoff, Edith William. 1978. *Fabled Past: Tales of Long Island*. Empire State Historical Publication Series: Kennikat Press.

Yale, David. 1997. "Law and Order in Early New Haven: The Forgotten Colony." http://www.dcyale.com/law_papers/new_haven_history.html.

Young, Susan D. 2013. *Kent Online Parish Clerks; Dutch Refugees in Maidstone, 1585.* Nov 5. http://www.kent-opc.org/Parishes/Manors%20and%20more/MaidstoneDutch.html

INDEX

446

geners
John, 223, 269
generss
Thomas, 269
Gennors
John, 217
George Nelson, 407
gibb
Andrew, 272
Gibb
Andrew, 273, 275, 277
Gibbons
Will, 68
Gibbs
Andrew, 274
Benjamin, 99, 233, 234, 235
Gilbert
Samuel 3rd, 347
Samuel Jr, 347
Gloucester
St. Nicholas, 30
Glover
Henry, 89
Goldhatch
Alice, 19, 37, 50, 146, 147, 149
Robert, 38, 39, 60
Goldhatch Tritton
Alice, 36
Goldhatche
Alice, 39
William, 39
Goldsmith
Tho, 122
Goodman Edwards, 140
Goodman Myles
Goodman, 88
Gosmer
Mr., 107
gould
BenJamen, 266
benJemen, 269
Gould
Benjamin, 237, 274
gouldsberry
Robart, 270
Gouldsberry
Robert, 266
Gouldsberry
Robert, 275
goulsbery
Robart, 276
Governor Andros, 239
Graves

Hannah, 267
Great Awakening, 336, 337, 339
Great Migration, 23
Green
Agnes, 15
Thomas, 336
Greene
Agnes, 29
Agnete, 29, 37
Margaret, 15
Gregory
Goodman, 97
Griffin
Hugh, 224
Griggs
John, 172
Groue
Goodman, 93, 96
Groves
Philip, 97
Hadley Town Clerk, 403
Haines
Benj, 155
James, 153, 154, 155, 156, 157, 166
James Haynes, 155
John, 155
Jona, 155
Mary, 155, 165
Sarah, 155
Thomas, 155
Hall
John, 68
Mary, 207
Rlaph, 207
Hallefax
Simon, 248
Hallett
John, 280
Hallifax
Simon, 247
Hallock
Iasiah, 334
Noah, 334, 336
Halsey
Thomas, 107, 108, 109, 118, 122, 127
Hames
Goodm, 68
Hammond
Elisha, 384
Hampshire, 127
Hand
John, 127, 132, 137, 141, 143, 145, 147, 206

John Sr, 126
Stephen, 319
Hanmer
Sarah, 284
Harck
William, 119
Harker
[Wm], 127
William, 118
Harlow
Thomas, 192
Harris
George, 197
Harrogate, 12, 13
Harvard University, 75
Harvey
Josiah, 224
Matthias, 212
Haskell
David and Edythe, 394
Haughton
Sarah, 302
Hawkings
Zachary, 253
Hawkins
Zachariah, 217
Zachr., 217
Zakery, 217
Hawxhurst
Christopher, 202
Haynes
James, 209
John, 154
Mary, 154, 214
Mary [Knight], 153
Hayward
James, 91
Heathrow Airport, 14, 34
Hector, 44, 45
Hedges
Stephen, 129
William, 145
Helme
Tho, 277
Thomas, 254, 292, 334, 360
Hempstead, 208
Joshua, 302, 303, 305, 308, 309, 311
Manhasset, 106
Henry VI, 11
Henry VIII, 15
Herbert
John, 154
Mr., 157
Hercules, 42

447

Walter, 244
Manhansett Indians, 73
Manhasset
    Cow Bay, 72
Manhattan Island, 106
Manor of Deighton, 10
Mapes
    Thomas, 192, 195
Marden
    Robert, 110
Margareta de Dighton, 12
Marsh
    Johnath, 77
Marven
    Robert, 152
Mary Davis, 167
Massachusetts
    Boston, 22, 28, 29, 30, 44,
        49, 50, 51, 52, 53, 54,
        55, 60, 61, 62, 63, 73,
        75, 99, 173, 175, 176,
        192, 233, 235, 262,
        300, 353, 365, 372, 387
    Boston Harbor, 44
    Chesterfield, 393
    Dorchester, 63
    Lynn, 49, 50, 51, 52, 72,
        73, 74, 102, 118, 126,
        127, 129, 140, 181, 192
    Middlefield, 392
    New Bedford, 391
    Roxbury, 62
    Salem, 124, 126, 154, 155,
        262
    Saugus, 50
    Wenham, 251
    Worthington, 391, 392,
        393, 400
Massachusetts Bay, 2, 22,
    50
    Lynn, 2
Massachusetts Bay Colony,
    23, 63
Mastic Beach, 389
Matares, 202
Mather
    Cotton, 53
    Frederic Gregory, 379
    Rev. Moses, 377
Meade
    Bennett, 39
Meaker
    Wm, 81
Mecar
    Robt, 77
    Will, 77

Mecham
    Jeremiah, 148
Medlin, 110
Meeker
    Sam., 81
    William, 81
Meger
    James, 336
Meges
    Goodman, 97
    Mr., 96
Meggs
    Mark, 110
    Vincent, 110
Melyn
    Catherine, 117
    Cornelius, 117
Menunkatuck plantation,
    55
Merino wool, 392
Merlesuan, 13
Merryman
    Nath, 68
Mervin
    Robert, 121, 122, 152, 153
Metcalfr
    Steven, 68
Middle Island, 336
Miles
    Richard, 63
Milford, 62
    First Congregational
        Church, 85, 86, 129
miller
    andrew, 248
Miller
    Andrew, 172, 230, 232,
        233, 234, 244, 283,
        292, 334, 335, 336
    Ebenezer, 334
    George, 169
    John Jr, 236
    Richard, 334
    Timothy, 334
    William, 334, 336
Mitchell
    Bro, 88
    David, 225
    Tho, 68, 88
Moger
    John, 244
Money
    Francis, 217
Monroe
    David, 371
Montauk, 112, 113, 116

Montauk Indians, 126, 236
Montaukett, 114, 201
Moody
    Lady, 87
    Lady Deborah, 86, 302
More
    Sir Thomas, 30
Morris
    Robert Hunter, 357
    Tho, 68
Mors
    John, 77
Morss
    Robert, 346
mosure
    John, 269
Mott
    Lawrence, 203
Mould
    Isaack, 77
Mounson
    Thomas, 68
Mulford
    goodman, 138
    Goodman, 183
    John, 86, 125, 126, 127,
        129, 134, 135, 139,
        143, 147, 176, 214
    Samuel, 236
Mullford
    John, 136, 161
    William, 136
muncy
    francis, 235
Muncy
    Francis, 227, 230, 237, 262
Munsey
    John, 253
Myles
    Rich^h, 88
Naish
    Thomas, 55
Nash
    John, 68
    Reverend Sylvester, 61
Needham
    Edmund, 118
New Amsterdam, 106, 111,
    197, 212
New Haven, 34, 53, 63, 77,
    156, 188, 203, 305, 306,
    411, 435
    Morris Cove, 90
    Oak Street, 69
    Solitary Cove, 90

451

www.ingramcontent.com/pod-product-compliance
Lightning Source LLC
Chambersburg PA
CBHW080353030426
42334CB00024B/2855